MANAGEMENT COMMUNICATION

ARTHUR H. BELL, Ph.D.
and
DAYLE M. SMITH, Ph.D.
McLaren School of Business,
University of San Francisco

John Wiley & Sons, Inc.
New York • Chichester • Weinheim • Brisbane • Singapore • Toronto

ACQUISITIONS EDITOR	Ellen Ford
MARKETING MANAGER	Carlise Paulson
SENIOR PRODUCTION EDITOR	Christine Cervoni
SENIOR DESIGNER	Harold Nolan
ILLUSTRATION EDITOR	Ann Melhorn
COVER DESIGNER	Harold Nolan
COVER PHOTOGRAPH	© Fred Collins Photography

This book was set in Times Roman by Matrix Publishing and printed and bound by Malloy Lithograph. The cover was printed by Lehigh Press.

This book is printed on acid-free paper. ∞

Library of Congress Cataloging-in-Publication Data
Bell, Arthur H. (Arthur Henry), 1946–
    Management communication / by Arthur H. Bell and Dayle M. Smith.
        p.   cm.
    Includes index.
    ISBN 0-471-23971-2 (pbk. : alk. paper)
    1. Communication in management.   I. Smith, Dayle M.   II. Title.
    HD30.3.B448   1999
    658.4′5—dc21   98–46670
                                                                                CIP

Printed in the United States of America

10 9 8 7 6

Preface

Management Communication serves a new generation of managers in a new century by answering the questions beginning with "How?"—How can communication tools help organizations achieve their missions? How can business writers and speakers adapt their communications to the specific needs of their audiences? How can managers make the best use of new communication technologies? How can rising executives prepare for intercultural communications challenges? Above all, how can workers at *all* levels develop sincere, ethical approaches to upward, lateral, and downward communication in their organizations?

Through clear explanations and contemporary examples, this text answers these questions and others. This book is different. Throughout, this book emphasizes the ethical imperative of doing the right thing for business communicators, not simply doing things right. This expands the discussion beyond traditional and conventional issues to the issues of strategy and style. Business writers pressed for time learn how to generate ideas on the spot instead of waiting for inspiration. Business speakers with sweaty palms read a noted psychiatrist's advice for dealing with speaker's nerves. Managers preparing for intercultural business service find discussions of actual documents and presentations from major trading cultures.

There are frequent opportunities to practice what the book preaches. Managers and managers-in-training who use this book will find themselves engaged in the exciting challenge of thinking through various business dilemmas and communications solutions. In the process, students will develop their own "voices" in writing and speaking—personally appropriate styles that they can use with confidence and commitment throughout their careers. Special features include:

- Twenty-five cases keyed to chapter topics pose real-world business dilemmas that can be resolved by strategic communication.
- A concise, bound-in handbook answers questions about grammar, punctuation, usage, and documentation.
- A variety of exercises for each chapter allows for a wide range of learning styles and course orientations.

- Dozens of full-length examples of business documents, some in before/after versions, show editing and revision possibilities.
- Helpful shortcuts and acronyms (for example, the SALES and ACTION patterns for letters) help writers achieve professional results quickly.
- New communication technologies are not merely described; students learn strategic ways to achieve their goals through specific techniques and tricks-of-the-trade appropriate to e-mail, fax, videoconferencing, the Internet, and other electronic communication channels.

This book is unique in other ways as well. First, it is co-authored by a man and a woman, both of whom bring balanced treatment of their points of view. Second, it includes optional Internet exercises and cases tied to the book's Web site, which includes a powerful Internet Resource Guide, an annotated directory with links to more than 800 Web addresses directly related to management communication. Third, it supplements lessons in management writing, speaking, and listening with thorough coverage of many emerging issues for advanced business students, such as, how to communicate during a company crisis, how to present and ineract on camera, how to conduct behavioral hiring interviews, how to seek career opportunities electronically, how to lead and participate in effective meetings, how to meet the media, how to write and speak for intercultural audiences, how to work collaboratively, and other important topics. We offer a global focus. In addition to a full chapter dedicated to intercultural communication topics, the book integrates a global perspective into the discussion of virtually all aspects of management communication. Above all, this book is written with *enthusiasm for management communication* and is targeted to students who intend to enjoy their academic studies and management careers.

An Instructor's Manual is available that includes quizzes and tests, supplemental cases, a guide to video and audio teaching materials, sample syllabi, marking guides, and other useful aids. PowerPoint presentation slides can be viewed and downloaded from the book's Web site at http://www.wiley.com/college/bell. The Internet Resource Guide is available on the Web.

ACKNOWLEDGMENTS

The lessons organized here grew out of the authors' own research and teaching with MBA, EMBA, and upper-level undergraduate business students as well as from extensive conversation and consultation with practicing managers and executives. Of the more than 100 companies and government organizations that provided access to people and documents for this book, we single out twenty for special thanks: Price-Waterhouse, PaineWebber, TRW, Lockheed Martin, Citicorp, Sun Microsystems, Charles Schwab, American Stores, Cost Plus World Markets, China Resources, Guangdong Enterprises, the U.S. State Department, the Colonial Williamsburg Foundation, the Central Intelligence Agency, the U.S. Coast Guard, New York Life Insurance, IBM, Pacific Bell, British Telecommunications, and Deutsche Telekom.

We also thank our many supportive colleagues and friends at the University of Southern California, Georgetown University, and the McLaren School of Business at the University of San Francisco, where Dean Gary Williams encouraged our efforts and offered valuable insights. Our interactions with Professors Tom Housel, Bill Murray, Kathy Kane, Zhan Li, Steve Alter, Karl Boedecker, Dan Blakley, Barry Doyle, Heather Cowan-Spiegel, Ofelia Alayeto, Peggy Takahashi, Carol Graham, Caren Siehl, Dave Bowen, Mary Ann von Glinow, Norman Sigband, Doug McCabe, Denis Neilson, Steve Huxley, Alev Efendioglu, Heather Hudson, Roger Chen, Richard Puntillo, Eugene Muscat, Rex Bennett, and Ming Xian Liu added significant perspective to our work. We appreciate and respect them all.

Thanks also go to those who reviewed this work in various stages of development and offered suggestions for its improvement. We appreciate the constructive feedback from: Judi Brownell, Cornell University; Heather Cowan-Speigel, University of San Francisco; W. Tracy Dillon, Portland State University; Francine S. Hall, University of New Hampshire; Rhonda S. Palladi, Georgia State University; Erik Skopec, West Coast University; William Sonnenschein, University of California, Berkeley; and Anthony Townsend, University of Nevada, Las Vegas.

Finally, we thank Ellen Ford, Ann Pulido, and their many colleagues at John Wiley & Sons for their expertise, patience, ideas, and encouragement during this project. Only authors know how much a good publisher can add to a book.

ABOUT THE AUTHORS

Arthur H. Bell is Professor of Management Communication at the McLaren School of Business, University of San Francisco, where he directs the Management Communication Program and teaches communication strategy at the MBA, EMBA, and undergraduate levels. He holds his Ph.D. in English from Harvard University and is the author of 36 books on a variety of management communication and business-related topics. His most recent book is *A Framework for Knowledge Management,* forthcoming in 1999.

Dayle M. Smith is Professor of Management at the McLaren School of Business, University of San Francisco. She teaches leadership, communication, organizational behavior, teambuilding, and human resource topics at the MBA, EMBA, and undergraduate levels. She is the author of several recent books on motivation, leadership, interpersonal communication, and work/family issues. Her book, *Women at Work: Leadership for a New Century,* is forthcoming in early 1999. Bell and Smith consult separately and together for more than forty Fortune 500 companies.

Dedication

The authors dedicate this work with love to their parents, Arthur and Dorothy Bell, and Owen and Hinda Smith.

Introduction

We make three important assumptions in this textbook:

- *You probably don't have time to read these pages.* Like most busy managers or managers-in-training, you face information overload as a daily reality. Consequently, we have tried to get to the point and stick to the point. We want each sentence you read here to *matter* to your business and academic success.
- *You will rely less and less on books in the years ahead.* The Internet has probably already become an important resource in your educational and business life. Therefore, we have accompanied this textbook with what we believe to be the most complete guide to management communication resources available on the Internet. In addition, we have based many of the textbook's exercises and assignments on Internet exploration and use.
- *You care more about communicating than learning about communication.* Because excellent communication skills are already a "must-have" in your business and academic life, you are no doubt eager to focus on specific techniques to improve those skills. In this textbook, therefore, we follow the "explain it—try it—evaluate it—perfect it" approach to communication instruction. We believe that what you can *do* as a communicator is more important to your career than the number of terms you can list.

The great majority of students using this textbook will not major in communication nor will they become communication directors within their organizations. Instead, they will find success in fields such as accounting, finance, marketing, management, information systems, telecommunications, and human resources. For this reason, we have *applied* the communication concepts and techniques in this textbook to business situations outside the area of communication itself. A quick glance at the Cases in Appendix A will make the point concretely. There, and throughout the text, you will find the opportunity to apply communication skills and insights to such fields as retail sales, manufacturing, biotechnology, transportation, food services, real estate, personal and corporate financial management, personal planning and supervision, and many other areas.

Finally, we want to express appreciation to the professors who have chosen to use this textbook and to the students who have purchased it. Your questions, comments, and suggestions are welcomed by the authors and publisher. We invite you to e-mail us (Art Bell's e-mail: bell@usfca.edu, Dayle Smith's e-mail: smithdm@usfca.edu) or write to us at the McLaren School of Business, University of San Francisco, San Francisco, CA 94117. You *will* receive a prompt response.

Contents

PART ONE

FOUNDATIONS FOR MANAGEMENT COMMUNICATION

Communication Directions for a New Century

Let's not mince words: you probably cannot attain your complete career objectives without good communication skills. Put positively, you can achieve much for your organization and yourself by using the full range of your communication abilities.

"Employment Opportunities" advertisements in the *Wall Street Journal*, *National Employment Weekly*, the dozens of internet job sites now available, and elsewhere regularly call for "excellent presentation skills," "well-developed writing abilities," and "interpersonal communication strengths" as primary requirements for management positions at all levels. Recent surveys published in *Harvard Business Review*, *Business Week*, and *Fortune* point to communication skills as one of the most important determinants for upward career mobility across industries. In the words of Don Karcher, former president of the large chain of Carl's Restaurants, "real advancement in my own career didn't begin until I had developed a facility for written and oral expression, and that facility becomes more important as my responsibilities increase."

You are now studying at an advanced level to participate meaningfully and profitably in business, and probably to lead others as well. You no doubt want to equip yourself with the communication tools you will need to achieve personal and professional goals. But which communication abilities really matter for a fast-track professional?

There's the rub in a time of rapid technological change affecting all aspects of management communication. Which communication skills will matter most for you in the years ahead? How do you make sure you are preparing for the future, not the past?

We cannot assume that "the basics" of business communication remain unchanged from decade to decade. For example, an employee trained only in the basics of traditional letter-writing skills may have difficulty adjusting to the informality and brevity of e-mail messaging. At the same time, an employee adept at writing only for e-mail may let the company down when it comes to sending a formal business letter by mail or fax.

This textbook attempts to emphasize only those communication lessons from the past that bear significantly on your likely communication needs for the future. No matter how sophisticated word-processing and presentation software packages become, you will continue to be served well by many traditional communication values, including sound reasoning, insightful audience analysis, clear written and oral expression, and careful listening.

But in these pages equal weight is also given to new and emerging communication lessons. For example, what techniques should you use to send e-mail or voice-mail messages in a time of information overload—a time when businesspeople routinely scan rather than read their dozens of daily messages, or simply delete many of them entirely? How will the style of business documents change as we begin to speak our words into the computer (using automated speech recognition systems such as IBM's Via Voice) rather than using a keyboard? What new verbal and nonverbal lessons must we learn to work successfully with audiovisual teleconferencing or video telephone? What adaptations must we make in vocabulary, idiom, and format when writing or speaking to international audiences? What new communication techniques must be mastered to lead or participate in a collaborative writing group or presentation team?

Just as important for your consideration are the ethical issues bound up in virtually all communication relationships. More than style should be involved, after all, when a manager communicates orally or in writing with his or her workgroup. Has the manager used language with integrity or deceit? Do messages invite and deserve trust? Can the manager be relied on to mean what he or she says? Such basic concerns, the subject of Chapter 19, are part of the ethical foundation on which professional communication of all kinds is built.

These are but a few of the questions and lessons that matter most for real managers, and hence occupy center stage in these pages. The author/publisher team responsible for this textbook has rigorously applied one standard to literally every sentence in the book: Does this material provide valuable insight for advanced students preparing for management careers? Your feedback to the authors is welcome as you test each paragraph of this textbook against the real-world communication needs you face in your academic and professional life.

WRITING FOR YOUR PRESENT AND FUTURE

Good writing has always been easy to define for any era: "proper words in proper places," as Jonathan Swift proposed two centuries ago. That sounds simple, but how do you know what will be proper—appropriate, timely, necessary—in business messages? Consider three factors (among the several treated in depth in Chapter 3) that determine the appropriateness of your words for your audience:

- *Tone*   No matter what the *content* of our messages, we inevitably communicate a *context* of personality, intention, and image through the words we choose. When the tone of our communication is overly formal ("It has come to my attention that . . ."), our readers may feel an air of superiority or haughtiness in our message. Their response, in turn, may be negative or at least guarded. An inappropriately casual message ("Hey, boss, about that raise . . .") can backfire if the reader resents our apparent lack of respect or seriousness.

- *Word Choice*   Your selection of words also influences the willingness of your readers to grasp your message and act upon it. For most business purposes, sesquipedalian vocabulary ("long words") is unnecessary for clear writing and speaking. Mark Twain remarked that "I never write 'metropolis' when I get paid the same for writing 'city.' "
- *Length*   Even when you have struck an advantageous tone and chosen suitable words for your audience, your message can still go unread if its length is inappropriate. Test your own response to message length the next time you receive an e-mail that takes two or three screens to view or receive a fax of a dozen pages or more. Length translates as "more work" for busy professionals; we are willing to put out extra effort for such work only when we believe it to be unavoidable. Long messages that could have been shorter add to our workday and subtract from our patience.

Notice in the cases of tone, word choice, and length that our reader *matters* to our communication choices. Before beginning our message, we consider the best way to approach our audience. We call to mind our purpose in sending the message and plan how to achieve that purpose. Above all, we try to view our message not only through the lens of *intention* (what we're "trying to say") but also through the lens of *perception* (what our audience understands us to say).

The new global communication possibilities of electronic bulletin boards, internet chat rooms, e-mail networks, and fax availability all rely on good writing skills to reach their potential. A poorly written message does not improve with speed of delivery. No matter what technologies you have used in the creation and transmission of your message, you must still win your reader's attention and approval by your choice of tone, diction, length, and other important aspects of good business writing.

SPEAKING FOR YOUR PRESENT AND FUTURE

Pronunciation, enunciation, vocal variety, gestures, eye contact—these speaking *manner* skills were some of the key training topics for generations of traditional business presenters. As important as these skills remain for every professional speaker, modern managers must also master new lessons concerned with the *medium* of their oral and visual communications. Just as actors and politicians learn to manage camera angles and staging to their advantage, so businesspeople are now involved in mastering new techniques for eyes, hands, facial expressions, and voice. These new lessons equip managers for successful participation in video teleconferences, radio and television appearances, videotape roles (including training tapes), video internet contacts, and many other emerging communication channels.

An often overlooked aspect of business speaking is our day-to-day telephone work. In many businesses, most sales and technical support contacts are handled entirely by phone. You have certainly had thousands of hours of experience in using the telephone over the years, but you may never have taken time to evaluate the effectiveness of your telephone voice, manner, and strategy.

**Communication
Checkpoint**
*Prepare to Listen
Your Way to
Success*

- Listening requires you to do more than just hear. To listen you must literally think along with the speaker. This is actually quite complex: You must think about what you heard while still listening to new information.
- Listening requires you to seek out the whole message. Speakers communicate by their pauses, nonverbal gestures, dress, and expressions of feeling, in addition to the words they choose for their message. Effective listeners attend to the whole message being communicated.
- Listening requires you to overcome barriers to communication. These barriers can include almost every aspect of the listening experience. For example: you don't like the speaker, you're bothered by the hum of the air-conditioning or heating, you're not interested in the topic, and you think you know what's going to be said. All these obstacles can impede your understanding.

We can all think of people who don't present themselves or their ideas well by phone. Perhaps they sound abrupt or impatient; they may drone on endlessly without a break; or they may talk too softly or too loudly. Are we perceived as having some of these same problems by people with whom we talk by phone? Chapter 15 explains in detail how to evaluate and improve your telephone presentation and conversation skills.

LISTENING FOR YOUR PRESENT AND FUTURE

Like most of us, you probably have spent the vast majority of your total classroom hours engaged in an activity for which you have never received training: how to *listen*. It's no surprise, therefore, that many students enter the business world ill-equipped to listen effectively.

Whatever listening skills we have acquired on our own will surely be put to the test by new listening challenges of the future. Increasingly in business, we will find ourselves having to pay attention to voice messages generated by software, voice chips, and electronic recording in other forms. In addition, a significant portion of our business day will no doubt be spent "keeping up" with our voice mail. One sales manager at Sun Microsystems reports returning from a three-day business trip to find 256 messages waiting on his voice mail. Faced with the sheer volume of listening required in management careers, we cannot afford to listen inattentively.

Nor can we listen unintelligently. We may have to learn—and practice—new skills to listen for what's *not* said or what is overstated. We can learn to listen "through" the slickness of a presentation or advertisement to determine its real content, or lack thereof. We can develop listening skills that pierce through a boring presentation or uninteresting conversation to grasp its core facts. Because of the central importance of listening in business life, Chapter 13 focuses on ways to evaluate and improve your listening habits, including the ways gender influences our business communications.

COMMUNICATION TECHNOLOGIES

The Communication Revolution, underway throughout the industrialized world since the late 1970s, has gone through at least five stages to date. In its first stage, the *look* of business documents changed for the better. A variety of fonts and formats allowed business

VOICE MAIL

It happens to everyone in business—usually several times a day. You call someone who isn't in.

For some companies, voice mail—telephone technology that manages messages without paper—may be the solution. The simplest form of voice mail is an answering machine. Connected to your office phone, an answering machine lets callers leave any kind of message, . . . and you can retrieve your messages by calling in from wherever you are. If both you and the person you are trying to reach have answering machines, you can even have a dialogue of sorts.

But answering machines are . . . limited in what they can do. A business alternative is a complete voice-mail system. Here's what such a system can do.

- **Serve many people.** Every person with a phone in effect has a private answering machine with a personalized greeting.
- **Record personal messages.** You can record messages that will be played back only to persons who have been given a special access code.
- **Forward messages.** When you are away from your usual phone, a voice-mail system can record an incoming message, then call you wherever you are and play the message back.

- **Distribute messages.** You can record a message and have the system route it to several people.
- **Screen and hold calls.** A few systems greet incoming calls with a recording [which allows you] to answer the call or direct the voice-mail system to take a message. . . . Callers who are put on hold are told how many people are waiting.
- **Provide a bulletin board.** Employees can phone in for messages of general interest, such as office closings or the date of the company picnic. Bulletin boards can be open to everyone or restricted to authorized persons with an access code.
- **Furnish access to a computer data-base.** An elaborate voice-mail system can be tied into a company's main computers [allowing sophisticated retrieval of information].
- **Serve as an automatic attendant.** Most voice-mail systems can go beyond taking and routing messages, answering all phone calls automatically with a standard recording. Many calls can thus bypass the receptionist. An automatic attendant can also eliminate the need for a special [after-hours arrangement].

Reprinted with permission, by Goldhirsh Group, Inc. 38 Commercial Wharf, Boston, MA 02110.

writers to produce book-quality documents at their desktop personal computers. Thanks to spell-check and grammar-check programs, these documents were easier to edit and proofread than ever before.

Word-processing and desktop publishing software raised standards for how we expect a business document to appear. Traditionally typed memos, letters, reports, and proposals looked amateurish by contrast. Companies rushed to install computers and laser printers that could enhance the corporate image, as reflected in business documents.

The second stage of the Communication Revolution dates from the early 1980s. Using e-mail and facsimile technologies, companies were finally able to bypass the post office bottleneck and transmit documents throughout the company or around the world in seconds.

But with this new ease of communication transmission came unexpected problems. Companies used to a "buffer period" of days or weeks in corresponding with customers and suppliers now had to answer the question, "Why can't you e-mail or fax me the document right now?" In an effort to respond to this sense of urgency, managers at all levels were pressed into service as communicators with external stakeholders. Suddenly, good communication skills became necessary throughout the company.

COMMUNICATION FOR A NEW CENTURY

FAX: NEW RULES FOR A NEW COMMUNICATION MEDIUM

Communication technology shows every sign of challenging the U.S. mail by the year 2000 as the most common way to send and receive brief printed messages. In 1991, prices for fax machines with a few basic features had dropped to the mid-$300 range, putting this technology within the budgets of individuals, as well as businesses.

The fax revolution has suggested the need for some still-evolving loose guidelines for effectively using this powerful communication channel.

1. Provide your recipient with full sender information on a fax cover sheet accompanying your message pages. The cover sheet should include the following:
   - Your name
   - Your company's name and address
   - Your fax/phone number.
   - A voice telephone number to contact in case of questions or transmission trouble
   - Your recipient's name
   - Any necessary information about the recipient's location (office number, etc.)
   - Date of transmission
   - Number of pages being transmitted (including the cover sheet)
   - Any directions or instructions regarding delivery of the message or other matters
2. Consider the sensitivity and confidentiality of your message before deciding to send it by fax. Will it matter that one or more secretaries or other staff members may read your message as it comes out of the fax machine or when it is being delivered to your intended reader? You may want to use a sealed envelope and traditional delivery for this more private communication. This applies particularly to matters regarding personnel action, highly sensitive new product information, and anything that could affect stock prices.
3. Try to send only clear, dark, large-print, legible documents. Fax transmission reduces the quality and the crispness of documents, so they must be very clearly readable. This is especially true when the same page, with added notations, is sent back and forth by fax several times.
4. Ask your recipient for permission before sending long documents by fax. After all, the receiver has to pay for the fax paper on which your message is printed. That usually amounts to about five cents per page. In addition, a transmission of several dozen pages may unnecessarily tie up the recipient's fax machine.
5. Prefer off-peak transmission times for sending low-priority fax messages. You can save telephone-line charges by transmitting nonurgent message after business hours. Also, your recipient may appreciate your courtesy in not tying up the fax connection during the business day.

Beginning in the mid-1980s, the third stage of the Communication Revolution brought high-quality graphics and visual aids into business documents and presentations. Graphs, charts, pictograms, and many other forms of business graphics could now be created with ease at the PC. Spreadsheet programs such as Excel and Lotus 1-2-3 took the lead in providing graphic capabilities linked directly to database information. The report or proposal without several attractively rendered visual aids quickly became the exception in business practice rather than the rule.

By the early 1990s, the fourth stage of the Communication Revolution had taken visual enhancement of business communication to a new level: full-motion audiovisual teleconferencing. For the first time, businesspeople could choose not to send their bodies where only their minds and images needed to go. During these exciting years, futurist John Naisbett reminded the business world that "hi-tech" advances must always be accompanied by supportive "hi-touch" features for a new technology to be widely embraced.

The slow acceptance of audiovisual teleconferencing across industries can be explained primarily as failure in "hi-touch" aspects of this communication development. Expecting themselves to look and sound like professional anchormen and -women, businesspeople often were displeased with how they appeared and sounded in teleconferences. And no wonder: in most cases, they had received no media training to help them use this new technology to their best advantage.

With the advent of AT&T's affordable video-telephone in the mid-1990s and the rapid growth of interactive motion-image transmission via the internet, seeing the person to whom you are speaking (with all the advantages of extra messaging through nonverbal cues) has come out of the boardroom into offices and homes throughout the world. In a 1998 television interview, Andrew Grove, president of Intel, predicted that the popularity of motion imaging would soar in the near term and bring with it a sea-change in our expectations for business documents and presentations. According to Grove, by the turn of the century even the most common business documents will be making use of sophisticated, full-color graphics to help communicate their messages with impact and pleasure. Even the most routine oral presentation will employ multimedia visual aids. Why? Because technological advances have put such attractive and persuasive communication tools into the hands of managers at all levels. As digital cameras and high-resolution color printers become commonplace, the day will soon arrive when we can easily produce a proposal or report with all the visual excitement and energy of a professionally printed travel brochure.

The fifth and most problematic stage of the Communication Revolution involves "wizards" (expert system helpers included in office software) ready and willing to take over a large part of the intellectual work in developing a successful document or presentation. Wizards already exist, for example, in recent versions of PowerPoint to "help" presenters settle on key points in order to be used in a variety of speaking situations.

Certainly, such wizards are welcomed by managers who dislike the hard work involved in thinking through what they want to say and to whom they are directing their message. At their best, wizards can rescue such managers from presentation disasters by offering orderly if somewhat standardized points for use right "out of the box." But at their worst, wizards can short-circuit the important creative work involved in assessing audience needs and tailoring communications to meet those needs precisely. In these cases, wizards offer one-size-fits-all formats and argument structures for documents and presentations that need the sophisticated fine-tuning of a human touch. The reliance on software wizards is most unfortunate among entry-level employees or business students who learn how to let the wizard produce a slick document or presentation, but who do not learn to think for themselves.

The sixth stage of the Communication Revolution is sweeping the United States as this book goes to press. For the first time, writers are learning to link their spoken words directly to their written words by automated speech recognition (ASR) computing. Managers who "hate to write but love to talk" are empowered to talk out their messages rather than wrestling with the elaborate and often arcane rules that have come to surround the act of writing. For the majority of employees and students who regularly experience Writer's Block (but have never experienced Speaker's Block), ASR capability comes as a godsend.

How the style of business discourse will change as a result of widespread ASR messaging remains an open question. Inevitably, it would seem that the writing style used for memos, letters, and other common documents will become more conversational. Previously sacrosanct language structures (such as "the complete sentence") may give way over time to more spontaneous utterances, of the sort used in ordinary conversation. As a result, documents may grow more lively at the same time that they grow less and less "correct" by previous writing standards. (In e-mail messages, we already see this trend developing. E-mail writers permit themselves wide latitude in omitting capital letters, mixing conversational and casual phrases with more businesslike prose, and inserting emotional icons to communicate personality and humor.)

Where will the Communication Revolution lead in its further stages? Given the rapid pace of development on many frontiers of science and technology, even the most imaginative vision of the next ten years will probably prove too conservative. Two developments in particular, however, bear watching for their special relevance to business communicators.

Natural Language Processing.   With simultaneous dramatic advances in computer memory and processing speed, the holy grail of natural language processing (a computer that can understand unrestricted human conversation, conceive its own thoughts and responses, and convert them into human language) is now within our reach, if not our grasp.

Just as the game of chess changed forever when IBM's "Deep Blue" computer began to beat human grand masters of chess, so our place as the intellectual overlords of the material and animal world will be shaken by the advent of machines that think and talk. At first, we will gladly turn over mundane languaging functions to these artificial intelligences (as we now use voice chips to remind us to close our auto doors and computer voices to deliver "411" telephone number requests). We may turn over teaching and training functions with more reluctance, knowing that students shaped by such instruction will be forever different from us, for better or worse, in their range of imagination and expectations for language interaction with others.

Finally, we may turn over our highest levels of decision making and political dialogue to those who, in an odd twist of Matthew Arnold's great phrase, have mastered "the best thoughts of the best minds"—that is, the artificially intelligent computers linked to complexities of conception and quantities of data entirely beyond individual human capacity. Who would choose not to manage the most important decisions—medical diagnosis, environmental management, economic policy—by employing the most intelligent means? As one science fiction writer puts the case (with some hyperbole), when that ultimate computer knows all and controls all, we will have at last discovered (or invented) God.

Virtual Reality.   Now in the game stage (as were photography and electromagnetism at first), virtual reality speaks directly to humankind's long-felt need for environmental control. Walking through a real jungle admixes the thrill of adventure and new sensations with the threat of poisonous snakes and stinging insects. Walking through a virtual jungle, however, is quite different; it can be electronically cleansed of all objectionable aspects, as might a virtual tennis partner, teacher, or lover. What we discover in a virtual world, of course, has been planned for us or by us—and therein lie both the glory and the prison of this new form of experience.

At the far edge of virtual reality lies image manipulation of human faces and forms. The 1996 movie *Toy Story* showed elementary possibilities for creating dimensional cartoon figures from mathematical rather than analog or photographic models. The same technology that can prance a digitized toy dog across the screen with considerable verisimilitude can eventually present the full-motion face and body of a company executive, or national president, or you or me. In short, our individual appearances can be digitized for re-creation in ways and for purposes that we do not control.

Several Navajo and Hopi tribes to this day do not permit photographs to be taken of their members, for fear the soul or specialness of its people will be carried away and displayed out of context and out of the control of the authentic human beings represented in the photographs. In similar fashion, may we not all be concerned when a famous actor, professor, or politician licenses his or her digitized form to be used indistinguishably from "live" appearances? Especially as advanced holographs present such images before us in three-dimensional form, we may have to redefine the notion of "reality" itself.

Could it be that our grandchildren, surrounded by absolutely accurate visual imitations of human forms animated intellectually and emotionally by artificial intelligence, will find our concept of the "real" hopelessly quaint? Will one of those artificial forms, eternal in the precision of its programming, be you or me? Will we say and do things typical of us, and hence be "real" participants in the lives of countless generations to come? Will Christmas in 2075 bring a new Microsoft release of Virtual Grandmother or Grandfather to adoring descendants we never saw with our (apparently) limited biological eyes? Finally, will the prospect of perpetual virtual "life" be a balm to the disappointment and pain of fading biological life for each of us? Will we draw strength or terror from the knowledge that our image and form may have its own electronic life far beyond our years, living on ghostlike to delight, puzzle, or accuse those for whom perception is indeed reality?

SPECIFIC CHALLENGES OF THE COMMUNICATION REVOLUTION

For businesspeople, one of the most striking effects of the dizzying pace of technological change in the Communication Revolution will be more words, more information, and more ready-made messages and documents (or wizards at hand to assist us in making such communications). Consider the impact of each of these developments on your own professional life:

More Words.   You may already have noticed over the past decade a dramatic increase in the number of words you are expected to process (by reading, writing, hearing, remembering, revising, filing, and so forth) each business day. Faster word processors allow us to produce more words more quickly. High-speed copy machines make it possible to reproduce those words for the entire office and beyond. E-mail and internet connections allow us to distribute messages across continents to limitless numbers of individuals at the press of a key. Massive data storage in a small hard-disk drive in our desktop or notebook computer allows us to shelve words for future use.

Every business communicator must take seriously the implications of a business world awash with words. The final pages of this chapter suggest several ways to survive as an effective communicator in an era when words are not only cheap but omnipresent.

More Information.   Thanks to the thousands of academic and commercial databases (and to additional thousands of useful Web sites) now available to business, every personal computer becomes a gateway to vast stores of information. But are you prepared, by your education, experience, or other means, to *use* this information effectively? A grade school teacher in Ohio outlined this problem succinctly: "With our new internet computers, my students can access reams of information on even the smallest topics. One youngster ordered up 420 pages on the goldfish for a class report. He brought the pounds of paper up to my desk. 'Now what?' he asked."

All of us may well ask "Now what?" when faced by the daunting task of assembling, analyzing, organizing, and limiting the pertinent data available from information sources at our disposal. "Data isn't information," warns Victor Walling, senior strategic planner at SRI International. "You need to have information assembled in a way that will help you make decisions. The communication experts of the future will be good not only at gathering information, but at interpreting it with intelligence."

More Ready-Made Messages and Documents. As more and more business documents are stored in various forms of computer memory, the temptation will inevitably grow for businesspeople to recycle old language rather than to generate new language tailored to the situation at hand. After all, writing (together with the thinking that goes into writing) is hard work. It is much easier to call up an old document, rearrange a few sentences and insert new names, then to pass it off as a contemporary communication. In some cases (such as collection letters and order responses), such a strategy may be appropriate. But in more complex business communications, each word in the document must be selected for its suitability for your intended audience, purpose, and circumstances. These important messages can't be cut out of the old dough of past documents. They must be made fresh.

Resist the temptation, therefore, to reuse tired business prose from the past. The authentic, in-the-moment human voice (whether conveyed through writing or speaking) remains the single most potent communication tool in business. Find that voice within you and learn to trust it.

THRIVING IN AN ERA OF MORE WORDS, MORE INFORMATION, AND MORE STORED DOCUMENTS

Skilled business communicators can practice six techniques to survive and thrive in an age of ever-quickening communication change:

1. *Grab attention early.* To cope successfully with the growing problem of more and more words in business, try to catch the reader's eye early with your main message. You must make sure that the glance given to your e-mail message or memo by busy executives draws them in to a thorough consideration of your full message. Use subject lines in memos and letters, executive summaries in reports and proposals, and first sentences in e-mail and fax messages to capture an irresistibly important or urgent point about your topic. In short, skip the "front porch" with which so many business documents begin ("As you know . . ."). Take your reader immediately into the most interesting room in the house.

2. *Write concisely.* Each year, business reports and proposals get shorter on average—but few would claim that less communication is taking place. The "word market" in business simply demands that writers get to the point without wasting words. To communicate your full message in fewer words, follow the techniques explained and exemplified in Chapter 4.

3. *Consider the impact of format.* Your documents must not only be readable but, at a first moment's glance, *appear* to be readable. Use white space, headings, bullets, highlighting techniques, and other approaches discussed in Chapter 3 to attract and hold the attention of your reader. Simply from the "look" of your document, your reader should have the impression that "this report looks well-organized and professional." Beginning with that favorable mindset, your reader will be disposed to approve not only the appearance of your document but its content as well.

4. *Find the right tone.* Although the tone of business messages in memos, e-mail, and letters should not be exclusively personal (as, let's say, in diaries), that tone should be friendly and approachable in most cases. Chapter 6 shows several techniques for communicating warmth and appropriate regard for your reader.

5. *Write efficiently.* As a businessperson, you don't want to follow old school habits of taking writing tasks home for completion at the eleventh hour. You want to finish work *at* work. To do so, you must learn to break Writer's Block and get on with communication tasks in an efficient way. Chapter 9 describes proven techniques you can use to generate and organize your ideas, then convert them to a valuable first draft.

6. *Write naturally.* Don't use overly difficult or bureaucratic language in an effort to impress your reader. Busy executives have little time to wonder what you're trying to say. Write and speak naturally in your own voice, valuing your ability to express more than your temptation to impress. Chapters 7 and 14 discuss techniques for achieving grace and honesty in your communications.

PREPARING FOR CEASELESS CHANGE

Past communication revolutions happened at a slower pace, with an old technology gradually giving way to a newer one. Handwritten documents of the sort produced by Melville's Bartleby the Scrivener were gradually replaced over decades by more automated technologies culminating in the typewriter. Businesspeople had several generations to master and improve the technology of the typewriter before computers came along.

But the Communication Revolution we inhabit sweeps us all along at a much faster pace of change. Just when we adapt to the "butterfly" keyboard on our notebook computer, the industry standard becomes automated speech recognition computing. Just when we perfect our skills in telephone communication, a moving image pops up on our video phone and the whole game changes again.

In short, our Communication Revolution promises perpetual and unpredictable change. What business documents or presentation forms will be used in 20 years when your career is in full blossom? We can only guess. Perhaps many traditional forms will be vastly changed or entirely extinct.

How do we prepare for such rapid change? First, we can identify those aspects of business communication that remain relatively constant: among others, the right of an audience to have its point of view taken into consideration; the obligation of a writer to present ideas clearly; and the advantages of choosing appropriate styles, diction, arguments, examples, and formats to suit your audience, purpose, and circumstances.

Furthermore, we can resolve to be lifelong learners sensitive to the demands of the future and the necessity to create new solutions for communication problems. For many of us, such learning may carry us "outside our field" as we read and hear about new com-

GUIDELINES FOR WRITTEN AND ORAL WORK

WRITTEN WORK

1. Make sense.
Express your ideas in a coherent, orderly way. Don't rely on verbal padding to take the place of clear thinking.

2. Back up your assertions.
In most cases, an assertion is not true simply because you claim it to be so. Consider the use of examples, anecdotes, citation of authorities, statistics, and other forms of support to lend credence to your assertions.

3. Write for your audience.
Select language, length, and levels of argumentation and evidence that suit your audience.

4. Edit and revise.
Eliminate deadwood, provide solid transitions between ideas, and repair every last error in grammar, spelling, and mechanics. Often a second set of eyes can catch errors to which the writer is blind.

5. Format for readability.
Use the word-processing technologies available to you to create easy-to-read, attractive documents.

6. Write to express, not to impress.
Business language has little place for puffery. Get to the point.

7. Prefer common language to difficult verbiage.
Mark Twain vowed "never to write 'metropolis' when I get paid the same for writing 'city.' "

8. Give credit to your sources.
Ideas, sentences, phrases, and terms that aren't your own must be footnoted. APA and MLA documentation styles are standard.

9. Use graphic aids where necessary to capture and highlight ideas.
Don't use graphic aids as decoration.

10. Write with energy and conviction.
Business writing can be as interesting as the world of business itself.

ORAL PRESENTATIONS

Following these additional guidelines for oral presenting:

1. Speak up.
Audiences resent having to lean forward in an effort to catch your words.

2. Achieve rapport quickly.
Use the first few moments of your presentation to orient audience members and show them that you feel comfortable with them.

3. Look at your listeners.
Indicate by your eye contact that you are talking *with* your listeners, not *at* them (or, *worse*, to the ceiling, floor, or walls).

4. Use gestures to express your ideas.
Appropriate hand gestures and facial expressions add energy and communicate sincerity.

5. Move freely, without pacing.
Use the available space to move naturally.

6. Use notes (if necessary) as unobtrusively as possible.
Notes function best as "thought triggers," not as verbatim transcripts of a presentation.

7. Highlight key ideas.
Voice volume, pauses, graphic aids, and "headlining" (telling listeners that a point is particularly important) can all be used to emphasize key points.

8. Channel nervous energy into an enthusiastic delivery.
Accept nerves as a natural form of excitement and use that energy to deliver your points with appropriate passion.

9. Watch your audience for signs of comprehension or misunderstanding.
True communication is not a one-way lecture. Pay attention to the facial expressions and body language of audience members to determine if you're "getting through."

10. End with a bang, not a whimper.
Your concluding words should be memorable for your listeners.

puter developments, experiments in artificial intelligence, and advances in computer graphics. The pursuit of lifelong learning may take us back to the classroom regularly for seminars and extension classes. No matter what route we take to new learning, what matters most is our resolve to preserve what remains useful from the past and invent what we require for the future. The years ahead promise astounding change in how we communicate with one another—an exciting journey indeed for business communicators equipped with courage, curiosity, and not a little patience.

SUMMARY

1. New communication advances extend our influence over one another and the environment.

2. Writing habits will change as writing technologies change.

3. Like writing, our speaking will have to adapt to the possibilities and limitations of new communication links such as the teleconference and modern telephone.

4. Listening involves far more than just hearing. To listen is to seek out the whole message, by paying attention to both verbal and nonverbal cues. Active listening overcomes barriers to full understanding.

5. Modern computer-based technology influences writing habits by making it easier to revise, print, and save documents.

6. Electronic mail has reduced the number of letters and paper memos in corporations. This new technology creates its own forms and rules for writing.

7. Audio and video teleconferences break some of the ordinary conventions of person-to-person conversation. We must learn new ways to speak and listen to use these technologies successfully.

QUESTIONS FOR DISCUSSION

1. What is revolutionary about the Communication Revolution?

2. Why can we refer to writing, speaking, and listening as "social glue"? What would life be like without them?

3. Why should you consider tone, diction, and length when composing business communications?

4. Why is it necessary to master the medium of your communication? What common communication media do businesspeople regularly use?

5. How would you define effective listening skills?

6. How much should you rely on standardized checklists to determine good or bad communication? Explain your response.

7. List five key communication machines for the twentieth century.

8. How might the easy recall of computer-based writing technologies affect your writing style?

9. What are the shortcomings of traditional mail delivery?

10. What unexpected problems might you face as a user of electronic mail?

11. In what ways does quick access to information both benefit and challenge business communicators?

12. What kinds of new technologies do you look forward to using? How might you prepare yourself to use them effectively?

EXERCISES

1. Imagine what a world without words would be like. Describe how people would communicate.

2. List the kinds of information you shut out in the following situations: watching television, listening to a friend or family member describe his or her day, and listening to an instructor's lecture. In each case, what kind of input startles you into paying attention again? What characteristic of that information—the method of presentation or the subject matter itself—overcomes your tendency to filter out nonessential information?

3. Photocopy a graphic aid (a chart or graph) from one of your textbooks and bring it to class. Without providing its accompanying written interpretation, trade graphic aids with a partner. Now, try to write text reflecting the information contained in the graphic aid. Is this picture "worth a thousand words"?

4. Photocopy text summarizing information contained in a graphic aid. As you did in the preceding exercise, trade samples with a partner, and try to generate a graphic aid reflecting the information contained in the text. Compare your graphic aid with the text. Which is most useful?

5. What are the implications of computer phones and teleconferences for business communicators? Envision yourself in an environment where your picture can be transmitted along with your voice over the telephone lines. What new considerations will you have to make each time you reach for a ringing phone?

6. Explain why some businesspeople resist using audio or video teleconferencing, even though the technology can save them time, travel, and money. Also explain how, in your opinion, such resistance can be overcome.

7. Managers usually receive no formal training in listening. Assume that you have been given the task of providing such training in your company. Describe how you would teach managers to become better listeners.

8. The workstation concept began with the idea of putting a coordinated set of necessary work tools at one comfortable location for a manager or other office worker. Consider your life as a student, then describe the components you would include in your own personal workstation. Assume that you have an unrestricted budget for this project.

INTERNET ASSIGNMENT

You're new in your position as an entry-level associate with a major consulting firm. Typically, the company provides a period of 90 days for orientation and training before you are assigned to projects as a member of a team with experienced senior consultants. Your mentor in the company, Susan Williams, asks you to spend a few hours exploring management communication resources on the Web, then to write up a one-page memo to her in which you

- give your evaluation of the usefulness of Web materials for the kind of training you are now undergoing in the company
- select five websites on different aspects of management communication (Ms. Williams will look at these personally. She wants you to comment on why you think they deserve her special interest.)

After conducting the Internet exploration described above, write the memo addressed to Susan Williams, Director of Management Training.

CHAPTER 2

Communication Theory and Architecture

Just as an electrical contractor can plan a complex system of electrical service lines for a building, so a manager well versed in organizational communication principles and practices can plan conducive channels for communication within a company. This process involves much more than installing a company newsletter and more e-mail terminals. If corporate communication is to drive profits and progress in the organization, it must infiltrate every aspect of company culture.

In too many companies, after all, communication "pipelines" from lower-ranking employees to upper management do exist, usually in the form of e-mail access, "open door" policies, suggestion boxes, and occasionally "town hall" meetings. But the mere presence of these channels does not guarantee their *use*. Employees may get the message loud and clear from the dominant culture or subcultures in the company that "we don't ever send unsolicited messages upstairs. Let sleeping dogs lie."

Conversely, some companies have opened so many communication channels to top management that CEOs and Executive VPs spend half their time wading through "FYI" memos, e-mail messages, and phone calls. Clearly, communication architecture must be planned to coordinate with company needs, resources, and mission.

This chapter provides theoretical grounding for managers who understand, or want to understand, the importance of carefully planned communication architecture within their organizations. By grasping what communication is, how it functions in principle and in practice, and what barriers it must overcome in organizations, managers are well equipped to select types of communication media and map out channels for intended communication in their companies.

Chapter 1 introduced the revolution in business communication, and it described many of the revolutionary business-communication technologies. Clearly, you'll have to become acquainted with all of these technologies as you launch your career in business.

However, as Chapter 1 suggested, the technologies alone won't affect you as much as the changes that the technologies are causing in business communication. Even if you had a team of personal secretaries to do all your word and data processing, faxing and electronic mailing, and even your telephoning (video, audio, or otherwise), your daily business activities would still be changed by the business-communication revolution.

The biggest revolutionary change is the huge amount of information that the new technologies make available. Actually, it may seem more as if we're drowning in a constant flood of letters, reports, faxes, electronic mail, junk mail, and data of every kind and in every form. This onslaught of information means that you and other businesspersons must be able to

1. Handle more business documents and other business messages
2. Sift through more information to choose the information you need
3. Understand more information
4. Communicate information more effectively to customers, coworkers, suppliers, and others (after all, they too have to sift through more information, to choose whether they need yours)

To do all these things, you must be a highly skilled communicator. This brings to mind three questions: (1) What is a skilled communicator? (2) What does a skilled communicator do? (3) How can you become a skilled communicator?

Before answering these questions, we have to define what *communication* means.

WHAT IS *COMMUNICATION*?

Communication springs from the Latin verb *communicare*, which means "to make common." Notice that the primary meaning of *communication* is *not* to recite, deliver, speak, write, or sermonize. All of these activities fall short of "making common" the flow of ideas and feeling. Mere speaking is a one-way activity, while communication involves *common* ("communal") interests shared by all parties involved in the communication.

Skilled communicators share in the give-and-take of ideas and feelings. Even when they give speeches, communicators notice responses from their audiences. For example, a man smiles in the front row. An older woman leans forward to hear from the back row. Two teenagers yawn and squirm. All of these responses show that others actively participate in the speaker's communication process. The speaker alone can only make speech noises. The audience alone can only wait to hear or see something. Together, they can communicate in the mutual activity of making thoughts and feelings common to the group.

WHAT DO WE KNOW ABOUT COMMUNICATION?

Philosophers have been studying communication for centuries, and modern researchers have been studying it scientifically for decades. Though much of communication still remains a mystery, a great deal has been learned about just what it is and how it works.

What we now know about communication can be described in terms of answers to the following eight questions:

1. Can words describe everything we see, feel, and know about our experiences?

2. When you say a word, does it mean the same thing to you that it means to your listener?
3. What keeps us from hearing and understanding one another?
4. How can you find out whether I understand what you tell me?
5. How should your listeners' (or readers') needs affect what you say (or write)?
6. What keeps us from communicating information to one another?
7. How does the *medium of communication* (such as a telephone, telegram, thank-you card, or billboard) affect the message being communicated?
8. How does technology affect communication? Do we communicate to it, with it, or through it?

Unfortunately, we don't have clear, precise, final answers to these questions, but highly talented researchers have come up with some good ideas that give us keen insights into (1) how we usually communicate and (2) how we could communicate even better.

Can Words Describe Everything We Experience?

Early researchers studying communication noticed that specific cultures used words that didn't exist in other cultures. For example, they noticed that Eskimos had many words for snow, but tropical cultures had not a single word for it. When they noticed this, they asked a very intriguing question: Can we see, feel, and know about our experiences if we don't have words to describe them?

What they have concluded is that if we don't have the words we need to communicate something, we make them up. This doesn't mean that we're never at a loss for words, though. Particularly at the height or depth of emotion, you may say that "words can't describe how I feel." If much of what we experience lies outside the boundary of words, how is it possible to communicate—or even to think—about those ideas and feelings?

Let's say, for example, that one-dollar bills were distinguished from ten-dollar bills only by color: the one-dollar bills were a lighter shade of green than the ten-dollar bills. What would we do if we had only one word to express greenness—the word "green"? We would probably create a new word to make that distinction. When people feel strong needs, they change their language to express those needs. In short, we use words to point to things we care about.

On the other hand, language sometimes limits how we think. We risk seeing and thinking only about what we have words to describe. For example, the words *mailman*, *fireman*, or *policeman* give the expectation that a male adult will be doing those jobs. In this case, language becomes a blinder that keeps us from seeing or thinking about many aspects of our experience. ("Mail carrier," "firefighter," and "police officer" have become more widely used for just this reason.)

The limitations of the language we use may even keep us from noticing things in our environment. For example, tourists visiting Eskimo villages look out and see only miles and miles of ice—while Eskimos looking at the same terrain see much more. Their language provides dozens of words to name different colors, ages, densities, and configurations of ice. They may see more because they can name more. By the same token, Eskimos looking at an urban street might well see much less than we do. Our language provides us with a wealth of words for stores, shops, delicatessens, stands, markets, booths, boutiques, and so forth.

It's up to us to make sure that we shape our language according to our needs and that we avoid letting language limit our awareness and our thinking.

Are You Saying the Same Words That I'm Hearing You Say?

Everything we say and write in words is based on the idea that the words I tell you have the same meaning to me when I say them that they have to you when you hear them. If either of us has any doubts about the meanings of the words, all we have to do is look in the dictionary—right?

Early dictionary writers often wrote that they hoped that their uniform definitions of words would once and for all settle confusion and misunderstanding in the world. Unfortunately, despite their grand hopes, they were wrong. Even the most carefully defined words can produce unexpected responses at times.

Consider the word *dimple*, for example. By dictionary definition—the *denotative meaning*—it is "a small, natural hollow on the surface of the body." But its *connotative meanings*—the associations and emotions aroused by the word—differ radically from person to person. One person may consider a dimple adorable. For another person, the word may conjure up painful years as a pudgy child.

Business communicators should remember the connotational pitfalls of language. As Roger Brown reminds us in his book *Words and Things*, we can never assume that the saying or writing of a word automatically brings our intended thought or image into the mind of the audience. Words may be a stimulus to thought, like a knock at the door, but they are by no means the guest that comes to call. The art of business communication lies largely in focusing on what your readers or listeners will probably *receive*, not solely on what you want to *send*.

A BUSINESS APPLICATION

We can apply the ideas about the necessity and the limitations of words to a business dilemma at Melrose Insurance. Franklin De Grange, operations manager, took on the job of writing a brochure for filing clerks at the company. Previously, trainers had led clerks through the large filing room, pointing out banks of files. "Premium receipts go over there, but expiration notices belong in these files," the trainers would say. *De Grange faced the task of giving each of the files an identifiable reality by assigning a name to each one.* Then, and only then, could new clerks be expected to find the right file without a personal guide.

De Grange's brochure clearly described the main task of clerks, but it didn't mention the many and varied other activities that they were supposed to perform during the business day. De Grange had considered those tasks too trivial to mention.

The brochure immediately resulted in problems with the new clerks. The new clerks clung to the *language reality* of their job described in the brochure. Because De Grange had so clearly specified the main tasks and hadn't even hinted at the possibility of additional tasks, the new clerks considered the imposition of other tasks to be "outside my job classification." De Grange bemoaned the fact that "we used to tell them too little about their jobs, and they did whatever they were asked. Now we tell them too much!"

The point: Many important aspects of your business practice will need the clarification and definition provided by words. Be prepared to find ways to say necessary things. On the other hand, language can become a mental straitjacket for creative thinking and perceiving. Remain open to the realities of business beyond the buzzwords and catch phrases.

A
BUSINESS
APPLICATION

You have to draft a report to major stockholders on Academy Mortgage's new plans for Southbay Park, a forested tract being developed by Academy for use by employees. Your own feelings are clear to you: You think the park is a great idea, and you look forward to hiking, rowing, and generally relaxing in the healthful environment. As you draft the report, you notice the prevalence of certain key words: "recreation," "leisure," "peaceful," "relaxing," "calm," and "refreshing." These are all "plus" words for you—words that would persuade you to support the development of the park. However, you begin to mentally reread your draft from the perspective of Stockholder Mortimer Creed, a millionaire who hasn't taken a day off in 20 years. You wonder, with foreboding, what Creed understands the word "leisure" to mean (laziness?). You call to mind Stockholder Jill Benforth, the child genius. She graduated from Yale at 17 and made her fortune by 25. She wants the company "to push employees on toward excellence—push, push, push!" What will "peaceful" and "calm" mean to her?

The point: Words are not miniature trucks that deliver preformed packages of meaning from our heads into our audience's heads. The same words can produce different meanings in each of your readers or listeners. As a communicator, learn to plan for those differences.

Why Don't I Understand You?

Communication researchers have identified five aspects of the communication process:

1. An **information source** (usually called a "message"—an idea or thought or fact)
2. A **signal** (a stream of words or images or gestures that express the message)
3. A **transmittal** (an act of sending, delivering, or transferring the message)
4. A **channel** (usually called a "medium," such as a report, TV image, or speech)
5. A **destination** or **receiver** (usually called an "audience"; may be listeners, viewers, or readers)

The way in which this works is that (1) an *information source* is translated into (2) a *signal* that is (3) *transmitted* through a (4) *channel* to a (5) *destination* or *receiver*. This description of communication is deceptively simple.

For business communicators, this simple description poses a key question: Why do the signals we send in our written and spoken words often seem to bounce off our readers or listeners? They read or hear us, but they don't seem to understand. According to communication researchers, "noise" could be the culprit. **Noise** in communication theory is broadly defined as a signal interference—everything from literal noise (clinking dishes, traffic, and so forth) to mental noise, including preoccupation, prejudice, or presumption on the part of our audience.

However, just as interference can be reduced or eliminated in electronic transmissions, so noise in written and spoken business communications can be identified and removed. In written documents, generously used **white space** (white areas on a page, created by adding space around key parts of the text, such as headings or lists). This can reduce the visual noise produced by all-print pages. In speeches, use a pace-changing story or *visual aid* (picture, map, or something else that the audience can look at to receive your message). These can restore "signal reception" distorted by lagging attention spans.

Different age groups are prone to different forms of noise. Young people may receive your signals through a haze of *semantic noise*—the interference of assigning different connotations to your words. Your use of *scam* to mean "subterfuge" or "deception" may differ from their meaning for the word. Older audience members may experience noise if you talk too quickly or too softly. In written documents, poor formats, as well as grammar, punctuation, or spelling errors, can produce signal-distorting noise.

The source of the signal may itself be a form of interference and influence. A signal sent from the boss to the secretary—"Let's keep this area a bit neater"—may be heard as a distinctly different message when compared to the same words spoken by the janitor. Some communication theorists emphasize the role of the social setting in the signals we send. We don't usually send new thoughts that don't relate to anything the receiver already knows. If we do, the receiver probably won't understand our message. For example, if you attended a calculus class without ever having studied algebra or geometry, the teacher's messages would be 100 percent new—and 100 percent incomprehensible.

Effective communicators don't really send 100 percent new information. Rather, they use words to jog and massage patterns of meaning already in process within the minds of their listeners. Usually, these meaning patterns help in understanding the message. Sometimes, they create noise that interferes with the message. The boss's message, for example, is interpreted by the secretary through the influential noise of associations and feelings regarding the boss, most of which help the secretary to understand what he means by "this area" and "neater," but some of which may interfere with the reception of the boss's message.

These forms of noise that are internal to the receiver are called "filters." In 1979, Werner Severin and James Tankard suggested that messages have trouble "getting through," due to a series of conscious and subconscious **filters.** Filters can distort a message. For example, the *exposure filter* allows message receivers to ignore all aspects of a message except those they want to hear. Receivers literally don't expose themselves to messages they don't want. For example, managers have been known to "bury their heads in the sand," reading only those reports and evaluations supportive of their efforts. Other, more negative documents are dismissed.

Similarly, the *perceptive filter* picks and chooses the material to notice from the material to which the receiver has been exposed. That is, the receiver is *exposed* to the information but doesn't *perceive* it. In business introductions, for example, some people pick up some insignificant detail about a person's life (a smudge on his or her jacket, perhaps, from changing a flat tire) while hardly perceiving information that could be much more important, such as the person's name and company affiliation.

Finally, a message receiver can filter out aspects of a message by means of the *retention filter.* That is, even if the information is *perceived*, it may not be *retained* in memory: Does the message feel good? If so, remember it. Does it hurt? If so, forget it.

To Severin and Tankard's list can be added other filters: *the experience filter* (have I experienced what the message is talking about?), *the personal filter* (is the message about me in some direct way?), *the age/sex/race/religion filter* (does a message come from "that" sort of person?), and so forth. No matter what the list, the point for the communicator is clear: Powerful psychological forces operate to distort the message we intend to send. Knowing what these filters are can be a first step in planning our messages so that they can't be filtered beyond recognition.

Clearly, the process of communication can be hindered by various kinds of "noise" and by the presence or absence of conducive social contexts and bases of shared knowledge. We send out a configuration of thoughts for our audience to compare with similar thoughts

Dean Harrison Edwards at Midwestern University thought he had a happy faculty. The three or four cronies he ate with regularly seemed supportive of his efforts. In fact, the faculty was on the verge of mutiny over a number of issues including delayed salary increases, class cancellations, and tenure denials. Faculty "filters," therefore, were especially active as professors read the following memo from Dean Edwards:

> In my position as Dean of this university, it gives me deep pleasure to announce the Visiting Scholars Lecture Series. Four established and respected experts will present lecture/discussion sessions in the fields of computer science, literature, history, and art. Representatives from our faculty will serve as university hosts for these scholars.

The Dean was dumbfounded to learn that his faculty had decided to boycott the lecture series, calling his memo "insulting."

What aroused the faculty filters to pick out of this memo for emphasis:

1. *"In my position as Dean . . . it gives me great pleasure . . ."* He's patting himself on the back again. Who cares what gives him pleasure?
2. *". . . established and respected experts."* He's as much as saying that none of us are established and respected!
3. *". . . in the fields of computer science, literature, history, and art."* How expected that the Dean should choose the fields of his cronies!
4. *". . . faculty representatives will serve . . ."* Notice that he doesn't ask us—he tells us what we'll do. The guests are called "scholars" while we're just "representatives."

If we wish to place blame for this communication disaster, the faculty certainly could be more charitable in its interpretation of the memo. However, the primary responsibility probably falls upon the Dean—a leader who failed to consider the presence and activity of powerful filters that distorted the message he meant to send.

The point: It is not enough to mean well in sending a message. We must design messages well to counter the effects of powerful and often subconscious filters active in our readers and hearers.

already brewing in their own minds. *Understanding* is not really the reception of new signals and resultant new thoughts: instead, we sense a likeness as our internal thoughts come into harmony with the pattern of thoughts suggested by the signals coming to us. We usually indicate this harmony through such phrases as "I'm with you" and "I understand" (literally in its Old English root, I "stand among" your ideas).

How Can You Find Out Whether I Understand You?

In 1949, Norbert Wiener described the concept of "feedback." The act of communication, Wiener argued, isn't a one-way delivery of goods from speaker to hearer. Instead, true communication takes the form of a loop. The speaker delivers a message to the hearer, who in turn interprets the message and, by word or expression, sends **feedback** to the speaker. If the communication continues, the speaker uses the feedback received to adapt any new messages. The feedback, for example, may have communicated, "I think you're being devious and snobbish"—in which case the speaker can choose to be more direct and common.

Feedback does not wait for obvious pauses in a speech. An audience flashes signs of understanding, approval, disapproval, curiosity, frustration, pleasure, and so forth on a second-by-second basis. Wiener calls this form of feedback "immediate" and credits good

If you've told them once, you've told them ten times—and you're getting angry. As manager at Efton Shipping, you insist on one-hour lunch breaks for your employees. You've posted a general memo, in fact, demanding "compliance with company procedures regarding punctuality." Some workers have gotten the message, but others, particularly the bunch down on the loading platform, don't seem to understand you.

Notice in this example how "noise" may be interfering with the signal carrying your message. The "semantic noise" of difficult vocabulary and the "channel noise" of the posted memo make it harder for some receivers to get your message. At the same time, consider the mindset of your workers. How would you redesign your message if you considered it not as a "new thought" but as a partner to meanings already present in their minds? Perhaps you could make more sense talking about how all workers in the company depend on one another—hence the importance of getting back from lunch on time. The message can still be strong in tone, but its method of development will no doubt change.

The point: Oral and written signals do not produce automatic responses in human receivers. The process of making meaning is not the same as physically moving new thoughts into the mind of the receiver.

communicators with the ability to respond to it almost unconsciously. A presenter at a business meeting, for example, watches the eyes, faces, and physical gestures of his or her audience. Feedback in the form of sleepy eyes and drumming fingers can tell the speaker to speak more forcefully, or perhaps to add an interesting story or a visual aid.

In this regard, eye contact with an audience is crucial. Of course such attention makes the audience feel that you are talking *to* them, not *at* them. Just as important, eye contact keeps open the feedback channel. The audience can tell you in subtle and not-so-subtle ways whether they are enjoying your speech. Key feedback indicators are physical posture (watch for the "deadman's slump"), active hands (scratching, drumming, flexing), averted eyes, and of course yawns and physical stretching. Experienced communicators do not interpret such signs as negative criticism; rather, they are efforts by the audience to share in the communication. Members of the audience are signaling you to take action that will make communication more successful. By adjusting your content and delivery to such cues, you will give your audience the pleasure of genuinely sharing with you in the communication.

In many communication situations, feedback arrives too late to make on-the-spot adjustments. In the case of a business letter, for example, you may not know for days or weeks—or perhaps will never know—whether the letter found or missed its mark. For Wiener, this often-overlooked form of feedback is called "delayed feedback." We often ignore it, unfortunately, because we feel that communication has ceased when our voices cease or the letter or report has been drawn up and delivered.

To ignore delayed feedback is to miss an opportunity to learn and improve as communicators. Some writers and speakers take a proactive approach to delayed feedback by concluding their documents and presentations with a sincere invitation for comments and questions from the audience. In the case of a report, the writer can phone readers to hear suggestions and comments. Some writers attach a brief "opinion check" or questionnaire to important proposals and reports. Readers like to feel that their opinions matter and that they have a way to make their opinions known. Similarly, speakers can offer to stay for a few minutes of informal conversation after an address. These gestures remind the audience that true communication involves work on everyone's part—no one sits back as an uncommitted spectator.

How Can You Communicate to Meet Your Audience's Needs?

Feedback from your audience (receiver[s]) gives you valuable clues for figuring out how to meet your audience's needs. Feedback isn't always available when you need it, though. For example, before you speak, and whenever you write, you have no immediate feedback to use as your guide to your audience's needs. How can you figure out your audience's communication needs when you don't have feedback?

There are as many different assortments of audience needs as there are people who receive communication. What's more, each of us has different needs at different times and in different situations. Who could possibly hope to meet the diverse needs of audiences?

Fortunately, you do not have to meet—or even address—all of the needs of your listeners or readers. You have only to target a few key needs that your audience has for your particular information. For example, if your information is about a new software program for the accounting department, you don't need to know about your audience's family, health, and private needs. You need only know their needs regarding the work they do with the accounting department. However, if you are describing a change in the company

---

A BUSINESS APPLICATION

Gwendolyn Pontelli continued to lead an important fashion design house at the age of 72. Once a month, she met with her 18 unit managers; the meeting usually began with Gwendolyn's 20- to 30-minute overview of agenda items.

Over the past several months, Gwendolyn felt her notorious blood pressure rising over these presentations. Certainly, her employees were polite during the speech. "Just beef on the rack," Gwendolyn complained to her secretary. "They all sit there letting me do all the work."

Gwendolyn tried a bold experiment. In the middle of her next overview presentation, without changing her tone of voice, she repeated the same sentence again and again:

- Button prices, of course, seem to rise each summer.
- Button prices, of course, seem to rise each summer.
- Button prices, of course, seem to rise each summer.
- Button prices, of course, seem to rise each summer.

- Button prices, of course, seem to rise each summer.

No one in the group looked up or gave a glance of special interest after the second repetition of the sentence. After third and fourth repetitions, some of the brightest managers looked at her quizzically—but well over half absent-mindedly went on with their doodling and daydreaming. Not until the fifth repetition of the sentence did she have every eye solidly, though curiously, on her.

"Now," she said, "let's reach an understanding. At 72, I'm up here working hard to communicate with you. By the way you sit, the way you nod, the way you look at me, I want you to work hard, too. Make decisions about what I'm saying. Send me your reactions in your faces and eyes. If you don't communicate with me, I'll go my own way. If you do communicate while I'm up here speaking, there's a good chance I'll go *our* way."

The point: Feedback completes the communication act by letting the message sender know whether the message got through and how it was received. That information lets the message sender plan for the next stage of communication.

A BUSINESS APPLICATION	You direct credit services for a large furniture company. For the past year, you've argued that the

company's collection letters are sadly out of step with the times. Finally, the company president has given you the go-ahead to draft better letters for review by top management. As you plan the letters, you find yourself thinking less and less about what you want to say ("pay up!") and more and more about what your overdue accounts are thinking and feeling.

Most of your debtors, you conclude, expect a bitter or angry letter from you. They've let you down, but what do they need to hear? How can that need be used to your advantage? Gradually the letters take shape. Top management reviews them and congratulates you on your shrewd psychological insight and your persuasive rhetoric. You shrug off the compliment: "Really I didn't write the letters—they did." Some of the managers understand what you mean. Only a few need your explanation that the needs of your overdue accounts dictated the words in the letters. You focused on the "you" in communication rather than the "I."

Six months later, you are able to show management a 36% increase in collections due to the new series of letters.

The point: Speakers and writers can count on the presence of certain basic needs in any audience. Messages can be structured to fulfill those needs—the art of rhetoric—and in so doing win the support and approval of the audience.

health plan, you may very well need to know about their family and health information, but you don't have to know about their software needs.

Figuring out how to communicate in ways that meet the needs of your audience is not revolutionary—it's not even somewhat new. In fact, since the heyday of ancient Greece, communicators have been successfully doing just that. The Greeks developed **rhetoric** (a method of expression calculated to get an intended response from the audience) to help communicators figure out how to meet audience needs so that the audience would welcome what the communicators had to say.

Greek schools of rhetoric drilled students in hundreds of specific ways to produce emotional and rational responses in their hearers. In our century, we do not train writers and speakers in such precise rhetorical modes. Instead, we discuss general persuasional strategies in the hope that students can develop a personal rhetoric that is both effective and sincere. Chapter 7 ("Persuasive Letters") describes specific ways in which to tailor your communication to your receivers' needs.

What Stops You from Communicating to Me?

Just as the receiver's filters and other noise may keep messages from getting into the receiver, sometimes the speaker has difficulty getting messages out. The barriers to outgoing messages are **censors.** The message that finally comes out of a communicator's mouth or pen sometimes differs in important ways from the message he or she intended to express.

What forces take a message in its free-formed internal state and censor it for public consumption? Some psychologists suggest that we each carry around parentlike judges inside. When we begin to speak or write, these voices shout, "Wait! Is that a safe move? Have you accidentally revealed how dumb you really are? Have you opened the door to questions you can't answer?" These critical voices make us think about our statements again and again before actually speaking or writing. We try it this way and that. Ironically, we sometimes have to create crisis moments (such as the night before a deadline) to quiet the internal censors enough to get a few thoughts onto paper.

No wonder we often feel awkward about the words that we write and speak. As with many things, the solution is easier to say than to do. Don't try to be someone you're not, and don't mentally beat yourself because you're not perfect. Don't let internal censors make you uncomfortable because you fall short of some mythical standard of excellence.

At some point, every speaker and writer should give himself or herself permission to simply *be*. The real you can speak out, for better or for worse. Almost without exception, the experience proves for the better, not for the worse. We all respond to someone's straightforward, open effort to communicate. We are far less critical of slips and hesitancies than most speakers imagine. What counts most is a communicator's best effort to touch us with his or her thoughts and, in turn, to be influenced by ours.

How Does the Medium Affect the Message?

Earlier centuries viewed messages as words carried to the audience by conveyor belts of various sorts: speech, writing, song, and so forth. The message, notably, was thought to be *carried on* the conveyor belt or medium, not *part of* it. To improve your message-sending in those days, you would be told to study words themselves—how they are spelled and joined together into sentences (hence, the emphasis on traditional grammar study in past years).

With a famous rallying cry—"the medium *is* the message"—Marshall McLuhan led a group of theorists who changed our ideas about the perception of messages. For McLuhan, the medium by which the words are conveyed participates in the creation of meaning, along with the words for the recipient. For example, McLuhan points to the vast difference in a message created by a dot-matrix printout as compared to one that has been typeset. Judge the differences for yourself:

> Barclay Jewelers proudly announces the opening of its Western Hills branch. This new addition to the Barclay family will specialize in diamond, sapphire, and emerald creations for both men and women.

> Barclay Jewelers proudly announces the opening of its Western Hills branch. This new addition to the Barclay family will specialize in diamond, sapphire, and emerald creations for both men and women.

At first glance, we're tempted to say "both sets of words communicate the same message." Do they? Which set of words would you send out to customers if you were president of Barclay Jewelers? The typeset version's words communicate all that you mean by "proudly" and "diamond" and "creations." In contrast, the printout version actually detracts from such words, as if to say that the sender is not proud enough to put these words in an attractive medium. McLuhan's point is that words have different meanings when they appear in different media: Words together with their medium create the eventual message communicated.

You have many media to choose from. For letters and reports, you must choose what kind of paper to use, such as linen stationery or crisp, bond paper. You choose a suitable printer, preferably a letter-quality or laser printer. You set wide or narrow margins. You decide how much white space to use on the page, and how to distribute it effectively.

A
BUSINESS
APPLICATION

Sharon Montoya directs the Dealer Sales Team for a major automobile manufacturer. Each month Sharon publishes the "Dealer Update," a bulletin/newsletter informing dealers of special policies and programs authorized by the manufacturer. This month, Sharon has special news for her dealers: They will receive free automatic transmissions on all cars ordered from the factory during the month of December. The factory has authorized this special program as a Christmas bonus to dealers to help stimulate Christmas buying.

Sharon writes copy for the "Dealer Update" but isn't happy with the impact of the words. She adds a few exclamation marks and boxes the whole story with a bold line. Still, the words seem rather pale, considering the special nature of the factory offer. In this case, Sharon's words alone cannot create the whole message she wants to send to dealers. She must change the medium. Then the words, together with the new medium, may have a better chance of scoring a sales success.

Sharon contacts a local printer and has 1000 formal announcements printed—the sort that are sent out for weddings and formal parties. Sharon sends one to each dealer and is thrilled to hear soon that orders are pouring in. Words that could easily have been overlooked in the medium of the monthly newsletter created a powerful message when set in the medium of a special announcement.

The point: Words alone do not create messages. Words always appear in the context of a medium of some sort; together with that medium, words make messages. By choosing both your words and your medium with care and insight, you can communicate the whole message you intended to send.

In the case of speeches, you determine a suitable length. You incorporate visual aids. You decide how to dress, where to stand, how to move, and when to pause. In all these ways, you surround your words with a medium of one kind or another. The message you send is a blend of the words and the medium. Your readers and hearers usually are not aware that the meaning they are perceiving is created by far more than your words. However, you, as a communicator, must be aware of this fact. This awareness gives you more tools at your disposal to communicate ideas effectively.

How Does Technology Affect Business Communication?

The talking machine has been the focus of adoration through most of the twentieth century. Thomas Edison began the love affair with the radio and phonograph. Later came the television, tape recorder, and video cassette recorder. It was almost as if another human being were inside the box talking to us—almost, that is, because we could not interact with the voices and images coming from the first talking machines. Jackie Gleason and the Honeymooners would not answer back when we spoke to them.

Computers changed this one-way communication channel. Though the first computers did not speak or show pictures, they had one key advantage over the radio and television: We could enter our own directions and comments into the computer and be "heard." The machine would change its course of action based on our input.

By the late 1970s, the voice chip, an electronic circuit that can generate the sounds of the human voice, was on the market. Now the computer could begin to speak to us, much as a radio did, but with a great difference. No human being had ever prerecorded the sounds coming from the voice chip. They were generated afresh from the building blocks of language itself—ideas, words, grammar, sentences.

By the late 1980s, more-advanced computers were providing ways for us to speak to the computer by voice instead of by fingers on a keyboard. We were coming closer to the dream spawned by Edison—a machine that talked as we talked, and responded intelligently to our speaking. Existing computers—even the most advanced prototypes—can't do this.

However, that possibility is now coming close to reality. Computer scientists and linguists working in the field generally known as "artificial intelligence" are perfecting incredibly complex programs that allow computers to "process"—in effect, deal with in a reasonable way—the language as it is commonly spoken (hence the term *natural language processing*). The development of artificial intelligence has gone hand-in-hand with dramatic improvements in the computer's memory capacity. For effective processing of language, the computer must have almost immediate access to a staggering amount of information: the words of English, including the various shades of meaning created by different contexts. (For example, consider the different meanings of "hold" in these sentences: "Hold my hand" vs. "Hold my order.")

At the same time, the computer must contain information on how words join together in English to form sentences and paragraphs—a system called the "grammar" of the language. This systematic description of English (in effect, a recipe book) is an enormous undertaking and now occupies the day-to-day efforts of thousands of computer theoreticians, designers, programmers, and linguists around the world. At this time, no complete machine version of English grammar has been completed. In the near future, though, computers will begin to sound human. They will process information in a way that is close to what we mean by *thinking*.

We have taken time in this chapter to discuss the matter of machine communication because, of all developments in contemporary communication theory, it now occupies the greatest amount of scholarly attention and seems to offer promise of substantial advances in theory and application. In addition, the prospect of not just a talking machine but also a thinking machine must give every business communicator a chill half of excitement and half of foreboding. From the dawn of human civilization, words have been the primary bond between people. Soon—have you checked today's mail?—we will receive letters generated entirely by machine. Not long after, we will communicate orally, by phone or in person, with machines programmed to handle routine matters of business. You may have already heard the use of voice-chip computers in the telephone company's "Information" service. After that, who knows? Will we be interviewed by computers for employment positions? Will we find ourselves doing final polish work on reports and proposals generated by computers? Will we cease to "believe" in language altogether when so much of what we receive comes from an unfeeling machine?

These questions are no longer the stuff of science fiction. Visit your local computer store or read a current computer magazine to see how fast the world of tomorrow's communicating machines is coming toward us all.

This chapter hasn't completely answered all eight of the questions posed at the beginning of the chapter. Unfortunately, though the rest of the book offers additional answers, and researchers continue to study these questions in greater depth, complete answers simply aren't available now or in the foreseeable future. In fact, some of the answers you'll count on most will come from your own careful and thoughtful observations and analyses.

The next section may help you to fine-tune your observational skills as you notice your own communications, as well as the other communications that surround you.

A BUSINESS APPLICATION

Bud Jenkins has received a request from an important client for information in his company's "Utility Economiser" device, a machine that monitors utility use in large buildings for maximum efficiency.

Jenkins speaks to the computer occupying a small cabinet in his office. "We need to explain to Nathan Financial Associates how the Economiser can save them money. Enter the information they've sent about their headquarters building. Generate a report, with action steps for their approval. Explain on a nontechnical level the major components of the Economiser system. Let's keep it to within eight pages. Try to hit about a tenth-grade reading level, with illustrations where you think they're appropriate. I want to pick up my copy from the laser printer in ten minutes. If it looks OK, you can send a copy to the Nathan people immediately by electronic mail."

The ability to carry out this command may be years in the future for business computers—but not as many years as we might guess. At the University of California Irvine, the Navy is developing a computer system to "understand" and summarize reports received from nuclear submarines. Programs such as *RightWriter* and *Grammatik* demonstrate ways in which the computer can quickly check our writing for correctness in some areas of spelling and grammar.

The point: The future of business communication is intimately bound up with technological change. We can expect an ever-more-rapid increase in chip-driven changes to the ways we communicate. Such changes will require all business communicators to adapt old skills to new uses and new devices.

COMMUNICATION PATTERNS WITHIN AN ORGANIZATION

In some time/motion studies, employees wear chalk-laden booties so that their habitual "trails" in the workplace can be traced. Words that pass within a company cannot be "chalked," but patterns are nonetheless noticeable in any business environment. We explore the most common of these patterns so that you can learn to recognize the communication patterns within your organization, and use them to your advantage.

Structured Versus Unstructured Patterns

Communication patterns are either structured or unstructured. Examples of **structured communication** include the company newsletter, the weekly meeting for midlevel managers, and the annual stockholders' meeting. **Unstructured communication** includes the grapevine by which rumors spread through the workforce, the after-hour chat between employees, and the water-cooler conversations.

Structured Communication

You can learn to recognize and assess structured forms of communication within a company by certain clues. Structured communication is usually

1. Recorded or documented in some form. This may include printed copies of a newsletter, the written minutes of a meeting, and the printed agenda for a conference.

2. Less subject to change than unstructured communication. The messages in a newsletter, for example, are usually fixed in a way that a chat over coffee is not.

3. More widely known and more easily accessed. Structured communications such as quarterly financial reports are visible to a broad public and open to scrutiny. Private conversations, on the other hand, are generally unknown and unremarked on by other employees—and certainly cannot be accessed without eavesdropping.

Unstructured Communication

Though less fixed as to time and place, unstructured communication is just as important as structured communication to the effective functioning of a business. Notice these three characteristics about unstructured communication.

1. Dependent upon personal emotional factors. For example, John and Frank both receive a structured communication such as a company memo whether they like one another or not, but their conversation over a cup of coffee depends almost entirely on their attitudes toward one another.

2. More flexible and open-ended than structured communication. Conversations tend to raise questions and express attitudes and feelings more than to pose arguments and answers.

3. More personalized than structured communication. Most memos, newsletters, reports, and speeches for a general audience are necessarily couched in general terms. However, unstructured communication can change the message to suit individual interests and attitudes. The rumor of an impending layoff based on seniority, for example, can be told in very different ways to Jan Fernandez, a long-term company vice-president, and to Bill Victors, an employee hired just last month.

Communication Insights

Channels of communication are sometimes the chess board on which organizational games are played. These kinds of exercises undermine the effectiveness of the manager. But it does pay to be sensitive to the needs of various people within the organization . . . who would get copies of a particular memo, or when it's the right time to place an important phone call.

The Effective Manager DELTAK, Inc.

Of all the forms of unstructured communication within a company, one of the most useful—and potentially most destructive—is the company grapevine. Somehow, good news never gets better, but bad news always gets worse when it travels along the grapevine. Inevitably, each hearer adds his or her own prejudices or anxieties to the rumor before passing it along. Motives are attributed, often without cause, to the decision-maker involved in the news.

Learn to involve yourself in the company grapevine for positive ends. The grapevine exists, after all, because people without knowledge in a company are people without power. You can use this perfectly understandable need to know to build team spirit and mutual trust rather than crippling suspicion and jealousy. Here are three concrete suggestions for nurturing a fruitful grapevine:

1. Make sure, in your own involvement with the grapevine, that you make contact in several different places. If you are a midlevel manager, for example, don't restrict your casual knowledge of what others say to the bits and pieces you hear from other midlevel managers. Find interesting associates at other levels in the company.

2. Make time (don't just wait for a convenient time) to tune in to the grapevine. In the same way that you block out time for reading important structured communications such as reports and letters, set aside time for regular contact with key people in the company grapevine. These contacts need not, and probably should not, be scheduled as formal meetings of any sort. Instead, mark your calendar with likely times to find your key people at coffee or relaxing after work.

3. Participate in the grapevine in a natural way. Don't lecture or spy. The grapevine grows through trust and mutual need. It will not include you if you openly stand on a soap box or take notes on opinions being expressed. Take your lead from others in the grapevine, and be yourself. Both the information you get and the influence you exert will be richer for your effort.

Communication Patterns

The following diagrams apply primarily to structured communication patterns within business, though several also can be found in unstructured communication settings.

The Barbell

In this pattern, both partners to the communication depend on the other's confidence. Typically, neither wants to stand alone and isolated, so each relies heavily on the communication partner. When involved in a *barbell* pattern of communication, recognize the importance of discretion, confidence, and trust.

The Triangle

Three people or work units joined in a triangle pattern face the challenge of dealing with different points of view without making any one party to the triangle feel left out. Communication triangles work well in an atmosphere of mutual trust. You can recognize the breakdown of communication triangles when they begin to take this shape:

The Broken Triangle

In this case, two of the parties have severed communication. With time, they may also sever connection with the one party they have in common. Usually, it is difficult to remain the one trusted associate of two enemies.

The Pyramid

In pyramidal communications, one party usually assumes the top leadership role. In some cases, this party generates or obtains much of the information received by the group. In other cases, the leader acts as a clearinghouse and distribution point for information to be shared among members.

The Series

A chain of linked parties presents the challenge familiar in the party game called "Gossip," "Telephone," or "Rumor, rumor." In the game, one person whispers a sentence or two to the next person, who then passes it on down the chain. By the time it gets to the last person in line, the message has usually changed—often with hilarious results.

If linked chains of communication are necessary in your business structure, keep the chains as short as possible. One way to shorten the chain of command is to have direct contact with parties farther down the line. Many executives, for example, make it a regular practice to hold open office hours on Friday afternoons, a time when anyone can stop by for a business-related chat.

The Circle

This pattern helps to avoid the distortions possible from communication chains. The message is sent around the circle, but eventually finds its way back to the initiator. He or she can then alter the message, if necessary, or start a new one on its way around the circle.

Hub and Spokes

This pattern combines aspects of the pyramid—the hub resembles the peak of the pyramid—and the circle. The leader initiates a message that is then disseminated throughout the business group. At any point, however, individual parties can respond directly to the leader (feedback) or to one another.

Legs

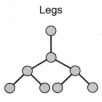

In this organizational communication pattern, messages are communicated through levels of responsibility to more and more workers. The legs pattern has distinct advantages. It frees the time of the central decision-maker: he or she need only explain the message once, instead of many times to many parties. The pattern also puts midlevel managers in a position of authority over the workers entrusted to them. These managers have important knowledge to dispense and are therefore seen as important figures by the workers they supervise. The legs pattern also promotes credibility in company messages as long as the employees consider the immediate supervisor a credible figure. "I wouldn't have believed it," a worker may say, "but I heard it from my own supervisor."

The legs pattern, when misused, can isolate company leaders from important feedback from lower levels within the company. Especially if the first or second tier of control is populated by "yes" men and women, executives at the top may find themselves disastrously out of step with the workforce.

The Crossfire

Freedom is the key word for this pattern. Members can speak freely to anyone in the group. The pattern works especially well for a brainstorming session, in which the goal of the meeting is to get a broad range of ideas out on the table. The pattern has the danger, of course, of leading to communication chaos. In business environments where an agenda and leadership responsibility are crucial, use the crossfire pattern only for brief periods.

UPWARD, DOWNWARD, AND LATERAL COMMUNICATION

Each of the preceding patterns, when translated into actual business contexts, could be described in terms of direction. Were lower-level employees talking to upper-level employees? Were employees on the same level talking to each other? The direction of communication becomes important insofar as it reminds us of possibilities and pitfalls.

Upward Communication

Possibilities:

- Allows upper-level managers to keep informed of concrete progress and problems regarding company projects.
- Gives lower-level employees the chance to participate in the decision-making process in the company

Pitfalls:

- Can cut heavily into a chief executive's time, especially when many parties demand time to express a variety of viewpoints
- Can involve upper-level managers in petty decisions that should be handled at a lower level of decision making

Downward Communication

Possibilities:

- Comes naturally because communication to less-empowered individuals in the company is nonthreatening to those in control
- Builds a sense of team spirit and mutual dependence through shared knowledge

Pitfalls:

- May lead to a sense of expectation on the part of lower-level employees to be informed of all company matters, however sensitive
- Can devolve into a command structure in which bosses send down orders to lower employees; communication may cease as these employees grow increasingly resentful of their powerless positions

Lateral Communication

Possibilities:

- Helps to create social bonds between employees—a powerful force in preventing turnover and disruptive behavior
- Builds credibility for company messages because they are heard from an employee's equal rather than from an upper-level manager, who might be seen as having ulterior motives

Pitfalls:

- Sets the stage for mutinous groupings of workers
- May be used to isolate certain individuals or classes of workers who are purposely excluded from lateral communication by their peers

You don't have to wait for your first day in your new business career to observe the fascinating working of upward, downward, and lateral communication. Watch for these communication directions in your everyday experiences. Do people put on different personalities as they speak upward, downward, or in a lateral direction? Does their use of language change? Do they choose different media for communicating in different directions? Pursue these questions in your own observations and speculations. The answers you discover will help you use upward, downward, and lateral communication to your business advantage.

TEN BARRIERS TO COMMUNICATION

Finally, we consider specific obstacles to communicating in business. Volumes could be written on each of the obstacles treated briefly here. For our purposes, it is enough to recognize that the obstacles exist and to suggest a few ways to overcome them.

1. Physical Barriers

After we have given a substantial amount of work to a speech or business document, we have the inevitable tendency to feel that the world "owes" us polite attention. Not so. The members of our audience are under bombardment by several physical forces that can ruin our effort to communicate. Such physical barriers relate to time, to the audience's physical environment and physical comfort and needs, and to the physical medium of communication.

Time, for example, puts pressure on each individual with whom we wish to communicate. For example, say that I have prepared a 20-page report. Do you (or others in my audience) have time to read so many pages? In the case of a speech, do you have time to hear me out?

Environmental conditions such as heat, cold, noise, and drafts can subvert communication. Environmental engineers working for major television studios find that they can control the mood of a studio audience by manipulating the thermostat. A chilly room will often lead to a hostile group; a warm room produces a lethargic, unresponsive audience.

In written documents, physical barriers include the amount of print bunched together on a page. Must the reader's eye find its way through a page-long paragraph? Fuzzy or irregular type can cast an unprofessional look over a document, posing yet another physical barrier to conveying your message.

2. Cultural Barriers

An entire chapter in this text is devoted to the barriers that can exist between cultures. Recognize, however, that communication can also break down between subcultures and the dominant culture. For example, the Old Money Club may list among its members the industrial magnates of a particular region. How will they receive a financial presentation from a nonmember, perhaps a young upstart just out of business school? Learn to assess the cultural barriers that you must overcome to communicate with a social group to which you do not belong.

3. Experiential Barriers

Whenever we present new information to a group, we're tempted simply to spill out the new information with the unspoken advice, "Trust me—I've been there." Unfortunately, the members of our audience are seldom so willing or gullible. They have trouble believing what they have not seen for themselves. Therefore, whenever you plan to take people on a mental journey beyond the limits of their own experience, relate your new material to something the audience has experienced. The astrophysicist Carl Sagan, for example, regularly won over nontechnical audiences by such descriptions as the "fried-egg" shape of our galaxy. We've seen a fried egg and can relate to Sagan's communication.

4. Perceptual Barriers

Be aware that your audience may be filtering out major portions of your communication, as discussed earlier in this chapter. At the same time, recognize that individual audience

FIGURE 2–1   **Perceptual Barriers**

members may be seeing other meanings than you intend. What, for example, do you see in Figure 2–1? Might another viewer just as certainly see something different in the same figure? (*Hint:* if you saw a young woman with her head turned away from you, try to see the profile of an old beak-nosed woman—or vice versa.)

In the same way, your audience may draw conclusions that you did not intend. Whenever possible, let another person preview a communication you want to send on its way to a larger group. Your reviewer can help you spot areas where unintended conclusions can be drawn by your eventual audience.

5. Motivational Barriers

Your audience may simply not want to be set into motion by your communication. Once they do begin to move with your thoughts, they may need help to keep going. This mental inertia is increasingly common among hassled businessmen and -women. "Just give me some peace and quiet!" they seem to plead by their postures and facial expressions. You can use many of the motivational devices suggested in this text (in the various writing and speaking chapters) to wake up and motivate an uninterested audience.

6. Emotional Barriers

Business situations rarely are able to entirely avoid the personal element. People's feelings get hurt. On a more positive note, people also develop strong emotional attachments. When you send messages to people with strong negative or positive emotions, you cannot expect the message to sail undisturbed through the heavy emotional weather. Often, your best alternative will be to face up to the presence of strong feelings early in the message—and then to proceed with communication. For example, a letter to a disgruntled client might well deal first with his or her anger:

You have expressed your disappointment with this company. I'm writing in an effort to mend fences with a client we respect and want to serve.

7. Organizational Barriers

Business practices, such as projects, are scheduled in distinct stages. Construction projects happen according to a carefully organized scenario of trades.

Be forewarned that your communication, no matter how well constructed, can fall flat if it is not synchronized with the organizational schedule in the minds of the audience. A typical example is an impassioned speech at a business meeting—a speech that earns only the reply, "That's well and good, George, but we're past that point."

You can test the organizational timeliness of a communication with the *Need Test:* Simply ask yourself, "Does my intended audience know they need the message I intend to bring them?" If the answer is "no," you must first convince them that they need your message. If the answer is "yes," design your messages to address as closely as possible the need they perceive.

8. Linguistic Barriers

This is not a compliment: "I didn't understand much of what he said, but it was an excellent speech." Effective communicators do not use vocabulary and sentence structures beyond the limits of their audiences. Language is neither a hammer with which to beat your audience nor a mirror in which to admire your own intelligence. Use words to create mental windows through which you and your audience can see your message clearly.

9. Nonverbal Barriers

As discussed in the text's chapters on speaking skills, your nonverbal gestures can create serious barriers to be overcome by your words. Sagging posture can undo the effect of the most enthusiastic words, telling the audience "I don't really feel or believe what I'm saying." Lack of eye contact communicates embarrassment or insecurity over the words you are saying. These and other nonverbal signals are discussed in detail in other chapters.

10. Competition Barriers

Your audience seldom is "captive" to you alone. Members can choose other activities, some more exciting, perhaps, or less work than the communication activity you propose. Your long business letter, for example, may arrive in someone's daily mail along with the monthly issue of a favorite magazine, a pressing bill, and several short business letters. No matter how persuasive your words, your letter may not even be opened for several days—because of competition for the reader's attention. Remember, your words have to fight for attention. Use attractive, readable formats and energetic, eye-catching beginnings to place your communication ahead of the competition.

COMMUNICATION ARCHITECTURE

Based on our discussion of communication principles, practices, patterns, and barriers, what practical conclusions can a manager draw for establishing a successful communication architecture in his or her organization? Will a monthly company magazine for employees be more useful than a weekly newsletter? Should the CEO send regular "talking head" videotapes of his or her opinions to each work unit for viewing? Should interdepartmental meetings be held, and if so, how often? What can be done to ease the crush of e-mail messages taking up so much time for employees? How can voice mail be scanned quickly to sort out urgent messages from less important matters? The answers to such questions vary, depending on a company's culture, mission, and resources. But these and similar questions are *worth asking* in the difficult but enormously productive process of designing a communication architecture for the organization. Although the details of such architecture are necessarily different from company to company, at least five architectural components appear in virtually all successful corporate communication plans:

- *Need-based Communication Planning*   Who needs to talk to whom in the organization? Why? What barriers stand in the way of their present efforts to communicate?

- *Sufficient Bandwidth*   What quantity and quality of communication can various channels carry within the organization? Can marketing use electronic means to send full-color mockups of new advertising materials to other divisions, or must hand delivery still be used? Can a collaborative writing team in several locales do their work efficiently by means of groupware, or must they travel to a central location for in-person work sessions? Can the CEO get a message out to all company employees through existing audiovisual channels, or must the old system of memos and bulletins be used?

- *Scalability and Convertibility of Communication Media*   At times of company crisis or sudden opportunity, can various types and channels of communication be quickly expanded to reach all stakeholders, including customers, regulatory agencies, television and radio representatives, and others? Can the standard company press release, for example, be quickly converted to a video news release beamed by satellite to news agencies and business television and radio throughout the world? Can an already overloaded e-mail system sustain a period of company crisis, where urgent messages must not be caught up in electronic bottlenecks?

- *Sensing Systems*   Like seismic sensors placed in earthquake-prone locales, systems of information-gathering can be developed to predict and prevent the ground from shaking in organizations. These include liaison individuals whose job duties include regular and candid communication of "what the rank and file are saying" to upper management. Sensing mechanisms can be as formal as a regular questionnaire soliciting employee opinion on company developments or as informal as Sam Walton's famous Friday afternoon barbecues to get to know his Wal-Mart employees.

- *Monitoring and Maintenance of Communication Channels*   Skilled communicators in the organization must be given the task (and rewarded accordingly) of looking after the health and planned growth of communication channels in the organization. Installing suggestion boxes, for example, is an empty gesture if employees doubt that their contributed ideas influence management or are even read. Even the most attractive in-house magazine fails as a communication channel if workers consider it the "voice of management" and are suspicious of its motives and content.

SUMMARY

At the beginning of this chapter, we asked three questions: (1) What is a skilled communicator? (2) What does a skilled communicator do? (3) How can you become a skilled communicator?

Now that we've explored what communication is and how communication works, we can begin to answer these questions. *Communication* means "making common" your thoughts and feelings with your audience and receiving the response of your audience to your thoughts and feelings. Skilled communicators do this well.

That is, *skilled communicators* are able to transmit (send) their information to the intended receiver so that the receiver understands the information. To do this, they are aware of each aspect of communication: (1) the *information source* (the idea or message they want to communicate), (2) the *signal* (the stream of words or images they use to send the message), (3) the *transmittal* (the sending of the message), (4) the *channel* (the medium in which they send the message), and (5) the *destination* or *receiver* of the message.

Once highly skilled communicators identify a message (#1) to be communicated, they usually focus on the receiver's (audience's) needs (#5) and work backwards from there. That is, first, they notice the audience's needs, as well as filters and background noise that might interfere with communication. Next, they choose a medium or channel of communication (#4) that will be understood by the audience and that will also effectively convey their message.

Skilled communicators also think carefully about transmitting the information (#3), and they find ways to avoid or minimize the many barriers to communication. Finally, they carefully choose the words and images (#2) they'll use for their message, always keeping in mind the specific audience to whom they're communicating.

Skilled communicators think about the answers to eight key questions about communication:

1. Can words describe everything we see, feel, and know about our experiences?
2. When you say a word, does it mean the same thing to you that it means to your listener?
3. What keeps us from hearing and understanding one another?
4. How can you find out whether I understand what you tell me?
5. How should your listeners' (or readers') needs affect what you say (or write)?
6. What keeps us from communicating information to one another?
7. How does the *medium of communication* (such as a telephone, telegram, thank-you card, or billboard) affect the message being communicated?
8. How does technology affect communication? Do we communicate to it, with it, or through it?

You can become a highly skilled communicator by doing what skilled communicators do: Constantly observe the communication going on around you. Notice structured and unstructured patterns of communication and the ways in which each pattern (barbell, triangle, pyramid, series, circle, hub and spokes, legs, and crossfire) works best. Observe the communication flow in each pattern: lateral, upward, or downward. Notice the barriers to communication: physical, cultural, experiential, perceptual, motivational, emotional, organizational, linguistic, nonverbal, and competition. Find ways to overcome—or at least minimize—these barriers.

QUESTIONS FOR DISCUSSION

1. Define *communication*. What qualities do true communicators possess?

2. How might knowing a theory of communication help you to be an effective communicator?

3. Is language always adequate for our needs, or are there times when words simply can't express our thoughts? Explain your answer.

4. What is the difference between *denotative* and *connotative* meanings?

5. What are some effective ways to overcome *noise* in business communication?

6. What role does *feedback* play in determining your communication strategies?

7. Why is it helpful to maintain eye contact with your audience?

8. Why do speakers and writers censor themselves? What is the best way to overcome excessive self-censoring?

9. How do listeners and readers filter messages? How can you construct effective messages that can penetrate these filters?

10. Do you agree with Marshall McLuhan that "the medium *is* the message"? How does the communication affect the message?

11. What are the various features of structured and unstructured communications?

12. How can you nurture a fruitful company grapevine?

13. Make a list of communication patterns, dividing the list into two columns; the efficient patterns versus the inefficient patterns. Is there any pattern which might be correctly listed in both the "efficient" and "inefficient" columns? What pitfalls might users of this pattern encounter, and how can these pitfalls be overcome?

EXERCISES

1. Before you must write or speak, listen carefully to internal censors telling you what *not* to say or write. Where did those censors come from? Are they a help, a hindrance, or both? Write responses to these questions, illustrating your points with details and examples.

2. Visually represent the grapevine among your acquaintances or fellow workers. Discuss in writing the speed, accuracy, and motives of the grapevine.

3. List the various forms of feedback you receive during a typical day. Which influence your actions the most? Why?

4. Think about a familiar person or object—perhaps someone or something in your home or workplace. Describe the person or object verbally to a friend. Now do the same thing in a letter to your friend. Compare the two descriptions. How did your strategies change? Which description was more effective, and why?

5. "The medium *is* the message." Compare two advertisements for the same product—perhaps a billboard and a television or radio commercial. In what ways have the marketers of this product adapted their message to each medium?

6. Play the rumor game. See whether it's true that a message changes substance drastically when carried by word of mouth. Choose a somewhat complex piece of information, and involve as many "rumor-mongers" in the game as possible. Record your findings.

7. "What unique qualities do you possess which you feel distinguish you from your peers?" Practice answering this question by writing a personal biography. Imagine that you are writing it for a prospective employer. Do you feel compelled to censor yourself? How can you overcome self-censorship and yet present yourself in the best possible light?

8. Sometimes, an organizational arrangement can itself become a barrier to communication. Describe in writing any organizational barriers to communication that you perceive at your workplace, school, or other organizational setting. Go on to suggest ways in which such barriers can be reduced or eliminated.

9. Assume that you supervise ten other employees in an insurance company. On what occasions would you use the crossfire pattern of communication with your workers? On what occasions would that pattern be inappropriate? Explain your answers in writing to these questions.

10. In XYZ Insurance group, the company president sends a long (six to eight pages) memo each week to each employee. Evaluate in writing the pros and cons of this downward arrangement. Following your evaluation, suggest other forms of downward communication that involve fewer drawbacks.

11. Consider how lateral communication occurs among your colleagues. Describe in writing the process by which messages on important topics get communicated to everyone. Discuss potential problems with this process, including the spread of misinformation and the distortion of truth as it passes from person to person.

12. Many companies prefer that employees communicate upward only through channels of the company hierarchy. An entry-level employee, for example, would be advised to speak with his or her supervisor before communicating directly with senior management. Evaluate in writing the reasons for this preference. Include in your evaluation both the advantages and disadvantages of restricting upward communication to hierarchical channels.

INTERNET ASSIGNMENT

You are a mid-level manager in a computer firm that, in the past four years, has grown from a "garage" operation with eight employees to a publicly traded firm with more than 2000 employees. Unfortunately, communication channels and links among employees have not kept pace with the explosive growth of the company. You are asked by senior management to explore communication design options for increasing company efficiency and profitability. You decide to begin your research by investigating Internet resources (many listed in the Communication Theory section and the Organizational Communication section of the Internet Guide). After exploring these resources, draw together your thoughts in a relatively short document (2 to 5 pages) describing several options the company should consider in improving its internal and external communication channels.

CHAPTER 3

Guidelines for
Management Writing

Even experienced business communicators sometimes fall prey to the "inspiration fallacy"—that is, the belief that wonderful ideas for a business document will come at last to those who wait . . . and wait . . . to the last minute before beginning to write. Such procrastination is a habit well rehearsed through college years, when major writing tasks were often accomplished (or at least attempted) in the late night hours the day before the assignment was due.

Few other occupations allow such brinksmanship. Contractors and architects, for example, develop elaborate site plans, renderings, and blueprints before a single shovel of dirt is turned for the foundation of a new building. Before takeoff, pilots file detailed flight plans and think through all weather conditions and other factors affecting their flight. Lawyers prepare well-researched briefs before going to trial or meeting with adversaries. Teachers work out lecture notes and lesson plans before stepping in front of their classes.

Managers who want to write well must also *focus on planning* as the essential first step for any writing project. When managers don't plan, the result is Writer's Block—those agonizing minutes or hours when words simply won't "flow," usually because the planning process is missing in action.

To avoid such problems, carefully plan (preferably, in writing, but at least mentally) what you'll write. In your plan, you should consider five questions related to five key aspects of writing:

1. Purpose—What are you trying to communicate?
2. Audience—To whom are you writing?
3. Exploration—What ideas should you consider?
4. Patterns and Outlines—How can you best arrange your ideas?
5. Details and Examples—How can you support your points?

This chapter examines each of these questions.

PURPOSE: WHAT ARE YOU TRYING TO COMMUNICATE?

Moving targets are hard to hit with arrows or words, and nonexistent targets can't be hit at all. Therefore, be sure to decide on your target or purpose *before* taking aim with your words, sentences, and paragraphs.

This notion may seem little more than common sense—but, as Will Rogers liked to point out, "common sense just isn't very common." In general terms, your purposes will probably fall within one of the purpose circles shown in Figure 3–1. You'll notice that the circles overlap, suggesting that you can certainly have more than one purpose in a document or speech.

Decide at the outset of any communication task which of these purposes you wish to fulfill. The following communication checkpoint should help you figure out your purpose for communicating.

**Communication
Checkpoint**
*Understanding Your
Purpose*

1. Why are you communicating?
2. What do others expect you to accomplish with this communication?
3. What do you expect to accomplish?
4. What do you want your audience to know after your communication?
5. What do you want your audience to feel after your communication?
6. What do you want your audience to do after your communication?
7. What situation, circumstance, attitude, or event will be affected by your communication? In what ways?
8. What people, other than those in your audience, will be affected by your communication? How?
9. How does your short-range purpose in this communication differ from your long-range purpose?
10. Will this communication serve more than one purpose? Specify the various goals you want to achieve.

AUDIENCE: TO WHOM ARE YOU WRITING?

When we write friendly messages to people who like us, we usually have no difficulty writing the message. On the other hand, when we want to complain, to give bad news, or to say almost anything to someone who doesn't want to hear our message, it's much harder

**FIGURE 3–1   Purposes of
                Communication**

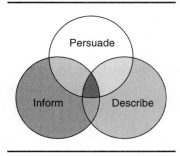

to figure out what and how to say the message. If we believe that the reader is hostile to us or to our message, we agonize over what and how to write the message.

For example, when you wrote in high school, you probably struggled to write term papers for any teachers who criticized everything you wrote. In contrast, wasn't it easy to write notes to your friends during class time?

Imagining Your Audience

Unfortunately, not all of your business writing will involve communicating with your personal friends. You can't count on your business readers to be as eager to hear what you have to say as your high school chums were. In fact, business writers must often write to a hostile audience. Frankly, some of your readers may even want to find as much fault as possible in what you write. For instance, you may have to say "no" to Raymond K. Beasley (who is outraged over the loud engine noise produced by your product, the Grasswizard, and wants a full refund after using it for six months). You may have to draft a termination letter for Grace Cotton, who is furious over an evaluation that documented her low productivity.

At these times, words are hard to find. Writing begins, then stops, then starts again only to reach a dead end. We all stall on these occasions because our minds drift away from what we want to say toward how our audience will react to our words. When writing to hostile or negative readers, take a moment to think through their feelings. This process may be described as "taking aim." The way to do this is described in the next subsection, "Analyzing Your Audience."

Next, turn your energies toward your purpose as a writer. Send a message as effectively as you can. Don't endlessly worry about each frown, grimace, and sneer that a negative reader *might* show when reading what you write.

Most audiences, of course, aren't either friends or enemies. Most readers are neutral toward you: interested if you interest them, bored if you bore them. Nonetheless, even neutral readers can prove intimidating. If you imagine writing to a blank-faced reader, you may very well feel your whole mind go blank. How do you write for faceless, emotionless, and unpredictable readers?

When you must write to unknown (faceless) readers, recall how easy it was to write to friends. As you wrote, you could almost see their smiles as they read the news and warmth in your notes.

Just as you imagined the faces of your friends, you can give the blank faces of a neutral audience whatever faces you would prefer to see—and why not the faces of friends? When you imagine that your readers are your friends, you relax. In every way, the language that springs from you in that mood is more natural, more vivid, and more persuasive than writing born of hesitation, fear, and doubt.

In the following two letters, notice the drastic change in tone, all because the writer chose to be friends with a neutral audience.

(The circumstances: Frank Wirten prepares to open a tire store in a new community. Unsure of how to express himself to people he has never met, he writes a stiff and nervous promotional letter to the community.)

Our market analysis demonstrated that the northern suburbs of Seattle lacked a full-service tire store. We have decided to open such a store at 41120 N.E. 88th St. We are prepared to handle general tire problems, as well as specialized needs such as alignment, spin balancing, and chassis adjustment.

Note Frank's choice of language. He clearly feels distance from his audience. He doesn't sound friendly because he doesn't know how they feel about him. In part to shield himself against their disapproval, he chooses formal language—"analysis" and "demonstrated"—and defensive arguments. He doesn't risk showing enthusiasm toward his new store or his prospective customers.

Notice the crucial change in the letter when Frank takes a new attitude toward his readers. He decides to look at his readers as friends:

> The northern suburbs of Seattle have deserved a full-time tire store for years. Friends, we've arrived! Visit us at 41120 N.E. 88th St. just to say "hello" and to look us over. We'll take pride in providing you with the best tire at the best price. Alignment, balancing, and chassis work? Right up our alley. We look forward to meeting you. At Wirten Tire, we're new neighbors, but good neighbors.

This revision might seem too schmaltzy for you and your readers. For Frank, however, this friendly version of his promotional letter came as a vast relief after his efforts to write a stiff and formal letter.

To sum up, your perception of your audience (whether hostile, neutral, or friendly) influences your ability to write with ease. *You* control those perceptions. No audience holds you captive to an unproductive set of mental images. Instead of picturing threatening audiences, real or imagined, substitute the faces of friends.

Analyzing Your Audience

After making this initial, crucial attitude adjustment, you must consider other aspects of your audience. Most of your considerations will stem from common sense and not a memorized list in this text or another. Nonetheless, the following checkpoint may help you think about your audience in ways that help you communicate effectively.

One way to describe this analysis of your audience is to call it a "market analysis"—which is exactly what it is. You are analyzing your audience as a market for your message. Once you have analyzed your market, you are ready to design your "product." That is, you are ready to tailor your message to your audience. Just as a manufacturer must design a product before deciding how to package the product, you must design your message (that is, your ideas) before you can design your idea package (that is, the words and phrases you'll use).

Communication Checkpoint
Analyzing Audience

1. Who is your primary audience? (the first people to read or hear your message)
2. Who is your secondary audience, if any? (a group such as senior management, which may also read or hear about your message)
3. Is your audience made up of similar individuals or groups of distinctly different individuals?
4. How big is your audience? How will audience size influence the channel and pattern of communication you choose?
5. What does your audience know about you?
6. How can you increase your credibility with your audience?
7. What do you already know about your audience?
8. What do you need to learn about the background or previous experiences of your audience to help you communicate your message effectively?

9. Based on how you answered Questions 7 and 8, what does your audience already know about your message topic?
10. What do you think your audience should know about your topic?
11. What more does your audience want to know about your topic?
12. In what ways will your readers demonstrate that they have understood your message? How can you plan for such feedback?
13. How will the situation, circumstances, time, or place influence the way your audience receives your message?
14. What do you want your audience to do with the information you provide?

EXPLORATION: WHAT IDEAS SHOULD YOU CONSIDER?

Once you have determined the purpose of your message and you have analyzed your audience, you are ready to design your message for your audience. This means that you must come up with the ideas that communicate your message to your audience. There are two phases of the idea-design process: (1) **exploration** (finding and creating ideas), and (2) **selection** and **organization** (choosing and ordering ideas in a way that makes them easy

---

A BUSINESS APPLICATION

How does a business writer assess his or her audience? We asked two experienced writers, and summarize their responses here:

Shirley Housholder is an account executive for a large midwestern stock brokerage. She had just completed a prospect letter to be mailed to 5000 potential clients.

To tell the truth, I prepared to write by sitting down and paging through my present accounts. I asked myself, "What kind of people are these? What do they want for themselves? What do they want from me?" I suppose I thought along those lines for 10 or 15 minutes. Looking back, those were probably the most valuable minutes I spent on the whole letter. The writing got easier when I convinced myself that I was writing to real people.

Roman Chavez is a loan officer at a Dallas savings and loan. Roman had the responsibility of writing a quarterly report for the Board of Directors on an uncomfortable subject: bad or shaky loans made by the bank.

Our loan record was generally good—but, yes, there were some rotten apples. I had never met any of the members of the Board of Directors for the bank, though I had seen them in the bank from time to time. At first I kept starting the report, then tearing it up, starting over again and again. I couldn't forget that old saying, "They kill the messenger who brings the bad news." It came to a crisis one night about midnight. I had paper strewn all over the kitchen table at home and was nearly berserk over my inability to write a decent report. I knew how, but the words just wouldn't come out.

My wife helped me. She said, "Look, these people on the Board aren't ogres. They're probably just like me—willing to understand. Write the report to me, Roman, and see what happens."

I did just that. The writing came quickly because I didn't have to con anyone. I just told both sides of the story—our many loan successes and the few failures. I did my best to show how we could avoid the failures in the future.

The report went over big. I got a phone call from the Chairman of the Board thanking me. She asked me to handle a couple other writing tasks. I think it's a good sign.

to understand). It may seem trivial to say that this involves two phases, but if you try to do both things at once, you may not do either one well.

In this section, we discuss the exploration phase of designing your message. We call this the "exploration phase" because for most writers, getting ideas involves an expedition of sorts. Unfortunately, ideas rarely present themselves in a top-down, A, B, C order. Instead, they arrive like cards in gin rummy—all in a jumble awaiting some final sorting and ordering.

Resist the temptation to reject ideas or to impose final order on them too early in your idea-design process. Let a wide variety of ideas come to you—mixed up, sideways, upside down, in any form. The relatively simple task of arranging ideas can be done later. For now, open yourself to the possibilities.

Business writers particularly must guard against the temptation to lock in ideas prematurely. The competitive nature of business life pressures business writers to sound *definite* in all pronouncements. Too often, business writers respond to such pressure by putting aside valuable competing ideas so that their writing can sound simple and certain.

For example, consider what single-minded obsession produces in business writing. This memo, in two versions, comes from a laboratory supervisor in a large chemical corporation.

> This laboratory pursues pure research, not applications of known results. Our work has been hindered in the past year by demands for applications by other divisions within the company.

The supervisor wrote this memo while obsessed with a single idea: His lab is for pure research only. However, he wisely decided to let the memo sit for a day before sending it to his superiors. This practice often leads to improved messages. Two competing ideas came to mind:

1. He had to admit that the demands made by other divisions gave two of his less productive workers something to do.
2. One of the demands, though irksome at the time, led to a new and exciting route of inquiry among his pure researchers.

The supervisor, aware of the danger of single-idea thinking and writing, revised his memo.

> This laboratory's mission and primary contribution lie in pure research. As time and personnel allocations permit, we welcome inquiries and requests for assistance from other divisions within the company.

Good business communicators distinguish themselves by their ability, from the very beginning of a writing project, to escape the tempting traps of single ideas.

Idea Circle

One useful way in which to generate ideas is to use an **idea circle.** Here's how this idea generator works. Whenever you seek a variety of ideas on a topic, simply write the topic on a sheet of paper accompanied by an "idea circle." Figure 3–2 illustrates an idea circle with eight wedges, but the number of slices you draw is entirely up to you.

FIGURE 3–2   Idea Circle

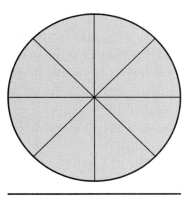

As ideas occur to you, fill in the slices of the pie. Notice that the circular arrangement of the slices allows each idea to exert equal weight as we mull over which pattern of ideas makes the best sense.

Figure 3–3 represents an idea circle for marketing vinylized paint; it illustrates how the mind can freely mix the topics in various orders in search of the best marketing approach. In the advertisement that actually grew out of this set of ideas, notice how the copywriter saw her central theme in the idea circle:

> Brighten up the kids' room this Saturday with the rainbow colors of Vinyl-Brite. This one-coat, lead-free, all-purpose interior paint lasts for years. Handprints wipe off with a sponge. Worried about that painting mess? No problem—Vinyl-Brite rolls on, and cleans up with water. Hurry! It's on sale now for $9.99 a gallon!

FIGURE 3–3   An Idea Circle of Marketing Ideas for Vinyl-Brite Paint

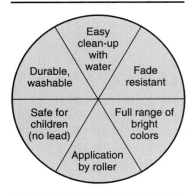

The Classic Questions

There are times, alas, when the idea circle sits empty on the page before you. On such occasions, practice the technique perfected by Greek orators—the classic questions—presented here in adapted and modernized form.

Mentally fill in the blank in each question with your topic. Ask the question aloud, if possible. The odds are high that most of the questions will produce usable ideas for your business writing.

1. Why do I/others even care about _____?
2. If I had to divide _____ into parts or stages, what would they be?
3. What forces/circumstances led to _____?
4. What kind of person is interested in _____?
5. If _____ did not exist, how would things be different?
6. What aspect of _____ do I (or would my readers) like best? Least?
7. What larger movement, field, or situation provides background for _____?
8. What are the principal benefits of _____?
9. If _____ fails or is ignored, what barriers were to blame?
10. How could _____ be explained to a 10-year-old child?

Don't feel that you must answer every question thoroughly. Don't laboriously work our prose answers. Rather, use the questions as mental prods to get your mind moving and your ideas flowing.

As ideas come to you, jot them down within an idea circle. The entire process may take no more than four or five minutes. Certainly that investment of time is preferable to staring at a blank sheet of paper waiting for inspiration. The classic questions claim to deliver inspiration by the installment plan.

Consider the idea circle on profit-sharing plans, shown in Figure 3–4. For convenient reference, the number of each classic question appears next to each idea. Notice that some questions didn't pan out at all. That's fine. The classic questions are intended only to suggest some possibilities. At times, several questions will not apply directly to a given topic, yet these questions may lead to your own questions, which do give you ideas for your message.

In addition to idea circles and the classic questions, another way to explore ideas is to use computer software that has been designed to help you with this process. Usually, this idea-processing software is used with other software, such as word processors or software generally known as "outliners." This outlining software might help you with the next phase of designing your message: organizing your ideas.

PATTERNS AND OUTLINES: HOW CAN YOU BEST ARRANGE YOUR IDEAS?

In the last decades of the eighteenth century, businessmen and -women served their culture as inventors of technological devices—all the buzzing, whirring, pumping, ticking machines that made up the Industrial Revolution. In the last decades of this century, businesspeople must increasingly invent ways in which to use that technology to create and communicate meaningful information.

FIGURE 3–4 Idea Circle for a Profit-Sharing Plan

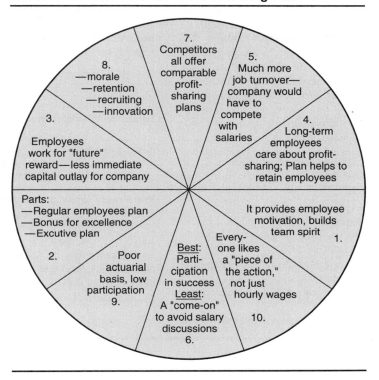

Data banks and high-speed information retrieval techniques already make it possible to call up most of human knowledge on almost any topic. In business, information access through such massive data banks as Dialogue and ERIC gets less expensive in time and money each year. Such developments bring problems and challenges for communicators: Surrounded by stacks of computer printouts, someone has to make *meaning* out of the data. Someone has to formulate and organize ideas.

How to Organize Ideas

When faced with chaos—usually on fanfold computer paper—and asked to develop an idea, we must find a silver thread that runs through the chaos, to bind it together in an orderly, understandable way.

A large part of the art of good business writing lies in finding (or inventing) the right pattern to make sense out of the data at hand. These patterns can be simple commonsense frameworks for thinking. While these patterns may seem natural and obvious, we certainly complain when they are absent: "This report rambles," or "This letter just doesn't say anything."

In your business career, you are often handed chaos in a basket. No colleague or writing instructor is present in the wings to whisper, "Psst! Here's an organizing pattern to use . . ." Acquaint yourself with the following 16 common organizational patterns or

> ### A BUSINESS APPLICATION
>
> At Remson Office Supply Wholesale, for example, Personnel Manager Ron Chavallo was given chaos in a basket by a corporate vice-president. "Ron, we've had an unusual run of resignations in the past six months—twelve in production, six in accounting, and three among supervisory staff. Here are all the exit interview records. Work up a report for the Board on the 'whys.' O.K.?"
>
> Ron Chavallo jotted down an organizational listing for himself—
>
> My Goal: to explain the unusual frequency of resignations.
>
> 1. Needs: What data do I want?
> 2. Resources: Are the data available? Where?
> 3. Input: Read all available data
> 4. Evaluation: Locate common factors and themes among resignations
> 5. Organization: Order my points with appropriate evidence
> 6. Presentation: Write the report in an effective way
>
> For now, let's look specifically at Ron's handling of Points 4 and 5 on his list: Evaluation and organization. As Ron read the exit interviews, he organized reasons for resignation according to a pattern.
>
> | | |
> |---|---|
> | *The Most Common Reason* | Cost of living in this region is too high in relation to salary |
> | *Significant Minority Reason* | Poor chance for advancement |
> | *Isolated Reasons* | Return to school, spouse's relocation, illness |
>
> We already know where Ron got his evidence—from the exit interview records—but where did he get his organizing pattern? From his own understanding of the data.
>
> The point: The crucial pattern came from Ron's own thinking, not from the data. He imposed his orderly pattern on the data. His pattern fit the data and did justice to its complexity.

"skeletons of thought." Used with judgment, they can provide useful frameworks for shaping the meaningful structure of a memo, letter, or report.

Sixteen Patterns of Organization

Each example for the following patterns appears in paragraph form. In addition, you can use the same patterns to organize longer messages. Naturally, you should feel free to change these patterns (or to invent new ones) according to the audience, situation, and purpose at hand. Like good recipes, these patterns suggest a way—but not the only way—to combine ingredients in a meaningful and successful way.

When using the patterns to organize sentences into paragraphs, use each step in the pattern as one or more sentences in your paragraph. (Examples of such paragraphs are provided for each pattern.)

To organize paragraphs into longer documents, you can use steps in the patterns to form topic sentences in consecutive paragraphs. (A topic sentence is usually followed by related sentences that explain, clarify, qualify, or give examples of the topic sentence.) In the time pattern, for example, the first step, "In the past," could become this topic sentence: "From 1992 to 1998, Lloyd Industries faced a continuing series of setbacks in its efforts to modernize telephone communications."

In very long documents, you can use each step in a pattern as a major heading in a report, proposal, or extended memo or letter. (Major headings are typically followed by paragraphs explaining and exemplifying the major heading.) In the space pattern, for example, the "Far away" step could become this heading: "I. Foreign Markets for Laser Disks."

The Time Pattern
In the past
At present
In the future

Example (from an annual report)
In the past, we supplied local retailers with prescription pharmaceutical articles. At present, we have expanded our line to include toiletries. In the future, we want to break into the over-the-counter pharmaceutical sales.

The Space Pattern
Far away (at a
   considerable distance)
Close at hand
Right here

Example (from a sales letter)
For busy brokers in Trent, time means money, especially in choosing an escrow company. Twenty miles north in Atlanta are the old-name escrow firms. Closer at hand, but still twenty minutes by freeway, are their sattelite branches, offering limited services However, beginning January 1, Jenson Escrow is pleased to open a full-service escrow office right here in Trent.

Cause
Situation A caused
   event B
Event B can be
   described as
Event B can be
   undone/repeated/
   furthered by

Example (from a claims letter)
Misdirections in the instruction manual to accompany my Starflite Moped caused an expensive mishap. Because you neglected to specify that oil had to be mixed in with gasoline for the moped, I had to pay $182 to have a frozen engine repaired. Please send me reimbursement in that amount. May I also suggest that you issue an amended copy of the Starflite instruction manual.

Emotion
Once I felt
Things changed
Now I feel

Example (from a resignation letter)
As a new engineer here at CLT in the 1990s, I felt that my work would earn me respect and financial rewards. However, twice in the past three years, I have been passed over for raises. Therefore, I resign effective December 20.

Logic
All A situations have B
   characteristics
C is an A situation
Therefore C has B

Example (from a memo)
All new accounts feel hesitancy as new hands take over the books. Our latest new account, Winston Lumber, is no different. We must try to be sensitive to Mr. Winston's initial hesitancy to show all his financial dealings forthrightly.

Relative Significance
What matters most
What must also be
   considered
What we can safely
   ignore

Example (from a letter of recommendation)
Above all else, Janice Jobren can *sell*, as demonstrated by her stellar track record in wholesale hardware since 1992. She has also distinguished herself as an accurate record-keeper and field supervisor. The fact that she has little formal education interferes in no way with her productivity.

Hidden Significance

A has obvious
  characteristics
A also has seemingly
  insignificant
  characteristic
Why this seemingly
  insignificant
  characteristic is
  important

Example (from an internal personnel memo)

Certainly Mr. Lance Nash presents himself in an assured,
groomed, and socially comfortable way. I noted, however,
his passing remark that his college grades were always
"right up there." His transcripts reveal only a "C" average.
This slip, I think, cuts deep into my favorable impression
of Mr. Neal as a candidate for head teller at the bank.

Perspectives

One way to look at
  the topic
A second way to view it
Finally, a third
  revealing view

Examples (from a proposal)

We all agree that L&M Auto needs more exposure. The
sales staff recommends a freeway sign. Our advertising
consultant favors a flyer tucked in with the daily newspaper. The approach outlined here takes a new tack: a
huge hot air balloon tethered to the roof of our dealership.

Doubt

Others say that A
  will happen
We doubt that A
  will happen
Here's why

Example (from a real estate sales letter)

They're singing the old lament again: Housing prices are
bound to fall, so wait to buy. At Merton Realty, we just
don't believe it. We point out that land, materials, and labor
costs continue to rise at 13 percent or more per year. A
better buy next year? Don't bet your money on it.

Contrast

A is not like B
A has _____, but B
  has _____
Only A has _____

Example (from a relocation report)

Seattle differs from L.A. in several ways. In Seattle,
commercial office space rents for 35 cents per square foot;
in L.A., comparable property rents for 60 cents per square
foot. Only Seattle offers clean air, reasonable housing
costs, and all the rain you'll ever wish for.

Comparison

Both A and B
  have _____
Neither A nor B
  has _____
Only A has _____

Example (from the same relocation report)

Both Seattle and Spokane have a variety of commercial
banks. Neither has a regional stock exchange. Seattle,
however, does offer an international airport and harbor.

Reputation

A is reputed to
  have _____
In actuality, A does
  (does not)
  have _____
A's reputation is
  deserved/must
  be adjusted

Example (from a consumer report)

A new pain reliever, Loado, claims to provide four potent
painkillers in addition to common aspirin. Our laboratory
analysis reveals only the presence of inert dyes in addition
to aspirin. Loado offers more hype than common aspirin,
but not more pharmaceutical power.

Variety
Item A comes in these
  sizes/shapes/aspects
  1., 2., 3.

Example (from a health club promotional letter)
Beauty comes in different forms: first, the irrepressible natural glow of the teen; next, the warmth and fire of young adulthood; and finally, the cultured radiance of maturity.

Opinions
Some people say
Others claim
But most will admit

Example (from a sale report)
Some of my clients feel that it is a mistake to restock inventory during the next quarter. Others claim that prices will fall still lower in the coming months. However, most will admit that all retailers will have to make major purchases before the traditional fall surge.

Preference
We see the merits of A
We also recognize
  the merits of B
But we prefer C
  (because)

Example (from a Grants Committee report)
We admire the fine work done by Dr. Merrick's team at Mayo Clinic. We also have the highest respect for M.I.T.'s computer simulation of inheritable diseases. We chose, however, to award the 1998 Research Grant to Boston Hospital's heart team for its advanced work in cardiology.

Likelihood
A is possible
B is likely
But C is certain

Example (from a reply to an order)
While truck express may be able to deliver your parts by April 4, a somewhat later date is more likely. However, air express could guarantee delivery in time for your assembly deadline.

Communication Checkpoint
Three Ways to Use Organizing Patterns

1. How do these patterns suggest logical, coherent ways for you to organize sentences into paragraphs, paragraphs into pages or sections, and sections into larger documents?
2. How can you use these patterns to link consecutive paragraphs with logical transitions?
3. How can you use these patterns to create logically ordered headings in long documents?

These brief patterns help to create order out of chaos. They serve as reminders, too, that every well-written document has a basic and easily stated chain of argument or "pattern" at its heart.

To sum up: when you have successfully filled an idea circle with ideas, find or invent a pattern to organize the ideas in a straightforward way. Next, write down your pattern of ideas as a rough working outline.

Outlines

Almost all professional business writers use some sort of outline early in the writing process. However, these outlines don't necessarily follow the strict I, II, III, A, B, C order that you were taught in school (illustrated later in this section). Business writers' outlines are more like a rough working framework, which allows the writer (you) to put the ideas and idea patterns into some logical sequence.

Why Should You Outline?

Although patterns of organization provide the essential backbone for business documents, they don't have enough meat on their bones to guide you through long paragraphs of writing. When you're in a rush to write something (which is usually the case in business), you may be tempted to skip writing an outline in your haste. Don't yield to temptation.

Without an outline, you may waste valuable time staring at a half-started document, wondering "What on earth do I say next?" Worse yet, you may come to the end of your rough draft and realize, "This doesn't make any sense." At that point, you'll be stuck trying to rearrange sentences, to cut and paste paragraphs, and to make some order—an outline—out of the text you've scrawled. After frantic reshuffling and finally figuring out an outline for your document, you'll have to rewrite all your transitions and all your logical steps, to fit your new order.

Like builders following a blueprint, writers need clear outlines to write efficiently. When points on an outline are expanded to full or even partial sentences, much of the hard work of drafting is already over. The major phrases you've written in your outline grow into headings and topic sentences in the first draft. By filling in details, examples, definitions, and explanations, you quickly build an organized, coherent first draft.

How Might You Outline?

Once you decide on a master pattern for your ideas (your own pattern or one of the patterns listed in this chapter), you are ready to create your outline. Most writers figure out their own personal systems for outlining. If you use idea-processing software—or even just word-processing software—to organize your ideas into patterns, the software may offer ways to help you develop an effective outline. Also, whether writing with a computer or a pen, you might find that the following system, which you may have learned in school, helps you. (Notice that the ideas at each level are vertically lined up with the other ideas at the same level.)

Master Pattern
> Topic: Changes in How We Communicate

Past
> I. Fastest forms of communication over longer distances survived slower forms
>> A. The natural world
>>> 1. Carrier pigeons vs. human runner
>>> 2. Visual signals (smoke, etc.) vs. voice
>> B. The technological world
>>> 1. Telegraph vs. pony express
>>> 2. Telephone vs. telegraph

Present
> II. New fast modes now compete with familiar slower modes
>> A. What we send and receive
>>> 1. Word processing vs. typing
>>> 2. Computer modem vs. traditional mail

B. What we store and retrieve
    1. Computer memory vs. file drawers
    2. Database vs. booklike directors

Future

III. More speed lies ahead, with inevitable changes in how we communicate
  A. How messages are generated
    1. Artificial intelligence devices that help us find appropriate words
    2. Model documents stored in computer for our use
  B. How messages are transmitted
    1. Satellite networks for worldwide communication
    2. Speech-driven computers to free us from the keyboard

This sample outline may not reflect your precise outlining habits. You may find it helpful to put down more or fewer words. The point is this: find a personal outline method and *use it* to guarantee orderly, logical thought development in your speeches and written documents.

If you are using a computer to create your outline, you'll find it easy to move ideas around and to add and subtract ideas and idea patterns. If you don't have a computer, however, another way to do this is to use large (4″ × 6″ or 5″ or 7″) index cards for each idea and then to spread out the cards on a large surface (a table or even a floor), gradually moving them into the general order of your outline. Once you have found the general order that you like, you can pick up the index cards in the correct sequence. If you want to, for each index card with an idea, you can create another set of index cards to fill in the smaller ideas that support that big idea. You can add as many cards as you need to make your outline as detailed as you need it to be. (In fact, you can use the index cards for filling in supporting details and examples.)

DETAILS AND EXAMPLES: HOW CAN YOU SUPPORT YOUR POINTS?

Once your outline states your major and supporting points clearly, begin to develop what I call the "hidden persuaders" in business speaking and writing—the actual details, examples, and stories that give life and substance to your claims.

Three Roles of Details and Examples

Details and examples play three important roles in business writing:

1. To provide information
2. To *verify* (show the truth of) an assertion
3. To *illustrate* (give an example of) an *abstraction* (an idea, concept, or principle)

Inform

A trip report to a major client's office includes precise details of who visited whom, when, where, and what was said. These details and examples are provided in the memo or report to supply data for future planning. The goal of the writer is to give an instant snapshot of sorts, recording as many of the key details of the meeting as possible for later review and assessment.

Verify an Assertion

Abstract propositions such as "hard work pays off" must rely on evidence for their truth value. True, we do not always require the writer to supply actual proof. As a general rule, in fact, we require less proof from those we like and trust than from those we dislike and distrust. Often, however, business writing must substantiate its assertions by demonstrating, through detail and example, the concrete reality supporting the abstract statement or idea. For example, I now assert that at Jackson Engineering, "hard work pays off." In order to decide which examples to provide as proof, I must resolve two questions:

- What do I mean by "hard work"?
- What do I mean by "pays off"?

In this example, I decided that "hard work" means working at least 20 hours overtime per month for the past year. I determined that "pays off" means receiving a 14 percent pay raise.

I'm now prepared to develop an appropriate example to prove my assertion.

At Jackson Engineering, hard work pays off. (Example:) Thirty-one of our ninety engineers worked at least twenty hours overtime per month for the last year. All thirty-one men and women received a 14 percent pay raise in recognition of their commitment to the company and its goals.

Notice that I have not really proven that "hard work [always] pays off," but merely that hard work (by my definition) pays off at Jackson Engineering. Note also that I've fudged a bit: I have actually demonstrated that hard work has paid off (in the past) at Jackson Engineering. However, my original assertion—"At Jackson Engineering, hard work pays off"—not so subtly suggests that present and future hard work will meet with the same reward as that received by the 31 engineers.

In business writing, you must distinguish between true proof and what may be called overclaim. This is important to you both as a reader and as a writer. For example, Can you spot the logical overclaim in each of these advertisements?

If Brighto can clean this brat's clothes, it can certainly get your wash spring fresh and super clean.

More than 100 dentists of those surveyed found Stiki-sweet perfectly safe for children's teeth. (Note: 4532 dentists were surveyed.)

You can trust your home to General Insurance. Our local agent, Mark Tiers, pitched in to rebuild the Boys' Club in Lincoln, Nebraska, when the building was lost to fire last summer.

While business writing doesn't usually bother to formally prove each and every one of its assertions, it cannot afford blatant overclaim. No reader likes being led down the path of half-truths and hype. When you feel your details and examples may be misunderstood as overclaim, insert a qualifying remark (underlined here):

> Morgan Trust protects your money. <u>While our money market accounts are uninsured</u>, our passbook savings accounts are backed by FSLIC insurance for up to $100,000.

Your qualification prevents people from making the easy assumption that all accounts at your bank are insured to $100,000. A qualification maintains your integrity and credibility by pointing out that your example is not to be taken as universal proof.

Illustrate an Abstraction

Often, business writers want to show that abstract thoughts and propositions actually work on common, day-to-day situations and materials. Consider the following principle, followed by an illustration:

> Relatively small towns usually can supply a wide variety of talented personnel. [Illustration:] When our drilling project began in Marysville last year, we were able to hire all our secretarial help, half of our laborers, and more than one third of our white-collar staff from among the townspeople.

Notice that the example does not prove that a labor supply exists in most small towns. At best, the example merely illustrates or supports the assertion. Business writers often use illustration in this way to create the *impression* of proof without having to take the time and effort to provide actual proof. To formally prove the writer's assertion, many small towns in the nation would have to be reviewed in an effort to statistically measure their ability to provide a talented labor pool—clearly a prohibitive task.

The writer has chosen to trade on *trust*, not *fact*, with the reader. We are willing to accept illustration in place of formal proof whenever the writer has established credibility by his or her credentials and/or common sense. If we doubt the writer's integrity or acumen, we often refuse to allow illustration to stand in place of proof. Consider the following bit of bluster:

> The employees in this company have no sense of loyalty. Last week, Jack Friedkin quit without giving even a week's notice.

We find ourselves protesting that one employee's quick departure has no relation to general employee loyalty. We refuse to take this illustration as proof.

Readers appreciate frequent details and examples in your business writing just as they love pictures in a book. Even an elegant chain of abstract assertions gets hard to follow without frequent concrete examples. Whoever we are, we understand and trust the physical world of flower pots, crying babies, bicycle tires, and burnt toast. That's where we live. If a business writer wants to "sell us" on the reality of his or her arguments, these propositions have to seem real in the way a flat tire is real.

Four Ways to Persuade Readers to Believe Your Message

In at least four ways, good business writers manage to persuade us that their details and examples have the ring of real life. Good details and examples are (1) specific, (2) clearly understandable, (3) brief, and (4) focused.

Specific

Notice how each vague detail in the following example gains strength when transformed to a specific detail.

VAGUE | Some classic automobiles have risen steeply in price in recent years.

SPECIFIC | Such auto classics as the gull-winged Mercedes, the MGTD, and the Porsche Speedster have risen 400 percent in real dollar value since 1965.

Part of our pleasure in reading specific details lies in the mental images they produce. "Gull-winged" and "Speedster" certainly evoke more powerful images in our minds than more general words such as "automobiles."

Clearly Understandable

Your readers want to hold onto the expected and familiar. The secret for good business writers lies in always allowing readers to hold onto the old world as they reach for the new. Lucid examples reveal new thoughts by referring in part to old, familiar images and experience.

Consider an astrophysicist's description of our galaxy:

DIFFICULT, UNFAMILIAR | Our galaxy, a protracted spheroid mass of stellar bodies and vaporous amalgams arranged primarily along a single plane, revolves in space.

UNDERSTANDABLE | The Milky Way, its countless stars drawn together into a shape not unlike an immense fried egg, revolves in space.

Strive to keep your business details and examples in touch with the common things of daily existence.

Brief

In business writing, an example should be short. Writers purposely condense examples in order to fulfill the larger purpose of their writing task. In her report on employee theft as Krayco Department Store, for example, Security Officer Jean Torson condenses the following scenario into a crisp, telling example.

TOO LONG | Since her promotion to night shift Manager Level 4, employee 20114, Barbara Conway, has had the responsibility to lock up the south loading ramp door adjoining the Women's Wear department. Inventory control checks ordered by Sarah Martin, Corporate Vice-President of Krayco, revealed the loss of the following items over a period of nine months in Women's Wear:

32 dresses (average $34 each)
16 pairs of jeans (average $28 each)
42 blouses (average $22 each)
12 belts (average $9 each)
18 pairs of socks (average $3 each)
2 cloth coats (average $105 each)
1 ski jacket ($79)

Investigation was initiated with approval of Henry Martinson, Krayco store manager. On Oct. 4, Oct. 7, Oct. 12, and Oct. 16, I established a surveillance point in Women's Wear. On each date, I observed Barbara Conway setting aside unpurchased merchandise in plastic garbage bags identical to those used for department trash. At closing time, she set all bags, both trash and merchandise, alongside the south loading ramp, ostensibly for trash pickup. She herself was observed picking up the bags containing clothing on two of the four nights in question. She was apprehended and now awaits the decision of management regarding prosecution.

BRIEF

The night manager in Women's Wear, Barbara Conway, was arrested in mid-October for stealing clothing. She stashed dresses, jeans, and blouses worth more than $2000 in trash bags behind the store. After closing, she picked up the valuable trash bags. Prosecution is pending.

If a security report contained many such cases, and if the writer expected the report to be read by management, the examples would have to be condensed. That shortened version should still contain vivid detail ("trash bags," "dresses, jeans, and blouses"). However, it may omit all information that is marginal to the basic purpose of the report.

Focused

Business writers probably overestimate the care and attention their work receives. Studies of attention spans and eye-to-print reading patterns show how often readers pause, lose track, retrace, and even skip large passages of writing. Therefore, good business writers go out of their way to focus on their key points. They use examples to direct the reader toward their intended meaning. Notice how the first example lacks such guidance.

AIMLESS

Few coal miners participated in the Grants-for-Education program. "I worked until six o'clock every night. Saturdays, we drove to my parents' house. Sundays, I watched football. I didn't have time, that's all."

FOCUSED

Few coal miners participated in the Grants-for-Education program. *Bret Jolleson, 28, explains why he turned down a $2500 grant:* "I worked until six o'clock every night. Saturdays, we drove to my parents' house. Sundays, I watched football. I didn't have time, that's all."

The crucial directed transition between the major point and the example itself can be called the "shoehorn." The directed transcription slips the reader painlessly into the heart of the example. It tells the reader in advance what the example contains and why it is important. Notice the transitional "shoehorn" (italicized) in the example. Use such directed statements to make the intended meaning of your examples unmistakably clear to the reader.

WRITING THE FIRST DRAFT

Because you have taken the time to develop a working outline and a set of well-developed supporting details and examples, writing the first draft may be surprisingly easy. You know generally what you want to say, and somewhere in the back of your mind, the actual words have already begun to form during the outlining process.

The trick to writing the first draft is letting go. Of course, you will make mistakes. Of course, you will use unnecessary words. Of course, you will wander at times. Nonetheless, bravely let the words flow. You will discover what most professional writers say:

Quite a bit of the very first draft is usable material. The sentences may have to be trimmed and patched, but the essential message is intact.

You may have to turn off internal editors and censors to write an effective first draft. There's the voice, perhaps, of a former English teacher somewhere inside whispering "Stop! Have you spelled correctly? Stop! Have you punctuated correctly?" There may be the voice of a parent or sibling: "That sounds awkward. Shouldn't you sound more intelligent?"

To all such voices, the effective writer says "Wait." There is a time and place to edit and polish, but that time is *not* while you are writing the first draft. If you are using a word processor for writing, don't use your spell-checker, your grammar-checker, or any other editing features while you are writing your first draft. Don't worry about any of these details until you are ready to revise what you wrote.

If you find this very difficult, you could take a bold step to keep yourself from editing what you write: Turn off (or down) your monitor—be sure not to turn off your computer, though! If your monitor is turned off, you won't be able to see what you write, and you'll focus on letting your ideas flow freely. (You could also do this at the beginning of writing, when you're trying to generate lots of ideas without criticizing any of them as being too wild.)

If you aren't writing with a computer, you could use a different technique to keep from editing yourself at this early stage. Put your pen and pencil tip onto the paper and do not lift it until you have finished a paragraph. Try to keep your pen or pencil moving across the page, even if you have to draw a line to mark places where a particular word or phrase should occur but doesn't. At the end of each paragraph, lift your pen or pencil, stretch and relax, then tackle the next paragraph.

Another technique can be used with any kind of writing tool. It employs your considerable powers of conversation to motivate effective writing. Talk out a sentence or two before trying to write it. Once you have written for a while, read it aloud, and try to continue the thought in your speaking voice. (You may want to imagine yourself talking to a friend about your idea.) After you speak out what you have to say, write it down (not necessarily in the same words you used in speech).

More than a few famous writers (such as Wordsworth and Tolstoy) were thought by the townsfolk to be crazy for frequently talking out loud while they wrote. Take the risk. Your success in effective first drafts will answer the occasional raised eyebrows of those watching you work.

REWRITING, REVISING, AND EDITING

According to most professional writers, it's much more fun (though still challenging) to revise than it is to write the first draft. The rough diamond lies before you, ready to sparkle as you cut, trim, and polish.

Like your personal approach to writing the first draft, the actual steps you take to revise your work may differ in order or substance from the following steps. However, if you have no systematic method for revision, you may want to practice these steps until they become a habit.

Step 1. Check for Logical Connections.   In the heat of argument, written or spoken, we may make logical errors. These can prove fatal to our effect if they appear in the final draft of a speech or document. Three logical errors in particular often surface in business communication:

1. Either/or thinking: "Either this company buys new equipment, or it faces a long and inevitable decline." (Are there really no other solutions? Should you confine your argument to a black/white, either/or presentation?)

2. Circular reasoning: "The sales manager's poor social skills prevented him from working successfully with people." (Think about the logical circle here: the second half of the sentence repeats the meaning of the first half.)

3. False cause: "Johnson joined this company in 1998, and we've had nothing but problems since then." (It may be true that Johnson joined the company in 1998; and it may even be true that there have been nothing but problems since then. Does it necessarily follow that Johnson *caused* the problems? Of course not.)

Step 2. Check for Appropriate Transitions.   Readers or listeners should not feel a mental lurch as you move from one sentence or paragraph to the next. When your thoughts take a significant step forward, provide a bridge by using transitional words and phrases. Notice how an appropriate transition ties these two sentences together.

> Videotape rentals increased 80 percent last year. Revenues at movie theaters dropped by 15 percent.
> Videotape rentals increased 80 percent last year. At the same time, revenues at movie theaters dropped by 15 percent.

The transitional phrase "at the same time" shows that the two thoughts are related.

Here are transitional words that you may wish to tie your thoughts together. (*Note:* Don't use *or* or *and* to start sentences. All others may be used in almost any position where they sound all right to you.)

but, or, and	still	in short	inevitably
yet	because	in sum	consequently
however	although	in brief	gradually
furthermore	thus	first, second	increasingly
therefore	hence	by contrast	more and more
similarly	nevertheless	of course	for example
in addition	for instance	probably	in effect

Transitional words serve as traffic signs to your reader or listener, providing early warning of the direction in which your thought is heading. Like traffic signs on a highway, however, too many of these words can create more confusion than they resolve. Read aloud your transition words, listening to both the rhythm of your sentences and the flow of ideas. Be on the lookout for too many and too few transitions.

Step 3. Eliminate Unnecessary Words.   As you read your rough draft, you will find "fat" words that contribute little or nothing to your message. Cut them out. Watch, in particular, for these common forms of unnecessary words:

Repetitious language: "We trusted the <u>unfounded</u> misrepresentations." (Notice that the underlined word repeats the substance of a following word.)

Meaningless language: "<u>It was</u> the manager <u>who</u> decided which plan to accept."

Wandering language: "My uncle's company (<u>founded in 1937 by my uncle together with Al Bennett, an insurance salesman</u>) earned $.98 per share last quarter." (Note that the underlined words draw us away from the central point.)

Step 4. Test Your Diction for Power and Propriety.   As mentioned in Chapter 1, *diction* means the choice of words. Some words may be too weak to use. The word *nice*, for example, pales in comparison to more descriptive words:

"The corporate headquarters were nice"—"The corporate headquarters were luxurious."

When reviewing your choice of words, consider both the *denotative* meaning (dictionary meaning) and *connotative* meaning (emotional shading) of the language you use. Would you, for example, want to refer to the unmarried female president of your firm as a "spinster"? That word, no matter what its narrow dictionary definition, reeks with negative connotations. Exercise similar care in the words you choose.

Step 5. Check for Grammatical and Mechanical Errors.   Slips in grammar and **language mechanics** (spelling, punctuation, word usage, capitalization, etc.) distract readers from your message. Many of these errors in your writing may lead readers to feel that you either did not know or did not care about the rules that the rest of the English-speaking and -writing world abides by. Often, these slips lead to mistrust. Readers, for example, may be justly suspicious of someone's claim to expertise as an "acountant" (notice the missing "c") or as a "bookeeper" (notice the missing "k").

Here is a checklist of grammatical and mechanical categories. Each is treated in Appendix B.

Spelling	Semicolons
Sentence structure (fragments, run-ons, comma splices)	Colons
	Apostrophes
	Quotation marks
Dangling sentence parts	Italics
Subject–verb agreement	Dashes
Correct parts of verbs	Parentheses
Pronoun agreement	Hyphens
Pronoun form	Capitalization
Commas	

Step 6. Make Stylistic Improvements.   The next chapter concerns business style and its improvement. When you understand each of the stylistic suggestions in Chapter 4, you may find the following checklist a useful summary.

Use active verb patterns	Avoid very fancy or formal style
Vary sentence types	Avoid unacceptable contractions and abbreviations
Emphasize important words through placement	Use parentheses correctly
Be specific	Avoid unnecessary questions
Eliminate wordiness	Choose words carefully
Create parallels	Avoid awkward constructions and repetitions
Choose pronouns carefully	
Control paragraph length	
Avoid trite and slang expressions	

By applying these six steps in your own way, you can shape a polished document out of the roughest of first drafts. At times, you may have to be brutal in cutting long strings of words that have no place in the final draft. At other times, you may have to be willing to give up a particularly interesting phrase or idea for the sake of general logic and clarity. Such revision will reward you and your readers with a clear and stylish piece of writing.

Communication Insights	Winston Churchill gave immortal expression to the pleasures and frustrations of writing:
	Writing is an adventure. To begin with, it is a toy and an amusement. Then it becomes a mistress, then it becomes a master, then it becomes a tyrant. The last phase is that just as you are about to be reconciled to your servitude, you kill the monster and fling him to the public.

SUMMARY

1. Every communication has a purpose. Knowing that purpose before you begin to write helps you to shape your words and ideas for your purpose.

2. What you write depends in part on your audience. Analyze that audience with care.

3. Write naturally and with confidence by getting to know and feeling friendly toward your audience.

4. Ideas do not usually come by simple inspiration. The techniques of the idea circle and the classic questions can help to generate ideas when you have time pressures.

5. Ideas must be arranged in a logical, persuasive pattern in order to communicate effectively.

6. Ideas can be made more persuasive and memorable by supporting them with details and examples.

7. Writing the first draft should be a free, no-holds-barred attempt to get your major thoughts down on paper.

8. Revising involves a careful look at each word, phrase, sentence, and paragraph for conciseness, clarity, and mechanical correctness.

QUESTIONS FOR DISCUSSION

1. Why is it important to answer the question, "To whom am I speaking?" before writing a letter or memo?

2. What characteristics of your intended audience should you evaluate?

3. List the purpose circles shown in Figure 3–1. Might there there be times when you will want to fulfill more than one of these purposes?

4. What are the dangers of locking in ideas prematurely?

5. How can using an idea circle and the classic questions help your business communication?

6. Is it possible to organize business documents effectively without first outlining your message? Defend your response.

7. What are the hidden persuaders in business speaking and writing?

8. What are the dangers of overclaim, and how can they be avoided?

9. When are readers likely to accept an illustrated assertion in place of formal proof?

10. List four ways in which business writers manage to persuade us that their details and examples have the ring of real life.

11. How does the shoehorn help business writers to communicate clearly?

12. What advice would you give to a friend who has trouble starting the first draft of an assignment because she or he is afraid to misspell words and make grammatical mistakes?

13. What techniques do professional writers use to generate successful early drafts?

14. Which process do you find most enjoyable—generating the first draft or revising it? Explain your response.

15. List some steps in the revision process. Which of these steps in particular might help you to create a clear and stylish piece of business writing?

EXERCISES

1. Things have been a little tight lately, and you need some money to get you through to the end of the school term. Write three letters asking for a loan of $500 (1) to a friend, (2) to a parent, and (3) to a bank loan officer. How do your approaches to these audiences differ in tone, style, and content?

2. In three paragraphs, describe a product or service with which you're familiar. In the first, merely describe its physical characteristics; in the second, inform people about it; in the third, persuade people to buy it.

3. Of the paragraphs written for Exercise 2, which required the most "outlining" (whether mental or written)? Why was this paragraph more difficult to organize and to write than the others? Explain.

4. Find a merchandise catalog from any major department store or merchandise outlet. Are there any items that you would hesitate to buy because they are not described in great enough detail? What information would you like to have seen included in the catalog description?

5. Choose an article, letter, or document that doesn't have enough formal proof to back up the author's assertions. On a separate sheet of paper or marginally, point to passages where the author clearly needs to add further proof. What has the author substituted in place of the needed proof? Be specific.

6. Select an article, letter, or document that needs more transitions between ideas. Edit the document. What shoehorns would you insert, and where would you insert them?

7. Use the time pattern discussed in this chapter to describe in writing your first week in a job (any job).

8. Find a way to make this undirected example fit into a short report on college dropouts, as a directed example: "In 1998, more than 60 percent of college students had personal debts in excess of $5000." (*Suggestion:* Relate this statistic to the question of why college students sometimes drop out.)

9. Use the emotion pattern discussed in this chapter to describe in writing your impressions of some important experience you had within the past three years.

10. Make up three specific examples to support the following assertion: "Stores can be arranged to encourage impulse buying."

11. Use the logic pattern discussed in this chapter to argue in writing for higher salaries for entry-level employees.

12. Find a communique you consider to be poorly structured, and restructure it. Compare the two versions and consider the revision process you underwent. Why is the new version superior?

INTERNET ASSIGNMENT

You have quickly risen to fame and fortune as a fast-track manager within an investment banking firm. You now supervise 12 account executives, all of them well-versed in their technical skills but less skilled as business writers. In fact, you cringe at times when you review their correspondence (as you insist on doing) before it goes out to important clients.

You know that something must be done to upgrade the writing skills among the people you supervise. You don't hold out much hope that a consultant can be brought in for a day-long seminar or two to "cure" your employees of their writing ills. Since all your people are adept at using the Internet, you hope to discover sufficient training resources on the Web for their use. To begin the process, explore writing topics treated on the Internet (see the Principles and Techniques of Business Writing section of the Internet Guide). Pick approximately eight sites that link together to form a curriculum of sorts with which your employees can begin to resolve their writing difficulties on their own time. Write a memo to your employees in which you emphasize the importance of the Internet writing training they are about to undertake, the sites you have selected, the way in which these sites relate to one another, and specific directions for how you want the employees to use these websites.

CHAPTER **4**

Management Writing Style and Collaborative Writing

Following the principles and techniques described in Chapter Three, you can write a well-organized, cogent business document. Now let's polish it to near perfection by applying the special ingredients of your personal voice and personality.

Managers want their writing to capture the unique flavor of their personal characteristics as business leaders, just as their verbal communicating conveys *who they are* in addition to what they say. This approach to organizational leadership could be called MBBR—Management By Being Real. Those who read and hear the words of the MBBR manager recognize the authenticity and sincerity of the message by its direct stylistic ties to the manager's own nature. Put simply, managers have to find a style that doesn't sound fake.

The search for one's authentic communication style as a manager has many barriers to overcome through years of formal education, where each teacher seems to have new priorities and particular taboos for student writing. As a result, students retreat to a safe mode in writing style—bland, uninspired writing that risks little in class but lends little to real-world enterprises.

One form of such stylistic retreat lies in the Encyclopedia Voice (one well-practiced from grade school days for many American students). This cardboard creation sounds detached from any human speaker, and therein lies its main advantage for the writer-in-retreat. When we disengage ourselves from the "voice" heard in our writing, we can't be personally hurt when others criticize or ignore that writing. It wasn't "us."

THE ENCYCLOPEDIA VOICE

Characteristics: stiff, unemotional

Example: It is possible to define the term *headquarters* as the central location or primary residence of a corporation. In general, such a definition may be said to include geographically propinquitous peripheral satellites of the central base, as in the case of Kodak, the headquarters of which are in Rochester, New York.

At the other end of the stylistic spectrum, we may revert to a voice that is entirely us at our most childish moments. This is the Emotional Voice, which obviously is no more appropriate for business purposes than the Encyclopedia Voice:

THE EMOTIONAL VOICE

Characteristics: blunt, childlike, repetitive, often slangy
Example: I can't believe that I wasn't promoted. Look, my sales were up this year. I didn't miss a day of work. I worked overtime. I came in early. What else can a guy do? It's just unbelievable to me that I wasn't promoted.

Somewhere between these polar opposites lies the voice that will serve you best throughout your business career—your own way of expressing what you think and feel with the needs and communication preferences of your audience fully in mind. Although no one but you can specify the precise qualities of your own "Business Voice," we can generalize the following attributes of mainstream business style:

THE BUSINESS VOICE

Characteristics: direct, controlled, reasonable, clear, personal but not self-centered.
Example: For six months, we have sought a new headquarters for Dynavision without asking one basic question: Do we all share the same meaning for the word *headquarters*? Do we mean several floors in an urban high-rise? A single building of our own? A cluster of buildings in a town?

As discussed in Chapter 2, your purpose, audience, and circumstances influence the voice you choose for your messages. Admittedly, some business messages find a legitimate place for strong emotions, particularly when expressing disappointment or excitement in memos and e-mail. But management communicators must remember that emotion can easily be misunderstood by readers. When you suspect that your writing voice is overly emotional, let a trusted associate read your communication before sending it. Listen to his or her response to the voice and tone of your writing, and revise accordingly.

E-mail messages have been particularly prone to a phenomenon called "flaming"—an inappropriate outburst of emotion (sometimes contained in name-calling and swearing) that the writer usually wishes he or she could recall. But once sent, the flaming e-mail message is irretrievable; recipients often print out copies to show to others as the professional reputation of the message writer figuratively goes down in flames.

To prevent "flaming" in business messages, make it your habit to turn most often to your standard Business Voice for written communications. In this voice, you speak directly to the issue and respectfully to your audience. As Brent C. Ernst, founder of the Big Six accounting firm bearing his name, points out:

> My managers each speak and write in a personal, unique voice. At the same time, they all speak with one voice—the voice of the company. Particularly when they are involved in stressful, high stakes situations, I remind them that each word in their communications to clients comes from the company.

Even the courts (not always known for forthright language) have ruled that business writing must be clear in contracts. The Sixth U.S. Circuit Court of Appeals found that a loan agreement violated the Truth in Lending Act because of "indecipherable" language, including the following sentence: "A deferment charge may be made for deferred payments equal to the portion of the regular finance charge applicable by the sum of the digits methods to the installment period immediately following the due date of the first deferred installment times the number of months of deferment."

WORDS WITHIN THE SENTENCE

To this point, you have learned to overcome "Writer's Block" by assessing your audience, exploring ideas, developing a plan, arranging examples, and choosing an appropriate voice.

Now what comes out on the page?

Words. One at a time, these small building blocks line up to create larger and larger language structures. By looking closely at words within the sentence, you can assure yourself that the basic building blocks of business writing are sound and true to form.

Making Language Specific and Concrete

Readers have only one motive in reading your writing. What's here, they ask, that can be put to use? When you use specific and concrete words, you give your reader useful tools instead of airy approximations. The following passage from a memo announces a client–staff meeting first in a vague way and then in a specific way. Observe the important differences.

> A client wants a brief overview after lunch tomorrow. Bring along anything we can use to show off our company.

Consider the vague, abstract language:

VAGUE	"a client"—Which client?
SPECIFIC	Allyson Royce, Operations Manager for Norton Hotels
VAGUE	"brief"—20 minutes? Two hours?
SPECIFIC	45 minutes
VAGUE	"overview"—A lecture? A slide-show?
SPECIFIC	A presentation of our services
VAGUE	"after lunch"—1 P.M.? 3 P.M.?
SPECIFIC	2:30 P.M.
VAGUE	"anything"—Drapery? Pictures of the kids?
SPECIFIC	Letters of appreciation, files from open accounts, and photos of current buildings we manage
VAGUE	"company"—The building? The logo?
SPECIFIC	our maintenance and rental services

Revised in a specific form, the memo passage makes its point clearly.

> Ms. Allyson Royce, Operations Manager for Norton Hotels, can meet with us for 45 minutes tomorrow at 2:30 in my office. Please bring letters of appreciation, files from open ac-

counts, photos of the buildings we now manage, and any other items that demonstrate the quality of our maintenance and rental services.

One way to test for unnecessary abstractions in your writing is to watch for nouns ending in *-tion, -sion, -ance, -ence,* or *-ness.* While no writer avoids all such words, their overabundance can cloud your writing. In the following examples, abstract words are transformed into more direct, specific words.

VAGUE	The *definition* of leasing at Boylston Leasing is the investment of a small amount of money to gain the use of large dollar amounts of equipment.
SPECIFIC	Boylston Leasing *means* large value for small dollars.
VAGUE	The *expansion* of Tri-City Freight has progressed at a pace in step with the *expansion* of the West.
SPECIFIC	Tri-City Freight *grows* with the West.
VAGUE	Our firm exhibits excessive *dependence* on a single supplier.
SPECIFIC	Our firm *depends* on a single supplier too often.
VAGUE	It was her *experience* that it was easy to make friends among her clients.
SPECIFIC	She makes friends easily among her clients.

This abstract language is called "Latinate" because so many vague words stem from Latin roots. No business writer avoids all Latinate words. Still, try to limit your use of *-tion, -sion, -ance, -ence,* and *-ness* nouns, and be more specific whenever you can.

The vague word *very* and its speech twin *really* weaken business writing. Often, a business writer uses *very* in a feeble effort to turn up the volume on another word: very nervous, very upset, very hungry, very good. Business writers who know the power of specific words prefer to amplify the *content* of the word at hand, not its volume. Instead of "very nervous," they write "frantic"; instead of "very upset," "furious"; instead of "very hungry," "ravenous"; and instead of "very good," "outstanding." Specific words help the business writer say more with fewer words.

Using Active Versus Passive Verb Patterns

A verb communicates action. For example, *dropping* is the action in the sentence. "The manager *dropped* the vase." In general, English sentences work best when they pulse with action. Readers appreciate the sense of energy in the sentence. Also, sentences with active verbs are easily readable. Who *did* what to whom stands out loud and clear in action sentences. In addition, action sentences usually take fewer words (hence, less work for the reader) than nonaction sentences. Compare the length of these two sentences:

ACTION	The manager delegates tasks well.
NONACTION	One of the manager's skills is her ability in the delegation of tasks.

Readers seldom feel much energy or motivation from sentences containing only an "is," "are," "was," or "were" at their heart. Writers, too, grow tired of these actionless verbs. As a business writer, you want to recommend, develop, suggest, argue, refute, substantiate, summarize, begin, continue, grasp, reveal, glimpse, fulfill, and all the other activities that make up business life.

One variety of the *is* construction requires a special note: passive verb forms, such as, "The cash register is/was fixed by Henderson." These forms dilute the sense of action in business writing. Instead of telling *who* did *what* to *whom*, passive sentences awkwardly unfold who got done what by whom, if you pardon the grammar.

That is, the *victim* or object appears first in the sentence: "The crown was crushed by the beauty queen." Not until the final word of the sentence does the reader discover the *actor*, in this case the beauty queen. While we can tolerate this reversal occasionally for variety, we prefer the native English pattern of *actor → action → object*.

Another difficulty with the passive form lies in its irritating habit of dissolving key figures in the sentence. An active sentence tells us that "Betty embezzled the money." When that news appears in a passive sentence, notice who's missing: "The money was embezzled." Betty, if she wishes to hide behind the grammar of the passive sentence, can disappear entirely (perhaps to Costa Rica).

Observe in the following sentence how the central *actors* have misused the passive form to conveniently step out of a negative personnel evaluation.

> **Ms. Bradford is generally disliked here. Her work habits are frequently criticized. Prior to beginning work as supervisor, she was rated poorly as a leader.**

Wait a minute, Ms. Bradford has a right to insist. Who dislikes (active) me? Who criticizes (active) me? Who rates (active) me poorly? Rewrite my evaluation in active form, not passive, so I can confront my accusers.

Business writers will never completely eliminate passive and is/are constructions from their writing, nor should they. For occasional emphasis and variety, the passive form serves well. We can, however, learn to look upon every is/are/was/were and passive verb as a taunt: "Change me if you can."

Choosing Positive Language

Business writers and speakers recognize that happy, optimistic people are more open to new ideas and change than are discouraged, cynical people. Therefore, such communicators lose no opportunity to accentuate the positive.

Notice in the following pairs how a dreary, guilt-ridden message is recast into a brighter form by the choice of positive language:

NEGATIVE	Your complaint is being dealt with by Mr. Flores.
POSITIVE	Mr. Flores will answer your inquiry promptly.
NEGATIVE	Ten percent of the sales force failed to attend the conference.
POSITIVE	The conference attracted 90 percent of the sales force.

No one needs a list of the negative words in the English language. They are among the most memorable words from our upbringing: *no, don't, can't, won't, shouldn't, failed, forgot, omitted, destroyed, complained, ruined,* and so forth. These words, though, sometimes quite accurate for the situation at hand, rarely have the power to *change* the situation for the better. Business writers wisely choose positive language whenever possible to motivate an audience to new courses of thinking and action.

Notice in the following example (written to a customer who has always paid on time) how the change from negative to positive language influences your perception of the writer, your motivation to follow the advice, and your emotions.

NEGATIVE   We are taking time to write in order to notify you that you failed to pay your September VISA bill, as required by your card contract.

If we don't receive this overdue payment by October 6, 19—, your credit rating will be adversely affected.

POSITIVE   Thank you for checking to see whether you have mailed your September VISA payment due by Oct 6.

Your continued on-time payment record assures you of an "A+" credit rating from our company.

Avoiding Noun Clusters

In the section on "Making Language Specific and Concrete," nouns ending in *-tion*, *-sion*, *-ance*, *-ence*, or *-ness* were found guilty of making your sentences vague and weak. In this section, we accuse them of bunching together to cause confusion.

A *noun*, as you know, names a person, place, thing, or quality. *Computer* is a noun, and so is *difficulty* and *pebble*. Readers of English expect most nouns either to do something ("the computer beeps") or to have something done to them ("Spot swallowed the pebble.").

Business writers sometimes short-circuit this expectation by surrounding nouns not with action but with other nouns.

Be sure to attend the business opportunities youth guidance session.

The what? If you attend, you undoubtedly will receive a copy of the "Business Opportunities Youth Guidance Session Report." Back at your office, you may have to discuss the report with colleagues. Don't call your meeting a "business opportunities youth guidance session report evaluation."

The simple solution to the problem of noun clusters lies in using adjectives and verbs.

Noun Cluster	Revision with Adjectives and Verbs
the franchises investment opportunity	the opportunity to invest in franchises
the candidate interview patience measurement	the measurement of a candidate's patience in interviews

Closely related to noun clusters are prepositional strings (*to* the park *by* the lake *with* four ducks *under* the bridge). As a general rule, never string together more than two prepositional phrases in a row.

NOT   the receipt *of* the package *of* tools *by* the supervisor *at* Benson Mechanics Center.

INSTEAD   the supervisor at Benson Mechanics Center received the tools.

Replacing Vague Pronouns

Business writers would never send out a memo, letter, or report pockmarked with penny-sized holes in the typed page. Yet vague pronouns (*this, it, that, these, those*) can leave gaps of meaning comparable to actual holes in the page. Consider the gap in meaning left by the vague use of "this":

> At its last meeting, the Employee Safety Committee's discussion focused on the buddy system for particularly hazardous duty. This met with opposition from management representatives.

This what? The possibilities are many:

- this discussion met with opposition
- this meeting met with opposition
- this system met with opposition
- this duty met with opposition

The page has a huge gap of meaning.

To spare readers an annoying guessing game, we could place an identifying word or phrase immediately after "this," and revise the sentence to specify that "this safeguard met with opposition from management representatives."

The problem of the vague *it* often can be solved even more easily. Rephrase the sentence to remove the meaningless "it" entirely.

NOT   Johnson's perpetual questions make *it* impossible to concentrate.

INSTEAD   Johnson's perpetual questions make concentration impossible.

Controlling Emphasis

In a business conversation, have you stopped to listen to the first sound out of someone's mouth when he or she begins to speak? Quite often, no word is said at all. Rather, a short cough, a clearing of the throat, or the taking of an audible quick breath signals a person's intention to speak. If the speaker actually says a word, it often turns out to be a nonword—a verbal cough—such as *well* or *uh*.

Business writing, like speaking, has its rituals of introduction. Like *well* and *uh*, these sentence openers have little or no meaning. They exist merely to get things underway. Good business writers learn, though, that business prose gets underway quite well, thank you, without such empty words and phrases. Notice that we lose no meaning but gain considerable sentence strength by eliminating the meaningless openers, "it is" and "there is/are":

NOT   There is an oak beam supporting the roof.

INSTEAD   An oak beam supports the roof. (Actor → Action → Object)

NOT   It is possible that Williams will apply for section leader.

INSTEAD   Williams may apply for section leader.

Such revision also has the virtue of making the sentence shorter for the reader. More important, by removing meaningless words from the beginning of the sentence, the opening slot—the *strong slot*—is free to contain significant words.

Your chance to emphasize key words can be lost entirely when sentences grow too long. No precise word limit can be set, of course, for business sentences. A better measure of length than an arbitrary word count is grammatical *part* count. Do your sentences usually contain more than one subject and one main verb? If so, your sentences probably are running too long for proper emphasis.

Readers are understandably eager for the first word or two in each sentence. There, after all, lies the first clue to understanding the meaning of the entire sentence. The strong-slot words are like a compass arrow providing orientation for the reader. Hence, words placed there receive special attention and emphasis from readers. For that reason alone, waste-words such as "it is" and "there is/are" should be removed entirely, or at least placed later in the sentence.

Such removal is painless. In almost all cases, meaningless phrases can simply be snipped out of the sentence.

NOT	There are meaningless words that should be removed.
INSTEAD	Meaningless words should be removed.
OR	Remove meaningless words.

Using Words Correctly

English presents the business writer with many pairs of problematic twins, a few of which are listed here. Be careful to choose the word you mean rather than its lookalike or soundalike double.

disperse–disburse	*disperse* means to scatter; *disburse* means to pay out
site–cite	*site* is a location: to *cite* is to point out
lead–led	*lead* is a heavy gray metal; *led* is past tense of the verb, *to lead*
lose–loose	to *lose* means to be without; *loose* means not tight
bear–bare	to *bear* means to carry a burden; to *bare* means to expose
principle–principal	*principle* is a truth; *principal* is a school official, an amount of money excluding interest, or the main concept, object or person (principal idea, principal violinist, or even principal principle)

Spell-checking software programs will not flag soundalike words that are used incorrectly. These programs check for spelling, not meaning. For example, the relatively sophisticated spell-checking programs built into business word-processing software can't tell you to correct *if* when you meant *is* or *by* where you intended *be*. Some of the very advanced grammar- and style-checking software can do some of this, but even these programs have limitations. Thus, even with powerful computer tools, you must proofread with care, checking all lookalike or soundalike words.

Eliminating Wordiness

Wordiness has little to do with the length of a document. After all, some reports are long simply because they have a great deal to say. In contrast, even a one-paragraph memo can be guilty of excessive reliance on the use of somewhat redundant and often repetitive terms—in short, *wordiness*.

Watch for wordiness in these three disguises:

1. Unnecessary doubling. Notice how the following sentence states, then restates, its point by doubling each key word.
   Not: If and when we can establish and define our goals and objectives, each and every member will be ready and willing to give aid and assistance.
   Instead: When we define our goals, each member will be ready to help.

2. Unnecessary modifiers. Are the italicized modifiers really necessary in the following sentence?
   Not: In this world of today, official governmental red tape is *seriously* destroying the *motivation* for financial incentives among *relatively* small businesses.
   Instead: Governmental red tape is destroying financial incentives for small businesses.

Avoiding wordiness is especially important now, when most decision-makers find themselves with too much to read. Each document must compete for its share of attention—and unnecessarily wordy documents lose out.

Avoiding Sexist Language

Not long ago in this country, these sentences seemed perfectly proper:

A lawyer must choose *his* clients carefully.
Every surgeon washes *his* hands before operating.

Some grammar handbooks still allow "his" to stand generically for humankind instead of just males. Other handbooks (and the author of this text) recommend that you avoid even the appearance of sexist assumptions by conscientiously providing "his or her" in place of "his" or "her" by itself, when the gender of the person is not known.

A lawyer must chose his or her clients carefully.
Every surgeon washes her or his hands before operating.

Admittedly, the phrase *his or her* can become stylistically awkward when repeated several times in a paragraph. In that case, consider making your subject plural:

Lawyers must choose their clients carefully.
Surgeons wash their hands before operating.

Notice that the plural form manages to avoid the gender issue altogether.

SENTENCES WITHIN THE PARAGRAPH

If, as we mentioned earlier, words are the building blocks of communication, sentences are the rows of blocks. These rows must be well laid out and properly planned. Before reviewing several plans for laying out sentences in your business writing, we should take a stand on a sensitive issue: sentence fragments.

As you may remember from English instruction, a sentence fragment lacks either a subject (actor) or a verb (action).

FRAGMENT	Fixed mortgages lasting 30 years.
SENTENCE	Fixed mortgages lasting 30 years have disappeared.
FRAGMENT	Being thoroughly reviewed.
SENTENCE	His loan application is being thoroughly reviewed.

You may also remember from English instruction that sentence fragments are often treated as the almighty no-no in formal writing. However, for business writing the context of the fragment may permit some exceptions. Automobile advertisements, for example, use sentence fragments freely.

Powerful expressive devices:

- The luxury you've earned.
- Plush bucket seats.
- An incredible powerplant.
- Lines to lure da Vinci.
- Yours at last. Enjoy.

Nonetheless, without disputing the appropriateness of sentence fragments in such ads, business writers usually choose to avoid fragments in memos, letters, and reports. In these contexts, sentence fragments can sound either wrong, glib, or crude. Consider the effect of the highlighted fragment in this short paragraph from a report:

> When the security officer pointed out to the manager that his actions were against store policy, he simply laughed. **Showing his degree of respect for the company.**

Because most readers of English do not expect sentence fragments in business writing, they consider them to be mistakes. Therefore, writers do well to avoid fragments entirely in most business writing.

One other sentence construction causes the reject light to flash on in readers' minds: the comma splice. This error occurs when two perfectly content English sentences are unceremoniously married or "spliced" together by a comma.

NOT	Profits were down in 1998, the Board blamed the recession.
INSTEAD	Profits were down in 1998. The Board blamed the recession.

Comma splices ring such wrong bells that they are rarely if ever found in even the most casual advertising copy. If a period seems inappropriate, use a semicolon, not a comma.

Business writers who cherish the *strong slot* at the beginning of each sentence have a special reason to dislike the comma splice. The construction takes two strong slots and reduces them to only one. Like sentence fragments, comma splices should not appear in your business writing.

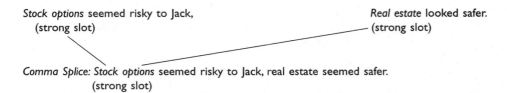

Stock options seemed risky to Jack,
   (strong slot)

Real estate looked safer.
   (strong slot)

Comma Splice: Stock options seemed risky to Jack, real estate seemed safer.
   (strong slot)

Let's turn from such linguistic disasters to positive, practical techniques for developing strong sentences in business writing.

Life would be simple (but boring) if all sentences followed the actor–action pattern:

The whistle blew. We dressed. The coalcart came. We rode. It stopped. We worked. We stopped. We ate. We talked. We worked. We stopped. The coalcart came. We rode. It stopped. We showered. Then, man, did we break loose at Rosy's Bar and Grill.

Except for the last sentence, these short sentences have little to fault them. They are direct, clear, and orderly, but they are *boring* in the repetitions of the actor–action pattern.

Business writers achieve interesting variety in their writing by mixing sentence patterns. Without involving elaborate grammatical descriptions in our discussion, we can describe five useful sentence patterns.

1. The action → action → object sentence
   Example: The balance sheet showed a significant loss.
2. The *-ing* or *-ed* opening with a comma
   Example: Rifling through his papers, the salesman found the missing receipt.
3. The *-ing* beginning without a comma
   Example: Joining Ralph meant everything to Sarah.
4. The middle break (marked here by an arrow)
   Examples: If she takes her vacation in July, ↓ I'll have to schedule mine in August.
   Few employees noticed Ms. Adams, ↓ but her genius showed as the yacht neared completion.
   Traffic snarled in front of the plant; ↓ Mr. Todd had been playing policeman again.
5. The guide word beginning
   Examples: Consequently, Burton took his invention to an engineer.
   Reluctantly, the manager ordered the plant closed.
   By contrast, the two youth groups in Salem won civic awards.

Among the many possible guide words, some are listed here:

for example	on the other hand	often	recently
for instance	frequently	however	inevitably
by comparison	moreover	nevertheless	unfortunately
in addition	notably	on one hand	
increasingly	hence	therefore	

These initial words provide guidance to the reader; they function much like traffic signs, telling of conditions that lie ahead in the sentence. The transitional words and phrases mentioned toward the end of Chapter 3 (Step 2) also guide readers.

Developing Effective Sentences

Effective sentences *begin strong*. Readers are eager to know at the beginning of each sentence, "Who did what?" Writers satisfy that interest by providing the subject or a key transition word as soon as possible.

Notice what happens in the following sentence when the subject (highlighted) is delayed:

Of course, without knowing the full circumstances or complete terms of agreement between the two parties, my **client** cannot . . .

As readers, we feel a growing edginess as the writer piles more and more words up before giving us the subject. How much more satisfying to find the subject early in the sentence.

My **client**, of course, cannot act without knowing the full circumstances. . . .

Transition words can also appear early in the sentence, with powerful effect.

Nevertheless, Morton kept his goal solidly before him.
On the contrary, Maxine spoke highly of her.

The advice to "begin strong" must be tempered by stylistic considerations. Sentences that *all* begin with subjects would soon make the writing sound like "Dick and Jane" fare. For occasional variety, begin with an *-ed* phrase ("Rated first among colleges, Harvard . . .") or an *-ing* phrase ("Bracing for a hard winter, the village . . .")

Strong sentence beginnings should be followed by the *central verb* in the sentence as quickly as possible. When the verb is delayed, readers begin to squirm. Consider:

VERB DELAYED   The vacation so well-deserved by Ms. Kaye but postponed by her supervisor, Ms. Virginia Ward, for petty reasons, finally took place.

We have an almost insurmountable need as readers to know "Who did what?" Once the information has been given (in other words, once we are oriented to the meaning of the sentence), we will be content with long stretches of related information:

VERB UP FRONT   Virginia Ward denied Ms. Kaye her well-deserved vacation for petty reasons.

Finally, effective sentences *vary in length.* As readers, we like variety in sentence rhythm, as well as in content. By mixing short, medium, and long sentences, a skilled business writer keeps us from falling into a humdrum stagnation. By "long sentence," we do not mean a multilined monster. In modern usage, a "long" sentence can extend to three typed lines, but rarely beyond. Short sentences, by contrast, can be as short as one or two words. Sometimes, the most potent sentence in a paragraph contains the fewest words. Brevity counts.

Effective Paragraph Development

Too many business writers create paragraphs by looking at the number of lines on the page and saying, "Well, that should be long enough." A paragraph is not a measurement of length; paragraphs can properly be as short as two or three sentences or, under some conditions, longer than a page. *Paragraph* names an *internal organization of parts.*

Business writers find three traditional patterns particularly useful. Although the following examples provide only one sentence to illustrate each part within the paragraph, that part can and often should include more than a single sentence.

Exposition Pattern

Sentence 1: sets for the *topic* or *main idea* of the paragraph.
Sentence 2: expands the meaning of the major terms in the topic sentence.
Sentence 3: provides an example or illustration of the topic sentence.
Sentence 4: answers the question, "So what? So what if the rest of the paragraph is true? What can be said in conclusion?"

The *exposition* plan serves as the standard paragraph model in reports and proposals. Observe how each sentence plays its part in this paragraph from a marketing proposal for a new kitchen utensil.

TOPIC SENTENCE EXPANSION OF MAJOR TERMS EXAMPLE CONCLUSION	All nutcrackers now on the market in the United States, Canada, and Europe require extraordinary grip strength from the user. Traditional nutcrackers, as tested by Underwriters' Laboratory, can demand up to 110 lbs. of hand pressure to crack an average walnut. In testing the West German "Nut Jaws," for example, the laboratory staff cracked 100 walnuts and 100 pecans with an average grip pressure of 105 lbs. per nut. One staff member dislocated a thumb in the effort. Because such grip requirements far surpass the average grip strengths in the general population, the market may be ripe for a gear-ratioed device.

Enumeration Pattern

Often in the course of a memo, letter or report, you may wish to list items, events, or circumstances. The following pattern of sentences offers a model.

Sentence 1: presents topic sentence announcing the nature of the list.
Sentence 2: expands or qualifies the key terms occurring in the topic sentence.
Sentences 3–5: First . . . _____
Second . . . _____
Finally . . . _____
Sentence 6: concludes by answering the question, "so what?"

Like the exposition plan, the *enumeration* plan can be useful throughout the broad range of business writing. Observe the role of each enumerative sentence in the following paragraph from a job description.

MAIN IDEA

EXAMPLE

CONCLUSION

> The position of sales manager requires academic preparation and practical work experience in general retail sails. While a college degree is not mandatory, at least one year of successful sales experience in each of three capacities will be required. First, the candidate must evidence a knowledge of cash and register management. Second, the candidate must have demonstrated in past work experience superior leadership and supervisory abilities. Finally, the candidate must present a record of reliability and diligence. After interviews have been concluded, the company will make hiring decisions within seven days.

Inquiry Pattern

A substantial portion of business writing asks rather than answers questions. The *inquiry* plan organizes the sometimes difficult task of asking questions in an orderly and tactful way.

> Sentence 1: Here's why I need to ask a question.
> Sentence 2: Here's my question.
> Sentence 3: Here are specific aspects of my question.
> Sentence 4: (so what?): Here's what I can do when you give me your answer.

Observe how the inquiry paragraph develops in this example from a commercial property manager's letter to a client.

> (1) We're unable to rent Unit 4 in the Ashbury Warehouse until we determine the status of the previous lease. (2) Did you formally release a Mr. Robert Duncan from his three-year lease on the unit? (3) Specifically, we need to know if you possess written proof of that release, or if Mr. Duncan has signed a forfeiture of any kind. (4) When we receive your response, we can act quickly either to lease the unit again or to locate Mr. Duncan for a resolution to the current problem.

Business writers find that clients prefer to know both the reason (Sentence 1) and the use (Sentence 4) for most inquiries. These crucial sentences have the additional rhetorical value of imposing a sense of urgency on the inquiry: "I need your answer."

At the risk of overworking our building block analogy, we can observe that in paragraphs, connectives and adhesives hold the parts together in a unified way, just as mortar holds bricks together. The most powerful of these adhesives is the force of connected, logical ideas, as developed in the preceding sentence patterns. Certainly, you will develop variations on these basic patterns and invent new frameworks of your own. The key to tight, smooth connections between sentences lies in starting the thought of one sentence where the thought of the previous sentence left off. At no point within a paragraph should the reader be startled by a new and unexpected point of beginning.

The advice to start one sentence where the previous sentence left off cannot be applied to the actual words you use. Avoid using the last word of one sentence as the first word of the following sentence.

NOT

> We received notice that Boston was sending down a *Geiger counter. The Geiger counter* was supposed to help us evaluate the waste dump in the East Yard.

INSTEAD   We received notice that Boston was sending down a *Geiger counter. The device* was supposed to help us evaluate the waste dump in the East Yard.

Be careful not to use the same word over and over within a paragraph. If you have used the word "Geiger counter," for example, switch to "this instrument" or another variant in the next reference to the device.

Questions.   Use questions in your business writing with discretion. Readers can be made to feel set up or even foolish when the writer stages what could be called "mannequin questions." These have the look of real questions but are actually dummies arranged by the writer for purposes of show and effect. Observe the unnecessary and mildly insulting effect of such mannequin questions in this paragraph from an industrial report.

Our purchase of the 904 sheetmetal press has increased output of ductwork and connectors. *But did we know what we were doing? Did we think the matter through? Did we take our time?* No. We will have to run the press for 30 years at full speed to recoup our expenditure for the new equipment.

The writer of this passage knows the answers to each of these questions before he or she asks it. The reason, then, for casting the matter in question form is manipulative: The writer wants to raise eyebrows and perhaps tempers artificially.

Readers don't enjoy such prods and charades. Faced with unnecessary questions, readers may well mutter, "If you know the answer, just tell me."

Sincere questions, of course, are very appropriate. Notice how the mannequin questions from the previous example can be rewritten as a sincere question.

Our purchase of the 904 sheetmetal press has increased output of ductwork and connectors. In the past three weeks, though, we have tried to answer an important question: Has our investment been justified by increased profits due to the new machine? We have determined that, in present market conditions, we will have to run the press at full speed for 30 years to recoup our investment.

Sincere questions are distinguished from mannequin questions in one essential way: Writers ask sincere questions also of themselves; they ask mannequin questions only of their readers.

Checking for Paragraph Unity and Coherence

As we have seen in the foregoing examples, the primary ingredient holding a paragraph together is the glue of logical development. Certain stylistic techniques, however, can help to bond ideas together.

First, use transitional words generously. If one idea grows out of a preceding idea, tell the reader by using *therefore*. If an idea contrasts with an earlier idea, signal the difference with *however*, *but*, or *in contrast*. In similar ways, you can signal the flow of meaning within your paragraphs with such words as *nevertheless*, *of course*, *in short*, *consequently*, and others listed earlier in this chapter.

Second, trace the relation among key words in your paragraph. In drafting, some writers go so far as to underline every subject in a paragraph and then to ask, "how do these subjects lead from one to another?" Notice in the following paragraph how the underlined key words, including several subjects, form a meaningful progression:

Funeral homes in America have endured a decade of criticism since the early 1980s. Their elaborate decoration of death, some say, is grotesque and unethical. Critics point to smooth-talking morticians who present their sales pitch (often involving thousands of dollars) just at the time when bereaved relatives are least able to make wise financial choices.

Third, examine each paragraph to make sure it treats one central idea, not two or three. After announcing a central point, a paragraph may go on to examine two or three aspects of the matter. However, no paragraph should include two distinct, separable ideas. When such combinations appear in your writing, devote a separate paragraph to each.

LEADING AND PARTICIPATING IN COLLABORATIVE WRITING TEAMS

"I was surprised," says Senior Account Manager Victor Olsen of General Electric, "to discover how often I worked with others on writing projects when I began my career. My MBA and earlier college studies prepared me to write alone, not as a member of team." By some recent estimates, team writing accounts for as much as 60 percent of all managerial writing.

Collaborative writing involves sharing responsibilities for a writing project with at least one other person. Whether you work in dyads (pairs) or as a member of a larger project team, you will need to understand

- what can go wrong when groups write together
- what advantages accrue from the team approach to writing
- how group problems can be avoided
- how to participate as a member of a writing team
- how to lead a writing team

The Hazards of Collaborative Writing

"A camel is a horse designed by committee," goes the old corporate joke. Many managers have a deep distrust of shared responsibility and shared decision making when it comes to writing projects. These men and women have witnessed delays, poor compromises, and uneven work on collaborative writing projects all because of personality squabbles or lack of leadership in the group. (Many MBA and college students have had equally negative experiences in trying to produce a group paper or presentation.)

Four complaints about collaborative writing echo across industries:

1. "One person ends up doing all the work." Many teams quickly divide into spectators and a single gladiator doing battle in the arena. Of course, those watching usually have plenty of advice and criticism for the person doing the work.
2. "We can't keep things moving forward." Each team member often has a different idea of how the project should develop. Planning meetings turn into exercises in frustration as each member tries to pull the group in a different direction.

3. "We can't harmonize our different styles." When team planning begins to break down, group members each grab their preferred piece of the project to work on. The result is usually unsatisfactory: group members bring back fragments of writing that can't be unified into a single, organized document.

4. "We're wasting time by trying to work together." The time misspent on chaotic meetings and misdirected writing leads group members to despair of the team approach to writing. They urge management to assign writing tasks to individuals, never to teams.

These negative judgments are often deserved—collaborative writing often does go astray. But why shouldn't it? Managers have typically spent their school years perfecting the art of working alone. Writing has been taught as an individual sport, not a team activity.

The Advantages of Collaborative Writing

The practical world of management writing can't afford to keep each writer/manager in a private ivory tower. Real-world business problems usually require a team approach to writing for four reasons:

1. One writer can't do it all. Documents dealing with large problems often demand the shared skills and insights of several writers working in close coordination.

2. Time is money. Even when one writer can accomplish a major writing task over an extended period of time, few companies have the luxury of providing that time. Deadlines loom, and only a writing team can produce the required volume of work in the time allotted.

3. The team provides a safety net. What happens to an important writing project when an employee falls ill or quits? Nothing disastrous, if the project has been assigned to a team instead of to an individual. Companies ensure continuity and reliability by using the team approach to producing major documents.

4. Collaborative writing teams provide "buy-in" from many constituencies. If for this reason alone, companies rely on team writing for politically or organizationally sensitive projects. When a writing team is made up of a member from marketing, a member from finance, a member from administration, and a member from production, the eventual document that emerges has a better chance of support throughout the company because each major division has had a voice in its composition.

Avoiding the Pitfalls of Collaborative Writing

If team writing at its best is both productive and politically desirable, how can managers prepare to work effectively as participants in and leaders of collaborative teams? To answer that question, let's provide constructive responses to the four major areas of criticism for team writing discussed earlier:

1. "One person ends up doing all the work." To resolve this problem, divide work fairly among team members, abiding by individual preferences where possible. Each member in a well-chosen team has particular strengths. Discover those abilities and assign work accordingly. Here's how one collaborative team divided ini-

tial writing responsibilities for an extended report on total quality management (TQM) for their company:

Pablo: Determine which databases will be most useful for a computer search for relevant books, articles, and case studies. Gather key descriptor terms from team members. Make arrangements with the company Informational Technology Services (ITS) supervisor to conduct the computer search.

John: Interview senior managers to determine their recommendations for length, format, and style. Obtain examples, where possible, to illustrate their expectations. Distribute these examples and a summary of your interviews to all team members.

Susan: Work with a company graphics specialist and our budget liaison to determine the kinds of graphics that are within our financial means. Distribute samples of such graphics to all team members along with your cost analysis.

Maria: Make sure that all team members are trained in the use of Lotus Notes [the groupware used for this project].

Chin: Obtain a copy of *The Chicago Manual of Style*, 14th ed., for each team member and distribute it. Determine company deadlines for draft approval and for final publication. Determine production time and costs from word processing and duplication. Distribute a summary of your findings to all team members.

2. "We can't keep things moving forward." Keep the project moving along by developing a shared game plan. In its initial meetings, the writing team must decide on target dates for completion of work and on the review process that will take place when the work is handed in. The writing team introduced above agreed on the following schedule. Their shared commitment to meeting these dates exerted peer pressure on all team members to complete their work on time:

Sept. 1	Completion of idea generation (brainstorming)
Sept. 5	Completion of initial idea selection and organization.
Sept. 10	Completion of computer search #1 (data gathering).
Sept. 17	Completion of working outline.
Sept. 22	Completion of computer search #2 (additional data gathering)
Sept. 25	Completion of final working outline and assignment of drafting tasks.
Oct. 2	Completion of first drafts of assigned sections.
Oct. 7	Completion of initial graphics (rough).
Oct. 12	Completion of revised drafts and final graphics.
Oct. 15	Completion of final editing/revision.
Oct. 20	Completion of document, including presentation strategy.

3. "We each have a different style." Decide on issues of style and organization before team members begin to write, not after. Team members should decide on matters of voice, tone, and support techniques. Each writer needs to know, for example, whether "I," "you," or "we" will be used in the document; to what degree statistics will be used to support assertions; to what extent footnotes will be added; and so forth. Team members also should agree in advance on a master outline of key points.

The writing team discussed above decided on this statement agreement to guide their individual writing activities:

> "As a writing team, we have agreed to avoid the bureaucratic style commonly found in this company's formal reports. Instead, we will emulate the direct, concrete, and appropriately informal style found in such business publications as *Fortune*, *Business Week*, and *Forbes*. Specifically, we will each strive for short sentences and paragraphs, common diction, active voice, and frequent headings. Because our work will be read by a wide audience, we will avoid jargon and unnecessarily complicated charts and graphs."

4. "We're wasting time by trying to work together." Writing teams must learn to value the time spent in comparing ideas and in coordinating effort. The time devoted to the process of team writing is as important as the individual time given to the product of putting words together on paper. The company wants the eventual document to speak for a consensus in the company, not just an individual. That consensus can be forged only by patient, active participation by team members as they share insights, resolve conflicts, and coordinate work activities.

Consider the experience of one writer on the team we have discussed:

> I'll admit that I wasn't happy at first to be assigned to a writing team for an important report. As a veteran engineer in the company, I'm more comfortable working on my own projects, where I have more personal control and accountability. But after a few meetings with the team, I began to see one of the advantages of group writing. Even though our specific work was writing a document, our more general work was getting to know and trust one another. Until I worked with this team, I had little to do with employees outside of Engineering. Now I know how other people from other departments think and work. When our document is eventually published in the company, I'll be in a position to explain or even defend it to the people I work with in Engineering.

Participating as a Member of a Collaborative Writing Team

Getting ready to work effectively as a writing team involves, first, a shift in attitude. A manager fresh from MBA or college writing experiences must be prepared to listen well at the first organizational meeting of the writing team. When each member shows sincere interest in the opinions of other members, an environment of trust quickly develops. Team members aren't tempted into prima donna roles or competitive rivalries.

Second, team members should express ideas and reactions candidly and provisionally, not in an absolute way. All team members have to speak up if the project is to take shape. It does little good for one team member to tell another, "Your idea just won't work." Such absolute verdicts drive team members apart. If negative judgments need to be expressed, they should be phrased constructively: "I want to understand how your idea fits this project."

Third, team members have to avoid sole ownership of ideas. Once a suggestion is made to the group, it becomes the property of all. Ideas should not be labeled permanently as "Cal's opinion" or "Barbara's notion." That kind of ownership limits discussion to little more than interpersonal politics. The team should agree in advance that there's "nothing personal" in positive or negative comments about ideas. The goal is simply to come up with the best writing plan possible, no matter whose ideas won or lost.

Finally, team members must respect and value one another's differences. It's not uncommon for each member of a writing team to look at the work of others and say, silently, "I could have done it better." In fact, the final document reflecting the work of all team members will probably not be completely pleasing to any one team member. There will always be a turn of phrase, an elaboration here, or a condensation there that will raise an eyebrow among some members of the writing team.

Such differences are inevitable and should be expected. They don't prove that team writing is mediocre writing; instead, these differences demonstrate that we each have our own opinions about what makes good writing. A major writing project shouldn't be held captive to any one vision of writing style. The strength of team writing lies in its ability to harmonize somewhat different voices into a shared chorus.

Leading a Collaborative Writing Team

The coordinator or leader of a collaborative team has the often difficult task of keeping the project moving forward while simultaneously "putting out fires" involving disputes between group members, failure of some members to contribute, and inability of members to agree on common purpose or method. Every collaborative team leader will at some time encounter these common complaints from team members:

1. "No one listens to me." Your job as team coordinator is to make each team member feel valuable to the project and respected by other team members. Inevitably, some team members will contribute more than others. But the team leader should do everything possible (including personal conferences and negotiated duties) to prevent malaise, withdrawal, or resentment from disrupting the work of the team.

2. "Who says you get to make the rules?" Occasionally, a frustrated team member will directly challenge your role and authority as leader. In such cases, let others in the group speak for you, or you can remind the complaining team member that you have the support of the other team members. It may also be helpful in some situations to explain that your leadership duties are professional, not personal. You're simply fulfilling a necessary job, not seeking inappropriate power or glory.

3. "Why can't we just get the project done right away?" In any process involving the work of several people, occasional delays will occur as one team member waits for another to complete his or her work. Make sure that your team understands both the inevitability of glitches in the team approach to writing and the importance of completing work on which others depend.

4. "Where does he get off telling me I'm wrong?" We are all sensitive to negative criticism about the way we speak or write. That sensitivity carries over to the workplace, especially when one team member criticizes our work as "too wordy," "unclear," or "disorganized." We respond defensively—"do it yourself, then"—instead of understanding and possibly profiting from the interchange. As coordinator, emphasize that criticism is directed at the passage, not the person who wrote it. Conducting revision and editing sessions in a good-humored way goes far in alleviating the potential hostility that can develop when team members spar over language choices.

5. "I don't understand the changes you've made." Especially as deadlines approach, the team leader may change the work of other members in what may appear to be a high-handed way. If a team member requests an explanation, it's important for the coordinator to provide one. Never simply say that a passage is "better my

way." Doing so breeds ill will in the team and fails to teach preferable alternatives to the objecting team member.

Using these guidelines can help a team leader deal quickly and fairly with some of the most common interruptions to the smooth functioning of a collaborative writing team.

SUMMARY

Business writers choose voices appropriate to their audience. In general, the proper voice for business documents is the business voice. Having settled on a voice, the writer looks to individual words within the document, striving to make them

- Specific and concrete
- Active, not passive
- Positive, not negative
- Distinct, not clustered
- Clear, not vague
- Emphatic
- Correct
- Lean
- Unbiased

Such words create effective sentences, which, in turn, find their place in paragraphs ordered by the exposition, enumeration, inquiry, or other pattern. Paragraphs achieve coherence and unity through transitional words, linked key terms, and organization around central ideas.

Collaborative writing teams must have a thorough understanding of the process by which their work can be accomplished most successfully.

QUESTIONS FOR DISCUSSION

1. What does business style generally emphasize, and why?

2. What three "voices" are available to you as a business communicator?

3. How do these three voices relate to each other in psychological terms? Which one is the voice you want to strive for?

4. Should Latinate terms be avoided in your text?

5. Is it more important to amplify the content of a word or its volume? Why?

6. How do readers respond to active verbs?

7. In passive constructions, where does the object appear in the sentence? What is the preferable native English pattern?

8. What is a noun cluster? How can you avoid it?

9. How can you solve the problems created by vague pronoun references?

10. Where are the strong slots of sentences located? How can you make use of them to create impressive business prose?

11. What are the three disguises of wordiness?

12. How can sexist language be avoided?

13. When are sentence fragments or comma splices acceptable in business writing?

14. What problems do collaborative writing teams often encounter?

EXERCISES

1. Find a writing sample containing either the encyclopedic or the emotional voice, and rewrite it, using the business voice.

2. Rewrite the following vague sentences, providing specific information: (a) He was tall for his age. (b) The company took a big loss last year. (c) Henderson quit because he needed more money.

3. Transform the following passive sentences into the active voice: (a) It was decided by the committee that parking fees should be raised. (b) The job was performed well by them. (c) The library was staffed by only two librarians this weekend.

4. Substitute positive words for negative ones in the following sentences: (a) I absolutely deny any involvement with union activists. (b) She refused to work overtime, claiming that she wanted to spend the weekend with her family. (c) Don't make the mistake of coming to work without the proper attire again, please.

5. Change vague pronouns to strong-slot words in the following sentences: (a) This is the most productive time of year for us. (b) It must seem like you've gone through a time warp when you visit Williamsburg, Virginia. (c) That she would agree to go out with him on Friday night was all he wanted.

6. Write a paragraph about your preparation for a business communication course, following the exposition pattern.

7. Write a paragraph listing your best qualities as a communicator, following the enumeration pattern.

8. Write a paragraph requesting information about a class lecture that you missed, following the inquiry pattern.

9. In general, business writers prefer the active voice to the passive voice. Describe in writing an occasion or situation in which the passive voice would be more appropriate than the active voice for communication. Give an example to support your point.

10. Revise the following sentences so that they begin with the subject, as discussed in this chapter.

   After carrying the heavy package up the subway stairs and across Sixth Street to his office, Tom Evans breathed heavily.

   Although she was not at first the company's favorite candidate for the position, Jill Foster got the job.

> When reporting on the measurement of distances for European and Asian clients, remember to use the metric scale.

11. Revise these noun clusters by rewriting these sentences:

> We were particularly impressed by her Grand Canyon soils erosion measurement study.

> Last Friday, he obtained his state training orientation instructor certification.

> Few managers attended the senior citizen home-maintenance seminar planning session.

12. Rewrite the following sentences to replace Latinate vocabulary with more common English words:

> In order to ameliorate the circumstance, we facilitated the involvement of a counselor.

> Subsequent to her departure from the company, Linda Smith was assigned to an administrative position in a management capacity for the accounting division.

13. Rewrite the following sentences to repair sentence fragments and comma splices. Add words where necessary.

> When deciding whether to enter the military prior to college.

> The most likely successor to Helen Wald, the present chairperson of the committee.

> Both managers appreciated the opportunity to attend the convention, neither was willing to travel by car.

> The specifications for the new factory wing contained several errors, these included a mistake in the type of concrete required for the floor.

14. Create a "T"-chart showing the pros and cons of a collaborative writing experience in which you have been involved. For each of the con points, write a sentence or two suggesting how the difficulty could have been resolved.

15. Interview one or more fellow students who have served as leaders of a writing team either for a school project or in business. Determine what the person found most challenging and most rewarding in the capacity of team leader. Ask what the person would do differently in a similar leadership role for a writing team in the future.

INTERNET ASSIGNMENT

In your university studies, you had many opportunities to work on projects in a team environment. Now that you're in your first professional position, you're surprised that many of your colleagues have never worked as team members on a major writing or presentation project. This lack of experience on their part poses a special problem for you when you receive word from your boss that you've been chosen to head up a collaborative writing team to produce (under tight deadlines) an important report to a government regulatory agency. You know that the people assigned to your team will never be able to produce the product required if they are not skilled in the process of collaborative work. Investigate Internet resources in the Principles and Techniques of Business Writing section and the Meeting Skills section of the Internet Guide. Write a memo addressed to your team in which you summarize for them what you've discovered on the Web and recommend specific ways in which they can use these resources to learn more about the collaborative writing process.

PART TWO

CORRESPONDENCE

CHAPTER 5

Form and Style of Business Letters

This chapter discusses the most important written communications seen by your company's customers and the general public—your business letters. By the words you choose, by the way you arrange them on the page, and even by the letterhead stationery you select, you create for your reader an image and impression of your company and of yourself. Customers form opinions about whether your company is friendly or snooty, efficient or lazy, modern or old-fashioned, fair or arbitrary, organized or chaotic, based in large part on your letters. To see how quickly (and deeply) such impressions are formed, decide what you think about the company that allowed the letter in Figure 5–1 to be mailed to the customer.

SHOW YOU CARE ABOUT YOUR READERS

The letter in Figure 5–1 clearly puts Haeber Financial Services at a disadvantage in winning Bob Thomas and his pension fund as an account. At his first glance at this letter Mr. Thomas may justly conclude that Haeber Financial Services itself is a slipshod organization. Otherwise, how could one of their investment specialists be allowed to send such a sloppy communication?

The problem lies not only in the glaring punctuation and spelling errors. The letter does not express its points fully and clearly. Its tone is self-centered and hurried. Above all, the letter lacks appropriate respect for and attention to the reader's interest. The focus of the letter is on what "I," the writer, want instead of on what "you," the reader, want. The following examples illustrate the significant difference in effect between an "I emphasis" and a "you emphasis":

FIGURE 5–1   A Poorly Written Letter with Many Errors

HAEBER FINANCIAL SERVICES, INC.
3892 Western Avenue
Baltimore, MD 29832 (123) 555-1234

Jn. 4th, 19__

Mister Bob Thomas
Administater, Public Teachers Pension Fund
193 Lincoln St.
Baltimore, MD 29833

Dear. M. Thomas:

Per my call to you a couple days ago, I think we can put together a package for your membership that will earn in excess of the figures you quoted me from your experience with your previoius money management consultant.

Call me so we can move on this. I'm out of town for several days starting this coming Friday, so ring me before then, please.

Sincerly,

Burton Cay
Investment Specialist

Emphasizing *You* More Than *I*

As a business writer, you must show empathy for your readers, particularly in documents as personal as letters. To show empathy in your letters, you must focus on your reader's needs more than on your own needs. In this book, we call this the *you emphasis* in business writing. The following two examples illustrate the difference between an *I emphasis* and a *you emphasis:*

I EMPHASIS | I am sending information on peripheral devices suited to the computer I sold you.

YOU EMPHASIS | You'll receive complete instructions with details and capabilities and prices of optional add-ons suited to your new computer.

The difference in these two statements may at first seem slight—both do get the message across. Yet the recurring use of *I* in a complete business letter causes your reader to lose interest in the letter—and lose connection with you as well. Show your genuine concern for your reader by emphasizing *you* and downplaying *I* as much as possible.

Showing a Warm, Friendly Tone

Another way of describing this feeling of concern is to say that you use a warm, friendly **tone.** (*Tone* was described in Chapter 1.) Two other techniques help you to convey a warm, friendly tone to your readers:

1. Focus on people more than on things.
2. Include feelings as well as facts.

Focus on People As Well As

Concentrate on *people* as much as you do on things. In the following passage, a supervisor tries to compliment an employee on a well-written report. Notice how the emphasis of the message falls on the document rather than the person and hence ends up sounding hollow and cold.

VERSION 1   "Alternatives in Pension Planning" presents four popular pension plans, each with advantages and disadvantages. The report evaluates the plans in relation to specific company needs. The report is clear and orderly.

Notice how much better the following version sounds, when the supervisor focuses on the *person* instead of the *product*.

VERSION 2   Thank you, Mary, for your good work in "Alternatives in Pension Planning." You've analyzed the four competing plans in a clear, orderly way—just what we need to help us choose the best plan for our company.

When you concentrate on objects, your praise falls on the object instead of going to the person. Readers can hardly be expected to care when an object receives praise. When you move your emphasis to people, however, you create human warmth, and you get more positive responses.

Include Feelings with Facts

In addition to focusing on people more than on things, another way to show a warm, friendly tone is to include some of your feelings when you're telling your reader your facts. This doesn't mean that your letters should gush over with feelings that don't belong in a business letter. The following feelings generally would be inappropriate in a business letter:

- Personal feelings about your personal life
- Personal negative feelings about your company, your supervisor, your coworkers, your customers, your suppliers, or anyone else with whom you work
- Negative feelings toward your reader or any of your reader's associates
- Intense emotions, such as love, hate, anger, or fear

You can probably add many other feelings that you know are inappropriate for a business letter. A helpful guide to figuring out what these would be is to think about what your supervisor wouldn't mind overhearing you say personally to your reader. Your common sense should guide you as to what feelings don't belong in your business letters. When you aren't sure about what doesn't belong, ask someone else to read your letter and give you an objective opinion.

Don't make the mistake of leaving out feelings altogether, though. In modern business writing, your readers expect you to show your feelings in an appropriate way.

Unfortunately, business writers tend to fill their letters with long strings of facts, presented in complex ways. For example,

Trace elements no. 5 and no. 7 appeared in 14% of the Westbury samples, as summarized in Report no. 22, dated May 2, 199_ of the Soils Chemistry Laboratory.

Don't let yourself forget that business writing takes place in a people-centered world. Businessmen and -women are deeply interested in what others do, think, and feel. For example, when reminding a client about a 3 P.M. meeting, don't hesitate to reveal your feelings:

NOT   We will meet at 3 P.M.

INSTEAD   I look forward to talking with you at our 3 P.M. meeting.

Feelings are certainly not out of place in the midst of the hard realities of business. Together with describing the facts, tell the reader how you feel about those facts.

Readers understand the force and importance of feelings in business letters and accurately translate feelings into a significant part of the business message:

The manager writes: "The Sundance Peak project shows some promise."
The reader interprets: "The project sounds tentative, iffy."
The manager writes: "You'll probably share my excitement about the potential of the Sundance Peak project."
The reader interprets: "Excited? There's something worth looking into here."

Writers, of course, can overdo the inclusion of personal feeling. A helpful guide is this: Be as personable in business writing as you would be in a face-to-face business meeting. While your business associates and customers may never know you as well as your best friends do, you can still show many of your feelings in your business writing. Just as important, you can be sensitive to the feelings of your readers.

PREPARING TO WRITE A BUSINESS LETTER

Once you've come to understand the needs of the reader (your audience), you must decide how you're going to speak (write) to him or her. In reading your words, your audience should hear the voice you intend, a way of speaking that is probably very close to the voice you use in conversation. In other words, if you were to read your letters aloud, they should sound like you.

Letters as a Printed Conversation

Prepare for writing a business letter, then, by imagining yourself speaking to your reader face-to-face. While you probably won't use all the words of an actual conversation, you can catch up the natural spirit of conversation in your written words. Chapter 4 described more fully how to choose an appropriate voice and style for business writing.

Though a conversational tone and style is desirable, your written words in letters differ significantly from the actual words you use in conversation. In general, letters are more organized than conversations. Sets of similar and related ideas are set apart as paragraphs. Sentences flow smoothly, without the "uhms," "ahs," and repetitions that mark spoken conversation.

Letters as a Legal Record

Business letters also differ from conversations in a way that isn't obvious at first. Because business letters are written in a printed, permanent form, they can be considered legal documents. Anything you promise or even hint at promising might be considered an informal contract obliging your company to fulfill that promise.

In addition, your company can be legally obliged to make sure that it lives up to anything you state as a fact about your company's services or products. When you "put it in writing," you do more than just "give your word." You are committing your company to a legal obligation. That's quite a responsibility for an entry-level employee. For that reason, businesses large and small now often require that letters leaving the office first be reviewed by an authorized manager. For example, at the Newport Beach office of a commercial real estate brokerage, the office manager each day faces the substantial task of reading, and often rewriting, each and every business letter directed to a client.

Naturally, the manager is eager to catch misspellings, poor grammar, improper punctuation, and so forth. Even more important, however, the manager weighs the legal implications of each business letter. Do the writer's assertions to the client constitute a binding promise—a contract, in effect? Do the words in the letter fairly reflect the truth of the situation at hand, or do they leave the door open for later legal challenge? Are the words clear, or can they be misinterpreted?

After a few months of this kind of editing, managers develop a built-in danger-detector that sounds off when company business writers stray into legally hazardous territory. In the letter by Helen Townsend, in Figure 5–2, note the changes penned in by Helen's manager before it could be reprinted and sent to the client. Helen's manager has wisely revised those claims that may leave the salesperson or the company open to charges of misinformation.

In the original version of the letter, Helen had forgotten that letters stand as signed, permanent legal records of assertions, claims, and representations. Imagine the potential problems Helen would face if the unedited version of her letter had been sent to the client. If the roof had leaked disastrously, Helen could be called to account for misrepresenting the property "the roof is in fine shape"). If the neighborhood turned out to be unbearably noisy, the new owners or their attorney would have every right to question Helen's assurance that "the neighborhood is as quiet as the country."

The words you write on company stationery create lasting impressions of the company and of you. They stand as permanent legal records of representations you have made. Chapter 21, "Ethics and Law for Business Communication," discusses the legal pitfalls business writers must avoid in such areas as personal matters, credit and collection communications, and product representations.

Letters as a Modern Business Tool

Before the widespread use of computers and word processors, business communication had a straightforward way of guarding against problematic misstatements in business writing: guide letters and letter recipes. Business writers had only to follow the standard recipe line-for-line, word-for-word. Many writers kept a guidebook to business letters. When they

FIGURE 5–2   Letter Edited by a Manager

Martindale Realty, Inc.

4422 Trendville Lane
Des Moines, Iowa 50332-5190
(515) 555-3698

May 2, 199_

Mr. and Mrs. Ralph Crown
532 Lincoln Boulevard
Benchton, Iowa 77342

Dear Mr. and Mrs. Crown,

Together, we have searched for the "right" family home for you. As you remarked last week, 1942 Ridgecrest Drive seems to be just what we've been looking for.

I checked into the two matters that concern you.

                  only ten years old
   1. The roof is ~~in fine shape.~~ It was replaced in 1988 by Standard Roofing of Everly-ville.

      Neighbors on both sides of your chosen home
   2. ~~The neighborhood is as quiet as the country.~~
     told me they enjoyed the country–like neighborhood.

Let's plan to see the house once more this Thursday morning. I'll stop by at 10:30 A.M. Please phone if you would like to arrange an alternate time.

Sincerely,

Helen

Helen Townsend
Realtor

---

had to send a letter, they simply looked in the index and found the correct model letter to use as pattern for their letters.

Today's business letters are expected to be friendlier than these impersonal business letters of the past. Writers try to present themselves as gracious, tolerant, understanding, and even witty rather than dry, machinelike, and rigid. Modern readers know the importance not only of stating the message in a letter, but also of motivating the reader to understand the message and to act on it. To be effective, the modern business letter must be empathetic, warm, and friendly. (Figure 5–3 shows a business letter that conveys this warm, empathetic, and friendly tone.)

In addition, modern business letters are much shorter than business letters from the past. Today's letters rarely exceed one or two pages. If more needs to be said, the writer usually encloses additional materials, perhaps in the form of a brochure, a report, or a proposal. Modern readers seem to have less patience for long reading expe-

FIGURE 5–3   Audience-based Business Letter

111 Murphy Street • Salt Lake City, Utah 84106-7324
(801) 555-6744

August 4, 199_

Ms. Millicent Owens
4533 Sanborn Lane
Salt Lake City, Utah 45338

Dear Ms. Owens:

THE CLIENT ASKS: At 9 A.M., Friday, August 22, our analysis team will drop by your home to evalu-
"WHAT DO YOU WANT?"   ate your use of electricity, as you requested. Their work will be neat, quick, and
                           thorough. You need not move furniture or carpets.

THE CLIENT WONDERS: By Monday, August 25, you will receive a computer-developed assessment of your
"HOW DO I PROFIT?"   electrical usage patterns. The report contains recommendations for achieving
                           savings without sacrificing comfort or convenience.

THE CLIENT FEELS SPECIAL: You are a valued customer, and we are eager to help you get the most out of your
"ALL THIS FOR ME?"   utility dollars.

FINALLY THE CLIENT ASKS: Mail in the enclosed registration card to confirm the date and time of your elect-
"WHAT SHOULD I DO?"   rical analysis. Or, if you prefer, phone in your reservation to Kabel by calling
                           1-800-423-3456

Sincerely yours,

Graham Trevor

Graham Trevor
Operations Manager

GT/pm
Enclosure: Registration card

---

riences. They want the message to be brief—and business letters reflect this preference.

Modern business letters are also expected to be more attractive and more error-free
than letters used to be. Word processing, desktop publishing, high-quality printers, spell-
checkers, and grammar-checkers have all contributed to documents that look very professional. The look of a modern letter shows the author's professionalism even before the
reader sees the actual message.

A key feature of the professional look of a modern business letter is its format.

Parts of the Standard Business Letter

Now that you're familiar with the overall tone and appearance you should use for business letters, you're ready to explore each part of the letter. The following are the individual parts of the standard business letter, some of which you must include, some of which

COMMUNICATION TOWARDS 2000

FORM LETTERS

With the appearance of modern computers, preprinted guide letters have almost completely disappeared from business offices. Form letters have *not* disappeared, though. In fact, modern word processors make it even easier to use form letters. Many software programs even provide an entire repertoire of form letters to suit almost any standard business-letter purpose. Also, many companies have a *letter bank*—a software directory of form letters the company uses for routine letters.

The increasing ease of using form letters has made it much easier to send more letters to more people more often. The volume of your incoming mail can certainly testify to the ease of sending a lot of mail to a lot of strangers a lot of the time. When it's mail you didn't want, from someone you don't know and don't want to hear from, you call it "junk mail."

However, as a business writer, you don't call the letters you write "junk mail." The letters you write are important. When you use form letters, you have a good reason to want your readers to read your letters, not toss them into the trash bin.

For example, suppose that your company wants to inform its 5000 customers that an earthquake may have shaken your office building but not your company's solid foundation. You're moving to new temporary offices and will have a temporary mailing address and phone number extensions until more permanent offices can be located. Within three days, you must notify more than 5000 customers. You can't possibly write a personal letter to each one. Business computers allow you to send an individually addressed letter—with a few personalized items in the body of the letter—to many thousands of people within hours.

If you just released or updated a product, added a new service, or need to warn customers about a product defect, these mass-mailing form letters can help you contact countless people right away.

Don't kid yourself, though. Even the most sophisticated, individualized form letters can't replace the personal warmth you can add to the letters you write to a specific person to show that you care about her or his individual business needs. When you send a personalized letter, your readers will recognize your personal concern. Don't use unmodified form letters when you want to show business readers that you genuinely care about their individual needs.

This doesn't mean that you have to write every letter from scratch. It does mean that you must rewrite and revise your letters with your specific readers' needs in mind. Whenever possible, take the time to personalize your letters to meet the specific needs of your readers. They'll notice the difference.

you should include, and some of which are *optional* (you don't need them, but you might want to include them):

- Letterhead (or return address)   (must be included)
- Date   (must be included)
- Inside address (of your recipient)   (must be included)
- Subject statement   (optional)
- Attention line   (optional)
- Salutation   (must be included)
- Body (of the letter—your message)
- Complimentary close   (must be included)
- Signature   (must be included)
- Final notations   (optional)
- Postscript   (optional)

Letterhead

When your reader unfolds your business letter, the first image to greet the reader is your letterhead. Ideally, it attractively displays the image your company wants to convey. Its style and information should tell your reader exactly who you are. Knowing who you are helps your reader to decide whether to read what you have to say.

The letterhead on business stationery always identifies the company, either by name, company logo, or both. The letterhead usually includes the address, city, state, and zip code of the company, as well as one or more telephone numbers and a fax/cable/telex address code or phone number. In some contemporary letterheads, the company name stands at the top of the letter, with all other information arranged at the bottom of the page. Figure 5–4 on page 104 illustrates three kinds of letterheads.

Sometimes even the most artful letterheads leave out information the recipient needs in order to write back: the street address, the full company name, or the zip code. In such cases, be sure to include the missing information in a return address. This block of information about the sender appears first in the order of business letter parts, as illustrated in Figure 5–7. Note that the writer's name and title do not appear in the return address. They are reserved for an identifying line after the signature at the end of the letter. Return addresses and letterheads always append a zip code after the city and state.

Date

Place the date of the letter two line-spaces below the return address; then leave two more line-spaces between it and the inside address. (If several days pass between when you write the letter and when you mail it, you should type the date the letter is to be mailed, not written.) Keep in mind several dont's when you write the date:

- Don't mix letters and numbers in the date (not Feb. 2nd).
- Don't just use numbers (such as 8/21/98 or 9-27-98).
- Don't abbreviate the names of months that have only five or fewer letters. (Standard abbreviations for Jan., Feb., Aug., Sept., Oct., Nov., or Dec. are fine, though.)
- Don't use unusual abbreviations or unusual sequences for the date.

Inside Address

Address your reader by his or her full professional name in the inside address, even if you plan to use a more informal name in the salutation.

Ms. Margaret Finch
Vice-President
Bennington Savings and Loan
381 Fifth Ave.
Princeton, NJ 30283

Dear Margaret,
    (or)
Dear Ms. Finch:

FIGURE 5–4   Samples of Letterheads.

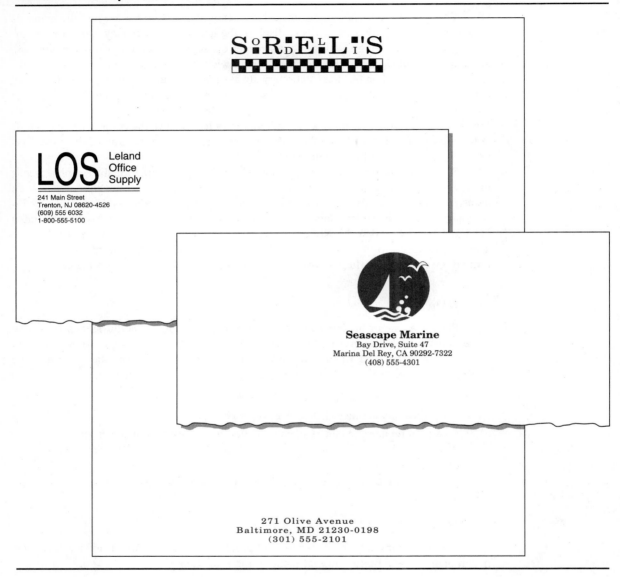

When you don't know the reader's name, use the job title both in the inside address and salutation:

Director of Marketing
Victory Products, Inc.
300 Buena Vista St.
Ft. Worth, TX 46839

Dear Director:

If the person to whom you are writing has no professional title, simply type the name and the company affiliation:

Mr. Ralph Nelson
Sunrise Auto Sales
498 Parkway Drive
Minneapolis, MN 79382

Dear. Mr. Nelson:

The abbreviation *Ms.* is the feminine equivalent of *Mr.* and should be used when addressing women. Do not use *Miss* or *Mrs.* unless your reader has expressed a preference for one of these. It is also accepted business practice to address both men and women without the prefacing abbreviation of *Mr.* or *Ms.*

Barbara Fischer
Sales Manager
Pets International
17 Westmoreland Ave.
Tampa, FL 59030

Notice the titles (Sales Manager) usually appear on the line beneath the reader's name. It is also permissible to attach a short title, following a comma, after the name and on the same line:

Walter Fredericks, Supervisor
Office of Social Welfare
400 State of Iowa Building
Dubuque, IA 40230

In such cases, the writer's goal is to produce an inside address that looks somewhat balanced, with lines of approximately the same length. When the job title is more than one word, place the entire title on the line following the recipient's name.

Next, type the department or division (if any) within the company where the reader is employed. On the next line, type the company name, followed on the next line by the street address. On the next line come the city, state, and zip code. If you abbreviate the state, use the capital-letter postal abbreviations (don't add a period after the abbreviation; for example, CA is California and FL is Florida). A complete, detailed inside address would look like this:

Mr. Harold Robley
Head of Engineering
Division of Mechanics
Raycon Scientific, Inc.
4 Brenton Place
Bellevue, WA 92683

Subject Statement

A subject statement briefly describes the topic of your letter. It should always have two line-spaces above it and below it, to make it stand out. It may be placed between the

FIGURE 5–5   Block Style

Williams Electronic Supply, Inc.
3892 Breston Place
Ft. Collins, CO 80525-4061
(303) 555-9540

January 7, 199_

Mr. Frank Devlin, Manager
Devlin Industrial Wiring, Inc.
55 Leavitt Street
Denver, CO 80216-3113

SUBJECT: Upcoming Industrial Arts Fair, May 15-17, 199_

Dear Mr. Devlin:

Your booth at last year's Industrial Arts Fair certainly made a hit. No doubt your creative staff is already planning surprises for us at this year's fair.

Williams Electronic Supply wants to team up with Devlin Industrial Wiring for this year's fair. Together we can put on a fascinating demonstration of recent advances in domestic and industrial uses of electricity. You and I spoke briefly of this possibility at last year's fair, Mr. Devlin. We agreed then that our mutual efforts would be great for the fair and, of course, good advertising for our companies.

I'm planning to visit Denver on January 18, 199_. Can we meet to discuss our common interests? You can reach me weekdays at the number above. If we haven't made connection by January 15, I'll give you a call before my trip to Denver.

Until then, best wishes from all of us at Williams Electronic.

Sincerely,

Cindy Galloway

Cindy Galloway
Advertising Director

CG/woi
Enclosure: "Planning for the 199_ Industrial Arts Fair"

P.S. We have reserved the booth space next to yours in hopes that we can expand both booths into one large display area.

inside address and the salutation, as shown in Figure 5–5, or between the salutation and the first paragraph of the body of the letter. In formal letters, instead of **Subject:**, business writers sometimes used the abbreviation **Re:**, for the Latin phrase *in re*, which means *in regard to*. Modern business writers are more likely to use **Subject:**, which is usually capitalized for emphasis. A colon follows the subject notation. The words you use to describe the subject of your letter don't have to make a sentence. Try to say precisely what your letter is about in as few words as possible. For example,

SUBJECT: Flood insurance
SUBJECT: Tax considerations of the proposed merger

Subject announcements have the advantage of setting forth in a bold, clear way the topic of your letter. Therefore, they can be particularly useful in business dealings when it is necessary to catch and hold the reader's attention in a direct, if somewhat blunt, way. Because subject headings announce the content of a letter as in a headline, they can also help you to quickly file your business letters.

Subject headings often have the disadvantage of sounding too urgent and impatient, especially in a relatively friendly business letter where personal warmth plays a key role. In addition, subject headings can rob the crucial first sentence of your letter of its importance. After you have announced the subject, you shouldn't restate the same idea in the first sentence of the letter. Therefore, use a longer subject line or an entire sentence only when your meaning requires it.

Attention Line

When you address your letter directly to the company, use the attention line to name a person, position, or department whose attention you are calling to the message. The word *Attention* is often capitalized for emphasis. The use of a colon after the word *Attention* is optional. Place the attention line after the inside address:

Bondaroy Paving Contractors, Inc.
173 Highway 95
Tucson, AZ 60023

ATTENTION: Personnel Director
 (or)
ATTENTION: Personnel Office

Salutation

The traditional greeting (such as "Dear Mr. Bevins:") appears beneath the inside address and occurs in almost all major business-letter formats. By convention, we continue to address business correspondents as *Dear*, even when our feelings are far from fond. No one attaches emotional meaning to it any longer. Therefore, feel free to address even stern collection letters to "Dear" without fear that you are softening your message.

The salutation should be addressed to the same person whose name appears on the first line of the inside address. This doesn't mean that you can't use a more informal version of the name, though. For example, if your inside address was to "Juanita Jimenez," your salutation might read, "Dear Juanita:" However, if your inside address was to "Ms. Jimenez," you would use "Dear Ms. Jimenez:" as your salutation. That is, if you didn't use your reader's first name in the inside address, don't use it in your salutation. If you used a first and last name in the inside address, you may use just the first name, if appropriate, in the salutation. (Note also that modern business letters usually end the salutation either with a colon following the name or with no punctuation at all.)

Correct:	**Correct:**	**Incorrect**
Mr. J. Kelly	James Kelly	Mr. Kelly
Educational Services	Educational Services	Educational Services
1234 Orchard Avenue	1234 Orchard Avenue	1234 Orchard Avenue
Sunnyside, CA 92109	Sunnyside, CA 92109	Sunnyside, CA 92109
Dear Mr. Kelly:	Dear James:	Dear James:

When you don't know the name of the person to whom you are writing, use the job title on the inside address as the salutation. For example,

Personnel Director	Purchasing Agent
Fundamental Equipment Corp.	Garrish Garments
5678 Pinkerton Lane	6789 Robertson Way
York, PA 17404	Hopkinton, MA 01748
Dear Personnel Director:	Dear Purchasing Agent:

Body of Your Letter

The body of the letter contains the message you want your reader to receive. This is the message that motivated you to write the letter in the first place. If there were no body, there'd be no letter. To make your letter immediately pleasing to your readers, though, even the body of the letter may have parts. To grab your reader's attention at a glance, show that your letter has a beginning, a middle, and an end. Figure 5–6 shows how your letter would look if your words took the shape of the empty boxes.

The boxes, of course, are only roughly suggestive of what a letter with a distinct beginning, middle, and end might look like. The importance of the pattern lies primarily in its effect on readers. They perceive at a glance that the beginning of the letter will be easy: it requires the reading of only a sentence or two. Similarly, they notice that the ending, too, is easy—again, requiring that only a sentence or two be read and understood.

They figure that the larger middle paragraph must contain the *heart* of your message. Though some work will probably be required there, they trust that your brief introductory paragraph and brief concluding paragraph will guide their efforts to make sense out of the middle paragraph. Readers resist having to figure out meanings that the writer could and should have helped them to understand.

Of course, some letters have more than three paragraphs. Even your long business letters can show the reader a distinct beginning, middle, and end, with the rest in the middle. The pattern shown in Figure 5–7 shows how this still creates at-a-glance appeal on the page.

When readers see a letter with these three parts in the body of the letter, they believe that you'll help them to make sense out of your points. In addition, you may want to glance back at the advice from Chapters 3 and 4, which described how to write clear messages in an appropriate business voice.

FIGURE 5–6   Visual Appearance of a Business Letter

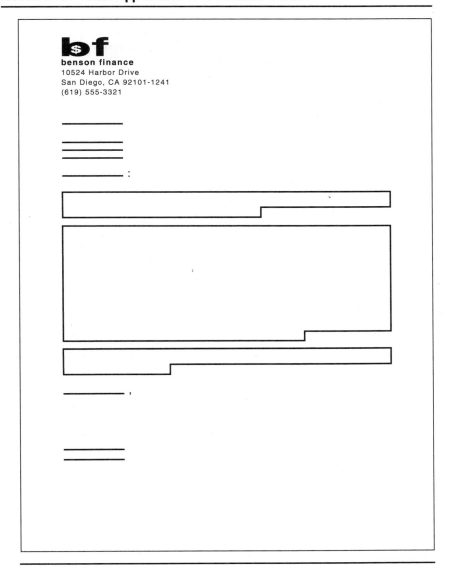

A helpful idea mentioned previously is to use the white space on the page to show off key information. For example, use displayed bulleted or numbered lists to set off long lists of things you want your reader to pay attention to. The following communication checkpoint uses a displayed numbered list to show you some other key ideas for writing the body of your letter. Notice how much easier it is to tune in to each idea when the items are set off in a displayed list (compared to a very long paragraph).

FIGURE 5–7   Parts of a Longer Letter Arranged for Easy Reading

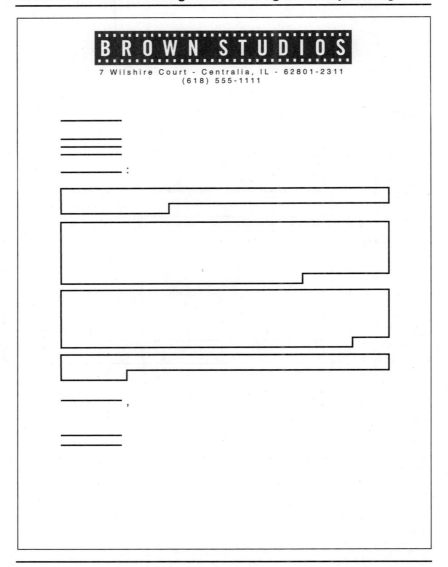

1. *Complete:* Is the body of your letter *complete*? Have you included all the facts, arguments, examples, and details you need to make your point?

2. *Coherent:* Are your letter's points *coherent*? Do they link together in an organized, logical way? Have you helped your reader move from point to point with transitions? (Transition words such as *therefore*, *however*, and *but* may help your reader.)

3. *Concise:* Is the body of your letter's points *concise*? Have you used the fewest words you can? Have you cut out any padding that your reader doesn't need to get your message?

4. *Concrete:* Is your letter's language *concrete*? Do you use easy-to-understand words that give your reader specific mental pictures about your message? Do your verbs show actions (such as *direct, send, produce*) instead of just being (such as *is, are, were, was*)?

5. *Convincing:* Does your letter sound *convincing*? Is your letter ordered logically so that you persuade your reader to understand and trust in your message?

6. *Considerate:* Is your letter and its message *considerate*? Do you show your readers you care about their needs in the message you send and the way in which you send it? Have you looked at your letter from your reader's point of view? Have you used a warm, friendly tone that tells your readers you care about their needs?

Complimentary Close

This brief word (such as *Sincerely*) or phrase (such as *With best wishes*) is your last chance to show regard for your reader. After the body of the letter, insert two line-spaces and then type the complimentary close that seems most appropriate to you. A century ago, the complimentary close was extremely flowery:

I am, believe me, dear Sir, your devoted servant,
   With deepest regards for your well-being.
      Most Sincerely,

In contrast, modern business writers usually use just one word to close most business letters.

Sincerely,

When businesspeople know and like their readers, they feel an urge to express personal regard. This friendliness should show in the tone of the entire letter, but the complimentary close offers a chance to show genuine feeling. For example, in place of *Sincerely*, you may want to type *Cordially, Best wishes,* or *Warm regards*. However, not all closings are suitable for most business readers. Complimentary closings such as *Cheers!* or *Greetings to all* might not be appropriate for most clients, most companies, most writers, or most messages.

How do you know when to use a warmer complimentary closing than *Sincerely* in a business letter? To a large degree, your own feelings will guide you correctly. When you weigh those feelings, keep in mind these common business practices:

1. A first letter to a new client or unknown reader usually closes with a conservative ending such as *Sincerely*. Warm personal regards in such an initial letter can be seen as insincere because the reader has no basis yet for judging your feelings.

2. Business letters that begin with a first name—Dear Jenny—can close with a warmer ending than *Sincerely*. In fact, *Sincerely* may make the reader feel that you have chosen a rather traditional, noncommmittal closing for what may have been a warm and somewhat personal letter.

Your common sense should guide you, and when in doubt, ask for a second opinion.

Signature

Because your typed full name and professional title (optional) appear beneath your signature, you don't need to take pains to ensure that your signature shows perfect penmanship. Most business signatures have a bit of personal flair—a hint regarding the personality of the signer. Also, it isn't always necessary to sign your name exactly as it is typed on the business letter. In a particularly friendly letter, you may wish to sign with just your first name:

Best wishes,

Frank

Franklin J. Clinton
Director of Sales

In a more formal letter, you may sign your entire name.

Best wishes,

Franklin J. Clinton

Franklin J. Clinton
Director of Sales

Signatures are the only nonmachine mark on a typed letter. As such, those few strokes of the pen provide valuable clues to the reader about your temperament, vitality, and even your reliability. For example, notice your own responses to this signature:

Franklin J. Clinton

Take a moment to evaluate your professional signatures in the same way you look at the rest of your letter. Beginning writers often find they try too hard when signing an immaculately typed letter. You may want to practice your signature several times on scratch paper. Use a signature that pleases you, and sign your letters naturally and confidently.

Final Notations

A series of notations often appears at the bottom of business letters, always below the signature and along the left-hand margin.

Copy notation. The *cc* notation, followed by a colon, stands for *carbon copy*, though carbons have long since been replaced by photocopies in most businesses. Writers place these notations at the bottom of letters to tell their readers to whom copies of the letter have been sent. It is also appropriate, especially for emphasis, to use *copy* instead of *cc*.

Sometimes, you may want to send a copy of a letter to a third party *without* the knowledge of the original reader. (For example, you may want a manager or supervisor to keep a copy.) If so, you may note *bc* for *blind copy* on the copy you send to the third party as well as on your own copy. Do not, of course, also include the *bc* notation on the original letter.

Enclosure simply records on the business letter the list of additional items you have included with the letter. In the letter in Figure 5–8, this brief notation tells the reader what Mr. Clinton sent along with the letter. If a secretary prepares Mr. Clinton's letter for mail-

FIGURE 5–8   Letter with Final Notations

Mortan Building Supply
253 Lansdon St.
Cheyenne, WY 82009-1323
(307) 555 2839

September 12, 199_

Ms. Barbara Wilkins
Manager, Supply Group
Lakston Wholesale Supply
2493 Peterson Blvd.
Santa Fe, NM 87501-0982

Dear Ms. Wilkins:

For the past four years, we've been a steady customer of yours for R-19 insulation. But in the future, we'll be using R-24 insulation.

Wyoming has just changed its building code requirements regarding insulation in residential properties. From now on, only R-24 or better insulation meets state and local codes.

That leaves us with a problem: we have 117 units of R-19 now in stock. May we return them for credit?

Please let me know if you plan to stock R-24 insulation, and what our volume price will be.

My thanks.

Sincerely,

Franklin J. Clinton

Franklin J. Clinton
Director of Sales

cc: C. Busrin, D. Henderson

FJC/dc
Enclosure: "199_ Insulation Requirements"

ing, the enclosure notation serves as a reminder to also enclose the materials specified. When the reader files the letter, the enclosure note stands as a record of pertinent related materials that came with the letter. To help remind yourself and your reader what you enclosed, list enclosures by title whenever possible.

Reference initials identify both the author of the letter—Franklin J. Clinton—and the typist (*dc* for David Collins). Note that the author's initials are all-capitals and precede the typist's initials, which are lowercase. The writer's initials can be separated from the typist's by a colon or slash. An identifying code number for word processing may also be included with, or may take the place of, the reference initials.

When mailing copies of a letter to others, attach a brief note to the copy or clearly label it COPY. Photocopy machines have made copies look so much like originals that many business readers can't tell at a glance whether they are reading the typed version or a copy. They become disconcerted to read halfway through the letter (often in confusion) only to realize, "Oh, this letter isn't for me. It's just a copy." You can prevent this misunderstanding by attaching a note of guidance: "For your information" or "For your files." You may also simply circle the *cc* line to make it clear that the letter is a copy.

Postscript

Located below all other matter on the letter, a postscript identifies a message that you want to add to the letter—often a thought or a request that deserves the reader's special attention. The postscript is marked by the letters *P.S.*

P.S. If you act now, we'll include a free Map Atlas with your set of encyclopedias.

Historically, postscripts were used to set down afterthoughts. In modern business practice, though, if you discover that you have omitted an important sentence or two from your letter, retype it to include the message in the body of the text. Reserve postscripts for occasional use to highlight an idea or action step you wish to emphasize. Used with discretion, postscripts can serve the writer as a highlighting technique. Used too often, they make business correspondence seem hasty and disorganized.

Standard Formats for Business Letters

When seeing your letter for the first time, a reader is impressed first by overall appearance and only thereafter by actual words. The format—the shape, arrangement, and order of letter and envelope parts matters not merely as a nod to business tradition but as a crucial component of letter-writing success. The preceding parts of a letter can be arranged into one of four common format styles for business letters. These formats are so familiar to business readers that if a letter arrives on your desk in any of these formats, it will probably take you no time at all to figure out the format and move immediately to the message of the letter. Figures 5–5, 5–9, 5–10, and 5–11 illustrate each of the four major format styles. As you read the description of each style, refer to the figure that illustrates the style.

Block Style (Figure 5–5). In this popular business format style, all parts of the business letter are printed (or typed) beginning at the left margin. Paragraphs are separated from one another by one or two extra line-spaces. This is a relatively modern-looking style and gives you an impression of being up-to-date. The writer may choose to use a colon or a common after the salutation and a comma after the complimentary closing, or the writer may choose to use **open punctuation** (no common or colon after the salutation or after the complimentary closing).

Indented Style (Figure 5–9). Three elements of the indented style are moved to the center margin: the return address (if letterhead stationery is not being used), the date, and the signature block, including the complimentary close. Paragraphs are indented, usu-

FIGURE 5–9   Indented Style

Williams Electronic Supply, Inc.
3892 Breston Place
Ft. Collins, CO 80525-4061
(303) 555-9540

DATE MINDLINE
January 7, 199_

Mr. Frank Devlin, Manager
Devlin Industrial Wiring, Inc.
55 Leavitt Street
Denver, CO 80216-3113

SUBJECT: Upcoming Industrial Arts Fair, May 15-17, 199_

Dear Mr. Devlin:

     Your booth at last year's Industrial Arts Fair certainly made a hit. No doubt your creative staff is already planning surprises for us at this year's fair.

INDENTED

     Williams Electronic Supply wants to team up with Devlin Industrial Wiring for this year's fair. Together we can put on a fascinating demonstration of recent advances in domestic and industrial uses of electricity. You and I spoke briefly of this possibility at last year's fair, Mr. Devlin. We agreed then that our mutual efforts would be great for the fair and, of course, good advertising for our companies.

     I'm planning to visit Denver on January 18, 199_. Can we meet to discuss our common interests? You can reach me weekdays at the number above. If we haven't made connection by January 15, I'll give you a call before my trip to Denver.

     Until then, best wishes from all of us at Williams Electronic.

SIGNATURE BLOCK MIDLINE

     Sincerely,

     Cindy Galloway

     Cindy Galloway
     Advertising Director

CG/woi
Enclosure: "Planning for the 199_ Industrial Arts Fair"

P.S. We have reserved the booth space next to yours in hopes that we can expand both booths into one large display area.

ally five spaces. This common style is somewhat more traditional and literary in appearance than the block style. It requires more care and effort on the part of the typist, however, and partly for that reason is less popular in business today than the block style. The open style of omitted punctuation is rarely if ever seen in this more conservative format.

FIGURE 5–10   Modified Block Style

Williams Electronic Supply, Inc.
3892 Breston Place
Ft. Collins, CO 80525-4061
(303) 555-9540

DATE MINDLINE   January 7, 199_

Mr. Frank Devlin, Manager
Devlin Industrial Wiring, Inc.
55 Leavitt Street
Denver, CO 80216-3113

SUBJECT: Upcoming Industrial Arts Fair, May 15-17, 199_

Dear Mr. Devlin:

Your booth at last year's Industrial Arts Fair certainly made a hit. No doubt your
creative staff is already planning surprises for us at this year's fair.

NO INDENTION   Williams Electronic Supply wants to team up with Devlin Industrial Wiring for this
year's fair. Together we can put on a fascinating demonstration of recent advances
in domestic and industrial uses of electricity. You and I spoke briefly of this possibility
at last year's fair, Mr. Devlin. We agreed then that our mutual efforts would be great
for the fair and, of course, good advertising for our companies.

I'm planning to visit Denver on January 18, 199_. Can we meet to discuss our common
interests? You can reach me weekdays at the number above. If we haven't made connection by January 15, I'll give you a call before my trip to Denver.

Until then, best wishes from all of us at Williams Electronic.

SIGNATURE BLOCK   Sincerely,
MIDLINE

Cindy Galloway

Cindy Galloway
Advertising Director

CG/woi
Enclosure: "Planning for the 199_ Industrial Arts Fair"

P.S. We have reserved the booth space next to yours in hopes that we can expand both
booths into one large display area.

Modified Block Style (Figure 5–10).   In this formation, elements of both the block
style and indented style appear. The return address (when not using letterhead), the date, and
the signature block are moved to the center margin. All other letter parts are placed along the
left margin. Paragraphs are not indented. Open punctuation is commonly used. The modified

FIGURE 5–11 AMS Simplified Style

Williams Electronic Supply, Inc.
3892 Breston Place
Ft. Collins, CO 80525-4061
(303) 555-9540

January 7, 199_

Mr. Frank Devlin, Manager
Devlin Industrial Wiring, Inc.
55 Leavitt Street
Denver, CO 89483

UPCOMING INDUSTRIAL ARTS FAIR, MAY 15-17, 199_

Your booth at last year's Industrial Arts Fair certainly made a hit, Frank. No doubt your creative staff is already planning surprises for us this year.

Williams Electronic Supply wants to team up with Devlin Industrial Wiring for this year's fair. Together we can put on a fascinating demonstration of recent advances in domestic and industrial uses of electricity. You and I spoke briefly of this possibility at last year's fair. We agreed then that our mutual efforts would be great for the fair and, of course, good advertising for our companies.

I'm planning to visit Denver on January 18, 199_. Can we meet to discuss our common interests then? You can reach me weekdays at the number above. If we haven't made connection by January 15, I'll give you a call before my trip to Denver.

Until then, best wishes from all of us at Williams Electronic.

Cindy Galloway

Cindy Galloway
Advertising Director

CG/wol
Enclosure: "Planning for the 199_ Industrial Arts Fair"

---

block style is less common than block style and indented style, but it can be useful when the writer is trying to strike a modern look that still appears balanced on the page.

AMS Simplified Style (Figure 5–11).   This style uses a subject line, often without the "Subject:" notation, at the head of the letter. The salutation is omitted entirely, or worked into the opening sentences of the first paragraph. The complimentary close is also omitted, with the writer's signature appearing three or four blank lines between the end of the letter text and the writer's typed name. All other conventions of the block letter style are maintained.

This relatively new style is gaining popularity particularly in companies where correspondence is often sent to customers or prospects with names that are ambiguous with regard to gender (Pat, Chris, Lee, and so forth). Because the salutation is omitted, the writer doesn't have to decide whether Mr. or Mrs. is appropriate. The somewhat stark appearance of the letter can be softened by a personable tone.

When the letterhead supplies the address of the sender, that information need not be repeated in a return address. When using blank paper, supply any addresses or division/unit/group/office numbers that your reader may require to reply to your letter. The date appears above the inside address, usually separated by double-spacing.

Block, indented, and modified block are all used frequently in contemporary business. The block style is most popular. It is easy to type (and easy to instruct new typists to use) because all lines are **flush** (straight in a vertical line) on the left margin. For some writers and readers, this style has a bold, urgent appearance.

Others still prefer the softer, more balanced patterns in the indented and modified block formats. These writers and readers like the way this style emphasizes the reader's name and address without visual interference from the date and, in some cases, the return address. They like the placement of the complimentary close, feeling that it has more impact when set on a margin with the date and the return address. Some advocates point to the symmetrical balance of these formats.

Other experimental formats appear from time to time. However attracted you may be to such innovative forms, consider the risk that some of your readers may expect traditional business formats as a sign of traditional business practices. Such readers may react negatively to experimental formats.

Whichever business format you choose, check for the shape and the print quality of your letter:

SHAPE   Does the body of your letter have at-a-glance appeal? Does it look balanced, attractive, and organized on the page?

PRINT QUALITY   Have you chosen type that looks professional? Have you avoided smudges, half-printed characters, uneven spacing, and the printer-problem look?

Beginning business writers may use these guidelines to revise the rough draft of a business letter. With experience, these standards can become almost second nature to the writer—good habits that make the task of letter writing fast, effective, and satisfying. The following communication checkpoint suggests a summary of the points you should look for before you let your letter go out the office door.

Communication Checkpoint
Effective Letters

1. From your point of view as the writer:
   - Have I expressed my message clearly?
   - Have I supported my points where necessary?
   - Have I arranged my ideas persuasively?
2. From your reader's point of view:
   - Is the language of the letter easy for your reader to understand?
   - Is the message directed to your reader's needs?
   - Is the length of the message appropriate?

- Is the tone of the letter appropriate for the message and the relationship between the writer and the reader?

3. From your company's point of view (correctness and completion):
   - Is the letter free of surface errors (grammar, mechanics, spelling, usage, and so forth)?
   - Does the letter follow standard business letter conventions (block form, modified block, simplified style)?
   - Has the letter been signed?
   - Have you made copies of the letter, if necessary?
   - Has the envelope been correctly prepared?

SUMMARY

1. Both your company's image and your career advances can depend on your business letters.

2. Combine a clear message with a clear understanding of your readers' needs.

3. Business letters have important legal implications for the writer and for the company.

4. Effective business writers emphasize the *you* perspective in letters.

5. Appropriately expressed feelings are important in business letters.

6. Form letters and guide letters must be personalized to be effective.

7. Business letters usually appear in block, indented, or modified block style.

8. Conventions of folding letters and the placement of address information on envelopes are important to the success of business letters.

9. The way in which the parts of business letters are arranged on the page should allow for easy reading.

10. The major parts of the business letter are the letterhead, date, inside address, salutation, body, complimentary close, and signature.

11. Minor (optional) parts of the business letter include final notations such as subject line, attention line, reference initials, enclosure, copy information, postscript, and others.

QUESTIONS FOR DISCUSSION

1. Do the expectations of your readers influence the format you choose in business letters? How? Why?

2. How do the three major letter styles differ?

3. How can the salutation and complimentary close emphasize feelings of friendship?

4. Name and discuss six basic considerations to bear in mind when composing the body of a business letter.

5. How should a business letter be folded?

6. How would you define the following abbreviations and describe their placement on the business letter: cc, pc, bc, enc, AHB/sra, AHB:sra, WP30465, P.S.?

7. What is a letterhead? What is its importance on the business letter?

8. Why is an appropriate business signature important?

9. Why can't business correspondence always be written according to fixed recipes?

10. How would you define the *you* perspective in business correspondence? Give an example of this perspective.

11. What are some of the legal implications of letters sent from your company?

12. Consider "junk letters" you receive. In what ways do they abide by and/or ignore the principles discussed in this chapter?

13. List at least six common complimentary closes. Which do you prefer? Why?

14. What should a company consider when developing a letterhead for all stationery?

EXERCISES

1. Collect at least three letters that you think may reflect negatively on the writer or the company. On a separate sheet or in marginal notations, show why. Then rewrite the letters to repair the problems.

2. Find a business letter that you think is well done. With a red pen or pencil, locate (by underlining) places where the writer really showed concern for the reader's needs.

3. Write a short business letter announcing the opening of a new student clothing store. Address your letter to area residents. In the first version of the letter, express your message from the *I* point of view. Then rewrite the letter to emphasize the *you* perspective. Compare the two letters. Write a short statement explaining which is most successful and why.

4. Find a business letter written in block form. Rewrite the letter in indented or modified block style. Compare the results in a written statement.

5. Fold the letter in exercise 4 or 5 (or a blank sheet of paper), and place it correctly in an envelope. Address the envelope.

6. Find a business letter that looks unattractive to you. Rewrite it for a more pleasing effect.

7. Write a business letter on a subject of your choice, using any of the three major styles. Use all major letter parts in your letter. Also using the following final notations: cc, enc, P.S., reference initials, word processing code.

8. Conduct a brief survey of responses to block, indented, and modified block style. Which style do your classmates prefer? Which style do businesspeople prefer?

9. Read the following postscript to a business letter addressed to a prospective client. Evaluate in writing the effect such a P.S. may have on its reader.

P.S. I forgot to mention the third advantage of our RiDex office systems: a 24-month guarantee, including repair labor or replacement. Sorry.

10. Write an appropriate subject line for each of these situations:
    a. A letter informing the reader that his life insurance policy #29832 will expire soon, due to nonpayment of premium.
    b. A letter to a bank suggesting that a separate deposit window be opened for merchants from 3 P.M. to 5 P.M. each workday.
    c. A letter to the company personnel director, requesting information on resource and referral programs for employees' elderly relatives.

11. Find three examples of letterhead stationery. Evaluate each in writing, pointing out the positive or negative impressions it communicates about its company.

12. Rewrite and expand each of these neutral messages to include an appropriate expression of feeling.
    a. In the last general election, Paul Carson was elected to City Council. [*Note:* Paul is a manager in your company. You are writing a memo to all employees, informing them of Paul's election.]
    b. Kevin Johnson's mother died yesterday. He will be out of the office for a week. [*Note:* Kevin Johnson is your personnel director. You are writing a memo to inform employees of his mother's death and his absence from work.]
    c. The company president has increased profit-sharing bonuses by 10 percent following a favorable third-quarter report. [*Note:* You are writing a memo to communicate this good news to employees and to share the president's appreciation.]

13. Rewrite this informative message to show your concern for your readers' needs, as explained in the chapter. Specifically, you want to emphasize the importance of this visit to the company without explicitly telling employees how to behave.

The message: "On January 3, company leaders from four Pacific Rim countries will visit our plant. Each of these men and women represents companies that are potential customers. The visit will include a luncheon with employees who would like to attend."

INTERNET ASSIGNMENT

You've landed your ideal job as a mid-level manager in a prominent commercial real estate brokerage. In your opinion, however, the firm has not been well-represented by the quality of the letters sent to clients. These communications are often poorly organized, incorrectly formatted, and flawed in tone. You don't have time to counsel each of the firm's employees on better writing skills. But you can refer them to Internet sites where they can see models of professional letters, memos, and other documents. Research some of these sites (in the Specific Business Documents section of the Internet Guide). Then write a memo in which you describe what you consider to be the most useful of these sites for improving correspondence in your company. Address your memo to all brokers within the company.

CHAPTER 6

Saying "Yes" and "No" in Letters

Companies build goodwill, keep old customers, and win new customers not only by appropriate warmth in saying "yes" to orders, requests, adjustment letters, and credit applications but also by their skill in saying "no" when they must.

Let's begin with a short case study of *yes* communication. Assume that Louisiana Carpet Supply places a first order for 400 boxes of "Tack-strip" carpet bonding from the company you manage. Your options include the following:

- Ship the order and bill without comment.
- Ship the order and notify the client by sending a copy of the shipping order that the boxes are on their way.
- Ship the order and respond briefly in writing to a manager at Louisiana Carpet Supply, a new customer.

It may not be possible to respond to each and every order with a special letter or note. But you should do so often. Any order you receive shows your customer's trust in you; the order shows your customer's belief that you can fulfill a need. As often as possible, therefore, you should respond to that expression of trust by a brief letter, such as the one in Figure 6–1. It contains not only a *yes* message but also an expression of appreciation and goodwill.

Sometimes, you will have to respond with a partial *yes* to an order that you were unable to fill completely. The letter in Figure 6–2 tells in the first paragraph what you were able to do and goes on to suggest a timely solution for filling the rest of the order.

Your readers look forward to hearing you say "yes" to orders, inquiries, requests, invitations, and credit applications. As such, this good news should appear first in your letter. Conditions, qualifications, provisos, and other information should generally follow your clear statement of a positive response.

When clients hear "yes," they value your company's participation in their own progress. You are letting them have their way rather than standing in their way. We all

FIGURE 6–1   "Yes" Letter that Builds Goodwill

 National Carpet Company Inc.
45 Express Way • Louisville, Kentucky 40207-0571
(502) 555-4838

February 12, 199_

Ms. Martha Cummings
Wholesale Manager
Louisiana Carpet Supply, Inc.
6783 Lowry Street
Baton Rouge, LA 70808-1230

Dear Ms. Cummings:

Your order of February 10, for 400 boxes of Tack-strip was shipped to you on February 12, by Southeastern Trucking. They promise delivery to your store no later than February 16.

Please note on the enclosed invoice that you qualified for a 10 percent discount because you agreed to pay C.O.D. for the shipment.

A catalog of our most recent line is enclosed, with several specials marked in red.

National Carpet Company, the volume leader in carpet supplies, appreciates your business. We'll do everything we can to ensure that our products and services keep you coming back.

Sincerely,

Lennis Smythe

Lennis Smythe
Regional Manager
National Carpet Company, Inc.

LS/ow

Enclosure: National Catalog

---

like to have our way, and we like the people and companies who make *yes* possible. In fact, we translate our liking into action. We tell others about the company that helped us. We return to the company for future business.

FORMAT FOR *YES* LETTERS

Yes letters come in a wide variety of forms, but all rely on a simple four-point plan:

1. *Deliver the "yes" message as soon as possible in the letter.* After all, you have good news you're eager to tell the reader. Reserve all the specifics and additional information for a later paragraph.

FIGURE 6–2 Partial "Yes" Letter

Builders Supply _____ 422 W. Main Street
Missoula, Montana 59802-1249
(406) 555-9302

April 9, 199_

Mr. Henry Morgich
Manager, Ace Homes, Inc.
495 Trent Street
Miami, Florida 33148-3179

Dear Mr. Morgich:

Your April 5 order for 650 Tube-Chime Doorbell units (#49592) was shipped that same day and should reach you by April 10.

The remainder of your order, for 100 Choose-a-Tune Doorbell units (#49852), will be shipped on April 15. This popular item has been backlogged since the Christmas holidays.

Be assured that we will ship the Choose-A-Tune units by express as soon as they are in stock, and in no case later than April 15.

Thank you for choosing Nutonic Builders Supply for your wholesale construction needs.

Sincerely,

Roberto Laiso

Roberto Laiso
Assistant Manager

RL/ce

2. *Keep the "yes" message simple.* If at all possible, let the *yes* statement stand by itself without a clutter of conditions, comments, and qualifications in the same paragraph. Good news, when left to itself, establishes a moment of joy for the reader. Don't spoil that moment.

NOT

> At the last meeting of the loan committee, your application no. 4705 for a construction loan in the amount of $70,000 was approved, provided that you acquire and maintain fire insurance in the amount of the loan on the construction project.

INSTEAD

> We're pleased to approve your construction loan for $70,000.

[conditions appear in later paragraphs]

3. *Tell the client exactly what you are saying "yes" to.* Be specific. Especially in contractual matters and questions of credit, it is wise to spell out the exact commitment you are and are not making by your yes response. Has the client, for example, asked for an extension of credit? After granting the request in the first paragraph, spell out in the second paragraph the precise details and conditions of your credit program.

> To protect your project and our investment, we require that you acquire and maintain fire insurance for the amount of the loan.

4. *Sell your company's service, product, image, or relationship.* A customer who has just heard you say "yes" to his or her request may be quite receptive to sales information. Here are several ways in which you can weave your sales message into your *yes* letter:

- Mention a related *product or service* your client might need.

> Our construction loan department offers an inexpensive voucher plan by which you can keep track of construction expenses and subcontracted work.

- Describe the future *relationship* you look forward to with the client.

> We look forward to a solid partnership with you in the development of the Seven Seas resort. Consider our participation, we ask, in future projects.

- Thank the client for past business and promise continued good *service.*

> Since 1995 you have been the kind of client we consider a company friend. We all will do our best to maintain our high level of service to you.

- Compliment the client on his or her current projects, and rehearse the *company's capacity* to assist.

> You deserve congratulations on seeing this project from initial design stage to this exciting time of construction. Keep in mind that Midwest Bank offers full-service banking to builders like you. We also offer loan bookkeeping, cash flow management, commercial checking, and computer payroll services.

- Mention *current developments* at the company and how they will affect the client.

> As you may have noticed, Midwest Bank is undergoing its own construction project with the building of three automated night tellers. If your checking needs occasionally require an after-hours deposit or withdrawal, keep our automated tellers in mind. They will be ready to serve you by January 8.

Saying "Yes" to Orders

Begin the *yes* letter to an order by stating exactly what you are saying "yes" to. You need not repeat the customer's entire order, of course, but do be sure to provide all the information the customer needs to understand what order has been approved. In the next paragraph, explain any conditions, delays, product specifications, and shipping or billing information that the customer needs to know. Conclude with a statement of appreciation and, where appropriate, a sales message.

In Figure 6–3, notice how the writer seems pleased to say "yes" to the order. He says "yes' quickly in this letter, reserving details and the sales message for later para-

---

FIGURE 6–3   Positive Response to an Order

Remington Galleries

Four Smith Place
Homestead, Florida 33034-1431
(305) 555-4960

March 17, 199_

Belinda McNeil
Director, Human Resources
Tennebrach Petrolem, Inc.
3939 Industry Avenue
Miami, FL 33149-6095

Dear Ms. McNeil:

On or before March 22, 199_, we will be pleased to ship 27 art posters from our series "Spring Morning" to your Miami headquarters.

The posters will arrive by United Parcel, C.O.D. Although we take extreme precautions against damage in the packaging of our framed posters, you should check all packages you receive with care. If you discover damage, please notify us immediately, including the insurance number marked on the damaged package.

We trust that you will find pleasure in seeing varieties of "Spring Morning" in your corporate offices. When making plans or decoration elsewhere in your facilities, please consider the beautiful oil paintings and watercolors now available in our fall catalog. These investment-quality art pieces would be a handsome addition to your growing collection of quality works.

Our sincere thanks and best wishes.

Cordially,

Morgan Fairmont

Morgan Fairmont
Sales Director

MF/eis

Enc.: *The Remington Fall Catalog*

graphs. Notice how the writer expresses feeling in words like "pleased," "enjoy," "thanks," and "best wishes." The writer wisely compliments the reader on her order and on the company's growing collection of art works.

Positive responses to orders can build goodwill and pave the way to frequent re-orders. Even if you use a guide letter to suggest appropriate phrases, take the moment or two it requires to respond positively and persuasively to orders.

Saying "Yes" to Inquiries

Like positive responses to orders, these short letters begin with the *yes* statement and then proceed to other paragraphs containing additional information and expressions of feeling. If the inquiry was complex or if a long time has passed since you received the inquiry, you may wish to preface your *yes* response with a brief restatement of the inquiry. You risk repeating information the reader already knows—but that risk is often preferable to the larger risk of saying yes to a forgotten inquiry.

In Figures 6–4 and 6–5 two responses are exemplified, one with an explanation and one without. In the first, the writer repeats the essence of the inquiry before answering it. In the second, the writer simply answers the inquiry without repeating it. Notice how columns and white space are used effectively in the center of both letters.

Saying "Yes" to Requests and Invitations

To often, business writers handle these brief responses without giving them the attention they deserve. The result can be missed opportunities at best and miscommunication at worst.

For example, notice how easily a response to a request can be misunderstood, particularly if a week or two has passed between sending the request and receiving the response. The following invitation is an excerpt from a longer letter.

> Could Mr. Brady attend either the Democratic Committee meeting on Thursday, May 4, or the Regional Caucus on Friday, May 5? If so, could Mr. Brady speak on one of three topics?
> —Should the party endorse a primary candidate?
> —Should the party take a stand on tax reform?
> —Should the party favor import regulations?

Judge for yourself the effect of Brady's terse reply:

> Dear Mr. Slather:
>
> Yes, I believe I can attend. I prefer your second topic, though the third is also acceptable.
>
> I look forward to meeting you.

Brady's brief *yes* answer left Slather confused. Will Brady attend one meeting or both? Will he choose the second topic or the third? Slather, in fact, must hunt up his own copy of the invitation (if he retained a copy) to find out just what the second and third topics were.

You can avoid this sort of confusion by including a brief summary of the request or invitation after the *yes* statement. In the positive response to an invitation in Figure 6–6,

FIGURE 6–4   Positive Response to an Inquiry without an Explanation

9789
Fifth Ave.

Montgomery
Entertainment, Inc.

Chicago, IL
60605-2228

March 20, 199_

Calvin Murphy
30205 West Port Lane
Terminal Island, CA 92930

Dear Mr. Murphy:

(312)
555-4950

We're happy to send along the true names of stars under our management:

Stage name	Actual name
Trixie Rocklin	Patricia Rockinski
Troy Fields	Mortimer Schoel
Bronc Attlington	Bertram Attlington
Sissy Torrell	Sistine Torrellini

We hope this information serves your needs. Best wishes with the research you described in your letter.

Sincerely,

Harvey Montgomery

Harvey Montgomery
Owner/Agent

HM/tel

---

the writer reminds the reader about the nature of the invitation. The letter concludes with an appropriate expression of goodwill.

In some answers to requests and invitations, the *yes* response must be accompanied by qualifications and conditions. For example, suppose that Mr. Brady wanted to include conditions having to do with his introduction at the convention. A paragraph can be inserted after the initial *yes* paragraph in the letter:

I am pleased to accept your kind invitation to the Friday meeting of the caucus.

May I ask, however, that I be introduced to the audience in my capacity as president of a construction company, not as a board member of television station KYEX. I wish to speak freely about my political views without involving the editorial and managerial positions taken by the station.

FIGURE 6–5   Positive Response to an Inquiry with an Explanation

---

Montgomery
Entertainment, Inc.

9789
Fifth Ave.

March 20, 199_

Chicago, IL
60605-2228

Calvin Murphy
30205 West Port Lane
Terminal Island, CA 90731-0052

Dear Mr. Murphy:

(312)
555-4950

In response to your inquiry regarding the true names of actors and actresses under our management, we are happy to provide the following information:

Stage name	Actual name
Trixie Rocklin	Patricia Rockinski
Troy Fields	Mortimer Schoel
Bronc Attlington	Bertram Attlington
Sissy Torrell	Sistine Torrellini

We're glad that you're interested in these stars and wish you well with your continuing research.

Sincerely,

Harvey Montgomery

Harvey Montgomery
Owner/Agent

HM/tel

Here's another example, this time of a qualification on the part of the writer:

> I am pleased to accept your kind invitation to the Friday meeting of the caucus.
>
> In fairness, however, I must remind you of my continuing political support for Assembly-woman Linda Vollens, a Republican. In spite of my long-time Democratic ties, I feel she is a superb legislator. I mention this matter now to prevent possible misunderstanding or embarrassment at the caucus.

Saying "Yes" to Credit Applications

Before you write *yes* to someone who's waiting to hear your answer to a credit application, consider some of the issues at stake. The applicant to whom you are writing has revealed personal and business matters to you in confidence. You know, for example, how

FIGURE 6–6   Positive Response to an Invitation

**Brady
Construction
Inc.**

Trackson Park No. 5
Beverley, Delaware 19930-0444
(302) 555-1072

April 2, 199_

Mr. Ralph Slather, Director
Democratic Convention Committee
254 W. Third Street
New York, NY 10023-3095

Dear Mr. Slather:

I am pleased to accept your kind invitation to the Friday meeting of the caucus.

As you suggest, I'll speak for about forty minutes on tax reform (one of the topics you offered).

I look forward to meeting you.

Sincerely,

James R. Brady
President, Brady Construction, Inc.

JRB/eg

---

much the applicant makes and what debts he or she owes. Hopes have been aroused. The applicant looks forward to a positive answer from you. In some cases, his or her financial stability may depend on your credit approval. In other cases, his or her dreams—a new car, perhaps a new home—depend on your answer.

In these situations, you must choose your words carefully and sensitively. In addition to dealing with the company's money in credit approvals, you are also dealing with people's problems, fears, hopes, and dreams.

Therefore, don't tease the reader with ambiguous messages at the beginning of the credit approval letter. Write a succinct *yes* message that includes the precise terms of the credit granted. Like paper currency, a letter approving credit is virtually a form of money, at least for all transactions between your company and the customer whose credit you approve. Like a paper bill, the letter must bear exact notation of its "denomination" or limits to be of worth. The letter of credit approval, like other *yes* letters, concludes with a paragraph that sells your company.

In the approval letter in Figure 6–7, notice the brisk *yes* beginning, the main details in the heart of the letter, and the restrained sales message in the final paragraph.

The writer delivers good news to the reader and, on the strength of that good news, proceeds to less easy reading: the precise terms of the credit arrangement. In a concluding paragraph, the writer tries to build goodwill and to express appreciation. A final sales message concludes the letter.

It is especially important to read over a credit approval letter before you mail it. Some companies recommend that the writer put initials in the margin beside key amounts and provisions described in the letter. As Chapter 21 explores in detail, such letters, to-

FIGURE 6–7   Credit Approval Letter

597 Cactus Drive
Phoenix, Arizona 85040-1751
(602) 555-7964

October 9, 199_

Mr. Robert Ortega
Best Home Products
4949 W. Thomas Road
Glendale, AZ 85234-0211

Dear Mr. Ortega:

After reviewing your application, we are happy to approve your request for a 90-day credit limit with us for $10,000.

Our credit agreement, enclosed for your approval and signature, provides that wholesale orders may be charged to your credit account for a period not to exceed 90 days. Interest on the unpaid balance during that time will be 18 percent per year. We request that you do not exceed your credit limit of $10,000. You will find additional terms and conditions of this agreement, including billing and payment procedures, in the "Credit Purchaser's Handbook" we have enclosed for you.

We welcome you as a new customer and look foward to your company's continued growth and success. We'll do our part to provide you with the very best in fine lighting products.

Sincerely,

Cary Mellon

Cary Mellon
Credit Manager

CM/wu

Enc.: Credit agreement, "Credit Purchaser's Handbook"

gether with the documents they summarize, often become legally binding documents. An accidental misstatement—$100,000 instead of $10,000—can cause misunderstanding, mistrust, and even significant legal problems.

WRITING *YES* WHEN YOU'RE UNDER STRESS

It's relatively easy to write *yes* and to share good feelings and goodwill, and it's particularly easy to share these messages with those who like you. Sometimes, though, you're going to have to write to people who are angry with you—dissatisfied customers who are frustrated with your products or services, furious suppliers who aren't satisfied with your payment, angry co-workers who don't like their performance evaluations.

Responding Positively to Criticism

It's particularly hard to force yourself to write a response to someone who has let you know that he or she is angry with you or your company. For example, a client may have tried to get information about her account with your company by telephone. Someone in your company (whose name you don't know) apparently told her bluntly that account information was not released by telephone. Incensed, the client writes to you:

> After being put on hold for more than ten minutes, I was told by a very rude man that he was not allowed to give me information about my own account. So I've had to take my extremely valuable time to write this letter.

You realize that her complaint is probably accurate. Your company does have a policy of not releasing some account information by telephone in order to protect your customers' privacy and your accounts' confidentiality. In responding to this customer, you have a choice: On the one hand, you could self-righteously tell her that your company's policy is justifiable, so her feelings are inappropriate. On the other hand, you could acknowledge her feelings and then give her some good news:

> I apologize for any inconvenience you experienced in contacting our company. In matters involving account balances and transactions, we make every effort to protect your privacy by using only written communications, though we regret any delays this policy may have caused you. I'm happy to be able to answer each of your questions at this time.

What's the good news here? (1) You're not angry, responding blow-for-blow to her letter. (2) You can do what she wants. (3) Your company is doing its utmost to serve her interests.

In writing this kind of letter, begin by establishing the good news tone before bringing up any of the details that provoked the original bad feelings. By "starting fresh," you get the communication (and the relationship) off to a new start.

Notice in Figure 6–8 how the writer builds a spirit of sincere goodwill as a means of overcoming negative feelings on the part of her correspondent.

FIGURE 6–8 Positive Response to a Negative Letter

CORPORATION
3728 Clifton Avenue • Columbus, OH 43278-3728
Phone: (614) 555-3304 • Fax: (614) 555-3305

[This reply is in response to a complaint letter from Evan Foster. He wrote that, in several phone calls to the company, he was unable to make contact with anyone who could give him information about summer internships.]

July 8, 199_

Mr. Evan Foster
1898 Sixth St.
Jennifer, Ohio 28932

Dear Mr. Foster:

Your letter was fowarded to me by Ms. Covington, who asked that I contact you immediately with complete information regarding summer internship programs at UniTel.

Our internship coordinator, Margaret Wesley, is presently on maternity leave; we're sorry that your calls weren't routed correctly in her absence.

When you have reviewed the enclosed brochure, "A Summer at UniTel," we hope to receive your application. The deadline for this coming summer's program, you will note, is December 10.

Thank you for your interest in UniTel. Please call me directly at (305) 893-9834 if you have questions.

With best regards,

Phyllis R Wilson

Phyllis R. Wilson
Assistant Coordinator for Internship Programs

Encl: "A Summer at UniTel"

Positive Adjustment Letters

In business, a client occasionally has bad luck with a product or service you provide. A microwave oven suddenly stops waving, a television becomes just a radio, or a waterbed turns into a fire hydrant. The customer writes you a letter in the heat of anger and disappointment, full of woeful descriptions of the product failure and the inconvenience and frustration *you* have caused. The letters often end with vague or not so vague threats about "further action" and "courts of law."

Prepare to write the positive adjustment letter by answering each of the following questions to yourself. You need not answer yes to each question to justify the writing of a positive letter. You may decide to settle the issue by a positive response even if the customer is not right or cannot clearly prove fault on the part of the company. Your decision will be based on a complex set of factors, including your own judgment on a case-by-case basis and company policy.

1. Is the customer right?
2. Is the problem the company's fault?
3. Can I admit that fault?
4. Can I resolve the problem satisfactorily?

Begin your positive response by getting directly to the good news: "Yes, this company grants your claim." You need not repeat the details of the claim itself, except in a brief way to make clear the nature of the positive response. Especially if the details of the claim cause anger for the reader, avoid repeating what went wrong.

Let your *yes* statement be direct. It should satisfy the demand made against the company once and for all. Business letters cost money, and a half-yes merely invites further expensive correspondence, especially when lawyers become involved.

In the letter in Figure 6–9, the writer makes reference to the claim itself only in the SUBJECT line. Thereafter, the claim is quickly granted in the *yes* paragraph that begins the letter. Necessary details are provided in the second paragraph. The writer tries to restore goodwill and customer confidence in the final paragraph.

Businesses do not make a regular practice of sending blanket *yes* letters in response to any and all claims against them. Later in this chapter, we will discuss the *no* letter that must often be sent. Somewhere between these two answers is a middle ground: the positive adjustment letter that nevertheless takes time to educate the customer.

Let's say, for example, that Ms. Malloy's refrigerator is no longer under warranty when you receive her claim letter. Let's say, further, that your company nonetheless decides to fix her refrigerator. In your positive adjustment letter, you take time after the initial *yes* paragraph to educate Ms. Malloy, in a diplomatic way, about the realities of consumer purchases.

Although your refrigerator is no longer under warranty, we will do our best to see that it is restored to good working order. At no expense to you, Garson Appliance Service in your city will be glad to inspect your refrigerator and resolve the problem to your satisfaction.

You may want to know, Ms. Mallow, that you have purchased one of the most reliable refrigerators in the industry, according to Consumer Reports. We're confident that the problem you are experiencing can be easily repaired. At the same time, we urge you to read warranty information carefully for each appliance you buy. In most cases repairs are the responsibility of the purchaser after expiration of the warranty period.

Does such education do any good? Companies hope so. If the buying public begins to expect businesses and manufacturers to grant every claim, few companies can operate profitably. By including a brief paragraph of education for Ms. Malloy, Reston Appliances is making an effort to retain the meaning of important business concepts such as *warranty*.

FIGURE 6-9   Positive Adjustment Letter

45 Harbor Street
Lowell, MA 01888-1376
(617) 555-4857

April 6, 199_

Ms. Anna Malloy
4536 Oak Lane
Beaverton, MA 01223-2214

SUBJECT: Your letter of April 3, 199_: refrigerator malfunction

Dear Ms. Malloy:

According to our records, your refrigerator is still under warranty. At no expense to you,
Garson Appliance Service in your city will be glad to inspect your refrigerator and resolve
the problem to your satisfaction.

Please make arrangements for their visit by calling 427-3842.

You may want to know, Ms. Malloy, that all Reston appliances—including the revolutionary
micropulse dishwashers—are on sale beginning April 15. We've enclosed a sales catalog
for your review.

Thank you for giving us the opportunity to live up to our reputation for quality and service
in refrigeration products.

Sincerely,

Morgan O'Neill

Morgan O'Neill
Customer Relations

MO/wo

Enclosure: Sales Catalog

Finally, the positive adjustment letter provides a good opportunity to mend fences
with disappointed customers. Obviously, a problem has led to the claim against the company. Your positive adjustment letter goes a long way toward repairing the feelings of disappointment and frustration. Buoyed by your *yes* response, in fact, the customer may be
eager to learn of new products, services, sales, promotions, and so forth offered by your
company. Include that information near the end of your positive adjustment letter.

HUMANIZING THE COMPANY

By legal definition, a *corporation*—meaning, literally, a *body*—is empowered with many of the same rights and responsibilities as an individual. Also, like an individual, the company (for better or worse) comes to have a personality of sorts for its clients and the general public. Call to mind the different "personalities" you associate with the following companies: Neiman Marcus, Sears, Prudential, J.C. Penney, Montgomery Ward, Saks, K-Mart, and Exxon. In each case, notice that your impressions have been created in large part not only by your direct experience with the company, but also by its advertising, the reputation of its products, and the events (such as athletic contests) or other social activities with which it associates itself.

The hundreds of business letters that flow out of the company each day also play a key role in creating (or destroying) the company image. A company like Allstate, for example, insists that its business letters, in tone, courtesy, and helpfulness, support the company's image as "the Good Hands People." Despite millions spent on national advertising, that image would quickly fade if Allstate's clients received nothing but stiff, insensitive correspondence from the company.

In choosing positive approaches to your correspondence, bear in mind that each letter that goes out to a client contributes to the big picture—the client's image of and trust in your company.

SAYING "NO" DIRECTLY AND POLITELY

Recognize that many business inquiries, requests, and invitations ask you a simple question: can you or can't you? These businesspeople who ask that question may not want to hear the reasons and justifications for your answer. "No" may be all they have time to hear before setting out in new directions. In short, don't explain your negative answers on all occasions. Your audience may not care about your explanation.

Most of the time, of course, your correspondent may want to know why you've answered "no." A good test for such occasions is to put yourself in your reader's shoes. Would you appreciate an explanation of a negative response? If so, include such an explanation in your letter. This consideration on your part builds goodwill in the long run, even for customers to whom you say "no" in the short run.

Compare the examples of negative response letters in Figures 6–10 and 6–11. The first, though maintaining a friendly tone, does not try to explain the "no" answer. The letter does not spell out specifically why this applicant was denied. It would not have been helpful to tell Francine Gillings that "your grades and test scores qualified you for aid, but your letters of recommendation, in our judgment, seemed somewhat hollow and restrained in their praise of you." In this case, the office chose not to tell all the reasons that led to its negative decision.

By contrast, the letter in Figure 6–11 explains the negative response. The writer wisely chooses to explain in detail why the reader's application for employment was turned down. Consider her reason for doing so: the company has a long-range interest in hiring the applicant at a later date—after his doctoral studies, perhaps, or when he has mastered

FIGURE 6–10   Negative Response without an Explanation

Delvin University Office of Student Aid

4 Callings Building • Kent, Utah 84037-3152 • (801) 555-3363

May 7, 199_

Ms. Francine Gillings
4983 Wilton Place
Boise, Montana 59316-1020

Dear Ms Gillings:

This year the Office of Student Aid reviewed many excellent applications, including yours, for scholarships and grant assistance.

We regret that we are unable to offer you financial aid at this time. You will find enclosed, however, a brochure describing the many low-interest student loan programs now available through local banks working in cooperation with the federal government and this university.

Best wishes for a successful academic year.

Sincerely,

Xavier R. Reyes
Director, Student Aid

XRR/wor

Enclosure: "Low-Interest Student Loans"

UNIX. The explanation for the negative response lets the applicant know what he can do to change the *no* to a *yes*.

In short, you must decide when to explain your *no* response. As a general rule, explain a negative response whenever it will help build goodwill or make possible future contacts. Do not explain if the reader clearly does not care for one, or if your explanation will unnecessarily complicate future contacts with the leader.

In your business career, you will face a steady stream of inquiries and requests. As a manager, for example, you will be asked about job reassignments, promotions, raises, and a host of other matters. You'll be asked to fire Charley, transfer Helen, fund the volleyball team, and sponsor a jog-a-thon. If you intend to support each of your *no* answers

FIGURE 6–11   Negative Response with an Explanation

Peterson Microsystems, Inc.
12 Graves Road
Fostoria, Ohio 44830-0372
(419) 555-8934

January 3, 199_

Mr. Geoff Beams
7895 Trevor Lane
Henderson, Ohio 44862-3414

Dear Mr. Beams:

Thank you for your thorough application for the position of programmer at Peterson Microsystems and for the time you spent in interviews. We certainly enjoyed meeting you.

We regret, however, that we cannot offer you the position you seek at the present time. Our decision, made after long deliberation, is based on two factors:

1. All programmers here must often work with the UNIX operating system from the first day on the job. You have not had experience with UNIX.

2. Our programmers must often work overtime on high-priority projects. Your time commitments as a doctoral student, we feel, will make overtime impossible for you.

You must know, Mr. Beams, that we are interested in your abilities and thank you for contacting Peterson Microsystems. Please keep us in mind as an employer when the preceding matters no longer present obstacles to our mutual association.

Sincerely,

Berta Kiely

Berta Kiely
Personnel Director

BK/ogi

---

with a watertight web of explanations, you will find little time for any other activity in business.

Learn to say "no" simply, politely, and firmly.

USING A BUFFER STATEMENT

A *buffer* is a positive or neutral statement—not a negative one—that serves as a starting place for your negative response. Buffers allow the reader to feel comfortable with you before experiencing the discomfort of the *no* message.

1. Choose a positive aspect of the subject at hand.

We were frankly surprised when our small advertisement drew over 350 responses.

2. Praise the reader for personal or professional qualities.

In your interviews, Mr. Johnson, we came to know your extensive managerial skill and good business instincts.

3. Concentrate on special needs.

At Vector Direct Mail Sales, we have limited our new product acquisitions to cosmetics, electronic games, and jewelry.

4. Use time factors as explanations.

Our production schedule demands that we settle upon a computer system that can be on-line no later than February 7, 1996.

In using buffers, writers try to prepare the reader to receive the *no* response. Of course, you cannot avoid disappointing the reader entirely. *No* means *no*, despite buffers. However, your effort to soften the blow of the negative response often builds goodwill that goes beyond the momentary disappointment.

NEGATIVE RESPONSES

You can prepare for the writing of negative responses by considering your reader. What language and tone will be most appropriate? What alternatives can be offered without compromising your position? How much empathy should you express, and in what form? How much can or should you explain your negative decision? The answers to these questions will guide you in organizing and wording your *no* answers to orders, inquiries, requests, invitations, and other matters.

Negative Responses to Orders

Businesses must often say "no" to orders. The buyer's credit may not be good, or the item ordered may be out of stock. At such times, use the following model in your letter saying "no" to the order.

1. Begin with a positive buffer (perhaps a statement of appreciation for the order).
2. Go on to a clear statement of what you can and cannot provide.
3. Include any explanations or qualifications you feel will be helpful to the reader.
4. Conclude with a statement of goodwill, appreciation, or a brief sales message.

In Figure 6–12, Better Carpets regretfully must decline a huge carpet order. Notice how the writer leaves the door open for future business. He begins with a buffer of

FIGURE 6–12   Negative Response to an Order

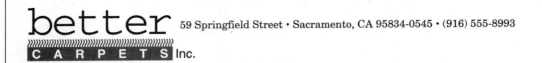

59 Springfield Street • Sacramento, CA 95834-0545 • (916) 555-8993

March 19, 199_

Ms. Hanna Morley
Director, Interior Design
Western Homes, Inc.
273 Ghent Drive
Sacramento, CA 95830-3661

Dear Ms. Morley:

Thank you for choosing Better Carpets as carpeting subcontractor for the 385 homes in your
Sierra Madre subdivision.

Unfortunately, we must decline your order as it now stands. Our decision, made reluctantly,
is based on two considerations:

- As a relatively small carpet business, we have a limited work force. A job as large
  as the Sierra Madre project would require their full energies for at least two full
  months. We could not continue to serve the rest of our customers during this period.

- We would have to make substantial capital investment in new equipment to accomplish
  the Sierra Madre job in the time frame you specify. Such equipment would be idle
  after the job was finished.

We would like to suggest another plan for you to consider. Better Carpets will carpet the
22 model homes in the Sierra Madre tract at the discount rate you requested for the 385 homes.
We would be pleased to work with you selecting another competent carpeting contractor
for the larger job.

We appreciate the confidence you have shown in Better Carpets, Ms. Morley, and I look foward to
meeting with you soon to discuss our participation in the Sierra Madre project.

Sincerely,

Ronald C. Horton

Ronald C. Horton
President

RHC/iow

appreciation. The *no* message is explained in some detail. The reader understands *why* the small carpet company must decline the order. She may then be disposed to accept the compromise plan: a carpet order for 22 homes. The letter concludes with appreciation and an action suggestion ("meeting with you soon").

Negative Responses to Inquiries

As with orders, writers can say "no" to inquiries in a polite but firm way. Notice that the writer of the letter in Figure 6–13 chooses not to provide elaborate explanations for the *no* response. He does provide a buffer emphasizing a positive aspect of the inquiry (the professor's interesting research). The *no* message follows, supported by a brief explanation ("security regulations"). The writer is able to offer an alternative in the form of a booklet. Although it does not meet the professor's need for U.S. Army data, the booklet does provide a concrete expression of goodwill to close the letter.

Negative Responses to Requests and Invitations

Busy professional people often have to choose which things they can do from among the things they ought to do. They often find themselves saying "no" to worthwhile projects and causes.

Don Lyman had a successful import business. The price he paid, he felt, was high blood pressure and an on-again-off-again ulcer. Relief from job pressure came on the golf course every Wednesday. Don played with friends. He loved these moments, and he realized they were good for him.

Don received a request from the local Rotary Club to lead a two-month seminar for high school students interested in business careers. The seminar met for only one hour per week—but on Wednesdays. Don knew he should accept the invitation. He knew equally well that he didn't want to sacrifice golf. He wrote the *no* response that appears in Figure 6–14.

Has Don made up excuses? No, he has told the truth. Should he have offered more cogent excuses? No, he has the right to decline an invitation by the same token that the Rotary Club had a right to ask him. Were his friends at the Rotary Club outraged by his refusal? Of course not. Life moves on, especially business life, more quickly than we like to admit. The Rotary Club simply found a new seminar leader.

To deny a request or an invitation, follow the model suggested for responding to orders and inquiries. Please also see the following Communication Checkpoint, "Handling Negative Responses."

Communication Checkpoint
Handling Negative Responses

1. Begin with a buffer statement that suggests, "here's a positive thought we can share." Often, the buffer helps to prevent disappointed readers from thinking, "She [or he] probably didn't understand." You do understand and must say "no."

2. Clearly say "no," and then explain the "no" if that would be helpful. You might also suggest some alternatives.

3. Conclude with a positive message, perhaps a statement of appreciation, goodwill, or a sales message.

When you conclude your negative responses, you can express goodwill or well-wishing for the reader and for the reader's project or request. Take care not to sound hyp-

FIGURE 6–13   Negative Response to an Inquiry

Ft. Ebson Station
Boulder, CO 80303-0424
(303) 555-7834

April 12, 199_

Professor Andrew Higgins
Department of Biology
Northern State University
Wiley, CO 80731-2446

SUBJECT: Your inquiry regarding stress testing

Dear Professor Higgins:

Thank you for your letter of April 6. We especially enjoyed hearing of your research work
and wish you well on its successful outcome.

We cannot, however, provide the data you requested from U.S. Army files because of national
security regulations.

However, you may find interesting a recent booklet by the Army, published for civilian
researchers. I enclose it for your review.

Sincerely,

Nathan Ramirez

Nathan Ramirez
Staff Sergeant
Medical Research Unit

MR/cox

Enclosure: "Universities and the Army: Partners for Peace"

ocritical. For example, when you really cannot wish the applicant or the project well, you
can conclude by simply thanking the reader for contacting you.

Negative Adjustment Letters

Another common occasion for a businessperson to write a *no* answer is when a customer
makes a claim of damage, defect, or negligence against a company. No business lasts long
by granting every customer claim lodged against it. In learning to write *no* responses to

FIGURE 6–14 Negative Response to a Request

Lyman Oriental Imports, Inc.

2358 Bureau Street
Westport, Connecticut 06880-1919
(203) 555-6789

March 23, 199_

Mr. Jack Baily
President, Rotary Club
2554 Seventh Street
Westport, Connecticut 06881-2720

Dear Jack,

Thank you for your invitation to lead a business seminar for high school students for the next two months.

Unfortunately, I've already made other commitments for those dates.

With you, I recognize the importance of this worthwhile project. Please let me know how else I might support the present seminar.

Sincerely,

Don Lyman
Lyman Oriental Imports, Inc.

DL/cc

---

claims, use the customer's own reasonable expectations as a framework or agenda for your letter. The customer expects

- To be heard (the positive "sharing" in the opening buffer statement tells the reader, "I heard you")
- To be answered decisively, not put off (the clear, direct *no* statement does this)
- To understand the grounds for your decision (your brief explanation helps the customer understand)
- To be treated with respect (your polite style of writing shows this)

These reasonable expectations form a blueprint for *no* letters.

No single recipe can or should be the only way to say "no" to claim letters. Much depends on the consumer protection regulations and company policies that apply to the product or service you sell. Four general guidelines, however, can serve you well in your writing:

1. Without bias, assess whether the claim is justified. Make an honest effort to see the situation from the customer's point of view.

2. If the claim merits it, give what you are able to give, both in words and in replacement merchandise or payment.

3. Take care not to use language that may cause you and your company future problems. Some of the simplest phrases can cause the trickiest problems if a case is brought to court. In general, don't suggest company responsibility or liability for a mishap, unless you have authorization for doing so.

4. No matter how angry and abusive the claim letter is, keep your answer polite and businesslike. Don't get caught up in your customer's anger. Your goal should be to dispense goodwill, act fairly within your limitations, and put an end to the problem.

Observe how these guidelines can be used to deal with a messy, sticky customer claim.

In 1998, Maynard Manning bought a pressure cooker. He took it home to cook a beef stew for friends in his newly wallpapered kitchen. About 20 minutes after the pan was put on the burner, the pan's top shot up with a roar of steam, carrying with it all the beef stew, atomized now to a fine, greasy spray. The wallpaper was ruined. Maynard checked the pressure cooker and discovered that the entire escape valve unit had blown off the lid of the pan. In his letter to the company, he asserted his claim:

> I demand that you replace not only my pressure cooker, but also reimburse me in the amount of $554, representing what it cost me to re-wallpaper my kitchen after your product failed in such a dangerous and destructive way.

The company, Presley Cookware, has a strict policy on customer claims. It will grant any claim involving replacement of a returned product; it will grant no claim for cash outlay; it will accept no liability under any circumstances. The customer relations representative operates under these guidelines. He knows, therefore, that he will say "no" to Mr. Manning's claim in his letter (Figure 6–15).

Notice that the writer avoids telling Manning that he is wrong or has not followed directions with care. Such direct confrontation will lead only to anger and an end to communication. The writer takes a firm but not a hostile stand regarding the money demanded by the customer. Subtly, the writer never mentions the exact amount, allowing it to slip from attention.

A form of compromise is held out in the offer of a new pot, a slight but wise concession by the company. Many angry clients seek to save face more than recover money. Manning may well feel that receiving a new pot, though far from his original demand, at least shows the company is willing to make amends.

Notice, too, that at no time does the writer admit fault on the part of the company. Such an admission of liability (fault assigned to someone) might be used against the company in a later lawsuit. In showing professional concern for the cause of the accident, the writer invites the customer to send in the damaged pressure cooker for examination.

Instead of expressing outright sympathy, the writer tries to move the focus to positive present and future events ("you weren't injured," "a new cooker," "absolutely no charge") rather than dwelling on the event causing Manning's claim letter. Expressing sorrow for each detail of the incident would only stir up bad memories for the reader. Therefore, the expression of sympathy is general and brief.

FIGURE 6–15   Negative Adjustment Letter

PRESLEY COOKWARE•
456 Yolda Boulevard
Baltimore, Maryland 21218-2075
(301) 555-4859

December 5, 199_

Mr. Maynard Manning
4932 Seventh Street
Ft. Worth, Texas 76180-1876

Dear Mr. Manning:

Thank you for your letter of December 2, in which you describe a most unfortunate cooking incident. We are glad you weren't injured.

Decision   Although we are not able to pay the amount you suggest, we will replace your Presley Cooker at absolutely no charge to you. Please send your damaged cooker to us for replacement.

Explanation or   Our product engineers will inspect the returned cooker to discover the cause of your
interpretation   accident. When you receive your new cooker, may we remind you to read the accompanying directions—particularly those involving temperature control—before using the cooker. Steam cooking requires special precautions.

You can count on receiving years of satisfying service from your new cooker. Please contact us if we can be of further help.

Sincerely,

Brad Wilcox

Brad Wilcox
Customer Relations

BW/wv

At times, you may choose to explain your decision *before* announcing your *no* response in a direct way. Consider this rearrangement of the body of the letter to Maynard Manning:

Thank you for your letter of December 2 in which you describe a most unfortunate cooking incident. We are glad you weren't injured.

Our product engineers will inspect your cooker to discover the cause of your accident. Please return it (we will pay postage) at your earliest convenience to the address above. We will then replace your Presley Cooker at absolutely no charge to you. When you receive your new cooker, be sure to read the accompanying directions—particularly those involving temperature control—before using the cooker. Steam cooking requires special precautions.

You can count on years of reliable service from your new cooker. Please call on us if we can help you further.

You must judge whether to explain the grounds for your decision before or after the *no* response. In either case, the goal is to help the reader understand and deal with your decision.

Denials of Credit

Many people feel that their ability to qualify for credit reflects the degree of their morality, reliability, and even intelligence. Therefore, saying "no" to credit applications requires special skill and care.

Applications for credit buying are typically reviewed by staff members trained for such work. They forward their recommendations to the credit manager, who makes a final decision on each case. As a business writer, you may find yourself in such a managerial role. You no doubt will have to say "no" to a large percentage of applicants for credit with your firm. How you say "no" can make or break future business relations with these clients.

Before considering what to say to such applicants in a letter, consider your assumptions about them. Is an inadequate credit record *today* absolute proof of poor credit *forever*? No. Some of your best future clients may be among the list of applicants receiving *no* letters today. Choose language that will not alienate or offend these clients.

Will clients with an inadequate credit record stop buying from your company on a cash basis as soon as they receive your *no* letter regarding credit? No. The experience of major department stores such as Sears and Penney's proves that if credit applicants are turned down in a polite way, customer buying habits do not change. Choose words, therefore, that encourage rather than discourage patronage.

Finally, are the names on your list for *no* letters the dregs of society, misfits, losers, and scoundrels? Emphatically no. By and large, these are ordinary citizens. The verdict of inadequate credit often comes from living too short a time in one area, working too short a time on a new job, or recovering financially from crises such as illness or divorce. No client on your *no* list deserves to be offended.

When you begin to write a *no* letter regarding credit, you may have the applicant's full credit history, including the details of outstanding loans, missed payments, and so forth. You will be guided by your company's policy regarding how much or how little explanation you should give in your letter of credit denial.

Figure 6–16 shows a typical letter denying credit from a company that, for legal reasons, does not choose to specify in exact detail why credit was denied. Notice that the reader *can* find out the reasons for denial but must call a credit service to do so.

By contrast, the letter in Figure 6–17 tells the customer precisely why credit was denied. (It is not within the scope of this text to offer legal advice on which method is preferable. In all communications regarding credit, writers should have access to the advice of an attorney.)

Most *no* letters regarding credit have three sections, usually written as separate paragraphs.

FIGURE 6–16   Letter Denying Credit without Explanation

Constant Attention Clothing, Inc.

33 Breeze Street
Carefree, AZ 85377-4343
(602) 555-9843

July 19, 199_

Mr. William Connelly
5894 Sixth Avenue
Phoenix, AZ 85013-0523

Dear Mr. Connelly:

We at Constant Attention Clothing were pleased to receive your application on July 10, for a $3000 credit line.

At this time, we regret that we cannot approve your application. If you wish more information on this action, please contact TRW Information Services at (893)555-3893 to review your credit history with a credit counselor. This service is available without charge to you for 60 days from the date of this letter.

Thank you, Mr. Connelly, for looking to Constant Attention Clothing for the latest in affordable fashions. We will continue to welcome your business and look forward to your reapplication for credit at some time in the future.

Sincerely,

Victoria Y. Felton

Victoria Y. Felton
Manager, Credit Division

VYF/riw

---

1. Tell the client *how your company felt* when he or she made the effort to apply for credit. Mention the dates of application and the amount of credit requested.

    Luxe Women's Wear appreciated your inquiry of May 2 and your application regarding a credit line of $2500 at our store.

2. Without undue stalling, *get to the heart of your action.* Say "no" politely and firmly.

    After careful review of your application, we are not able to extend the credit you request at the present time.

FIGURE 6–17   Letter Denying Credit with Explanation

STUNNING KITCHENS Inc.

6869
Highway 9
Frontier
Nevada
89406-5370
(702) 555-3849

May 7, 199_

Ms. Barbara Devon
3894 Western Walk Lane
Frontier, Nevada 89406-1246

SUBJECT: Your credit application, April 25, 199_

Dear Ms. Devon:

We appreciated receiving your application for $5000 credit with this company and have given your request careful consideration.

Based on your salary and credit history, Ms. Devon, we are unable to extend credit to you at this time. May we call your attention to two items on your credit record that influenced our decision:

  • You are delinquent in payments to Harvest Furniture Co., Las Vegas, Nevada, in the amount of $585.

  • Your extra income in the amount of $750 per month from real estate investments cannot be verified by public records.

If you have information that does not appear in your credit record regarding either of these items, please contact us.

Thank you, Ms. Devon, for considering Stunning Kitchens, Inc. for the remodeling you contemplate. We'll be happy to serve you as a cash customer or, if the matters listed above can be cleared up, as a credit customer.

We send you our best wishes for your building project.

Sincerely,

Nancy O. Joplin

Nancy O. Joplin
Credit Manager

NOJ/poe

If you wish to *qualify your action* in any way, add additional sentences.

> You do qualify, however, for our Spring Shopper's Card, allowing purchases up to $500. Because we hope you'll become a Spring Shopper at Luxe, I have taken the liberty of enclosing a credit agreement for your signature. Your card will be mailed out the day we receive the signed agreement.

3. *Conclude by thanking the client* or by selling the merits of the company.

> Luxe Women's Wear would like to express its gratitude for your patronage. We do hope to be able to act more favorably on your credit application in the future.

> Luxe Women's Wear wants to invite you to its Priority Sale, available only between 9 A.M. and 12 P.M. on May 10, for special customers like you. Please bring the enclosed pass to be admitted to this outstanding sale.

Clients *can* take "no" for an answer, especially when you don't overly emphasize it with solemn, funereal overtones. Judge, for example, the effect of this heavy "no":

> It is with regret that we must inform you that your application for credit has been denied.

The phrases "it is with regret" and "we must inform you" are too grim and somber for a denial of credit.

When holding out hope for future credit, make sure that the hope you express is realistic. Asking a client to "reapply in a month or two" merely sets the stage for future disappointment if it is clear to you that the client has little chance of qualifying for credit at that time.

A credit manager for a Tucson jewelry store has a healthy approach to "no" credit letters.

> I imagine that my client has just asked me if I carry baseballs in my jewelry store. "No," I say, "but I have other lovely things." In the same tone, when I have to deny credit I simply say, "No, but I welcome your business and I'll do my best to serve your needs."

That straightforward, respectful spirit goes a long way toward preventing the hurt pride and disappointment that can stem from letters denying credit.

FOLLOWUP LETTERS OF EXPLANATION

Even your very polite, sympathetic letter saying "no" will often result in a rude, quite unsympathetic reply: "What do you mean, 'no'? I demand that you explain your reasons and reconsider!"

It's tempting at such moments to become defensive and to fire off a blunt, angry, or sarcastic letter. Resist the temptation. The test of your business maturity will be to keep your head when others are losing theirs.

Begin to assess your situation by reviewing the circumstances. What did the person originally request? What were your reasons for saying "no"? What explanation did you provide at that time? What further explanation is being demanded?

Then decide what you want to accomplish in this followup communication. You have no obligation, of course, to "jump" at their demands for further explanation. In many business situations, no amount of explaining will satisfy angry, disappointed correspondents. However, simply ignoring the demand for explanation seldom resolves matters, and it often complicates them.

Faced with a demand that you justify a *no* answer more completely, you can choose one or more of these alternatives:

- Repeat your explanation in different words.
- Provide the additional information requested.
- Refer the matter to someone else.

The following example illustrates how this might be done.

Original:
The repairs you request are no longer covered under warranty, which expired last year. Our factory service center estimates a parts-and-labor cost of $485 to repair the unit. (It would then be covered under warranty again for a period of three years.)

REVISION 1: **Repeat your explanation in different words.** Add appropriate clarifying information. Your reader will feel insulted, and rightly so, if you simply repeat your exact words from an earlier letter. Notice in the following example how the original explanation is reworded in a followup letter (after the customer demands further explanation):

We're happy to provide further information regarding your warranty, as you requested in your letter of June 15. The warranty on the Savage 307 unit extends from date of purchase (in your case, Dec. 2, 1987) for a period of three years (expiring Dec. 2, 1990). All factory repairs after the expiration of warranty are charged at industry-standard rates, with reinstatement of warranty following such factory repairs.

In this case, the writer does not try to "sell" the customer on having the factory make necessary repairs to the unit. Such a strategy might be misunderstood as manipulation ("we have you over a barrel, and here's your only way out.")

REVISION 2: **Provide the additional information requested.** You may often decide to "go the extra mile" to salvage a business relationship. In the following example, the writer researched the customer's complaint and reports the results:

In response to your letter of June 15, I met with the head of our testing division for her evaluation of the breakdown you experienced with your Savage 307 unit. She reports three similar cases in the past two years. All three were associated with the customers' inadvertent use of graphite oil instead of the 30-weight oil specified in the maintenance manual. I do not know, of course, whether this circumstance is applicable to your case, but I offer the information in the hope that it will be useful to you in evaluating your difficulties with the Savage 307 unit and your plans for repair.

In this case, the writer is fairly certain that the customer has simply used the wrong oil in the unit but stops short of saying so directly. This spares the customer loss of face and avoids false accusation. The customer will probably appreciate the writer's research efforts and willingness to supply helpful information.

REVISION 3: **Refer the matter to someone else.** "Passing the buck" is helpful only when it truly helps the reader. Don't pass on a complaint to a "dead letter desk" in the company—someone who never answers the phone or responds to letters. In the following example, the writer refers a customer to a company employee specifically trained to deal with product complaints:

> In your letter of June 15, you asked for additional information regarding warranty on the Savage 307 unit. I've asked Linda Richmond, Customer Relations Manager, to respond to your request within the next 7 days. She and I have discussed the details of your earlier letters and I trust that the additional information she provides will prove helpful to you.

In each of these alternatives, the writer did not emphasize personal feelings of remorse or pity ("I'm so, so sorry that our hands are tied in repairing your unit," etc.). Such expressions may be less than sincere and may only lead the reader to feel that the request was unjustly refused. (Why else would the writer feel such emotion?)

Communication Insights

The more we practice writing, the faster the writing process becomes. We accustom ourselves to certain ways of expressing ideas—our own "style," we begin to call it.

Skilled business writing, like fine carpentry, can become a craft in which we take just pride. When we begin to enjoy building good memos, letters, and reports, we understand what Hemingway meant when he insisted that all good writing "is architecture, not interior decoration."

FINAL CONSIDERATIONS IN SAYING "NO"

Business communicators can be sensitive to disappointment and anger without feeling responsible for it. If Ted asks you for a raise and you say "no," with appropriate explanation, you have no reason to feel responsible for Ted's ensuing tantrum or tirade. That is, your actions should not be held captive by Ted's potential emotions. How Ted responds is his business; what you decide is yours.

This is not to say, however, that you should say "no" in a cold, uncaring manner. The key to saying "no" and maintaining goodwill is to allow for the feelings of others while remaining true to your own responsibilities.

SUMMARY

1. The occasions for *yes* letters are also occasions for building goodwill and communicating sales messages.

2. In making positive responses to orders, convey the *yes* message and any related details. Then provide a closing statement of appreciation, goodwill, or a sales message.

3. In making positive responses to inquiries, decide whether you need to repeat the substance of the inquiry in your reply.

4. Positive responses to requests and invitations should specify exactly what the writer is saying "yes" to.

5. In writing positive adjustment letters, the writer should announce the good news, explain any conditions or qualifications, and then express appreciation, goodwill, or a sales message.

6. Credit approvals must be precise in their statement of details and conditions.

7. Your positive constructive response to hostility and criticism can salvage business relationships.

8. Saying "no" does not have to offend the reader.

9. Negative responses to orders should provide explanations and, where possible, alternatives that build goodwill.

10. Negative responses to inquiries might not need accompanying explanations, depending on the circumstances.

11. Negative responses to requests and invitations should be truthful. Such statements often begin with a buffer statement.

12. Negative adjustment letters begin with a buffer statement and then provide a rationale for the negative decision. The decision itself may appear before or after the explanation. The letter concludes with a message intended to maintain goodwill.

13. Business writers must handle credit denials expertly and sensitively. These messages might not specify the grounds for the denial, depending on the circumstances and the company policy.

14. Followup letters can repeat the original message in different words, provide additional information, or refer the matter to someone else.

QUESTIONS FOR DISCUSSION

1. Why might you want to repeat the substance of an inquiry, request, or invitation in responding positively?

2. In general, should the *yes* message stand on its own or be attached to qualifications and conditions? Explain your answer.

3. How would you advise a writer to provide a partial *yes* response to a request or order?

4. What is the relation between the *yes* message and a sales message in a positive response letter?

5. In general, where should the good news of the *yes* message be placed in positive response letters? Why?

6. What considerations must be called to mind when writing credit approvals?

7. In what three ways can a sales message be woven smoothly into the *yes* letter?

8. What risk do you run when answering *yes* and not providing details explaining the content of your positive answer?

9. How can goodwill be increased through *yes* letters?

10. Why should the details of credit approval be stated precisely? Which details matter most of all?

11. Why must the *yes* letter sometimes be accompanied by conditions and qualifications? Give an example to illustrate your point.

12. What questions should be asked when preparing to write the positive adjustment letter?

13. What emotions are readers likely to feel when reading *no* letters that are too blunt?

14. What is a buffer? How is it used in negative responses?

15. Must every *no* answer be explained thoroughly in business communications? Explain your answer.

16. Is it a good practice to write all negative responses without *any* explanations?

17. What are three types of buffers that may be used to begin *no* letters?

18. How can you say "no" to an invitation if you have no good excuse?

19. When you provide an explanation, should it appear before or after the *no* statement in a negative response letter? Discuss the pros and cons of each placement.

20. Why is denial of credit an emotionally difficult matter for many people? Describe ways in which writers can avoid angering the reader who receives a credit denial.

21. Describe your own feelings aroused by reading a *no* letter at some time in the past. How could those feelings have been influenced by different words in the letter?

22. In your opinion, why do many *no* letters have an unfriendly and even hostile tone? Support your answer with reasons.

23. In addition to moral considerations, why should explanations in *no* letters be truthful?

24. When is a buffer statement unnecessary in a *no* letter?

EXERCISES

1. You're the manager of Frederick Trucking, Inc. Write a *yes* response to an inquiry from a local farmer who wants to ship produce to market. Include a sales message.

2. A professor writes to ask you, now a successful businessperson, to speak to a business class. Write back, accepting the invitation and repeating key details of the invitation.

3. The town mayor requests that your company hire unemployed teens. Respond with a partial yes to the request. Include a sales message and maintain goodwill.

4. A customer complains that your product has failed. Create the circumstances, then write a positive adjustment letter.

5. Approve the credit application of Ms. Frances Allison for a credit line of $5000 with your company. Include whatever conditions or qualifications you feel are necessary.

6. Write a positive response to a large order for your company's product.

7. Write a positive response to an invitation on the condition that some key detail of the invitation can be changed. Create the circumstances.

8. Write a partial *yes* response to an order for your company's product. Explain how the remainder of the order will be filled.

9. Assume that you, as president of a college organization, have received a request from the Dean's office to change the date and location of your annual new members initiation. Write a letter confirming the change of plans and agreeing to a new date and location.

10. As manager of a chain of restaurants, you have received a request from the Children's Charities organization to advertise their fund-raising activities by means of posters placed in your windows. The organization also wants to use part of the parking lots of your restaurants for fund-raising car washes. Write a response letter in which you agree to the placement of posters but not to the use of the parking lots. Cite reasons for your answer.

11. You manage a large furniture production facility. A customer writes to say that drawers have warped so badly in your model #293 dresser that they will not slide in and out. The retail outlet where he bought the dresser has instructed him to contact you, the manufacturer. Write a letter addressing this customer's concerns and instructing him on how to receive an adjustment. Make up any facts necessary for a complete response.

12. You are the credit manager for a wholesaler of beauty supplies. Write a letter granting $20,000 in commercial credit to a new customer. In the same letter, make the new client aware of several products you're trying to promote.

13. Assume that you, as a customer service representative, must write a partial adjustment letter saying "yes" to a part of a customer's claim, but "no" to the remainder. Should the *yes* message come before or after the *no* message? Write out your answer, and explain your position on this question.

14. Create a dialogue—as in a comic strip—in which one character makes a request and the other says no. Write down what they actually say beneath your drawing of the characters. Write down what they are thinking above the characters.

15. Write a negative response to an order while maintaining goodwill. Make up the circumstances.

16. A local political group has sent you a long questionnaire asking for your political and ethical judgments on a number of subjects. Write a negative response to the group, indicating that you will not answer the questions. Include only a brief explanation. Then rewrite the letter, including a lengthy explanation for your decision. On a sheet attached to this assignment, assess which of the two letters you prefer, and explain why.

17. Write a negative response to an invitation. Begin with a buffer. Offer alternatives to the reader.

18. In the role of a claims supervisor, write a negative adjustment letter to a customer who complains that your company's plant food killed his houseplants. Make an effort to maintain goodwill.

19. Write two negative responses to a request for your donated services as honorary chair of a local charity. In the first version of your letter, explain your reasons before stating the *no* message. In the second version, explain your reasons after the *no* message. On an attached sheet, explain which of the two letters you prefer and why.

20. Write a negative response to a credit application, explaining the grounds for denying it. Maintain goodwill.

21. Write a negative response to a credit application. Do not explain the specific grounds for your action; instead, refer the applicant to a local credit service for counseling. Maintain goodwill.

22. You manage the credit office for a large food distributor. A new merchant wants to buy from you on a credit basis. Based on the merchant's limited credit history, you must say "no" to the request. Do so in a polite letter aimed at nurturing a business relationship on a cash basis.

23. Your local business association invites you to serve as chair of this year's benefit fund-raising drive. Write a letter in which you turn down the request without indicating lack of regard for association members or their charitable work.

24. Provide buffers for each of the following *no* messages.
    a. The Student Loan Committee cannot grant your request for a $3500 tuition loan.
    b. Your application for a credit account at Lindsay Clothiers has been turned down.
    c. You have not been selected for one of the four summer internship positions available at Price-Waterhouse.

INTERNET ASSIGNMENT

You direct a large non-profit organization that considers grant applications from a wide variety of community, religious, and social organizations. Your employees have little trouble writing "yes" responses to such applications. But their "no" letters (by far the preponderance of their correspondence) are often unnecessarily abrupt and unsympathetic. You worry that applicants who are turned down in a less-than-professional way will not make applications in the future and may think and speak negatively about your organization. To help your employees help themselves in writing "no" correspondence, investigate several useful Internet sites (in the Specific Business Documents section of the Internet Guide). Prepare a brief oral presentation or write a memo that persuades employees to use these sites to improve their ability to say "no" with grace and professionalism.

CHAPTER 7

Persuasive Letters

NATURE AND PURPOSE OF PERSUASIVE LETTERS

A strong ability to sell your ideas at work, whether to superiors, co-workers, employees, or clients, will greatly enhance your chances for a successful career. One definition of *selling* is, simply, to persuade someone to buy what you are offering. To *persuade* someone is to influence the person's thoughts or actions, often by demonstrating reasons for the person to accept your influence. For example, you might persuade homeowners to buy fire insurance by showing them that if they don't have insurance, their property will be lost entirely in the event of fire.

When known facts are purposely distorted or hidden in persuasive appeals, selling is manipulative and unethical. The selling of fire insurance would be manipulative, for example, if homeowners were told that they stood a 90 percent chance of losing their homes by fire, which is untrue. Ethical persuasion rests on a truthful presentation of facts or beliefs as they are known to the presenter.

Effective persuasive business letters must influence readers by truthfully presenting written information. If the letter is to influence the reader, it must demonstrate that the position or action it suggests serves the needs of the readers. The range of those needs is broad, and readers often have many overlapping needs that effective persuasion may address, such as needs for

Money	Health
More free time	Comfort
Productivity	Entertainment
Importance	Security
Power	Knowledge
Attractiveness	A desired skill
Friends	Reputation

These and other needs describe what *interests* the reader. If your product or service is to prove interesting as well, it must be linked in some way to a *need already felt by the reader.* In other words, persuasive letters make readers understand not merely that the product or service is good, but that it is good for them.

FOUR TYPES OF PERSUASIVE LETTERS

In this light, the majority of business letters are persuasive in the best sense. They present ideas, evidence, and beliefs in an effort to win agreement (and perhaps action) on the part of the reader by considering the reader's needs, point of view, and background. In this chapter, we discuss four important forms of persuasive letters.

1. *Sales or promotional letter*, which persuades readers to buy a product or service
2. *Direct-mail letter*, a form of sales letter, which persuades readers to shop for products and services by mail
3. *Claim letter*, which persuades the reader, often a company employee in charge of customer service, to make requested adjustments because of a flaw or a failure in a product or service
4. *Collection letter*, usually one in a series, which persuades the reader to pay money he or she owes

THE SALES AND PROMOTION LETTER

The terms *sales letter* and *promotional letter* mean the same thing in common business use: letters intended to sell a product or service. Occasionally you will find the term *promotional letter* reserved for selling *programs* and *product lines* rather than specific products and services. In common use, however, and in this text, the terms are synonymous.

The work of creating an effective sales letter begins in your head, not on paper. First, decide to concentrate on *you* (the reader) rather than *I* (the writer). In the following example, notice how the focus of the sales concept changes.

"I" EMPHASIS   The new Chevette features a four-cylinder engine, revolutionary new suspension, and tinted windows.

In the "you" example, the writer has used the reader's needs (for economy, comfort, and security) to sell the product. "The product is not just good," the writer seems to say to the reader. "It's good *for you.*"

"YOU" EMPHASIS   The new Chevette features a four-cylinder engine to save you money on gasoline, a revolutionary new suspension to take the bumps away, and tinted windows for glare-free driving.

Arousing the Needs of the Reader

Do readers always know what their needs are? Should you take time at the beginning of a sales letter to remind the reader of those needs?

It's an important question. On the one hand, sales letters that serve no felt need on the reader's part fail in their purpose. "It looks like a nice product," the reader says, "but I don't need it." On the other hand, you risk alienating your readers by assuming a set of needs in your letter that they may not feel at all.

That's where market research comes to the rescue. Either through professional research organizations or your own efforts, you must test *your market* in order to know your readers. Are they aware of their need for your product? If so, begin your sales letter by showing how your product meets their need. Are they unaware that your product can help them? If so, begin by reminding them in a sentence or two of a problem they have been experiencing. Then let your product come to the rescue in the letter by providing an answer to that problem. It may help to illustrate each of the two options: (1) product/ service first or (2) need first.

Product/Service First

In the letter in Figure 7–1, sent to experienced boaters, the writer assumes that the audience is well aware of the problems of corrosion involved with metal boat propellers. She moves immediately into information about the product at the beginning of the letter. The rest of the letter is used to demonstrate how the new product meets the needs of the reader—for a reliable, profitable item and so forth.

Here are two more examples of sales openers that assume the reader's awareness of a need related to the product or service offered for sale:

> You'll be glad to know that, at Crestline Commercial Brokers, all rental units are maintained by a property manager.

This opening would be appropriate for investors who know the problems of owner-maintained buildings. In the next example, the jeweler addresses a sales letter to experienced gem buyers:

> Francis Jewelry is proud to be the only wholesale jeweler in this city to offer a free X-ray with each gem it sells.

The opening would be ineffective for an audience that was unaware of the need for an X-ray to reveal characteristics and flaws in a gem.

Needs First

For audiences that must be made aware of a need, begin the sales letter by describing the need that your product or service fulfills. For example, suppose that you want to market a product called "Handi-File," an organizer for household and business receipts. A letter describing the need before announcing the product is shown in Figure 7–2. Notice that the writer *creates* the need for Handi-File by reminding the reader of important government regulations. A reader who otherwise might say "my filing is in reasonably good shape" could be led, by the first paragraph, to reconsider: "Files for the past three years? Maybe I should look into Handi-File." The writer lists the advantages of Handi-File *to the reader* and concludes with an action the reader can take (the phone call) to bring Handi-File to his place of business.

FIGURE 7–1   Sales Letter with Product/Service First

470 East Bay Drive
San Franscisco, CA 94109
(415) 555-8932

May 30, 199_

Ms. Glenda Forbes, Manager
Pier Marine Supply
44 Dock Road
Oakland, CA 98392

Dear Ms. Forbes:

Jensen Marine proudly announces an all-plastic propeller.

First, consider the product:

> • Tested and approved by Nautical Labs
>
> • Guaranteed for a *lifetime*
>
> • Can't corrode, chip, break, or dent

Second, consider the price:

> • Less than half the wholesale price for comparable brass propellers
>
> • Rings, pins, and fittings come with the propeller at no extra cost

You can save money for your customers while still *making more profit per propeller yourself.*

Finally, consider the terms:

> • Jensen Marine will place an attractive stand-alone display rack of new plastic propellers in your store *on a consignment basis*, without cost to you.
>
> • Purchasers of plastic propellers during the introductory period (ends July 15) will receive a 15% discount.

You've looked to Jensen Marine over the years for the technological advances that matter in boating. Thank you for considering the new plastic propeller as a good business move—and a good move for boating.

Order information and forms are enclosed. Feel free to contact us (call collect) if we can help you.

Sincerely,

Patricia Olloway

Patricia Olloway
Marketing Director

PO/wod
Enclosure: Order Information Packet

FIGURE 7–2 Sales Letter with Need First

Underwood Office Supply
1948 W. Sixth Street
Spokane, WA 99212
(509) 555-8923

August 18, 199_

Mr. Thomas Barth
Manager
Comfort Retirement Home
385 Bedford Place
Spokane, WA 89283

Dear Mr. Barth:

As manager of Comfort Retirement Home, you probably are aware that tax records must be retained for three years, as required by Federal law.

Maintaining organized records can be easy with Handi-File, a bookkeeper's dream come true.

Handi-File lets you

- file documents by subject, author, and date simultaneously

- call up just the file you want by using Dial-a-File

- preserve your files through fire and flood

Frankly, we're excited about the product and we want you to see what the excitement is about. The Handi-File display van will visit your area on August 25–27.

Call 555-8923 for your personal appointment with a Handi-File representative. The van will pull up to the curb in front of Comfort Retirement Home. You can take as much or as little time as you wish to see the Handi-Files on display inside.

You'll be glad you called for a visit from Handi-File, Mr. Barth. Won't you do it today?

Sincerely,

Mildred T. Reynolds

Mildred T. Reynolds
Manager

MTR/oie
Enclosure: "Handi-File: The Filing Revolution"

Developing the Sales Letter

Once you have analyzed the reader's needs and determined how much or how little to assume, you can begin a step-by-step planning process for each part of the sales letter. One easy-to-remember pattern for the sales letter follows the letters *S-A-L-E-S:*

S—Spark the imagination and curiosity of the reader.

A—Announce the product or service.

L—List the advantages to the client.

E—Express appreciation and goodwill.

S—Specify exactly what the client should do—and when.

S—Spark the Imagination.   The introductory sentence in the sales letter should get the reader's attention and then guide it meaningfully to consider a worthwhile product or service. Here are several ways to spark imagination and arouse curiosity.

1. Suggest in the first sentence that *you can do something unique* for the reader. Few of us can resist reading on to find out what that "something" is.

Lesborn Tire Company offers you a new way of buying tires.

2. Drop an impressive name, if appropriate, and then associate the reader with that name.

Astronaut Luke Seaborg, like you, knows the importance of regular eye examinations.

3. Mention local people, places, and events, if possible.

Hinton, Iowa, had dirt streets when my grandfather built Higgins Drug Store—and his reputation—at the corner of Lake and Main.

4. Empathize—feel *with*—your reader.

Cash emergencies occasionally catch us all off guard, especially as the holidays near.

In most sales letters, the imaginative beginning should not be more than a sentence or two long. A short, pointed opening provides an easy entry for the reader and helps to create the attractive "beginning, middle, and end" shape discussed in Chapter 3.

A—Announce the Product or Service.   In this section of the letter, do your business in a frank, specific way. The reader has had his or her curiosity piqued in your opening sentences and now wants it satisfied. This portion should first advertise the product or service; only then can you afford to go on to such matters as the history of your company or your product, or the expertise of your personnel.

At Lesborn Tire, just your signature, address, and driver's license number let you drive away on a high-quality set of Lesborn tires—with 24 to 36 months to pay.

Each November, we celebrate Grandfather's Month at Higgins Drug Store. This November, we offer a two-for-one sale on all cosmetic items, with large reductions on all other store merchandise except pharmaceuticals. For example, school supplies have been marked down 40 percent.

Establish in this section of your sales letter an honest, assertive voice. Speak up for what you have to offer, naming it in specific terms. Where space permits, provide a persuasive example or two.

L—List the Advantages to the Client.   Because the second paragraph of a sales letter often turns out to be rather long, this section can profitably be written along inset margins, with major points set off as a list.

Floral Display, Inc., will take charge of the interior landscape of your office.

- by placing gorgeous tropical plants to advantage throughout your workspace
- by maintaining these plants at the peak of condition and beauty
- by helping you make inexpensive but stunning decorating decisions using fresh, fragrant plants

This section of the sales letter convinces readers that your advertised claims in the second paragraph have practical applications. You have a chance to demonstrate the wide variety of needs your product or service can fulfill.

Like all sections of your sales letter, this one should avoid the pitfalls of insincerity. Don't try to *sound* sincere—simply *be* sincere about what you say your product or service can do.

E—Express Appreciation and Goodwill.   So far, your reader has faithfully followed your train of thought through most of the sales letter. It is time to thank him or her for considering your ideas, to praise the reader's company, or to express goodwill. While compliments may seem to be unnecessary to you, they are high-interest items to readers. You want interest to be high and dispositions to be rosy at this point in the letter because just around the corner lie the final sentences that matter most: the call to specific action. The following are typical examples of compliments and expressions of goodwill.

In its advertising and public offices, your firm is known throughout the industry for its continental flair.

We admire the standard you have set for yourself and others.

S—Specify Exactly What the Client Should Do—and When.   Finally, tell the reader in a clear, specific way what you want him or her to do—and when—to bring about the advantages described in the letter. Maintain the upbeat "yes" attitude. Be careful not to use threats: "Your life depends on your tires. Buy Safe-T tires now before. . ."

Instead, define an easy and appealing path of action for your reader. If the action is at all complicated, break it into separate steps.

Call Marci at 555-2451 to arrange for a free decorating analysis without obligation. If you prefer, mail the enclosed card to receive our color decorating catalog—with no strings or plants attached.

Present the enclosed coupon on or before May 10 at your local Safe-T Tire Store, 1325 South Olive Street. You'll receive $40 off your new set of four Safe-T tires.

Specific action statements often consist of an action verb (*call*, *present*, *visit*, and so forth), a specific address and telephone number, a specific time ("now" or "on or before May 10"), and perhaps one final advantage (free decorating analysis, color decorating catalog, $40 off) if the reader does what you suggest.

Observe each of the *S-A-L-E-S* sections working together in the complete sales letter shown in Figure 7–3.

DIRECT-MAIL LETTERS

The broad range of letters that try to sell by means of the mail are called direct-mail letters: subscription letters, luggage offers, insurance discounts, restaurant specials, and so forth. Try to estimate the number of such letters you throw away each month. Many never get opened or are only half opened to satisfy the beginnings of curiosity ("Is there anything free inside?"). Now consider how often you respond to the sales pitches contained in direct mail. Do you actually send off a check after reading one letter out of five? One out of ten? One out of a hundred?

The direct-mail sales letter presents formidable obstacles. Readers *usually* throw your message away without reading it. Postage rates, paper costs, and printing expenses continue to escalate. The public becomes increasingly resistant to direct-mail techniques (such as including a tiny pencil with a magazine-subscription appeal).

Having faced the dark side of direct-mail sales, we can go on to name its merits and extraordinary potential. Direct mail allows the consumer to shop in the privacy and comfort of the home. Direct mail involves relatively little business expense for you, the entrepreneur. You don't have to provide a showroom for your products. You literally can do business out of your garage as long as your image to your readers is maintained by the literature you send out. Direct-mail marketers usually have few problems with returned merchandise. Even if the buyer is not entirely pleased with product, the practical task of rewrapping the merchandise and sending it (at the buyer's expense) back to the marketer becomes too troublesome for average purchasers. Stick the thing on the shelf and forget it, they seem to say.

There are techniques for getting potential customers to read sales letters once they arrive in their hands, and these techniques are important weapons in the direct-mail sales arsenal.

These techniques include

- Using envelopes to invite curiosity
- Getting attention in the opening line
- Personalizing the direct-sales letter

Using Envelopes to Invite Curiosity

Writers of direct-mail sales letters often forget the role played by the envelope. No matter how stimulating your sales appeal, readers will never see it if they do not first open

FIGURE 7–3 Complete Sales Letter following the S-A-L-E-S Pattern

4982 Brooks, Suite 4 • Toledo, OH 43606 • (419) 555-9049

FLORAL
DISPLAYS

April 10, 199_

Mr. David Jenkins
District Manager
Coleberry Financial Services, Inc.
324 Wall Avenue
Toledo, Ohio 69587

Dear Mr. Jenkins:

S   Do you sometimes wish you could bring the park—trees, flowers, shrubbery—back to the office with you after lunch?

A   Floral Displays, Inc., makes wishes come true. We rent out and maintain gorgeous tropical plants for your office and reception area. For less than $2 per day, we can surround you in lush philodendron or hide you behind an elephant plant.

L   Plants make business more pleasant and more profitable.

> • Clients appreciate your thoughtfulness and admire your taste in softening the bare edges of business life with lovely plants. Happy clients spend more, more often.

> • Employee turnover (the great hidden expense for most businesses) is drastically reduced. Employees come to think of the office as an attractive, inviting place.

E   Your reputation in Toledo as a leading financial services company can only be further enhanced by a modest investment in a more healthful, attractive and impressive office environment.

S   Take a moment right now to call Marci (555-9049) for a free floral decoration analysis of your office. She will come at your convenience, finish her work quickly, then dazzle you with affordable decorating ideas. If you prefer, mail in the enclosed card for our latest color catalog of decorating ideas.

With best wishes,

Sandra T. Lansdon

Sandra T. Lansdon
Marketing Director

STL/bck
Enclosure: "Your Catalog Reservation" (return postcard)

the envelope. Most of us do not conscientiously open and read every piece of mail. We reach for personal letters, bills, and only then anything that looks interesting to *us*.

In designing your strategy for direct mail, you must make a decision. Should your envelope look personalized? If not, how can it look interesting enough to gain the reader's attention? By "personalized," we mean an individually typed, high-quality envelope (no address labels) that imitates the look of a letter that might arrive from your university or your lawyer. In past years, this approach proved too expensive for direct-mail merchants because of typing costs. However, with the advent of word-processing and high-speed laser and letter-quality printers, thousands of envelopes—all neatly and individually addressed—can be turned out in a short time. Because the letter cannot be distinguished from important mail by the envelope alone, the recipient opens it. If the letter catches his or her attention and imagination in the first sentence, the direct-mail merchant has won the first battle.

Or we can choose techniques to make the letter look especially interesting, even though it is label-addressed and enveloped in less expensive paper. *Time* magazine marketers hit upon a technique to get letters opened when they included a tiny pencil, costing the company only a fraction of a cent, in each letter. Interestingly, the slight bulge in the envelope piqued the curiosity of readers. Once they opened it to find a pencil, they were primed to mark "yes" in the subscription coupon for *Time*.

Other direct-mail merchants have made good use of an envelope window. Through the window they reveal not only the reader's name and address, but also the beginning of a highly stimulating message: "Congratulations! You have won. . ." Of course, the reader cannot see what he or she has won until opening the letter.

Other techniques include the use of bright colors and dramatic graphics on the envelope itself. While these patterns do catch the eye, they do not necessarily motivate the recipient to open the letter. In one case, an envelope so perfectly framed a graphic of a country scene that readers hesitated to tear open the envelope and damage the picture.

No technique remains fresh for long. What worked for *Time* last year may not work next year. If you are involved in direct-mail sales, try to come up with a fresh approach that would work on you when opening your own mail. If you do this, your chances of success using such a technique will be better than relying on standard formulas.

Getting Attention in the Opening Line

Once the reader has been tempted to open the envelope, the first sentence of the letter must grab and hold the reader's attention. Any of the techniques we have already reviewed for the first sentence of the "yes" sales letter may be used. In addition, consider the "give-away" opening. If you have enclosed a free sample of your product, mention it in the first sentence. If the reader can send for a free gift, say so in the first sentence. If wonderful prizes can be won in a contest, describe the competition right away. All of these techniques try to make the reader want something so much that he or she can't help but read on to find out how to get it.

A note of caution: Be aware that a broad range of federal, state, and local laws now regulate the claims and business practices of direct-mail merchants.

Personalizing the Direct-Sales Letter

From your mailing list, you may have first and last names for each of your readers. By using a merging routine on a word processor, you can merge the reader's name not only in the inside address, but also in the salutation and, if you wish, at points throughout the text of the letter.

... the prize. All you have to do, Mr. Scott, is ...

If you do not use name merging in your direct-mail letters, you can imitate the look of a traditional business letter without actually having a name for the inside address and salutation (Figure 7–4).

Make a habit of saving direct-mail letters that for one reason or another cause you to open the envelope and actually read the letter. Analyze those letters that work. Discover the techniques, cues, attractions, and temptations that worked on you, the reader. The prac-

FIGURE 7–4   **Direct Mail Letter without Inside Address or Salutation**

Remingford
CUTLERY

3355 Lakeview Drive
Orlando, FL 32826
(407) 555-7654
1-800-967-8978

May 15, 199_

Dear Neighbor,

We know lucky people like yourself who have already received the finest set of kitchen knives in the world—at incredible discount prices.

How much are you now paying for the best knives in your kitchen? $45? $50? $65? Even these prices seem reasonable for a top-quality knife, one made from Belgian stainless steel, triple-tempered to hold a razor edge.

But Remingford Cutlery has good news for you: the Heritage Collection can be yours for *less* than you are used to paying for a single, high-quality knife. Included in the Heritage Collection are

- two paring knives
- one broad knife
- two fillet knives
- one citrus fruit knife
- one heavy chopping knife
- two dicing knives

Each of these gourmet-quality knives is fashioned in Belgium by artisans for whom excellence is a tradition. Each comes with a two-year unconditional money-back guarantee.

The price? For the next ten days, you can purchase the Heritage Collection at the premarketing price of $49.97.

Soon you'll see these fine knives in better department stores at $89 and more. Act now! Check "YES" on the enclosed postcard and drop it in the mail today.

With compliments to the chef,

Reginald H. Rosenbaum

Reginald H. Rosenbaum,
Remingford Cutlery

tice of learning from your own experience will help you plan effectively to write direct-mail sales letters for others.

PERSUASION BY ELECTRONIC MAIL INTERNET SITES

Through computer connections to e-mail and Internet commercial sites, consumers can be reached by on-screen sales appeals, as shown in Figure 7–5. These differ from traditional sales letters in three important ways:

1. Electronic sales messages are usually shorter than word-processed letters.
2. Electronic messages can make use of innovative advertising formats (such as animated graphics)
3. Electronic messages have greater freedom to refer to additional information the user can call up at the press of a key.

Word-processed letters, by contrast, usually must enclose extra information in the form of brochures, reports, and so forth.

CLAIM LETTERS

A *claim letter* is a persuasive business letter in which you state and explain your demand for repayment, restitution, or replacement because of a failure in a product or service. Along with the sales letter and proposal, the claim letter is one of the most powerful tools in a business writer's workshop.

Imagine, for example, that your company purchased a Model 61 photocopy machine for $4000. It was delivered with several bottles of photocopy toner, which you poured into the machine according to instructions.

The toner, you discover too late, was the wrong kind. It has gummed up the ma-

FIGURE 7–5 A Persuasive Message from a Computer Bulletinboard

MaxVent 3000 speakers, shipped UPS to you at the below-wholesale price of $428 per pair! Speakers will be shipped same day that order is received.

VISA, MasterCard, and American Express accepted.

chine; no copies can be made at all. The salesperson who sold you the machine says you should have noticed the error before pouring in the toner—the bottles were marked, "For Model #41." He refuses to replace the machine or to pay for its repair. Meanwhile, your office work grinds to a halt for lack of a copy machine.

If you can imagine your own anger in such a situation, you know how difficult it can be to compose a steady, decisive, action-oriented letter in times of emotional stress. Without denying the validity of your feelings, set your course of *action*. The letters of the word (conveniently) remind you how to write a claim demand letter that bring results.

PREWRITING   **A—Assess the entire situation.** Exactly what happened? Where do you place blame? Is there another side to the story? What would remedy the problem? When must action be taken? Who must take action?

PREWRITING   **C—Consider your audience.** What do you know about the person who has caused the problem or the person who can solve the problem?

WRITING   **T—Tell your side of the story in a clear, organized way.** Avoid depicting those who made the mistake in derogatory terms, such as "idiots" or "incompetents."

WRITING   **I—Insist on specific, timely action.** Don't leave the remedy to the imagination of your reader (as in the appeal to "Do something!"). Spell out what you want done and when.

WRITING   **O—Offer your cooperation.** Assist in the effort to correct the situation.

WRITING   **N—Name specific actions to remedy the situation.** Be specific, to the point of setting down dates and times of the day when you want to see something done. Name alternatives you plan to pursue, such as contacting higher levels of authority or turning the matter over to your lawyer.

Observe the *A-C-T-I-O-N* pattern in the claim letter shown in Figure 7–6. Notice how the writer first assesses the situation by reviewing the facts and circumstances surrounding the photocopy incident. Next he considers the audience. Addressing a letter to the obstinate sales representative probably will do little good, so our writer decides to send the letter to the manager of the photocopy store.

Claims and adjustment letters, written well, can often resolve day-to-day business problems without the expensive and time-consuming involvement of lawyers, agencies, and regulatory commissions.

A final reminder on how to write successful claims letters comes from one who sees them fail every day. Leland S. manages the consumer complaint division for a major auto company. He describes the kinds of letters that get little or no attention from his office:

> Some people are so mad they can't make sense. From their letters, you cannot discover what went wrong, when it happened, or what they tried to do about it.
>
> Others begin with elaborate threats regarding government agencies, lawyers, and even congressional representatives. We often withhold action on those letters. Any words we do send can be used against us if the customer does go to court.

FIGURE 7–6   Claim Letter

Levi & Willard Accountants, Inc.
3829 East Fourth Street
Buffalo, NY 14215
(201) 555-2943

March 15, 199_

Ms. Wendy Johnson, Manager
Target Photocopy Supply
3499 Lincoln Blvd.
New York, NY 19332

Dear Ms. Johnson:

On March 9, my firm purchased a model # 61 photocopy machine from your salesman, Mark Trebley. As your records will show, we paid $4021 for the machine (invoice #29843). That price included a six-month supply of toner, delivered to us with the machine.

Tell

I personally poured the toner into the machine in the way that Mark Trebley showed me. Only when the machine stopped making copies a few minutes later did we discover that the wrong toner (for model #41) had been delivered to us with the machine.

I phoned Mr Trebley that same day. He claimed to be "swamped" with customers and promised to phone back. After my repeated efforts to reach him by phone, I called personally at your store and confronted Mr. Trebley with the error regarding the toner. He made these points:

1. Someone "in the showroom" sent the wrong toner.
2. In his opinion, I was largely responsible for the problem since the toner bottles were labeled "For model #41".
3. The machine would need an extensive and expensive overhaul for which neither he nor your store would be responsible.

He and I have had no further contact.

Insist

I insist that you remedy the problem caused by your personnel by replacing our photocopy machine with a free loaner during the period of overhaul. To the detriment of our accounting business, we have been without a copy machine for almost a week. Therefore, please have the loaner sent over no later than March 19.

Offer cooperation

We will not insist the loaner be a new model #61. In fact, we are willing to make do with any serviceable model so long as it arrives by March 19.

Name specifics

Please call me (555-2943) no later than 5 p.m. tomorrow. I am confident that you are as anxious as we are to put this problem to rest. If I have not received your call by noon on Friday, March 17, I will reluctantly turn this entire matter over to both my attorney and the Better Business Bureau for action against you.

Sincerely,

Thomas Levi

Thomas Levi
Partner

c.c. Mr. Mark Trebley

TL/eb

A few letters leave absolutely no possible solution open to us. A man in Florida, for example, had recurring problems with his car cigarette lighter—and would settle, he said, for nothing less than a new replacement car. Of course we can't act when no reasonable course is left open to us.

Finally, there are letters we call "mazes." They wander about the topic, never really saying what the customer wants to complain about. Usually near the end of the maze, the letter writers invite us to call them so they can describe their problems in person. Scrambled letters get little or no response.

Learning from such experience, you can write demand letters that are *controlled*, *realistic*, and *organized*. That simple prescription proves easier said than done, however, when your temper is boiling regarding an injustice.

COLLECTION LETTERS

Many people regularly fail to make payments due on mortgages, consumer loans, and credit cards. Of these, about half simply have a variety of money management problems: unexpected expenses, illnesses, layoffs, poorly planned budgets, and so forth. They mean to pay and will pay but have had temporary upsets. The remaining hardcore debtors, for many reasons, may have decided never to pay. Some have resources on which they can draw to pay their bills. They simply prefer to live on borrowed money from you instead of their own earned money.

When you first send a collection letter to someone, you may not know whether you are writing to an unintentional or an intentional debtor. Collection letters must be written in such a way that both groups are motivated to pay what they owe.

We can learn to write effective collection letters by considering a story from each of the two aforementioned groups.

The *unintentionally delinquent debtor* can be illustrated by James P., who is 39 and married with two children. He has missed one payment on his 1991 Ford pickup. He may miss the next payment, due in two days.

Well, I'm a carpenter and when we have rain like we've had lately, there's just no work. When there's no work, there's no money. I can't sell my truck because I need it for my livelihood. I've got a part-time job at the lumber company, but my wages there don't come near making the house payment, truck payment, and putting food on the table. Someone just has to wait for their money until times get better.

The *intentionally delinquent debtor* can be illustrated by Peggy W., who is 26 and single. She works in the public relations sector of a large real estate development firm. She has many unpaid bills.

I look at it like this: You live life once, and nobody says that living has to be neat, you know what I mean? I admit that State Oil is after me for $206 I haven't paid on my gas card. Modern Ms. wants $96 for a crummy dress that practically fell apart after I charged it, and there are some other bills here and there.

But what do they all stack up to? I get different colored letters in my mail that I don't even open—I can tell a bill a mile away. They keep sending them, and I keep throwing them away. My credit rating isn't A plus, but so what? I can always buy a car somewhere, even with poor credit. And I can usually get an apartment without a credit check. So they can keep sending their pink, yellow, and red letters. I'm probably never going to pay. I don't need to.

Different collection letters are certainly required for down-on-his-luck James versus irresponsible Peggy. Unfortunately, you as a business manager will not know in advance whether you are dealing with a James or a Peggy.

The Appearance of Collection Letters

Before discussing techniques for writing the first collection letter, recognize that the delinquent debtor never even sees your carefully written words unless he or she chooses to open the envelope. Too often, well-designed collection letters go out in cheap pulp envelopes with a machine-addressed label pasted unevenly across the envelope face. The envelope shouts "junk mail" or "collection letter" and is promptly trashed.

Put your collection letter into a good-quality, letter-sized envelope—the kind you would use for regular business communication. The address on the envelope, whether written by hand, typed, or printed by a word processor, should look as though it could appear on an important letter which, of course, is exactly what your collection letter is.

Style of Collection Letters

In any collection letter, you as a business writer must make up your mind on five factors:

Assumed cause	Why has the debt not been paid?
Emotional stance	What tone will your letter use?
Specific action	What do you want the reader to do?
Time and place	When and where must the action occur?
Motivator	What motivational force inside the reader do you plan to address?

The Friendly Collection Letter

In the collection letter shown in Figure 7–7, the writer assumes that the debtor simply forgot to make the payment and needs a friendly reminder. Business managers approach debtors in such a nonthreatening way for good reason. The first collection letter can bring more than a 50 percent response rate from delinquent debtors. Those who pay are relatively good customers who will provide future business if they are not chased away by brusque, surly collection language.

The emotional attitude of the letter, therefore, is friendly. Though the action statement names a specific amount to be paid, the time is stated generally ("now," "as soon as possible," "right away") and no specific place or person for payment is named. The writer tries to motivate the debtor based on his or her sense of responsibility.

In beginning the letter, the writer strives for a sentence that makes its point in a somewhat friendly or even humorous way. An outright joke will not do, because it negates the urgency to pay or backfires as sarcasm or satire. The letter is brief because clients will not read more. It relies on goodwill and mutual respect to produce the payment of the debt.

FIGURE 7–7 Friendly Collection Letter

5000 Brent Place
Ogden, Utah 84409-3487
(801) 555-5000

August 6, 199_

Ms. William Forest
91 Cross Road
Ogden, Utah 39523

Dear Ms. Forest:

Did you forget us this month?

Your regular monthly payment of $71.54 has not arrived. Please check your records to make sure that it was sent.

If not, consider this a friendly reminder to a client of value.

Don't forget, by the way, to visit us during August for our Clearance Sale on barbecue equipment.

Sincerely,

Boyd Richards

Boyd Richards
Assistant Manager

BR/we

THE FIRM COLLECTION LETTER

If the first collection letter brings no response, we can assume that a simple slip of memory is not to blame. Instead, we assume that some problem (illness, layoff, travel, and so forth) has interrupted the regular flow of payments. Our emotional attitude becomes firm with a hint of urgency. The specific action is spelled out in unmistakable terms, with a time and place named. We attempt to motivate the reader on the basis of a sense of fairness and business decency.

In the collection letter shown in Figure 7–8, notice that the product, a lawn chair costing $71.54, is not mentioned. If the letter reminded the debtor of the lawn chair, the seed of a defense might be planted in mind: 'What about that chair? I never really found it comfortable. Do I really want to pay $71.54 for it now?'

Similarly, the writer doesn't offer to answer questions or adjust the payment schedule. A debtor who has questions or wishes to adjust a payment schedule will seek assistance; others will read the offer of assistance as a chance to talk their way out of the debt entirely.

The color of the second collection letter may be changed to distinguish it from the first collection letter for the reader. Perhaps with good purpose, many collection letters get a deeper and deeper shade of red as they proceed through the series, like the growing

FIGURE 7–8   Firm Collection Letter

WESTWINDS Patio Furniture

5000 Brent Place
Ogden, Utah 84409-3487
(801) 555-5000

August 18, 199_

Ms. William Forest
91 Cross Road
Ogden, Utah 39523

Dear Mr. Forest:

Your account with us is seriously past due.

Please take a moment right now to write a check for $71.54 payable to Westwinds Patio Furniture. We have enclosed an envelope for your payment.

You are no doubt eager to resolve this problem. So are we.

Sincerely,

Boyd Richards

Boyd Richards
Assistant Manager

BR/we

---

shades of irritation in a human face. Other companies prefer to maintain the formality of white stationery for their collection letters.

Quality envelopes, again, are crucial to the success of the letter. On the collection letter, a signature should appear in ink, so that at least the illusion of personal attention is created.

At your discretion, a pre-addressed return envelope may be included as an additional prod to put a check in the mail. Some businesses even include a stamped envelope, reasoning that the money spent on postage is a good investment to reclaim a bad debt.

The Urgent Collection Letter

If payment still is not received, we now must assume that the debtor cannot or will not pay without strong motivation. Our emotional tone is now resolved, urgent, and straightforward. We name a specific time, place, and person to whom payment must be made. We attempt to motivate the customer by guilt, pride, and the beginnings of fear.

The urgent collection letter shown in Figure 7–9 includes a name for the debtor to contact. This creates the possibility that the debtor will call and arrange payments of some kind. Note, however, that a two-month payment is now due ($71.54 + $71.54 = $143.08), and it is unlikely that the debtor will write a large check when he could not or would not write a smaller one. The looming alternative is to turn the debt over to a collection agency, which may retain as much as 50 percent of the debt if it collects the debt.

FIGURE 7–9   Urgent Collection Letter

WESTWINDS
Patio Furniture

5000 Brent Place
Ogden, Utah 84409-3487
(801) 555-5000

September 10, 199_

Ms. William Forest
91 Cross Road
Ogden, Utah 39523

Dear Mr. Forest:

Contact Mr. Valenzuela at 555-3434 immediately regarding your delinquent account in the amount of $143.08.

You must act on this matter by 12 o'clock noon, Friday, Sept. 18, to avoid action by our attorney. Bring your payment to 5000 Brent Place, or mail it—today, please—in the enclosed envelope.

With your attention to the debt of $143.08 today, we can avoid future action.

Sincerely,

Boyd Richards

Boyd Richards
Assistant Manager

BR/we

A major U.S. bank has had some success in sending third collection letters (particularly on overdue VISA cards) by Mailgram. These look urgent among the other letters in the daily mail and do get opened. The recipient feels that the sender who uses a relatively expensive means of communication is serious about collecting.

The Final Collection Letter

By now, the company has invested a considerable amount of time and expense in trying to rescue a bad debt. The last collection letter (before the collection agency begins its own series) assumes that the debtor will not pay and will make no effort to arrange partial payment. The letter in Figure 7–10 illustrates the characteristics of the final collection effort: its emotional stance is determined, tough, but not offensive. It names a last-ditch time, place, and person for payment. The principal motivator now is fear of legal action (not Mafia extinction!). The company no longer cares to consider future patronage from the debtor. It wants its money.

If this letter is not sent by Mailgram, it can be given a semiofficial look by sending it via certified mail, a somewhat less expensive technique. A registration number is pasted on the envelope by the post office at the time of certification. Hence, the letter arrives with more impact than an ordinary letter.

Chapter 21 describes the narrow limits within which debts may be legally collected in the United States. Such legislation as the Equal Credit Opportunity Act (1974), the Fair

FIGURE 7–10   Final Collection Letter

WESTWINDS Patio Furniture

5000 Brent Place
Ogden, Utah 84409-3487
(801) 555-5000

September 20, 199_

Ms. William Forest
91 Cross Road
Ogden, Utah 39523

Dear Mr. Forest:

Seventy-two hours from the date of this mailing, your delinquent account for $214.62 will be turned over to our attorney, Ms. Lela Vincent, for collection by legal means.

You can still avoid legal proceedings against you by paying your account in full no later than 12 o'clock noon, Friday, Sept. 22, to Mr. Valenzuela at 5000 Brent Place (phone 555-3434).

Your cooperation at this late date can benefit you in two ways: You will avoid legal action against you, and you will not further harm your credit rating. Please act immediately.

Sincerely,

Boyd Richards

Boyd Richards
Assistant Manager

BR/we

Credit Billing Act (1974), and the Fair Debts Collections Practices Act (1978) have set forth strict guidelines for collection. For example, a collector cannot call the debtor before 8 A.M. or after 9 P.M., cannot make a series of calls in rapid succession, cannot threaten to make the debt public knowledge, and cannot continue to contact the debtor by telephone after receiving written notice from the debtor to stop.

Before sending a collection series that you wrote, therefore, ask an attorney to review your words for possible violations of federal, state, or local codes. Modern laws reflect an effort to protect debtors from harm at the hands of powerful merchants and lenders.

FINAL CONSIDERATIONS WHEN WRITING PERSUASIVE LETTERS

In arranging your arguments and evidence for a persuasive letter, remember that your reader has already faced dozens of persuasive appeals that day. Television, radio, magazine, and newspaper ads (which were created by professional ad designers) have screamed or whispered "Buy me!" Many business memos, letters, conferences, and conversations have been attempts to persuade: "Accept me! Approve me!" Your letter arrives in competition with these other persuasive appeals. To be effective, it must distinguish itself in a number of ways: by its readability, responsiveness to the reader's needs, persuasive logic, engaging tone, and honesty. Making good use of these qualities is "being yourself" in writing—that is, demonstrating in writing the same qualities that would distinguish you in a face-to-face meeting.

SUMMARY

1. Effective persuasion is based on needs perceived by the reader.

2. Sales letters, like other forms of persuasion, emphasize the reader's interest—"you"— over the writer's interest—"I."

3. A writer must get to know his or her audience in order to write a successful sales letter. What do the readers need? How much do they already know? What information should be provided in the letter?

4. The *S-A-L-E-S* pattern provides a guideline for developing persuasive sales letters.

5. Direct-mail letters should be based on the needs and interests of the reader.

6. Claims letters may be developed according to the *A-C-T-I-O-N* pattern. Writers use claims letters to inform the reader of a problem and to call for action regarding it.

7. Effective collection letters depend on timing and persuasive language. The collection series communicates the writer's growing concern and resolution.

8. Persuasion should not be manipulative.

9. Electronic technologies such as computer bulletin boards and electronic mail offer new formats and approaches for persuasive messages.

QUESTIONS FOR DISCUSSION

1. What is the "you" emphasis in sales writing? How does it differ from the "I" emphasis?

2. Discuss the assertion, "Persuasion is based on need." What should that mean to writers of persuasive letters?

3. Discuss the *S-A-L-E-S* pattern. Why should these steps be relatively short?

4. Some sales letters begin by reminding the reader of a need of some kind. Evaluate this approach to persuasive writing. When is such an approach appropriate? When is it inappropriate?

5. In what four ways can you spark the imagination of a reader in a sales letter?

6. What are direct-mail sales letter? What challenges face those who write for this market?

7. What is a claim letter? How does the *A-C-T-I-O-N* pattern apply to the writing of such letters?

8. In what ways does anger undercut a writer's success in developing an effective claim letter?

9. Discuss the importance of timing and persuasive language in collection letters.

10. Describe the three stages in collection letters. How do they differ?

11. Why does the first collection letter avoid blunt language?

12. How do the writer's assumptions change during the course of writing a series of collection letters?

EXERCISES

1. Write down three needs perceived by your reader. Call to mind a product or service that relates to those needs. Then develop a sales letter, based on the *S-A-L-E-S* pattern, that addresses those needs in a persuasive way.

2. Choose a sales letter you received recently. Find three common human needs that the letter proposes to satisfy. Note them in the margin of the letter. Then rewrite the letter based on three different human needs.

3. Choose a product or service. Write a sales letter to an audience that knows about that product or service. Write a second version of the letter for an audience that might be expected to use the product or service, but that knows little about it.

4. Develop a direct-mail letter for warm pajamas.

5. Write a claim letter based on the *A-C-T-I-O-N* pattern. Base your letter on some product or service in which you have been disappointed.

6. Write a series of three collection letters trying to motivate Walter Nesbitt to pay the $68 monthly payment he owes for a television set.

7. Contact a collection or credit agency in your city. Ask for information on its methods for collecting from overdue accounts. Describe these methods in writing and give your opinion of their effectiveness.

8. Use the letters you have at hand from Exercise 6 or 7 above. For each, write down how you would respond to the letters if you were an intentional debtor. Then write down how you would respond to the letters if you were an unintentional debtor.

9. Select three television or radio commercials, and evaluate in writing each one's approach to persuasion. What audience needs do they address? How do they catch and maintain attention?

10. Your organization is sponsoring a ski weekend for members. Write a letter to members, "selling" them on the idea and telling them how to sign up.

11. Assume that a major product—an appliance, computer, automobile, and so on—has broken down. Even though the warranty on the product has expired, you feel that the manufacturer should know about the breakdown and perhaps do something about it. Write a claim letter in which you describe the breakdown and seek some kind of remedy from the manufacturer.

12. Assume that you are a business broker interested in selling a business. Write a sales letter to an interested investor regarding this business. Make up all the specifics you need.

13. Find a particularly effective magazine advertisement. Evaluate in writing its persuasive appeal. Then translate the techniques it uses into a sales letter for the same product or service. You can address your letter to a general audience or a particular person.

INTERNET ASSIGNMENT

It wasn't quite the position you had in mind while you were completing your academic studies, but here you are as regional campaign manager for a political candidate. In addition to print, TV, and radio ads, you have decided to launch a well-targeted letter-writing campaign intended to solicit support and financial contributions for your candidate. Investigate Internet sites that present models and methods for writing persuasive letters, including marketing and sales letters. Use the insights you discover to write a one-page letter to potential supporters of your candidate. Make up whatever details you require for the letter. On a separate sheet, list the Internet sites that were most useful to you in completing this assignment. Comment briefly on the features you liked most in each of these sites.

CHAPTER 8

Memos and E-mail Messages

Second only to phone calls, memos (whether sent as hard copy or e-mail transmissions) are the primary means of in-house communication in American business. Memos convey queries, comments, replies, announcements, policy statements, direction, statistical information, clarifications, reminders, authorizations, and a host of other routine but vital communications.

Despite their obvious importance, memos and e-mail messages are treated too casually by many business writers. Those who would not think of sending a letter containing even one typo to a client may nevertheless dash off memos and e-mails marred by garbled language, half-formed sentences, and hit-and-miss spelling and grammar. After all, they reason, "it's just a memo." Unfortunately, poor memos and e-mail messages quickly create negative impressions of the writer for recipients of those messages throughout the company—including the writer's boss.

This chapter describes professional techniques for writing memos and e-mail messages that are clear, correct, and persuasive. Every word matters in a memo as much as it does in letters, reports, and proposals.

IN-HOUSE COMMUNICATION PRINCIPLES

The following principles may guide you in writing in-house correspondence:

- Give in-house writing your best effort
- Exercise judgment in sending in-house communications
- Use positive language to produce positive results
- Use appropriate procedures for transmitting, routing, filing, initialing, and presenting in-house communications
- Send the whole message when you send a memo

Give In-House Writing Your Best Effort

No business writer should allow sloppy writing to leave his or her desk with the excuse that it's just for in-house readers. An immensely successful executive with an East Coast computer firm privately calls his in-house memos his "promotion tickets":

> I've had corporate officers look up when my name is mentioned at a business meeting. They know me not by my face, but by my memos. I've tried over the years to write good memos, emphasizing the progress we're making as a company. The executives I mentioned appreciate hearing from me; they use the information I send in their own conversations and planning.

Every word you write helps to create your business identity within your company. If your writing is abrupt, sloppy, inaccurate, or long-winded, your associates can't help but question your professional abilities. On the other hand, your conscientious effort to write stimulating, persuasive, and skillful memos, letters, proposals, and reports reflects positively on your capabilities. Although each of your memos may not actually be a "promotion ticket," your written work can drastically hurry or halt career advancement. Dr. William F. Bauhaus, chief executive officer at Beckman Instruments, has seen it happen again and again:

> Executives must be able to convince not only their superiors but also their colleagues and subordinates that their programs make sense and are understandable. It takes precise communication to convince. It takes convincing to get proper action. Pure ability without the capacity to communicate and to convince is oftentimes wasted ability.

Exercise Judgment in Sending Memos

When you write memos about your personal opinion and sensitive records, use discretion and tact. One guide to help you decide whether your memo is tactful enough is the "next-week rule." Evaluate every memo, letter, proposal, and report against a wise criterion: Will I want to see these words above my signature *next week*—after the waves of anger, excitement, rush, and personal feeling have passed?

Here are specific occasions when the next-week rule spared unnecessary hard feelings and contributed to effective leadership.

Situation	*Initial Reaction*	*Next-Week Rule*
Tracy Clete, a new programmer, stretches her lunch hour each day. You, as her supervisor, have mentioned the problem to her, without result.	You feel like writing a direct, no-nonsense memo to Tracy, with a copy to her personnel file. You want to tell her to obey the rules or face firing.	You decide to send a general reminder to all staff in Tracy's unit regarding the lunch hour regulations. On Tracy's copy you handwrite, "Please see me if there are circumstances I should know about."

Bret Thomas, a real card, continues to tell offensive jokes about ethnic minorities at work.	As Bret's supervisor, you feel like writing a scorching memo to Thomas regarding his insensitivity and prejudice.	You send a copy of the company's Affirmative Action and Professional Dignity manual to Thomas. You ask him to read the manual, then speak to you privately.

The next-week rule does not force you to withhold communication entirely. Instead, you use your discretion and judgment in your use of words. This marks you as a responsible, farsighted leader. You recognize that not every business situation needs to be or should be recorded in words.

You will have to judge what situations, facts, and opinions should be put into writing. For example, think about how you would handle each of these sensitive issues:

- Seven reams of paper have simply disappeared from the office supply room (to which six employees have regular access).
- One of your key supervisors, Nancy Lincoln, has talked to you about her continuing mental health problem. She is under a psychiatrist's care, but you must lighten her duties without angering the other supervisors.
- As a city building inspector, you have contact with many developers. A few of them are unscrupulous. Developer Davon Trebley took you aside at his Seagate Resort project to hint at—not actually offer—a bribe: "One of these condos could be yours. I'm not talking about money changing hands. What could change, of course, is the City's insistence on copper plumbing here at Seagate."

As you consider your options in each of these sensitive situations, you can see the potential power of words. At times, you might say too much in writing; at other times, you must put things in writing, if only for the file, to protect yourself from later accusations.

Use Positive Language

The meaning of your written words depends on more than their dictionary meanings (or *denotations*). Words also carry feelings or *connotations* to your reader. You must choose words that have both denotative and connotative meanings that suit your purpose.

Unintended connotations can often warp or misplace the intended meaning of your message. Notice how negative connotations distort the message in Figure 8–1.

Unfortunate connotations occur in two principal ways. First, the writer's tone can be unnecessarily pushy, abrupt, or inappropriately personal.

ABRUPT   Don't reorder item #2076.

TOO PERSONAL   You probably oppose my plan because of your son's unfortunate experience.

Second, the negative slant of individual words can give a negative cast to an entire document. Notice the difference between these negative and positive statements:

FIGURE 8–1   Negative Connotations Distorting the Message

Negative	Positive
You failed to notice	May I point out that
You neglected to mention	We also can consider
You overlooked the fact	One additional fact is
You missed the point	From another perspective
If you persist in	If you choose to
I see no alternative but	Our clear plan of action

Negative language usually addresses what the reader did *wrong* (failed, neglected, overlooked, or missed). Positive language emphasizes what the reader can do *right* or what you and the reader can do together. Certainly, no one likes to be reminded of failure or to be threatened with negative consequences. Your readers are motivated and persuaded by encouragement, not by accusation and discouragement.

Use Appropriate Procedures

Over time, each company develops a set of standard operating procedures for most in-house communication. Take the case of the memo.

Routing

Use judgment in routing memos throughout the chain of command. Often, just the right memo for your fellow employees may prove to be just the wrong memo if circulated to other groups within the company. If something you describe could prove embarrassing to others, don't route it to them or to those who evaluate them or to their co-workers. Also, be careful to give full credit where it is due; don't forget to mention all those who helped in achieving a success when routing a memo describing the success.

Although it is true that solid writing skills can get you noticed in business, use judgment in routing communication beyond your immediate supervisor. Before distributing your work to a broad audience in the company, take the time and the courtesy to seek your supervisor's advice.

Filing Considerations

Recognize that your business communication will probably become part of a file, a long-term reservoir of business matters (and a lasting record of your abilities). Therefore, avoid heat-of-the-moment emotional comments in your communications. Don't let emotion-filled memos work against your career.

You should also provide a brief framework of background knowledge that may help to place the memo or report in some context at a later date. A memo dated February 3, 1998, to the effect that "we have Air Force approval" might not mean much months later when an auditor tries to establish which of 27 Air Force contracts you signed on that date. Take time to spell out the essential details necessary to make sense out of the central message.

Initialing

It is customary to sign your name or initials alongside your typed name on a memo. This notation signifies that you have read over and approved the typed copy of your communication. In this way, no one else could circulate a typed or word processed memo and say that you wrote it. In addition, you have one last chance to think, "Is this really what I want to say?"

Presentation Considerations

Memos routinely are sent through company mail or hand-carried to appropriate offices. You may want to evaluate how to deliver and present substantial in-house communications. Consider the comments of Frank Francisca, vice-president of planning for a major developer, regarding two reports he received.

> Before a meeting at the bank, I had five minutes free to shuffle through two or three days' worth of company mail in my in-basket. There, among the usual clutter, was Ed Beal's report on utility costs at our Twin Lakes subdivision. I had been waiting for the report for days. Why didn't he let me know he was sending it?
>
> Kathy Blake made a brief appointment for 10:30 A.M. She was right on time, handed me her report on condo conversions, and told me where she would be if I had questions. As it turned out, we chatted about her findings, and she was able to give me a good understanding of the report before I began reading. Ms. Blake left me with a good impression of herself and her work.

Whenever possible, treat important work you have done by delivering or presenting it in a special way.

ELECTRONIC MAIL: A BIG HELP, WITH A FEW HEADACHES

Across business, industry, and government, electronic mail ("e-mail") has cut down the volume of paper (reports, memos, letters, and photocopies of all kinds) piling up on the desks of workers. Using an e-mail system such as TeleNet, the sender can key in a message on his or her computer and forward it, at the press of a key, to another computer across the office or the world (assuming that they have a link by means of telephone lines or local area network). The message receiver can then open her or his electronic "mailbox" to find the message the others have sent.

Unfortunately, it's not easy for message receivers to figure out quickly which of their electronic mail messages are important. The junk mail that comes in envelopes can be separated quickly from the important correspondence by looking for automatic mailing labels, poor-quality stationery, fourth-class mass delivery postage, and so forth. It may take only a few seconds to toss out the junk mail from a large stack of letters.

Those telltale cues are missing, however, when a businessperson opens an electronic mailbox. Each message must be read, at least in part, to determine its relative importance. Discovering which messages matter, and then separating them out from a dozen or so unimportant messages, can take many minutes, not seconds, when using mail.

The e-mail junk mailers are also learning to disguise their messages as important communications. Although the junk-mail gimmicks ("Open Immediately." "Winning Tickets Enclosed") don't work very well on printed letters sent by U.S. mail, they may seem serious—at least for a moment—when found at the beginning of an e-mail message. For example, what about an "Urgent communication from the National Award Registry"?

Junk e-mail comes from both the usual advertisers and in-house sources. Because it's relatively easy to send an e-mail message to all office recipients on the e-mail system, electronic mailboxes frequently are jammed by "For Your Information" messages, redundant announcements, and "Does Anyone Know. . . ?" queries.

As this powerful communication technology matures, both senders and receivers of messages will learn to use and to spot cues, signals, and formats that immediately distinguish serious messages from the clutter of daily mail.

Send the Whole Message

Business communications in memos have at least four levels:

Past meaning—what has happened?
Present meaning—what is happening?
Future meaning—what will happen?
Emotion—how do I feel?

When business communication focuses too narrowly on any one aspect of the total message, the writer's message can go astray.

Notice, in the following example, how a series of incomplete messages proves ineffective until, at last, a complete message brings productive action.

The Situation: Operations Manager Rita Collins has to deal with a breakdown of discipline in Unit 6. Employees there have regularly been leaving work long before quitting time. She writes a memo to Unit 6 supervisor, Terry Carston.
Aug. 1 Ms. Collins to Supervisor Carston

I just received a summary of your unit's time cards for the past six months. Your people regularly left work fifteen to twenty minutes early.

Supervisor Carston's reaction to this memo was lighthearted. He quipped to his workers, "Well, our time cards didn't win us any awards for the past six months, gang."

Notice that Ms. Collins's message concentrates solely on *past* events, which her readers easily dismiss as ancient history.

> Aug. 8 Ms. Collins to Supervisor Carston
>
> I stood by the door today from 4 p.m. to 5 p.m. More than half of your employees left work early.

Carston again treated the matter casually when he spoke to his employees: "Some of you kind of blew it on August 8."

Notice that Ms. Collins's message concentrates solely on *present* events. Her readers can discount the importance of the message because it seems to deal with only a one-time event.

> Aug. 15 Ms. Collins to Supervisor Carston
>
> We're going to have to develop some new procedures for strict enforcement of working hours.

Supervisor Carston interprets this message to his workers in a facetious way: "Ms. Collins is thinking about developing some new rules. Isn't that swell?"

Notice that Ms. Collins's message emphasizes only *future* implications in her message. Like all projections, these can be put out of mind by readers as an "I'll-believe-it-when-I-see-it" experience.

> Aug. 20 Ms. Collins to Supervisor Carston
>
> I'm extremely upset at you and your entire crew. What makes you think you can flout the rules around here?

Carston is dumbfounded. He confides in his workers that "for some reason, Ms. Collins is really on our case. I don't know why."

Notice that Ms. Collins's message focuses solely on the *emotional* content of her message. Such an outburst can cause readers to wince but not to respond in productive, directed ways.

> Aug. 29 Ms. Collins to Supervisor Carston
>
> Since January, more than half of your employees have been leaving work early. I noticed in spot checks this week that the problem continues. From now on, I insist that your people follow personnel procedures to the letter regarding quitting time. This on-going problem deeply concerns me; let's end it now.

In this statement. Ms. Collins finally achieves her whole message. She leaves her readers no loopholes.

Whole communication does not always have to contain elements of past, present, future, and emotion. However, these divisions may help to remind you to think about your whole message before you send memos.

Communication Insights

Brevity matters more and more in business documents. Paul Dillingham, vice-president of Coca-Cola, comments:

> I can recall a chief executive officer who expected that any memo to him be no more than two pages and preferably one. In unusual situations where longer memos and reports are essential, I find it useful to prepare a one-page Executive Summary and attach it to the longer report, which may be referred to if the reader's time and interest permit.

Whole communication reduces the *ifs*, *ands*, and *buts* in your reader's mind. As a business writer, you want to leave no room for misinterpretation or for the reader to postpone taking action because of confusion about your message.

Emotion in business communication generally has an important role in motivating action. Your deep feelings about an idea or project can be contagious, as in this closing sentence from a real estate sales letter: "We are proud to offer houses that only need *you* in order to become homes."

On the other hand, your irritation and even outright anger, used appropriately, can stir up a stagnant situation: "We placed our order four months ago. We waited patiently and now are waiting impatiently. Please ship the order today, or consider it canceled."

Even your emotional ambivalence can be used to awaken caution in your readers: "Certainly the planners are right that historic old Henderson pier has the visibility and accessibility necessary for a restaurant site. I have my misgivings, though, about the public's response to this alteration of the old landmark. I recommend further study."

A frank statement of your emotions—never a gush or a whine—announces your priorities loud and clear. Business writers who express their emotions appropriately rarely hear a reader respond, "I didn't know it meant that much to you." Readers may choose not to follow your emotional lead, but they cannot claim you failed to take a stand.

We can now turn to specific forms of in-house writing and to the techniques that build success in these forms.

Communication Checkpoint
Check Your Messages for Completeness

One way to check the completeness of your message is to step into your reader's shoes for a moment. Ask these questions of your message:

- What can be misinterpreted?
- What options does the message allow me?
- What response does the message seem to ask for?
- Does the message ask for that response in a specific way?

Four Common Memo Mistakes

Many business writers manage to ruin memos through casual, thoughtless mistakes. Their errors fall into four categories. Make sure you avoid each in your own writing:

1. The telegram writer
2. The scrawler
3. The windbag
4. The tease

The Telegram Writer

Some business writers who otherwise speak and write well show an odd problem when they write memos. They leave out major portions of sentences—sometimes even the subject itself:

To: Sandra Phillips

From: Natalie Forbes

Date: April 22, 199_

Subject: National Association of Realtors convention

Attended the seminar on exchanges. Discussed ways to trade our New Haven building for an industrial site. Met Jerry Hausing of Dynaflite Corp. Mentioned being interested in such a trade. Eager to talk more about this.

What does this telegram form of writing communicate? *Who* attended? *Who* discussed? Most crucially, *who* showed interest in the trade—Hausing or Forbes? *Who* is eager to talk more? Writers who use this clipped telegram type of memo only complicate and confuse their messages, which slows the reader's ability to understand and respond to the memo.

The Scrawler

Because memos offer such an easy-to-use, casual format, some writers fall into making mistakes in spelling, grammar, style, and even handwriting (see Figure 8–2). Such informal language may be easy to write, but it destroys the credibility of the message and the writer. Readers assume that glaring little mistakes ("desines" for *designs*, "modles" for *models*) indicate underlying big mistakes in judgment and, possibly, limited intelligence.

FIGURE 8–2   Handwritten Memo Containing Many Errors

TO: Harvey

From:

Date: Wednes

Subject: Prelim desines will be ready for next yrs. modles by next Tues. or so.

Jo

The Windbag

Just as the word *memo* is short for *memorandum*, the messages in memos should be brief and to the point.

Consider this first paragraph from an eight-paragraph memo, which was intended to announce that brochures from a local trade fair were available from the memo writer:

> I'm writing this memo upon my return from St. Louis where, as you know, I represented the company in my role as Midwest sales supervisor at a trade show aptly named "Farm Expo '98." I saw many new techniques and products demonstrated at the trade show, all of which I plan to summarize at an upcoming seminar, which I will conduct for interested parties within the company.

Clearly, this writer is going to bore the readers long before they could find out about the brochures.

Communication Insights	At Ford Aerospace, Vice-President Louis Heilig gives this advice to his people:
	Write down on one sheet the objectives and criteria for the project you wish to carry forward. Make it so straightforward that it is essentially impossible to misunderstand.

The Tease

Some memo writers consciously or unconsciously irritate their readers by hinting at information that they should tell fully:

> Regarding that matter at lunch, I want to give you the green light, provided you clear it with the appropriate people.

Writers who hint at unstated but necessary information in this way are trying to sound intimate with their readers. They mistakenly think that the false sense of shared secrets makes memos work.

Memos are not treasure maps. Never try to build a sense of suspense or intimacy at the expense of your message. First, let the message be clear. Then add whatever social or personal remarks you wish to add warmth and intimacy. Figure 8–3 shows an effectively written short memo.

Four Common Business Memos

The following four memos are commonly used in most businesses:

1. Policy memo
2. Notice-of-change memo
3. Inquiry memo
4. Update memo

FIGURE 8–3   Short Memo

Memo

To: Brad Taylor
           Design Specialist

From: Katherine Fremont
           Vice-President

Date: March 1, 199_

Subject: City approval of solar panels on Burke project

I received a letter dated Feb. 26, 199_, from City Planner Richard Ortiz. He wants us to present exterior elevations showing all proposed solar panels on the Burke project.

Let's meet in my office at 2 P.M., Wednesday, March 3, to prepare this aspect of our presentation to the City.

Policy Memo

This memo is usually sent to a wide distribution list within the company to announce or clarify company policy. The memo typically begins with a background statement, then the policy statement, and finally a directive, if any.

To: All Supervisors

From: Linda Morgan, Vice President, Personnel

Date: January 7, 199_

Subject: Statements to the Press

The *Wall Street Journal* and other newspapers and magazines have recently reported takeover and/or merger rumors with regard to our company.

It is the company policy (#207.1) that "no employee shall make statements to press representatives regarding company products, personnel, planning, or other proprietary concerns without written authorization from the president or appropriate designee."

Please review this policy with each of your subordinates within the next 48 hours to ensure that misstatements and misinformation do not adversely affect the company's efforts to resist hostile acquisition.

Notice-of-Change Memo

This memo describes a change in method, personnel, procedure, location, or other matter. It typically begins with a background statement, then the change description, and finally an interpretation, if any, for those affected by the change. The notice-of-change memo often works to set the record straight in the face of rumors.

To: [*distribution list*]

From: Mikail Volsklov, Head of Engineering

Date: May 17, 199_

Subject: New Testing Schedule for F180 Project

New Department of Defense guidelines regarding the structural testing of tail components for the Air Force F180 project require that Air Force representatives be present for field testing.

We have therefore postponed tests A24 and A25 from June 6, 199_, to June 24, 199_, when Air Force Captain Leland Owens will visit our facility to oversee testing. All other arrangements remain unchanged.

We do not anticipate that this change in schedule will affect the ultimate delivery date of the F180 prototype on Dec. 10, 199_.

Inquiry Memo

This memo asks a question and may give guidelines for the reader's reply. The memo typically begins with a need-to-know statement that explains why the question is being asked. The question follows the explanation, and then a final, optional guidelines statement tells how the inquirer wants the query to be answered.

To: Fred Samson, Supervisor, Parts Department

From: Bernice Johnson, Accounting

Date: June 28, 199_

Subject: Inventory planning for third quarter

In the past, Fred, I know that you have closed your department down for two days each quarter so that you could use your own personnel to do inventory counts.

Do you want me to investigate professional inventory services that can handle this chore for us each quarter? Citywide Ford has apparently had good luck with this approach for the past year or so.

Please let me know today, if possible, (a) when you've scheduled third-quarter inventory, and (b) your approximate costs in salaries and lost business for the two-day inventory period. After I've received information from external inventory companies, you and I can meet to decide which route we want to take.

Update Memo

This memo tries to inform readers about developments, projects, and processes. The memo typically begins with an at-last-report statement, followed by the update statement, and concludes (optionally) with a forecast statement or a future-report statement.

To: [*distribution list*]

From: Kiko Yang, Director of Advertising

Date: July 8, 199_

Subject: Update on Advertising/Marketing Campaign for Hilo Hilton

In June, I reported to you that we had won a one-year contract to provide promotional ser-vices for the new, exciting Hilo Hilton.

Since then, our creative teams have been hard at work on an integrated but varied promo-tional package to meet and exceed our client's goals. The package will be demonstrated in a gala dress rehearsal at the corporate theater on July 12, 10:30 a.m. Attendance is manda-tory for Level 1 supervisors, with additional reservations available for other employees who wish to attend. Contact Milt Covington at ext. 3892 for reservations.

Following the presentation, the audience will be asked to complete an evaluation questionnaire on the promotional package. I'll compile the results and report back to you within ten days.

FIVE GUIDELINES FOR E-MAIL MESSAGES

In addition to the general writing advice provided earlier in this chapter, consider the fol-lowing guidelines when writing messages for e-mail:

1. *Abide by accepted conventions for spelling, capitalization, grammar, and punctu-ation.* Early use of e-mail tended to omit capital letters and allowed great latitude in spelling, grammar, and punctuation. In most corporations, those days are long past.

2. *Get to your point early in your e-mail message by making clear use of the subject heading and using your first sentence or two to communicate your central mes-sage.* One popular pattern for e-mail messages is the following:

   Paragraph (or sentence) 1: "Here's what I want."
   Paragraph (or sentence) 2: "Here's why."
   Paragraph (or sentence) 3: "Here specifically what to do."

3. *Read your e-mail message over at least twice before transmitting it.* Unlike tradi-tional memos which can be fished out of the boss's mailbox, e-mail messages are irretrievably on their way to their reader once you press the "Send" command. Take special care with e-mail messages written in the heat of argument or anger. You may want to practice the "one-hour" rule: let the passionate e-mail sit in your file for one hour, then read it again. You may save yourself embarrassment (or worse).

4. *Route the e-mail message only to those with a clear need-to-know.* Although still in its infancy as a corporate communication channel, e-mail has already achieved the dubious reputation of "glut-mail." Some companies have resorted to a color-coding system on the list of incoming messages to distinguish treasure from trash. But even these systems have not entirely saved managers from the burdensome and time-intensive task of sorting through dozens of (and, in extreme cases, a hun-dred or more) e-mail messages each day. More than one manager has let it be

known that "I don't check my e-mail very often. If you want to make sure you get through to me, use the phone." That alternative, unfortunately, causes voice-mail to load up with the same information overload experienced by e-mail systems.

5. *Make sure your correspondent can decode attachments, files, graphics, and other accompaniments to your e-mail message.* Don't assume that all e-mail systems can accommodate your supplements. It is both courteous and good business practice to call to check on the recipient's success in receiving your entire message package.

The Memo to File

A *memo to file* is addressed to no specific person and yet to everyone in general who happens upon the file. Therefore, the memo to file matters as much as any other business communication. Its audience may range from an auditor to the chairperson of the board. Therefore, choose your words with care. Be specific about names, places, dates, events, order numbers, and so forth.

Because the file cannot shoot back questions—"What do you mean here? Was the convention in Chicago or Detroit?"—be thorough, even to the point of stating what seems obvious at the moment of composition.

FINAL CONSIDERATIONS

It's difficult to overestimate the amount of writing you will do or its importance to your business career. In 1998, four midlevel managers from the media, insurance, aerospace, and real estate industries agreed to keep a two-month log of the various forms of written communication they personally produced. By far the most common form of writing for all four managers was the *memo*. A partial list of other documents they wrote is shown in Figure 8–4.

FIGURE 8–4 A Partial List of Frequently Written Documents

Letters of recommendation	Proposals
Trip reports	Cover letters
Work orders	Job descriptions
Performance evaluations	Letters of authorization for
Congratulatory notes	subcontracts
Sympathy notes	Sales and promotional letters
Quarterly reports	Adjustment and claims letters
Announcements	Statements of objectives
Instructions	Press releases
Procedures	Suggestions
Replies to inquiries and orders	Recommendations
Summaries of meetings	Edited versions of
and interviews	documents written by others

All four managers confessed surprise at the volume and variety of their writing tasks. "I think of myself as being on the phone half the day," said one manager, "but I guess I'm at my word processor much more than I thought."

You too will face a wide variety of writing tasks that will matter for your own professional future. The ability to write a crisp, clear, persuasive memo is an important step in becoming a skilled business writer.

SUMMARY

1. Most business writing is in-house writing.

2. Not everything that can be said *should* be said in written form.

3. Positive language can achieve positive results in written communications.

4. It is important to learn standard procedures for in-house communications within your company.

5. Effective in-house communications convey the whole message, not a partial message.

6. Style and form are as important in brief in-house communications as they are in longer documents sent out of the company.

7. Early orientation to your message and the use of topic headings are particularly important in longer memos.

8. The letter memo combines the directness of the memo form with the formality of a letter.

9. The memo to file creates a written record of business events.

QUESTIONS FOR DISCUSSION

1. To what kind of audience are the majority of business documents addressed?

2. What would you say to a colleague who writes sloppy memos because they're "just for the folks in our department"?

3. What is the "next-week rule," and how can it help you to exercise discretion and tact when writing memos?

4. Discuss the importance of using positive language to produce positive results.

5. Why is it important to exercise judgment in routing communications within your company?

6. What are some points to keep in mind when writing memos that will become part of a permanent file?

7. If you feel you have written a strong business document, how should you present and deliver it?

8. Will anticipating your reader's reaction to your message help you to create a complete message? Explain.

9. Define "memo." Why do business writers generally find the memo the easiest business document to write?

10. In what ways does the long memo differ from the short memo? What techniques for being clear and concise become especially relevant for writers of long memos? Why?

11. When might you choose to write a letter-memo rather than a regular memo for an in-house communication? Will audience considerations influence your choice?

EXERCISES

1. Assume that you've been passed over for a promotion you deserve. Experiment with the advantageous control of anger in this way: First, write an obviously angry first draft of a memo in which you communicate your outrage; second, revise the draft so that it still communicates your position in strong terms but does not alienate or insult the reader.

2. Assume that you have been asked to speak at the Young Achievers luncheon. To experiment with negative and positive language, write two versions of a turn-down letter for this invitation. In the first version, purposely use negative language to say "no" to the invitation. In the second (preferred) version, use positive language to communicate your turn-down message.

3. Write an update memo to your business communication instructor, updating him or her on some aspect of your school or work life. For example, you may want to update your instructor on your academic major—why you chose it, what classes you've completed, and so forth.

4. Write an inquiry memo to an administrator. Ask a question regarding policies, procedures, or other matters that affect your life. Explain why you are making your inquiry. (If appropriate, you may want to actually send the inquiry.)

5. Assume that you are a senior leader in a college or business organization. In that role, write a notice-of-change memo to your members or employees about some matter of significance to them.

6. In the role of a senior decision-maker in business, write a policy memo for your employees on one of the following subjects: on-site smoking, sexual harassment in the workplace, affirmative action, flextime, or early retirement.

7. For each of the following *past* meanings, write companion *present* and *future* aspects of the message.

> Past: "The company used to have 60 percent of the American market share in men's gloves."
> Past: "One president led the company for more than 25 years, until last year."
> Past: "Monthly federal inspections of the plant were required until 1988."

INTERNET ASSIGNMENT

Your firm is attempting to become "paperless" by conducting most internal correspondence by e-mail. Unfortunately, the paper blizzard formerly plaguing the company has now turned into an electronic information overload for employees who face one hundred or more e-mail messages per day. Many workers say privately that they ignore most of their e-mail messages or simply scan them for messages from the boss. You've been given the task of investigating ways to make e-mail work better within your organization. Use the Communication Technologies section and Organizational Communication section of the Internet Guide and whatever other resources you can discover on the Web to develop a plan for reducing unnecessary e-mail within your company and improving employee attitudes toward this communication channel.

PART THREE

REPORTING AND PROPOSING

CHAPTER 9

Short and Long Reports

OVERVIEW OF SHORT REPORTS

Short reports are usually less than ten pages long and can be read in one sitting. Business organizations of all sizes rely on these documents to learn what's happening (or what has happened or will happen) in two worlds:

1. **The internal world**—What are employees working on? How is it going? What resources are being used, or which are required? In what ways is the company growing or shrinking? What problems need to be addressed?

2. **The external world**—How is the company perceived by clients and the general public? What do clients want from the company? What is the company's competition, and how can it be met? How can the company attract skilled workers? What social responsibilities and political challenges does the company face?

These issues and others are discussed by means of all communication channels within the company, including meetings, interviews, memos, and letters. However, the report often addresses these issues more thoroughly, and with more formal organization than other forms of business communication.

Purpose of the Short Report

The purpose of the report may be informative (*what* is known about the topic), analytical (*why* circumstances have developed), persuasive (*how* readers should respond), or portions of all three. Because short reports are used for making decisions, they include enough evidence to support the option suggested in the report. Although short reports can refer to other written work, they should not just be cover letters to relatively disorganized collections of facts and figures.

The Audience for Short Reports

Reports in corporations and other organizations are typically requested when upper management faces a *problem* or a *question*. These concerns are then delegated to subordinates who, after necessary thinking and research, respond to the problem or question by means of a short report. In other words, the needs of the audience determine the purpose for a short report.

First, the report is read and approved by the person or persons (usually senior management) who requested it. Next, a report may be distributed to various levels of responsibility within the company, or it may be stored in a company library, where others may read it. In this role, the short report becomes a vehicle for getting information out to co-workers. In fact, a report writer may be asked to produce two versions of a report: (1) a complete version for the manager(s) who requested it and (2) a summary version for distribution to others in the company.

The specific details of the format of short reports differ somewhat from corporation to corporation. One company may insist on reports in memo format (beginning with a "To:/From:/Date:/Subject:" block), whereas another company may prefer the more traditional title page opening. Some firms bind all authorized short reports into special paper folders; others use colored papers to signify different kinds of reports. Across industries, however, the format of a short report can generally be described, page by page, as shown in Figure 9–1. The following paragraphs briefly describe the common elements found in most short reports.

Title Page

The title page contains key information: *what* the report is about, *for whom* it was prepared, *by whom* it was written, and the *date* of its completion or filing. **Pagination:** counts as a page in lowercase Roman numerals, but no page number is actually shown on the page.

FIGURE 9–1   Short Report Format

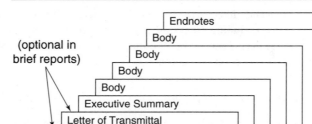

The Table of Contents

This page is optional in reports of six pages or less, but it is helpful to readers of longer reports. Because your goal (as always in business writing) is to help your readers understand your writing, include this element if it might be helpful. Don't include it if it only makes your document longer, not better. **Pagination:** counts as a page and is typed in lowercase Roman numerals, usually centered in the bottom margin.

The Letter of Transmittal

This optional page is a letter from the report writer to the report readers (see samples in Figures 9–2 through 9–10). It briefly provides the following: (a) reason(s) for the

FIGURE 9–2   Sample Short Report—Letter of Transmittal (optional)

   Executive Offices
903 Yates Road
Akron, Ohio 44305-1775
(216) 555-5409

January 6, 199_

Ms. Gloria Demers
Chair, Executive Board
EEW, Inc.
903 Yates Road
Oshkosh, WI 54986-3749

Dear Ms. Demers:

We are pleased to enclose "Policies on Maternity Leave at EEW, Inc.," the brief report requested by the Board for consideration at its mid-January meeting.

The report sums up our review of over 800 personnel cases involving pregnancies at EEW in the past two decades. On the basis of that evidence, we recommend that the Board consider a more liberal maternity leave policy, as detailed in the report.

We invite the Board's comments and questions regarding our findings. If you wish, we will be happy to attend the Board meeting to answer any immediate inquiries.

Thank you for this opportunity to investigate a problematic area of company personnel policy.

Sincerely,

Margery Vickers
Co-director, Personnel Department

Sheldon Ramirez
Co-director, Personnel Department

MIV, STR/epv
Enclosure: "Policies on Pregnancy at EEW, Inc."

FIGURE 9–3   Sample Short Report (continued)

Policies on Maternity Leave at EEW, Inc.

Submitted to
The Executive Board

by

Margery Vickers
Sheldon Ramirez
Co-directors, Personnel Department

January 6, 199_

report, (b) report authorization, (c) highlights of particularly interesting items, and (d) contact information for readers' questions or comments. Such letters usually appear in short reports that must be conveyed to their readers by mail or messenger rather than in person by the report writer. (The letter of transmittal may also be attached to but not included in the report, in which case it does not appear in the table of contents.) **Pagination:** counts as a page and is typed in lowercase Roman numerals.

FIGURE 9–4   Sample Short Report (continued)

TABLE OF CONTENTS

FIGURE 9–5 Sample Short Report (continued)

EXECUTIVE SUMMARY

From 1983 to 1988, EEW, Inc. granted no maternity leaves for pregnant workers. As a result, more than 50 pregnant workers per year quit their jobs. Less than 10 percent returned after delivery. Late in 1988 the company began granting selective maternity leaves, without pay, based on an employee's record of accomplishment. Because few employees applied for such payless leaves and fewer received them, resignations due to pregnancy still totaled 40 to 45 workers per year in the time period 1988–1990. Since that time, company policy has been liberalized to permit pregnant workers to take maternity leave, still without pay, but with no loss of position in seniority if they return to work within six months. While this policy has helped to stem the steady flow of resignations due to pregnancy, the company should consider a policy of maternity leave with half-pay as an effective way to retain trained employees and, in the long term, to save money.

The Executive Summary

This may also be called an "abstract" or a "synopsis" in technological and scientific work environments. This page summarizes the purpose, organization, methods, and outcomes of the short report. The executive summary usually runs no longer than one page and may be as short as a single paragraph. **Pagination:** counts as a page and is typed in lowercase Roman numerals at the bottom of the page.

The Report Body

These pages contain the actual information of the report, with major divisions of argument and evidence demarcated by headings. The development and organization of these report sections are treated in depth later in this chapter. **Pagination:** first page of the report body begins with Arabic number 1, continuing successively through all the remaining pages, including endnotes and bibliography, if any.

Endnotes, References, or Bibliography

Notes may be used in the text itself, placed at the *foot* of the page—that is, "footnotes"—or gathered at the *end* of the report as "endnotes." The References or Bibliography pages, usually last in a short report, always follow all notes and in-text references. These are described more specifically in Appendix B, "A Guide to Documentation." Many short reports don't include this documentation when the report does not cite sources or require other notes. **Pagination:** continuation of Arabic numeral series from the report body.

TEN STEPS TO WRITING A SHORT REPORT

Now that you've seen an overview of short reports, you're ready to find out how to write them yourself. Experienced report writers in business and industry usually develop individual approaches to the craft of report writing. Many prefer to read widely in their topic area,

FIGURE 9–6 Sample Short Report (continued)

I. Overview

Motivated by Federal and State legislation, union demands, and its own interests, EEW has assigned the Personnel Department the task of reporting on past, present, and future company policies regarding maternity leave among company workers. This report details past practices, summarizes present policies, and evaluates the factors that will guide future policy.

The report concludes that EEW should provide up to four months maternity leave, with half-pay. These measures, while not yet common among our competitors, are justified in the report on the basis of employee retention and long-term savings to the company.

II. Past Policies on Pregnancy at EEW

At the time of the company's founding in 1983, it had no written policy for pregnancy among the staff. Workers routinely quit their jobs when they discovered their pregnancy or were dismissed when the pregnancy became obvious to their supervisors. Company personnel files show that a few workers requested leaves of absence without pay for the period of their pregnancy and the months after. Without exception, these requests were turned down by the company.[1] In the words of an infamous internal memo from the now-deceased former president of the company, "Absolutely no. If she has one child, she'll probably have more. There is no end to that kind of thing."

Under pressure from union negotiators and women's groups, the company in 1988 began to grant leaves without pay to workers who had demonstrated a record of achievement and promise. While no statistics can be gathered to make the point in a concrete way, many pregnant workers still were dismissed in the late 1980's on the grounds that their records weren't "promising enough." Despite repeated efforts by the company's personnel director during those years, management resisted all efforts to set forth clear work standards by which "enough" could be measured. Pregnant employees well into 1990, therefore, found themselves dependent upon the whim of a supervisor for a leave of absence, of course without pay.

In 1991, a watershed event changed the company's policies overnight. Interestingly, this event came not from legislation or external pressure. A talented vice-president of the company proudly announced her pregnancy to a somewhat shocked Board meeting on June 2, 1991. She went on to speak of her commitment to the company and her earnest desire to take up her duties again as soon as possible after giving birth.

A discussion ensued, pitting the traditionalists in the company against those interested in finding new and more flexible policies. Traditionalists argued that profits, not parenthood, were the sole concern of the company. Pregnant employees, they said, could not be retained, nor could their positions be held open for them. More liberal minds argued that companies had far-reaching obligations to their employees and could not simply turn them out for choosing to bear children.

The pregnant vice-president brought both groups up short in a brief statement still recorded in the minutes of that meeting: "Let me put it this way, gentlemen. I led the successful company effort to attract over $4 million in contracts and grants last year. I have an offer to do that kind of work for your main competitor during my pregnancy and after. I spoke of my commitment to this company. Now you must decide if I'm worth your commitment. In the long term, will I make you enough money to compensate for my pregnancy leave?"[2] At that point she smiled and left the meeting.

usually while taking notes, as a start to the writing process. Others like to start by making a very rough guess about the form and content of their eventual report. These writers sketch outlines and other patterns for information as they shape their possibilities for research.

You, too, will develop personal approaches to report writing that work for you and your company. To give yourself a start on your own approach, consider ten steps that have

FIGURE 9–7   Sample Short Report (continued)

As a result of that meeting, she was offered a leave of absence without pay for the last three months of her pregnancy and the first three months of motherhood. (Incidentally, she left the company to accept an identical offer <u>with</u> pay from the competitor.) Leaves without pay were available from that time on throughout 1991 to other pregnant workers. Relatively few workers took such leaves, however, because they could not afford to live for that period without an income. They opted instead for unemployment compensation or other work that allowed them to earn right up to the week of delivery.

III. <u>Present Policies</u>

Since 1991, the Personnel Department sponsored a successful drive in the company to allow pregnant workers to stay at their occupations with the company as long as their personal physician would allow. Barring company-wide layoffs, these workers could return to their jobs within six months after giving birth, without loss of seniority or pay level.[3]

That policy continues to the present. No salary is paid during leaves of absence due to pregnancy. Benefits may be paid, depending upon the fringe package selected by the employee.

At present, the work force of EEW totals 1152 workers, of which 802 are women. While the Personnel Department does not claim to know of every pregnancy among the workers, we estimate that each year fifty to sixty workers become pregnant with the intention of bearing a child. Of this number, no more than 10 percent apply for a leave without pay for the period of pregnancy and delivery.[4]

IV. <u>Evaluation</u>

Those pregnant workers who do not request a leave of absence simply quit. Few return to the company in later months or years. As illustrated in Figure 1, these resignations result in a substantial loss to the company each year. Note in the chart that an employee usually requires at least five months to reach the production level of our average experienced employee:

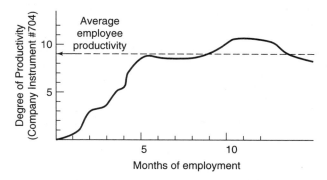

Figure 1. Productivity During First Year of Employment

During this period of learning, the company is paying out an average salary of $2000 per month, only a percentage of which is earned by employee production during the learning process. Thus, the company invests on average $5000 in the training of each employee, as demonstrated in the table at the top of the next page.

FIGURE 9–8   Sample Short Report (continued)

Month	Salary	Production %	Training Cost
1	$2000	10%	$1800
2	$2000	30%	$1400
3	$2000	50%	$1000
4	$2000	70%	$ 600
5	$2000	90%	$ 200
		Total	$5000

In addition to this $5000 spent in training, the Personnel Department spends on average $1240 in advertising, interviewing, and processing costs for each new employee hired.[5]

Therefore, if 50 workers quit per year due to pregnancy, the company cost in wasted training, advertising, interviewing, and processing is $312,000 (50 × $5000 + $1240).

For prudent policy decisions on pregnancy, that substantial sum must be weighed against the cost of simply providing half-pay for pregnant workers during the last month of pregnancy and the first three months of motherhood. Assuming that all 50 workers accepted such an arrangement, the company would pay 50 × 1000 (half-pay) × 4 months = $200,000.

The resultant saving to the company under such a plan would be $112,000. More difficult to measure but equally important are such advantages to the company as improved employee morale, enhanced company image for job-seekers, and fewer trainees in the work force.

VI. <u>Conclusion</u>

Over the nine years of the company's existence, policies on pregnancy leave have been steadily liberalized in favor of the worker. Based on the training and replacement costs set forth in this report, the trend toward partial salary during pregnancy leave is in the financial interest of the company. EEW will spend one-third less to retain pregnant employees through half-pay leaves than to lose them and pay for advertising, interviewing, processing, and training for replacements.

---

helped many report writers get from an initial idea to a polished report in an efficient manner. If these steps prove helpful, you may want to photocopy them and attach them to your word processor as a convenient report-writing road map.

Step 1: Think about the W-O-R-M

W	**W**ho will read the report?
O	What is the **O**bject of the report?
R	What's the **R**ange of the report?
M	What's the **M**ethod of presentation in the report?

Thinking about the W-O-R-M helps you to focus on important aspects of the report. It also helps to relieve your tension when you first start writing your report.

Who Will Read the Report?

Think carefully about your immediate and long-term audiences. What are their interests? their needs? their biases? The answers to these questions can help you determine what to discuss and how to shape your material to best effect.

FIGURE 9–9 Sample Short Report (continued)

APPENDIX: FIVE CASE STUDIES

All aspects of the following five cases are factually true. Names have been changed to protect privacy.

1984—Ruth

After six years with the company as an accountant, Ruth asked her supervisor for leave without pay during her pregnancy and first few months of motherhood. The request was routinely denied. Ruth resigned her position at EEW, had her baby, then found employment with EEW's main competitor, Technoelectric Designs. Today Ruth heads the accounting division at that company. Recently she was honored by the National Accounting Association for innovative and money-saving approaches to economic forecasting at Technoelectric.

1987—Jan

Fearing that she would be fired, Jan hid her pregnancy as best she could into the sixth month. Her supervisor recommended her dismissal at that time in spite of Jan's excellent work record at EEW. Jan's husband, a senior engineer at EEW, expressed outrage at the handling of the situation. Both found employment elsewhere.

1992—Francine

An assembly-line worker, Francine requested a leave of absence without pay. Her request was turned down because her work record, in the words of the rejection memo, "did not merit such concessions by the company." Acting through her union, Francine took the matter before the National Labor Relations Board and won a judgment against the company. After receiving back pay and a settlement, Francine voluntarily found employment at Micro-Circuitry, Inc. She now supervises an assembly unit there.

1995—Barbara

Barbara applied for and received a maternity leave without pay. She left EEW in the fifth month of her pregnancy. Faced with rising financial obligations, however, she found temporary work at Technoelectric Designs during the latter months of her pregnancy. A few weeks after delivery, she returned to the work force—but not at EEW. She manages the sales support team at Technoelectric Design today.

1998—Cathy

Cathy in early 1998 came to the Personnel Department for counseling. She and her husband planned to start a family, she said, but could do so only if she could be assured of returning to her job a few weeks after delivery. The personnel officer explained that she could return to her job up to six months after delivery. Cathy kept her job at EEW, returning two months after her baby was born. She resigned a few months later, explaining in her exit interview that she and her husband were making plans for another child. She wanted to find employment with a company that offered some kind of financial support during pregnancy leave.

What's the Object of the Report?

Learn as much as possible about the purpose (object) and intended use of your report before beginning to write. Don't be misled by the tentative title you or someone else has given to your report. Titles don't always reveal the true object of the report.

Before you start to write, find out what your report is supposed to help your key readers do. Should it help them to make a decision? If so, the report must analyze the

FIGURE 9–10   Sample Short Report (continued)

WORKS CITED

1. <u>Annual Personnel Summary, 1986</u>, Vol. IV, p. 68.
2. <u>Corporate Minutes</u>, Oct. 1997, p. 137.
3. For a full description of this policy, see <u>Personnel Policies and Procedures</u>, 1997, pp. 387–98.
4. This figure is based upon leave applications formally filed with the Personnel Department during the 1997 fiscal year.
5. For a detailed explanation of this estimated average, see <u>Internal Economic Report No. 7</u>, Jan. 1997, p. 204.

---

choices, and it might need to suggest a best choice. Should it rationalize a decision that was already made? If so, it should tell why that specific choice was made and should ignore choices that seem better now, with hindsight.

Many experienced report writers jot down their object on an index card, which they keep handy while writing. The card serves as a constant reminder that every aspect of the report must help to achieve the object. Any other writing, no matter how terrific, is wasted effort.

What Is the Range of the Report?

How broadly should you describe and cover your topic? Do you want to summarize facts? to interpret facts? to predict future patterns of growth?

Determine the range of your report before beginning to write. This means that you will often have to leave out interesting information. There will always be important topics that are fascinating but don't belong in the report you write. Like stones thrown into a pond, almost all business writing topics ripple out implications and suggest further areas of study. You cannot always follow the topic wherever it leads. Don't let your topic control you: the report would become unmanageably long and disjointed. Instead, you must control the range of your report by deciding what belongs and what does not belong within your area of study.

What's the Method of Presentation?

Words do not find their places automatically on the sheet of paper. Exercise extreme care in placing your words well on the page. First impressions are important.

Use topic headings, graphics, tables, and white space wherever they will help the at-a-glance readability of your report. Write for the reader who will merely glance through your report as well as the reader who will read it with care.

Step 2: Know What Your Audience Wants

In actual business practice, writers too often finish a report only to be told by upper management, "You missed the point." When such writers hear what the report was supposed to treat, they usually respond, "Why didn't you say so?"

On the other hand, why didn't the writer ask? The report writer bears primary responsibility for knowing what the reader wants. Upper management can be notoriously brief and cryptic in setting forth the topic for a report.

Thus, report writers have to learn to decode the short prescriptions of upper management. Usually, this decoding process involves limiting broad, unmanageable topics. In the following passages, notice how what was said gets translated by the report writer into a limited, manageable topic.

Executive Requests Report	*Report Writer Limits Topic*
On the minority hiring situation here at Plantron	Affirmative Action Hiring at Plantron Since 1992
On automated tellers for the bank	Four Highly Rated Automated Tellers Suitable for Installation at Salton Bank

The limiting process usually happens naturally and quickly in day-to-day business conversation. When the report writer formulates a limited version of an assigned topic, he or she checks it out with upper management—usually by means of a brief memo, conference, or phone call. These important few minutes help the writer avoid wasted days of effort on misunderstood or misdirected topics.

Often, report writers must also convert the newly limited topics to specific problems. If a vice president of a large air-conditioning manufacturer orders "a study of sick leave at Dynatemp," he or she may in fact want a report on the *problem* of rising numbers of sick days taken by workers at the company. Pity the fate of a report writer who fails to convert the topic to a problem and who merely summarizes the sick leave policies of the company.

Consider how each of the following topics has been converted into a specific problem for purposes of the report:

Topic	*Specific problem*
How well we get our product to our retail outlets	Four bottlenecks in Amax shipping procedures and routes
Plant security	Points of security vulnerability at the Southgate plant

Not all topics need to be converted into problems. Some topics are intended only to summarize and report existing conditions and situations.

Step 3: Brainstorm about Your Topic

Consider using the Classic Questions (see Chapter 3) as a brainstorming technique. For a report on the cost of employee training, this might work as shown in the following questions:

1. Why does the company care about the costs of employee training?

THE CLASSIC QUESTIONS

Costs have been rising dramatically in the last two years.

2. If I had to divide the costs of employee training into parts, what would they be?

New employee orientation
On-the-job training programs
Retraining veteran employees

3. What forces/circumstances led to the rising costs of employee training?

> Efforts to refurbish training facilities
> Acquisition of new electronic teaching aids

4. What kind of person is interested in the rising cost of employee training?

> Executives in the company who want to see positive results for the dollars spent.

5. If rising costs due to new equipment did not exist, how would things be different?

> The training program would be labor-intensive, relying on repeated lectures and workshops by company instructors. This method would be 30 percent more expensive than the present program.

6. What aspect of the employee training program do I like best? least?

> The CAI lab has been worth the investment because filmstrips and film loops become outdated too quickly.

7. What larger situation provides background for an investigation of the costs of training?

> The new president of the company has embarked on a systems analysis and projection of company needs in the next three years. He wants to make sure that the rising costs in training are a one-time occurrence, not a fixed feature.

8. What are the principal benefits of employee training?

> Faster transition to new jobs
> Increased safety
> Employer retention

9. If employee training is curtailed, what barriers are to blame?

> Shortsighted view of immediate profits
> Lack of understanding regarding the value of training

10. How could the rising costs of training be explained to a ten-year-old child?

> Our teaching tools were old-fashioned and worn out. We needed to buy new ones.

The time you spend with the Classic Questions can start your mind working in productive directions. You can better understand your manager's interest in the topic.

In order to select major ideas from among the many approaches conjured up by the Classic Questions, you could begin filling in an idea circle (see Chapter 3). As Figure 9–11 demonstrates, when arranged in circular fashion, the wedges of the idea circle allow you to change the order of your thoughts quickly and easily. You can easily mentally rearrange them when you're ready to outline.

FIGURE 9–11   Cost-of-Training Idea Circle

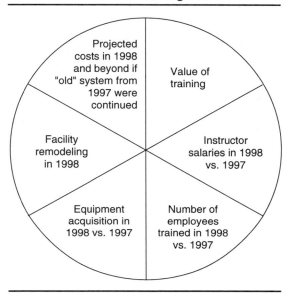

Step 4: Research Your Topic

Once you have brainstormed your topic, you know what to look for in the piles of records and files heaped on your desk. For example, for the cost-of-training report, you might look up the total amount spent on buying new teaching equipment in 1997 and 1998. You might then quickly locate a file containing final remodeling costs in 1998 for a training facility. You will find that research is no longer a needle-in-a-haystack experience. A firm grasp of what you are looking for provides a powerful magnet to draw together the facts you need.

In many business situations, reports are based on *primary research sources* (that is, first-hand information from surveys, interviews, measurements, and samplings, and so on). The following report-writing techniques show how to use *secondary research materials* (that is, second-hand information, from books, articles, and so on). Nonetheless, these procedures can also be used with primary research sources.

Use research cards to record the helpful information you find. Many researchers fill out both sides of 3″ × 5″ or 5″ × 7″ cards. If you follow this practice, on one side of the card, provide the full bibliographic data on the source of your information. (This sample shown in Figure 9–12 is for a book.)

FIGURE 9–12   Research Card

Blake, Karen. Effective Employee Training
   Programs. (New York: Windsor Press,
   1998).

FIGURE 9–13 **Notes on Key Points and Quotations with Page Reference**

Training costs save money for the Company

   "By hiring relatively unskilled workers and investing in their training, business and industry avoid the more costly alternative of attracting skilled workers at significantly higher wages." (p.94, Blake)

On the other side of the card, jot down the content information you may want to use. Also, write notes and reminders to yourself on the research card. To keep your notes to yourself from becoming confused with the words and notes from your source, separate the two kinds of notes in some way. See Figure 9–13 for sample notes.

When taking notes on internal company documents, such as memos, letters, reports, and proposals, you can use the index card system to identify documents by type, title, date, and file number and then, on the reverse side of the card, specify the key point you want to remember, as shown in Figure 9–14.

Inevitably, beginning report writers gather much more information than they can use in the report at hand. As your writing skills improve, you'll get better at picking the information to locate and copy down for your report. As you write more and more reports, you'll have fewer cards containing information that you end up not using.

For most of the twentieth century, business research took place in company files or in company, school, or public libraries. While those traditional sources are still valuable,

FIGURE 9–14 **Note Cards with References to Internal Documents**

Letter, from John Harns, CEO, to Linda Burtz, OSHA Director, June 6, 199__, file #6738

Key point:
   "As of Jan. 1, 199__, all reports of alleged OSHA violations will be reviewed by my office."
                                 [para. 3]

many new and powerful research tools have been developed. For example, many business and university libraries now use the computer to research topics.

For a computer search, the researcher provides a number of key words to the librarian, who uses the words as a guide while conducting the search. Several databases might be tapped. For example, the huge ERIC database contains hundreds of thousands of individual documents, representing millions of pages dealing with aspects of education and training.

Only minutes after the computer search begins, the titles of books and articles come spilling out of a high-speed printer. If you wish, the search can provide abstracts for the books and articles as well. For a few dollars, you can obtain hundreds of individual citations that it would ordinarily take days to ferret out.

Step 5: Arrange Your Major Points

There are many patterns of thought by which you can organize your work. (Several patterns are included in Chapter 3.) Think not only about what you want to say, but also about placing each aspect of your argument in its appropriate location. For example, after thinking through the logical, persuasive appeal of a pattern of thought about training costs, you might write an outline resembling the one shown in the following outline.

I. Overview
The purposes of the training program
The key question: Is the company getting its money's worth?

II. Past methods of training
What we used to do
Why we did it that way
How much it cost

III. Present methods of training
What we do now
Why we do it
How much it costs

IV. Evaluation
Old methods versus new methods
Old costs versus new costs

V. Conclusions
New costs are due to one-time equipment acquisition
New methods are worth this expenditure
Training per employee will cost less and less in the future

Some executives and managers prefer that the conclusions and recommendations portion of a report be placed at the beginning of the report. This rearrangement is especially common when the report does not begin with an executive summary.

Note that the use of Roman numerals to mark divisions within a short report is optional. In fact, very short reports can be overpowered by such formal enumeration of parts. If you don't use Roman numerals, don't number your major headings at all. However, you may find that Roman numerals help in organizing longer reports. They particularly help when you refer to different parts of the report (such as "See Part V").

Once your outline has been completed, sort your research cards into groups appropriate to each outline heading. Where evidence is weak or missing, return to the files for additional research.

Step 6: Write Your Rough Draft

Your outline sits ready before you. Your research cards are organized to support each major point in the outline.

Now you begin writing the rough draft. A helpful way to get started is to use an **overview** for the first section of your report. Overviews tell both the writer and the reader what to do with the report. Both look to the overview for a point of perspective, a view of the purpose of the report, and a suggestion of the approach it will take. Readers particularly like the word "overview," with its implicit promise of orientation.

Once the overview is written, write the rest of the report, according to your outline and your research cards. From time to time, remind yourself that your purpose is to communicate, not to impress. If you begin to experience Writer's Block, study the outline again. It will show you where you are in the total report and what comes next. Your research cards fall naturally into place throughout the report.

At the end of your report, write down both an evaluation section (how you and the reader may think about the topic) and a conclusion (what you and the reader may decide about the topic). The evaluation unfolds the *process* by which you compared, contrasted, weighed, and balanced the ideas. The conclusion reveals the *products* of your thinking.

Before beginning the revision of this draft, you may want to take a break from working on the report. Make some needed phone calls, do some other work, or even go out of your office for a few minutes. When you return feeling refreshed you'll be more ready to revise your report.

Step 7: Revise Your Rough Draft

Your completed rough draft—with cross-outs, erasures, asterisks, and arrows—is lying on the table before you. Now you must tackle the all-important task of revision. The following checklist should prove useful as you rework your rough draft.

Eight Revision Techniques

1. Organize the topics into a logical pattern (such as past–present–future).
2. Use headings to clarify and highlight the report's organization.
3. Use short paragraphs and short sentences to make the report more readable. However, you should also vary the sentence length, using some short sentences for emphasis.
4. Review your choice of words, substituting specific, vivid words for general, abstract words. Prefer short, simple, familiar words to long, fancy, or strange ones. See Chapter 3 for specific tips on words.
5. Check *all* spelling, grammar, and language mechanics. Appendix B provides specific tips for these areas.

6. Replace most weak verbs (such as *is, are, was, were, has, have, seems to be*) with strong, vivid verbs (such as *reveal, grasp, demonstrate, fall, strike, seize*).

7. Use the strong slot (the crucial first two or three words in each sentence) for meaningful words and phrases (not "it is," "there is/are," or "and").

8. Fix the vague, detached "this" ("*This* proves that we can begin to . . .") by placing an identifying word after "this" ("This *discovery* proves that we can begin to . . .").

To get an idea of how these techniques might be used, see both the rough draft and the final report in Figures 9–15 and 9–10.

Step 8: Review the Appearance of Your Rough Draft

Recognize that your report must please your readers' eyes if it is to please their minds. Arrange your words and visuals for at-a-glance appeal. Use varied margins, white space, underlining, and appropriate graphics to create a document that readers will *want* to read.

Pay particular attention to your use of quotations, tables, and charts. Do you provide helpful transitions into and out of them? The following sentence, for example, provides a transition to a chart:

In the following chart, note the sudden decline after 1979 in the price of imported wines.

FIGURE 9–15 A Portion of a First Draft of a Short Report (in need of revision). Compare with the Polished Draft in Figure 9–6.

The matter of whether or not EEW, Inc., should grant maternity leave with pay to workers has been a debate over the years involving many factors, stemming originally from the pronouncement by a prominent company vice president in 1992 that she would quit the company if not given maternity leave. Prior to this time, the union had begun raising the maternity issue as a potential negotiation point, since well into the early 1990s virtually every pregnant woman at EEW was dismissed on grounds that the personnel director at that time felt were unfounded, but were nonetheless enforced by the company—those grounds being that the performance records of said pregnant employees were not "promising enough," with "enough" being ill-defined or undefined. Historically, dating from the company's founding in 1983, pregnancy was considered a sign that an employee had no long-term future with the company. (See pronouncements on this subject by early company officials.)

The 1980s saw the liberalizational of maternity leaves at EEW, but with the stipulation that the affected workers not receive pay during the leave—in other words, maternity leave was leave without pay. It is not surprising that few workers took a leave on this basis. They felt it more lucrative to allow themselves to be terminated so they could receive unemployment compensation, etc. It was the Personnel Department that led a successful movement in the company to change this policy, so that pregnant workers were allowed to remain at their positions as long as their personal physicians felt it posed no health risk to either mother or unborn child. Their seniority and pay levels were frozen at the time they left the company for delivery, and they had the right within six months to return to reclaim said position and pay level, even though no pay was paid by the company during the interim period of leave. That remains the essential policy at EEW, Inc., to date of this report.

Step 9: Prepare Your Final Copy

Prepare a crisp, clean version of the report, with photocopies. If you wrote it at a word processor, be sure to make a backup of your file for future reference and revision. You may want to experiment with different printer fonts to make your report attractive.

Pay careful attention to the suggested format and other conventions of report writing specified previously. If appropriate, you may want to consider binding your report. Several inexpensive bindings are now available through print and photocopy shops.

Step 10: Present Your Report Advantageously

You may hold several copies of the finished report in your hand. You feel proud of your work, but you still have to consider how to present your report.

Instead of sending the stack of reports to your manager by office courier, for example, you may decide to deliver the copies in person. That way, if your manager has comments or questions, you'll be on the spot to deal with them.

COMMON TYPES OF REPORTS

The preceding ten steps for writing short reports may be used for a variety of business reports. Among the most widely prepared reports in business are the periodic report, the computer report, the progress report, and the trip report. These are known by various names from company to company. The periodic report may be called the "quarterly summary" or the "monthly update." The progress report may be called a "milestone report" or a "status report." No matter what they are called, these common report types have three common features. They must

1. Maintain a consistent format from period to period for ease of comparison
2. Use direct, concise language and clear descriptions of data
3. Highlight particularly important developments and trends

The Periodic Report

Senior management keeps its finger on the pulse of operations by requiring periodic reports from subordinate managers. These reports are usually written each month or quarter. They summarize business activity during the period and comment on noteworthy developments. At the request of senior management, the report writer may offer recommendations based on factors described in the report. These recommendations may appear at the beginning or the end of the report, but they always also appear in the executive summary. Figure 9–16 includes an example for a short periodic report.

The Computer Report

Many business operations, such as cash register sales, inventory accounting, and personnel timecards, can be monitored by computer. Management receives up-to-date results of that monitoring by means of the computer report. This document usually begins with summary statements of data and then provides specific data by date or category. Computer reports can be generated periodically or as needed.

When delivering a computer report to a superior in the company, it is customary to attach a brief cover memo that highlights particularly important aspects of the report. A sample cover memo and computer report are included in Figures 9–17 and 9–18.

The Progress Report

This report is written to bring senior management and other interested parties up-to-date on the current status of a company project or development. *Progress* suggests development or moves forward in accord with some established plan and schedule. Therefore, the report typically begins by specifying target dates or other accomplishment milestones against which progress can be measured. The report then sets forth specific evidence of that progress, including both positive and negative factors. If requested to do so by management, the report writer may conclude the progress report with a forecast for the future course of the development or project. See the progress report in Figure 9–19.

FIGURE 9–16   A Short Periodic Report

Quarterly Sales Report
State University Bookstore
for the period ending
April 15, 199_

Prepared for

The Board of Financial Management
Student Body Association
State University

Prepared by

Helen C. Witt
Bookstore Manager

April 30, 199_

FIGURE 9.16 cont.   A Short Periodic Report (continued)

EXECUTIVE SUMMARY

Total sales for the quarter amounted to $213,000, up 11 percent from the same quarter last fiscal year. This gain can be attributed directly to the inauguration on January 1, 199_, of the bookstore's in-house student charge card (the Bookstore Charge-it card). Of the 74,000 individual sales made during the quarter, 20 percent were made using the new charge card. (Visa and Mastercharge volume remained relatively unchanged from the eight past quarters at approximately 30 percent of all sales.) I anticipate further sales increases as more students apply for and receive the Bookstore Charge-it card. Therefore, I recommend the investment of $10,000 from the contingency fund for an aggressive advertising campaign to attract more student users of the Bookstore Charge-it card.

Overview of Quarterly Sales by Category
    Gross sales during the quarter totaled $213,000, made up of the following category subtotals:

Textbooks: $130,000.
Academic supplies: $34,500.
Clothing: $38,500.
Food items: $10,000.
Total: $213,000

All categories showed percentage increases in sales when measured against the comparable quarter last fiscal year:
Textbooks: + 11%
Academic supplies: + 10%
Clothing: + 12%
Food items: + 11%
Average increases: 11%

Business Developments during the Period
    The marked increase in gross sales can be attributed directly to the increasing use of Bookstore Charge-it cards by State University students. This promotional program, begun on January 1, 199_, offers Bookstore credit of $500 to qualifying students. To date, 4,231 students have applied for Charge-it cards and 3,255 cards have been issued. The great majority of State University students—a remainder of approximately 13,000—have not applied for these cards.
    During the quarter, 20 percent of the 74,000 total sales were made with Charge-it cards. Although management cannot assess losses due to late payment or collection action on these card sales until next quarter, we are encouraged by the Charge-it concept as a powerful sales tool.

Conclusion, with Recommendations
    The State University Bookstore continues to exceed sales goals set by the Board of Financial Management in its Bookstore Projections for this fiscal year. The important contribution of the Bookstore Charge-it concept can be enhanced by

1. authorizing a budget of $10,000 from the contingency fund for the purpose of promoting Bookstore Charge-it applications and use for all University students.
2. authorizing staff time for a statistical study of the relation between the use of Charge-it cards and the continuing rise in gross sales. Pending your authorization, this study can be completed to accompany next quarter's periodic report.

FIGURE 9–17 **Cover Memo for a Computer Report**

To: Alice Roth
               Vice President, Operations

From: Rachel Torres
               Warehouse Superintendent

Subject: July Computer Summary

Date: August 2, 199_

Attached, Alice, is the July summary of warehouse inventory. As we discussed, it shows slow movement in the Canned Fruits segment compared to last month and to July of last year. All other inventory categories are at or above target levels.

If I can offer input on the Canned Fruit situation, give me a call (ext. 3892).

FIGURE 9–18 **The Computer Report**

July, 199_, Computer Report
Warehouse Inventory Levels
ACE Provisioners, Inc.

Prepared for
Alice Roth
Vice President, Operations

Prepared by
Rachel Torres
Warehouse Superintendent

Data Computer Run Conducted: August 1, 199_

FIGURE 9–18 cont.   The Computer Report (continued)

Summary of Inventory Levels by Category
Period: July 1–July 31, 199_

Item Totals

Beginning of period: 6345

End of period: 4164

Percentage movement this period: 35%

Last month: 32%

July period, last year: 31%

Totals by Category	Beginning total	End total	% Change	Target Change %
Baked Goods	806	502	37%	35%
Beverages	704	431	38%	30%
Candy	925	722	22%	20%
Cookies	820	524	24%	20%
Dry Goods	460	211	54%	40%
Fruits (canned)	822	750	9%	30%
Meats (canned)	381	152	60%	50%
Spices	860	562	35%	30%
Vegetables (canned)	567	310	47%	40%
Totals	6345	4164		

The Trip Report

In 1998, American corporations spent an estimated $24 billion for business travel and trip-related expenses. Because companies want something to show for that investment, they request trip reports. These short reports provide details on the rationale, strategies, and results of a business trip. Although some trip reports include expense accounting, they usually focus on informational and analytic matters: Why did you travel, where did you go, whom did you see, and what was the result? Most companies handle expenses separately by means of an expense report form. A sample trip report is shown in Figure 9–20.

REPORT INVENTORIES

Given the breadth and range—and sheer number—of short reports, companies have good reason to guard and catalog their short reports. First, many reports contain sensitive company information about product developments, financial projections, personnel actions, and client data. Most larger corporations therefore code their reports, much like library books, so that they can be filed and tracked efficiently. Employees and others may be pro-

FIGURE 9–19 The Progress Report

The Bookstore Charge-it Campaign: a Progress Report

Prepared for

The Board of Financial Management
State University

Prepared by

Jon C. Richfield
Vice President
Peterson Management Consultants, Inc.

October, 199_

Executive Overview

Three months after its initiation, the Bookstore Charge-it advertising campaign has achieved three
of its four goals. First, the 13,000 State University students who did not hold Charge-it cards at
the beginning of the campaign have now each received two promotional mailings (attached). Second, a statistical study by Bookstore staff, in consultation with Peterson Management Consultants, has been completed on the relation between the number of Charge-it card holders and gross
sales. That study demonstrates that the Bookstore can expect a 3 percent rise in gross sales over
the next twelve months for every additional 1,000 Charge-it card holders. Third, a no-fee collections firm has been recommended by Peterson Management Consultants and retained by the
Bookstore to handle all late-pay and no-pay Charge-it accounts on a commission basis. The
fourth goal, as yet unachieved, involves a discount system at the Bookstore for Charge-it card
users. Initial plans for such a system have met with substantial resistance from University students and faculty. Further study of the issue is recommended.

FIGURE 9–19 cont.   The Progress Report (continued)

Background of the Charge-it Promotional Campaign

After a first-quarter, 199_, gross sales increase of 11 percent following introduction of the Bookstore Charge-it card, the Board of Financial Management on May 2, 199_ authorized the expenditure of not more than $10,000 for administration supervision of a Charge-it promotional campaign. The target population for this marketing effort was the remaining majority of University students—some 13,000—who had not yet applied for the Charge-it card. A secondary target audience was the University faculty.

Peterson Management Consultants contracted to develop and supervise the marketing campaign. On September 5, 199_ each non-card student received by mail the "You're Good For It!" mailer and application form (see attachment A). A follow-up mailing was sent out to the same recipients on September 20, 199_. (See attachment B, "A Card for All Seasons.")

Achievements to Date

As of the date of this report, a total of 5,283 applications have been received from the target audience of 13,000 students, and an additional 485 applications from a faculty of 820. Of these numbers, a total of 4,301 card applications have been approved for students and 438 for faculty. This number far exceeds the Board's enrollment of 2,000.

Simultaneous to the mail campaign, Peterson Management consultants worked together with Bookstore staff to understand what impact the Charge-it program was having and could be expected to have on gross sales. That report, presented to the Board on September 30, 199_, demonstrates a probable increase of 3 percent in gross sales over the next twelve months for every 1,000 additional Charge-it card holders enrolled.

To deal with the inevitable cases of late-pay or no-pay card holders, Tyson Collection Service was retained on a commission basis. Tyson will receive 25 percent of amounts collected from accounts 60 to 90 days in arrears, and 40 percent of accounts more than 90 days late.

Potential Obstacles

In its contract with the Board, Peterson Management Consultants agreed to develop a discount system for Charge-it card holders to encourage card use. That effort, after an initial pilot program conducted from September 5 through 10, has been stalled by heavy criticism on the part of students and faculty. As expressed in several recent editorials in The Student Voice, Bookstore customers who pay in cash feel they are being treated unfairly. An informal survey of 200 Bookstore customers in mid-September suggests that 70 percent of students and faculty (including card holders) agree with this claim.

Conclusion, with a Recommendation

The Charge-it promotional campaign has achieved its major goal of enrolling new card holders and has surpassed the target goal for such enrollment by more than 100 percent. The University community does not appear willing, however, to accept a discount program at the Bookstore for Charge-it card users. Peterson Management Consultants, Inc., urges the Board, therefore, to approve the following recommendation:

That Peterson Management Consultants be retained for an additional $2,500 fee to develop ways to encourage Charge-it card use without incurring significant criticism from the University community.

FIGURE 9–20 Sample Trip Report (Note: This report could be formatted as a typical short report. Because it is short, however, the writer has chosen the memo report format. Notice that headings have been omitted in such a concise report.)

To: Jackson Bennington
          Vice President, Sales

From: Cecil Williams
          Account Executive

Subject: Business trip to Conway Laboratories, Cincinnati, Ohio, Jan. 6–7, 199_

Date: Jan. 14, 199_

As discussed in our end-of-year sales meeting, I visited with purchasing agents Sheila Owens and Thomas Long at Conway Laboratories to apprise them of our 199_ product line and to ascertain their current and future needs.

Our discussions, lasting for three hours on January 6 and four hours on January 7, 199_, yielded the following useful information:

1. Due to the AIDS epidemic, Conway Laboratories faces unmanageable insurance premiums for its employees who draw blood and perform other blood-related procedures. Their insurance carrier has committed to a substantial reduction in premiums if the laboratory uses only protective catheters and related devices. Both purchasing agents showed genuine interest in our line of protective medical equipment. Action item: we should be prepared to provide them with cost comparisons with other brands.

2. Training in the use of new laboratory equipment has become a particular problem for Conway. According to the purchasing agents, the laboratory would be willing to purchase in large lots from a single vendor if on-site training in new systems were included for Conway staff without additional expense. Action item: we need to tailor our present training packages so they can be administered on-site at Conway Laboratories and other major customers.

3. Conway Laboratories is considering a new branch office located in the Washington, D.C., area. Set-up costs for equipment and supplies are estimated at $2.6 million, which the laboratory expects to award to a single bidder. Action item: as these plans develop, we need to stay in close touch with Conway Laboratories for an early look at their Request for Proposal. The purchasing agents have assured me that the bid will not necessarily go to the lowest bidder; Conway Laboratories wants to deal with a full-service provider.

In my view, this trip was well worth the effort and expense. If I can provide further details about my discussions, please give me a call at extension 3892.

hibited from photocopying particularly sensitive reports. Some of these sensitive reports in company files may be read only on a need-to-know basis for selected employees.

Second, companies keep close tabs on their reports because these documents are expensive to produce. For example, a short report that has used up a full week of work for three managers in a writing team may cost the company thousands of dollars in employee time. That expense will be paid again and again if other workers in the company don't know that the report exists and duplicate its research.

Federal, state, and local regulators also influence a company's careful recordkeeping when it comes to short reports. These agencies usually require regular filings of information on the part of the company. When questions or disagreements occur, the company must assemble information from past reports. Some reports are also regularly *purged* (destroyed) by companies eager to destroy disadvantageous evidence that might fall into the hands of outside examiners, regulators, or competitors.

BUILDING STRONG REPORT-WRITING SKILLS IN THE ORGANIZATION

"I would rather write 100 memos than one report!" That sentiment is shared by many businesspeople, who feel that memos are "easy" because they're short and relatively informal while reports are longer and more formal. When employees have these feelings about report writing, they compose reports only reluctantly—and at considerable cost to the company paying for their efforts.

In your organization, you can build both the willingness and the ability to write good reports by understanding why employees often dislike report writing. For some, the fear of readers' reactions causes Writer's Block and other writing problems, especially when writing for superiors who will be making decisions about the report writer's career.

In the face of fear, three things happen to our business prose. First, we begin using sesquipedalian verbiage—big words—to try to impress others. Next, we use stilted sentence rhythms. For example, instead of writing naturally, we might write the following awkward sentence:

> For your consideration when you find the time to, and knowing the importance you place on communication networks within the company, it is my purpose to act upon your appreciated suggestion.

Finally, we may even stop thinking clearly. If you let your mind flit compulsively to endless "what ifs" and images of the boss's frowning face, you'll find it hard to think, write, or speak clearly and logically.

For all these reasons, the most important principle to master when writing for upper management has nothing to do with form, stationery, phrases, or margins.

Simply *relax*. Relax—not because the writing task is trivial, but because it is important. You will need all of your word skills to do your best work. That state of readiness comes about only when you let yourself relax.

Especially in the middle of a hectic business day, business writers may find it hard to let go, to relax, to let language flow. Therefore, many successful report writers have relaxation routines they use before starting to write reports. A construction executive in New York takes five minutes for a brisk walk around his office building. He breathes deeply, swinging his arms freely. An administrator of a large Chicago hospital uses what she calls "gravity meditation." She consciously tries to imagine each major muscle group in her body growing heavier and heavier, drawn down by an irresistible gravitational force. Within two or three minutes, she reports feeling peaceful, clear-headed, and ready to write.

Whether you relax by walking, rubbing a pet rock, or simply drinking a cold glass of water, try to develop dependable ways to let yourself feel calm before beginning to write. It may also help to review the ten steps in the following Communication Checkpoint.

Communication Checkpoint
Ten Steps to Good Short Reports

1. Thinking about the W-O-R-M.
2. Know what your audience wants.
3. Brainstorm about your topic.
4. Research your topic.
5. Arrange your major points.
   Review logical, persuasive order
   Plan for topic headings
   Arrange research under appropriate headings
6. Write your rough draft.
7. Revise your rough draft, including the eight revision techniques.
8. Review the appearance of your rough draft.
   Eye appeal
   At-a-glance messaging
   Use of evidence
9. Prepare your final copy.
10. Present your report advantageously.

OVERVIEW OF LONG REPORTS

Consider the ingredients of a long report. First, it usually includes a number of prefacing pages called "front matter"—a title page, letters of authorization and transmittal, tables of contents and figures (even a table of tables!), sometimes even a preface and foreword, and usually an abstract or executive summary. The body of the report is usually 15 or more pages (often many more). Concluding matter includes appendixes, legal instruments (if any), endnotes, a bibliography, and perhaps a glossary and index. Few long reports in business number less than 20 pages, and most are considerably longer.

Every major business, professional, and governmental organization regularly generates long reports. In an age of burgeoning in-baskets and hectic schedules, why do businesspeople read or write long reports? Many long reports have to do with money: Some long reports tell the company or government agency what it got in the past for its money. Other long reports may look ahead to future planning for how to invest money and other resources. Still others report the present status of projects, processes, or resources on which the company is spending money. Whether discussing the past, present, future, or a combination of these three tenses, long reports provide key information to decision-makers regarding how effectively they have spent their money and used their other resources. Although many short reports also provide such information, most big expenditures (including expenses for personnel and supplies) require long reports for adequate justification.

KEEPING LONG REPORTS CLEAR AND READABLE

In many ways, long reports are extra-long versions of short reports. However, because they have few length restrictions, long reports can easily get sidetracked and confusing. Without very clear organizing strategies, long reports can become grab-bags of jumbled information. In no other business document are clarity and organization more important than in the long report.

Pay particular attention to paragraph beginnings and endings. Use these to provide summary introductions and conclusions, as well as helpful transitions. Readers should not have to wade through several sentences before understanding your message and how it relates to surrounding paragraphs.

Follow the suggestions for writing style taught in previous chapters, and avoid the "The Ten Fatal Ills of Business Writing" shown next.

Communication Checkpoint
Ten Fatal Ills in Business Writing[1]
. . . and what to do about them

1. **Anemic Verbs** (*is, are, was, were, seems to be*)
   Not: It is the policy of this company to promote creative thinkers.
   Instead: This company promotes creative thinkers.

2. **Impotent Verbs** (passive constructions)
   Not: The account was handled carelessly.
   (Perpetrators can escape visibility if passive constructions are used.)
   Instead: Jack Bevins handled the account carelessly.

3. **Atrophy of the Position of Emphasis**
   Not: There are two financial packages suited to our needs.
   (Initial strong position wasted on meaningless words)
   Instead: Two financial packages suit our needs.

4. **Distended Sentence Length**
   Not: While seven of our managers at the midlevel range object to the idea of corporate offices, the majority of our senior staff is agreeable to the move as an opportunity to live in the Sun Belt.
   Instead: Seven midlevel managers object to moving our corporate offices. Our senior staff, however, welcome the move as a chance to live in the Sun Belt.

5. **Hypertrophy of the Noun**
   Not: The unification of companies will prove beneficial to the establishment of arrangements more conducive to solvency and profitability.
   (Avoid swollen nouns.)
   Instead: Merging our companies will help solve our money problems.

6. **Slow Sentence Pulse**
   Try mixing Subject–Verb–Object sentences with other types:
   Frustrated, Jerry wrote a scorching memo. (-ed beginning before the subject)
   The storeroom, long an eyesore on the fourth floor, is scheduled for remodeling. (Subject, break, verb)
   His taxes were due, but his wallet was empty. (Subject/verb, then subject/verb)

7. **Obese Paragraphs**
   Try "easy in and easy out," using very short paragraphs at the beginning and end of business letters, memos and short reports.

8. **Noun Clots**

   Not: Please write a minorities opportunity evaluation report.

   Instead: Please write a report evaluating opportunities for minorities.

9. **Spastic Repetitions**

   Not: We reviewed the benefits package. The benefits package provided for . . .

   Instead: We reviewed the benefits package, which provided for . . .

10. **Contagious Prepositions**

    Not: We ran an advertisement in a trade journal in May for a manager of the sales division at our subsidiary in Wisconsin.

    Instead: "Sales manager," "Wisconsin subsidiary" (Combine prepositional phrases into adjective/noun combinations.)

---

[1]Arthur H. Bell from *Nation's Business*, November 1984. Copyright © 1984 by Nation's Business. Reprinted by permission.

ELEMENTS OF THE LONG REPORT

Long reports typically contain the following elements: cover, flysheet, title page, table of contents, table of tables, letter of authorization, letter of transmittal, executive summary (often called an "abstract"), the body of the report, notes (or endnotes), and bibliography. Following a description of each of these elements is a summary of the format for paginating the long report. Figure 9–21 illustrates the sequence of elements in a short report. A sample long report is shown at the end of this chapter.

Cover

Long reports may be bound like a softcover book. Less expensive binding (of the sort done at photocopy shops) uses vinyl or heavy paper covers, many with windows so that the title of the report appears through the cover. The cover has no page number.

Flysheet

A single sheet of blank paper separates the cover from the title page (unless a cover with a window is used). This sheet has no page number and bears no marks of any kind. In more formal documents, the flysheet is often parchment- or translucent-quality paper.

Title Page

On this important page, center the title of your report, your name (and the names of all other contributing writers, or the name of your workgroup or your supervisor) title, professional affiliation, and the date. The title page must clearly show the professional quality of your report.

FIGURE 9–21   Order of Pages in a Long Report

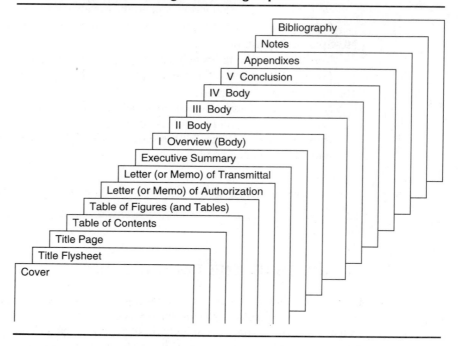

Table of Contents

This familiar directory simply lists topic headings with appropriate page numbers. If your report is well organized and uses informative headings, the reader can grasp your general approach to the topic from your Table of Contents.

Table of Tables

Although the repetition in the name might make you smile, this table can prove useful when the reader is trying to locate charts, graphs, and statistical breakouts throughout the text of a long report. The table also helps to show how much statistical information your report contains.

Letter of Authorization

You will probably *receive* this document more often than you will *write* it. It is usually (and unfortunately) written in the contorted jargon of militarese or legalese. The letter of authorization answers three key questions:

1. *Who authorizes work to be done?* Government agencies and large corporations will commonly refer not only to an authorizing individual, naming his or her position, but also to an authorizing or "enabling" document such as a work order, legislative measure, or appropriations bill.

2. *What work is authorized?* The letter briefly describes the work to be undertaken, referring in most cases to a more thorough description of the work contained in a request for proposal (RFP) or other documents.

3. *By whom will the work be done?* The letter names specific people and groups who will complete the work as described. Because the letter often serves as a binding contract, it is usually signed and dated by the authorizing official. The inclusion of the letter in a long report bears indisputable testimony that the writer has the backing of the authorizing agency.

Letter of Transmittal

Just as you would send your résumé with a cover letter, you should introduce your long report to your intended reader by means of a letter of transmittal. While this business letter can cover a wide number of topics, three areas of focus are crucial, and a fourth is helpful.

1. *To whom are you sending the report?* Address the letter of transmittal to that person or organization.

2. *What are you sending?* Name the report by title in the letter of transmittal, then go on to comment briefly on the highlights that might be especially interesting to your audience. You may want to mention your authorization to write the report.

3. *What do you want your readers to do after reading your report?* Spell out in specific detail any action you expect from them. (For example, "Please notify Ms. Jill Clayton, Director of Advanced Design, when you have read this report and are prepared to meet with the engineering panel.")

4. *What are you willing to do for your readers?* Offer to help your readers or to answer any questions they have, if this is appropriate and you are truly willing to do so.

Executive Summary

The executive summary (also called an "abstract") condenses or summarizes the matter of the report into one or more paragraphs (usually restricted to one page). This page typically answers five questions (though the answers appear, of course, in paragraph form).

1. What is the subject of the report?
2. What is the purpose of the report?
3. How is the report argued?
4. What kind of evidence is used?
5. What conclusions and recommendations are reached?

An executive summary should never be used to create suspense (omitting, for example, a statement of conclusions). Rather, it should leave the reader with an accurate overview of what your report contains.

Body of the Report

Beginning with the first page of text, numbers change from Roman to Arabic and start over again at 1. An example of the body of the long report appears in the sample long report at the end of this chapter.

Notes

This page differs from footnotes because the notes (also called "endnotes") contained here appear at the end of the report rather than at the foot of each page. The report writer may choose to use either footnotes or endnotes. If the notes are important to the reader, grouping the notes at the end of the report makes the reader's job harder. However, if the notes aren't important for readers, or the report must be written without a word processor that automatically manages footnotes, endnotes are easier for the writer and may be fine for the reader.

Bibliography

Aside from slightly different punctuation and ordering, the references listed in the bibliography differ in three ways from similar references contained in notes:

1. A bibliography lists all materials the author found useful in preparing the report, not merely the works quoted or cited directly.
2. The bibliographic list of works appears in alphabetical order, not in the order of citation in the text.
3. Bibliographic citations do not include comments from the report writer.

You can follow several styles to prepare footnotes and bibliographies. Some of these styles require that brief notes be placed in the text itself. These notes refer by number to sources listed in a more thorough way at the end of the document. When trying to determine which style to use, check the predominant practice within your company. Also check on the reader's preferences or requirements. Once you have settled on a single convention for notes, stick with it closely. Don't mix styles. See Appendix B for guidelines on the most common reference systems.

FORMAT: PAGES AND PAGINATION

All the pages of a typical long report are noted page by page, first to last, in the following list (refer to Figure 9–21). Pay particular attention to pagination. Notice that some pages are numbered in lowercase Roman numerals (i, ii, iii . . .) and some in Arabic (1, 2, 3 . . .). Following the chart of pages is an item-by-item description of each element in the long report.

Cover	Don't count it, and don't type a page number.
Flysheet	Don't count it, and don't type a page number.
Title Page	Count it, but don't type a page number.
Table of Contents	Count it, and type a Roman numeral as the page number.
Letter of Authorization	Count it, and type a Roman numeral.
Letter of Transmittal	Count it, and type a Roman numeral.

Letter of Transmittal	Count it, and type a Roman numeral. (Note: Especially when no Letter of Authorization is included, some report writers attach the Letter of Transmittal to the report but do not bind it into the report or include it in the Table of Contents.)
Table of Tables or Figures	Count it, and type a Roman numeral.
Executive Summary or Abstract	Count it, and type a Roman numeral.
First page of the body	Count it, and type an Arabic numeral 1.
All succeeding report pages	Count them, and type Arabic numerals in series.
Placement of page numbers	Numbers are usually centered vertically and horizontally in the bottom margin or, less often, in the top margin. Once you have chosen a location for numbers, be consistent throughout the report.

SUMMARY

1. Short reports are vital business documents that communicate information about internal and external events, processes, and circumstances.

2. Reports flow up, down, and sideways in organizations.

3. The process of writing a short report can be described as a ten-step process.

4. Typical short reports common in business are periodic, computer, progress, and trip reports.

5. Reports within a company are carefully filed, which allows easy reference and avoids duplication of effort.

6. Long reports contain extensive front matter, in addition to the report's body and concluding materials.

7. Particularly because of their length, long reports must be clear, well-organized, and persuasive or informative.

8. Pagination in long reports follows a conventional order, using both Roman and Arabic numerals appropriately.

9. The audience for long reports may be quite large. Therefore, reports should be written with an appropriate degree of detail and background information.

QUESTIONS FOR DISCUSSION

1. What topics are typical in reports directed to in-house audiences?

2. What topics are typical in reports directed to external audiences?

3. Why is it important to have a planned approach to the writing of a short report?

4. What is a report inventory?

5. How can the aspects of short reports suggested by the W-O-R-M acronym help the report writer?

6. Why do report writers usually complete a working outline before beginning the rough draft?

7. When should you consider using Roman numerals in your report?

8. What information should be included on the report title page?

9. What is a periodic report?

10. What is the function of an executive summary in a report?

11. What are the objectives of a trip report?

12. Why is relaxation necessary to achieving a natural writing style for reports?

13. What is a *stilted* writing style? How can it be avoided or revised?

14. What is a progress report? How does it differ from a periodic report?

15. What is a computer report? Why does it usually require a cover memo or letter written by a human being?

16. How can converting a topic to a specific problem help business writers to organize reports effectively?

17. Why is an overview preferable to an introduction?

18. What distinguishes an evaluation section from a conclusion?

19. How important is at-a-glance appeal in reports? What techniques create at-a-glance appeal?

20. Why do business writers add front matter and other materials to long reports?

21. What important features should you include in the letter of transmittal introducing your long report?

22. What purposes does the letter of authorization serve?

23. Why is the executive summary (or abstract) important in the long report?

24. Do you prefer the use of footnotes, endnotes, or parenthetical in-text references in long reports? Respond first as a reader, then as a writer. Did your responses differ?

25. Cite several differences between a long report and a short report.

26. Why do long reports continue to be written when businesspeople have so little time to read and write them?

EXERCISES

1. List as many methods as you can think of that you have found to be useful tools for relaxation or for relieving the fears of public writing or speaking. Share these with your classmates; in turn, copy down any of their suggestions that you think might be useful.

2. Generate a list of broad topics you would like to know more about such as job possibilities in your community. Trade lists with a partner. Limit the broad topics your partner gives you to more manageable ones. The first topic, for example, might become "job openings in the local aerospace industry," or better still, "engineering opportunities in the local aerospace industry." Get together with your partner and trade notes. Explain to one another the limits you imposed on the broad topics.

3. Now trade back the lists of manageable topics that you wrote for Exercise 3. Convert each topic into a specific problem to be solved. For instance, you might want to determine how to make the right personal contacts for getting an entry-level engineering position in the local aerospace industry.

4. Take a report or essay you've written previously, for school or for business, and rewrite it in the form of a long memo. What differences in the two forms do you see? How does your old introduction differ from your new overview? How does your old conclusion differ from your new evaluation and conclusion sections?

5. Find a letter or other document that doesn't have at-a-glance appeal. Rewrite it, providing the missing appeal.

6. Create an outline for a short report on the need for affordable housing in the area surrounding your college.

7. Write the executive summary for a short report that recommends that your company should participate in an energy-conservation campaign.

8. Write a cover letter to a company vice-president to accompany your short report on energy savings. (See Exercise 7.)

9. Limit each of the following concepts to a specific report topic.
   a. Motivation
   b. Loyalty to the company
   c. Causes for employee turnover

10. Write a letter of transmittal to a corporate vice-president to accompany a long report on the status of employee training and education programs. (You need not write the report itself.)

11. In the role of a corporate vice-president, write a letter of authorization for the report on employee training and education programs.

12. Write a working outline of first- and second-level headings for the long report on employee training and education programs. Make up the specifics you need.

13. Based on your outline in Exercise 12, write an executive summary for the long report on employee training and education.

14. Create a table of contents, including all elements of your report on employee training and education programs.

15. Study the long report included in Appendix D. Locate a suitable place for a graphic of some kind. Create the graphic, then write out appropriate transitions leading into and away from the graphic.

16. Assume that the long report in Appendix D must be shortened by 50 percent without eliminating major headings. Rewrite one page of the report to show you could cut down the sentences and paragraphs.

17. Write good titles for long reports on these subject areas:
    a. Employee theft
    b. Medical benefits
    c. Speaking skills for managers
    d. Conflict resolution among employees

18. Write the conclusions and recommendations section of the long report on employee training and education programs.

INTERNET ASSIGNMENT

As one of the country's most successful pharmaceutical development firms, your company generates hundreds of reports for clients, investors, government regulators, and in-house use. You have noticed, however, that these documents vary dramatically in format, organization, and writing style, all depending on which employees in the company have worked on them. You resolve to investigate standard report formats to see if one format and style can serve the great majority of reports written by people in your company. Use the Specific Business Documents and Organization Communication sections of the Internet Guide to discover one or more useful report formats that could serve as a model for company report writers. Also, find dictionary and style-guide reference materials for your writers in the Business Writing Aids section of the Internet Guide. In a memo addressed to these writers, describe the format you recommend, tell where it can be found on the Web, and explain why a uniform report format and style will improve the company's image and communication effectiveness with its various audiences.

SAMPLE LONG REPORT

Memo of Authorization

To: Robert Johnson
           Chair, Honeywell Work and Family Task Team

From: Linda Roberts
           Senior Vice President
           Corporate and Community Responsibility
           Minneapolis Operations

Subject: Compilation of a Task Report on relations between worklife and family life
           at Honeywell

Date: August 1, 1998

The Corporate Executive Council voted unanimously on July 30, 1998, to authorize the development of a major company report by your task team. I have attached specific budgetary information and staffing details to this memorandum.

The working title of this project will be "Managing Work and Family Life." The Executive Council is particularly interested in learning as much as possible about

- how Honeywell employees now manage their worklife in relation to family life,

- how the changing nature of family life and responsibilities influences employee productivity,

- what specific action the company can take to heighten worker productivity and the effectiveness of the family unit.

The Executive Council requests a preliminary draft of your report by December 1, 1998, and the final draft by March 15, 1999.

Thank you for your willingness to chair this important study. I look forward to working closely with you and your task team in its development.

Letter of Transmittal

To: Linda Roberts
           Senior Vice President
           Corporate and Community Responsibility

From: Robert Johnson
           Chair, Work and Family Task Team

Subject: Final draft of "Managing Work and Family Life"

Date: Feb. 15, 1999

On behalf of the sixteen members of the Work and Family Task Team, I am pleased to present to you the work authorized in your August 1, 1998, memorandum: "Managing Work and Family Life."

We trust that the Executive Council will be particularly interested, as we team members were, at the striking correlation between family stress and reduced productivity. Furthermore, we are confident that the Council will recognize both the urgency and importance to the company of the recommendations put forth by the task team.

The task team will be happy to meet with you or other members of the Executive Council following your considerations of "Managing Work and Family Life."

Thank you for your help and guidance in the preparation of this study.

Note: These samples of a memo of authorization and a letter of transmittal were not included with the real Honeywell report. Names and company information in these documents are fictitious.

Managing Work and Family Life:

A Honeywell Task Team Report

TABLE OF CONTENTS

I EXECUTIVE SUMMARY

"Trying to juggle a career, schools, family, friendships, and caring for a recently widowed parent can be overwhelming. You can only concentrate on one thing at a time while trying to accomplish several. The most serious comes first." (Single female)

"I think employers such as Honeywell need to understand better the changing roles in dual career couples. When our children are sick or require emergency attention, I need to share these responsibilities with my wife who is also employed full-time outside the home. Too often, people and companies perceive those functions to be the sole responsibility of the wife/mother." (Male in dual career family)

"There are unique problems to my being single—living away from support groups, financial concerns, too few social demands, and loneliness—these have a real impact on my job performance and career satisfaction." (Single male)

"Being a working mom isn't easy. I am very committed to my job, but I'm very concerned about plans for my children when they're sick or on vacation. In addition, I feel guilty when I have no leave or miss work because of my kids. I wish I didn't feel so guilty." (Female in dual career family)

These comments from Honeywell employees reflect an important reality. Creating a balance between work and family demands challenges employees of all ages, genders, income levels and phases in the family life cycle. The issues are not limited to young working parents with small children, to women or to hourly employees.

These employee comments also suggest that Honeywell, like other corporations, must seek a clearer understanding of the changing dynamics between the company and its workforce around work and family issues. It must analyze the implications of these changes on worker productivity. If Honeywell is to stay competitive in its markets and even flourish, it must create a sensitive work environment which acknowledges the multiple roles employees play.

The Task Team believes these are the significant issues to address in 1987:

- Employees are experiencing more stress due to pressures to increase their commitments to work and to family.

- Employees desire more flexible work practices to help mitigate time conflicts caused by their work and family demands.

- Employees in several locations have problems locating child care, including after school care, which is affordable, dependable, and of a high quality.

- Employees particularly find it difficult to make arrangements for the care of sick children.

- Employees increasingly express concern about the impact of two-career and single working parent families on their children.

To guide its responses to these issues, which are at the very heart of how employees manage their day-to-day responsibilities, the task team developed this mission.

"Honeywell will affirmatively develop policies and services which support employees in achieving their work and family goals."

In their recommendations, fully stated in Section IV, the task team urged:

- Senior management to create a climate of greater sensitivity to employees' work and family demands.

- Development of training seminars and materials so supervisors can help employees deal with their own dilemmas.

- Implementation of informational seminars and resource materials which help employees balance work and family responsibilities.

- Consideration of plans to develop near-site child care for employees and others in the community.

- Exploration of a total time off policy, combining holidays, vacation, and casual sick days to be managed by employees.

II   INTRODUCTION

In August 1986, the Work and Family Task Team was convened by the Corporate and Community Responsibility Department and Human Resources Council for Minneapolis Operations on the premise that employees who successfully maintain the intricate balance between work and family are likely to be more satisfied and productive employees.

Honeywell, like many other American corporations, recognizes the interdependence between companies and their workforces. As Sheila Akabas, Director of Columbia University's Industrial Social Work Force Center says, the workplace needs families to supply and produce the current and future workforce. The family, on the other hand, needs the workplace for income, benefits and much of its identity.[1]

The Work and Family Task Team set out to develop a strategic and coordinated approach to help employees as they attempt to balance their dual commitments. This document will:

- explore the changing relationship between corporations and families, and specifically, Honeywell and its employees

- describe the business rationale for Honeywell's commitment to addressing work and family issues, and

- recommend policies and programs to heighten worker productivity and family effectiveness.

New Norms in Work and Family Structure

Changes in the American family over the last three decades are dramatically altering the profile of the American work force. Well into the 1950s, men and women in the typical American family had clearly defined roles. The male breadwinner who provided sole financial support for his family was the norm. Meanwhile, his wife was caring for the children full-time, chauffeuring them to after school events, nurturing the family's relationships with relatives and friends and, perhaps, volunteering in the community as well.

Now, however, women have entered the labor force at an accelerated rate, diversifying the profile of the work force. The "typical" male breadwinner constituted 70% of the American workforce in 1950. By 1984, women were in the majority, with 54% working outside the home. The Department of Labor estimates that 60% of all women will be employed by 1995. Further, a large majority of these women have young children. Women with children under the age of five are the fastest growing portion of the workforce.[2]

These employees face many challenges as they enter the workforce. The story of a young Honeywell employee, who testified to a Honeywell task force, deserves reporting.

A single parent, she leaves home at 5:30 a.m. to begin working on a factory shift at 6:00 a.m. As soon as she arrives at work, she calls her two children, ages 6 and 9, to wake them. Shortly after, she calls to make sure they're awake and that they're getting dressed and eating breakfast. Next, one of them calls her at work because he can't find a lost school book. Finally, she calls to make sure they leave in time to catch their school bus. Occasionally, if they miss the bus, she has left work to drive them to school. By 8 a.m., if she hasn't heard, she assumes they're on the way to school and, emotionally exhausted, she applies herself to work. She told the task force that she feels guilty about leaving her children at home to fend for themselves. She feels guilty that she has not been worth much to Honeywell. She hasn't been able to resolve the conflict and she really wants to do well by both, she says.

These same kinds of concerns affect Honeywell people with management responsibilities, as another story illustrates.

An engineer, whose wife works as a lawyer in another corporation, tells about waking during the night to the cries of their young toddler. She's got a fever, is coughing, and wants to be held. Both he and his wife try to sort out the next day's schedule for which each have serious responsibilities to other people. They argue about whose meetings are most important, who should have the privilege of going to work, and who should stay home to care for their sick child. Their baby continues to cry and cough. They don't feel she should go to her child care center and don't know who will come in to care for her. There are no grandparents available to step in. As dawn comes, each makes a flurry of phone calls to reschedule some meetings, they divide responsibility for the care of their child, and both begin the day feeling angry, guilty and anxious about attending to their daughter's needs and their work responsibilities.

Dual wage earner couples, single parents and employees in other non-traditional families have become the norm. Data from a 1986 survey of salaried employees at Honeywell's Military Avionics Division reflects these national trends. Seventy percent of the married participants have working spouses. Only 12% were from families with mothers at home with children.[3]

Growing Conflicts

As a result of this changing family structure, growing numbers of employees face conflicts between their work and family responsibilities. In some cases, employees are unwilling to subjugate their family responsibilities to job functions. A large percentage of survey respondents who are married with children said that their concentration and judgment at work are often affected by concerns over family responsibilities and that these concerns are likely to limit achievement of their work or career goals. Job pressures, such as excessive overtime and schooling for career advancement, were reported to have an adverse effect on the family relationships of respondents, especially dual earners and single parents with children. Further, persistent efforts to meet both work and family demands are causing a large proportion of employees to feel increasingly more stress.

III   TASK TEAM APPROACH

Chaired by Mannie Jackson, Group Vice President, Marketing and Sales, Commercial Building Group, the Work and Family Task Team was comprised of senior management, directors, managers and employees representing most Minneapolis divisions. Members included those who manage business operations and others whose job functions focus on human resources, labor relations, communications and finance. It was staffed by the Corporate and Community Responsibility department.

Guided by its executive committee, the task team's work plan included an analysis of issues facing both the company and its changing workforce, other corporate approaches, the status of current Honeywell programs and policies, the company's decentralized structure and current business climate, and assumptions about the relationship between the company and employees.

The task team heard testimony from national and local experts, assessed the concerns and suggestions raised by Honeywell employees and Honeywell's Work and Family Survey, and reviewed significant literature about other programs. Perhaps most significantly, team members drew on their own personal experiences and professional observations regarding work and family dilemmas.

Assumptions About Work and Family

While the task team reacted with widely differing perspectives on many issues, they reached consensus on these assumptions:

1. Social and economic conditions and the demographics which drive the current work force dilemmas will continue. Whether or not the company provides greater support and flexibility, working parents will continue to be a large part of the work force.

2. Work and family issues concern both men and women at all stages of their family life cycles. While the task team agreed that working parents have significant responsibilities, it soundly rejected the view that other members of the workforce are unaffected by dual demands.

3. Employees want to be productive at work and be responsible, caring family members. Most are committed to resolving conflicts between work and family demands so they can be effective in both roles.

4. No single program or policy will solve the work and family dilemma. Rather, employees have varying needs, concerns and circumstances which require multiple solutions.

5. Employees need information, support and flexibility from the company to empower them to make good decisions about managing their work and family lives. They do not want the company to assume responsibilities for them or their families.

6. Children of working parents are a valuable resource not only to their families but to the broader community which includes corporations. The quality of parenting and child care they receive will affect their potential to be effective parents, citizens and future members of the workforce.

Understanding the Honeywell Context

As it began to develop recommendations, the task team gave careful consideration to program and policy options that are consistent with Honeywell's current business climate, its decentralized structure and its unique corporate culture.

These factors were viewed as significant:

1. Honeywell's highly decentralized structure requires flexible policies and programs which can be adapted to a variety of business settings and workforces.

2. The restructuring of Honeywell's business operations and cost reduction measures were considered possible constraints on company work/family initiatives; yet, there was consensus that, especially in difficult times, the corporation must develop measures to enhance employee satisfaction and productivity.

3. Because of current business conditions, management needs employees to work harder, often longer hours, and more productively. At the same time, more employees have increased responsibilities for family and home demands. Tension and conflict are inevitable.

4. Honeywell and its employees have enjoyed a strong reciprocal commitment to one another. At the very time the company most needs to remain competitive in a difficult business climate, their good relationship appears to be eroding. The company ought to preserve this spirit of reciprocity, and when necessary, develop new ways to rebuild it.

5. One of Honeywell's Principles says people are the company's "key to success." While this principle does not explicitly address the family, it reinforces many of the task team's assumptions about how individuals and the company relate to one another. Understanding the competing stress between work and family, flexibility in policy interpretation and dealing with employees as individuals are themes which should be stressed.

IV WORK AND FAMILY TASK TEAM RECOMMENDATIONS

Summary of Recommendations

After analyzing issues facing the company and its workforce, other corporate approaches, the status of Honeywell's current programs and policies, its decentralized structure, its current business climate, and the changing relationship between company and employees, the task team made these recommendations:

A. Honeywell's senior management must take initiative to enhance management understanding and acknowledgment of the issues surrounding employees' conflicts between work and personal life and to create an atmosphere which fosters management sensitivity throughout the company.

B. Work and family training modules and reference materials should be developed and included in supervisory training sessions such as the new supervisor orientation, the affirmative action, and the diverse work force programs currently held in all divisions.

C. Honeywell should design and implement a series of informational programs and resource materials for employees which build on their capacity and desire to manage their work and family demands. These workplace seminars would complement the supervisory training programs.

D. Honeywell should consider sponsoring the development of a child care center for the children of employees and others near an operating division but owned and managed by an outside child care organization. It should be operated as a pilot or demonstration program and monitored for its effect on employee productivity and morale.

E. Honeywell should consider a total time-off policy, combining holidays, vacations and sick days into a lump sum managed by individual employees according to their own or family needs. While the model may be developed by Corporate, its implementation would be subject to specific business demands and work force consideration of divisions.

Recommendations

"American management is not on top of things today. You just look at the labor force demographics. They tell you that industry needs women and that women need work. As more women go to work, more men have to play a more responsible role in their families' lives. And that is just a fact of life."[5]

Recommendation A

Honeywell's senior management must take initiative to enhance management understanding and acknowledge the issues surrounding employees' conflicts between work and personal life and to create an atmosphere which fosters management sensitivity throughout the company.

Rationale

The Task Force believes that policy direction or lack of it will not, alone, resolve work and family stresses for Honeywell employees. The cultural and business pressures of each business unit, along with the management styles and practices of each division, play larger roles in creating the environments for flexibility and support required by employees. Involvement and support of General Managers throughout the company is critical.

Responsibility for Action

- Task team findings and recommendations will be presented to General Managers by their chair and members of the executive committee. In addition, the task team will provide suggestions for divisional initiatives, resource material, and communication vehicles.

- Divisional management should have primary opportunity and responsibility to address issues in their organizations. Management messages summarizing the Task Team Report and appointment of employee action committees at divisional levels are suggested.

- General Managers should be commissioned to complete formal reviews of divisional policies which affect employees and their families. Both the language and the implementation should be analyzed to reaffirm the policies' purposes and to remove barriers to their appropriate application. Supervisors should participate in these work teams.

- Corporate management has an obligation to clarify the corporation's principles and values in the context of these issues. In this recent period of extraordinary change at Honeywell, creating hardship for many employees, there is a significant need for this clarification. It is also appropriate and important to understand these issues in the context of other major issues confronting this corporation—the need for heightened productivity and changing demographics of the workforce, for example.

- At the Corporate level, acknowledging the impacts of Corporate restructuring on Honeywell employees provides a good opportunity to clarify the principles of the organization as they affect work and family issues. Actions include: incorporating language sensitive to work and family issues into the Honeywell Principles, communications programs, sponsorship of management luncheon speakers and corporate executive visits to divisions to discuss these issues.

"My boss at Honeywell expects high quality work and a high degree of commitment. He also understands that at times family illnesses will test our abilities to balance demands. When my mother went into surgery last fall, he said, 'Take whatever time you need.' That statement helped ease my concern, and solidified my commitment to the company as well. Who wouldn't be loyal to a company that expresses such concern?"

Recommendation B

Work and family training modules and reference materials should be developed and included in supervisory training sessions such as the new supervisor orientation held in all divisions.

Rationale

The task team observed and recent survey findings documented that supervisors play a critical role in the effectiveness with which employees are able to manage their work and family responsibilities. Employees whose supervisors are sensitive and flexible in working out suitable arrangements which enable them to meet both work and family demands report a high degree of loyalty to the company and a sense of productive work behavior. Employees report that rigid supervision heightens their tension and feelings of ineffectiveness at work.

Supervisors have not been trained to deal with work/family issues which employees face and may be uncertain how to balance employee needs and business priorities. Honeywell supervisors should be given management encouragement and guidelines which empower them to adapt and apply corporate policies to the special circumstances of employees consistent with the cultural and business environment of their operation and which fit each supervisor's style. Finally, it should be recognized that supervisors also are affected by work and family stresses.

Program Description and Responsibility for Action

Corporate Human Resources Department, with assistance from the Work and Family Task Team, should develop a work and family module for adaptation by divisions in their supervisory training packages. The following elements should be included:

- Rationale for Honeywell interest, from corporate or divisional senior management perspectives.

- Nature and scope of issues being addressed, based on national and Honeywell specific data.

- Summary of task team findings and recommendations and access to all reference materials.

- Clear policy guidelines with work sessions focused on adapting them to multiple situations.

- Role-playing sessions on how to manage both common and unusual employee problems.

- Session on how to use available resources, both within Honeywell and in the community.

"The availability of educational programs would allow employees to manage their own work and family life; employees would be in control."

Recommendation C

Honeywell should design and implement a series of informational programs and resource materials for employees which build on their capacity and desire to manage their work and family demands. These workplace seminars would complement the supervisory training programs.

Seminars

Rationale

Many Honeywell employees report high stress over persistent conflicts between work and family demands. They say they want to function effectively on behalf of the company and their families but often feel overwhelmed by the dual demands. Workplace seminars would aim to reduce the tension and help employees construct manageable plans to integrate their dual responsibilities. Programming would be based on the premise that effectiveness in one role enhances performance in the other.

Workplace seminars are inexpensive vehicles with potential benefits for both employees and the company. Employees would:

1. Understand more clearly the nature of the demands that cause their tension;

2. Learn how to effectively balance multiple obligations;

3. Identify their personal strengths, develop confidence in them and learn to build on them;

4. Learn how to identify and use resources;

5. Gain support from others who are becoming proactive problem solvers, rather than just "copers."

Benefits to Honeywell

- Enhanced morale among employees who appreciate the company's acknowledgment of the daily challenges they face.

- Increased productivity from employees who are less distracted by family obligations and more focused on work.

- An opportunity to learn the nature and extent of conflicts facing employees and how they solve them, so it can continue to develop appropriate methods to assist them.

Program Description

Since work and family conflicts affect all employees depending on the type of family, stage in the family life cycle, age, particular family concerns, work responsibilities and particular work units, seminars would focus on a wide variety of themes.

Subjects which have surfaced in employee surveys, in personal interviews, and at task team meetings, include:

- Making anticipatory plans for the care of sick children and other dependents. (See Appendix A.)

- Making after school plans for children, appropriate to their age and maturity level and family circumstances. (See Appendix B.)

- Communicating concerns and suggested solutions to one's supervisor.

- Caring for an aging parent.

- Developing personal support networks.

- Identifying and effectively using company and community resources.

Responsibility for Action

- Honeywell executive management should communicate its support for workplace seminars.

- Corporate or divisional Human Resource Departments should develop pilot initiatives, models for other divisions to follow or adapt to their own circumstances. Pilot seminars would allow Honeywell to evaluate usefulness to employees and their families and their value to the company before implementing seminars more broadly.

- Several models have been used throughout the company: Programs developed by Corporate and Community Responsibility Department, The Women's Council, the ACE programs, and divisions could be updated and adapted. Further, new courses could be developed relatively inexpensively.

Resource Materials

Rationale

Employees currently lack sufficient awareness of the many resources available to them which could help them manage work and family responsibilities. Additional resources may not be needed beyond those now available through human resource representatives, supervisors, the Employee Assistance Program, peers, the medical staff, the union, Human Resource Development, training and planning, community relations, ombudsmen and top management. However, Honeywell can more effectively promote the services so employees can take the initiative to utilize them.

As employees become more aware of resources, utilization of services, productivity and individual performance may also increase. Additionally, the company may see cost-savings as an inventory of existing programs reveals redundant services which may be consolidated.

Program Description and Responsibility for Action

- Corporate and Divisions should strive to consolidate information about corporate and community resources and services.

    1. Review and obtain available resources, both internal and external.

    2. Disseminate this information. Examples include:

    - Literature racks near cafeteria and recreation areas.

    - A list of resources on a wallet-size card.

    - A "help" hotline as currently exists in Military Avionics Division.

    - Expanded employee orientation with information on available resources.

    - Continue funding and supporting community services through divisional community action committees, contracts with service providers, and the Honeywell Foundation.

"I hope the company will look very hard at the feasibility of a child care center. Productivity of people is better when they're not worried about their kids."

Recommendation D

Honeywell should consider sponsoring the development of a child care center for the children of employees and others near an operating division but owned and managed by an outside child care organization. It should be operated as a pilot or demonstration program and monitored for its effect on employee productivity and morale.

Rationale

At some facilities, employees lack access to quality, affordable child care. For many employees, scarce child care is a major burden which leads to stress, decreased productivity and increased absenteeism. These employees would feel more secure if they had near-site company sponsored child care, to reach their children quickly in emergencies, to insure closer observation of center's programs, and to have the option to work later if necessary.

Two major goals would be achieved with the development of a Honeywell-sponsored child care facility. High-quality professional child care by a professional staff addresses the development needs of each child in care. Children need nurturing, stimulating and well-supervised programs which enable them to grow socially, physically and intellectually. Parents cannot perform well at work while worrying that the needs of their child are not being met. Therefore, a high-quality program should be the primary goal of a near-site center sponsored by Honeywell.

Secondly, the child care program should be consistent with corporate goals. Company-sponsored child care services could reduce work hours lost when child care problems force employees to make personal phone calls, leave work early or not come to work at all. An employer who offers child care services is more attractive to potential applicants, and significantly reduces turnover. If the center enables employees to be more productive at work, reduces turnover, and enhances productivity, Honeywell benefits.

Responsibility for Action

- Corporate Human Resources should develop systematic and efficient models for divisions to use as they explore development of child care near their locations.

- Interested divisions establish feasibility and cost studies.
- Divisions work with childcare organizations to develop programs owned and operated by organization.
- Divisions consider providing technical assistance and some start up costs.

In other locations not chosen as the pilot site, employees should continue to have access to resources for locating adequate child care. This should include an updated Honeywell brochure on how to locate child care as well as continued funding of the Child Care Information Network (CCIN).

Honeywell should also continue supporting quality, affordable child care in communities with Honeywell locations through:

- Grants to child care organizations or advocacy groups.
- Supports for programs to upgrade training and pay for child care professionals.
- Lobby for legislation aimed at improving the availability of care.

"Let's say both parents work for Honeywell, and each has used up the normal allowed number of sick days. Now the kids start to get sick and the daycare service doesn't allow sick kids. Your parents and hers are all working. You want to stay home and watch the kids, but you know you might get in trouble if you call in sick. Shouldn't the company be more understanding? What is the solution?"

Recommendation E

Honeywell should consider a total time-off policy, combining holidays, vacations and sick days into a lump sum managed by individual employees according to their own or family's needs. While the model may be developed by Corporate, its implementation would be subject to specific business demands and work force consideration of divisions.

Rationale

Establishing a total time-off policy with individuals responsible for managing their own time off would benefit the company as well as the employees. The principal advantage of such a policy, according to companies currently using this system, is that employees may use the enlarged block of time to accommodate personal needs—temporary illness, personal appointments, illness in the family, problems with child care arrangements and others.

Absenteeism due to unplanned time off will be reduced by giving the employees greater latitude in justifying and scheduling their time. There would be less need to compensate for absence through the use of overloads. Supervisors will be able to hold employees accountable for time off for casual illness, which currently is inadequately reported and tracked. Also, total time off could help eliminate perceived inequities in how time off is granted by minimizing differences in supervisory practice.

Supervisors and employees can be more honest with each other, with the resulting trust extending into the total working relationship. Additionally, employees may be motivated to use their casual sick time more carefully to avoid applying the majority of their time off to illness days.

When designing the policy, consideration must be given to several factors which are potential barriers to its success. It may be most effectively implemented in a highly-structured working environment, where tracking time off is possible without new regulations. In a less structured setting, supervisors would have additional administrative burden of tracking and monitoring the time off.

Another concern is the policy could cause some employees to reduce voluntary overtime due to the continuous tracking of their time. Also, some employees may take more days off than they now do.

Despite its potential drawbacks, the Task Team feels that the positive implications of a total time-off policy outweigh these disadvantages and thus recommends further investigation by the company.

Program Description

Typical total time-off policies in other companies generally combine the number of vacation days available to an employee based on established company guidelines with a number of additional days previously considered sick leave. Thus, the total time off an individual employee receives varies, depending on years of service to the company. The days are banked in a time-off account and are drawn upon by the employee to accommodate personal needs.

Within Honeywell, both SSED and Marine Systems Division have successfully adopted the total time-off concept.

Responsibility for Action

As with all time-off policies, application of this policy must fit the particular needs of the business. Therefore, policy guidelines should be developed at the Corporate level with divisional implementation based on applicability:

To implement the policy, Corporate must first promote and establish a total time-off policy through the following actions:

- The Corporate Vice-President of Human Resources should commission a subcommittee of the Human Resources Council to study the current applications of total time off within Honeywell. The subcommittee would also review existing divisional policies at SSED and MSD, SSED and MSD should be asked to identify appropriate experts from their operations to facilitate the review process. The subcommittee should report its findings and make recommendations to the full Council.

- Based on the subcommittee's recommendations, the Human Resources Council should
  a) Encourage pilots in Honeywell division (or)
  b) Incorporate total time-off concepts into corporate benefits redesign (or)
  c) Develop total time-off guidelines after which divisions could model their own policies.

- If appropriate, divisions should survey employee interest/need.

- In a timely manner, divisional decisions should then be made and communicated to all employees.

V   CONCLUSION

The company's workforce will continue to undergo change. It is imperative that Honeywell understand the nature of these dramatic changes and their implications on its ability to meet its business objectives. The company must make some significant changes in its practice if it is to continue to recruit, maintain and manage a highly productive work force.

Not long ago, Honeywell was considered a national leader among corporations in its development of practical programs and policies which helped employees manage both major commitments. Dramatic changes at Honeywell in the last several months make it even more important for the company to increase opportunities for employees to reach their full potential as workers and as family members.

VI FOOTNOTES

1. Peter Coolsen et al., *Strengthening Families Through the Workplace* (Chicago, IL: National Committee for the Prevention of Child Abuse, 1985), p. 3.

2. The Conference Board, *Corporations and Families: Changing Practices and Perspectives* (New York: The Conference Board, 1985), Report No. 868, p. 4.

3. "Honeywell Work and Family Survey: Productivity Issues and Family Concerns" (Minneapolis, MN: Honeywell, Inc., 1986), p. 3.

4. Ibid., comments from employee respondents.

5. Excerpted from employee comments on Honeywell Work and Family Survey and employee remarks to Work and Family Task Team, 1986.

VII   APPENDICES

APPENDIX A

Module for Employee Seminar on Sick Child Care

Sick child care is an example of an issue which should be addressed in employee seminars. Honeywell is negatively affected by a high degree of absenteeism, need to pay temporary help in some cases, or decreased productivity of employees who come to work feeling their sick child care plans are inadequate.

The implications of their illness are often negative for the sick children themselves. Left with an irritated child care provider who worries about the risk of contagion to other children, or home with a frustrated parent who feels he or she should be at work, the child often feels burdensome and guilty. Left at home alone, the child often feels lonely as well as sick.

A divisional pilot program could be developed which provides guidance to working parents for developing a practical plan for the inevitable and unexpected crisis or illness. Its components include:

- Explanation of company or divisional policies, either explicit or implicit, regarding time off to care for sick children.
- Inventory at available community services for sick child care.
- Exposure to developmental needs of children at varying ages.
- Opportunity to learn how to negotiate with current child care provider, spouse, other family members, friends or neighbors in developing plans.
- Opportunity to communicate one's proposed plans to supervisor in anticipation of an illness.

APPENDIX B

Module for Employee Seminar on After-School Child Care

After-school child care is an issue which should be addressed through Honeywell courses. Employees with school age children often worry about their children during the hours after school when the children are home alone. This has a negative impact on Honeywell as employees often do not give their full attention to their work during these hours, resulting in decreased efficiency and productivity. Children may also be adversely affected when left to care for themselves. Research on these children shows that they are more likely to feel lonely, depressed and anxious than other children who are supervised.

A divisional pilot program could provide education on after-school care for both working parents and their children. Such a program would ease the tension for both parents and children as they become better able to manage the issues. Its components include:

- Domestic survival techniques for children, enabling them to better accept responsibility for themselves when left home alone.

- Developing contracts to clarify guidelines and expectations between parents and children.

- Opportunity for children to develop personal and social skills so they can cope with being home alone.

- Exposure to after-school scheduling techniques.

Additionally, a brochure on after-school care should be published and made available through the seminar or through general distribution.

APPENDIX C

Materials Used by Task Team

1. Axel, Helen, *Corporations and Families: Changing Practices and Perspectives*, Report No. 868, New York: The Conference Board, 1998.

2. Bell, Connie, *Child Care Center Feasibility Study for Honeywell's Commercial Aviation Division*, Minneapolis: Greater Minneapolis Day Care Association, 1998.

3. Coolsen, Peter, et al., *When School's Out and Nobody's Home*, Chicago: National Committee for the Prevention of Child Abuse, 1998.

4. Coolsen, Peter, *Strengthening Families Through the Workplace*, Chicago: National Committee for the Prevention of Child Abuse, 1998.

5. Copeland, Tom, *The Sick Child Care Dilemma: Solutions for Business*, Report of the Saint Paul Area Chamber of Commerce Child Care Task Force, St. Paul: St. Paul Area Chamber of Commerce, 1998.

6. Greater Minneapolis Day Care Association, *Sick Child Care!*, Minneapolis: Parents in the Workplace, 1998.

7. Hedin, Diane, et al., *Summary of the Family's View of After School Time*, Minneapolis: Center for Youth Development and Research, University of Minnesota, 1998.

APPENDIX D

Honeywell's Work and Family Initiatives

Honeywell's workforce increasingly is comprised of women, dual-wage earner couples, and single parents who have responsibility for the care and development of children and other family members.

Recognizing that conflicts between work and family roles limit productivity, Honeywell developed a series of corporate policies and programs. Each was designed to build employees' confidence in their own ability to use personal, company, and community resources to manage their work and family demands.

- The **Child Care Information Network (CCIN)** is a computerized information and referral service designed to help employees and others locate current openings in licensed family day care homes and day care centers throughout Hennepin County. As an initiator of CCIN, Honeywell provided start-up costs in addition to managerial and technical assistance for its establishment in 1980. Honeywell currently covers the annual cost of providing the service for its employees.

- **"Honeywell's Working Parents Guide to Child Care"** is a complement to CCIN, developed by the Corporate and Community Responsibility and Occupational Environmental Health departments. Honeywell has distributed more than 8,000 of these guides, designed to help persons locate the type of child care which meets the needs of their particular children.

- **Seminars and classes for employees** offer information, resources and the opportunity to learn skills to help balance work and family responsibilities. These seminars and classes have included ACE Work and Family classes, a work/family forum and a single working parents workshop, among others.

- Honeywell has a **corporate-wide flex-time policy**, opted in 1982, which allows employees to start work within a given range of time. Honeywell's goal was to insure that business and personal needs were, to the maximum extent possible, satisfied in an efficient and compatible manner.

- A **dependent care option** is included in Honeywell's flexible benefits plan adopted in 1986. The dependent care option allows employees to use pretax dollars, deposited to a special account through payroll deductions, to pay a portion of their costs for dependent care. Dependents include children under the age of 15 and physically or mentally disabled adults who are unable to take care of themselves.

- A **child care discount program** is available to all Honeywell employees in the Minneapolis-St. Paul area with discounts available at Learning Tree, Building Bloc and New Horizon day care centers. Employees receive a 10% discount.

- **Parenting fairs** were held to connect Honeywell working parents with community resources for families. Participating organizations included child care centers, the police and fire departments, and arts organizations for children.

- Corporate and Community Responsibility Department implemented a **Work and Family Survey** of salaried employees at the Military Avionics Division. Developed to update a data base about the needs and concerns of employees, the survey findings will be used to develop more effective policies and programs. Earlier surveys have focused solely on child care.

- Honeywell provides assistance to community organizations and projects which strengthen family functioning, particularly in working families. Honeywell provides financial contributions, technical and managerial assistance.

- Honeywell serves as a **resource** to the nonprofit community, public sector, academic institutions and other corporations on strategies to address work and family issues. Activities in this area range from addressing Senate hearings to chairing national councils and participating on issues task forces.

APPENDIX E

Other Honeywell Reports on Work and Family Issues

Honeywell Women's Task Force, *Child Care Recommendations for Honeywell Employees*, Minneapolis: Honeywell Inc., 1998.

Honeywell's Working Parents Task Force: Final Report and Recommendations, Minneapolis: Honeywell Inc., 1998.

Commercial Aviation Division Ad Hoc Day Care Team, *On-Site Child Care at Honeywell Commercial Aviation Division*, Minneapolis: Honeywell Inc., 1998.

Honeywell Work and Family Survey: Productivity Issues and Family Concerns, Minneapolis: Honeywell Inc., 1998.

CHAPTER 10

Graphic Aids

If you were to compare 50 business reports and proposals from the 1950s with 50 comparable documents from the late 1990s, the most obvious difference would not be formality of style, length of paragraphs, or use of headings. What would leap to your eye from the late 1990s documents are their graphics—those interesting, attention-getting, and often entertaining forms of visual information. Despite this obvious change in business documents, many otherwise skilled business writers and presenters feel uncomfortable when it comes to creating and using visual aids. On the one hand, these communicators acknowledge the importance of graphs, charts, illustrations, photographs, and other visual aids in making a point. On the other hand, many writers and speakers wilt when they think about creating good graphics. They assume that creating the graphics will be time-consuming and difficult.

"I'm afraid," confesses a financial counselor in Dallas, "that my artistic efforts will look amateurish. Yet I don't have the time, money, or patience to work with a professional artist."

NEW TOOLS FOR NONARTISTS

Advances in word-processing and computer graphics technology have put the artist's pen in every business communicator's hand. Tables, line graphs, bar charts, wedged pie charts, flowcharts, maps, and many other visual aids are now easier to produce than ever before. A huge variety of graphics software is now available for every computer and company budget. This software makes it possible to prepare professional visual aids in a short time.

What has not changed, however, is the necessity to *think* about whether you want or need visual aids. You still must decide where they should be placed, what kind you need, and how your words and visual aids together can form a mutually supportive package of meaning.

REASONS FOR USING VISUAL AIDS

Although visual aids attract the reader's print-tired eyes, there are even more important reasons for using visual aids. Consider five key reasons for using visual aids in your business documents and presentations.

1. To *clarify* your point. A visual aid can show a process, procedure, relationship, cross-section, or quantitative view of topics.
2. To *emphasize* your point. Visual aids call attention to key ideas much more vividly than words do.
3. To *simplify* your point. Relationships among ideas, facts, and statistics can be shown simply in graphic form.
4. To *unify* your points. Several ideas can be brought together in one visual aid.
5. To *impress* your reader. Readers are swayed by your imaginative approach to the communication of ideas.

WHERE TO BEGIN: THE AUDIENCE'S NEEDS

Which graphics you use, if any, depends entirely on your audience's *need* for such visual supports to meaning. Begin, therefore, by asking yourself what passages in your document or presentation should be enlivened and clarified for the sake of your audience. This requires reading your work as if for the first time, watching and listening objectively for those portions that will seem difficult, vague, or complicated for your audience. Look also for *emphasis* opportunities—places in your communication where a visual aid would make a key point more memorable.

Having found these possible locations for visual aids, you're ready to choose which graphics belong where. The discussion of the many visual aids depicted in this chapter can help you make an informed choice. Be cautious with graphics, though. Graphics by themselves can hurt a business communication as easily as help it. A chart or table that appears out of context can perplex readers, drawing their attention away from your text and undercutting your credibility.

To avoid misusing visual aids, follow five commonsense *dos* and *don'ts*:

1. *Do* point out the conclusions you want your reader to draw from a visual aid. *Don't* expect a reader to automatically see your point in a chart, graph, or illustration.
2. *Do* locate your visual aids next to the text that explains them. *Don't* expect your reader to hunt for the text that explains a visual aid or vice versa.
3. *Do* simplify your visual aids so that they make their primary point within a second or two of the reader's attention. *Don't* cram visual aids so full of information that they cannot be interpreted by the reader.

4. *Do* provide keys, legends, captions, and titles as required by your visual aids. *Don't* assume that the reader will understand the intent and symbols of your visual aids.

5. *Do* scale your graphic aids and place them on the page so that they can be seen and interpreted easily. *Don't* frustrate the reader with postage-stamp-sized graphs and charts.

DISTORTION AND DECEPTION IN VISUAL AIDS

Like words, visual aids can be used to lie or, put more politely, to "shade the truth." This text does not investigate in detail such misapplied uses of visual aids, but three deceptive practices appear so frequently that you should be aware of them.

DISPROPORTION   The visual representation of statistical data is disproportionate to the data itself. *Example:* A pie chart showing a large wedge identified as "welfare cheaters" when the proper wedge should have been no more than 6 percent of the circle.

MISALIGNMENT   The measurement scales along the axes of graphs and charts have been misaligned, often by moving or omitting the zero point, to create more dramatic graphic effects than the data deserves. *Example:* Profits at an automobile company grew only by 2 percent. By changing the measurement numbers along the vertical (*y*) axis, the upward curve of profits seems much more substantial than a mere 2 percent rise.

OMISSION   Visual aids are simplified representations of data. As such, they are especially vulnerable to distortion by omission of neutral or unfavorable data items. *Example:* A software company has had several rocky months, but because of tax write-offs, it is able to show somewhat steady growth at the end of each fiscal quarter. The roller-coaster nature of the company can be masked entirely by a bar chart showing only quarterly results.

The following Communication Checkpoint may aid you in your use of graphics.

Communication Checkpoint
Using Graphic Aids

- What are the key points of my talk? Which of these should be underscored by visuals? Will the graphic aids achieve my objectives?
- Will my visual aids clarify my ideas, or will they merely support them? If they only support them, should I still use them?
- Are my visual aids appropriate and concrete? Are they informative?
- Have I considered the cost, time, and thought any of these visuals will take? Does the particular presentation of my topic justify these? Can I manage just as well without them or without some of them?
- Is each of my graphic aids consistent with my objectives? Do they add up to a consistent basic structure and unity? Are they free from complicating typefaces, art techniques, and symbols?
- Can my audience easily grasp what they see, or is an added explanation necessary? Are my graphic aids direct and to the point?
- Should my graphic aids be representational, pictorial, or symbolic? Which treatment is best for my topic? Which treatment is best from the standpoint of the audience?

- Is the sequence for my visual aids logical? Are they so organized that they add strength and relevance to one another and to my overall topic?
- Are my graphic aids as effective as they can be made? Did I put enough thought and effort into the planning of my graphic aids? Did I consider all the ways in which the topic could be reinforced and clarified by my graphic aids?
- Are my graphic aids believable in terms of the overall topic? Will my audience appreciate and understand them? Will they be completely readable?
- What kind of graphic aids should I use?

VISUAL AIDS FOR BUSINESS DOCUMENTS AND PRESENTATIONS

To be able to choose the very best graphic aid for your documents and presentations, read the following gallery of commonly used visual aids. Be sure to look at the illustration of each type of graphic aid. Note that storyboards, flip charts, and physical objects are exclusively used in oral presentations. In addition, most of these could be used as overhead-projector transparencies, as slides, or even in filmstrips, films, or videotapes.

Photograph

While certainly a powerful visual communicator, the photograph can be difficult and expensive to reproduce. Depending on the distribution you intend for your work, you may also need to obtain written releases from all of the humans pictured in the photo. Nonetheless, photographs can prove invaluable in communicating product descriptions, geographical information, and personalities. For that reason, they are the most common graphic technique used in annual reports.

Line Drawing

Because of the advanced state of line drawings (including cartoons) today, public standards for line drawings are quite high. If your abilities with a pen don't measure up, ask a professional artist to create your line drawings. These can add emphasis and attraction to your documents and presentations (Figure 10–1).

Line Graph

This is the simplest of graphic aids; it shows trends at a glance (Figure 10–2). Note that only the dots (the data points) represent accurate measurements. The line between the dots does not portray, point for point, an accurate measurement of data.

Multiline Graph

By differentiating lines by color, size, or texture, a multiline graph portrays simultaneous trends, allowing easy comparison (Figure 10–3). Care must be taken not to include too many different lines (three are usually the maximum advisable) or to portray lines that intersect one another too often for easy visual interpretation.

FIGURE 10–1   Line Drawing

Effective marketing managers define their job as creating and delivering the proper market impact to well-defined market targets. This is a rifle approach that aims at a specific market target. This marketing manager does not waste resources and effort on the nontarget area of the market.

Bar Graph

The bar graph creates strong visual statements for comparative measurement (Figure 10–4). Trends can still be gauged but without the sloping (and often inaccurate) lines of a line graph. The simple bar chart compares two or more values and can be drawn either horizontally or vertically. Exact quantities represented by each bar are often written inside or at the top of each bar.

A gallery of graphic aids appears on the following pages to show various ways of conveying ideas and statistics.

Grouped Bar Graphs

A grouped bar graph is, in effect, a series of simple bar charts, each measuring two or more values at specified intervals (Figure 10–5). It allows comparison of a single element across the chart or among elements at each place on or across the chart.

FIGURE 10–2   Line Graph

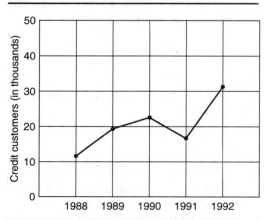

Six Graphs Based on the Same Data

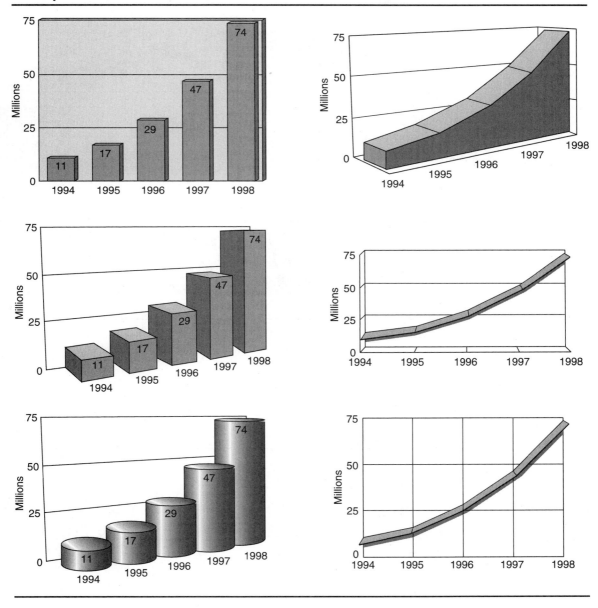

Flowchart

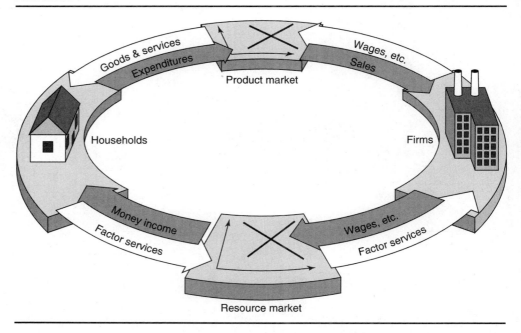

Grouped Bar Graph

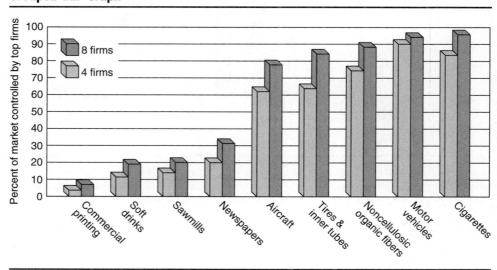

Map

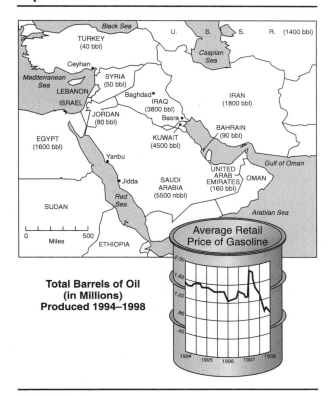

Total Barrels of Oil
(in Millions)
Produced 1994–1998

Bar Graph

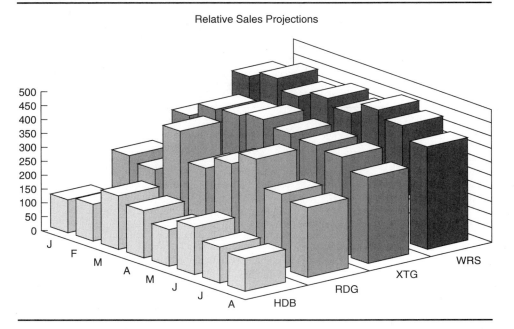

Organizational Chart

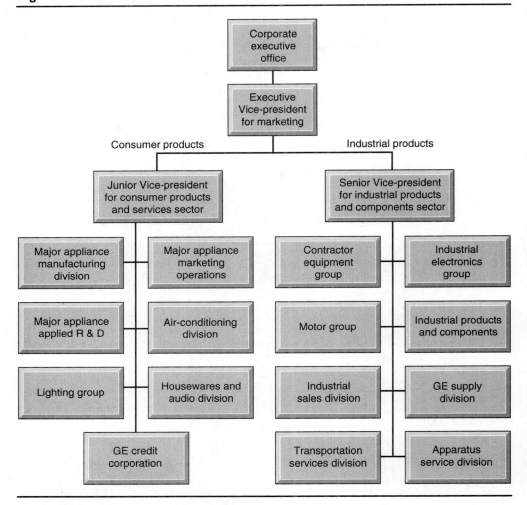

Time Chart

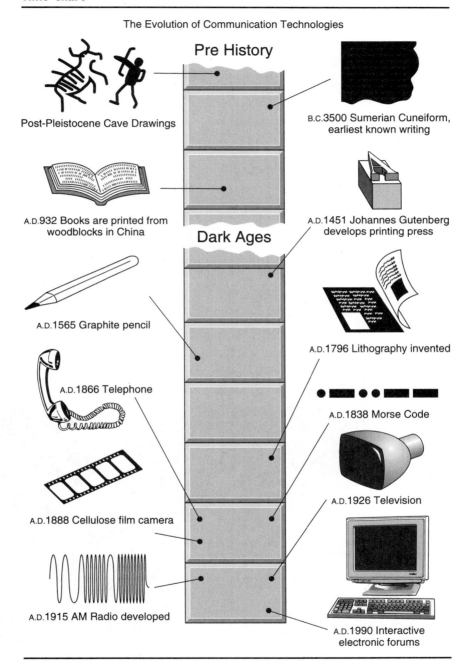

The Evolution of Communication Technologies

Pre History

Post-Pleistocene Cave Drawings

B.C.3500 Sumerian Cuneiform, earliest known writing

A.D.932 Books are printed from woodblocks in China

Dark Ages

A.D.1451 Johannes Gutenberg develops printing press

A.D.1565 Graphite pencil

A.D.1796 Lithography invented

A.D.1866 Telephone

A.D.1838 Morse Code

A.D.1888 Cellulose film camera

A.D.1926 Television

A.D.1915 AM Radio developed

A.D.1990 Interactive electronic forums

Line Drawing

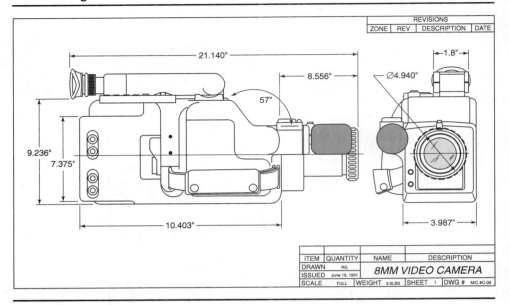

Cutaway

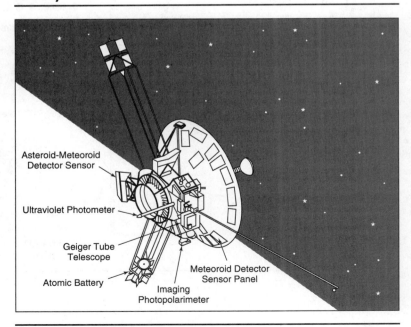

Pie Chart Generated from Selected Data

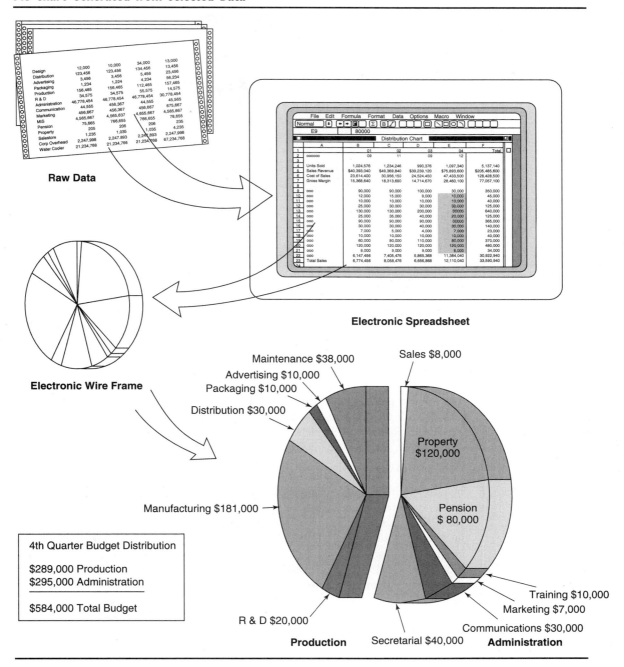

Raw Data

Electronic Spreadsheet

Electronic Wire Frame

Maintenance $38,000

Sales $8,000

Advertising $10,000

Packaging $10,000

Distribution $30,000

Property $120,000

Manufacturing $181,000

Pension $ 80,000

4th Quarter Budget Distribution

$289,000 Production
$295,000 Administration

$584,000 Total Budget

Training $10,000

Marketing $7,000

Communications $30,000

R & D $20,000

Production   Secretarial $40,000   **Administration**

FIGURE 10–3   Multiline Graph

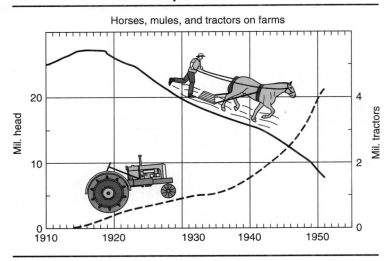

Horses, mules, and tractors on farms

Segmented Bar Graph

The segmented bar graph distinguishes different parts of the whole by color or texture (Figure 10–6). Each bar is segmented into parts corresponding to amounts represented. This highlights the cumulative effect of the parts while still permitting comparisons among the parts.

Line Bar Graph

The line bar graph simultaneously emphasizes individual measurements and trends (Figure 10–7). It may offer the advantages of both bar and line graphs. However, it may also overly complicate the effects or make the graphic aid appear cluttered.

Pie Chart

In a pie or circle chart, each portion represents part of the total amount (often, the total is 100%) depicted in the full circle (Figure 10–8). Portions represented must be proportionate in size to the value they represent. To prepare the pie chart, compute percentages of the total for each portion and then multiply each percentage by 360 degrees. Using a protractor, mark the degrees for each part starting with the largest portion at the top of the circle. Proceed clockwise to smaller and smaller divisions. In general, the pie chart should not contain more than eight parts, to avoid clutter and confusion. Group some categories, as needed, to reduce the number of wedges. For example, "apples" and "oranges" might be put into one wedge as "fruit." Names for segments can be placed inside or outside the chart itself. However, try always to have the names appear horizontally on the page.

Pictogram

Pictograms usually combine line drawings with graphics such as line, bar, and pie charts to make a point in an attractive, eye-catching way (Figure 10–9). Pictograms are often

FIGURE 10–4   Bar Graph

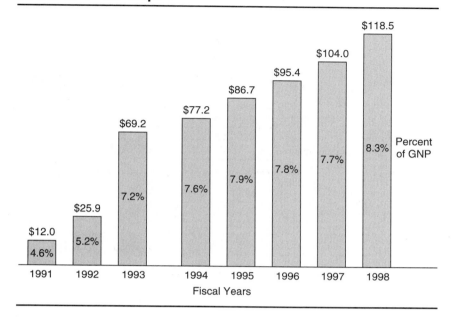

FIGURE 10–5   Grouped Bar Graph

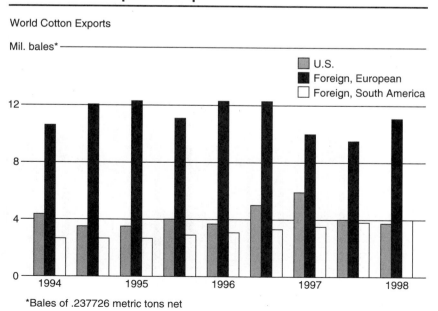

FIGURE 10–6 Segmented Bar Graph

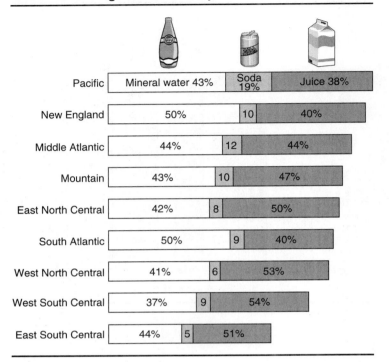

Pacific	Mineral water 43%	Soda 19%	Juice 38%
New England	50%	10	40%
Middle Atlantic	44%	12	44%
Mountain	43%	10	47%
East North Central	42%	8	50%
South Atlantic	50%	9	40%
West North Central	41%	6	53%
West South Central	37%	9	54%
East South Central	44%	5	51%

FIGURE 10–7 Line Bar Graph

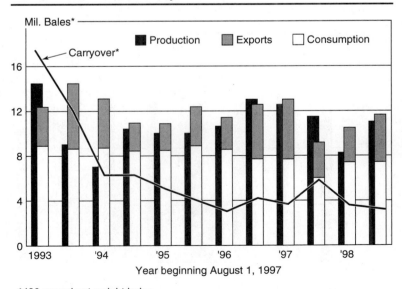

Mil. Bales*

Production Exports Consumption

Carryover*

Year beginning August 1, 1997

*480-pound net weight bales

FIGURE 10–8   Pie Chart

Expenditures for school lunches
(Fiscal year 1998)*

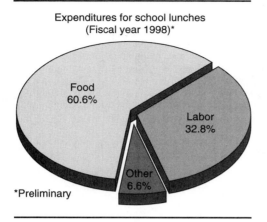

Food
60.6%

Labor
32.8%

Other
6.6%

*Preliminary

FIGURE 10–9   Pictogram

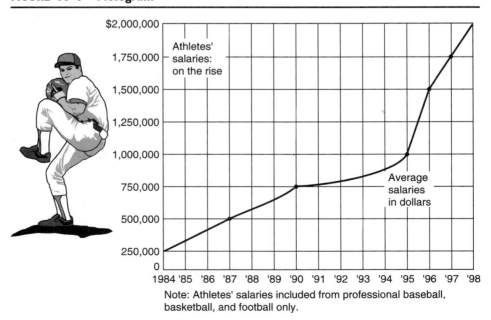

Athletes'
salaries:
on the rise

Average
salaries
in dollars

Note: Athletes' salaries included from professional baseball,
basketball, and football only.

FIGURE 10–10   Flowchart

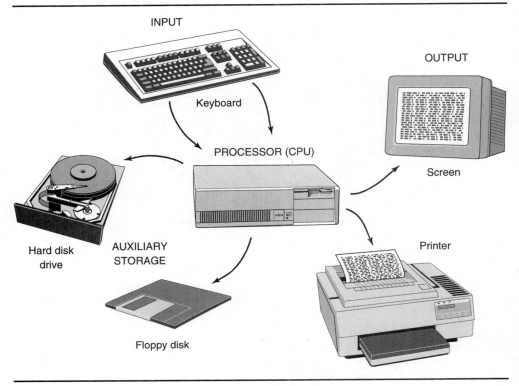

used to try to influence emotions and attitudes. Be careful not to let your creativity involved in a pictogram become your only objective. If so, it might distort or hide the central point of the statistics you want to show.

Flowchart

Flowcharts present a process or procedure (Figure 10–10). Examples include the steps involved in the procedure for applying to college or the stages of a chemical process. Each
step should be labeled clearly and may be differentiated by shape to suggest different functions. Some scientific and technical fields use specific shapes for specific elements. If you
are using flowcharts for scientific or technical audiences, find out and use the correct flowchart symbols.

Cutaway or Exploded Drawing

The cutaway or exploded drawing lets the viewer see into a structure to observe the relationships among its parts (Figure 10–11). Such representations are often used in product
descriptions and technical discussions.

FIGURE 10–11   Cutaway

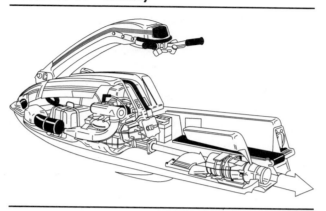

FIGURE 10–12   Time Chart

Activities	Time periods—week beginning							
	Jan. 14	Jan. 21	Jan. 28	Feb. 4	Feb. 11	Feb. 18	Feb. 25	Mar. 4
Review absentee files in personnel office	▨							
Interview supervisors and operations personnel		▨	▨					
Collect data on absentee plans from professional journals and books				▨	▨			
Organize and evaluate the data						▨		
Write the report							▨	
Type and proofread the report								▨
Submit final report to personnel manager								▨

FIGURE 10–13 Organizational Chart

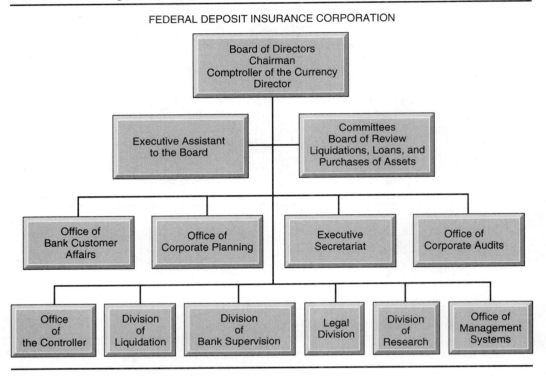

FEDERAL DEPOSIT INSURANCE CORPORATION

Time Chart

Time charts use bars or lines inside a work–time matrix, to show when jobs, tasks, or other activities begin and end (Figure 10–12). Used often in reports and proposals, the time chart serves as a work progress schedule for projects. Many businesses have special software that generates this type of chart, often referred to as "project management" software.

Organizational Chart

Organizational charts are similar to flowcharts but represent hierarchies of relationships among people rather than processes or procedures (Figure 10–13). An organizational chart, for example, could show related functions or departments within a corporation.

Map

Maps present geographical representation of data (Figure 10–14). Family incomes, for example, could be represented on a state-by-state or region-by-region basis using a United States map. Shading, coloring, or texturing can distinguish different regions on the map.

FIGURE 10–14   Map

Comparison of Sales Potential (1)
with Sales Penetration (2)
Southwest Region

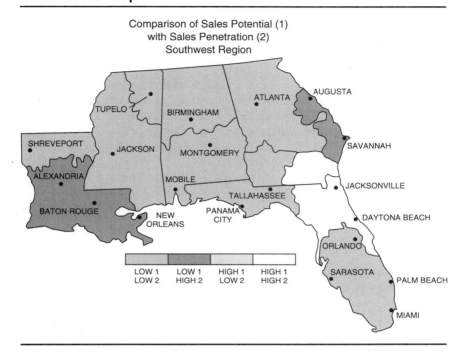

LOW 1	LOW 1	HIGH 1	HIGH 1
LOW 2	HIGH 2	LOW 2	HIGH 2

FIGURE 10–15   Storyboard

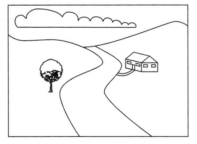

VIDEO: LONG SHOT House on
Deserted Highway and
Streakin Panther
AUDIO: "Faster than a Speeding
Bullet...Able to leap
Tall Buildings in a..."
SFX/MUSIC: SOUND OF JET
TAKING OFF MIXED
WITH PANTHER'S
ROAR

VIDEO: LONG SHOT House on
Deserted Highway
AUDIO: ....
SFX/MUSIC: WIND SOUNDS

VISUAL AIDS FOR ORAL PRESENTATIONS

Storyboard

Storyboards may be presented on cloth or on computer screens or other media. They allow the presenter to prepare in advance a series of words, shapes, and pictures that literally "tell the story" of the presentation as it unfolds (Figure 10–15). These words, shapes, and pictures can be put up, rearranged, or removed as the speaker makes his or her point. In addition, on the computer screen, the pre-prepared screens can be called up at the press of a key. Presentation software packages that allow storyboarding to be done easily are widely available, often also as computer-aided instruction software design packages.

Probably most familiar among such software products is PowerPoint, included within Microsoft's Office software package. PowerPoint gives the presenter the ability to format attractive screens, call up bullet points as needed (with sophisticated movement and "dissolve" features), include sounds in various forms, and integrate images and graphs. More

FIGURE 10–16   Flipchart

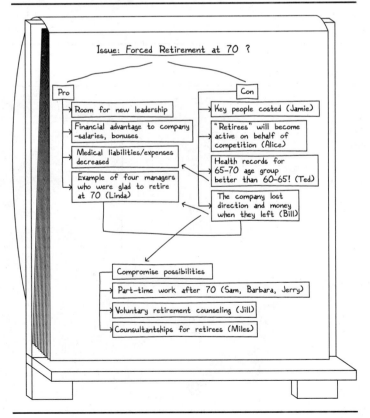

extensive multimedia software products such as Director make it possible to include animated figures in the presentation and even some 3-D effects. Producers of popular presentation software packages recognize that users usually do not want to read an extensive manual in order to put together visual displays. Therefore, a variety of on-screen "wizards" and short-cut tutorials are included for ease of use.

Flipchart

Flipcharts are pads of large-sized paper mounted on a display stand (Figure 10–16). Pages can be prepared in advance, then *flipped* as the speaker goes from point to point. The speaker can choose to create visual aids on the spot, using bold-stroke pens in a variety of colors. Sometimes, a speaker may extemporaneously (while speaking) highlight key items on a readymade flipchart.

Physical Object

Physical objects can be held up and even passed among the audience. These serve presenters well in making ideas, descriptions, and functions concrete, particularly for product or component demonstrations or for "hands-on" workshops.

SUMMARY

1. Computer graphics software allows nonartists to create professional-looking visual aids.

2. Visual aids can clarify, emphasize, simplify, and unify your points, as well as impress your audience.

3. Visual aids must be specifically introduced and identified in nearby text.

4. Those who create and use graphic aids should not attempt to deceive readers and audience members by using disproportionate, misaligned, or incomplete graphic aids.

5. Common graphic aids are photographs, line drawings, line graphs, bar graphs, pie charts, pictograms, flowcharts, organizational charts, time charts, maps, and cutaway drawings.

6. Common graphic aids used by oral presenters are storyboards, flipcharts, and physical objects.

QUESTIONS FOR DISCUSSION

1. Discuss the relation between words and graphics in business documents. How do they support one another?

2. Why do readers like graphic enhancements in the form of photos, charts, graphs, pictograms, maps, and so forth? Explain in detail.

3. On what basis would you decide to use a bar chart instead of a line graph? Give an example.

4. Discuss common errors in using the following graphics:
   Pie chart
   Bar Chart
   Line Graph
   Pictogram
   Map

5. Discuss the impact of computer software packages for generating graphics. How have such packages influenced the look of typical business documents?

6. Are graphics always appropriate? If not, discuss a situation in which words are more appropriate than graphics.

7. Discuss the placement of graphics on an $8\frac{1}{2}$ by 11 inch page. What guidelines can you suggest? Explain the reasons for each guideline you mention.

8. How can even a low-budget office operation make use of graphics in its documents? Discuss.

9. In what ways can particular parts of a graphic be made to catch the reader's eye?

EXERCISES

1. Choose a short document (perhaps a letter or brochure) that has no visual aids. Create a visual aid, and retype or cut-and-paste the original document to place the graphic into the document with any additional words you require. Write a paragraph justifying your selection and handling of the visual aid you chose.

2. Visit a local computer store and learn about graphics packages for business use. Write a brief report of your findings, adding any literature you receive from the store.

3. Create a portfolio of at least eight different kinds of visual aids used in a business context. You may find such graphics in magazines such as *Fortune*, *Forbes*, *U.S. News and World Report*, *Business Week*, and *Nation's Business*. Write one paragraph evaluating each item in your portfolio. Assess the success or failure of the graphic at hand.

4. Obtain a photograph and then include it in a business document at least one page in length. Take particular care to identify and introduce the photograph using the words that surround it on the page.

5. Assume that you want to graphically represent the income levels of various neighborhoods, areas, or towns in your region. (Unless your instructor specifies otherwise, you may make up statistics for the purpose of this exercise.) Show at least six different income groups by number, annual income, and any other distinguishing characteristics you wish to include. Choose three different visual aids by which to represent your statistics, and create each visual aid with pen and paper or a computer software package.

6. Photocopy a map of the United States. Use it to create a statistical map in which you point out regional differences in a category you've chosen. (You may, for example, show population differences for states or regions; education differences; age differences; and so forth.)

7. Create a flowchart showing the step-by-step progress of a process or procedure of your choice. Your chart should have at least eight distinct stages.

8. Create two transparencies for use in an in-class presentation. Write one or two paragraphs in which you explain what you are attempting to achieve in the transparencies. Deal particularly with your choice of words, shapes, and pictures, including their placement.

9. Investigate computer storyboard software. Write a brief report in which you discuss the uses of these programs for business presenters. Attach any literature you are able to get on the programs.

10. Find an example of distortion or deceptive emphasis in a graphic aid (perhaps from a magazine or newspaper). Photocopy the graphic, then write a memo explaining how the graphic distorts information and how it can be repaired for accuracy. Assume that one of the your employees created the graphic; address your memo to that person.

11. Decide what kind of graphic aid you would use to visually depict each of the following. Explain your choice for each.
    a. The number of foreign cars sold in the United States each year, compared to domestic cars sold here
    b. The average length of employment for employees in these salary categories: to $20,000, to $30,000, to $40,000, to $50,000, to $60,000 and to $70,000
    c. The number of departments within your company and the number of employees in each department
    d. The interrelation of parts in a new bicycle design

12. Select a graphic aid in a recent business news magazine. Study the relation of the graphic to the text of the surrounding article, including the sentences leading into the graphic and those leading away from it. Evaluate in writing how well the use of the graphic is coordinated with the article text.

13. Call to mind several graphic aids that you've seen used in your college classes. Which of those graphics was most effective? Why? Record your opinions in a written response.

14. Find a graphic aid that you consider too complicated for easy understanding. Show how the graphic can be simplified or divided into two or more graphics for clarity and effect.

INTERNET ASSIGNMENT

Your small company is preparing to develop its first catalog for direct-mail sales. You know that the quality, placement, and quantity of graphic elements in this catalog will in large part determine its success. Unfortunately, no one in your company has much expertise in the development of effective graphics. Use the Visual Aids section of the Internet Guide to discover resources that can guide your employees in their self-education on how, where, when, and why to use graphics in the upcoming catalog. Write a memo or prepare a brief presentation addressed to your employees. Describe which Internet sites you believe to be the most useful and why. Conclude with a specific action plan your employees can use to improve their skills in graphic design and placement.

Proposals and Business Plans

OVERVIEW OF PROPOSALS

Contracts do not simply arrive on a company's doorstep, or—despite advertising—come marching out of the Yellow Pages. Contracts are usually earned through words, most often cast in the form of a business proposal.

A business proposal describes ideas in such a way that they appear to fulfill the client's needs. Sometimes clients don't have a clear idea of their needs. In that case, the proposal must not only provide solutions but also describe the problem. In the words of an old saying, "Give them the answer, but first make sure they know the question."

The power of your proposal ideas depends on a powerful need being felt by your client. A proposal for a miracle cure can bring yawns and shrugs to an audience unconcerned about the disease.

Business proposals may be almost any length, from a single typed page to several bound volumes (as in the case of a proposal to the military from an aerospace contractor). A proposal must be long enough to do the work it is supposed to do—no more and no less.

3 KEYS TO PERSUASIVE PROPOSALS

What are the parts of a proposal? Although proposals differ according to use and length, most are made up of an overview, a problem analysis, proposal specifics, a budget, and a conclusion. These five parts are treated in detail later in this chapter.

How is a proposal arranged? Parts find their place according to one criterion: the role they play in the overall purpose of the document. In the case of the business proposal, the central purpose is to persuade an audience to act. All parts of the proposal, then, must be arranged to serve this purpose. Consider three powerful forces to persuade your reader(s) to act on your proposal:

1. Logical order
2. Psychological order
3. Solid evidence

Logical Order

The parts of a proposal must be arranged in such a way as to appeal to the reader's sense of reason. Readers who can follow an argument point-by-point feel confident that the writer has thought through the material with care. Such readers are much more likely to say "yes" to the ideas proposed in the document.

Logical Chain

The chain of logic in a proposal can be viewed as a row of dominoes. Each acts on the next in an onward movement toward the conclusion of the proposal. Only a missing link—a logical flaw—can halt the onward movement of the reader's mind. (See Figure 11–1.)

By carefully reviewing the logical order of ideas within a proposal, the writer makes sure that the reader's thoughtful consideration of the document is not interrupted or frustrated by logical errors.

Consider, for example, the sequence of logical steps at the heart of a proposal to install brighter street lights in a residential neighborhood.

FIGURE 11–1   Logical Flaw

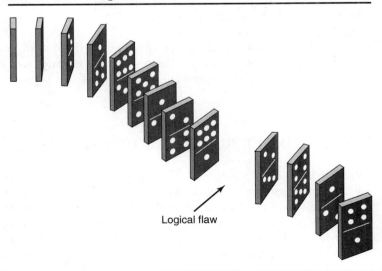

Logical flaw

Point 1:   Residents care most of all about safety and property values.

Point 2:   Brighter street lights discourage crime (thereby making the neighborhood safer).

Point 3:   Brighter street lights increase property values (because safer areas have higher property values).

Point 4:   Residents can be expected to support the proposal (because it gives them what they want—safety and higher property values).

This logical design is not complex, but it serves to illustrate the domino effect of solid logical argumentation. One point leads to the next, which in turn leads to a related point. Taken all together, the points lead to a conclusion that appeals to common sense.

Logical Flaws

Too many proposals (and other messages) fail because they don't have an understandable logical design. Be on guard for the "Ten Most Unwanteds" in logical ordering of ideas.

1. **Circular Reasoning.** What was supported to be an explanation turns out to be a mere restatement.

   > All employees are encouraged to participate in after-hours company recreation programs because such programs are especially for the use of employees after the workday has ended.

2. **Hasty Generalization.** The conclusion reached is based on too little evidence.

   > Democrats can't win the election because of their stand on animal rights.

3. **Non Sequitur.** A conclusion is reached that does not follow from the evidence presented.

   > Johnson owns two homes, a boat, and a sports car, so I trust his investment advice.

4. **Bias.** Personal opinions and viewpoints become the standard for evaluating objective arguments.

   > Ms. Wilmington has every right to apply for the new position, but she won't get it. I just don't want to work with a woman.

5. **Either/Or Thinking.** Two alternatives are presented as the only alternatives when others should be considered.

   > Either he apologizes or I quit.

6. **False Cause.** An earlier occurrence is incorrectly presented as the cause of a later event.

   > We switched to leased cars instead of company-owned cars in 1996.

   > No wonder we have so many auto repair bills each month!

7. **Straw Man.** A false target is set up for the main thrust of an argument. Knocking over the straw man creates the illusion that the argument has succeeded.

> This company's problems can be blamed on poor benefits. How can anyone expect workers to concentrate on their jobs when they have doubts about their medical and dental coverage?

8. **Faulty Syllogism.** A flawed pattern of thought leads to an unjustifiable conclusion.

> All managers wear mustaches. I wear a mustache. Therefore, I must be a manager.

9. **Stacking the Argument.** Presenting evidence on behalf of one side of the argument while ignoring evidence on the other side.

> Undersea mining operations are dangerous, expensive, time-consuming, and unreliable. We should not consider undersea mining in deciding how and where to mine for gold.

10. **False Elimination.** From an array of possible alternatives, one by one is eliminated until only one alternative remains. The illusion is thereby created that the final alternative is the best.

> In reviewing cities for our company move, we've seen why Toledo, Miami, Dallas, Chicago, and Milwaukee won't meet our needs. That leaves Phoenix as our new company home.

Such logical flaws can collapse the credibility of a proposal. Eliminate them from your own proposal writing.

Psychological Order

Skilled proposal writers try to influence feelings as well as thoughts. They want readers to *want* to agree with the ideas of the proposal. One technique used by such proposal writers is the careful placement and timing of *good news* and *bad news* in proposals.

The Placement of Bad News

Bad news can be defined as a message that threatens our welfare, stability, or reputation. A manager may hear the bad news that his or her division is being reduced in size and influence. A company may hear the bad news that it faces a major lawsuit.

Proposal writers don't shy away from bad news. Instead, they recognize bad news as the stage—the necessary precondition—for good news. Bad news forms the question, in a sense, that good news (the proposed idea) attempts to answer.

Consider, for example, a major proposal for road improvements on a mountain pass highway. The bad news is that several accidents have occurred because of poor road conditions, particularly during bad weather. The proposal writer explains the causes of the accidents in detail, all in preparation for the proposed solution of repaving, posting better signs, and setting speed limitations.

The Placement of Good News

Good news may be welcomed by every reader, but that does not mean it will be believed by every reader. Good news must be presented in such a way as to seem not only *possible* but *probable*. This entails careful analysis of what the reader may resist in the good news being presented.

In the case of a proposal for land development, for example, the proposal writer might point to three items of potential good news for those interested in investing in the venture:

- Housing prices are higher than ever before
- The exclusive area in question has only a few remaining tracts for development
- The architect has worked up creative initial renderings of the kinds of homes that can be built

Each of these items of good news falls flat, however, if the proposal writer does not take into account the *resistance* that may be felt by readers. If housing prices are higher than ever before, will there be a market for the finished homes? If the exclusive area has only a few undeveloped tracts, have they remained undeveloped for a reason, such as permit problems, drainage, and so forth? Finally, will the architect's creative plans prove economically feasible?

Delivering good news, then, requires timing and sensitivity to surrounding issues. Bright, desirable ideas must face and overcome whatever obstacles are present in the reader's mind before they become influential ideas.

Solid Evidence

Readers are swayed to accept ideas by the skilled use of evidence in the form of examples, illustrations, statistics, and details. Such evidence can be *general* or *specific* in nature.

General evidence is made up of a great number of specific examples gathered together (or "generalized"). "The air in metropolitan areas is 16 percent cleaner this year because of federal pollution legislation" is general evidence.

By contrast, *specific evidence* treats precise details in a single case. "Air quality measurements during the month of July in Los Angeles show a 16 percent improvement in overall air quality." Specific evidence, especially when supported by reputable and knowledgeable sources, helps to convince the reader that the proposal writer's major ideas are sound.

Successful proposal writers mix both general and specific evidence to create a case for their ideas. Too much general evidence will make the proposal sound vague and unfocused. Too much specific evidence can make the proposal sound narrow, local, and parochial in its concerns. When they are balanced, however, general and specific evidence can earn the reader's acceptance of ideas within the proposal.

PROPOSAL-WRITING STRATEGIES: A "HOW-TO" GUIDE

You will probably write proposals often in your business career to attract contracts, obtain research money, change in-house procedures, fund new facilities, or argue for product or policy revisions. Use this step-by-step guide to construct practical, successful proposals.

1. Determine Requirements for Your Proposal

Specific guidelines may already exist for developing your proposal. For example, many government agencies have strict requirements for the way topics are described, the order in which they are treated, the length of the proposal, and so forth. Some of these requirements may strike you as unnecessary and even inane. However, you should never purposely break the assigned guidelines issued by a granting agency or client without written permission. If you ask for and receive written permission, attach it to the proposal itself as a convenient way to remind reviewers why your proposal has not followed the prescribed form.

2. Determine Who Will Evaluate Your Proposal

Find out whether your work will be read by content specialists or by a more general audience. Choose language designed to communicate clearly to your readers.

3. Create an Outline for Your Proposal

Jot down ideas, examples, and details for possible use as you work your way through each section of the outline. Look at the parts of this common model used by many professional proposal writers to help you develop an outline specially suited to your own topic.

I. Overview

Provide the background information your reader will need to grasp the significance of your proposed idea. You should probably explain these briefly: Why is the proposal needed? Who needs the proposal? Why should the proposal be accepted? When should the readers act on the proposal? Once you have made the reader aware of the need for your proposal, you can go on to define your approach. What are your objectives? How does your approach differ from other approaches?

II. Problem Analysis

If you want your proposed idea to strike the reader as necessary and timely—an action item—set the stage by analyzing the problem with care. What caused the problem? Who suffers from its effects? What measures have failed in an effort to deal with it? What is the current scale of the problem? What will be its future scale? These questions suggest the kind of analysis to do in this section of the proposal. Use both general and specific evidence to let bad news influence your reader.

Communication Insights	Like mastering the fundamentals of tennis, golf, or sailing, learning to communicate involves taking one step at a time. Learn a technique, then practice; learn another technique, then practice. Along the way, surprising things can happen.

We find ourselves enjoying what we previously resisted. Erasmus knew it in 1508:

"The desire to write grows with writing."

III. Proposal Specifics

Describe in detail your proposed plan of attack. Are your methods proven? If so, by whom? What personnel will be involved? What is their training? What time schedule have you established for your work? What are major checkpoints in that schedule?

Also discuss how you plan to evaluate your proposed enterprise. What significant indications of progress will you look for? When? How will you measure success? Will your research results be observable? Preservable? Repeatable?

Conclude this section with a *summary estimation*—a convincing statement of the likelihood that your plans will produce the results desired. Often, proposal writers describe their ultimate goals as a series of achievement plateaus, any one of which justifies the work proposed. In this way, writers allow funding agencies to feel that even if the highest predictions of their proposals bear no fruit, important results can nonetheless be accomplished at plateaus along the way.

The summary estimation is the writer's last chance to persuade the audience before introducing the key part of your proposal: the budget.

IV. The Budget

Outline the costs of your proposed work, including the following items if applicable

- Equipment acquisition
- Facility rental
- Salary and wages, with benefit allowances if applicable
- Supplies
- Travel expenses
- Research expenses
- Contingency funds

In less frugal times, proposal writers padded their budgets as a hedge against inevitable slashes during the approval process. The "Two for One" rule applied: Determine what is really needed, ask for twice as much, and hope to end up with what was needed in the first place. That game is being played less and less in the late 1990s. One reason is that a dramatically padded budget simply doesn't slip by the shrewd evaluators now reviewing important proposals in business, science, and government.

You also should avoid purposely underbudgeting your proposal (with the false hope of presenting a real bargain to evaluators). An underbudgeted proposal makes promises it cannot keep, and no evaluator chooses to approve something that will be an exercise in frustration.

Perhaps the best advice is Will Rogers's: "Well, there's always the truth." State to the best of your ability what you will need to spend if your proposal is approved. Manipulative efforts to distort budget truths are unwise.

V. Conclusion

A proposal should never begin or end with a dollar sign. Conclude your proposal by expressing your willingness to help your readers: offer to answer questions and to provide further information, to meet with or speak by phone to the evaluators, referees, or others, even to consider reshaping your proposal as necessary to meet the needs of the client or agency.

4. Revise and Polish Your Proposal to Make It Attractive

Because proposals are often judged competitively, they must win attention and respect by how they *look* as well as what they *say*. Wandering margins, bleary type, and smudged graphics all say "amateurish" and "unreliable" to an evaluator trying to get value for money invested. Here are five ways to give your proposals a crisp, professional appearance:

1. Use your word processor's most attractive, proportionately spaced fonts.
2. Use heavy-bond white paper. Beware of pastel shades, especially if you plan to photocopy the work.
3. Use strict margins on all sides of the page. If you can do so without creating oddly spaced lines, use your word processor to right-justify your margins.
4. Decide whether your proposal will have a more powerful effect in bound form, with a vinyl or heavy paper cover (usually in a conservative color). Proposals of just a page or two, of course, are not bound. Most photocopy and fast-print businesses can bind your work inexpensively.
5. Make sure that photocopied versions of your proposal are comparable to your original in clarity and crispness. Copy machines in most photocopy businesses produce clean copies, at times almost indistinguishable from the original.

Advice on Writing Proposals

We have discussed how to make proposals logical, orderly, persuasive, accurate, and attractive. Finally, consider using a few final touches to help you create winning proposals.

1. *Use topics headings and indented material to show off your information.* Look at Figure 11–2, and judge for yourself the difference in effect.
2. *Never bury crucial information in appendixes or footnotes.* If the reader needs to know a fact to make sense out of your proposal, include that fact in the text itself. If necessary, state the fact briefly in the text, elaborating elsewhere in a footnote or appendix. However, never just tell the reader to see a footnote for important information.
3. *Be direct and specific, not vague and general.*

   Vague, General: Production has been hampered by the physical separation of related work units (from a proposal to remodel the floorplan of a factory).

   Direct, Specific: The company loses $400 per day in lost time as employees from the graphic and the word-processing units walk the 70-yard path between their two related work areas.

   Vague, General: In the past, our company has had success marketing floral fragrances (from a proposal to market a new perfume).

FIGURE 11–2   Using Topic Headings and Insert Material for Effect

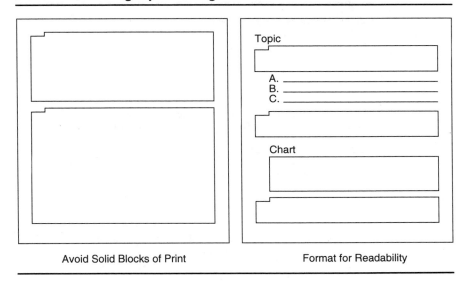

Avoid Solid Blocks of Print   Format for Readability

Direct, Specific: Since 1995, our company has marketed "Orchid Memories," "Gardenias in May," and "Roses Are Red." Each of these flower fragrances produced a profit margin of well over 56 percent in the first nine months of sales.

Proposals are the primary means by which businesses ask for work to do, for money to earn. The proposal requires the writer's sharpest writing skills whether it be long or short. Business writers who demonstrate the ability to write winning proposals reap substantial professional and financial rewards. These writers quickly make themselves indispensable in businesses small and large. A sample proposal appears at the end of this chapter.

The Form Proposal/Contract

In many trades and professions, a standard proposal form is used for making bids and giving estimates on jobs. This form is often worded so that, once signed by the client, it becomes a contract. The words for the proposal can be stored on disk and altered as necessary to meet the needs of individual bids. For very standard proposal/contract forms, a company may use a form such as the one shown in Figure 11–3.

Business Plans

A wide range of proposals for creating or restructuring a business are called "business plans." These documents may be as short as a few pages (communicating a business concept, for example) or as long as a thick book (including financial information, product or service descriptions, corporate officers' biographical sketches, etc.). Whether short or long,

FIGURE 11–3 Combined Proposal Contract

Combined Proposal and Contract

Date: _____

To: _____
  _____
  _____

The undersigned contractor hereby proposes to supply all necessary materials and perform labor required for the completion of the following:

_____

_____

_____

_____

_____

_____

_____

_____

It is furthermore provided that the proposed work shall be completed in keeping with standard industry quality standards and

_____

_____

(fill in any inspections or certifications required for completion)

Upon completion, the undersigned contractor shall be paid the sum of

_____($_____).

The terms and specifics of this proposal are valid until _____ and may not be altered except by mutual agreement in writing by the under-signed parties. Work will begin no later than _____ days after acceptance of this proposal/contract. The estimated completion date is _____.

This proposal and contract is submitted by:

_____

_____

_____

License no. _____

Acceptance of the Proposed Work
The work proposed by the above-named contractor is hereby accepted, in-cluding the terms described herein together with any attachments included by reference.

_____

(signature)

_____

(printed name)

_____

_____

(address)
Date of acceptance: _____

all business plans attempt to answer seven questions for the prudent investor or authorizing executive:

1. What is the key information that I *need* to know about your business plan?
2. What is the basic idea of your business?
3. What products or services will your (proposed) business produce or provide?
4. How will you sell your products or services?
5. How will you organize and manage your business?
6. How will your company's finances be handled?
7. What do you want from me (your reader)?

Key Information

In the executive summary of the business plan, you describe the following information as concisely as possible:

- What kind of business activity you intend to pursue
- Why your business appears financially attractive
- Who will manage and staff your organization
- Where you will base your business
- How much money your business will require for start-up and other costs
- What an investor or authorizing company can expect to gain for its support.

Basic Idea

Begin the body of the business plan by explaining and justifying the business concept itself. Describe the parts or processes involved in the concept. Relate the concept to all necessary background information about how the concept was started. Be sure to mention how your product or service compares with your competitors' and show why yours will be more profitable.

Products and Services

Specifically describe the products or services generated by your business concept. Pictures and other graphics may be particularly useful in this portion of the business plan. Really sell your product or service. Bear in mind that if you don't sell it in your business plan, you may never sell it anywhere else.

Marketing and Sales

Give a detailed account of your marketing strategies for the business. Tell who will be likely to buy your products or services and why. Back up your assertions with marketing data, demographic information, and other supportive evidence. The more specific you can be about the clients or customers to whom you will sell your service or product, the more your reader(s) will be tempted to buy your business plan.

Business Organization

Describe what kind of organization you will establish to produce your products or services. Define how the company will be managed and run. If your officers or managers have exceptional qualifications, be sure to mention them. Show that the efficient and intelligent management of your company will maximize the profits from your company.

Company Finances

Specify how much money will be required, and at what stages, for start-up costs. Provide a rationale for how money will be spent. Describe how profits and potential losses will be treated with regard to investors. Be as specific and realistic as you can possibly be, but be sure to highlight the positive aspects.

What You Want

Give specifics of the business offering itself, including how much money you are seeking from investors and in what installments. Describe the investors' degree of liability for company operations and the terms of their financial participation in company profits.

In a business world in which more than four-fifths of new businesses have gone broke by their fifth anniversary, a business plan must forcefully persuade attractive investors to take a risk. One venture capital firm received 1200 business plans over a period of months for funding consideration. Of that number, the firm selected only 45 for serious interest, and of that number, only 14 were eventually funded—a little over 1 in 100. In that kind of competitive environment, only the strongest business plans survive.

SUMMARY

1. Effective proposals depend on accurately analyzing the readers.

2. Both logical and psychological order are crucial to successful proposals.

3. Good news and bad news must be placed strategically in proposals.

4. A business plan provides information that potential investors need in order to decide whether to invest.

5. A business plan answers the questions what, who, where, why, when, and how much?

QUESTIONS FOR DISCUSSION

1. What does a business proposal do?

2. Why is logical reasoning a crucial part of any proposal?

3. What are the psychological effects of bad news and good news in a proposal?

4. Where should bad news and good news be placed in a proposal for persuasive effect?

5. Why should the proposal writer steer a middle course between general and specific evidence in supporting points?

6. Why should a proposal writer follow existing guidelines published by the person or organization requesting the proposal?

7. Why is it important for proposals to be visually attractive?

8. In what ways are proposals crucial to the process of winning contracts and promoting new ideas?

9. What is the logical flaw of "non sequitur"? Give an example.

10. What is the logical flaw of "straw man"? Give an example.

11. Why does the problem analysis usually precede the proposal's specifics?

12. What are the purposes of a business plan?

EXERCISES

1. Create an outline for a proposal to provide some product or service.

2. Write an executive summary for the proposal described in Exercise 1.

3. Write a cover letter (or letter of transmittal) to accompany the proposal described in Exercise 1. Address your letter to an appropriate reader.

4. Define some problem in your community (traffic bottlenecks, poor street lighting, industrial noise, etc.). In the role of a contractor, write a short proposal to your city government or some other agency for solving the problem.

5. A federal agency has advertised its request for proposals to provide durable eye-shields for military personnel. List five questions you would want answered before developing your proposal to meet this need.

6. In the role of a city administrator, write a letter accepting the proposal submitted in Exercise 4.

7. In the role of a city administrator, write a letter turning down the proposal submitted in Exercise 4.

8. In the role of a city administrator, write a letter asking for revision of certain terms in the proposal submitted in Exercise 4.

9. Write the last paragraph of the proposal described in Exercise 1.

10. Create a title page for the proposal described in Exercise 1.

INTERNET ASSIGNMENT

Unlike many of your classmates who entered traditional careers upon graduation, you and two friends are determined to carry through an entrepreneurial dream to produce a consumer product (of your selection—make up details as necessary). You have the expertise you require, but you lack the cash to undertake the development of a prototype and to put your idea into production. To learn how to write a successful business plan to present to potential investors, use the Specific Business Documents section of the Internet Guide. Since you will also be presenting your ideas orally to investors, also explore the Oral Presentations section. Then write the outline for a cogent business plan designed to convince investors of the worth and profitability of your proposed venture.

A Shuttle Service for State University

proposed to
The Board of Trustees
State University

Submitted by

Student Body Association

*May 16, 199_*

EXECUTIVE SUMMARY

The Student Body Association urges the Board of Trustees to approve the expenditure of $36,000 for a one-semester pilot test of a student/faculty shuttle bus at State University. The shuttle would alleviate parking problems, increase safety, reduce air pollution, and save money both for the university and for its members. The Student Body Association offers its human and financial resources in support of the pilot project.

Overview

Each year university administrators, faculty, staff, and students share a common complaint: too little parking on campus. Because most student living quarters and faculty homes do not lie within comfortable walking distance, particularly during the winter, most members of the university community drive a car to campus. A Student Body Association survey during fall semester, 199_, showed 2945 automobiles being driven to campus each weekday. Sixty-eight percent of those automobiles traveled less than two miles to campus from home. The great majority (82 percent) contained only one person. Arriving on campus, these drivers found limited and expensive ($138 per semester) parking.

The Student Body Association proposes a shuttle bus service from student and faculty living areas within a two-mile radius of the campus.

Aspects of the Parking Problem at State University

Bounded as it is by residential properties, State University has little chance to expand auxiliary parking areas in the coming years. Nor can a significant portion of campus land be converted to parking because of building plans already approved in the university's master plan.

Therefore, we must consider the university's 2475 student/faculty/staff parking places relatively fixed for the coming years.

Too Many Cars for Too Few Spaces

These 2475 spaces cannot accommodate the estimated 3000 cars per day driven to campus, even though 96 percent of this number have purchased on-campus parking permits. The overflow of approximately 350 cars per day (allowing for half-day parking use of spaces) must currently find parking in residential neighborhoods. This necessity has led to sixteen written complaints by university neighbors to City Hall in the past six months. Clearly, the neighborhoods surrounding State University do not wish to become auxiliary parking lots for students, faculty, and staff.

Walking Is Impractical for Most Students

At recent public hearings on the parking problem, university administrators have cited the Student Body Association survey showing that 68 percent of university commuters drive less than two miles to campus. Could not a substantial portion of those commuters, administrators asked, simply walk to school?

On April 7, 199_, the Student Body Association completed a poll of 500 such university members, selected randomly. Only 9 percent indicated a willingness to walk to campus and, of that number, 76 percent said they would walk only occasionally. Reasons cited by 91 percent who said they would not consider walking include

- difficulty in transporting books and school materials.
- discomfort in bad weather.
- use of an on-campus car for storing books, calculators, gym clothing, and so forth.
- time constraints (leaving campus for a job, etc.).

The parking problem, we can safely conclude, will not be resolved by a sudden willingness of State University students, faculty, and staff to walk to campus.

A Proposal to Relieve the Parking Problem

The Student Body Association urges the Board of Trustees, at their next regular meeting, to approve the expenditure of $36,000 for a one-semester pilot test of a shuttle service. As detailed below, the shuttle bus would serve students, faculty, and staff within a two-mile radius of the campus.

Transportation consultants donating their services to the Student Body Association estimate that such a shuttle service, operating from 7 a.m. to 7 p.m. weekdays, could provide transportation for approximately 400 students per day. That number exceeds the overflow now using neighborhoods around the university for parking.

A student, faculty, and staff survey completed April 30, 199_, by the Student Body Association showed that 86 percent of a random sample of 500 participants indicated a strong willingness to use shuttle transportation to the university if the cost per ride were 50 cents or less.

We project with some confidence, therefore, that a shuttle pilot program would be accepted by members of the university and would relieve the current parking problem. If the pilot program proves successful, the concept can be replicated for several shuttle busses, each earning its own way from rider revenues.

Budgetary Considerations

An expenditure of $36,000 will allow the Student Body Association to take the following steps:

1. Rent a state-approved 35 passenger shuttle bus for six months . . . .$ 6,000.

2. Pay two drivers' wages and benefits for six months . . . .$24,000.

3. Pay for garage expenses, upkeep, and contingencies . . . .$ 6,000.

$$\text{Total Expenditure} \qquad \$36,000$$

We project that a conservative rate of 400 paying rides per weekday at 50 cents per ride, the bus will produce gross revenues of $1000 per week, netting approximately $400 after gas and oil expenses. It is the intention of the Student Body Association to apply this net profit to the repayment of the $36,000 pilot fund. Over the course of six months (26 weeks), this repayment can amount to as much as $10,400 (26 weeks × $400 net profit per week). If the shuttle bus becomes more popular than we have estimated, the repayment figure will be even higher.

The Student Body Association agrees to repay the $36,000 expenditure in full from profits arising out of a shuttle service growing out of a pilot program before any profits are distributed to the Association itself.

Conclusion

Because it offers the best alternative for alleviating the severe parking problem faced by members of the university, the Shuttle Pilot Program deserves the serious consideration of the Board of Trustees.

The Officers of the Student Body Association will be happy to elaborate upon aspects of this proposal and to answer questions of the Board. We look forward to working with you in serving the needs of our mutual constituency.

EXAMPLE BUSINESS PLAN

TeleCycle

A Business Plan

prepared for

Armstrong Funding Associates
Salt Lake City, Utah

by

Richard R. Foster
Michelle Ames

January 15, 1998

(Proprietary)

EXECUTIVE SUMMARY

Americans will purchase 5,500,000 new telephones in 1999 for business and residential use. In the process, they will dispose of approximately 3,000,000 telephones in good working order. These are typically the black or white telephones popular in the 1980s. They are literally thrown away in the trash or stored in perpetuity on back shelves of American garages and storage rooms. This trend can be expected to continue throughout the 1990s as new advances in telephone technology and design cause increasing numbers of Americans to replace their present telephones.

TeleCycle, as proposed in this business plan, represents a highly profitable channel for recycling these telephones to foreign markets and both domestic and international industrial uses. Just as glass, paper, and aluminum recyclers have popularized the profitable reclamation of these materials, so we believe that the TeleCycle plan will persuade Americans by the millions to trade, not trash, their present telephones.

The method of operation is straightforward. TeleCycle representatives will contract with major telephone suppliers (GTE, The Phone Store, Circuit City, Home Depot, Builder's Emporium, K-Mart, and major department stores) to advertise $5 off the purchase price of a new telephone with the trade-in of an older phone in any condition. TeleCycle will reimburse these suppliers on a 50 percent basis—that is, $2.50 for every telephone delivered to TeleCycle. (Extensive test marketing has demonstrated that major suppliers are quite willing to absorb a $2.50 per sale expense if they can easily dispose of the traded telephones.)

TeleCycle will, in turn, refurbish and repair these telephones before selling them, in lots of 100, to foreign markets. Unrepairable telephones will be disassembled for usable materials to be sold for domestic and international industrial use. Market research has defined a large and untapped foreign market for working telephones in the $6 to $8 range per unit.

Based on this market potential, TeleCycle will begin proposed operations with an initial capitalization of $400,000, 25 percent of which is already on deposit as the contribution of the principals to the business. The business seeks twelve investment units of $25,000 each to accrue the remaining $300,000. Each unit will earn 4 percent of the company's net profit per year, in perpetuity, for a total investor interest in the company of 48 percent. The principals will retain a 52 percent share of profits.

I. The Business Concept

Recycling has proven to be one of the most popular and profitable industries of the 1990s, as Americans become more sensitized and motivated by environmental concerns. Glass recycling, for example, has grown to a $2 billion business, with average profits per major firm in the 12–14 percent range. Aluminum recycling showed a $234 million total profit for six companies in fiscal 1998.

The TeleCycle concept involves a similar appeal to the American people to recycle what they are no longer using—their old telephones. These units are omnipresent on the storage shelves of American homes and businesses. By the Consumer Report estimate of 1998, Americans are now storing over 11 million telephones. The vast majority of these will find their way eventually to the trash.

At the same time, Americans are buying new telephones in record numbers. Consumer Reports estimates that 5.5 million telephones will be sold by major distributors in 1999. In most cases, these customers could—and generally would like to—carry in their old telephones for a $5 credit toward their purchase.

Working closely with major distributors acting as collection centers for these telephones, TeleCycle will then repair or disassemble the units for resale. We project primary markets for repaired telephones to be Central America, South America, Africa, China, and Russia.

II. TeleCycle Products and Services

TeleCycle will contract with major new telephone distributors to pay a flat $2.50 rate per traded unit and to pick up these units from the distributors' central collection site.

Based on test market studies, we estimate that 70 percent of the traded telephones will be in good working order and will require only cleansing before being packed for shipment and sale. Of the remaining 30 percent, we estimate that half will be easily repairable (less than $2 in parts and 10 minutes in technician time) and the other half valuable only for parts and raw materials.

All evaluation, sorting, repair, and packing of telephones will take place at TeleCycle's proposed dockside warehouse in San Francisco.

III. The Business Process

At least eleven foreign countries maintain open orders, through governmental and private sources, for as many telephones as they can purchase in the $6 to $8 range. Depending on international availability, used telephone prices in the period 1988 to 1998 have ranged from a low of $4.50 to a high of $14. For the next five years, we project an average wholesale price per unit to be $8 and have based our financial structure on that conservative projection.

TeleCycle will make contact with major buyers of telephone equipment in selected foreign countries through their commercial officers, attached to embassies in Washington, D.C. Preliminary contacts with ten such officers have provided us with several bona fide purchase offers for used telephones in large lots. We also have had strong interest in the purchase of telephone parts and recyclable materials from domestic and international industries.

IV. The Marketing Plan

TeleCycle will market its services in four distinct ways:

1. Decision-makers at a wide range of new telephone distribution sources will be initially contacted by a professionally prepared prospectus and proposal, delivered by express mail.

2. Followup calls will be made by the TeleCycle principals and their representatives to bring these distributors aboard as contracted partners.

3. Advance advertising through foreign trade journals, magazines, and other media will alert foreign buyers to this new, substantial source for used telephones. The wave of their interest, in turn, will be used as evidence to further convince American distributors to join the program.

4. As soon as a limited number of distributors have contracted with TeleCycle, the company will begin a nationwide publicity campaign, primarily through newspaper and radio advertisements, to alert Americans to recycle their telephones. Our initial contacts with the Environmental Protection Agency and the American Advertising Council have given us strong reason to believe that many of these advertisements may be carried as low-cost public interest ads.

Once a stable network of distributors is in place, TeleCycle will employ a field staff of commissioned salespeople in carefully selected countries and regions to seek out quantity buyers of used telephone equipment.

V. Financial Information

Capital Outlay

Of the first-year $400,000 capitalization, approximately equal fourths will be assigned for the following uses:

$100,000	Staff salaries for two technicians and two secretaries. (The principals will not draw salary during the first year of operations.)
$100,000	Warehouse and office leasing and furnishing, two transport vans, overhead.
$100,000	Printing, advertising.
$100,000	Operations.

Projected Income

Based on a profit percentage of 60 percent (after repair and shipping expenses) for each used telephone unit sold, TeleCycle projects the following volume and revenues for the next three years:

Year	Units Sold	Gross Income	Net Profit
Start-up	90,000	$ 720,000	$ 432,000
2	200,000	$1,600,000	$ 930,000
3	340,000	$2,720,000	$1,632,000

Based on these projections, an investor holding a 4 percent share of net profit could expect, for the $25,000 investment, a first-year payout of $17,280, a second-year payout of $37,200, and a third-year payout of $65,280, with successive years following a similar upward curve.

VI. Management

TeleCycle will be directed by two MBAs with substantial experience in the telephone industry.

(Brief bios appear here for Richard Foster and Michelle Ames.)

VII. Specifics of the Business Offering

For investors interested in one or more units (at $25,000 per unit) of this venture, we will be pleased to provide copies of a contractual limited partnership agreement. Upon investor approval of the document, we request payment in the form of a cashier's check payable to TeleCycle, Inc. Individual investors may each own up to four units. The company seeks to place a total of twelve units with investors.

Thank you for your interest in the TeleCycle business concept and plan. The principals will be pleased to meet with individual investors or their representatives.

PART FOUR

CAREER
COMMUNICATION

CHAPTER 12

The Career Search, Résumés, and Interviews

The first decade of the new century promises to be an ideal period for finding the right job. The U.S. Bureau of Labor Statistics estimates that 21 million new jobs will be filled during this decade. Two-thirds of all new job applicants will be women. The members of the "baby-bust" generation, that relatively small group of college graduates from the one- and two-child homes of the 1960s and 1970s, are likely to be hired in large numbers. However, even when there are many career opportunities, you'll still have to know how to find the job and the company that are right for you. Also, you may have to work hard to find the job you want, and you'll definitely have to write well in order to get it. Your first step is to find the job you want.

FINDING THE JOB

Your training, interests, and abilities determine the general field of your job search. However, because jobs and job descriptions often change, you may not know exactly what job you want to get. The very process of job hunting may help you to decide on a career. A finance major, of course, rarely strays into a career as a surgeon. Still, finance majors often do find themselves in a wide variety of interesting jobs that they might not have expected to have. Look at the help-wanted ads, and try to find as many different kinds of jobs that you might qualify for. Broaden your horizons.

Keeping Track of Your Job Leads

Create a systematic way of keeping track of your job search. For example, you might keep a file of $3'' \times 5''$ cards modeled after the card shown in Figure 12–1. Use this file to prevent yourself from accidentally applying to the same place twice or making other em-

FIGURE 12–1   Record Card for Job Search

Position _____ Date _____

Company _____

Address _____

_____

Phone_____

Contact name _____

Action taken _____ (date)

Response received _____ (date)

Notes:

barrassing mistakes. You may, at any one time, have as many as 50 résumés circulating in the professional world. A file keeps your many fishing lines from becoming tangled.

If you have access to a computer, you may want to use it to store your job-lead information. Several recordkeeping software programs allow you to store names, addresses, and comments for each of your job leads. Most word-processing programs, spreadsheet programs, or database programs could also be adapted for this purpose. Contact a college computer center or a local computer store for recommendations. Once you have set up a system, consider various job sources.

Tips and Introductions from Friends

Personal referrals (that is, someone you know who might know someone who has a job opening) continue to work magic for job seekers. Managers who have no time at all for interviewing might find a few minutes to see you because "Frank" or "Sue" called to say how bright you were. The brief interview later turns into a job offer. One way to get these contacts is to let every one of your friends and acquaintances know that you are looking for a job. Speak freely about the broad range of your interests. Ask friends and acquaintances to let you know if they hear of an opening or of someone who is resigning or retiring from a job in your field.

Some job seekers have personal business cards printed up for this purpose. While friends may have your phone number and address, the large number of casual acquaintances in your life may not. If they have your card, they can let you know when a job possibility arises.

Career Opportunities with Former Employers

Review career opportunities in companies for whom you have worked part-time or during the summer. Even if your temporary or part-time job wasn't in your career field, don't overlook the career possibilities at that company. Many companies take pride in bringing someone along from the bottom of the ladder. Your experience even in the most mundane company responsibility may give you an important step up over the competition when it comes time for selecting management trainees. The company knows you, and you know the company.

Visit Personnel Offices

Stop by the personnel office of companies that interest you. Ask about job openings, and pick up application packets. Personnel officers do not mind seeing you as an uninvited visitor as long as you do not press them for what they cannot provide: instant evaluations of your chances for a job, definitive lists of what positions are available in the company, or a willingness to interview you.

You visit the personnel office of a company simply to express your interest in any openings they have and to pick up any materials they routinely give away to interested job seekers. Of course, you could also do this by mail, with less effort. However, that's just the point: by visiting for just a moment or two in person, you show more effort than the average job seeker. Secretaries in the office and perhaps even the personnel director see your face, shake your hand. Later, when your résumé arrives for review, they might remember you.

While visiting the personnel office, find out (and jot down the exact spelling) of the personnel director's name, or any other company official to whom you plan to write your letter. Record these names in your file. Mail that is addressed to a named person usually gets opened and read by that person. Mail that is addressed to a title or office (Personnel Director or Personnel Office) often is opened and read by a secretary.

You also have an additional reason to go to the personnel office personally: you might just get lucky and show up just when they need you. Many job seekers have literally walked into a job on their first visit to a personnel office. If the company's personnel office is within driving range of your home, stop by. The crucial key, again, is not to ask for too much.

College Placement

Make use of nearby college placement services. Participate in any workshops in interviewing skills, résumé preparation, and application procedures they may offer. Companies seeking new employees in your area work closely with the campus placement office. They often send representatives to your campus to interview prospective employees. Sign up for such interviews.

Find out whether the college department in your field maintains a file of help-wanted notices from business and industry. Departments such as marketing, finance, accounting, and management frequently receive invitations from local companies to send graduates for interviews. These notices sometimes are posted on bulletin boards for you to see, but often they are filed, and you'll have to ask about them.

Every year, *The College Placement Annual* lists more than 1000 employers who are seeking entry-level employees. For many of these companies, the annual contains specific job descriptions, salary ranges, and information on company projects and policies. Your local or college library or placement office will have the latest edition; if not, the annual can be purchased at major bookstores in the early spring of each year.

Using Ads

Advertisements are another helpful source of information regarding what jobs may be available in your field or in your community. In general, these ads fall into one of three categories:

1. Help wanted ads (usually in newspapers or other periodicals, such as magazines)

2. Job wanted ads

3. Public agency listings

Newspaper and Magazine Help-Wanted Ads

These advertisements can be read by anyone, but you have to be able to understand a few things they don't say in order to use them effectively. Essentially, there are three kinds of help wanted ads:

• Company ads

• Agency ads

• Blind ads

Company Ads.   The most common ads are *company advertisements*, in which the name and address of the company are clearly stated, sometimes accompanied by a contact name ("Ms. Barker") for those interested in making application.

COMPANY AD

> LANGSFORD MEDICAL CO., INC., an industry leader in hospital and doctor supply, seeks an Inventory Analyst. Experience in computer inventory systems required, with medical knowledge helpful. Salary commensurate with experience. Top benefits, potential advancement. Apply to Box 4563, Willowborough, New Hampshire 39574

Agency Ads.   Also common are *agency ads* placed by private employment agencies that receive percentages of the salaries of employees for whom they get jobs. Agency ads typically describe positions more glamorously than company ads: "Outstanding opportunity . . . unlimited potential . . . truly exceptional benefits package." They are much more like regular commercial ads. Often they aren't offering a job as much as they're trying to sell you the agency's services. Only answer agency ads if you know exactly what you're buying.

AGENCY AD

> READY TO TAKE CHARGE?
> Great opportunity for motivated person with sales background to head up regional commission sales group. Salary plus bonus incentives. Some travel. Call Gil Branch, 592-3942. Equal Opportunity Employer.

Blind Ads. You'll also see *blind ads*, some placed by the country's best corporations and some placed by fly-by-night liars and con artists. A typical blind ad does not specify a company, a location, or an agency.

National company seeks reliable management trainees for expansion territory in Sun Belt. Knowledge of mass marketing techniques essential, college degree optional depending on experience. Send resume to Drawer 92, *Los Angeles Times*.

Very reputable companies sometimes run blind ads for a number of good reasons. For example, they might not want their present employees to know that they're planning to hire supervisory staff from the "outside." The company may not want its competitors to know about their plans or their personnel. Perhaps the company is protecting its public image by not showing that it needs qualified personnel immediately. Hospitals, for example, often run blind ads when they seek nurses, administrators, and support personnel.

On the other hand, a blind ad can be used to snare unwary job seekers. Just how realistic do you suppose that blind ad #2 is?

BLIND AD #2

Don't read on unless you're determined to make at least $60,000 this year, and twice that amount next year. We're seeking men and women who fit in socially, who present themselves well, who like to set and meet their own goals. We provide full training. Write to Box 523, *New York Times*, for an appointment with Mr. Blackley.

If you checked into it, you would discover (after investing time and energy) that the ad was placed by Mr. Blackley himself, who—virtually out of a briefcase—runs a business he calls "Psychonetics." He meets you in the lounge of a fancy hotel and starts giving you his pitch. (He doesn't invite you to his office because he doesn't have one.) For $2500, he'll let you in on the ground floor of the greatest thing since sliced bread. "Psychonetics" teaches professional people to unleash their hidden psychic strengths, thereby mastering those around them. Your job? To offer "Psychonetics" franchises to others, on a commission basis. Mr. Blackley estimates that you could easily make $60,000 your first year.

Beware of blind ads. If you answer them, judge your first contact (whether a letter or phone call) with the advertiser with care. At the first sign of being asked to make "an investment" or "buy your samples" or otherwise spend your money to get a job, you may want to run in the other direction. Go back to your primary goal: finding a satisfying career.

Job-Wanted Ads

Some job seekers place ads on their own in such business publications as the *Wall Street Journal*, *Business Week*, and large urban newspapers. Although these ads are usually quite expensive, they occasionally bring worthwhile responses. Look over such ads in business newspapers and trade journals. Before advertising yourself, you may want to call one of the advertisers to ask whether they got the responses they wanted for their money.

Public Agency Ads

Public agencies (usually listed under *employment* in the white or yellow pages of your phone directory) provide free job listings. Often these offer temporary or day-labor positions. Don't ignore these altogether. If you can get a job lead from any source, take it.

WRITING YOUR APPLICATION LETTER AND RÉSUMÉ

Once you find the job you want, you'll have to take the time to write effectively to get the job. In fact, in questioning more than 20 chief executive officers of major corporations about their own writing attitudes and experiences, we asked "Do you recall a particular writing task that changed the course of your career?"

A few recalled particular letters, reports, and proposals that had marked career turning points, but most named the writing they did when trying to get a new job. For example, here are three typical responses:

I spent a whole day composing a bright, direct letter to accompany my résumé. That letter, along with good luck, started me on my way.

The time and effort I spent on my résumé probably made the single largest contribution to my initial career opportunities.

Believe it or not, the most important piece of writing I did at the beginning of my career was two paragraphs long: the brief essay I had to write as part of my job application. I took time to do it right and received praise—and a job—from those who interviewed me.

Like these executives, you may find that career communications are the most important business writing you'll ever do. It is no accident that so many aspects of searching for and applying for a job require you to write well. Once you have the job, you will be expected to write well in order to succeed in the company. Further, what you write will have the company's letterhead on it. What you write as a company employee will represent not only your image but also your company's image.

Naturally, a company that hires you wants to make sure that you know how to present a professional and competent image through your writing. Therefore, almost every company asks new job applicants to submit résumés and letters as part of the job-seeking process. In essence, the résumés and applications letters you send to prospective job-offering companies are sales letters—you are selling both your job skills and your writing abilities. The company that hires you is buying both.

The Application Letter

The personnel directors of Fortune 500 companies strongly prefer that people who want to apply for jobs should do so in writing before they try to get telephone or face-to-face interviews. That preference makes sense. Without looking at your résumé, they can't really tell you anything. Whatever they say before they see your written application may have to be taken back, once your record lies open.

Begin the application process, therefore, not with a telephone call but with an application letter accompanied by a résumé.

Letters of application, like other business letters, are typed on $8^1/_2''$ by $11''$ white or off-white bond paper. Don't use colorful stationery. When your materials are photocopied by the company, such stationery does not reproduce well.

The Invited Application Letter

An *invited* application letter (one that responds to a company advertisement or other offering of a job opening) opens by making reference to the position described in the ad and where the ad was seen. See the letter in Figure 12–2, for example.

Note that the letter of application typically has three parts:

1. Clear response to a clear invitation. The invitation is mentioned, in case the company has several job openings advertised in various places.

FIGURE 12–2 Invited Letter of Application

4857 Birch Road, Apt. 3
Glenview, IL 59684

August 9, 199_

Ms. Gloria Hrief
Personnel Director
Benway Manufacturing, Inc.
400 Railway Center Drive
Glenview, IL 59684

Dear Ms. Hrief:

As a June graduate in Accounting from Illinois State University, I am delighted to answer your advertisement (*Register*, August 8) for an entry level accountant in your farm equipment division.

You may be interested not only in my accounting preparation and experience, as described in the enclosed résumé, but also in my summer employment driving Benway tractors on my uncle's farm.

If my application merits an interview for this position or another in your company, please write or call (555-3948). I look forward to meeting you.

Sincerely,

Robert Collins

Robert Collins

2. Reference to the attached résumé, with a highlight or two pointed out in a polite way.

3. Appeal for an interview, with contact address and phone number.

Communication Insights	Does the business world care about the level of your writing skills? Listen to Paul Dillingham, vice-president of the Coca-Cola Company:

> In today's complex society, the ability to communicate effectively is essential. I am appalled at the number of graduates coming out of our universities in recent years who cannot compose a simple, readable letter. I recently saw an application for employment by a college graduate who neglected to answer a number of important questions on the form. Surely he will have difficulty finding a job.

Application letters, according to personnel directors, should be short and to the point. The reader is eager to get on to the résumé where your story will be told in close detail.

The Uninvited Application Letter

An *uninvited* letter of application requires a more creative opening. You are writing, after all, to a company official who has not told you that a job is even open. You begin, therefore, by breaking the ice, as shown in the letter in Figure 12–3.

The uninvited application letter moves immediately to the "you" perspective—something in the first sentence that interests or involves the reader. That you are seeking a job and you work hard is not particularly interesting to the reader who has not even asked you to apply for a job.

The following are some ways of beginning with the "you" perspective:

- Mention a common name, such as someone who may have put you in contact with the reader.
- Mention common professional interests or products.
- Mention developments in the company that you have observed, either from your reading or from your experience with company products or services.
- Express appreciation for the moment or two of the reader's time necessary to consider your qualifications.

The letter of application can demonstrate to the reader that you are a polite, literate, and persuasive person. The letter should not try to outdo or redo the résumé itself by rehearsing a number of work experiences or accomplishments. Select one or two of your most impressive or interesting achievements, and weave them smoothly into the course of the application letter so as not to appear to brag.

In the final paragraph of the uninvited letter of application, consider leaving the door open for something less than a job interview. If a company has no openings at the moment, the manager may still wish to make your acquaintance with an eye toward future openings. Make it clear that you would enjoy meeting even though there may be no openings right now.

FIGURE 12–3 Uninvited Letter of Application

Brenda Noel
247 Levitt Street
Walston, AL 66644

June 2, 199_

Mr. Herbert Reid
Manager, Software Systems
ATC Autonetics
577 First Street
Walston, AL 66644

Dear Mr. Reid:

Your advertisements in *Byte* magazine during the past few months reveal rapid expansion in ATC software products. If your need for state-of-the-art software specialists is also expanding, my enclosed résumé may interest you.

My senior project was written in LISP—a language offering great potential for ATC's work in artificial intelligence—and I also have worked extensively in systems using FORTRAN 77, COBOL, and various forms of BASIC, which may be needed for interfacing with and updating various existing software programs.

I would like very much to meet with you to discuss how I may be of service to your organization. Perhaps we can also discuss your vision of the high-tech advances that interest both of us. I will call next Friday to see whether we may arrange to meet at a time that is convenient for you. Please feel free to call me at 555-7689, to discuss any questions or comments you may have or to arrange a meeting. I look forward to speaking with you.

Sincerely,

Brenda Noel

Brenda Noel

The Résumé

The most important guidelines for the job-application process can be summed up as follows:

1. Use a cover letter of application
2. Keep your résumé to one or two pages if possible.
3. Eliminate typos and other mistakes.
4. Use "at-a-glance" appeal to attract attention to your résumé.
5. Match the style of your résumé to the job and the company you want.
6. Highlight the major categories of the résumé.
7. Choose the form of the résumé that fits you best.

8. Tailor the résumé to the job you're trying to get.
9. Use your résumé to highlight your best features for the job you want.

Use a Cover Letter of Application

If you mail your résumé, always cover it with a letter of application. A letter of application helps to provide the friendly opening that a handshake might provide in a face-to-face meeting. The preceding section described the other benefits of a cover letter of application.

One Page Is Best

Keep your résumé limited to one page if possible. Use two pages only if absolutely necessary. You want to highlight your best features in order to get an interview. Don't bore the reader with details that you can give in your interview if they seem appropriate.

Eliminate Typos and Other Mistakes

Don't permit any typos or other mistakes to appear in your résumé. Recently, the head of a writing and editorial service received an application from a college graduate asking for work as an assistant. In the résumé describing her experience and her abilities, she included a spelling error. Needless to say, she was not even interviewed for the position.

Writing mistakes may not be quite that crucial to the job you seek. However, because your résumé is supposed to show you at your best, the people who look at your résumé might think, "If this person makes mistakes on the résumé, just imagine how many mistakes will be made on the job! I don't want this person on my payroll."

If at all possible, use a word processor so that you won't have to retype your résumé each time you notice a mistake or need to make changes. Ask a friend or someone whose opinion you value to proofread your résumé before you let prospective employers see it.

Use "At-a-Glance" Appeal

Attract your readers' attention to your résumé at first glance. Look at the résumé formats in Figure 12–4. Both clearly emphasize categories of information with subordinated details.

Here are some techniques used to create résumés with at-a-glance appeal:

• Make headings parallel in meaning also parallel on the page.
• Surround important headings with white space.
• Allow the eye to read separate sections of print, not large dense blocks of type.
• Use capitals only on one or two words at a time for special emphasis.
• Use lines and small graphic symbols (bullets, asterisks, dashes) to unify and organize the résumé.

FIGURE 12–4   Two Résumé Formats

NAME
ADDRESS
TELEPHONE

CAREER OBJECTIVE
_____

EDUCATION
_____
_____

EMPLOYMENT
_____
_____
_____
_____

ACTIVITIES
_____
_____
_____

REFERENCES
_____
_____
_____

NAME
ADDRESS
TELEPHONE

CAREER   _____
OBJECTIVE

EDUCATION _____
            _____
            _____
            _____

EMPLOYMENT
            _____
            _____
            _____

ACTIVITIES
[or other   _____
category]   _____
            _____
            _____
            _____

REFERENCES

   _____   _____
   _____   _____
   _____   _____

   _____   _____
   _____   _____
   _____   _____

Match Your Style to Your Job

If you are applying for a business position, use a business style. Don't try to attract attention by being overly creative. Most personnel directors prefer an attractive but traditional résumé to a flashy one. This is particularly true for traditional kinds of businesses or jobs, such as finances-related jobs and managerial positions. It may be less so for jobs in advertising or other industries in which creativity would be valued. If you aren't sure how important creativity is in getting a particular job, go with a traditional résumé.

Highlight Crucial Elements

On a résumé, the four crucial elements to highlight are (1) name and address, (2) career objective, (3) education, and (4) employment experience. Even if you include other elements, make sure that these four can be seen quickly at a glance.

A special note about your telephone: if you are regularly away from your phone during business hours and have no answering machine or service, identify two numbers at the top of the résumé—your home number and a message number where the employer can be sure to reach someone during business hours. Probably thousands of job offers are lost each year because employers (who hate to write letters) have no luck reaching job applicants by telephone.

Choose the Form that Fits You Best

You have two choices: the chronological résumé and the functional résumé. As explained in the following pages, the chronological résumé (see Figure 12–5 organizes your experience according to years. If you have quite a bit of education but not a great deal of work experience, the chronological résumé allows you to highlight your academic work.

The functional résumé (see Figure 12–6) suits those who have proven their abilities through years of professional activity. It groups work experiences under two to four (seldom more) major abilities you have demonstrated over the years.

Tailor Your Résumé to the Job

Not all companies are alike, and not all jobs are alike. Make sure that the details of your résumé are finely tuned to match the particular job you're trying to get. If at all

---

COMMUNICATION FOR A NEW CENTURY

TWENTY RÉSUMÉ ERRORS THAT CAN KILL A JOB APPLICATION

1. Typographical errors and misspellings
2. Punctuation and usage errors
3. Difficult-to-read formats
4. Disorganized information
5. The presence of information that by law, the company cannot consider in its hiring decisions (e.g., your religion or race)
6. Omission of necessary names, dates, and other information
7. Misstatement or exaggeration of your college and work record
8. Inadequate contact information for your references
9. Too little résumé data to create a favorable impression
10. Too much résumé data, with the result that important features of your record become obscured
11. Outdated references that can't be contacted at the addresses you provide
12. Failure to attach a cover letter identifying the job for which you are applying
13. Outlandish experiments in font, format, and other appearance aspects of the résumé
14. Unnecessarily stiff or jargonized language
15. Unfamiliar terms, acronyms, and abbreviations
16. Vague information about degrees received or anticipated, jobs held, and other important data
17. Failure to tailor résumé information for a specific job and company
18. Poor photocopying or other form of duplication
19. Unwarranted focus on extraneous information (such as some high school sports activities and club memberships)
20. Unnecessary addition to your résumé of other documents and support materials not requested by the company

FIGURE 12–5 Chronological Résumé

Kikanza Brown

7614 Traverse Drive
Hartford, CT 10287
Home: (312) 555-2784 Message: (312) 555-6784

CAREER OBJECTIVE — To join McCoy/Adams Advertising as an entry-level accounts representative; with experience and training, I want to progress to a supervisory role in creative projects.

EDUCATION — Degrees

B.A. in Marketing
University of Washington
Degree expected June, 1998

Pertinent Coursework

Professional Selling   Retail Economics
Marketing Management   Advertising Strategies
International Marketing

G.P.A. 3.5 on 4-point scale

Awards and Scholarships

Laketon Art Scholarship, 1990
University of Washington Marketing Award, 1997

Future Educational Plans

After completing my B.A., I plan to enroll in an M.B.A. program during nonwork hours.
I am now enrolled in a B.A. program at the University of Washington.

EMPLOYMENT 1998 **Field representative,** Rent-a-Treasure Art, Inc., Hartford, Connecticut (part-time)

Responsibilities: Call on upscale corporate clients; rent, deliver, hang art in their offices; especially enjoy providing decorating advice

1997 **Store clerk,** Computer Village, Hartford, Connecticut

Responsibilities: Demonstrate products and closed sales on home computers

1996 **Designer, painter of super-graphics,** Weston Playhouse, Hartford, Connecticut (summer)

Responsibilities: designed and painted eight wall-sized panels

REFERENCES — Furnished upon request

FIGURE 12–6   Functional Résumé

CLIFFORD OWENS
9215 Branch Drive
Los Gatos, CA 90432
Home: (515) 767-4857 Message: 386-4968

CAREER OBJECTIVE

To join the Business Publications group at Metropolitan; after experience as a writer, to work into an editorial position.

EDUCATION

M.A. in English, Southern Methodist University, 1998
B.A. in Finance, Lester College, 1996
A.A. Sage Community College, Bridgeton, Texas, 1994

DEMONSTRATED ABILITIES

Ability to write well
    Instructor, Business Writing, Southern Methodist University, 1996–to present. Taught business memo, letter, proposal, and report writing.

    Member, Association for Business Communication.

    Ability to edit publications

    Assistant editor, *Neighbors* (Texas lifestyles), 1996, 1997

    Editor, *News and Views* (campus newspaper), Lester College, 1995

Knowledge of the insurance business

    Office manager, Allstate Insurance, Bridgeton, Texas, 1993–1994. Supervised six sales people. Served as area manager for the sales region.

    Insurance sales representative, Allstate Insurance, Bridgeton, Texas, 1991–1992. Sold auto, life, and fire policies; handled client claims.

References will be furnished upon request.

---

possible, match your skills and experience to the specific company to which you're applying.

For example, suppose that you're applying for two bookkeeping positions. One of them is in a huge Fortune 500 corporation, and the other is in a small nonprofit agency. In the résumé for the big company, highlight how well your experience and skills fit into a large department of fellow bookkeepers. In the other résumé, highlight the ways in which you'd take initiative to single-handedly tackle all bookkeeping tasks that might come your way.

When tailoring your résumé in this way, word processing comes to the rescue. With your résumé stored on disk, you can tailor it to suit quite different employers. In stating your career objective, for example, notice how you can appeal to a conservative corporate audience through more general language, yet customize your résumé also for less formal environments through personalized language:

GENERAL ABSTRACT
VERSION

CAREER OBJECTIVE:
Restaurant management, with eventual progress into corporate responsibilities

PERSONALIZED
VERSION

CAREER OBJECTIVE:
Begin as a management trainee in Auntie's Kitchen chain, and progress with experience to Franchise Representative

Businesses, like people, love to see their own names and interests in print. Satisfy that need by personalizing your résumé in any way possible.

Create your Résumé to Highlight Your Best

Your résumé should select those qualities that represent you at your highest potential—what you plan to be—instead of trying to state all the details of what you have been. Consider leaving out such extraneous matters as these:

- A brief job that has little to do with your application
- Personal facts that don't concern your employer
- Insignificant responsibilities listed under particular jobs
- College affiliations, memberships, societies, and sports teams that go beyond making the point that you are a social, likable, and active person

We can now examine the two most useful résumés in close detail.

The Chronological Résumé

Place your name at the top of the résumé, followed by your mailing address and telephone number. Note that your name is usually centered for eye-catching emphasis (Figure 12–5).

Stating Your Career Objective

In a prominent heading, write, "Career Objective" or "Career Goal." If you want to state more than one goal, write "Goals" or "Objectives."

You may want to state a two-part objective that shows you are realistic about an entry-level position, but you also want to grow professionally.

CAREER OBJECTIVE:
Beginning as a salesperson, I want to progress with experience to supervisory work on a regional level.

CAREER OBJECTIVE:
In the short term, client portfolio analysis, evaluation, and recommendation; in the long term, management of a pension fund trust

By such "short-term, long-term" statements, you have the best of both worlds. As much as possible, personalize the career objective of the résumé on each résumé you send out.

CAREER OBJECTIVE:
To begin in Henderson and Schmidt's Accounting division; with experience and further education, to supervise tax analysis and planning for major corporate clients.

CAREER OBJECTIVE:
To learn Northwest Bank's operations in the management training program; later, to work in a supervisory capacity in Northwest Bank's real estate loan sector.

If you cannot obtain specific information about the titles and hierarchies of job positions within a company, write more general objectives.

CAREER OBJECTIVE:
To work in cash flow management and economic analysis, with growing managerial responsibility

Describing Your Education

Begin by listing your most recent degree or certificate or highest level of education, then list other degrees and significant academic work.

B.A. in Economics, University of Pennsylvania, 1998
A.A., Windsor College, 1996
Certificates of Participation in two National Science
 Foundation Summer Seminars:
 "Solar Energy Alternatives," University of California
  at Davis, 1997
 "Geothermal Resources and Their Applications," Harvard
 University, 1996

You may choose to group information pertaining to one degree beneath that degree before moving on. Mention special competencies or accomplishments.

B.A. in Economics, University of Pennsylvania, 1998
 Senior thesis: "A Comparative Analysis of Coin-vs.
 Ticket-System Mass Transit Programs"

Don't get bogged down in details, though. Highlight the things that make you perfect for *this* job in *this* company.

If you have a good grade-point average (G.P.A.), mention it on your résumé. If you worked while getting your good grades, mention it. That impresses some employers.

Listing Awards and Scholarships

List any awards and scholarships you received. Place those items first that will be most meaningful and impressive to your reader. If you won a scholarship to college at the end of your high school years, you can list the scholarship by name and date.

Awards and Scholarships

Outstanding First-Year Student, School of Business, 1996
Chevron Scholarships, 1996–1997
Dean's List, 1996–1998
Rotary Club Tuition Award, 1996

Mentioning Future Educational Plans

This category is optional on your résumé, but you should consider its advantages. Your employer may be even more interested in your future than in your past. If you plan to acquire a new business skill, master another language, or work toward advanced degrees, why not say so?

Future Education Plans

I have begun taking courses at night toward my M.B.A. at Occidental College.

Be careful, however, not to give your potential employer the wrong impression that you're going to quit soon to return to college.

Describing Your Employment History

Begin by listing your most recent work experience, then previous jobs. When your job had a title (such as "night manager"), use it. If your job had no title, feel free to name the job within the bounds of truth (a recreation job might be titled "Swimming Instructor," but not "Nautical Locomotion Consultant"). Title this section, "Employment," or "Employment Experience," "Work Experience," "Employment Background," or "Experience."

EMPLOYMENT

1998–to present	Accounting Intern, Bliss and Wethers, Accountants,
	Boulder, Colorado (Jan.–May, part-time)
1996	Night Manager, Cleaver Restaurant
1995	Assembly Line Supervisor, Jay-Ray Cosmetics
1994	Assembly Line Worker, Jay-Ray Cosmetics

If your employment has been steady year by year, emphasize the dates by placing them first, as shown in Figure 12–5. If, on the other hand, you have had long employment gaps, give the dates less emphasis by placing them after the job listing.

EMPLOYMENT

Accounting Intern, Bliss and Wethers, Accountants,
    Boulder, Colorado, Jan.–May, 1998–to present. (part-time)
Night Manager, Cleaver Restaurant, 1998

You do not have to account for each and every month of your employed life on such a list. Employers, too, want to get to the heart of the matter: what *significant* experiences have you had?

If you have had virtually no paid work experience at all, list volunteer experiences related to business concerns. You can rename the Employment category as Experience. Perhaps you have helped to manage the financial affairs of a club at school or a church organization.

Under no circumstances should you simply skip the employment section of your résumé. Employers will look for this category, even if it has only one work item listed under it.

Job titles alone often fail to give a clear picture of your employment background. You can use the subcategory, "Responsibilities," to list significant aspects of the job.

EMPLOYMENT

Accounting Intern, Bliss and Wethers, Accountants, Boulder,
    Colorado, Jan.–May, 1998 (part-time)

> Responsibilities: worked under the supervision
> of a senior accountant in preparing
> evaluations and audits; particularly
> enjoyed participating in the writing of
> financial analyses

Night Manager, Cleaver Restaurant, 1998

> Responsibilities: supervised staff of nine;
> managed cash and ordering of provisions;
> participated in hiring interviews

In listing your responsibilities (not "duties"), choose active verbs: *supervised*, *oversaw*, *managed*, *headed*, *assisted*, *helped*, and so forth. To give your job a spark of life, occasionally tell how you *felt* about what you did.

enjoyed meeting clients (or) liked preparing press releases

Take care not to overstate the responsibilities of past positions. Remember that you are writing for a streetwise business audience not likely to be easily fooled. They don't expect you to have the corporate background of a CEO.

Providing Information on Activities and Interests

Because of federal and state legislation on guidelines for hiring, most companies do not want you to place information on your résumé that they cannot legally consider in evaluating your application for employment. For this reason, omit pictures and references to your age, marital status, number of children or family plans, religious and political affiliations, and other personal information.

You may nevertheless indicate that you are a well-rounded person by the list of activities you cite. Record here any professional or industry associations (particularly leadership positions), volunteer work, civic involvement, and student government roles.

If space allows, consider writing out your personal information in *full sentences*. In a résumé otherwise composed of short, staccato phrases, the practice of writing out personal comments and facts can add a touch of sincerity and warmth to the page.

The Activities portion of the résumé is optional. The information it contains often appears under Different Category names such as Personal Background or Personal Information.

Listing References

You can simply state that "References will be furnished upon request." If you have room, though, and your references sound impressive, you might want to list three or four references as follows:

Dr. Alfred Williams
Chief of Internal Medicine
Central Union Hospital
88 Jensen Street
Topeka, KS 70589
(385) 555-6859

Note that the reference is identified by name, position, address, and telephone number. It is wise (and polite) to ask—not inform—your references if you intend to include their names on your résumé. You thereby provide time for them to call your qualities and accomplishments to mind well before the phone rings. By asking references in advance for permission to include their names, you also give them a chance to politely decline your request.

The Functional Résumé

Unlike the chronological résumé, which tends to emphasize your education and potential, the functional résumé emphasizes what you've proven you can do.

The functional résumé, too, opens with your name, and address, and telephone number positioned in an eye-catching way. The *career objective* and *education* portions are handled in the same way as in the chronological résumé.

However, in writing the employment section of the résumé, prepare for major changes. Instead of listing your jobs one by one in chronological order, decide what major abilities you have developed and proven in those positions. Let those abilities, stated as brief phrases, serve as categories under which you can place individual job experiences.

As shown in Figure 12–6, you need not keep such job experiences in chronological order. Put your most impressive jobs first, and your least impressive jobs last within a category. Let the emphasis fall on the job title and description of responsibility, rather than on the dates you held the job (though dates should always be specified).

Many employers favor the functional résumé, especially for experienced applicants, because the document gets right to the key issue: What can this applicant do? Note that those abilities, when stated in the "demonstrated abilities" or "major strengths" section, can be nouns—"Supervision," "Planning"—or verb phrases—"Supervise employees effectively," "Plan for task completion," or "Organize shipping procedures."

Once you have written your résumé, you can begin planning how to prepare multiple copies for distribution to prospective employers. See Figure 12–7 for an additional sample résumé.

FIGURE 12–7   Sample Résumé

Robert C. Ortega

Present Address: Permanent Address:
30 Wisconsin Ave   24 Fellow Road
Washington, DC 20016   Moore, NJ 08057
(202) 914-2152   (609) 214-3102

<u>Education</u>:
    Georgetown University   Washington, DC
    B.S. Marketing & International Management   May 1998
    G.P.A. in Majors 3.4

<u>Experience</u>:
    Marketing Research Assistant   Washington, DC
    Georgetown University Marketing Department   Present

        Operate PIMS Program for Global Strategy database; supplement publications with research examples; create file of current global strategies.

    Research Associate   Washington, DC
    Georgetown SBA Ethics Project   Summer 1997

        Reviewed curriculum; interviewed professors; researched ethical issues in marketing, accounting, business law, and management science; wrote report to Dean and Board of Directors.

    Assistant Area Coordinator   Washington, DC
    G.U. Office of Summer Housing   Summer 1996

        Supervised staff of 30; created weekly and daily maintenance schedules to provide hospitality services for a 300-room dormitory.

    Court Aide   Mt. Holly, NJ
    Superior Court of Burlington County   Summers 1994–95

        Directed records retention program; coordinated Bar Paneling program; managed courtroom preparation and communication, pooled juries, and supervised evidence. Recognized for excellent service by County Bar Association and County Clerk's Office.

<u>Leadership Experience</u>:
    DELTA SIGMA PI, International Business Fraternity,
    • 1996–98 Vice President Chapter Operations;
    • 1997 Chancellor; 1994 Historian.

<u>Honors & Awards</u>:
    • Georgetown SBA Invitational Leadership Retreat, 1997
    • Varsity Letterman, Georgetown Varsity Track.
    • LEAD participant, Darden Graduate School of Business, U VA, 1995

    References available upon request.

FOLLOWUP COMMUNICATIONS: BEFORE AN INTERVIEW

Successful salespeople know the wisdom of the "fourth-call rule": The sale is usually made on the fourth call or later, not the first. Your success in selling your services to an employer may well depend on followup communications—those calls, visits, and letters that politely remind an employer how much you want the job.

Marketing graduate Phyllis Riley recalls:

> I saw firsthand why followup communications are vital. During my senior year, I worked as an intern for a major advertising firm in New York. Résumés came in every day from job-seekers and were barely glanced at by management before being filed away. The people who eventually got jobs were those who took the time to make contact often, either by calling or by writing.

Let's say that you mailed out your résumé and cover letter last week. The phone hasn't rung, and the mailbox is empty. What do you do?

There is no precise number of days or weeks after which you should inquire about an unanswered application. Use your own judgment, being careful not to appear rude or impatient. Companies often appreciate your polite inquiries as a sign that you're actively interested in the job.

Followup Letters

The followup letter is a traditional business letter in which you do the following:

- Politely remind your reader of *when* you mailed your résumé. Mention any correspondence you have received from the company since that date.
- Repeat your willingness to be considered for a position, and name it. Ask your reader to let you know whether your application is still being actively reviewed.
- Conclude by expressing appreciation to your reader for his or her efforts on your behalf.

The letter in Figure 12–8 shows an example followup letter.

Sooner or later, your first response will come from your career application. You rip open the envelope to discover one of three words: *yes*, we'll interview you; *no*, but good luck; or, *maybe* we can find a position for you.

If the answer to your job search is "Yes, we'll interview you," write a letter of response by return mail. If the employer's letter directs you to, also notify the company by telephone.

Accepting an Invitation to Interview

Write a brief business letter to the person who invited you to visit the company for an interview. Repeat the time and date of the interview, and indicate your pleasure at the invitation. Offer to bring additional application materials (letters of recommendation, transcripts, college projects, and so forth) with you.

FIGURE 12–8   Followup Letter

14 Briarcliff Street
Lincoln, NE 80848

April 13, 199_

Ms. Beverly Brown
Personnel Director
Kraco Medical Wholesale, Inc.
125 Seventh Street
Omaha, NE 80422

Dear Ms. Brown:

You may recall receiving my application, dated March 20, for a position as an inventory specialist at Kraco. I'm writing to confirm that you received my application and to check on its status in your review process. I'm particularly interested in knowing whether there may be appropriate job openings at Kraco at this time.

Naturally, I'd be very pleased to answer any questions you may have regarding my application or my qualifications for positions available at Kraco. Please call me at 555-3875 before 8:00 a.m. or after 5 p.m., or leave a message for me at 555-3934 during regular business hours. I'll return your call as soon as possible.

I look forward to hearing from you.

Sincerely,

Lillian Morgan

Lillian Morgan

Conclude by thanking your company hosts for the opportunity to pursue your application. Express your eagerness to visit with them. Figure 12–9 shows an example of an acceptance letter.

Responding to "No"

If the answer you receive is "no, but good luck," you may want to write a "thank-you-and-I'm-still-interested" letter. Express your appreciation for their attention to your application. If appropriate, mention briefly that you felt understandable disappointment at their decision. Express your willingness to be considered for future openings. Ask that your application be kept in an active file. Conclude with thanks and your suggestion that your paths may cross again soon.

THE JOB INTERVIEW

Your résumé, application letter, and followup contacts may eventually open the door to job interviews, which can take place on company premises, at conventions, or elsewhere. The job interview provides an opportunity for both the company and the candidate to get to know more about one another than can be found on the printed information of the company brochure and the applicant's résumé.

Preparing for the Job Interview

You will probably have at least a few days notice before your interview. Use that time to learn as much as possible about the company—its products, locations, workforce, clientele, management, and current developments. Your local or college librarian can help you locate sources such as these for your investigation:

> The National Job Bank (Boston: Adams, 1997) [This book lists employers by state, with specific company information and types of positions.]

FIGURE 12–9   Letter Accepting an Invitation to Interview

6142 Southern Lane
Raleigh, North Carolina 67042

March 1, 199_

Mr. Frederick Range
Personnel Director
Forbes Financial Services
8802 Clime Street
Raleigh, North Carolina 64011

Dear Mr. Range:

I'm pleased to accept your invitation for an interview on March 9, 199_, at 8:30 a.m. If you wish, I can bring with me any additional information or documents you would like to see in support of my application.

Thank you for this opportunity to discuss with you my qualifications for a position at Forbes.

I look forward to meeting you.

Sincerely,

Bradley Morris

Bradley Morris

The company index in the *Wall Street Journal* [This index may guide you to recent articles about company developments.]

Peterson's Guide to Business and Management Jobs (New York: Peterson's Guide, 1997)

In addition to learning about the company, try to contact people who may know about the culture (social patterns and style) of the company and its current needs. These people may include friends or associates who have interviewed with the company or who are now working for the company. Perhaps you can speak with someone in the same industry who knows about the company's reputation and its prospects.

Practice does improve your interviewing skills. If you can, try to arrange some mock-interview sessions, with constructive criticism. You can also set up informal interview practice sessions with friends. After 15 minutes or so of questions, analyze your performance as an "applicant," according to the checklist shown in Figure 12–10, or one of your own design.

The Purposes of an Interview

In an initial job interview, the company wants to see how you handle yourself, especially with words. What can you do to succeed?

- Dress appropriately
- Establish a friendly rapport by your natural smile and comfortable eye contact.
- Be ready to carry the conversation for a moment or two after the first question. Don't answer the interviewer with curt yes/no answers. To prepare for interview openers, consider these typical questions.

Well, Barbara, tell us a little about yourself.
Why in the world did you decide to major in accounting?

FIGURE 12–10   Interview Checklist

☐ Were answers clear and direct?
☐ Was the pace effective—not too fast or too slow?
☐ Was the volume appropriate—not too loud or too soft?
☐ Was choice of words fitting—not too fancy or too unprofessional?
☐ Were pronunciation and enunciation correct?

☐ Did the applicant understand the questions?
☐ Did the applicant make sense?
☐ Did the applicant provide details and examples?
☐ Did applicant have a good grasp of subject area?

☐ Was the applicant comfortable to be with?
☐ Did the applicant try to relate to each member of the interview group?
☐ Did the applicant demonstrate a sense of humor?
☐ Did the applicant demonstrate maturity in handling difficult or sensitive questions?

☐ Did the applicant make good eye contact?
☐ Did the applicant use face, hand, and body language effectively?
☐ Did the applicant avoid disruptive mannerisms?
☐ Did the applicant appear well groomed and suitably dressed?

Why would you like to work here?

You've probably considered a number of careers. Tell us about some of them.

By answering such interview openers in a comfortable, direct way, you establish your confidence to handle any question or comment that comes. Concentrate on speaking clearly and personably.

Interview Situations

We usually think of job interviews as taking place in the personnel office of the company doing the hiring. However, you probably will actually find yourself in at least two of the following three common situations for a job interview:

1. Off-site interviews
2. On-site personnel interviews
3. Supervisory interviews

The first interview situation mentioned here might also be the first interview situation in which you find yourself.

Off-site Interviews

Many companies send representatives to job fairs, industry conventions, and college campuses to accomplish three goals:

1. To give the company exposure among the prospective employees
2. To maintain mutually supportive relationships within the industry or with the university and its faculty
3. To develop lists of prospective employees who might later be asked for on-site interviews with the company.

In some cases, the representative interviewing you off-site will be, in fact, an employee who has little to say or do about hiring decisions. Therefore, you should just relax and do your best in an off-site interview. You are not talking to the chairman of the board. The representative probably cannot offer you a position on the spot. Therefore, look at the representative as a human being, not a judge. Try to imagine his or her day, filled with interviews. Speak comfortably and sincerely.

On-site Interviews

In some instances, your résumé or your off-site interview will earn you an invitation from the company for an on-site visit. At that time, if you haven't already done so, you will be asked to fill out an application for employment. One or more personnel officers usually conduct your first interview. Be prepared to move quickly into a smooth, comfortable conversation, even if the first question is a stickler ("What did you think of our building as you drove up?") Try to avoid one-word answers.

At the on-site interview, expect to talk briefly about your specific field of training. Interviewers commonly get to this topic by asking one of the following questions:

- What aspect of your education and experience seems particularly valuable to you?
- Did you have a special area of interest?
- What one experience seemed of greatest practical value to you?
- What can you tell us about your educational preparation for this job?
- Well, what's going on in [your present college or company] these days?

What if, in the process of answering a question, you make an obvious mistake? Without making much ado over nothing, simply note your mistake and repair it:

> When I studied macrosystems interacting spontaneously to factors, well, involving . . . I'm sorry, I want to say this more clearly: I studied the way major markets responded to international inflation.

Your interviewer will be grateful for your clarification and impressed that you could catch and repair a problem so gracefully.

Be prepared at both off-site and on-site interviews to show interest in the affairs of the company. Your librarian can guide you to such publications as *Standard and Poor's* and *Valueline*, each summarizing the size, product or service line, and financial stability of the company.

Your questions and comments about the company are often invited by these kinds of questions:

- Do you have any questions for us?
- You've seen our operation today. Any questions?
- What's your opinion of our office arrangement here?
- What would you still like to know about the company?

Try not to just grin sheepishly and shyly answer, "Well, nothing, really." Also, don't stall for time by awkwardly asking, "Would you please repeat the question?" Prepare in advance some interesting questions about the company:

- Where is the company headed in the next five years?
- Is a new product line or service now under development?
- What are typical paths of advancement within the company?
- What are typical travel requirements for this position?
- What subsidiaries does the company own?
- What training programs are available to new employees?

Do *not* broach sensitive or self-serving questions such as:

- How many sick days can I take per month?
- How soon do I get a raise?

Conclude the interview by thanking the interviewer and, if appropriate, shake hands. Don't prolong this final moment or make it awkward by last-minute parting shots: "By the way, I forgot to ask whether . . ."

When you return home, write a thank-you letter to the interviewers, as shown in Figure 12–11, described in the next major section of this chapter.

Supervisory Interviews

On the same day as your initial on-site interview or at a later time, you may be invited to interview with a division manager or supervisor. Expect this interview to be much less slick than the session conducted by the personnel officers. Long pauses may fall in conversation. The phone may ring, interrupting your discussion for a few minutes. The secretary may pop in from time to time with urgent business.

In all such disturbances, maintain easygoing good spirits, letting the supervisor know that you can cope with the ragged edges of real business activity.

Prepare to answer questions about your field:

- Have you done any work setting up annual reports?
- What accounting procedure would you use in this case?
- How would you structure a decision-making team for this kind of project?

FIGURE 12–11   Thank-You Letter for an Interview

112 Smithson Street
Las Vegas, Nevada 35082

December 20, 199_

Mr. Richard Hall
Personnel Director
Tri-State Mills, Inc.
205 Cactus Way
Las Vegas, Nevada 35082

Dear Mr. Hall:

I enjoyed meeting you, Ms. Watkins, and Mr. Valenzuela last Thursday afternoon. You made me feel quite comfortable (not a common interview experience!). I was especially interested in our discussion of Japanese "just-in-time" scheduling procedures, and their possible application at Tri-State Mills.

I'm more eager than ever to join you at Tri-State and certainly will be pleased to supply any additional information you would like to support my application.

Again, thank you for a stimulating afternoon. I look forward to discussing possible opportunities for me at Tri-State Mills.

Sincerely,

Rose Ramirez

Rose Ramirez

When you don't know an answer, say so—but add that you could find out (name specific ways). No company wants to hire an employee who tries to disguise an area of ignorance and to fake competence.

Prepare specific questions for the supervisor, being specific about your job and its relationship to the company or the department. Ask about specific tasks if you can think of appropriate questions.

- How do you handle a client's personal desires for a certain color or design in an ad?
- Do you use computer-aided graphics?

Writing that Is Requested During the Interview

When you arrive (a little early) for a job interview, you may be surprised to find more crucial writing tasks awaiting you. Many job applications now ask the applicant to fill in more than the blanks. You might also be asked to write a short essay on a topic of the company's choosing. A sample of the candidate's writing can reveal much. A large real estate development firm in Florida, for example, asks interviewees for management positions to write a brief response to this question:

> Leaders often must make unpopular decisions. Discuss your own way of handling the social pressure occasioned by an unpopular decision you make.

These kinds of questions sometimes appear in your mailbox as part of an application form to be completed and mailed back to the company prior to your interview. In that case, you have time to plan your response, to work out a rough draft, and to revise your answer until it pleases you.

Other employers, however, also use such questions to test your writing abilities (and thinking abilities) in those nervous fifteen or twenty minutes before the beginning of the interview.

Meet this on-the-spot writing challenge by reading the question over at least three times. Each time, you should find yourself grasping the *content* and *intent* of the question more firmly.

QUESTION	Leaders must make unpopular decisions. Discuss your own way of handling the social pressure occasioned by an unpopular decision you make.
FIRST READING	Does this question require me to list and explain several unpopular decisions made by leaders in the past? No.
SECOND READING	Does the question require me to describe several unpopular decisions I have made as a leader? No.
THIRD READING	Does the question require me to suggest how I handle social pressure arising out of an unpopular decision I've made? Yes.

Once you have located the heart of your question, briefly plan a format, using as few as three major parts, for your response. Here are two patterns that might suit the preceding question.

Alternative One

- The easy way out of social pressure for a leader
- The more difficult way out of social pressure for a leader
- Why the more difficult way proves more successful

Alternative Two

- The effect of social pressure in the short run
- The effect of social pressure in the long run
- How leaders direct attention from the short run to the long run

These patterns are not usually written down at all or at best are simply jotted onto scratch paper as a working outline for the answer. Your two or three minutes spent in such planning are valuable in terms of the eventual outcome of your essay. Although your pen may not move during the planning process, you are directly involved in the process of writing. Your short outline will help provide an organizational framework for your response.

When you find yourself faced with an essay question before an interview, practice the following routine:

- Read the question three times, looking for its central issues.
- Plan a three-part (or more) framework for your response.
- Write in a conversational style.

FOLLOWUP COMMUNICATIONS: AFTER AN INTERVIEW

The days immediately following your interview are a period of intense evaluation on the part of the company. Several levels of managerial review will probably be involved in deciding whether you're right for the job. You shouldn't simply sit back waiting for an answer to your application. You can influence this evaluation process in a positive way through tactful and appropriate communication, which may include letters of thanks (Fig. 12–11) and followup.

Later, after you receive a job offer, you'll continue writing to the company: letters of acceptance (Figure 12–12), postponement (Figure 12–13), or refusal (Figure 12–14), and other career communications.

The Letter of Thanks

After the interview, be sure to write a brief letter of thanks. If a company has devoted two hours and three interviewers to the interview, the cost of the time alone may exceed $200 to the company. Even if the interview did not go well for you, demonstrate your gratitude for the company's interest and expense by writing your thanks.

As shown in Figure 12–11, begin by thanking the interviewers by name, if possible, and focusing on one or two particular aspects of the interview for special comment. Then express your eagerness to work for the company and your willingness to supply fur-

FIGURE 12–12   Letter of Acceptance

41 Wilmore Place
Boston, MA 02108

January 4, 199_

Mr. James Kennedy
Director, Advanced Design
Microtech, Inc.
28 Linden Street
Waltham, MA 02611

Dear Mr. Kennedy:

I am pleased to accept the application you offer in your letter of January 1: Systems Engineer Step 3, with an annual salary of $56,000.

As you know, I have arranged to leave my present position on January 20. I will be able to report to my new job at Microtech on January 21. Prior to that time, I will be happy to begin the process of filling out employee documents and security clearances. In addition, I would like to pick up your division training manual to acquaint myself with Microtech policies and procedures.

You must know how happy I am to be joining Microtech. Please communicate my thanks to Mr. Langley, Ms. Crawford, and Mr. Thomas, who showed me every consideration during the application and interview process. I especially appreciated your help and look forward to working as your colleague.

Sincerely,

Duncan Phillips

Duncan Phillips

---

ther information. Conclude in a complimentary way, mentioning the company name if possible.

Now the w-a-i-t-i-n-g begins. During this difficult time, be sure that you can be reached by telephone. As personal judgment dictates, decide when the waiting has become excessive, and then write a polite letter of inquiry.

The Letter of Acceptance

If the answer to your job search is "yes," and you decide to accept an offer, write a brief letter of acceptance, as shown in Figure 12–11, covering each of these key points and others that seem important to you:

- Accept the job offer, repeating exactly what you are accepting. This practice helps to prevent misunderstandings on both sides.
- Describe the arrangements you have agreed upon for the position.

FIGURE 12–13 Letter of Postponement

960 Lake Way
Tacoma, WA 40211

April 9, 199_

Ms. Willa Frank
Personnel Director
AKF Industries, Inc.
9210 Cranston Street
Tacoma, WA 40211

Dear Ms. Frank:

I was pleased to receive your letter of April 7, in which you offer me the position of Assistant Inventories and Supplies Accountant at AKF, with an annual salary of $53,000.

May I consider your offer open until April 20? I will send my written response to you no later than that date.

Thank you for your favorable action on my application. I hope the time extension I have requested will be acceptable to you.

Sincerely,

Lisa Tomlinson

Lisa Tomlinson

- Thank your new employer (by name) for acting favorably on your application. Express your eagerness to begin work and to face new challenges.

The Letter of Postponement

You may find yourself faced with two or more job offers at once—or holding one job in expectation of another. In either case, you can often postpone offers for a short time while you make up your mind.

Do not feel traitorous in requesting an extension of time from a company you seemed so eager to join. Businesses understand that good candidates have many options. Usually, these businesses are willing to cooperate with you.

As shown in Figure 12–13, touch each of these key elements in your letter of postponement.

- Express appreciation at receiving the job offer. Repeat the substance of the offer in this letter.
- Request an extension of time for a specific period while you make your decision.
- Communicate gratitude for favorable action on your application.

FIGURE 12–14   **Letter of Refusal**

214 Riverdale Drive
Banning, CA 92004

February 9, 199_

Mr. Travis Freeman
President
Freeman Furniture Wholesale, Inc.
20 Bleyer Road
Beaumont, CA 92084

Dear Mr. Freeman:

Thank you for your letter of February 7, in which you extend a job offer as Marketing Director at Freeman Furniture. Although I appreciate the opportunity, I am not able to accept because I have accepted a position at another company.

Thank you for your interest in my application and your personal kindness during my interview. Best wishes for a prosperous future.

Sincerely,

Kenneth Williams

Kenneth Williams

The Letter of Refusal

At times, you will have to decline a job offer. Do so in a way that burns no bridges. After all, you may want to find a position with the company again in the future.

As suggested in Figure 12–14, include each of these key elements in the letter of refusal:

- Politely decline the job offer. You don't have to mention its specific details. You can decide whether to explain your decision. Don't try to sound more sorry than, in fact, you are.
- Communicate thanks for the company's interest. Express goodwill for their people and projects.

OTHER CAREER-RELATED LETTERS

Assuming that at least one of these interviews leads to your acceptance of a job offer, you'll eventually end up in a job in your career field. As Chapters 1 through 11 showed, this is certainly not the end of your business writing; it's only the beginning. In addition, if you are like most workers, you will probably also do much more career-related writing, including letters of resignation and letters of recommendation.

FIGURE 12–15 Resignation Letter

1140 Seally Drive
Wichita, KS 35011

August 8, 199_

Ms. Catherine Brown
Director
Trend Design
84 South Street
Wichita, KS 35011

Dear Ms. Brown:

After seven very satisfying and productive years with Trend Design, I am resigning to take over the directorship of another company. I wish to make my last day at Trend Friday, September 2. This date can be adjusted somewhat, as needed, to aid you in training my replacement and in making a smooth transition.

This decision was difficult, especially considering how much you and the other talented people at Trend have encouraged my professional development and have provided me with rewarding relationships. Together, we have certainly enjoyed our share of winning projects.

I wish you and the others at Trend all the success you so richly deserve.

Sincerely,

John Bradshaw

John Bradshaw

The Letter of Resignation

How quickly time passes. You have been on the job for quite a while, and the time has come to resign. Many important points must be covered in this, your final communication with your employer. Include the following:

- Express your intention to resign. Give the effective date of your resignation.
- Reflect upon significant projects and people during your career with the company.
- Decide whether to reveal the new position you are accepting.
- Offer to help provide a smooth transition, if possible, for your successor.
- Express thanks for the professional and personal associations you have enjoyed in your old job.

Tact is especially important in a resignation letter, even when the circumstances of your resignation are less than rosy. Some resignation letters even end up leading to job promotions and raises. A company hates to lose good employees to the competition.

Realize that your letter of resignation may be read as a challenge by upper management—a challenge to offer you new projects and financial rewards to keep you with the company. However, you should never plan on using your resignation letter to get management to give you a raise or promotion. It seldom works more than once per company, and frequently not at all.

Nonetheless, you should keep this possibility in mind. Write a tactful resignation letter that doesn't anger the reader. Notice in Figure 12–15 that the letter subtly suggests how valuable the resigning employee has been to the firm.

The Letter of Recommendation

You not only leave a letter behind when you leave—the letter of resignation—but you take letters with you to your new employer—letters of recommendation. When you are asked to *write* a letter of recommendation, tell the requester frankly whether you can write a favorable letter. If not, the requester then has the chance to ask someone else.

In writing the letter, you have considerable freedom to treat any aspect of your personal and professional relation with the person you are recommending. In general, do not guess about job requirements in the new position for which you are recommending the person. Rather, focus on the past and the present facts of your relationship. The following Communication Checkpoint may help you.

Communication Checkpoint
Topics for a Letter of Recommendation

- How long and in what capacity have you known the person?
- What can you say about the person's character and personality? Does he or she work well with others? Is he or she responsible? Creative?
- If possible, describe one or more specific occasions on which the person excelled. What did he or she do? How did it turn out?
- How does the person stack up against others you have observed in similar roles?
- What success can you predict for the person? Summarize the factors that make your prediction more than a wild guess.
- Conclude with an appropriately warm compliment to the person. Offer to elaborate on your recommendation by letter or phone. Provide your name, title, address, and phone number.

At least 90 percent of all letters of recommendation generally support the person recommended. The key, then, is to write favorable things that provide enough detail so that the reader can come to agree with your high opinion of the person you recommend.

USING THE INTERNET TO FIND CAREER OPPORTUNITIES

Wouldn't it be splendid if domestic and international employers simply entered their job openings on a computer bulletin board that you could access anytime, anywhere in your job search? Even more, wouldn't it be terrific if you could enter your résumé and career wish-list so that international employers could look you over electronically? Finally, it would be the icing on the cake if the computer would simply match up your career desires with available jobs, and send you a list each week or so of international jobs that seem particularly right for you.

That day, happily, has arrived. As this chapter will make clear, the Internet is the repository of literally hundreds of thousands of current job openings around the world. An earnest plea: if you're not now an Internet user, don't skip over this chapter. Getting on the "Net" is easy through one of the many user services such as America OnLine, Microsoft Network, and others. Your local computer store can help you get on-line with the Internet, or you can access the Net using computers increasingly available at work, college computer facilities, libraries, and, of course, friends' homes.

The Internet is changing the way companies do business and the way they hire. On-line commerce and e-mail connections offer companies, clients, and job-seekers instant access to global products, information, and opportunities. In 1996, there were over 30 million users on the Internet, with 100,000 more joining each month.

From 1989 to 1993 the "Net" was used primarily by scientists, engineers, and hobbyists. With the advent of the World Wide Web and powerful search software, the doors to global communication from your PC keyboard have been thrown open.

Proprietary services (listed above) are the primary means by which most PC users (now 30 percent of all U.S. households) connect to the Internet. This chapter will assume that you now have access to the Internet or are motivated enough by what you read here to get access as soon as possible.

Searching for Company Job Listings

Thousands of companies now make use of the Internet, by means of "home pages," to provide basic company information, advertise products and services, and post current job listings. To find your target company on the Internet, simply enter its name using one or more of the more "web crawlers" or search mechanisms. The best of these are:

- Architect, Mountain View, CA
  http://www.atext.com
- InfoSeek, Santa Clara, CA
  http://www.infoseek.com
- Lycos, Pittsburgh, PA
  http://www.lycos.com
- McKinley Group, Inc., Sausalito, CA
  http://www.mckinley.com
- Open Text, Waterloo, Ontario
  http://www.opentext.com
- WebCrawler, San Francisco, CA
  http://www.webcrawler.com
- MetaCrawler, Seattle, WA
  http://www.metacrawler.com
- Yahoo! Mountain View, CA
  http://www.yahoo.com

Others that you may want to investigate are Excite, The Electric Library, Alta Vista, A2Z, HotBot, Magellan, AccuFind, Point, IBM InfoMarket, and DejaNews. For those new to the Internet, there's good reason to use more than one search service: each will turn up somewhat different lists of job sites. Yahoo!, for example, yields 39 responses to the search term, "international jobs." The same search term on Excite yields more than 500 responses.

A "response" is simply a place you can look, described by its computer address on the World Wide Web (www), for listings of international jobs. To access these job sites, you type in the computer address and, voilà, you're sitting with sometimes thousands of current job possibilities before you from employers around the world.

Getting Where You Want to Go Quickly

This chapter will list the brightest and best of the current domestic and international job sites now available on the Internet. Some of these sites are specialized for particular occupations; others are massive collections of job listings of all types. Using the addresses provided here, you'll have to "surf the Net" a bit to discover which domestic or international job sites are most pertinent to your needs.

All search programs will ask you to enter search words or descriptor terms. By entering the name of your target company—Nippon Telephone and Telegraph, for example—you will quickly find dozens of "hits," that is, places to look on the Internet for information about the company, including its employment needs. Charles Schwab, Inc. is among the companies that make a practice of listing all their job openings on the Internet. Schwab feels it has nothing to lose and everything to gain by letting the whole world know about its employment opportunities. Or you can enter more generic search words in combination, such as "international employment" and "investment banking." This entry may bring back literally hundreds of hits, some of which will be just what you're looking for: current job ads for careers.

Certainly, one of the quickest ways to sort through the dozens of job sites to find the most current, complete, and reliable is to use (for free) the services of professionals at career centers at colleges and universities. These job counselors review available job sites on an ongoing basis and list the best as part of their university's home page.

Here's a concrete example. If you type in the address http://www.usfca.edu, you will be connected with the home page of the University of San Francisco. That page offers you several menu choices. By clicking on the "Career Center" item, you will be routed to an astounding collection of all kinds of domestic and international job listings. For our purposes, let's say that you are eager to find an international job experience, if only for a year or two. From the list of topics provided, click on "International Jobs" to see these categories:

Asia

- AsiaNet
- Asia Pacific Management Forum
- Malaysia
- Project Aspire
- TKO Personnel, Inc.

Australia

- Australian University Jobs
- Employment in Australia

Canada

- Canadian Association of Career Educators and Employers (CACEE)
- The Career Centre

Europe

- Employment in Ireland
- The Employment Network
- EuroJobs
- More European Jobs
- Russian and Eastern European Internships
- Swiss Jobs
- Work in France

Global Resources

- Contact: International Nonprofit Information
- Council on International Educational Exchange (CIEE)
- The Directory: Global Academic Recruiters
- The Employment Network
- Internet Job Surfer
- Job Hunt
- Overseas Job Express
- The Riley Guide Masterlist
- Working and Living Overseas

By clicking on any of the bulleted items, you can quickly be connected to literally thousands of current job openings, arranged for easy searching according to the country and type of job you're interested in. If you want to go directly to the University of San Francisco's international job listings without visiting its home page, use this address:

http://www.usfca.edu/career/International.html.

Many other universities and colleges have similar job services available for free through the Internet. Visit the home page of the university or college to be directed to these career services.

Using the Monster Board

By far the largest collection of current job ads can be found at the address http://www.monster.com. More than 55,000 job ads, both domestic and international, are gathered here by job category, region, and company. You can spend many hours harvesting outstanding job possibilities from this source. In many cases, you can apply electronically by registering your résumé at this job site (directions provided on the Monster Board) and having the service match up your abilities and background with likely jobs.

Be aware, however, that companies are more diligent about getting ads *on* the Monster Board than taking them off, once they have been filled or are no longer active. You will no doubt encounter a few dead ends on the Monster Board in your search for the right international position.

Other Valuable Jobs Sites on the Internet

Here is an address collection of other worthwhile sites you can visit to speed your search for the right job in the right place.

www.cyberss.com/software-source

This service specializes in placing data processing professionals in U.S. and international positions. The hiring companies pay all fees.

www.oai.com/jobs

Optical Access International lists its current jobs openings here.

www.indirect.com/spectra/legal.html

At this address you will find international jobs associated with the legal profession.

www.194.151.8.68/jobhunt/reader22.htm

This is a particularly valuable site for European jobs and contacts with headhunters.

www.camrev.com.au/share/jobs/html

Here are listed international academic jobs of all types.

www.snowmass.zdv.gov:8080/jobs.html

This site lists international job openings and also provides an extensive list of international job search resources.

www.expat.gulliver.frl

Here you'll find a wonderful resource—the *International Jobs Magazine* on-line. It contains not only current job listings but also helpful articles and testimonials by those who have found international careers.

www.netline.com

This is the justly-famous Career Center, with click-on connections to the following categories:

- Career Connections—direct connection between the candidate and the international job recruiter. The service is available 24 hours a day.
- California Career and Employment Center—international jobs, not just California listings.
- *Career Magazine*
- Career Mosaic—14,000 current job listings and profiles of employers
- Career Path—classified "help wanted" ads from major city newspapers
- Jobs—hundreds of international positions and contact information for recruiters
- Intellimatch Online Career Services—register your résumé here and specify companies and individuals (such as your current employer!) that can't have access to it.
- JobTrak—a superb site for college students and recent graduates. Three hundred colleges participate in this site in partnership with 150,000 employers.
- Recruiters Online Network—the largest site list of recruiters, employment agencies, and search firms

- Virtual Job Fair—a site specializing in domestic and international job placement for high-technology careers.

www.nationjob.com/rob half

This is the international job site for Robert Half International, one of the largest employment and search firms in the world.

www.kishbaugh.com

This site specializes in international jobs for executives and senior management.

www.renard-international/com/

Here you will find hundreds of listings for jobs in the hospitality industry (restaurants, hotels, tours, etc.) worldwide.

www.scopeinc./com/

A wide range of international jobs and employer lists are posted at this site.

www.icpa.com/

This site focuses on international jobs in technology, marketing, and finance throughout Asia and the Pacific Rim.

www.summerjobs.com/

At this site, you will find thousands of listings for domestic and international short-term and summer jobs.

www.jobsource.com

This collection of job listings and employer profiles also features a résumé generator so that you can enter your information efficiently for review by international employers.

www.espan.com

This site is rich in international job listings.

www.occ.com

Here at the Online Career Center is another collection of thousands of current job listings.

www.jobtrack.com/jobguide

This address takes you to Margaret Riley's Job Guide. You'll be amazed by the range and number of job listings and other career services available here.

www.kaplan.com

The Kaplan On-Line Career Center offers many international career possibilities.

www.peoplebank.com/

This is an international database of jobs and job-seekers.

www.oconnell.co.ok

This engaging site goes by the name "Searching the Universe" and focuses on recruitment for international finance positions.

http://Bizserv.com/greenlake/ERI/getjob.html

This site is called Executive International Employment and lives up to its name.

www.universal.nl/jobhunt/

At this address you will find the International Headhunters Guides, providing hundreds of headhunter addresses on the Internet, employment contacts, and current international job listings.

www.dmcl.com/it/

 This site is the International IT Recruitment Exchange specializing in information technology recruitment and job listings.

www.cegos.fr/

 This site, called Jobs Online, is limited to specific job offers from French and other European employers along with company profiles.

www.jobcontacts.com/ijc/

 The InfoHighway Job Contacts located at this address is Canada's largest database of international jobs.

www.itjobs.co.uk/

 This site, ARC International, specializes in technical job openings in the United Kingdom.

www.hway.net/kcswis

 This is the Directory of American Employers for International Professions. Look here for U.S. employers that will send you abroad.

http://hosea.atc.11.mit.educ.8000/jobs.html

 This site, called International Job Search Resources, is an excellent gathering of listings, employers, and recruiters.

http://asiafacts.kingston.net

 This is probably the best site for information about jobs, particularly teaching careers, in Japan, Korea, Taiwan, and other Asia countries.

www.tvp.com/jintl/html

 The name of this site, TVP's Job Information Center: International Job Opportunities, describes what you'll find here.

www.streamjobs.com/

 The Stream International Jobs site is yet another extensive collection of short- and long-term international job openings.

www.hway.net/jandl/jobs/jobs.htm

 This site is titled J & L's Job Classified, with thousands of current listings.

interbiznet.com/hunt/newsint.html

 Here you will find International Newsgroups, a site focusing on information exchange and shared job listings among those holding international jobs and those seeking these careers.

www.zynet.co.uk/bpark/bpchem.html

www.zynet.co.uk/bpark/bpoppo.html

 These addresses are but two of the several sites making up the UK Business Park. The first address specializes in careers in chemistry and pharmaceuticals throughout the United Kingdom. The second is a more general listing of international job opportunities.

www.purdue.edu/homes/swlodin/jobs.html

 Called Employment Resources on the Internet, this site (like the University of San Francisco example provided earlier in this chapter) provides a wealth of international career listings, résumé advice, and other resources.

http://phoenix.placement.oakland.edu/career/internet.htm

 This site is titled The Definitive Internet Career Guide and measures up to its name.

http://quintus.universal.nl/jobhunt

This is the Avotek International Home Page providing access to international jobs in dozens of categories and countries.

www.webcom.com/scope/correct.html

This is one of many sites maintained by 1-Stop Careers. By visiting this site, you can gain access to several related sites, all of which provide international job listings.

CHAPTER SUMMARY

1. The application cover letter is necessary each time you mail a résumé. It should be brief, tied to your résumé by references to highlights, and appropriately personalized.

2. The résumé is best developed by the job-seeker himself or herself in preparation for job interviews.

3. Chronological résumés often suit recent graduates, who have more educational credits to emphasize than work experience.

4. Functional résumés are more appropriate for those with extensive work experience.

5. Special letters or phone messages are called for in response to an invitation for an interview or a job offer.

6. The thank-you letter after an interview can be an important aid in securing a job.

7. When writing letters of postponement, refusal, or resignation, be tactful, honest, and brief.

8. Letters of recommendation should be descriptive, truthful, and sincere.

9. The Internet provides extensive resources for the job search.

QUESTIONS FOR DISCUSSION

1. Should you begin the application process with a letter of application accompanied by a résumé or by a phone call? Discuss your choice.

2. Identify the typical parts of a letter of application.

3. What strategies should you use in an uninvited letter of application?

4. Which of the nine guidelines for the résumé seem most important to you? Why?

5. What is meant by the phrase "at-a-glance appeal" when applied to the résumé? What is the importance of such appeal? How can you create it in your résumé?

6. What basic categories should always appear on a résumé?

7. How do the chronological and functional résumés differ? Which pattern will you choose for your own résumé? Why?

8. Is it important to tailor your résumé for each job? How can you do so?

9. Should references be listed at the bottom on your résumé, or simply offered as available? Why?

10. Why should you omit a picture of yourself and similar personal data from your résumé?

11. How important is it that your résumé contain no surface errors in grammar, mechanics, spelling, or printing?

12. Must you account for every month of your working life in the work experience section of the résumé?

13. What items can be included in the education section of the résumé?

14. Why should you take a personal hand in creating your résumé instead of turning the entire project over to someone else?

15. Why should a résumé be mailed with a cover letter to an employer?

16. What are the primary features of the followup letter? When should you write one?

17. What information should be contained in a letter accepting an invitation to interview?

18. Why might you write a polite letter expressing future interest after being rejected for a job opening?

19. What kinds of writing can you expect to do at an interview?

20. If you are asked to write a short essay at an interview, how should you begin your work?

21. What are the main features of the letter of acceptance?

22. What is a letter of postponement?

23. Why is it important to take time to write a letter of refusal for positions you do not accept?

24. What are the main features of a letter of recommendation?

25. Why should you be tactful in a resignation letter?

EXERCISES

1. Start a job-search file by listing companies or businesses with whom you would like to gain employment. Gather the relevant information on these companies, following the guidelines offered elsewhere in this chapter. How many prospective employers have you located? Which seem most appealing?

2. Write a letter asking an employer or professor for a letter of recommendation. Consider your tone and persuasive strategy when making the request. Remember, the way in which you ask for a recommendation might affect the recommendation itself.

3. Write a contact letter to the personnel director at a company with whom you have

worked part-time, requesting information about possible full-time employment at a later date. Place the director's response in your job-search file.

4. Visit the personnel offices of a company for whom you would like to work. Assume that you are not under great pressure to find a job at present, so you should be able to greet the office staff without feeling that you must walk out with a job. Simply introduce yourself and leave a résumé for consideration. Make sure that you write down the personnel director's name for inclusion in your job-search file. Later, record the experience and repeat this procedure at several attractive companies. Compare visits.

5. Visit the college placement service office at a local college or university. If the office keeps placement files, start one. Record your impressions and place any relevant information you gather in your job-search file.

6. Familiarize yourself with *The College Placement Annual*, available at a college career development center or library. What are the strengths and weaknesses of this annual?

7. Leaf through the help-wanted ads of the Sunday edition of a major newspaper in your area. Which ads seem like good leads? Which make you skeptical? Why?

8. Interview a friend or family member who holds an attractive job. Find out how difficult the job was to acquire. How long did your subject search for the job? How many applications did he or she send out? How many interviews did he or she carry out?

9. Write a letter of application in response to a job opening described in a newspaper advertisement.

10. Write an uninvited letter of application to a company with which you would like to gain employment. How will your strategy in this application change compared to the strategy you would use in writing an invited letter of application?

11. Create your own résumé. Experiment with several versions and layouts until you find the résumé form that best fits you and your goals.

12. As an experiment in résumé form, rewrite your functional résumé in chronological form, or your chronological résumé in functional form.

13. Find three job advertisements of different types (employer ad, blind ad, agency ad, and so forth), and write a cover letter for each.

14. Assume that you have not heard anything for 10 days since applying for a position. Write a followup letter asking about the status of your application.

15. Write a letter accepting an invitation to interview.

16. Assume that you receive more than one job offer at the same time. Write a letter of postponement asking for a specified amount of time to make your decision.

17. Write a thank-you letter to a company that interviewed you.

18. Use a friend's résumé as the source material for writing a letter of recommendation for that person.

19. Write an essay response to this question, as if it were presented to you at an interview: "What qualities define a superior employee?"

20. Write a letter accepting a job offer. Make sure to specify the terms under which you are accepting the offer.

21. Write a letter declining a job offer. Bear in mind that you may seek employment with this company at some future time in your career.

22. Assume that you have worked in one job for two years. A better opportunity has presented itself with another company. Write a tactful letter of resignation.

23. You receive a letter inviting you to interview. The letter gives several possible dates and times from which you can choose. Write back to the company to arrange the interview.

24. You are offered a job over the telephone. Accept the offer by letter, and confirm in writing the terms described to you.

25. You have been invited to interview on a specific date but can't because of important personal commitments (such as a wedding to attend). Write a letter asking for another interview date.

26. You are offered a job over the telephone. Decline the offer by letter.

INTERNET ASSIGNMENT

You've done well in your studies and now it is time to find a fulfilling career. Use the Résumés and Career Communication section of the Internet Guide to find sites well-suited to your career search. Choose your favorite three sites and explain in a two to three page document why these sites appear to be best suited to your needs.

CHAPTER 13

Listening

Each of us has spent up to 90 percent of our time in school *listening.* Yet few of us have ever received any training at all in how to listen effectively because we assume that being able to listen is as easy and natural as being able to see. We mistakenly assume that *hearing* is the same as *listening.*

Hearing is the physical capacity to sense sounds. Whether the speaker is speaking in Japanese, Greek, or Laotian, those present can *hear* the words being spoken. What those sounds mean, of course, and how they are to be understood makes all the difference for understanding them. The perception of meaning and the sometimes difficult task of achieving understanding both require the power to listen.

THE NEED FOR LISTENING IN BUSINESS

To make effective decisions, employees at all levels of a company must be aware of all the information—facts, opinions, and feelings—that affects and is affected by those decisions. Some of this information comes from reading letters, memos, reports, and other documents. But far more information influencing a business decision comes—or tries to come—by way of talking. The question is whether the decision maker truly listens to the many types of spoken information.

Because listening is so important to decision making, this chapter focuses on managers, who must constantly make all kinds of decisions many times a day. At some time in your career, you may end up supervising or managing other employees. Even if you don't, you'll still need to be able to listen effectively and to make informed decisions. In any company, at any level, it is important to practice good listening skills from your first day on the job.

For the rest of this chapter, picture yourself as a manager or supervisor in your career field. When managers fail to listen, companies quickly show the result in botched projects, unhappy employees, poor public relations, and weak earnings. For example, in the manufacture of an airplane brake system, a manager may hear but not listen to an engineer's warning about a substandard sealing ring. The product then goes to market with a hidden but dangerous flaw. The resulting problems on in-service airliners embarrass the company and endanger the public. The manager gets a bad reputation in the company, and the manager's whole department suffers. The situation gets worse as newspapers, radio, and television carry stories about the flawed brake system. Orders fall off, and so do company earnings.

This kind of slip-up occurs frequently across industries and can often be blamed on poor listening. Why don't managers listen, in order to avoid these problems?

WHY MANAGERS OFTEN FAIL TO LISTEN

If managers' careers depend on their decisions, and those decisions depend on the ability to listen carefully, why is poor listening so common? Unfortunately, five factors seem to get in the way of a manager's listening.

1. Overassertiveness
2. Internal mental competition
3. Assumptions about the speaker
4. Assumptions about the situation
5. Laziness

Overassertiveness.   Managers usually have assertive personalities. In business settings, they speak up more than others, usually with more definite opinions and more insistent ways of speaking. They move in the fast lane of business, making very few stops to listen. Too often, these personalities find it frustratingly difficult to listen to other people. By comparison with their own speed of thinking and expression, these other people may seem slow or disorganized or unclear. Many managers press ahead with their own agendas, sweeping away conversations with "Yeah, I know what you're going to say, but here's what I think we should do. . . ."

Internal Mental Competition.   A manager's head is often a beehive of competing ideas, facts, details, appointments, and worries. Even during conversations, the new information must compete with many other thoughts and feelings. Often, the other speakers in the conversation lose out—the manager's mind is elsewhere and thinking about other things.

The pace of ordinary conversation leaves plenty of time for extraneous thoughts to interfere with effective listening. The average person speaks at a rate of approximately 150 words per minute, even though most of us can comprehend at the rate of 600 words per minute. The difference leaves enough time for a wide variety of irrelevant thoughts to crowd in on our attention—and to crowd our listening.

Assumptions about the Speaker.   If we have already made up our minds about what the speaker is going to say, we don't really listen attentively. In the case of the engineer's warning about the defective sealing ring, the manager may have been thinking, "Frank's such a worrywart. He always makes mountains out of molehills." The manager then dismisses the engineer's warning—or never truly listens to it in the first place.

Assumptions about the Situation.   Similarly, we can fail to listen because we've already made up our minds about the circumstances being discussed. For example, a manager on a tight production schedule has a mental plan for how the project should proceed. Often, that plan is so vivid and preoccupying that the person doesn't listen to other voices, especially voices of disagreement or protest. In the case of the defective sealing ring, the manager may have felt—subconsciously, perhaps—that there was no time in the schedule for glitches. Those were supposed to be ironed out at an earlier stage. The manager can't listen to the engineer's warning because it doesn't fit the script etched into the manager's mind.

Laziness.   Unfortunately for their companies and for their subordinates, not all managers are enthusiastic and competent. Some, frankly, are simply putting in their time until retirement. They often don't listen because true listening would require that they do something. For the lazy manager, ignorance can be very comfortable.

IMPROVING YOUR ABILITY TO LISTEN

In a competitive business climate, lazy listeners waiting for retirement may find themselves waiting for unemployment checks instead. Few healthy businesses can afford the dangerous dead weight of managers who insist on closing their minds to what's going on around them. In order to listen effectively, managers and other listeners need to understand various aspects and types of listening.

Changes for Better Listening

Give the aforementioned five barriers to effective listening, it's clear that most of us need to change the way in which we listen. The road to effective listening includes significant changes in attitudes, in habits, and in techniques.

Changes in Attitudes

You can remove the five barriers to listening by (1) understanding the barriers, (2) noticing when they get in the way of your own listening, and (3) making a conscious effort to avoid them. This process of retraining involves giving yourself mental lessons. In effect, you must teach yourself new and more productive attitudes. That instruction may lead to personal resolutions, such as the following:

> I tend to shut Janice out whenever she brings up her problems in customer relations. I usually try to joke about it or change the subject. This time I'm going to try to understand what's she's saying as completely as possible.

You may even need to deal with a problem of being overly assertive. For example,

> I have a bossy personality—aggressive, energetic, and driven. Those traits can hurt me as a manager if I never give others a chance to really communicate with me. This time I'm going to let someone else have the floor—I'll be as energetic in trying to listen as I am in trying to talk myself.

Changes in Habits

Unfortunately, even after you've made up your mind about a new set of attitudes, your old habits—some of which you've practiced since childhood—may still interfere with your ability to listen. You may have the habit, for example, of cutting in on others whenever they say a word or phrase that sets off an interesting thought within you. You may habitually let your attention drift after the first sentence or two of someone's conversation.

Breaking old habits involves catching yourself in the act—or asking others to help you catch yourself. In the case of your habitual interruptions, tell the persons speaking to you that you don't want to interrupt them or get off the track. As them to let you know if they feel the conversation is straying from what they intended. Another idea—if it works for you—is to place a reminder to yourself on your desk: "Listen, don't interrupt!" or "Keep your mind on the message!" Though it's hard to get started in breaking bad habits, they go away more easily as soon as you start seeing the rewards for your new behaviors. Your new listening behaviors will pay extraordinary dividends in the respect others have for you and the wealth of new information you receive.

Changes in Techniques

The ways in which you listen—the techniques you use for receiving and interpreting others' words—may have to change significantly. For example, in the past, you may have shut down—and become entirely passive while others are active in speaking. However, to listen effectively means that you're as active when you listen as you are when you speak. That is, you are thinking with the speaker, straining to make connections between ideas and speculating about feelings, motives, and other matters. In short, you're working hard to make meaning out of the words you hear. The rest of this chapter suggests specific techniques you can use to improve listening in all its forms.

Types of Listening

Most of the listening required in business can be divided into four categories:

1. Passive listening
2. Attentive listening
3. Interactive listening
4. Empathetic listening

Passive Listening

In this form of listening, we are not required to make any response, either verbal or nonverbal. We are free to "tune in" or "tune out" as our mood strikes us. We often let our minds wander to associated ideas and images. For example, we often listen to the news and to music passively.

When attention wanders during this form of listening, it's often not a problem. Passive listening is fine for many forms of enjoyment. This type of listening, however, would be inappropriate in face-to-face conversations and other business circumstances.

Attentive Listening

In this form of listening, we consciously try to focus on what the speaker is saying. We make an effort not to let our attention wander. Examples of attentive listening include listening to instructions, a briefing, or other important information, such as a storm warning.

Interactive Listening

In this form of listening, we are expected to react verbally and nonverbally to what we are hearing. If the speaker says something surprising, we are expected to show our surprise. Not to do so would indicate a failure in interactive listening. Our faces, body posture, vocal noises ("Ah! Really? Uh-huh."), and hand movements all signal our intense interest in and understanding of the words we are hearing.

Examples of interactive listening include most business conversations, such as interviews and meetings.

Empathetic Listening

This most intense form of listening has all the characteristics of interactive listening with the addition of the listener's effort to understand and feel connected to the emotional content of the speaker's communication. In interactive listening, the listener is reactive—that is, the listener responds visibly and audibly to what he or she hears. In empathetic listening, the listener is not only reactive but is also participative—the listener attempts to share with the speaker the feelings and concerns that underlie the message.

Examples of empathetic listening include customer relations, counseling sessions, and some aspects of performance, hiring, and disciplinary interviews.

Strategies for Listening

For each of the preceding types of listening, you can use several techniques or strategies to improve your listening skills:

1. Listen to the whole message.
2. Listen for factual information.
3. Listen for feelings.
4. Give the speaker signs of interest and understanding

Listen to the Whole Message

Virtually all oral messages come to us with both attitudes and factual information. When we listen to another human being, we can perceive not only the *explicit message* (the information we would receive from reading the words)but also the *attitudes* (including feelings, mood, and suggestions of intent) that go with that message.

For example, if your company president tells you "I want you to attend the meeting," the attitude that goes with the explicit message is as important as the actual words themselves. By the expression on the president's face and the way the words are said, you could receive the attitude message that "I'm giving you the splendid opportunity of attending this important meeting—what an honor!" Given a different expression and tone, however, you could receive a different attitude message: "Now don't forget and show up late, as usual. I'm ordering you to be there on time!"

In most business situations, you should listen to both the attitudinal and informational aspects of what you hear. Sometimes, however, you should listen mostly to one aspect or the other of the total message. When you should be listening only for facts, you'll need to use techniques that differ from those used when listening for feelings or a mixture of facts and feelings.

Listen for Factual Information

When listening only for facts, try to find a pattern for the meaning so that you can connect all the individual details, statistics, and other items flowing to you from the speaker. Often, you can figure out the pattern simply by asking the question, Why? Why is the speaker telling me these details? Why is the speaker listing these facts? Why is the speaker quoting these authorities?

Such active mental work on your part lets you listen in on the key message instead of all of the many facts and details themselves. A helpful analogy may be a necklace of various beads. Seen as a necklace, the beads can be arranged and easily held in mind by their color and pattern. Without the necklace, though—that is, the underlying pattern—the beads scatter separately and are hard to hold in hand or in mind.

It will also be helpful to focus on key words that keep recurring in the conversation. Just as headings in this textbook help to organize chapters into manageable units, key words in a conversation or presentation help to mark stages of thought and relationships between ideas.

Listen for Feelings

Knowing how to spot and track all the key facts and terms in a spoken message is crucial for most business communication. But to fully understand what the speaker is trying to say, it's often more important to know what people feel and intend to say than to listen to the actual facts of what they say. Listening for feelings means opening eyes and ears to

- Tone of voice
- Facial expressions
- Gestures and posture
- Eye movement and eye contact
- Pace of speaking
- Indications of nervousness, excitement, depression, or other emotional states

These clues usually support the apparent meaning of a person's words, but they also sometimes contradict the words being spoken. For example, an employee may say "I guess you're right" to a supervisor. The supervisor may hear, "This employee agrees with me." However, if the employee snarls or whines those words angrily or sadly, a wise supervisor will continue the conversation to determine the person's real attitudes and opinions.

Give the Speaker Signs

When you listen to a business associate over the phone, even if you say very little, you occasionally chime in with "Uh-huh," or "Really?" "Hmmm," or "Oh," to let the speaker know that you're still there—the phone line hasn't gone dead, you haven't hung up, and the speaker isn't "on hold."

When you listen to an associate (or a client or supervisor or subordinate), you make the same kinds of "I'm still here, and I'm still listening" noises. When speaking to you alone or in a small gathering, the speaker appreciates these noises. However, when you are in a large group, many "I'm-still-here" noises could make the room so noisy that no one could hear the speaker. At these times, we use visual signs to tell the speaker, "I'm still here, and I'm still listening." For example, we keep our eyes focused on the speaker ("eye contact"), we nod our heads, we gesture with our hands, we take notes, and so on.

Most of us actually use eye contact, gestures, and "I'm-still-listening" noises even when we're talking face-to-face with one or two people. All of these signs also tell the speaker, "I'm interested in what you have to say, and I think you're an important enough person to pay attention to you." A few gestures can speak volumes.

All of these good listening techniques help the listener as well as the speaker. First, as effective listeners, we usually learn something—facts, ideas, opinions, or at least what someone else is feeling and thinking. Second, when we listen well, we encourage speakers to speak well. Knowing that we are listening with care, the speaker tries his or her best to make the words worth our attention. Finally, we build relationships. Friendship is impossible without sympathetic listening, and business friendships and relationships depend on its presence.

You may find the result of sympathetic, energetic listening quite powerful. Practice these suggestions in your day-to-day relationships with friends and coworkers. Notice how much more important you make them feel by your attentive listening—and, in turn, how much more important they feel you are for your interest in them.

The following Communication Checkpoint gives some tips on how to listen when you're in difficult communication situations involving conflict, disagreement, and misunderstanding.

Communication Checkpoint *Handling Difficult Communication Situations*	1. Focus on facts and issues, not on personalities. 2. Show by your facial expressions and your willingness to listen that you want to understand the other person's position and feelings. 3. Dignify and clarify the other person's position by repeating back in your own words what you understand the person to be saying. 4. Present alternatives in the form of possible options, not direct objections to the person's position. 5. Directly ask for the person's input on how to resolve matters of disagreement or impasse.

ASPECTS OF INTERCULTURAL LISTENING

Just as writing and speaking forms and approaches differ from culture to culture, so do listening habits and outward manifestations of attention. In Western cultures, intense listening is usually signaled by sustained eye contact the audience gives to the speaker along with responsive facial expressions (smiles, nods, and so forth). In many Asian cultures, however, the same degree of intense listening may be indicated by an averted gaze, with little animation of facial features. Western speakers new to such cultures must be careful not to judge the attention or interest level of an Asian audience by Western signs of listening.

In virtually all Western business environments, it would be considered impolite for an audience member to mill about, whisper to others, or leave the room entirely (except for emergencies) during a presentation. Not so in Japan and some other Asian business cultures, where it is commonplace for audience members in a business presentation to exchange notes, talk quietly in small groups, and come and go freely from the room as the presentation goes on. From a Western presenter's point of view, this behavior may be misunderstood as the audience members' lack of interest. But from a Japanese perspective, it is not necessary for all members of a decision-making team to be present for all portions of the presentation. The team trusts its members to gather the information needed from the presentation, even if no one team member heard the entire presentation from start to finish.

Another listening problem for a Westerner is often presented by Chinese hosts, for whom it is perfectly acceptable at meals or meetings including the Westerner to break into prolonged conversations in Mandarin or Cantonese. Even if a translator is present, these conversations typically go untranslated. The Westerner is left wondering whether to stare dumbly at his or her hosts, deep in Chinese conversation, to look to the translator for help, or to look elsewhere until the hosts again direct conversation to the Westerner in English or through the translator. Probably this last option is the best. The Westerner's visible signs of comfort during moments of untranslated conversation will come as a relief for Chinese business hosts. At the same time, the experience should alert the Westerner to feelings of being "left out"—feelings often encountered by Asian visitors to U.S. meetings and meals, where English buzzes on with little if any translation effort.

Cultures also have different conventions of *how long* audience members are typically willing to listen before offering reaction or input; *where* and *when* it is appropriate to listen to a sustained business presentation; and *what* they expect to hear in such presentations. See Chapter 18 for further information on the influence of culture on communication and for specific ways to prepare for listening habits that differ from your own.

FINAL CONSIDERATIONS

A Greek philosopher wrote, "The gods gave each of us one mouth and two ears. They should be used in that proportion."

When we meet superb listeners, we notice that their changing facial expressions show how carefully they are following each of our words. They indicate by a nod or a slight vocal noise that they understand and sympathize with what we are telling them. When we pause, they ask questions that get to the heart of the issue we've been trying to communicate.

We admit that such listeners are rare. More commonly, we talk at people whose eyes wander around the room, whose faces and body motions indicate that they are staying to hear us only out of courtesy or obligation.

Perhaps you can teach your co-workers how to listen by showing them how good it feels when you listen to them. Good listening can be contagious. By focusing on your own listening skills, you may start a trend that spreads throughout your company. At the very least, you'll learn more, and earn the goodwill of your business associates.

SUMMARY

1. Decision-makers at all levels of business must listen effectively to become aware of information they need.

2. Barriers to listening include overassertiveness, internal mental competition, prior assumptions, and laziness.

3. Basic types of listening are passive listening, attentive listening, interactive listening, and empathetic listening.

4. Different techniques can be used when listening for feelings than when listening for facts.

5. Good listeners give signs to the speaker to show that he or she is being heard and understood.

QUESTIONS FOR DISCUSSION

1. What is the difference between *listening* and *hearing?*

2. Why is listening important in business? Provide specific examples.

3. In what ways can overassertiveness prevent a person from listening effectively?

4. What is internal mental competition, and how does it affect the ability to listen?

5. What assumptions about the speaker or the situation can get in the way of listening?

6. What kinds of attitudes must often change for improved listening?

7. What kinds of habits must change for improved listening?

8. What is the difference between active and passive listening?

9. Define *empathetic listening*, and show how it differs from other forms of listening.

10. How does listening for facts differ from listening for feelings?

EXERCISES

1. Interview one or more managers regarding the importance of listening in business. Write up the results of your interview, or present your results orally to your class.

2. Collect stories from your friends and classmates about bosses who wouldn't or couldn't listen. Pay particular attention to the feelings of these friends and classmates. Determine how the bosses' inability to listen affected job productivity and employee satisfaction. Write up the results of your inquiry, or present your results orally to your class.

3. Write a dialogue between two or more characters in business in order to demonstrate how overassertiveness inhibits the ability to listen.

4. Write a dialogue between two or more characters in business in order to demonstrate how internal mental competition inhibits the ability to listen. You can place a character's thoughts (as opposed to spoken words) in parentheses.

5. Choose a speaker you listen to frequently. Without naming names, list your assumption about that speaker, and evaluate in writing how those assumptions influence your listening.

6. Call to mind a time when your assumptions about a situation prevented you from listening effectively. Evaluate in writing the effects of such assumptions on your willingness or your ability to listen.

7. Assume that you supervise a group of employees who don't listen well because of simple laziness. Describe in writing how you, as their manager, will go about building strong listening skills in the group.

8. Keep track of your own listening habits over a two-day period. List occasions when you listen passively, attentively, interactively, and empathetically. Evaluate in writing any insights you obtained into your own listening skills by this exercise.

9. Practice the techniques described in this chapter for listening for facts. Which technique worked best for you? In writing, evaluate your success in listening for facts.

10. Practice listening for feelings, as described in this chapter. Evaluate in writing the difference it makes to listen to the whole message, including feelings.

11. In a conversation with a friend or classmate, practice giving signs to the speaker, as described in this chapter. Evaluate in writing the results of this interactive listening technique.

12. Pick two or three people you consider to be excellent listeners. Describe in writing what qualities they share, and go on to evaluate how these qualities influence their ability to listen well.

INTERNET ASSIGNMENT

In your role as manager of a large work unit, you are frequently frustrated by having to repeat information and instructions to your employees. Weren't they listening at meetings? Didn't they hear you at briefings and planning sessions? You resolve to learn more about listening in the workplace so you can educate your workforce on this topic.

Begin by locating recent books on listening, especially those with a business focus. Sites such as *amazon.com* and *barnesandnoble.com* may be helpful in your search. Compile a list of these books, with whatever annotation you can find, describing their contents. Next, investigate Internet sites that provide information or consultation on listening. Write down the addresses of these sites and write a short content summary of each. Finally, include all these materials as supplements of a memo written to Michael Ortiz, Training Director at your company. In your memo, make your case for initiating a training program in listening for employees. Explain how the book list and Internet information attached to your memo can be helpful to Ortiz in his efforts to develop a curriculum for this training program.

CHAPTER 14

Gender Communication

In the last decade, several influential books (including Deborah Tannen's *You Just Don't Understand Me* (New York: Ballantine, 1991) and *Talking from 9 to 5* (New York: Avon, 1995) and Kathleen Kelly Reardon's *They Just Don't Get It, Do They?* (Boston: Little, Brown, 1996)) have argued that many aspects of women's verbal and nonverbal communication in business are distinctly different from those of men. Moreover, these authors assert, women's communication habits sometimes put them at a disadvantage for leadership roles, promotion, recognition, and full participation in decision making in corporate life.

In an oversimplified view, these arguments have sometimes been reduced to a latter-day version of Henry Higgins's complaint of Eliza Doolittle in *My Fair Lady*: "If only a woman could be more like a man!" But Tannen, Reardon, and others are making a much more substantial and sophisticated point: Women's communication habits in business exist for *reasons*; to understand those reasons is to put ourselves, both men and women, in a better position to choose mutually advantageous communication behaviors. In short, women and men must learn to listen to themselves and to one another, then make adjustments in communication styles to achieve fairness, make best use of human resources, and attain the organization's mission.

Some communication patterns used by women have been labeled "dysfunctional" (that is, disadvantageous to a woman's business welfare) because they apparently do not work well in a male-dominated, traditional business environment. That judgment, however, must be qualified and even refuted in many sectors of the rapidly changing business world of the twenty-first century. In the following specific description of language patterns used by women, rather than simply dismissing them as dysfunctional for the business environments of the past, in each case we note the positive ways in which those patterns may be useful to emerging business environments of the present and future.

HOW WOMEN TEND TO COMMUNICATE IN BUSINESS

Let us state at the outset that the following research observations are by no means applicable to all women in all business environments. No researcher of women's communication behaviors has claimed universality for results of quite limited studies. In Deborah Tannen's words:

> I do not imply that there is anything inherently male or female about particular ways of talking, nor to claim that every individual man or woman adheres to the pattern, but rather to observe that a larger percentage of women or men as a group talk in a particular way, or individual women and men are more likely to talk one way or the other. (p. 17).

At the same time, the science involved in this increasing body of research must be taken seriously. A number of studies have been carefully designed and critically analyzed. From such work we draw the conclusion that all businesspeople, men and women alike, should reevaluate their own communication styles and habits in the light of tentative findings from dozens of prominent linguists and social scientists.

Simply put, women do appear to communicate differently from men. Most often, because of this difference women have been judged negatively and have been instructed to "talk the talk" (i.e., the male talk) if they want to rise to positions of power in modern organizations. This effort to re-create women's communication patterns after men's image ignores the real contributions women bring to the organization through their ways of communicating. As a counterbalance, then, to the pervasive argument that women should learn to speak more like men, we offer brief interpretations of the first 20 gender communication differences in the following pages. These interpretations seek to point out the value of women's communication patterns *sans* alteration or repair for progressive organizations. We leave the last 10 gender communication differences in this list for the reader's own analysis, discussion, and interpretation.

Characteristics Associated with Gender Communication Patterns

1. Men are less likely to ask for information or directions in a public situation that would reveal their lack of knowledge.

   > *Man:* I don't need to stop at the gas station for directions. I can find the right street.
   > *Woman:* Why not stop and ask? It will save us time.

   This aspect of women's communication patterns can prove useful to what Peter Senge has called "the learning organization." The reluctance, out of pride or embarrassment, of "lone wolves" in organizations to seek assistance is counterproductive. The language habits of one gender can be extended throughout a company's culture as a way of encouraging openness to new information, reliance on team members as resources, and a constant readiness to ask questions and learn.

2. Women perceive the question "What would you like to do?" as an invitation for discussion and negotiation. Men perceive the same question as the stimulus to a direct answer.

Woman: We have to arrange a holiday party. What would you like to do? [expecting conversation about past holiday parties, anecdotes, personal memories, and possibility thinking]
Man: We have to arrange a holiday party. What would you like to do? [expecting places and times to be named]

Women's willingness to delay decision making pending a multidimensional review of background information and influences is sometimes portrayed as a deficit, especially for would-be leaders in an organization. But that same communication tendency can be valued as an antidote to a company's tendency to rush to judgment or to ignore relevant input. In modern organizations, leaders are cast less and less in the role of quick-draw decision-maker and more in the role of seer, with wisdom and patience implied. The gender communication approach of women in this case fits well with the requirements of leadership in complex organizations, where instant answers and quick decisions are often impossible or foolhardy.

3. Women misunderstand men's ultimatums as serious threats rather than one more negotiation strategy.

   Man: This is nonnegotiable. [a bluff]
   Woman: Fine, then. Have it your way. [doesn't recognize the bluff but accepts it as reality]

This may be a way of saying that women tend to attach meanings to words and assume that male speakers do as well. In the case above, the woman speaker believes that the man knows what "nonnegotiable" means and chooses the word to describe his position. If the man knows that his position is negotiable but chooses to dissemble by his choice of language, are we to praise his strategy and recommend it to both genders? In George Orwell's fine phrase, "The great enemy of language is insincerity." Women have much to teach about integrity in saying what you mean and meaning what you say.

4. In decision making, women are more likely to downplay their certainty; men are more likely to downplay their doubts.

   Woman: In making this recommendation, I think I've covered every base—at least the ones I'm aware of.
   Man: I make this recommendation with complete confidence.

Women's language tendency is sometimes portrayed as an inability to "stand strong" as a confident decision-maker. It can just as easily be regarded, and valued, as a reluctance to bluff the audience or to assume a posture of confidence that is neither felt by the speaker nor supported by the facts. The world may be seeking totems in which to believe, and men by their communication style may play into and even manipulate that need to believe in the all-confident, single-minded leader. Women, through their language of qualification and demurral, may be providing a necessary caution against the common need for simple answers and our leaders' proclivities for overclaim and totemism. In effect, women are telling it like it is: "I'm not entirely sure about my conclusions and I'm not going to pretend that I am, simply for the sake of your feelings of security. To do so would be to lie to you and, ultimately, to empower myself at your expense."

5. Women tend to lead by making suggestions and explaining those suggestions in terms of the good of the group. Men are more likely to lead by giving orders, with explanations (if any) based on rationales related to project goals.

> *Woman:* Let's proceed by dividing into teams. I think we can make the most of our individual talents by working with one another in smaller groups.
> *Man:* We're going to break into teams to divide up the workload and meet our deadlines.

Obviously, modern organizations require both approaches to planning and decision making as a way of dealing with rapidly changing business conditions. For every occasion when the team must be nourished and encouraged there is also a circumstance when someone has to call the shots without consensus (or relying on a trust bond that already exists with the group). The important point is that neither style is dysfunctional; both can be useful to serve different, though complementary, goals within the organization.

6. Women tend to apologize even when they have done nothing wrong. Men tend to avoid apologies as a sign of weakness or concession.

> *Woman:* I'm sorry, but I have to read you all this e-mail that just arrived from the boss.
> *Man:* Listen up. The boss just sent this e-mail . . .

In this case, only the most rigid literalist would interpret the phrase "I'm sorry" as an apology for a mistake of some kind. Instead, these words reveal a recognition that the listener's feelings may be bruised by the ensuing message and that the speaker is not unaware of or unresponsive to those probable feelings. In this way, women's communication patterns tend to insert emotional buffers into the push and shove of business life. What may on the surface appear to be unjustified apologizing is at a deeper level an effort to humanize the organization and its processes.

7. Women tend to accept blame as a way of smoothing awkward situations. Men tend to ignore blame or place it elsewhere.

> *Woman:* I probably didn't welcome our Japanese visitors exactly as I should have, but I tried to be gracious and sincere.
> *Man:* I met the Japanese visitors at the airport. Next time someone should tell me how and when to bow.

Business makes much of the need for "accountability" except when it comes to the language patterns illustrated here. The woman is clearly accepting responsibility for both what went right and what went wrong in her efforts to greet the Japanese visitors. The male, by contrast, seeks to avoid personal accountability and instead wants to pass it on to a vague "someone" in the organization. When less-than-ideal situations in business occur, the language habits of women in this case may be more likely depict the accountability involved rather than the language of denial men more typically use.

8. Women tend to temper criticism with positive buffers. Men tend to give criticism directly.

> *Woman:* You're doing a great job on this report, but you may want to look at page eight one more time. At least see what you think.
> *Man:* Fix page eight, then let me reread your report one final time before we send it upstairs.

As observed in number 6, an awareness of the listener's feelings is not a bad thing in business relationships. In the woman's example above, the speaker tries to preserve the relationship while changing the behavior. The man seems more willing to sacrifice relationship for the sake of behavior. In many organizations, that choice leads directly to low morale and excessive turnover.

9. Women tend to insert unnecessary and unwarranted "thank-you's" in conversations. Men may avoid thanks altogether as a sign of weakness.

> *Woman:* Thanks anyway, but I don't think I want to trade my parking place with Jack.
> *Man:* No, I don't want to trade for Jack's spot.

The facade of thanks is only part of a complex architecture of courtesy and civility that women may tend to prefer as their work environment. By contrast, the apparent tone of the male response here portrays the workplace as an arena for confrontation, victory, and defeat.

10. Women tend to ask "What do you think?" as a means of building consensus. Men often perceive that question to be a sign of incompetence and lack of confidence.

> *Woman:* What do you think about dividing my office into a work area and a waiting room?
> *Man* (thinks): It's her office. Can't she decide what she wants to do?

Let's assume that the woman in this example knows full well what she wants to do with her office. Her question is not a solicitation of permission (although the man takes it as such), nor is it a sign that she cannot make her own decisions. Instead, it is another demonstration of the tendency in women's language patterns to gather input and weigh opinions before acting.

11. Women tend to mix business talk with talk about their personal lives, and expect other women to do so as well. Men mix business talk with banter about sports, politics, or jokes (many of them sexually oriented).

> *Woman:* I don't mind traveling to Cincinnati, but it will mean finding overnight day care for our baby . . .
> *Man:* If I do go to Cincinnati, I'm taking an afternoon off to see a ballgame. That's the least they can do!

This question is worth asking: which gender is expressing most truthfully and accurately the impact of business responsibilities on personal life? Let's assume that the man in this case is a father and that he, no less than the working woman, has family matters to consider in arranging his business trip. He, too, must make provision for children, pets, and so forth. The point is that the woman tends to discuss with others how business duties influence her personal life, whereas the man is reluctant to do so. Businesses probably operate best in the daylight of knowing what problems, obstacles, and burdens their employees face. By knowing an employee's circumstances, the business can often adapt for "win-win" solutions.

12. Women feel that men aren't direct enough in telling them what they (women) are doing right. Men feel that women aren't direct enough in telling them what they (men) are doing wrong.

> Woman: I don't know how you feel about my work. [a request for more feedback]
> Man: Just tell me right out if you don't like what I'm doing. [a request to avoid mixed signals]

"Feedback" is a business buzzword that refuses to fade, perhaps because of its importance to employee motivation and quality management. Both genders in the example here are asking for feedback, but the woman's way of asking is more in line with the "360 degree feedback" systems currently in vogue for performance evaluations at all levels of organizations. The woman's communication pattern holds open the possibility that feedback may include both positive and negative aspects—that is, the full range of evaluation. The man's communication pattern closes the door to praise almost entirely and solicits only "trouble" feedback.

13. Women bring up complaints and troubles with one another as a means of arousing sympathy and building rapport. Men bring up problems only when they want to hear solutions.

> Woman: Our problem at home is just not enough time with each other. I get home just as Bob is leaving for his job . . .
> Man: We haven't been out to a show for months. Where do you find babysitters?

Sharing problems is not just an effort to build rapport and arouse sympathy. Perhaps more crucially, it is an effort to understand pain and thereby alleviate it. The woman's communication pattern in this example assumes that the group may have insights and experiences that will enlighten the nature of the pain or frustration at hand. The man's communication pattern is more cynical about the surrounding group's ability to provide in-depth perspectives or resonant ideas. The woman wants help in understanding the problem; the man wants help in postponing the problem.

14. Women's humor tends to be self-mocking. Men's humor tends to be razzing, teasing, and mock-hostile attacks.

> Woman: So I said in my charming way, "You forgot to plug it in."
> Man: So I said, "Do you notice anything strange about that cord lying on the floor?"

Freud wrote at length about "tendency humor"—our effort to disguise in humor what we really want to communicate. The tendency of the male communication pattern in this example is to emphasize the person's stupidity or foolishness. By contrast, the teller of the story is seen as smarter, less foolish, and more powerful. The woman defuses this potential power play in her softened version of the verbal transaction. She recognizes that the person will be placed "one down" by the incident, and so she consciously lowers her own status by self-mocking humor to avoid a breakdown in the relationship.

15. Women tend to give directions in indirect ways, a technique that men may perceive as confusing, unsure, or manipulative.

> *Woman:* You can handle this account any way you want, but taking him out to lunch might be a possibility. Or meet in his office. Whatever you think. Lunch, though, might be the way to go.
> *Man* (thinks): Is she telling me to take him to lunch or not? Is she setting me up for an "I-told-you-so" if I don't do it her way?

Organizations make much of "empowerment," which can take place only when the decision-maker-in-training has some options left open. In this case, the woman's communication pattern is conducive to empowerment because it leaves the decision-maker free to choose, learn, and grow within a range of options. The man's apparent preference for a "command" style of management may bring short-term efficiencies but does not encourage empowerment, with its allied benefits of creativity, motivation, and loyalty.

16. When women and men gather in a group, women tend to change their communication styles to adapt to the presence of the men. Women also practice "silent applause" by smiling more often, agreeing with others more often, and giving more nonverbal signals of attentiveness than men do.

    Audience adaptation is highly recommended in virtually all communication guides and textbooks, including this one. The apparent fact that women change their communication behaviors based on their audience is not a sign of uncertainty, deceit, or weakness. Instead, it is an effort to relate successfully.

17. Women in positions of authority tend to be less accustomed to dealing with conflict and attack than are men.

> *Woman:* Why is everyone mad at me?
> *Man:* This is an unpopular decision, but I've got to make it.

As consensus builders, women respond quickly and vocally to signs that consensus is failing and that relationships are threatened. For generations, this behavior has been interpreted negatively—"If you can't stand the heat, get out of the kitchen." It can just as well be interpreted positively for the purposes of modern organizations. Women are no less "tough" for recognizing and responding to conflict and attack. It can be argued that they are all the more tough for their willingness to confront and deal with those forces rather than stoically ignoring them.

18. Women are more often referred to by their first name than are men, sometimes as a sign of less respect for women and sometimes as a sign of presumed familiarity or intimacy.

> *Man:* Get Smith, Underwood, Connors, and Jill to go along with you on the sales call.

The use of the woman's first name in this example can also be interpreted as the male speaker's recognition that "Jill" is different from the gray functionaries Smith, Underwood, and Connors. Perhaps because Jill has expressed herself in more disclosing and honest communication patterns, she has risen to personhood and personality in the eyes of the speaker. He works with Smith et al., but he feels that he knows Jill. This is all said not to justify the unwarranted use of women's first names in an otherwise formal business environment, but to point out one additional reason why men so frequently opt to use women's first names and men's last names. Traditional notions of politeness may also explain men's reticence to use a woman's last name.

19. Men tend to be uncomfortable with female peers, particularly those who may threaten their power.

    "Working for a woman" is uncomfortable for many men primarily because they misunderstand the communication patterns explained throughout this chapter. The male employee may complain about the woman boss's seeming lack of direct supervision and mixed messages, while the woman boss may simultaneously complain about the male employee's unwillingness to discuss problems openly, to work well with others, and to share ideas.

20. Men tend to perceive a group of women in conversation as wasting time or hatching a plot of some kind. Women tend to perceive a group of men in conversation as doing business or working out power relations through bonding and joking.

    These at-a-distance impressions of gender-exclusive groups speak volumes about the core misunderstandings between male and female co-workers. Interestingly, women credit men with more positive activities (doing business, working out relations even in the midst of joking) than is the reverse case (wasting time, hatching a plot). Are women more sanguine about their co-workers generally than are men? Do women tend to see the corporate glass half full and men to see it as half empty? These questions grow directly out of research into women's communication patterns but cannot be answered by such linguistic research alone.

    We offer the remaining 10 gender communication patterns without interpretative commentary to allow breathing room for your own analysis, discussion, and insight.

21. Women tend to avoid direct confrontation about offensive behavior. Men tend to take stronger, more immediate stands in relation to stimuli they dislike.

> *Woman:* (shocked) I . . . guess that's one way to look at it.
> *Man:* (shocked) Wait a minute. You're way off base.

22. Women tend to react to disappointment by describing personal feelings. Men tend to react to disappointment by appealing to standards of fair play or by placing blame.

> *Woman:* I felt absolutely sick when I found out I wasn't promoted.
> *Man:* It's a raw deal. I deserved that promotion.

23. Women tend to express self-doubt and to seek affirmation after exhibiting assertive behavior. Men tend to repeat and reinforce their assertive behavior.

> *Woman:* I don't want to make a big deal out of this, but you've got to get here right when the office opens. Are we OK on this?
> *Man:* We open at 8:30 and that's when you have to arrive. Not 8:35 or 8:40. I don't want to have this conversation again.

24. Men tend to interrupt women much more often than women interrupt men.
25. Men tend to usurp ideas stated by women and claim them as their own. Women tend to allow this process to take place without protest.
26. Men tend to be more fearful of losing to a woman than to another man. Women tend to be more fearful of losing to another woman than to a man.

> *Woman:* I was up against Frank and Barbara for the two new job openings. I half expected to lose to Frank, but it killed me when they chose Barbara over me!
> *Man:* I was up against Frank and Barbara for the two new job openings. I understand why they chose Frank, but Barbara? What an insult to me!

27. Men tend to adopt patronizing behaviors in the presence of women. Women, in turn, may respond by finding father figures, knights, big brothers, and confessors in men.

> *Man:* I appreciate your interest in this project, Susan, but you've got enough on your plate. We'll let you know if we need more input.
> *Woman* (as if to a father): If that's the way you want it, it's fine with me. I've really enjoyed the times we've worked together.

28. Men value conversation primarily for information. Women value talk primarily for interaction.

> *Man:* What do you have going tomorrow? [seeks a point-by-point list of items]
> *Woman:* What do you have going tomorrow? [seeks conversation about job pressures, personalities, exciting or problematic situations]

29. Women appear to seek permission or validation by the addition of "tag questions" to their assertions. Men omit such tag questions or rephrase them as assertive challenges.

> *Woman:* Let's hold the executive committee meeting in Conference Room A, OK?
> *Man:* Conference Room C is obviously the best place for the executive committee meeting.

30. Women use softer voice volume to encourage persuasion and approval. Men use louder voice volume to attract attention and maintain control.

> *Woman:* (softly) I've read the files on the Henderson account and I'm wondering if . . .
> *Man:* (loudly) But have you read the files? I have! Here's what we need to do . . .

Kathleen Kelley Reardon sums up the conclusions of many researchers and social observers in the area of gender communication: "Patience and competence have proven insufficient to advance women to the top echelons of traditional business. More than two decades of research and study have convinced me that the problem lies not so much in discrimination (although it is part of the equation) but in the enduring nature of dysfunctional communication patterns and the stereotypes that accompany them" (p. 211).

In this chapter we are less ready to label women's communication patterns as dysfunctional. Instead, we have endeavored to counterbalance such judgments by showing how women's communication patterns align well with a new order of organizations in a new century, even though those patterns may not have served women well in previous centuries.

SUMMARY

1. Differences in communication patterns exist between genders.

2. Women in business have too often been counseled to "talk more like men" to get ahead.

3. Women's communication patterns have much to offer modern organizations, especially in the areas of leadership, team-building, employee motivation, and conflict resolution.

4. By recognizing their own and one another's communication patterns, men and women can equip themselves to use those communication patterns purposely and strategically to achieve business goals.

DISCUSSION QUESTIONS

1. Which communication patterns do you observe in yourself that accord with the list of gender differences in this chapter? Which do you observe that are at odds with the list?

2. Speculate about why communication patterns appear to differ between genders.

3. What is gained and what is lost by giving women the advice to change their communication patterns to a male orientation in order to get ahead in their careers?

4. How would one go about proving that the gender communication patterns listed in this chapter are shared by a vast majority of either women or men?

5. Are gender differences more or less pronounced in written communications, including e-mail? Explain your answer.

6. What differences in gender communication patterns have you observed beyond those listed in the chapter?

7. Do you believe gender communication patterns are in evidence during childhood years, or are they developed later?

8. To what extent do traditional power relationships in business help to explain differences in gender communication patterns? Would those patterns change in a business environment traditionally dominated by women?

EXERCISES

1. Take careful notes of gender communication differences at the next meeting (business or club) you attend. Report on your findings.

2. Read several articles in a magazine targeted to women readers. Then read several articles in a magazine targeted to male readers. What differences in style do you note between these sets of articles? How do you account for the differences you observe? Report on your findings.

3. Locate at least three gender-based communication patterns in your own communicating. Make a conscious effort to change those patterns over a period of days. Write or present a narrative of what you attempted to change, the difficulties involved in making the change, and the results of the change in terms of reactions you experienced from others.

4. Interview several classmates who have not seen the list of gender communication patterns listed in this chapter. Ask each interviewee if he or she believes differences in communication patterns do exist between genders. If so, ask the interviewee for specific examples. Report on your findings.

5. Of what practical business value is a knowledge of gender communication differences? Write or present your thoughtful response to this question.

INTERNET ASSIGNMENT

You supervise 26 men and women in a growing financial services organization. Your company's Board of Directors has mandated training for each employee in issues related to gender diversity and sexual harassment. Today you receive notice from your company president that such training will begin with your group as a pilot experiment. The president wants you to put together an effective but affordable training program for your people. To do so, you bring aboard a well-known consultant in the area. She admits that her one-day session with your employees will probably not be enough training to affect long-term behaviors. You and she discuss possible carryover activities that your employees can pursue to extend and reinforce the day of training provided by the consultant. In particular, the consultant refers you to the Internet to discover possible sites your employees can use to learn more about gender relations and productive inter-gender relationships. Investigate sites in the Listening and Gender Communication and the Communication Ethics and Law section of the Internet Guide. Write a memo or prepare a short presentation addressed to your employees. In your message, explain why and how to use the sites you have selected to enrich the training provided by the consultant.

PART FIVE

MANAGING ORAL COMMUNICATION

CHAPTER 15

Oral Presentations

Over the course of your career, you will speak hundreds of words for every one word you write. In phone conversations, one-to-one business conversations, meetings, and presentations, you will speak—for better or for worse—as your primary means to reach your own goals.

Because you want your spoken words to work well for you and for the company, you should make note of the following Communication Checkpoint.

Communication Checkpoint
Ten Tips for Effective Business Speaking

1. Do speak up, Don't mumble.
2. Do be brief. Don't talk on and on about your points.
3. Do look at your listeners. Don't avoid looking at your listeners.
4. Do organize your points. Don't ramble.
5. Do use visual aids when appropriate. Don't rely only on speaking.
6. Do use natural gestures. Don't be stiff.
7. Do maintain a comfortable pace. Don't rush or dawdle.
8. Do vary your volume, pitch, and tone. Don't talk without showing emotion or expression.
9. Do use pauses effectively. Don't stop and start.
10. Do listen. Don't ignore your listeners' gestures or comments.

LEARNING THE TEN TIPS FOR EFFECTIVE BUSINESS SPEAKING

Unfortunately, knowing what you should do does not by itself give you the ability to do it. If you are going to be able to follow the instructions in the Communication Checkpoint, you'll have to learn *how* to do these things. You'll probably have to practice doing them until they feel natural to you. When you're standing in front of your business associates or customers, you won't have time to recall checklists of dos and don'ts. You'll need to have the necessary speaking skills as part of you.

The key question, then, for this chapter is how can you make effective speaking skills become a natural, almost unconscious habit? The answer lies in understanding the "why" behind speaking principles, and then putting those principles to work in your business and public speaking.

Do Speak Up. Don't Mumble.

Why do business speakers so often mumble or speak so quietly that they can't be heard? They are responding to stress:

"I was so mad I *couldn't speak*," "I was so frightened I *couldn't even scream*," "I was *speechless* with surprise," "I *can't tell* you happy I am." Stress, whether negative or positive, acts directly on the muscles that make your voice work. In the first stage of stress, adrenaline tightens the vocal cords and muscles, shutting down the natural tones and pitches of ordinary speech. The voice gets high, squeaky, breathless, and cracked. Then the second stage of stress takes over: the wave of embarrassment. Because we feel unable to speak naturally, we try to hide our problem. We try to keep the words from leaving our lips. When we do speak, we dribble the words downward, not up and out to our audience.

Unfortunately, mumbling just makes the situation worse. The listeners who hear only mumbling may get irritated that they can't hear what's being said. If they show that they feel irritated, they make the speaker feel more nervous. Because the speaker is more nervous, the speaker mumbles even more . . . and so on.

Adjust Your Attitude

One of the first things you can do to stop the vicious cycle of nervousness and stress is to recognize that you don't have to be perfect to speak effectively. In fact, your listeners expect you to show that you're human and make mistakes. Your small mistakes may even make your listeners feel more comfortable around you because they know that they're not perfect either. If you show that you accept your own mistakes, you're letting them know that you probably can accept their mistakes as well.

Another secret that effective speakers have learned is to stop paying attention to themselves and to start paying attention to their listeners and to what they want to say to their listeners. When you concentrate on yourself—How do I look? How do I sound? How am I doing?—you don't pay attention to your listeners or to your message. Usually, your listeners have not come to see you; they've come to hear your message. How you look or how you sound isn't as important to them as what you have to say to them. Take your cue from your listeners and focus on your message, not on yourself.

**Communication
Insights**

Reaching the Unreachable Person

1. The *direct approach*, which requires you to:
   Confront the issue—for example, "I do not feel you hear me, and I don't know what else to do."
   Express a feeling—try saying, "It upsets me when you don't pay attention to me."

2. The *preventive approach*, which takes this format—"I know you have had trouble listening to me in the past, but would you try this once to hear a different point of view?"

3. The *therapeutic approach*, which requires you to say something like this—"You seem to have difficulty focusing on the discussion and often retreat behind a wall. This makes you unreachable—are you aware of it?"

4. The *punitive approach*, which requires posing an ultimatum: "If you can't discuss the issue without interruptions (or without changing topics, or whatever the person is doing), I will have to decide or act without your input."

5. The *indirect approach*, which can take these routes:

   - Writing a letter—some people communicate better through the written word than through face-to-face exchange.
   - Using a third party who has the confidence of the person.
   - Humoring and discounting.

When you focus on your message, concentrate on what you really want your listeners to learn or understand by the time you finish speaking. If you show your listeners your sincere interest in communicating a message to them, your listeners will be interested in hearing your message.

This doesn't mean that you'll never feel nervousness or stress. It just means that as soon as you stand in front of your listeners, you focus your attention on them and on your message, not on yourself. As you show your listeners that you care about them and about your message, you lose interest in your own nervousness. Amazingly, as you focus on your listeners and your message, the extra energy that you feel from the stress and nervousness will actually help you to be more active and enthusiastic in telling your message. Nervous energy becomes enthusiasm energy.

Adjust Your Vocal Cords

The second thing that you can change, to avoid mumbling, is your vocal cords. Changing your vocal cords is even easier than changing your attitude: yawn. Before you speak (not in front of your audience), open your mouth wide, tip your head back, and yawn deeply. This relaxes not just your state of mind, but also your vocal cords.

Once you are standing in front of your listeners (don't keep yawning!), look at the listeners farthest back in the room. Try to speak so that they can hear you. If they are craning their necks, leaning forward in their seats, tilting their heads, frowning, or squinting, you need to speak more loudly and more clearly.

The secret to speaking loudly is to project your voice from the deepest part of your lungs. Practice doing this before you speak by putting one hand over your vocal cords (in your neck) and one hand over your abdomen (beneath where you'd have a belt buckle). As you try to speak loudly, make your abdomen tighten up to force the air up through your lungs and out into your voice. The hand over your abdomen should feel your muscles tightening, and the hand over your vocal cords should feel your vocal cords loosening and vibrating more.

Practice this technique with a friend or co-worker who can tell you whether you're speaking loudly enough. As you practice more and get better, have your friend move farther away from you. Once you're good at the technique, you might try doing this in an open area such as a park. If your friend can hear you there, your listeners in an auditorium will be able to hear you easily.

One more tip will help you to keep from mumbling: speak as distinctly as possible, pronouncing each and every consonant, vowel, and syllable. It may seem awkward at first, but the more you do it, the more natural it will feel to do it. Several *articulation* (distinct speaking) exercises are given at the end of this chapter to help you further in speaking distinctly.

Do Be Brief. Don't Talk On and On about Your Points.

People ramble for three reasons:

1. They want to postpone the listeners' opportunity to react to what they are saying until they are reasonably sure the listeners will approve.
2. They enjoy the spotlight of attention and hate to give it up.
3. They're nervous about having pauses or silences and aren't sure what to say.

If you notice yourself rambling, or if your listeners give you signs that they're losing interest, try to figure out which of these may be your reasons for rambling. If it's for Reason Number 1, you might try asking leading questions to get the listener to say what you want instead of saying it yourself.

For example, if you were trying to convince listeners to spend money on safety equipment, you might ask, "What do you think we should do to make sure that [some awful disaster that the safety equipment could prevent] doesn't happen?" If you practice this skill, you can often get your listeners to make your points for you.

Two additional techniques may help you avoid rambling.

1. Ruthlessly cut your material to its essential message. Notice how the text of this speech has been improved by trimming away unnecessary fat.

> ~~Up to the present point in time, the employees and the management~~ To date, ~~of~~ Dartmoor Locks~~have agreed between themselves publicly and pri-~~ has restricted takeover bids. ~~vately to maintain the present independence of the company as an~~ ~~entity free from corporate entanglement with foreign financial~~ ~~and industrial organizations seeking to participate and even di-~~ ~~rect the interests and growth of the company through the control~~ ~~and manipulaton of its financial resources.~~

2. Frequently ask questions of your listeners. Though they may not be called upon to actually answer the questions aloud, the listeners will form answers for themselves. This will give them the feeling that they are participating in your speech. Observe the questions in the following excerpt:

> Our corporate headquarters fronts on the busiest thoroughfare in Atlanta. But what do those thousands of potential customers see as they look at our building? A gray, nondescript slab with an almost unnoticeable sign, "Wendselly Air Purifiers." Could

they enter our offices if they wanted to? Only if they discovered the side door, located on a one-way street with no parking. Before complaining about sinking profits at Wendselly, we have to ask a searching question: Does our building itself invite the business we say we want?

Do Look at Your Listeners. Don't Avoid Looking at Your Listeners.

Our eyes, more than any other facial feature, reveal our responses to others: awe, approval, skepticism, confusion, ridicule, and rejection. Insecure speakers naturally fear looking at the faces of the audience. That's perfectly natural at first. True bravery isn't being fearless—it's going ahead even when you feel afraid. When you do that, something amazing happens. When you look sincerely at the faces of your listeners, they become sincerely interested in what you have to say. When you show your interest in them, they become more interested in your message.

As you gradually feel more comfortable, so will your listeners. If you start to enjoy speaking to them, they'll enjoy listening to you. Let your audience know by direct eye contact that they can feel comfortable. You pay attention to their looks in an effort to make your message clear.

In addition to fear, another reason that many fail to look at their listeners is that they're too busy trying to read their notes—or even to read their whole speeches. Try to keep your eyes off notes or a manuscript and on your audience. Even on the most formal occasions, audiences appreciate a warm, conversational flow in speeches. For most speaking situations, therefore, don't write down every word you plan to say. You'll end up reading your speech, or—just as bad—delivering it with the zombie-glaze across the eyes that says to all, "I've mesmerized—I mean, memorized my whole speech."

You may be asking, "If I can't read my speech, how on earth am I going to be able to cover my points and remember to say what I need to say? I'll be so flustered that I'm sure I'll forget something important." Two techniques can help to make sure that you won't do this:

1. Organize your points well.
2. Use appropriate visual aids.

Sound familiar? These are the next two tips for effective speaking. If you have organized your points into a brief outline, as shown on the notecard in Figure 15–1, you can occasionally glance at it to see where you are now and what to say next. Notice that the notes in the figure are very brief, yet include a few key phrases or details to help jog the speaker's memory.

Another trick is to use visual aids, such as overhead projectors with transparencies. When you use effective visual aids, both your listeners and you can follow your outline, to see where you are and what you will talk about next. When you use well-organized visual aids, you and your listeners can follow your points together. You become allies in communicating your message.

Do Organize Your Points. Don't Ramble.

Chapter 3 described several patterns for the organization of written materials. These same patterns can be used to advantage by the speaker, with one addition: the overview.

FIGURE 15–1 Speaker's Notecard

> "The person with three hats . . ."
> —Managers as <u>judges</u>
>   (promotional procedures)
> —Managers as <u>organizers</u>
>   (job scheduling/formatting)—slides
> —Managers as <u>friends</u>
>   (personal support, advice, encouragement)
> Express appreciation to present managers,
> congratulations to new managers
> "When I began . . ."

Overview

Unlike readers, audiences have no chance to glance back to your earlier words in an effort to clear up confusion. The pattern of your thought must be clear from the beginning. Therefore, you should give a brief outline at the beginning of your presentation, as shown in the following examples.

> We have to choose the type of building we want for our proposed Seattle branch. Consider three alternatives with me: 1. the downtown remodel/renovation office; 2. the industrial park office; 3. the suburban office. Each has advantages and disadvantages.

Basing her speech on this overview, the speaker goes on to treat the advantages and disadvantages of each alternative.

Here is another example of an overview, this time using the past, present, future pattern of organization.

> We can plan most effectively by looking first at how we used to produce the K-14; then, at how we now produce it, using computer-aided design techniques; and, finally, at our production needs in the five years ahead.

This speaker will work from past to present to future. At every point in the presentation, listeners will know where they have been, where they are, and where they are going.

Reminders

Even highly intelligent and interested listeners have a hard time paying attention for more than 30 seconds at a stretch. Therefore, you should give occasional reminders of where you are in your outline. A good reminder looks both back to where the speaker has been and forward to what lies ahead. For example,

> So much for the urban remodel/renovation office. We can now discuss the second alternative, the industrial park office.

For longer presentations, handouts, projected slides and transparencies, and other visual aids can help both you and your listeners stay on the organizational path.

Do Use Visual Aids When Appropriate. Don't Rely Only on Speaking

Chapter 10 offered extensive suggestions for using visual aids, as well as quite a few good reasons for using them. Visual aids help to keep you aware of the points you want to be sure to mention. Words, words, words unrelieved by visual experiences can quickly lose your audience's attention.

Audience Attention

Figure 15–2 shows the typical attention-span curve for a business address. Attention drops off rapidly after the audience has heard about three minutes of the speaker's address. Attention perks up again from time to time, usually at moments when the speaker tells a brief, interesting story of some kind. When the speaker starts to come to a conclusion, attention rises again somewhat. Listeners hope to catch a summary of the points they have missed.

Figure 15–3, by contrast, shows the attention curve when visual aids are used. The initial interest level is higher when listeners expect to enjoy visual experiences. When those moments arrive, attention rises.

A Supplement to Words

Audiences love pictures, shapes, lines, and colors, in addition to words. Whenever possible, accompany your presentation with something visual they can hold in mind not only as you speak but after the presentation as well. The range of possibilities for visual aids is attractively large:

Handouts	Physical models
Slides	(architect models, scale models, etc.)

FIGURE 15–2 Typical Attention Curve for a Business Address

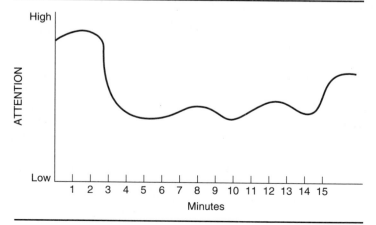

FIGURE 15–3 Attention Curve for a Business Address with Visual Aids

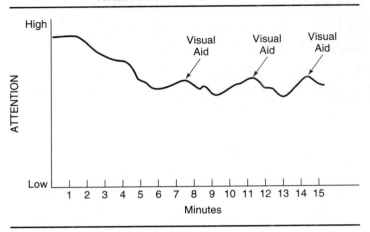

Overhead transparencies	Movies
Flipcharts	Maps
Blackboards	Television/videotape/videodisk
Felt-covered presentation charts	Computer presentation software, for projected or monitor viewing

Visual aids also make listeners feel that you have specially prepared for your speech. Your listeners feel that you must really care about them and about your message if you went to all this trouble.

Before you use visual aids, you should heed two warnings:

1. Make sure to coordinate your visual aids with the rest of your presentation.
2. Don't distribute a handout too early in a meeting if you think it might make all of your listeners become readers.

Do Use Natural Gestures. Don't Be Stiff.

Speaking without using your hands is like hiking without boots or shoes of any kind. It can be done. You can get where you're going. However, you are overlooking an easy way to make the hike more comfortable and the speech more effective.

Don't try to plan each of your gestures ahead of time. Your gestures must come naturally and be in close coordination with what you are saying and who you are. Notice, by the way, your own large variety of gestures that you use in everyday conversations with friends. You create emphasis, special meanings, and sincerity with your hands and body.

The goal, then, is not to learn gestures but to bring the natural gestures you already use into your business speaking. Your hands will do just the right thing once you give them a chance. They can't gesture at all, of course, if you hold them rigidly at your sides or you grip the edges of the *lectern* (the stand on which a speaker can place lecture notes). Free your hands to gesture by consciously placing them in a "takeoff position."

- As you begin to speak, touch your fingertips together in front of you. It doesn't matter where or how your fingertips touch. Once they meet, let your hands move where they will. When you're tired of gesturing, let your hands rest comfortably at your sides or on the lectern until you're ready to bring them to a new takeoff position.
- Touch a button on your coat, shirt, or blouse just for a second. Your audience will never notice, but you will have placed one hand in another good takeoff position for gesturing. At any time, the other hand can move to a button, then into action.
- Touch your cheek with the fingertips of one hand, then gesture. Most talented speakers keep their gestures relatively high on their upper bodies, so that they don't distract attention from eye contact (Figure 15–4).

High gestures help the listener look *through* the gestures into the speaker's eyes. The audience is hardly aware of the gestures at all and for that reason is all the more caught up in their effectiveness.

Though thousands of gestures are effective, a few gestures don't work well and actually distract the attention of your listeners:

THE POINTER
Don't point at your audience over and over with one finger. Instead, if you want to gesture toward your listeners, use an open hand. That way, you don't put anyone on the spot or make anyone feel singled out.

THE PUMPER
Don't raise and lower your arm in a repeated, energetic pumping motion. Any obsessively repetitious body movements distracts audience attention from what you have to say.

THE JANGLER
Some speakers fidget with objects in their pockets or with a piece of jewelry, such as bracelets or a necklace. The result can be a distracting jingle.

FIGURE 15–4   Gestures Appropriately High and in View

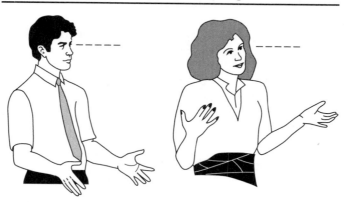

Low gestures distract attention
from eye contact.

High gestures supplement
eye contact.

THE SAINT

Don't deliver an entire presentation with your hands folded solemnly in front of you. Like an interminable prayer, this posture becomes increasingly uncomfortable for an audience. Your listeners pay more attention to your hands than your words.

You can study quite masterful gesturing by turning to religious or political presentations on television. Turn the volume down, and observe the natural way in which body movement, facial gestures, and hand motions work together to contribute to meaning. Although you may want to experiment with the gesturing techniques you see, don't try to copy another speaker's habits too closely. Build on gestures that you find natural and comfortable.

Do Maintain a Comfortable Pace. Don't Rush or Dawdle.

Most business presentations proceed at a pace slightly slower than ordinary conversation. The listeners, after all, must have time to fully understand the words of the presentation.

Mentally establish a comfortable pace by saying (silently!) the Pledge of Allegiance (reprinted here for good measure).

> I pledge allegiance to the flag of the United States of America, and to the republic for which it stands. One nation, under God, with liberty and justice for all.

The familiar pace we use for that pledge serves well for most business speaking occasions. You can use the rhythms and pace of the pledge to set a tempo for yourself, much in the way a band leader counts off before the band begins to play.

Do Vary Your Volume, Pitch, and Tone. Don't Talk without Showing Emotion or Expression.

Volume refers to how loudly or softly you speak. *Pitch* is the relative highness or lowness of your voice, as measured against a musical scale. *Tone* is a catchall category for the many moods and textures of the voice: harsh, sarcastic, sincere, whimsical, pleading, serious, goofy, and so forth.

When speakers fail to vary these key factors, the result is a relentless monotone. It vaguely recalls a mosquito buzzing on a hot night or your neighbor's power saw running for an entire day.

Listen to yourself to improve your natural speaking rhythms and changes. Read the following short sentences aloud. Listen to your natural rises and falls in volume and pitch, as well as your choice of appropriate tone.

MAD   You have no right to use my name in that way.

SARCASTIC   Well, you didn't wreck the whole car.

INNOCENT   I had no idea you already scheduled a meeting for that day.

ASSERTIVE   I feel that I've served this company well, and deserve a raise as much as anyone else.

DEPRESSED   OK, we'll try it just one more time.

Notice your own obvious changes in the volume, pitch, and tone of your voice. From our earliest years, we naturally change the volume, pitch, and tone of our speech. Now that you've heard the kinds of adjustments you naturally make when you speak, use those abilities to your advantage in business speaking.

Tape record one of your business or classroom presentations to check your progress in varying volume, pitch, and tone. Listen with care. If you hear a drone, stop the tape at a particularly flat sentence or two. Say those sentences aloud, this time adding the variations in volume, pitch, and tone you may have left out previously.

Do Use Pauses Effectively. Don't Stop and Start.

Just as new paragraph beginnings provide fresh starts for readers, pauses in speaking mark the end of one listening task and the beginning of the next for the listener. Many business speakers don't realize how valuable these pauses can be. They fear that a pause will be misinterpreted as a temporary loss of direction or a sign of poor preparation. Foolishly, they rush along at a steady clip without a pause.

Why to Pause.   As listeners would love to tell them, such speakers are dead wrong about pauses. Listeners appreciate the chance to let important points sink in; the chance to let the senses relax for a moment; and the chance to mentally take a deep breath before plunging into concentration again on the next portion of the speech.

How Long to Pause.   Pause can be learned in a simple, painless, and wholly reliable way. Simply swallow. The typical swallow takes a little less than two seconds to accomplish—the perfect length of time, by fortunate coincidence, for the effective pause.

The swallow has the additional advantage of soothing the vocal chords, helping to promote a clear, pleasant voice quality. Best of all, the swallow is virtually unnoticed by your audience. Remember that you, the speaker, are energized, while your listeners are much more relaxed. A two-second pause may seem to last forever to you, but it may be just right to your audience.

When to Pause.   Usually, these brief breaks can prove effective

- Before and after crucial points
- At the end of each major section of the address
- After especially significant or difficult names or terms
- After an important statement or a call to action. For example,

Finally, let me make a personal observation, (Pause) I feel strongly that . . .

How Often to Pause.   Pauses, like spices, can be overdone. Be careful not to fall into the habit of pausing after each thought. Your listeners will be left with the task of tying all your single sentences together into larger meanings.

Do Listen. Don't Ignore Your Listeners' Gestures or Comments.

Remember that the word *communication* means shared experience. Listeners find ways to share with you what they are thinking while you are talking:

- They shake or nod their heads, indicating approval or disapproval of your points.
- They reveal in their eyes and facial gestures such responses as acceptance, skepticism, resistance, and outright rejection.
- They use body language. Notice that some members of your audience sit comfortably, much as they would in a restaurant. Others slouch down in their chairs, seemingly weary of you; a few lean forward, their elbows on their knees; one or two rest chins-on-hands, eyes half open.
- They buzz, whisper, pass notes, and signal visually to others in the room.
- They break into your speech with questions.

COMMUNICATION FOR A NEW CENTURY

THE ART OF AUDIOVISUAL TELECONFERENCING

As new satellite links reduce the expense of audiovisual teleconferencing, some businesses, particularly large ones, are beginning to send their employees' images across the country or around the world rather than sending their bodies. A coast-to-coast audiovisual teleconference (with full motion video and audio, much like network broadcasting) now costs less than $800 an hour. Six businesspeople in Los Angeles, for example, could meet electronically with their colleagues in New York. Compare the cost of that teleconference with the much larger expense, effort, and interconvenience of transporting the same people on a typical business trip, including airfares, hotel expenses, and travel time away from the office.

Unfortunately, the communication skills necessary for participation in an audiovisual teleconference differ from the skills used in traditional business meetings. Much like actors preparing for television appearances, many U.S. managers are now receiving professional coaching on how to communicate more effectively in teleconferences. While such coaching depends on the needs of the individual manager, five guidelines are often emphasized:

1. Look through the camera to your intended listeners. As they look at your face on-screen, they must feel that your eyes are looking directly into theirs. If you don't look into the camera, your listeners may think that you seem awkward, uncomfortable, or disinterested.

2. Use facial expressions as you would in a conversation. It's tricky at first to produce natural facial expressions to a camera instead of to a person. For that reason, many first-time teleconferencers complain that they look stiff, expressionless, and boring. Before the actual teleconference, try to practice with videotape to see how well your facial expressions communicate your message.

3. Speak more distinctly and more loudly than in normal meeting conversation. Even the best audio transmission involves some distortion or omission of your vocal sounds. Compensate by consciously trying to speak clearly.

4. Plan in advance for graphics that will transmit well. If your meeting involves visual displays, work with your audiovisual technician to make sure that you are pleased with the way they appear on-screen.

5. Relax as you would for an in-person meeting. Remind yourself, therefore, to relax and to focus on your message and on your listeners. Your success as a teleconference speaker will be even greater if you can appear comfortable, warm, and naturally involved.

Don't let these cues and clues upset you. Don't forget your message, start mumbling, lose eye contact, forget gestures, and so forth. Instead, take these cues as responses to your message, and change what you say and how you say it, just as you would in a conversation.

After every business presentation, realize that your listeners were trying to tell you something, and force yourself to think about this question: What did I see, hear, or feel that let me know my listeners' response?

Here is one speaker's written response to this question.

> The drumming fingers and swinging legs let me know that I should be more lively. Dull, weary eyes told me that some kind of visual aid was needed to spark interest. The frowns and forward leaning of some of the older employees suggested that perhaps they couldn't hear me, and that I should speak more distinctly and tighten my belt muscles for better projection. The quizzical looks of almost half the audience when I referred to "our notorious Canadian problems" indicated I should have explained what I meant right then and there. The appreciative nods from many listeners indicated support for my recommendations.

By answering the question of what listeners are telling you, you sensitize yourself to the needs of your listeners. As you speak more often, you'll get better at responding to those needs *while* you speak, instead of analyzing what you could have and should have done after the speech.

UNDERSTANDING THE FEAR OF PUBLIC SPEAKING

Many businesspersons agonize over their 2 to 20 minutes (the usual limits of a short presentation) before an audience, even one made up of close business associates and friends. Figure 15–5 shows the relative anxiety of several forms of public speaking. We can condense their worries into one long moan:

> I know I'm going to forget my speech and make a fool of myself. They'll notice that I'm a bit overweight, that my upper lip shakes when I'm nervous, that my hands tremble. I feel like I can't breathe. I don't just perspire or glow: I sweat. I hate, hate, hate to make speeches.

Unfortunately, you must make speeches if you intend to move up in your company. Don Keough, president of Coca-Cola, put it well:

> As you move up through your career path, you're judged on your ability to articulate a point of view. Once you reach certain levels in an executive capacity, the ability to communicate perhaps a little better than others is a tremendous asset.

Thomas Swanson, M.D., psychiatrist, poses the question—"What are the causes of anxiety or fear associated with public speaking?" and offers the following answer.

ANTICIPATORY ANXIETY

> Basically, there is really only one process that causes fear of public speaking: *Anticipatory Anxiety.* This involves the process of saying "What if?" (What if I get nervous? What if I forget? What if the audience laughs at me? What if they think I'm stupid?) We learn to have anticipatory anxiety about speaking through previous bad experiences. We then live in dread

FIGURE 15–5   Progressive Steps in Oral Business Communication

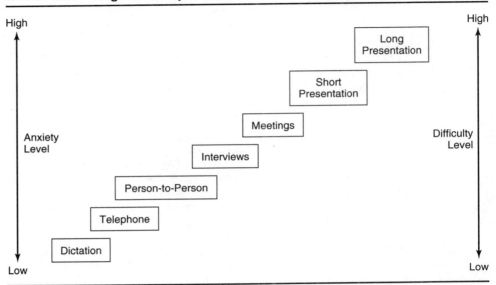

that the previous negative experience will repeat itself. For most of us the anticipation is far worse than the actual anxiety we experience while doing the activity. One of man's greatest assets—the ability to think and plan—actually becomes a liability in this kind of situation.

Dr. Swanson suggests the following techniques to self-treat or unlearn the fear or anxiety of public speaking.

1. Education
2. Experience
3. Attitude
4. Focus on the Present

Education.   Learning a few methods of writing, speaking, and communicating will help to decrease your anxiety. Knowing *what* to do helps. The principles in this book may help you to get started.

Experience.   For most of us, the more we do something, the more relaxed and the less fearful we become. This is the most common way that people lose their fears (we *learn* to relax, or we *desensitize*). An example is the anxiety that most of us feel during the first few days or weeks on a new job. If we hang in there and keep going to work, the anxiety soon fades.

Attitude.   *Think* differently about the situation. An important new concept in mental health is that successful people are able to change the way they think or believe about problems.

For example, two people in Anaheim, California, reacted quite differently to their situations when they each lost their house and all their belongings in a fire. In a TV interview hours after the fire, each was crying. The first said, "I can't stand it. I don't know what I'll do. It's the end. What's the point?"

The second said, "I'm upset. I don't like this, but I'm glad none of us was hurt. Oh, well. Life goes on." The differences in the way people think determine how they feel and cope with problems. Learning to talk to ourselves in more rational ways helps.

In the same way, you may be talking to yourself when you get in front of an audience. (If you are feeling *anything*, you are talking to yourself.) If you're anxious you're saying something like, "I *must* give a great talk and everyone *must* love it. If not, I'm a bad person in some way." (Notice how you're putting your whole self-esteem on the line simply by the way you think.)

In contrast, you might try to tell yourself the following: "I sure hope the audience likes the talk; but if they don't, it's okay. It's not what I prefer, but in any case, *I'm okay!*" In other words, your value, your worth, is not on the line.

There is another very important principle and consequence of talking to yourself positively: Because your self-esteem is not on the line, you're relaxed. If you're relaxed, you give a better talk!

Focus on the Present. Learn to concentrate on the here and now. Don't focus on the future, asking, "What if . . . ?" By definition, if you focus on the present, you're focusing on these what-if worries. Therefore, focus on what you're saying *now*. *Now* means this moment—this very second.

Take a moment right *now* to focus on the now. Focus on what you see, hear, taste, touch, smell. Pay attention to temperature, the feel of the book in your hand, noises in the environment, your breathing in and out, and so forth. It's important not to evaluate, but simply to be aware of your sensory experiences. When you do this, your anxiety, worry, and fear simply disappear.

THREE SITUATIONS FOR BUSINESS-RELATED SPEAKING

Although the variety of business-related speaking situations is great, the most common situations are as follows:

1. Brief appreciation and introduction speeches
2. Luncheon and dinner addresses (which may be almost any length)
3. Business presentations (which are usually relatively long)

The remainder of this chapter describes some specific strategies and techniques for making business-related speeches in these three common situations.

Brief Appreciation and Introduction Speech

As a business leader, you will probably be called on to "say a few words" about a company guest or colleague. In a short speech of appreciation, remember to do the following:

- Mention why the honored person deserves praise.
- Provide an effective example of the honored person's work or influence.
- Offer members of the audience the opportunity to participate in the appreciation (by applause, attending a party, or the like).

Before introducing a company guest or associate, determine from the person involved what educational attainments, work achievements, and positions of responsibility that person would like you to mention. In your introduction, be certain to suggest why the person is present with you (to look over the new office, to give a speech, for example). If your guest or associate is making a speech following your introduction, be careful not to steal the person's thunder, so to speak, by giving away a dramatic opening he or she plans to use.

Keep appreciations and introductions short, sincere, and warm. Except on very formal occasions, such speeches rarely are more than five minutes long.

Luncheon and Dinner Addresses

Somewhere after the main course and before the dessert, you may have to stand at the speaker's podium to speak for twenty minutes or so to your business associates or clients. These sorts of speaking occasions can be difficult. Waiters clink dishes as they clean off the tables; half the group lights up cigarettes for a relaxing after-meal attempt to choke the speaker. You haven't enjoyed your meal, feeling butterflies starting to flutter within.

Make the best of these circumstances by pleasing your audience in three ways.

1. Grab your listeners' attention right away.
2. Tell your listeners your central message.
3. Conclude your speech with a memorable emphasis of your point.

Grab Attention Right Away

The following techniques often help to get your listeners' attention immediately:

- Personal story
- Anecdote
- Pointed humor
- Unexpected statement
- Related fact or reference to location (linked to common audience interests or characteristics)

Additional techniques for getting attention are mentioned later in this chapter in the section on long business presentations.

The Personal Story.   Audiences respond to the intimacy and warmth of personal revelations that have a point.

> When I was a child, my father and I had a favorite pond hidden in the midst of small hillocks in northern Pennsylvania. We never caught many fish there, but we talked a lot. We got to know each other. One day, driving to the pond, we rounded the last corner to find the pond, the little hills, the trees absolutely gone—hauled away, it turned out, by huge coal trucks. We got out of the car and walked a short way on the raw, torn, scraped earth. My father's only words were, "Remember this, Sarah. Remember."

The speaker goes on to talk about the effects of technological change.

The Anecdote.   Closely related to the personal story, the anecdote makes a point about an incident, but it isn't personal about the speaker.

Americans have always enjoyed harpooning their political leaders. During Grover Cleveland's years in the White House, rumors flew regarding his extracurricular love relations. One cartoonist went so far as to depict a fatherless child on her mother's knee, imploring,

"Ma, Ma, where's Pa?"
The satiric answer followed—
"In the White House, ha, ha, ha."

The speaker proceeds to discuss why we sometimes hold political leaders in such low esteem.

Pointed Humor.   Not just any joke will do the trick. A joke that has no point ("Where does a general keep his armies? In his sleeves.") has no place as the opener in a speech. Audiences expect you to relate a joke to your essential purpose.

The poet Wordsworth, for all his genius, never mastered the art of humility. In discussing Shakespeare one day, Wordsworth remarked to Charles Lamb that "anyone could write like Shakespeare if he had a mind to." "Yes," replied Lamb quietly, "all he requires is the mind."

The speaker goes on to praise the quiet, inspired work of a company vice president who is retiring.

The Unexpected Statement.   Audiences lean forward in mild shock when they hear a speaker say just the opposite of what they expect to hear.

I've been asked to talk about the wonders of the computer revolution. Well, it's all a matter of dirty sand and dirty water.

The speaker soon makes clear that she is speaking of the use of trace elements in silicon—dirty sand—and similar elements in simple cellular structures—dirty water—as the basis for some computer technologies.

The Local Fact or Site.   You can choose to open a speech by reminding your audience of a local fact or nearby site with special bearing on your message.

Less than a mile from where we now sit, an Indian chief named Okanohok in 1837 signed over half of his tribe's 14,000 square miles of hunting territory for a government promise to supply the chief with 400 horses and 200 rifles.

The speaker goes on to disparage a takeover bid.

Tell Your Central Message

Once you have opened your speech and have earned the audience's attention, move immediately to your central topic. You can organize your thoughts by any of the patterns suggested in Chapter 3 or a pattern of your own. In a short speech, however, try to stress no more than three major points, or one point with three aspects.

Your speaking style should be energetic, direct, and conversational. Recall the common, simple style that Abraham Lincoln used in writing and probably in delivering the Gettysburg Address. Be just that human and approachable when you speak.

You may feel more secure with speaker's notes jotted on several cards. If so, don't let the cards interfere with your ability to look at your listeners and to gesture naturally. By setting the cards down on the lectern at the beginning of your speech, you free your hands for communicating.

Especially when giving informal luncheon and dinner speeches, do not try to read from a manuscript. If you find that writing out every word of your speech helps you, spend time reading and rereading the manuscript so that the speech can be delivered almost entirely by memory. When speaking the words you have memorized, try to make them sound natural and spontaneous.

A better idea than memorizing or reading your speech is to use visual aids in your speech. Each year, we rely more on what we see and less on what we hear for important meanings. By using such aids as slides, transparencies, charts, and objects, you appeal to your listeners' appetite for visual meanings.

Conclude with Emphasis

Close the short address by memorably bringing your thoughts to a conclusion. Each of the following closings provides that dramatic final moment (five more closings are treated later in the discussion of the longer presentation):

- Praise and Appreciation
- Call for Action
- Summary Plus
- Prediction
- Return to the Beginning

Praise and Appreciation.   You can close a short address by thanking your audience, praising all or some of its members for specific attributes or achievements, or expressing your appreciation in some other form.

> It has been my purpose to discuss two negative influences on company revenues. Let me conclude by paying tribute, though, to 100 very positive influences—those of you sitting before me.

Call for Action.   If you have tried to persuade your audience to take a particular course of action, close by specifically calling for that action.

> Theories of management are just that—theories—until real people take the time and effort to make them work. Together, we have discussed the importance of strong leadership in each of the company's divisions. In less than five minutes, each of you will return to your division and its people. Make the theory of effective management come to life through the words you say and the actions you take this very afternoon.

Summary Plus.   Listeners appreciate a concluding summary but also want to be left with something more, a "plus."

To sum up, we've seen three ways in which the San Moritz line of ski-wear can enhance profits at Leland Sports Supply.

1. The product line allows a healthy markup, with some advertising costs paid by the manufacturer.
2. Ski-wear will draw a new kind of customer into our store.
3. The introduction of ski-wear will give us a chance to test the market for other lines of sports clothing.

I leave you with one last bit of trivia—hardly worth mentioning. I suppose: The salesperson who sells the most San Moritz ski-wear this year gets an expenses-paid ski trip to San Moritz, Switzerland!

Prediction.   After marshaling facts and evidence for several minutes, you may conclude your speech by issuing a prediction or a prophecy.

If we invest this year in CAD/CAM equipment, here's my prediction for the next few years. In 2001, we'll still lag behind the competition as we pay for our new equipment. In 2004, we'll draw even. By 2006, we'll lead the pack, and we won't be overtaken for the foreseeable future.

Return to the Beginning.   If you began your speech in a rousing way, you may want to take your listener back to that moment for a wrapup.

We began this afternoon with a question: Why diversify our product line when we're doing so well? You've seen evidence and heard arguments to answer that question in two words. Why diversify? To survive.

A final note of caution: Some luncheon and dinner speakers, overcome by the appreciative applause, feel called upon to say a few additional words, something of an encore. Resist this temptation. No matter how much the audience liked your speech, they are probably glad it has ended. Their work of listening hard is over, and they can begin to relax and digest their food.

Business Presentations

Like luncheon and dinner addresses, business presentations should grab attention right from the start. Probably your range of openings will be more restricted when making business presentations. You may not, for example, want to tell personal stories. However, used with discretion, openers involving humor, anecdotes, and all the rest can work effectively even in a session that's business oriented.

Because business presentations often ask for financial decisions instead of applause, your pattern of organization must be absolutely clear to your audience. Consider, therefore, handing out an attractive outline of your major points. The page can contain especially persuasive charts and tables or a list of terms new to the listener.

Conclude the business presentation with a call to action, using specific language:

Based on the evidence we have reviewed today, I recommend that our company considers acquisition of Herder Printing within the next 60 days. I will remain after the meeting to talk with those of you who wish to help draft a resolution to the Board of Directors regarding this most attractive acquisition.

As you move up in your company, you will find yourself addressing larger crowds for longer periods. A company-wide sales meeting, for example, may want you to speak for an hour. A local university may invite you to deliver a 40-minute keynote address. A convention may honor you by requesting a speech to its 700 members. The stakes are high for you as a business leader and for the company's image. (A sample oral presentation is shown in Figure 15–6. This presentation was delivered to a group of 16 southern California property managers by a senior manager in the firm. The presentation exemplifies many of the qualities of a clear, interesting oral address. The names used in this transcript have been changed.)

After settling your nerves, turn your energies to the writing of a speech that has five distinct qualities:

1. It grabs attention from the start.
2. It takes the listener immediately into the main message of the speech.
3. It divides easily and obviously into natural steps or stages.
4. It works on the imagination by word pictures, examples, and actual visual aids.
5. It concludes so that the listener feels the end of a satisfying journey has been reached. It doesn't just seem as though the speaker suddenly quit talking.

Opening the Long Presentation

Begin the longer presentation by choosing one of the following common openers or one suggested for the shorter presentation, or even one that you come up with yourself.

- Striking visual aid
- Question
- Quotation
- Unusual definition
- Analogy

Communication Insights

Modern managers are virtually paralyzed without sound communication skills. U. J. LeGrange, former vice-president and controller for Exxon Corporation, puts it bluntly:

I cannot overemphasize the importance of communication skills for effective business writing as well as effective presentations. Most of your formal education will be to sharpen your analytical skills. However, let me just remind you that the most carefully thought out analysis even with the appropriate conclusion is worthless if not communicated in an effective manner. Also, remember that much of what your supervisor will see and use to evaluate your performance will be your written and oral skills. Keep this in mind and take every opportunity to polish these skills as you go along. Your success will indeed ride on your ability to communicate.

FIGURE 15–6 A Sample Oral Business Presentation

RECOGNIZE VIPs ANNOUNCE TOPIC GIVE TIME ESTIMATE	Jack Ortega [president of the firm, present at the meeting] asked me to talk to you for about 15 minutes—not a second longer, I promise—on the legal pitfalls lying in the path of the property manager in the next decade.
USE APPROPRIATE HUMOR OVERVIEW OF ORGANIZATION	Now, Jack knows exactly what these pitfalls are and where they're located—in fact, I think he's drawn up a private "pitfall map" he keeps locked in his top drawer. But instead of telling us what he knows, Jack passes out presentation assignments to faithful servants like me to see if we know what he knows. The trick in preparing this kind of presentation is to try to read Jack's mind. If my list of four dangerous legal pitfalls isn't his list, perhaps we'll ask him to fill in the missing pieces when I've finished speaking.
PROVIDE BACKGROUND	Those of us who have worked as property managers for a decade or more recall the days when the property manager could do little harm and never received calls from lawyers. We were the white knights in those days who rode in to evict bad tenants, find ideal tenants, and arrange to have broken water heaters fixed in the middle of the night. After we did our job, we rode away with the gratitude of the property owner and our commission.
CLARIFY PURPOSE	Those days, as you may have noticed by recent court cases involving property managers, are gone. Second only to physicians, we face almost daily risk of being sued for pursuing the customary and expected duties of our profession. I want to spell out four areas—four legal pitfalls, if you will—where we're each vulnerable to suit. My purpose in describing these pitfalls is not to scare you out of property management or to steer you away from some of your most common responsibilities. Instead, I want to show you how a few innocent false steps can cross legal boundaries and land you and the company in court. Simply knowing what these false steps are can help us each avoid them. If someone has to fall into pitfalls, it may as well be a competitor, right?
REFER TO EXPERIENCE OF AUDIENCE	Pitfall # 1—Eviction We've each had the difficult task of confronting tenants who don't pay their rent or fail to keep other terms of their lease contract. It's not a pleasant task, and tempers on both sides have a way of flaring. Be aware, however, that displays of temper on the part of the property owner or the property manager, as agent for the owner, may be construed by the tenant as an implied threat. Any angry or even terse messages you leave behind in writing can be used to bolster the case that the tenant was placed under duress. All sorts of legal action, including claims for emotional distress, can grow out of such charges.
	My advice is to remain absolutely professional in your dealings with even the most maddening tenants. Refrain from written messages, except those that are required by eviction law and worded according to approved models available here in the office. If you know you will face a confrontational situation with a tenant, take along another property manager as a witness to what took place.
USE VISUAL AIDS FOR EMPHASIS AND VARIETY	This chart shows the six steps to legal evictions, as recommended by the National Association of Realtors and the American Bar Association. Handouts of the chart will be distributed at the end of the meeting.
	Pitfall # 2—Tenant Recommendations When we find a tenant to rent one of our clients' properties, we make certain assertions about that tenant's credit-worthiness. We assert, for example, that we have contacted his or her previous landlord, present employer, and credit agency. It's no secret that, especially during the tourist rush in the summer, some of these "checks" don't get made, particularly when we're dead sure that a tenant is reliable and responsible.
PERSONAL ANECDOTE	"Dead sure" too often turns into dead wrong where tenant recommendations are concerned. I recall a television producer I placed in one of the rentals I managed. He drove a gorgeous antique Bentley and wore a $10,000 watch. I didn't take time to check references. Well, you can guess the result. He didn't pay a dime of rent after his first month, and it took us more than three months to evict him.

FIGURE 15–6 (cont.)   A Sample Oral Business Presentation (continued)

APPLICATION

In this case, the owner didn't sue me for false representation regarding the tenant I recommended—but the owner could have. That's the message for you. Make sure you perform due diligence in checking out a tenant's rental history and credit-worthiness. Document your findings and don't overstate the tenant's case to the owner. Whenever possible, simply lay the facts regarding the tenant before the owner and let him or her make the ultimate decision whether or not to rent.Pitfall # 3—the Uninsured Tradesperson   We're each responsible for maintaining the physical conditions of the rental properties we manage. That duty often requires us to employ carpenters, carpet layers, plumbers, and others to work on the property. The property owner has authorized us to employ these people as necessary, up to stated monetary limits.

VIVID EXAMPLE

But think about the list of people you regularly call to work on the properties you manage—the college kid who does such a good job with carpets on stairs, the retired guy who does plumbing part-time. These uninsured tradespeople are great when nothing goes wrong . . . but something *always* seems to go wrong eventually.

Picture this scenario, for example. You hire an unlicensed, uninsured electrician to make a few simple repairs. He manages to cross the wrong wires and start an electrical fire that does $50,000 in damage to the property and $20,000 in the loss of the tenant's property. The property owner has a $10,000 deductible on the fire insurance policy and the tenant has no insurance at all. Who is responsible for the amount of damages not covered by insurance—the $30,000? You guessed it—ultimately the property manager who authorized an uninsured tradesperson to do the work.

Insist that any workers you hire have proof of adequate, paid-up insurance before they step foot on one of your properties. You can ask, for example, that they provide you with written certification from their insurance agent as a condition of your contract with them.

APPEAL TO
COMMON
EXPERIENCE

Pitfall # 4—A Breakdown in Communication   No one works 24 hours a day, but property agents are expected to be ready to respond to property emergencies at any hour of the day or night. For that reason we wear beepers and pay plenty for a 24-hour answering service. It's also a fact that, especially when business is slow, some of us bury the beeper at the bottom of the drawer and take off on a long weekend. At one time or another, we've all reasoned that "if it's important it can wait until Monday."

Unfortunately, recent court decisions have interpreted our contract with property owners as an implicit contract to provide around-the-clock availability of emergency services. This doesn't mean that you personally have to wait by the phone each night. But it does require you to make arrangements so that someone in the company can respond to emergencies in your absence.

SUMMATION

EXPLANATION OF
HANDOUT

We've tried to address this problem by our "buddy" system, by which we cover for one another during holidays, vacations and other times. I urge you to be absolutely faithful about providing your tenants and property owners with a number that, come hell or high water, can be used to reach you or your stand-in. Otherwise, you and the company may be liable for damages sustained to the property and to its occupants during the time you were unavailable.

CONCLUSION

In the past 14 minutes, I've covered four dangerous pitfalls for the property manager—evictions, tenant recommendations, uninsured tradespeople, and breakdowns in communication. The handout I'll distribute now sums up the latest law in these matters.

FINAL THANKS

It's always somewhat unpleasant to discuss the pitfalls that seem to be lurking out there, waiting to swallow us up in backbreaking expenses. The bright side is that there's still plenty of high ground where we can go about our business profitably and happily. We just have to watch our steps.

QUESTIONS

Let me conclude by thanking Jack for bringing this topic to my attention. I've learned a lot about my business by researching these pitfalls. You probably have questions, so I'd like to invite Jack up here with me to answer them. Ask away!

Striking Visual Aid.   Some extremely effective longer presentations begin not with words but with pictures of some sort.

(The audience watches a brief 16mm film clip. In it, the camera moves down a crowded back street of New Delhi. Children in rags move toward the camera, their eyes and wretched physical features caught in momentary close-up as the camera moves along.)

When the speaker does begin the presentation, audience interest is high. Feelings have been powerfully aroused.

Question.   A direct question to the audience, followed by a pause for the question to sink in, can bring attention to a quick peak. The question also gets right to the heart of the speaker's message.

Aside from salaries, what can this company do to hold its best employees?

A long pause ensues while the audience considers the question.

Quotation.   Speakers can impart authority—and hence credibility before their audience—by beginning with a quotation from a recognized and admirable source.

John F. Kennedy could just as well have been talking about companies as countries when he said, "Ask not what your country can do for you. Ask what you can do for your country."

The speaker goes on to discuss the importance of employee loyalty.

Unusual Definition.   You can grab attention by altering common definitions in some way.

The word "profit" should be redefined. It's no longer what a company earns after expenses. Rather, it's what the government lets a company keep.

Analogy.   People find delight in making comparisons. If you suggest that pattern A is like pattern B in some way, the great majority of people will show some interest in discovering the points of similarity. Analogies are the speaker's way of drawing on this natural tendency.

An analogy is an extended comparison. The sudden sinking of the *Titanic*, for example, may be analogous to the sudden bankruptcy of a company hit by a crushing liability suit.

As long as analogies are not far-fetched, audiences find them handy patterns for thinking about more complex matters.

The Pied Piper promised to charm the rats out of the village. And he kept his promise. But that same magic also had the power to steal away the children, each and every one.

The speaker proceeds to compare the Pied Piper with an attractive government contract considered by the company. The contract brings relief from some problems, but it may bring unexpected problems later.

Developing the Long Presentation

After effectively opening your longer presentation, forecast your central concern and pattern of development. Audiences need a clear road map of where you are headed, especially when your shared journey will be long.

Choose a pattern of development from Chapter 3, or develop one of your own. Use the following checklist to guide your development of each stage in your argument:

1. Have you presented your point clearly?
2. Have you supported your point with interesting evidence, examples, and details?
3. Have you dealt with obvious objections to your point?
4. Have you shown the benefits of your point?
5. Have you summarized your point before moving on?

Like the short presentation, the long address usually has only one central concern, though it is often argued in three or more ways or phases. Speakers develop the long address not by casting their nets wider for more topics, but by fishing deeper for profound truths about a single topic.

Maintaining Interest in a Long Presentation

All speakers must use a variety of techniques to keep the interest of an audience during a speech lasting more than 15 minutes. A tire-industry leader stated the problem humorously: "In my business, the longer the 'spoke,' the greater the 'tire.' "

Consider using these interest-stimulators when delivering a long speech.

1. *Use visual aids*—slides, overhead projections, movie clips, or flipcharts—to spark interest. A hint; don't give away the interest value of your visual aid by using it too early or continuously throughout the speech. Often, the presence of a slide projector in the room will give the audience patience to hear you out for several minutes. They know that you plan to show them pictures during the presentation; they're willing to wait for you.
2. Build to a *climax* in volume and emotion, then pause for dramatic effect.
3. *Vary the content* of your speech. If you are rehearsing facts and figures, follow with an entertaining story. If you are speaking theoretically about ideas for a time, follow with a down-to-earth, practical matter.
4. *Move around.* No law says that you have to remain in one place behind a podium. High-quality microphones now clip onto your clothing, allowing you to walk comfortably as you speak. Avoid pacing. Make a point, then take a few steps (a visual breather for your audience), and begin your next major point. When you want to strike a particularly intimate note with your audience, move toward them, as if speaking confidentially.
5. Build in *wake-up noises* in the later stages of your speech. Laughter always wakes up an audience. So does a distinct noise, like a clap of the hands. Such noises must relate to your content, of course.

6. *Ask questions* in your speech, then pause as if actually expecting answers. An audience that is thinking along with you, trying to answer your questions, will work hard to pay attention.

7. *Take risks* by saying something a bit outrageous (but not offensive) in tone and content. For example,

> I've discussed the responsibilities of my position as chief executive officer of this company. I forgot to mention one reality of the job. I get lonesome. I need to see you all from time to time. I need to hear your ideas and to tell you mine.

8. *Vary the* kind and intensity of *gestures* you use. An audience tires quickly of any one movement repeated over and over. Consider beginning with rather modest gestures, becoming more and more communicative with your hands and body as your speech gains momentum. This will happen naturally as you and your listeners become increasingly enthusiastic.

9. *Summarize the points* you've made from time to time in the speech. A summary wakes up a sleepy listener, providing a chance to catch up and to begin paying attention again.

10. *Tell* your audience *how much longer* you plan to speak. When listeners know that the end is in sight, they perk up. For example,

> I see that I have less than five minutes remaining. Let me use that time to. . . .

The phrase, "In conclusion," serves the same function—"Wake up, listener! You only have one more chance to catch my message."

Concluding the Long Presentation

Conclude the longer presentation in any of the ways suggested for closing the short presentation or in one of these ways.

- Visual resolution
- Promise
- Challenge
- Reflective overview
- Appeal to emotion

Visual Resolution.   Especially if your presentation has begun with some stimulating or challenging visual display, conclude with a visual experience that somehow resolves the problems and issues posed in your speech.

> For the past half hour we have seen the faces of starving children in India. Let me leave you, however, with a different vision (slide comes up). These, too, are children in India. Yes, they are well fed, well dressed, well groomed. That's their school in the background—the private school for the children of government officials. Until every child in India has a chance to look as healthy and happy as these children, we will not cease in our labors.

Promise.   As an alternative to calling the audience to action of some sort, the speaker can make a strong commitment in the form of a promise or pledge.

> With your support, I promise a quick return to this company's historic policies of promotion within the ranks rather than hiring from outside for executive positions.

Challenge.   Speakers can try to verbally stun the audience at the end of the speech by means of a specific challenge, a bracing slap.

> We cannot rely on political help to stop foreign incursions into our sector of the automobile market. Whether we survive—no, triumph—as a company depends on our combined creativity and hard work. To put it bluntly, your financial future and mine start this afternoon: Are we willing to meet and beat the competition?

Reflective Overview.   A speech full of challenges can gain persuasive power by looking back in its conclusion to how far you and your listeners have come. You give the audience confidence that your proposed goals can be reached, given your past accomplishments.

> Yes, we face challenges in the new century, but don't lose heart. Our challenges are tame compared to those of the day in 1939 when Mr. Millstead mortgaged his own home to meet company payroll; the day in 1952 when a fire burned the main factory to the ground; the days in 1974 when new environmental laws threatened to shut us down completely. We met the life-or-death challenges of those days. Surely we can meet the challenges we face now.

Appeal to Emotion.   Used appropriately, the appeal to emotion can send a crowd out of the room buzzing with excitement and zeal. Used awkwardly, emotional ploys can ruin an otherwise fine speech.

The key lies in the word *appropriate*. The emotions you project as a speaker and the emotions you ask for from your listener must be a natural outgrowth of the rest of the speech. You cannot, for example, lecture for 40 minutes on the technicalities of the new tax laws and then suddenly plead for renewed, heartfelt dedication to the company and its goals.

The best emotional appeals occur after the speaker has made listeners feel important and strong. The audience can then afford to give the emotion asked by the speaker. An audience convinced of its weakness and vulnerability feels no strength to give emotion at all.

> We've talked about relative risks and margins of safety in relation to the pharmaceuticals we produce. We've seen impressive statistics about the strides we've already made in preventing adverse drug reactions—only one user in a hundred, and so forth.
>
> But stand with me by the hospital bed of that one patient experiencing an adverse drug reaction. Don't turn away from the suffering you see—the fright, the pain. That's the vision that keeps us working at our very highest level of commitment and skill. We want to remain the drug manufacturer that counts people, not numbers.

Following your extended presentation, the audience will probably applaud. It is customary to acknowledge their response by smiling and nodding in recognition. As a general rule, remember not to yield to the temptation to add just a few extra remarks to such an appreciative audience.

SUMMARY

1. Reduce your fear of public speaking by focusing your attention on the here and now—your message and your listeners.

2. Speeches of appreciation and introduction should be brief, sincere, and complimentary.

3. Luncheon and dinner addresses often involve an attention-getting opening, clearly defined points, and appropriate humor.

4. Business presentations are more formal than other short presentations and often make use of handouts and visual aids.

5. Longer presentations should be divided into parts, with frequent summations and interest-keeping devices.

QUESTIONS FOR DISCUSSION

1. What causes the anxiety or fear associated with public speaking?

2. What are some useful techniques for overcoming the fear of public speaking?

3. What are the features of the speech of appreciation or of introduction?

4. What are some common attention-getting openings for speeches?

5. What should you keep in mind when planning to use humor or jokes in your speech?

6. What speaking style is most effective for oral presentations?

7. What are the benefits and possible dangers of reading a speech or using notes?

8. If the audience seems pleased with your speech, should you consider saying a few more words after you have concluded?

9. What are the five distinct qualities of an effective long speech?

10. Why do audiences appreciate a forecast of the main points you'll be covering in a longer presentation?

11. What are some benefits and pitfalls that arise from appeals to emotion in speeches? What key should you keep in mind when appealing to your audience's emotions?

12. Why do direct questions help keep your audience's attention focused on your presentation?

EXERCISES

1. Attend a public speech given by a professional speaker. Note the particular strengths and weaknesses of this speaker. Report your observations to your class.

2. Interview your colleagues who have also given speeches and who have felt anxious about public speaking. Share your own experiences with them. As a group, determine some effective ways to overcome anxiety. One good way is to identify friendly faces in the audience to whom you address your speech. For your next speech, talk directly to some familiar group members and see whether your confidence grows. Be sure to thank your colleagues for their help.

3. For an upcoming speech, devise an appropriate effective opening. Try out a variety of possibilities before deciding on your final choice.

4. If you have written out a manuscript of your upcoming speech, practice it using a tape recorder. First, read the speech into the recorder. Next, deliver the speech, referring to your manuscript only when necessary. Play back the two versions, comparing your style of voice in each. Which delivery sounded more persuasive, and why?

5. To develop confidence in speaking without notes, practice giving impromptu speeches. Informally in a discussion group, develop and exchange possible topics for speeches with your classmates. Each group member should then speak spontaneously for about five minutes on the topic of his or her choice. Based on the group's feedback, determine the effectiveness of your speaking skills.

6. One way to overcome the fear of public speaking is to focus on the here and now. Resist the temptation to ask yourself, "What if my listeners don't like my speech?" Practice focusing on the present moment by describing in detail your sensory perceptions. Right *now*, what do you see? hear? smell? taste? feel?

7. Write a short speech of appreciation thanking your company executives for awarding you a plaque in recognition of your tenth anniversary with the company. The speech will be delivered at an informal luncheon in your honor.

8. Your company, Datatron Systems, Inc., has decided to install a new medical insurance program. Although the fees to employees are reasonable—$35 a month for complete coverage of individual employees and their immediate families—the program will not cover their visits to private physicians. Instead they must see doctors at a medical network. Many employees have expressed their dissatisfaction with the proposed plan, arguing that they will be treated like objects on an assembly line, never seeing the same doctor twice. You have been assigned the task of convincing them to accept the proposal. Prepare a speech to be delivered at the next union meeting a week from today.

   The following exercises ask you to imagine that you're conducting a "Better Professional Speaking" seminar for employees in your company. You can complete these exercises in writing or as an oral presentation.

9. What will you tell the participants about eye contact? How will you help those who understand the importance of good eye contact but can't master the skill itself?

10. Many of your participants are unwilling to use effective pauses in their speaking or attempt to fill a natural pause with "um" or "ah." How will you explain the value of pauses to the group?

11. Some participants can't seem to use their hands naturally while speaking. Are gestures necessary to effective speaking? If so, how will you help the participants free their hands to gesture naturally?

12. Your more nervous participants speak much too rapidly. Why is it important that they control the pace of their presentation? How can they become aware of their pace and control it?

13. Some participants speak too softly. Why is this a natural response to the stresses of public speaking? How can you help these speakers project their words more loudly?

INTERNET ASSIGNMENT

You didn't like making presentations as a student, and you certainly aren't looking forward to your fifteen-minute speech before the company meeting coming up in six weeks. Choose a topic that interests you, then investigate resources in the Oral Presentations section and Visual Aids section of the Internet Guide to help you accomplish the following:

- discover ways to overcome bothersome aspects of Speaker's Nerves
- find approaches for generating, organizing, and outlining the major points of your presentation
- locate guidelines for professional delivery techniques, including use of visual aids

Based on the Internet sites you discover, write up an outline of your presentation, make a list of ways in which you intend to overcome Speaker's Nerves, and list your personal goals for improving the delivery of your speech.

CHAPTER 16

Managing Interviews, Meetings, and Telephone Work

More than 40 percent of Fortune 500 companies and government agencies are now using a relatively new interviewing technique called behavior-based structured interviewing. But in spite of repeated research data showing this approach to be significantly more likely to distinguish winners from losers in the candidate pool, many companies continue to use the traditional, off-the-cuff approach to developing and delivering interview questions.

"Our interviewers like the unstructured approach to hiring," one personnel director told us. "It makes their job more interesting. You never know what you'll end up discussing with an applicant." He pointed out that experienced interviewers like to trust their intuitions—their "gut feelings"—to come up with the right questions and pick the right candidate. As this personnel director concluded, "it's an impossible task to plan what should be asked in all the various positions in the company. We have to trust our interviewers to come up with appropriate questions."

This set of ideas is the general defense for old-fashioned interviewing. In addition to the arguments made by the personnel director, traditional interviewing has the weight of history on its side—it's "the way we've always done it."

PROBLEMS WITH TRADITIONAL INTERVIEWING TECHNIQUES

Put yourself in the place of a job applicant. You and several other candidates sit in a lobby waiting to be called in to separate rooms for traditional interviews conducted by company personnel specialists. Does it matter which of these specialists interviews you? Of course it does. In traditional interviewing, the judgments of individual interviewers (and their relative clout in the company) can vary widely. If you're lucky, you will get an interviewer who likes you. If not, you're branded as an also-ran.

You are now called into an interview room—almost a closet compared to the more spacious offices being used for some of the other interviews. Does this cramped environment affect the outcome of your interview? Yes.

The interviewer begins his questions. Where do these questions come from, you wonder. Sometimes the interviewer glances at your résumé as a stimulus for a question or two. Sometimes he stares at the ceiling, as if stuck for the next question. Often he asks you to repeat yourself. He doesn't take any notes.

Note that in your unstructured interview, questions come "out of the blue," according to the whim of the interviewer. They are not formulated in advance in close coordination with job requirements. At best, they are conjured up by the interviewer in an attempt to "get an overall impression of the applicant" or to "see how the applicant relates and communicates." At worst, these questions are time wasters for both the company and the applicant—just "talk" that yields little valuable information about the candidate's suitability for the position.

After 30 or 40 minutes, you are dismissed from the interview room. You can't help but notice that some interviews in other rooms are often running much longer and others are much shorter than your interview. You suppose that it all depends on which interviewer an applicant happens to get—the luck of the draw. But you have good reason for concern about the length of interviews; recent research demonstrates that successful candidates invariably are granted longer interviews than unsuccessful candidates.

As you leave the building, you wonder what's going to happen to the answers you gave to the interviewer. Will they be recorded or noted in any way? Will they be conveyed accurately to other decision-makers in the company? Or will it all come down to the interviewer's gut feeling, a crude thumbs-up or thumbs-down based on personal impressions and vague criteria such as "the kind of person we're looking for" and "someone who will be a good fit"?

As you reflect on this interview experience, you feel you've just participated in a lottery of sorts. Your interviewer, the interview site, the length of the interview, the interview questions, and the recording and evaluation of your answers were all a matter of luck, not plan. No wonder that traditional interviewing so often produces the "halo effect" in which an interviewer simply hires the person who seems to be wearing a halo similar to the interviewer's. Given the freedom to make up questions and to evaluate candidate responses as he or she wishes, no wonder an interviewer's prejudices play such a major role in hiring. You can easily imagine an interviewer who consistently blocks the hiring path for women, or middle-aged men, or overweight applicants, or nonathletic types, or whatever other bias the interviewer applies in the hiring process.

THE LEGAL BASIS FOR STRUCTURED INTERVIEWING

To all such matter of chance, gut feeling, and potential bias, the law related to hiring says "Stop!" Specifically, the Uniform Guidelines arising out of Title VII and EEOC legislation insist that the interview be designed on the basis of specific job requirements. Both the content and method of the interview must be developed to reveal accurately and fairly which candidates are best qualified to fulfill the job requirements determined by the company. Employers must be able to show that interview questions are directly related to these job requirements. In addition, employers must afford each candidate equal treatment in the screening process.

WHERE STRUCTURED INTERVIEW QUESTIONS COME FROM

In creating interview questions, personnel specialists look to those who know the job best: those who perform it successfully or supervise its performance in the company. These "hands-on" experts list "critical incidents" involved in the successful performance of the job. (A critical incident is a specific problem or challenge presented by the job, together with a description of the behavior that solved the problem or met the challenge.)

Here, for example, is one critical incident from the analysis of a sales position.

> Problem: A client delayed placing an order because she had a technical question that the salesperson could not answer on the spot.

> Successful behavior: The salesperson validated the client's question, promised to find the answer promptly, and followed through in a timely way. Client proceeded with purchase.

This incident, drawn from actual work life and the job description for a salesperson, is one piece in the process of constructing job-based questions for use in interviews. If an employer knows what behaviors it takes to succeed in a given job, the employer can then develop interview questions and tests to locate people qualified to perform those behaviors. For some assembly-line positions, the job analysis may involve only a dozen or so critical incidents. For more complex positions in sales, management, accounting, and so forth, the number of critical incidents may rise to 50 or more.

These critical incident descriptions, once gathered, form the empirical basis for all the employer's assertions regarding "what it takes" to perform a particular job. By pinpointing the things that matter most, the employer has gone far to remove the element of guesswork from the hiring process.

DEVELOPING THE JOB ANALYSIS AND DESCRIPTION

A job analysis panel, usually composed of a personnel officer and managers deeply familiar with the job, meets to organize the many critical incident descriptions into a succinct description of job behaviors. The panel also considers

- information sources of particular importance for the job. Must the applicant, for example, be thoroughly familiar with a certain set of state or federal regulations? A flight or operations manual? A computer reference manual?
- abilities in decision making or information processing critical to job performance. Must the applicant be able to perform some mathematical operations in his or her head? Hold several numbers in mind at once? Read charts and graphs quickly?
- physical requirements, including coordination, stress, and dexterity. Must the applicant be able to lift certain weights? Handle volatile materials reliably? Sit or stand for long periods? Adjust to wide temperature variations? Endure sustained periods of unusual job pressure?
- social skills required for the job. Will the job entail the tactful supervision of others? Meeting clients in social contexts? Relating to co-workers as a motivational manager?

- scheduling and travel requirements of the job. Must the applicant be ready to make scheduling changes and travel plans on short notice? Is the candidate available for overtime and undesirable work shifts?

TURNING THE JOB ANALYSIS INTO INTERVIEW QUESTIONS

With the completed job analysis before it, the expert panel begins to formulate interview questions. These should be drawn from several different types of questions to provide variety and to measure an interviewee's ability to respond to different forms of questions, including the following.

DEFINITIONAL QUESTIONS	These are usually posed in a "What is a . . ." or "What does ——— refer to or mean?" format. They require applicants to demonstrate their knowledge of terms, concepts, and tools. Examples: What is a dado blade? What is meant by the pitch of a roof?
CAUSAL QUESTIONS	These are posed in the format of "What happens when . . ." or "What is the result of. . ." Causal questions ask the applicant to specify the consequence of some initial act or procedure. Examples: What happens when foundation concrete contains too much lime? What is the result of connecting iron pipe directly to copper pipe in a water system?
HYPOTHETICAL QUESTIONS	These questions take the form of "What would you do if . . ." or "What could happen if. . ." Hypothetical questions test the candidate's ability to handle future situations based on past learning and experience. Examples: What would you do if a heavy rainstorm was forecast during a period halfway through the framing stage of a building project? What could happen if wall studs are exposed to hot sunshine for several hours prior to use?
SITUATIONAL QUESTIONS	Related in some ways to hypothetical question, situational questions ask the applicant to put himself or herself into a realistic circumstance described in detail by the interviewer. These questions usually take the form of "Here's the situation . . . What would you do?" Example: You're laying the floor panels on the second story of a residence. Your helper suddenly screams in pain, and you look over to see that he has cut his hand badly with a power saw. Blood is flowing fast from the wound. What action would you take?"
SIMULATIONAL QUESTIONS	In these questions, the circumstance or situation is not described verbally to the applicant. Instead, the applicant is physically presented with some aspects of the job situation. Typically, simulation questions take the form of "To achieve the purposes of ———, you are now holding (facing, supporting, etc.) ———. Show what you would do to achieve your purpose." Example: The candidate is given a container of plumber's putty and asked to show how it would be used in installing a sink.
RELATIONAL QUESTIONS	These ask the applicant to tell, perhaps by role-playing, how he or she would handle interpersonal situations. Example: What would you say or do if a boss unjustly accused you in front of others of loafing on the job?
EXPLANATORY QUESTIONS	These usually take the format of "Why would you . . ." or "How would you explain. . ." Example: Why are cross-braces "let in" to wall studding?

Once questions and their answers have been selected according to the relative importance of job behaviors, the panel must arrange them for uniform delivery to job applicants. Questions are often arranged to follow the course of a typical workday or the work cycle from the beginning to the end of production. Or questions can be arranged in order of increasing or decreasing importance. In most cases, applicants will respond to questions more clearly and completely if the questions occur in a meaningful arrangement.

TRAINING GOOD INTERVIEWERS

One employment manager recently wrote that "getting honest information from our applicants is not nearly as big a problem as getting our interviewers to ask the questions we want answered."

Here she is referring to a widespread problem confirmed by recent studies at Duke University. Job interviewers are often reluctant to ask "hard" questions, particularly of applicants for whom they have an initial liking. Often in an effort to "help out" a congenial applicant, an interviewer may glide over such thorny areas as past firings, a succession of short job stays, or poor college performance. This quite human tendency on the part of the interviewer leaves an information gap for the company in its hiring process. The practice also discriminates against other applicants who, for whatever reason, aren't given special help from the interviewer.

For this reason, all questions developed for a structured interview are asked in order and verbatim for each applicant. In structured interviewing, the interviewer can repeat a question if necessary, but not paraphrase it, coach or prompt the applicant, give hints regarding the intent of or possible answers for the question, or otherwise influence the applicant's response. Nor does the interviewer indicate by verbal or nonverbal signals the relative success or failure of the candidate's answer.

SCORING THE STRUCTURED INTERVIEW

Unlike traditional interview results, structured interviewing offers a planned scoring system for each question used in the interview. At the time questions are developed for the interview, job experts (as described earlier) work out a rating scale for a continuum of possible answers, ranging from a great answer to a poor one. Such judgments as "great" and "poor" are tied directly to behavioral objectives in the job analysis, not to the flair or style with which the candidate can schmooze. A great answer is one that reflects probable success in performing the related job task. A marginal answer is one that reflects probable difficulty in performing the job task. A poor answer is one that reflects probable failure in performing the related job task.

But who is to say which answers are great, marginal, or poor? That judgment call is up to the same job experts who know the job best and are familiar with employees' relative success in accomplishing it. In most cases, rating scales for interview questions are developed in brainstorming sessions by job experts and personnel officers. Great, marginal, and poor responses are specified as "anchors" on a five-point scale. Even though applicants may not hit any of these predicted answers on the nose, their responses can nonetheless be placed meaningfully at some point on the continuum marked by these anchors.

Here are two examples of interview questions with accompanying rating scales. Note that these are not multiple choice questions. Only the interviewers see the suggested responses following the question.

Question 1: "When putting a piece of machinery back together again after repairing it, why would you clean all the parts first?"

5 (good) Particles of dust and dirt can cause wear on moving parts. Must have parts clean to inspect for wear and damage.

3 (marginal) Parts will go together easier. Equipment will run better.

1 (poor) So it will all be clean. I don't know.

Question 2: "Many of the tasks involved in this job require the use of a forklift. Please read this [90-word] forklift checkout procedure aloud."

5 (good) Reads fluently, pronouncing all words correctly.

3 (marginal) Can read most words, but hesitates often.

1 (poor) Reads with great difficulty.

Interviewees are not expected to say the precise words suggested in the anchor responses. Interviewers simply use these benchmarks to determine the appropriate numeric score of the applicant's actual answer. Panel members mark their scorecards for each question and take notes on the content of the applicant's answer. After all applicants have been interviewed, the panel begins the task of comparing, compiling, and reconciling their scores for individual applicants. If scores between raters differ by more than one number (for example, a "5" and a "3"), the panel discusses the applicant's response and seeks to bring the scores closer together. Ratings are then averaged for each question and totaled as a record of the applicant's performance.

This scoring system makes it relatively easy to compare several candidates on the merit of their responses. It goes a long way toward eliminating distortions caused by interviewer bias, differences in questions, and interpersonal factors such as attraction or revulsion.

DOCUMENTING THE STRUCTURED INTERVIEW

Companies and individual managers have good reason to protect themselves against potential charges of discrimination in hiring. Most plaintiffs to date are successful in such suits, and court awards regularly run into the millions of dollars.

If a hiring discrimination suit is brought against a company, the court will insist on knowing the following information. These items are "must-haves" for documentation of the interview process:

1. *Document the job analysis process.* How is the job defined? How did you determine the specific behaviors necessary for performing the job successfully?

2. *Document the process by which questions were created.* Who participated in their creation? Why were these people deemed competent to create the questions? How does each question asked in the interview relate to a behavior necessary for performing the job? In what ways do the number, type, and arrangement of questions reflect the proportionate importance of particular behaviors necessary to perform the job?

3. *Document the system by which applicant responses were scored.* What is the system? Who created anchoring responses? How do these anchoring responses relate to real levels of success among those actually performing the job? How were raw

scores handled statistically? What weighting, if any, was used in the analysis of scores?

4. *Document the process of interviewing candidates.* How did applicants find out about the job? What were the criteria for choosing those applicants who were invited for interviews? Where and when were interviews conducted? Who served as interviewers? What are their qualifications, especially in relation to the job at hand? How were questions delivered? How were responses noted? How long did interviews last? How did different interviews compare in time, content of questions, and method of evaluation?

5. *Document applicant responses and scores.* Notes taken by interviewers must be easily interpretable in reconstructing the approximate content of an applicant's response.

6. *Document the specific process by which one applicant was chosen over others.* What factors were involved? What was the weighting of those factors?

7. *Document the validity of the interview process.* Does the process predict job performance?

8. *Document the presence or absence of adverse impact against EEOC-protected groups participating in the interview process.* Are such groups being hired at a rate at least 80 percent that of nonprotected groups? (Companies will also want to consider recent court standards regarding the ethnic makeup of the surrounding labor pool in determining adverse impact.)

This kind of documentation may seem burdensome to managers and their companies. It compares favorably, however, to the more dangerous course of trying to construct or fabricate a legally defensible hiring procedure once the company faces a discrimination suit.

EXAMPLES OF BEHAVIOR-BASED INTERVIEW QUESTIONS

What an applicant has *done* is a better indicator of future job success than what the applicant believes, feels, thinks, or knows. The following questions are useful in getting applicants to discuss work realities rather than notions or suppositions.

Tell me how you increased teamwork among a previous group with whom you worked.

Describe what you liked and disliked about how you were managed in previous positions.

Recall a time when you made what you consider a mistake or a bad decision on the job. How did you handle the situation?

In your past worklife, what kind of people rubbed you the wrong way? How did you respond?

Tell me about a time when you set specific work goals for yourself. How did things turn out?

Describe a time when you had to criticize or discipline the performance of someone who worked with you or for you. How did you handle the situation? What was the result?

In the past have you had a preference for working mainly with men or women? Explain your answer.

Tell me about a time when you felt you went beyond the call of duty in helping a customer.

USEFUL PROBES FOR INTERVIEWING

Although probing for more extensive answers from candidates is not allowed in strictly structured interviewing environments, the practice is still widely used. It can be applied fairly if each candidate is given the advantage of approximately the same degree of probing by interviewers.

Please clarify what you mean by . . .

How did you feel when that happened?

Why do you think you reacted as you did?

Did you consider other options at the time?

Please give me more details about . . .

How do you think others felt about your actions at the time?

Looking back on the experience, how do you see things now?

What was going through your mind when you took that action?

Did the outcome of your action satisfy you?

FUTURE DIRECTIONS FOR INTERVIEWING

For legal and financial reasons, the movement is definitely on toward structured, behavior-based interviewing in American companies. Managers and personnel officers have to be able to defend their hiring decisions in court, if necessary. That defense becomes almost impossible if hiring criteria, methods, and records have been handled in an unplanned and disorganized way. At the same time, companies want to improve the quality and efficiency of their hiring efforts. A structured hiring process can be evaluated and improved through repeated testing of its components; an unstructured process, by contrast, changes according to the interviewer's whims. Those charged with bringing true performers into the company find it exceedingly hard to hit this moving target.

Many of the speaking skills you have developed for use in oral presentations will help you participate successfully in interviews and meetings. You know how to organize your material, express your points briefly, and use your voice and gestures to advantage. In addition to the skills for oral presentations, you must master several other important interpersonal skills for effective interviews and meetings. Most of these are conversational skills that you probably already practice.

INTERPERSONAL SPEAKING

When your turn comes to speak up in an interview or meeting, keep in mind the six qualities of an effective interpersonal speaker, as summed up in the C-H-E-E-R-S defined in the following Communication Checkpoint.

Communication Checkpoint

C-H-E-E-R-S Six Qualities of an Effective Interpersonal Speaker

1. *Compliment your listener.* Find something in his or her accomplishments, attitudes, or goals to say a kind word about.

2. *Headline your own points.* Don't leave listeners in the dark about what you're trying to say. Begin by briefly stating your main idea.

   > I'm concerned about the methods for handling layoffs in the company. [Your listener then knows the purpose of your other points.]

3. *Exemplify your points.* Don't ask your listeners to accept your point of view on faith alone. Point out supporting examples and details. For example:

   > Our current personnel document makes no reference to length of employment when layoff decisions have to be made.

4. *Enumerate your points for clarity.* For example:

   > I favor a three-part plan. First, layoffs would occur mainly according to length of employment. Second, sectors of the company with low-profit or with loss records would be subject to layoff first. Third, at least one executive earning over $45,000 would have to be laid off for every ten regular employees laid off. (Your listener can keep track of your idea.)

5. *Read your listener's face and eyes.* When a question or comment starts to appear, create a break in your own speaking, and welcome the listener's contribution.

6. *Speak sincerely.* This advice goes far beyond rules for communication to include ethics. To be *sincere* means not to lie to your listener, even in small ways. To be sincere means to show genuine emotions, not to fake an emotion to manipulate your listener.

COMMUNICATING VIA THE TELEPHONE

Depending on your position, you may find that many of your interpersonal conversations take place on the telephone. These telephone conversations include interviews of job candidates, meetings by conference call, contacts with clients and co-workers, and many other communications. For that reason, we should consider the special conversational skills required for the business use of the telephone.

Notice, first, how many advantages the telephone holds for business use. You can reach people inexpensively. You can break into a client's busy day without an appointment. You can argue or deliver bad news without the pain of seeing the client's face (or fist). You can get right to the point without the social preliminaries that we attach to in-person visits.

The phone also has limitations. Notice, for example, that you can't pause to think on the telephone. A pause of even a second or two produces the inquiry, "Are you still there?" All decisions made on the telephone are necessarily oral and often are later denied or reinterpreted.

As travel costs continue to rise, however, electronic communication must replace at least some physical contact. We can expect the telephone to play an even larger role in business life in the future. Already, some million-dollar-a-year firms can use an 800 number and an answering service for orders from national ads. All other work is conducted literally out of a warehouse or storage room.

The BLESS Guidelines

What do you sound like on the phone? One way to find out is to record your end of several conversations over a period of days. (Most answering machines offer this recording feature.) Play back the tape, and when you listen to it, ask yourself whether you sound pushy, monotone, long-winded, or confused. Figure out which qualities you would like to change. Then consider the guidelines summarized in this *B-L-E-S-S* (the telephone) list:

> B—Be likable.
> L—Lead the conversation.
> E—Explain your key points.
> S—Sum up.
> S—Say thanks.

B—Be likable

Because the person on the other end of the line cannot see your facial expressions, you must communicate through your tone of voice. Avoid being abrupt when you begin phone conversations. For business use, practice a smooth, friendly introduction to phone conversations. Greet the person you're calling, giving your own name as soon as possible.

Hello, Mr. Wilkins? This is Sally Jenson at the *Daily News.*

Consciously try to say the "hello" with a smile on your face. The smile will come through in your voice. Right from the beginning, the person you call will know that this will be a friendly call, not another hassle in the business day.

L—Lead the conversation

If you make a phone call, be prepared to lead the conversation to your important topics. In the case of important business calls, you may want to prepare a brief set of notes to which you can refer early in the conversation. Telephone conversation is much like dancing: It takes two, but one must establish the lead. Don't lose your listener by speaking too fast, but don't dawdle either. In most business conversations, you may want to lead until the listener comfortably starts to respond. Don't ask your listener to promise anything or agree to anything before you have stated all the key facts.

E—Explain your key points

In the five to seven minutes of an effective phone conversation, provide explanations and examples of your key points. Occasionally ask the listener, "Do you have any questions?" Ask whether your information or proposal suits the needs of your listener. Try to get your listener to take over the lead, mentioning concerns that you can answer.

S—Sum up

To make sure that you can briefly sum up your points for a conclusion, you should practice midconversation and end-of-conversation summary statements. These brief summaries pull together all the words that have been passing back and forth.

> "Well, just to sum up: You're willing to back Tracy for the position if she can demonstrate some track record of financial management. Have I understood you correctly?"

The last question "Have I understood you?" gives the listener the chance to answer. It also avoids one-sided decisions about the outcome of the conversation.

S—Say thanks

Appreciation can hardly be overdone. If you are grateful to your listener, say so as specifically as possible. Try to avoid clichés and implied thanks.

> *Not:* "Well, I guess you know how I feel. Bye."
> *Better:* "I want to express my appreciation for your help. Goodbye."
> *Best:* "Thanks, John, for supporting Tracy. It means a great deal to me. I'll talk to you again in a few days. Goodbye."

For many businesses, the telephone is the primary means of getting and keeping business clients. With good reason, employees "BLESS" the telephone when it rings or when they pick it up to call a client.

Eight Hints for Speaking and Listening on the Telephone

1. *Don't shout or whisper.* The amplification equipment in the average telephone has a limited audio range. Extreme volumes will either not be carried at all or will be transmitted in distorted, harsh tones.
2. *Call back to fix a bad connection.* Business calls are too important to risk not understanding what a client is saying. Instead, explain that you have a bad connection (such as one filled with static) and will call back.
3. *Don't talk while the person you're speaking with is still speaking.* If you can't seem to fit a word in edgewise, create pauses by approval statements. Your caller pauses to think about your approval, and you take the opportunity to begin speaking. Approval phrases: "I certainly agree," "You're right," "Good point."
4. *Provide support cues.* Your client will find it unnerving to speak for an extended period into the void of silence. Provide reassurance by occasionally murmuring "yes," "right," "OK," and "uh-huh." These supportive cues encourage your client to tell you more, and to trust that your response will be favorable and accepting.
5. *Vary the tone of your voice.* Telephone equipment tends to make monotones of us all. Counteract this by speaking with expression.

6. *Keep telephone conversations short and to the point.* Clients often hesitate to get too deeply involved in subject matter over the telephone, especially because there is no written record of the conversation. Therefore, use telephone conversation to establish general understandings and to make arrangements for more definitive meetings in person or in writing. Teleconferencing may greatly widen the use of the telephone for making decisions. This increases the likelihood that final details of negotiations can be made by phone.

7. *Avoid letting your office's background noise limit or hurt the effectiveness of either listener or speaker.* If you suspect that your client cannot hear you well, ask early in the conversation.

8. *Always set the telephone receiver down gently.* Don't let an abrupt crash of the telephone receiver ruin the pleasant ending to your business call. From your client's point of view, a loud crash may prompt the nagging question of why the receiver was banged down. "Did I say something wrong?"

Most telephone companies have business representatives who will be happy to provide your co-workers and employees with telephone-effectiveness materials and seminars. As telephonese and televideo equipment and computers become more important, successful businesspeople will use these free services more often.

VOICE MAIL: LEARNING TO TALK TO A CHIP

Voice mail is a sophisticated form of telephone answering machine and message service. The user can prerecord any number of helpful answer messages for callers. The message can tell the caller a forwarding phone number, the name of someone else to talk to, or the time when the user will return. Chapter 1 described some of the features of voice mail systems.

For all its convenience, however, voice mail has created a few problems for callers to some companies. "Now that our corporate headquarters has voice mail," complains a southern California training director, "I can't get through to anyone. Managers simply turn on their voice mail and check it from time to time throughout the day. Voice mail has turned out to be a way to avoid taking calls and to screen [the] calls received."

For this reason, when using the telephone, you should prepare yourself for the strong possibility that you will be talking to voice mail, not directly to the person you're trying to call. This preparation takes three forms:

1. *Prepare a clear, concise message.* In a person-to-person telephone call, your business message may come out a bit at a time in the give-and-take of conversation. However, when voice mail answers, you must be prepared to record your message without rambling or awkward pauses. To do so, think through or even jot down key points of your message before you call.

2. *Specify followup information.* After you have recorded your central message, be sure to tell the message receiver exactly what to do next. Do you want a return call? Where and when can you be reached? Are deadlines looming? Is the matter urgent or routine?

3. *Be courteous.* When you reach voice mail, you may feel somewhat disappointed at having to talk to a machine instead of a person. This is actually slightly misleading: You are talking *through* a machine, not *to* one. Therefore, include in your message all the signs of courtesy and personal warmth that you would use in a live conversation. These human touches can strongly motivate the person listening to your message, who is deciding how to respond to your call.

CONDUCTING INTERVIEWS

Although telephones are becoming increasingly useful, face-to-face meetings and interviews continue to be vital to businesspeople. You may feel that you are still many years away from having to conduct an interview of prospective employees, suppliers, and so on. That might not be so. In the late 1990s, employees in their first years with the company often also participate in hiring interviews. During your first year on the job, you may well be asked to sit in on a job interview, to ask questions of the candidate, and to offer your opinion of his or her qualifications. Your own managerial potential may even be judged in terms of how well you can participate in interviews. In some rapid-growth companies such as computer firms, it isn't uncommon for first- and second-year employees to conduct interviews when selecting their subordinates. In short, it's not too soon for you to learn how to skillfully conduct an interview. You'll be preparing yourself for a common managerial task. Meanwhile, you'll also become a better interviewee by understanding the interview process from both sides. (See Chapter 12 for more on how to be interviewed for a job.)

The Importance of Interviewing

As an interviewer, you help to determine how your company will grow. Through interviews and hiring, the company replaces lost employees, gains new expertise, and expands its workforce. Because this interviewing serves such important goals, companies devote many key resources to this activity. In 1998, American business spent about $40 billion preparing for, conducting, and evaluating job interviews. The American Management Association estimates that total hiring costs can go beyond $50,000 to find and sign up a manager for an $80,000 job. Even for entry-level positions, many companies in 1998 found themselves spending more than $1000 in advertising and interviewing expenses for each new employee they hired.

The Roles of an Interviewer

In addition to asking questions and taking notes, effective interviewing involves

- **Building a relationship**—Through your friendly manner and appropriate small talk, you help the candidate get over being nervous. This helps both you and your candidate present yourselves well. That is, while you help the candidate to form positive impressions about the company and its personnel, you also help her or him to impress you favorably.
- **Collecting information**—Job candidates usually speak at a rate of 250 words per minute or more. The job candidate pours forth all kinds of information about qualifications, experience, attitudes, goals, and preferences. As an interviewer, you must not only hear this information, but also decide which facts to write down for your later reference and evaluation.
- **Probing**—On behalf of the company, you ask the interviewee to clarify facts and to explain feelings, as well as to offer new information.

- **Giving information**—In a sense, the candidate is interviewing the company as well as vice versa. During the interview, you may be expected to briefly describe and explain company history, goals, policies, procedures, and other matters.

Bear in mind that you must do all of these things within the brief period of the hiring interview, usually about 30 to 45 minutes.

Interview Questions: Closed versus Open

When you prepare to lead an interview, you should make up a list of questions based on the company's hiring needs and the candidate's résumé, application letter, and other information. This list will include two types of questions: (1) *closed* questions, which can be answered simply by one or two words, such as "yes" or "no"; and (2) *open* questions, which require more than a "yes" or "no" or other one- or two-word answer. Here are examples of typical closed questions:

- Have you arranged for a health exam at the company health center?
- When will you graduate?
- Will you consider working outside this region?
- How long did you work at ABC Technologies?

Although these questions may be important to you in gaining needed answers, such closed questions tell you little about the candidate's communication, abilities, attitudes, personality, and intelligence.

Therefore, most of the interview questions should be open. These questions require the candidate to express more extensive answers, giving you some insight into how she or he thinks and speaks. Here are ten open questions that often can get a candidate to give you valuable information. Consider these carefully for use when you are an interviewer. You might want to practice answering them yourself in preparation for being interviewed:

- Tell me about the best boss you ever had. Why did you like him or her?
- How do you go about making important decisions?
- What risks did you take in previous jobs, and how did those risks turn out?
- Tell me about frustrations you've felt in your previous work experiences. How did you deal with those frustrations?
- Where would you like to find yourself professionally in three years?
- What did you do in your previous job to make yourself more valuable to your employer?
- How do you think people should be managed in business?
- What strengths would you bring to this job from the very beginning? What strengths would take time to develop?
- What kind of people rub you the wrong way?
- Do you consider yourself a loner or a team player? Explain your answer.

By preparing appropriate closed and open questions, you can use the brief minutes of an interview to maximum advantage in getting to know the candidate's thoughts, attitudes, feelings, and goals.

SPEAKING IN MEETINGS

Consider this common complaint about business meetings:

> If you want to see my company at its worst, listen in on our meetings. Certain know-it-alls do all the talking; others won't speak at all. The person chairing the meeting loses track of the agenda—if there was an agenda to begin with. Inevitably, personality clashes take over until someone finally moves to adjourn. Mind you, these are good professional people on their own. But together in a meeting, oh my word!

Despite the time they take away from your other work and the poor way in which they are often handled, business meetings are almost always unavoidable. There is no way of conducting business without occasionally participating in or leading meetings. Meetings may be centered on coordinating activities among departments or among the members of a department. Within a company, people must meet at least occasionally to plan how to coordinate their activities.

Businesspeople also have meetings whenever changes arise, such as market changes, internal company changes, or external changes in suppliers. To handle those changes, the company must alter its procedures and its policies. The best way to find out how to handle those changes is to have all the people affected by the changes meet to discuss them. Sometimes, the company personnel even have to meet in order to adjust the company's goals.

Another reason for meetings is to discuss how well everyone in a company or in a department is progressing in meeting the company's existing goals. Different companies have different needs for charting their progress, so these update meetings may occur quarterly, monthly, weekly, or daily.

Some meetings are also conducted with clients or with suppliers. Businesspeople often meet with the clients to tell them why to buy their products or services, how to use their products or services, or how to fix problems that may arise in their products or services. They may have similar meetings with their suppliers.

Because you will inevitably participate in meetings during your business career, you should know how to do so effectively.

Participating in Meetings

Several suggestions may help you to participate effectively in the meetings you must attend:

- Contribute information
- Show that you listen to others
- Notice nonverbal reactions
- When appropriate, suggest positive alternatives
- Praise whenever possible
- Use your social skills

Contribute Information

It isn't enough only to contribute or only to give information. Don't say something just to be able to say that you participated in the meeting, and don't provide information that really doesn't contribute to the overall purposes of the meeting. If the meeting's *agenda* (its stated purpose or its list of topics for discussion) is to discuss sales figures, information on a production process doesn't contribute to the meeting's purpose. On the other hand, don't keep silent when you have an idea or some information that might be valuable to the meeting.

The information needed in meetings isn't always just facts. Sometimes your ideas or opinions are the information needed in a meeting. For example, if the purpose of the meeting is to get everyone's opinion regarding how to respond to a change in your business's market, *do* contribute your opinion. Your opinion is exactly the information needed.

Show That You Listen to Others

In addition to speaking up and contributing to the value of the meeting, listen carefully to what others are saying. Write yourself notes about key ideas, hints, comments, or recommendations brought up in the meeting. Use your notes as a guide when you're deciding how to contribute to the meeting. Try to relate your ideas or comments to the information already given by others. You may also want to follow some of the other suggestions in Chapter 13, on listening.

Suggest Positive Alternatives

When you have listened carefully, you may hear something that you disagree with or that you question. If you aren't sure of something, try to word your question positively, avoiding criticism of the person whom you're questioning. If you disagree with something, try to suggest a positive alternative instead of focusing on how bad the original idea was. At all costs, avoid personally attacking the person whose idea seems wrong or questionable to you. Focus on how to improve the idea or how to achieve the same goal in another way.

Notice Nonverbal Reactions

While you are listening or speaking during a meeting, notice the faces and gestures of the other people in the meeting. Are they agreeing or disagreeing with the ideas? Are they worried about or delighted with the news of changes? Are they confused about what is going on, or do they understand what's being said? Are they enjoying the company of the people in the meeting or are they getting irritated that this meeting is taking too long? Use this nonverbal information to help determine how to contribute to the meeting's goals. In addition, watch your own nonverbal reactions, to make sure that you show support when you feel it.

Praise Appropriately

When someone says something particularly insightful or helpful, sincerely praise the person who did so—either during the meeting or afterward. Some of the things you might praise are things that you might wish you had done yourself, such as when someone

- Summarizes an idea particularly well
- Comes up with a compromise or a synthesis (integration) of several people's viewpoints

- Offers special expertise that gives everyone a new perspective on a problem
- Suggests a solution to a problem

Naturally, if you are the person who can do any of these things, do so.

Use Your Social Skills

As with many other communication experiences in business, your social skills greatly influence how effective you will be. If you show courtesy, cooperation, and appreciation of your co-workers during meetings, you'll probably do very well.

Leading Meetings

One reward for participating well in business meetings may be that you'll move up in your organization. If so, you may be asked to lead meetings. Consider the following hints and guidelines for conducting effective meetings.

- *Notify all participants about the meeting.* Include, if possible, an agenda—even a tentative one—so that participants can begin to gather their thoughts and notes for the meeting.
- *At the beginning of the meeting, if you have fewer than 20 people attending, ask all participants to introduce themselves.* These introductions not only let people meet one another by name, but also encourage free discussion. Simply by saying his or her name and company position, a participant has broken the ice. Speaking up later in discussion may then be easier.
- *State the purpose of the meeting clearly, but not in a bossy way.* This afternoon we'll discuss the sales commission structure now used in the company, and any other related matters that seem important to you.
- *State an estimated time for adjournment.* Try to stick to that ending time. We'll adjourn promptly at 4:00 so that several of you can keep other appointments.
- *Use informal rules of order.* Overly formal controls may discourage discussion in smaller meetings. Because many participants fear "being out of order," they stay silent.
- *Conduct the meeting by using commonsense methods:* Call on a variety of speakers, with fairness to each. Don't let one member of the group dominate discussion ("Let me stop you for a moment, Frank. Does anyone want to respond to the point Frank is making?"). If the discussion turns into a free-for-all, take control of it to reestablish order. ("Just a minute, please. Please. Frances, you had the floor, and Bill after you.")
- *Use a whiteboard, a blackboard, or a flipchart to show everyone the major ideas discussed thus far.*
- *Keep the meeting moving toward its goals.* Do this by providing occasional brief summaries, followed by a question.

  So far, we seem to agree that Wilford Advertising has been too conservative in its representation of our line of clothing. I suppose the next logical question is whether Wilford can come up with more creative approaches. Any comments?

- *Work toward consensus, not confrontation and early votes.* Try to prevent narrow majorities from dominating vocal and large minorities. Because the company usually has to move ahead with one voice, the meeting should proceed with discussion until compromises and understandings have been worked out that suit almost all members. When this meeting of minds is not possible, allow some outlet for minority opinion—a minority report, for example, or a later meeting to reconsider the issues.
- *Thank all participants for attending the meeting.* As soon as possible, distribute summary notes of the meeting, organized to highlight decisions made and actions recommended.
- *For your own growth as a chair, tape-record several meetings.* (Be sure to ask for the group's permission.) Listen to the tapes. Do you speak too much in the meeting? Are your decisions fair to all members? Can you be heard? Do you keep the meeting on course by occasional brief summaries?

Chairing meetings makes you more visible to upper management. Use this spotlight to showcase your ability, without self-consciousness.

SUMMARY

1. A growing number of companies are using behavior-based structured interviewing to increase the likelihood of choosing the best candidate.

2. Traditional interviewing techniques inevitably bring inequities to the interview process, including interviewer bias and dissimilar treatment of candidates.

3. Behavior-based interviewing focuses on what a candidate has done and can do as the best predictor of job success.

4. To use the telephone for business, pay attention to the B-L-E-S-S formula: Be likable, Lead the conversation, Explain your key points, Sum up, and Say thanks.

5. Successful person-to-person speaking depends as much on how you listen as on how you speak.

6. Good employee interview questions come from a clear description of the kind of employee you want to hire.

7. Interviews provide opportunities for you to demonstrate your abilities with words and ideas, especially in the area of explanation and problem solving.

8. Participating in and leading meetings requires careful attention to the purpose of the meeting, the attitudes of its members, and the moment-to-moment interactions.

QUESTIONS FOR DISCUSSION

1. What is behavior-based structured interviewing? How does it differ from traditional interviewing?

2. If you were interviewing for a position, would you prefer to be interviewed by the behavior-based structured approach or by traditional ways? Why?

3. How do you answer the charge that behavior-based structured interviewing inhibits the creativity and spontaneity of the interviewer?

4. Why do you think research has shown behavior-based structured interviewing to be a superior predictor of excellent candidates over traditional interviewing methods?

5. What are some of the benefits and limitations of communicating by telephone?

6. Summarize the guidelines suggested by the acronym, BLESS (the telephone).

7. How might it help to jot down an outline of the points you expect to cover in a telephone conversation?

8. Why is it a good idea to lead business conversation over the phone?

9. Why is it useful to occasionally summarize the points you've covered in a phone conversation?

10. What are some ways to ensure that others participate in and support one another at business meetings?

11. What responsibilities must meeting leaders accept? If you had to choose between leading a meeting and participating, which role would you prefer? Explain your choice.

12. Why is reaching consensus an important ingredient of a successful business meeting?

13. What different roles do you play as an interviewer for the company?

14. Why should you develop some interview questions in advance of an interview?

15. How can the nonverbal signals sent by the interviewer affect the attitudes and performance of the interviewee?

16. What is *probing*? How can this technique be used in interviews?

17. What does it mean to guide the conversation in an interview? Why is this technique often necessary?

EXERCISES

1. Do your own survey of attitudes toward business meetings among your classmates. Specifically, what do they like and dislike about meetings in which they have been involved?

2. Create a short "Guide for Better Meetings" addressed to meeting participants. Show what they can do to ensure more efficient, effective meetings.

3. Add a section called "Meeting Leadership" to the "Guide" in Exercise 2. Give step-by-step guidance to the meeting leader who is new to his or her role.

4. Take careful notes of the meeting process in the next extended business or club meeting you attend. What went well or poorly—and why?

5. Before making your next extended phone call, jot down an outline of the points you intend to cover. After the phone call, evaluate in writing or orally whether this technique helped you achieve your goals in the conversation.

6. Recall a bad experience you've had carrying out a business conversation over the phone. If you could begin that conversation again, how would you prepare for it to ensure that it went more successfully?

7. Recall a positive experience you've had carrying out a business conversation over the phone. Evaluate the factors that made this experience successful.

8. Carry out a mock hiring interview with a classmate. First act as interviewer, asking relevant questions of your applicant. Then change roles and play the part of the applicant. After the interviews, compare notes with your classmate. Exchange constructive suggestions on improving interview skills.

9. Interview a meeting leader at your college or in the business world. Record his or her ways to prepare for the meeting, techniques for conducting the meeting, and followup tasks.

10. Interview a classmate or other person who has just come from a job interview. Record the person's impressions of the interviewer, evaluation of her or his own performance, and memory of particularly difficult questions.

11. Interview a manager or other person who interviews job applicants. Determine what the interviewer looks for in a successful applicant, how questions are developed, and how interview results are recorded.

12. From the list of sample interview questions given in this chapter, choose five questions that you would find particularly difficult to answer. For each, write out an answer that is concise, well-reasoned, and well-supported.

13. Write two dialogues between interviewer and interviewee, to show correct and incorrect ways of phrasing interview questions.

14. Write ten open-ended selection interview questions that did not appear in the list of sample questions in this chapter.

INTERNET ASSIGNMENT

In your rapidly growing start-up company, you're bringing new employees into your workforce each week. A good portion of your own day as Director of Human Resources is spent in selection interviews. Thanks to your training in HR law and techniques, you feel that you are conducting your part of the interview process legally, fairly, and effectively. But you worry that other managers in the chain of interviews during the day are proceeding on a seat-of-the-pants basis, asking any questions (even illegal ones) that come into their heads.

To provide a learning resource for these company managers/interviewers, find several Internet sites in the Interviewing section and Communication Ethics and Law section of the Internet Guide. Prepare a short presentation or write a memo addressed to managers/interviewers in the company. In your message, explain the legal and strategic importance of conducting professional job interviews. Describe how your managers can use the Internet sites you have discovered to improve their interviewing effectiveness.

CHAPTER 17

Crisis Communication
and Media Relations

When your company finds itself in the spotlight by choice or circumstance, every word spoken or written by company spokespeople has great significance for the corporate image, public confidence, employee morale, and perhaps company survival. This chapter shows you how to plan for moments of crisis and for media relations before the cameras begin to whirr and the hard questions start to fly. Ralph Waldo Emerson remarked, "We tend to study geology the morning after the earthquake." By considering likely crisis scenarios and rehearsing possible media situations, we can help our companies prepare to handle the "real thing" professionally and responsibly.

LEARNING TO PREDICT THE UNPREDICTABLE

Company crises are often portrayed in newspapers, magazines, television, and radio as events that come as a complete surprise to those affected. In fact, most crisis situations can be foreseen to a remarkable degree by analyzing the range of disasters or business interruptions most likely to occur for a given company or industry. Among others, four categories of crisis origination must be considered:

1. **Natural Disasters.** If your company or organization is located in an area prone to hurricanes, tornadoes, earthquakes, forest fires, floods, or other natural disasters, you would be short-sighted not to develop detailed plans in advance (as described later in this chapter) for employee safety, damage control, security, customer relations, and many other matters. Any corporation headquartered along the eastern Florida coastline, for example, should have a plan in place for dealing with the severe tropical storms and hurricanes that plague that region almost every year.

2. **Product or Service Vulnerability.**   Before the moment of crisis arrives, you have a chance to determine the most likely problems you may face with regard to your company's product or service line. For example, a food manufacturer should prepare a crisis plan for actual or alleged food poisoning. A drug company should decide in advance how to deal with product tampering. An airplane or automobile manufacturer should develop plans for crises involving equipment failure (such as exploding gas tanks, faulty engine mounts, unreliable guidance systems, and the many other equipment problems that have made headlines in recent years). Similarly, service companies should prepare to answer public and regulatory criticism when crises occur owing to apparent employee negligence or other malfeasance. Intel's problems with the Pentium chip, Johnson & Johnson's Tylenol-tampering case, and Jack-in-the-Box's *E-coli* food poisoning dilemma are all examples of foreseeable company crises.

3. **Personnel Problems.**   These problems can range from workplace violence to union strikes to embezzlement to sexual harassment. No matter what the specifics, a company can decide in advance how to determine the facts of the matter, what outside agencies (detectives?, counselors?, security guards?) to involve, who will speak for the company, and how the company will act to protect its people, customers, and interests. The United Way, for example, could have developed a crisis plan to deal with negative press caused by the misdeeds of its senior leadership.

4. **Political or Social Upheaval.**   If the company thinks it stands in harm's way owing to possible political or social problems, it should work out thorough plans for protecting resources, relocating personnel, setting up temporary business headquarters, and other logical plans. More than a year before the Gulf War, for example, Shell Oil assembled executives to play out a scenario for how the company would respond if the tense relations between these countries erupted into actual warfare.

HOW TO PREPARE YOUR COMPANY FOR CRISIS

Begin by allocating time, money, and people to the important work of crisis planning. This vital activity requires financial and human resource commitment on the part of the organization.

Next, assemble a crisis coordination team (we'll call it the Crisis Task Force) made up of individuals from each major constituency within the company. You might, for example, assemble a group with representatives from finance, administration, new product development, production, marketing, and company security.

This group meets to study various forms of crises that have already struck the company, its competitors, its industry, or similar companies in other industries. The Crisis Task Force attempts to understand why these crises occurred, how the companies involved responded, and with what result. The team takes special note of strategies that could be put to use or altered in some way to help the company deal with future crises.

After studying what has happened to other companies, the Crisis Task Force develops a thorough list of crises, ordered according to probability, that foreseeably could impact the company. For at least the top four or five crises on this list, the group develops a narrative scenario—a story-like description—of the specific circumstances of a given crisis. A written document, the Crisis Communication Plan, is developed. (A sample outline appears later in the chapter.)

One or more disaster scenarios become the basis of a mock crisis response. Using its Crisis Communication Plan, the team meets to treat the scenario as if it were actually happening. Responsibilities are assigned, decisions are made, and action is taken.

After the Crisis Task Force has played through the scenario, it evaluates its success. What went right or wrong? What unexpected developments emerged? What could be done better next time? How might "the real thing" differ from the scenario? These and other questions form the basis of self-evaluation and revision for the Crisis Communication Plan and for the organization and actions of the Crisis Task Force. The mock scenario is then reenacted to test the validity of the revised planning measures.

It's hardly sufficient, of course, for one group of employees to know what to do in the event of company crisis. The learning that takes place in the Crisis Task Force must be disseminated to all company employees, so that everyone knows his or her role in the event of crisis. Such training can be facilitated by group meetings, videotape sessions, and employee access to crisis preparation websites on the internet or company intranet.

DIVIDING RESPONSIBILITIES FOR CRISIS PREPARATION

At a minimum, the following categories must be considered in shaping a successful company response to crisis:

External Communications with Wholesalers and Retailers

Whom will you contact in the event of a company crisis? By what channels? What typical messages should you "think through"? What can you expect retailers and wholesalers to do to help your company during crisis? What steps should you take now to prepare for rapid emergency contact with retailers and wholesalers?

Internal Communications with Employees

Which employees do you plan to contact in the event of company crisis? By what means? What are some typical messages you should prepare or at least think about in advance? How can employees be expected to react to various situations? Who should make first contact with employees? Who should handle followup questions and concerns?

Communication with Company Stakeholders, Including Shareholders

What kinds of communications should be issued to stakeholders? What typical messages might you prepare (or at least think through) in advance? What channels should you use? Who should handle followup questions and concerns? Who in the company should make first contact with these people?

Communication from the CEO's Office

What role(s) should the CEO play during the crisis? What typical messages should the CEO think through? By what channels will the CEO probably be communicating? How should the CEO prepare? Who should assist the CEO in preparation? Practice? With what groups will the CEO probably be communicating?

Coordination with Legal Counsel

How does the company intend to make use of its lawyers during crisis? With whom will lawyers communicate? What kinds of communications should be routed through legal counsel? What general kinds of crisis should you think through with an eye toward legal implications? Should employees and others be given legal counsel regarding what they should or shouldn't say during a time of company crisis?

Communication with the Public

How does the company intend to contact the general public? What potential crisis messages may have to be sent? By what means? By what people? In what areas? With what degree of saturation? At what expense?

Communication with Media Representatives

What media can you expect to contact you during company crisis? What will they want from you? Can you pre-package or practice your messages to them? Can you nurture relationships with media now that will pay dividends later? Can you plan now for damage control in terms of company image, market share, and so on? Who should speak to the media in a time of crisis?

Communication with Impacted Parties

What communication should be initiated with those who have been injured, disadvantaged, or otherwise impacted by a company crisis? Who should make the contact? Can you pre-plan how these matters can best be handled? How should legal counsel be involved? What sorts of somewhat predictable impacts can you discuss in advance?

Communication with External Expertise

What kinds of external expertise do you want "ready to go" in times of company crisis? Will trauma counselors be required? Security experts? Medical expertise? How can you acquaint external experts with the company and its needs? What should they prepare for the company in advance of a crisis?

Communication with Key People

At the first moment of crisis, which key people should be notified immediately? What plan can be put in place so that those key people can be contacted? What plans can you make now so that each key person knows what to do at the outset of a crisis?

SAMPLE OUTLINE FOR A CRISIS COMMUNICATION PLAN

The specific contents of a crisis communication plan will vary according to company needs and circumstances. The following categories, however, are standard in most such plans:

I. Introduction (explanation of the purpose and importance of the plan)

II. Contacts (names and access information for assigned crisis leaders and external consultants)

III. Potential Disasters (descriptions and rationales for foreseeable disaster or crisis situations that could impact the company)

IV. Action Priorities (detailed instructions on who should do what during the company crisis)

V. Media Relations (plans for interaction with the media, including designated spokespersons, responsibility for press releases, and advice concerning admissions of liability)

VI. Physical and Organizational Provisions (location of crisis command center within the company, map of resources and supplies, names of responsible individuals)

VII. Post-Crisis Planning and Evaluation (provision for cleanup, counseling, damage control, and organizational learning for future crises)

Perhaps because disasters and crises are not pleasant to contemplate, they are often put out of mind or downplayed until they actually occur. In that chaotic moment, unprepared companies inevitably make mistakes that threaten the welfare of their employees, their stockholders, their customers, and even their future business viability (as, for example, in Dow Corning's bankruptcy over the product disaster involving its silicon breast implants). The moral of the story is clear: crisis planning, though difficult, is crucial for companies that want to act in the best interest of all their stakeholders in times of crisis. In fact, the greatest risk most companies face lies in failing to prepare for the risks they can predict.

MEDIA RELATIONS

Related to crisis communication but far more extensive in its scope is the topic of how companies relate to the full range of media sources, including television, radio, newspapers, magazines, and the internet. Virtually everything the public knows about a company comes from one of two sources: direct experience with the company and its product line, or information and impressions gleaned from media coverage of the company and its products.

Media Relations can be divided into four categories:

1. Paid Advertisements.   In this common form of media exposure, the company has almost complete control over what it wishes to reveal about itself and its products. For example, a company may pay hundreds of thousands of dollars to an advertising agency to develop a single television commercial targeted to a carefully determined audience. The company controls what product to advertise, what aspects of the product to emphasize, and what audience to target. These forms of media relations can be categorized as high-control, low-risk for the company.

2. **Unpaid Notices, References, and Appearances.** Companies devote substantial amounts each year to information dissemination, often by means of press releases, video news releases, information services provided by the company's media relations employees, and appearances for speeches and interviews by company leaders. An example of an unpaid notice is, for example, a journalist working on an article for a computer magazine. He or she gathers the latest product information from computer manufacturers. When the journalist mentions Apple or IBM or Compaq in the article, he or she is obviously not paid by these companies for the reference. Nevertheless, the company has used media to its advantage, in this case by making relevant information available. This form of media relation can be categorized as medium control, medium risk. The company is not in full control of how reporters and journalists will use its information; therefore, the company runs some risk of negative media coverage.

3. **Investigative or Confrontational Media Relations.** These, the most uncomfortable for most businesses, involve "60 Minutes" or "20/20"-type probing into company actions, motives, or problems. Companies that choose the "no comment" response to investigative inquiries from the media do not avoid negative media exposure; reporters will broadcast a company door being slammed in their faces, and journalists will report that "the company would not respond to our questions." Furthermore, such stonewalling by the company can quickly lead to adversarial relations with media representatives. If thwarted, reporters' passion to get information can turn to less noble motives of "getting" the company.

Companies that do comply with media requests for information are not assured of favorable or even fair treatment. Interviews with company spokespersons are often edited by the media to minimal "sound-bites" that sensationalize the story while obscuring the facts. These media investigations and confrontations, of the sort faced by Exxon after the Valdez disaster and Odwalla after contamination of its fruit juice, are definitely low-control, high-risk for the company. Information, once released by the company, is almost entirely out of its control. The stakes are high, as the company finds itself in the headlines for better or worse.

GUIDELINES FOR SUCCESSFUL MEDIA RELATIONS

When appearing on television (as in a CNBC, CNN, or other network business news interview), five nonverbal behaviors should be practiced:

- Maintain eye contact with the interviewer if you are responding to a question.
- Maintain eye contact with the camera if you are making a statement to the public. Insofar as possible, do not let your eyes wander or drop to your notes, especially at the conclusion of your statement.
- Keep your head and upper body relatively still (as compared to public speaking, where you would show more physical animation).
- Keep your hands in view at all times. Hold them still in a comfortable position or, at the most, use a few conservative gestures to emphasize your points. (Hidden

hands arouse subconscious suspicion for the viewer, and overly active gestures are much less effective on television than they are in a live speaking situation.)

On the verbal level (whether speaking on television or radio), maintain a pace that keeps your listeners' interest. Too slow a pace can sound hesitant or boring on the "hot" media of TV and radio; too fast a pace can sound hucksterish and insincere. Whether answering questions or making statements, get to your main point right away. Reporters may interrupt you after a few seconds; you want to make sure that your central point gets heard.

Handle friendly and less-than-friendly media questions with these techniques in mind:

- Discover and use the reporter's name. (Notice the effectiveness of this technique in news conferences conducted by U.S. presidents.)
- Avoid a defensive attitude by reminding yourself that the reporter or journalist is a channel through which you can get your message to the public. Appreciate the media representative as a vital link in this process.
- Make your replies concise but not abrupt. Get to your point, provide quick supporting information if possible, then stop.
- Come prepared to cite up-to-date statistics, examples, or expert testimony on your topic. Media representatives are eager to quote what they perceive as factual material.
- Do not repeat inaccurate information or accusations. Begin by disputing the assertion ("That is incorrect . . .") and proceed to give your side of the story.
- Use "topic bridges" to move from a difficult area of questioning to a more positive area. Let's say, for example, that a reporter asks you to explain why your company has not hired more minority workers in recent months. You answer, "My company is committed to maintaining a diverse workforce. [Bridge] Here are the facts about our hiring practices for the last three years. . . ." [Notice in this case that you bridged to the record you knew you could defend—the three-year hiring record—instead of restricting yourself to the reporter's specified time period of "recent months."]

Above all, maintain sincerity, credibility, and a caring attitude. These qualities go far to dispelling even the most unfavorable company news and easing the tension with even the most hostile media representative.

SUMMARY

1. Planning for crisis communication begins by identifying likely crises for the organization.

2. Crisis communication must be designed and practiced well before the crisis occurs.

3. All stakeholders in an organization, including clients and community members, must be considered in an effective crisis communication plan.

4. Businessmen and -women can achieve good working relations with media representatives by understanding and responding to the needs of media.

5. Verbal and nonverbal skills necessary for effective media appearances by business representatives must usually be learned. These skills differ to some degree from public speaking skills.

QUESTIONS FOR DISCUSSION

1. Why do companies so often resist crisis communication planning?

2. What likely crises may occur in your academic environment? What provision, if any, has been made for those crises?

3. Recall a social or business crisis that, in your opinion, was handled poorly. What went amiss? What could have been done to improve the crisis communication?

4. Recall a social or business crisis that, in your opinion, was handled well. What did people do right in this situation?

5. What does a company or other organization risk by not planning for likely crises?

6. Why do you think media representatives seem to be "on the attack" when interviewing business leaders?

7. What aspects of a media interview are under the interviewee's control? Which are not?

8. How can a media representative influence the way a businessperson is perceived by viewers or listeners in a television or radio interview? In a newspaper or magazine article?

EXERCISES

1. Working together with a small group of classmates, describe three likely crises in your academic environment. For each, prepare a one-page summary of planning steps that should be taken to ensure effective communication should the crisis occur.

2. Contact a company to learn whether it has a crisis communication plan. (Such plans are often not available to the public because they include sensitive internal data.) Determine from the company how it prepares its employees to use the plan in the event of crisis. Report or present your findings.

3. Read several press accounts of a recent company crisis. From that media record, decide how well the company handled the crisis. Write or present your findings as a case study.

4. Watch a television interview of a business leader. Take careful note of obvious and subtle ways by which the interviewer and interviewee influence the course of the interview. What dominant impressions are left at the conclusion of the interview? What created those impressions? Write or present your findings.

5. Working together with classmates, create a short "Guide to Media Appearances" for use by students in your academic program. What media skills should they learn to prepare for radio, television, teleconference, and print appearances?

INTERNET ASSIGNMENT

You received a distressing e-mail this morning from a former classmate who took an upper-level management position with a food services company. Yesterday a bad batch of chicken salad caused a food-poisoning incident at a prominent meeting of business executives. The story is front page news today. Although none of the executives has died, many have been admitted to hospitals for observation and recovery. The reputation of your friend's company, of course, has sunk like a stone.

Even though such a crisis has not struck your company, you resolve to prepare for likely crisis situations and media confrontations before such moments actually occur. Choose an area of business, then use the Crisis Communication and Media Relations sections of the Internet Guide to discover sites that tell you how to construct a crisis communication plan. List the sites that have proven most useful to you, then make a detailed outline of the proposed contents of a crisis communication plan for your company.

PART SIX

GLOBAL ISSUES IN MANAGEMENT COMMUNICATION

CHAPTER 18

Communication for Intercultural Management

AN EVER-MORE-GLOBAL BUSINESS WORLD

Discussions of intercultural communication used to be intended for the few business graduates who would actually visit another country on business. For the late 1990s and beyond, however, *every* business communicator needs to know how to interact successfully with members of different cultures. As many as one-third of current business school graduates may have extended foreign business experience within the first five years of their careers. Virtually everyone in business will have business relations with a foreign company at some time. In addition, most businesspeople, during their careers, will be employed in multicultural workforces.

The opportunity for intercultural interaction may be right at hand in your own city. Urban areas such as Chicago, Los Angeles, Philadelphia, and New York City celebrate their cultural diversity. They can be viewed as cultural quilts, with enclaves of different ethnic groups set side by side. To do business in Miami, for example, you will want to know as much as possible about Cuban-American culture, for people of Cuban ancestry make up a major Florida market and represent an influential social force. In Los Angeles, many service industries and food-related businesses are dominated by Southeast Asian and Hispanic Americans. In New York, a day's walking tour will take you through a half dozen or more distinctive cultural neighborhoods.

You may find yourself working for an American company or a multinational corporation that employs people from several cultural groups in different locations in the world. Major business schools in the United States are already gearing up for what *Fortune* called a "global vision": "Students will have to master a foreign language and culture as well as the usual tough material on marketing and finance." In 1997, more than one-fifth of all agricultural and manufactured goods produced in the United States were exported abroad. That same year, we imported even more than we exported, for an import–export total of $600 billion. That level of trade spells thousands of jobs abroad for Americans each year.

Note at the outset that inter*cultural* communication involves more than inter*national* communication. *Intercultural communication* involves making connections between different views of the world, whether between countries or between cultural groups within one country. By contrast, international communication may involve parties of the same culture, as when an American businesswoman in San Francisco contacts her American colleague based in Paris.

This chapter is intended to help you prepare for communicating effectively with members of other cultures. Such preparation involves knowing your audience and knowing yourself.

THE MEETING OF CULTURES

When you and your own cultural background come into contact with persons of another culture, something new emerges—a middle ground, called a "transaction culture." In this new middle ground, sensitive and often unstated rules and understandings guide behavior. That is, if a member of Culture A interacts with a member of Culture B, neither the cultural rules of A nor those of B are the sole guide for behavior. Instead, a mixed set of rules—middle Culture C—develops for the purposes of the interaction.

For example, consider the cultural rules that would guide a business conversation between you and a manager from Japan. You would not speak and act entirely as you would when conversing with American co-workers, nor would the Japanese manager hold fast to Japanese conversational rules and behaviors. Both of you would consciously and subconsciously bend your own cultural habits and assumptions to accommodate the communication needs of the other.

In short, learning to be an effective intercultural communicator does not mean *becoming* Japanese, Russian, or African. In fact, it would be a big mistake to pretend to know more about someone else's culture than you really know. Nor should you pretend to understand or believe what you really don't understand or believe. For example, you should not pretend to understand or believe in the religion of a business associate. Instead, you should show your respect for the religion and try to understand it if it would help in your business interactions. To communicate with other cultural groups, you must be willing and able to adapt—but not discard—your own patterns of thought and behavior to meet the communication needs of your audience. That process begins with a sincere effort to understand another culture on its own terms.

RECOGNIZING CULTURAL MISCONCEPTIONS

Many forces can interfere with the desire to meet other cultures in a productive, mutually satisfying way. The most influential of these are internal beliefs and assumptions about other cultures—the *misconceptions* that may prevent successful intercultural communication. The following seven misconceptions frequently get in the way of successful intercultural communication:

1. *Everyone is essentially like me.* We too easily assume that others think as we think, feel as we feel, and therefore should act as we act. This egocentricity can blind us to very real differences in the way people of other cultures think and behave.

2. *Others lack my advantages.* Many people believe the reason that some people aren't like them is that there's something wrong with the people who are different. They explain away cultural differences as deficiencies. They call other cultures "disadvantaged" or "underdeveloped" when in fact they are simply advantaged or developed in other ways. A materialistic culture may judge a deeply spiritual culture as backward—and vice versa.

3. *All we have to do is just get together, and our differences won't matter.* Putting different cultures into contact will not automatically lead to mutual understanding and respect. The many examples of feuds between bordering cultures throughout the world shows that more is needed than shared spaces.

4. *Don't worry, I speak the language.* Unfortunately, the formal language training provided in typical academic settings does not guarantee successful intercultural communication. To know how to speak and write a language does not necessarily guarantee that you know the culture. However, knowing the language *is* a great way to start learning about a culture.

5. *They'll see that I'm sincere.* In our culture, sincerity can forgive a multitude of blunders; we like to see that a person's "heart is in the right place." Some other cultures, however, pay more attention to what you do than to what you intend. An old Greek saying, for example, advises us to "know a good man by the way he lives."

6. *They have to respect my knowledge.* Not so. Many cultures place more importance on mutual trust than on technical know-how. Your competence or knowledge may not even be considered in such cultures until a trust relation has been formed.

7. *We're all interested in the bottom line.* Americans are used to doing away with formalities and procedures when they threaten profits or efficiency. In some other cultures, however, you may never violate the established *process* of doing business—including working through a rigid hierarchy, observing customary waiting periods, and completing elaborate paperwork.

To expose these beliefs as misconceptions is not to say that American cultural assumptions are wrong or that other cultural assumptions are right. Instead, the message is that cultural assumptions can differ.

Examples of Intercultural Misunderstandings

In each of the following situations, observe the unfortunate interference of one or more of the preceding cultural myths. Notice also the sometimes devastating effect of crossed signals based on a misunderstanding of gestures, expressions, and innocent actions. The first set of situations is given in the following "Communication for a New Century" section.

Five additional examples may help to show the consequences of intercultural misunderstandings. First, in 1997, Carl Travis journeyed from St. Paul, Minnesota, to do business with Som Sharma at his huge clothing factory outside Puwahla, India. Carl wanted to propose a joint venture involving Sharma's money and factory and Carl's own American marketing contacts. Carl's proposal presented extraordinary opportunities for success by means of Indian import clothing shops in the United States.

As Carl presented his proposal, the taciturn Sharma shook his head from side-to-side. I'm not doing well, Carl told himself, and redoubled his persuasive efforts. Sharma shook his head back and forth more earnestly. After almost 45 minutes, Carl snapped his briefcase shut in consternation and stood up to leave. He apparently hadn't gotten to first base with his proposal.

Later, at his hotel, Carl learned an expensive lesson from the Indian concierge: Indians in many regions of the country express approval by shaking the head back and forth, the same gesture that Americans use for disapproval.

Second, Margaret Owens sat looking out at the Tokyo skyline from a managerial suite rented for the purpose of interviews. She wanted to find half a dozen enthusiastic Japanese representatives to market a line of pharmaceuticals in Japan. After completing ten interviews, Margaret was dumbfounded. Not one applicant spoke up in a direct, forceful manner, in spite of his or her stellar academic record and recommendations. Not one met her eye-to-eye for very long. None seemed comfortable speaking openly and frankly about accomplishments and aspirations.

Margaret reported her discouraging interview results to the Vice President of Asian Markets for the drug company—only to endure the most embarrassing lecture of her life. To speak up, she learned from the vice president, can be taken as impertinence, especially if one emphasizes personal accomplishments. To meet the eyes in some business situations is, in many Asian cultures, an indication of disrespect or even hostility.

Third, local mining magnates in Kajari, Pakistan, accepted Fred Revin's invitation to a business dinner at a local restaurant. Fred was pleased to begin the meal with nonbusiness small talk. But after 15 minutes of pleasantries, he wondered when the conversation would turn to business. He hesitated to broach business topics directly for fear of offending custom. The evening wore on in small talk, to Fred's immense frustration.

In fact, the Pakistani miners were wondering why Fred invited them to dinner. While several minutes of chat are ordained by Pakistani custom, the host—Revin—has the obligation to shift matters to business topics thereafter. Everyone was waiting for Fred to make his move.

Fourth, Jean Simonds was pleased to accept an invitation for dinner at the home of Klaus and Sonya Griegl, Belgian camera manufacturers. On her way to dinner, Jean spotted some lovely white chrysanthemums at a flower shop. She bought the flowers as a gift for her host.

To her dismay, the flowers brought a stiffly gracious response from her hosts, who set them aside quickly. White chrysanthemums, she learned later, are presented only to mark mourning in Belgium.

Fifth, in Venezuela, oil broker Cal Farnswell could not help but compliment Venezuelan manager Maria Ortiz on her gorgeous, flowing black hair. Obviously pleased, she received the compliment with a glowing smile. Carl then inquired if her hair was difficult to care for. The smile faded. The American had trampled on an important Latin American custom: Avoid personal questions about the private lives of acquaintances.

Eleven Common Areas of Intercultural Misunderstanding

Each of these American businesspeople initially reacted with shock: "Well, how was I supposed to know?" Avoid asking yourself the same question. Don't attempt to interact in a new culture before becoming aware of your own assumptions and blind spots. The following 11 questions relate to areas of cultural sensitivity around the world. The more you know about another culture, the harder you may find it to answer each of these questions. That's as it should be. Simple answers to complex questions can lead to stereotypes, the enemy of intercultural awareness.

The 11 areas of sensitivity are male–female interactions, respect, time and space, taboos, commitments, nonverbal cues, language and translation, dress, methods of persuasion, religious and political issues, and prejudices.

1. How do *men* relate to *women*, and women to men? Though you may not agree on the fairness of relations between the sexes in other cultures, knowing their ground rules helps you avoid disastrous social and business pitfalls.

2. How does the culture indicate *respect*? Consider the roles of silence, direct questions, seating arrangements (such as the infamous seating struggles before the Vietnamese peace talks), eye contact, gestures, gifts, compliments, and invitations. Also, find out whether specific categories of people (e.g., older persons, religious figures, more-senior staff) always receive some of these specific signs of respect.

3. How does the culture view human *time and space*? Does an appointment at 7 P.M. mean "7 sharp" or "sevenish" or, as in some Latin countries, around 8? Is one business day, once passed, gone forever (the American notion of linear time), or does the same circumstance repeat itself over and over (the Eastern cyclical view of time)? What of space? Should you stand a bit closer to Frenchmen than you are used to standing to Americans?

4. What are strict *taboos* in the culture? Is alcohol, for example, accepted, winked at, or absolutely unthinkable? Is your host's off-color joke an invitation for uproarious laughter or a subtle test of your own mores?

5. How are business *commitments* made in the culture? By oral approval? By a handshake? By signing of documents? Often, American businesspeople believe that a verbal agreement shows that the listener agrees to the proposal and is committed to it. When they discover that their hosts are merely being pleasant and agreeable, they feel deeply disappointed and may even feel cheated. Try to establish in advance the words and actions in the culture that will let you know that your deal is moving forward to commitment. Try also to find out how people say "no" or avoid saying "no" in the particular culture.

6. What *nonverbal cues* are used in the culture to pass information to you or to pass private understandings between members of the culture? How should you interpret the "V" sign in England? (Sometimes an obscene gesture.) How are you to understand an apology delivered with a big smile in Japan? (Utter sincerity, not a charade.) What does the eye pull mean in Italy and Spain? (Careful, I'm on to you.) Why does your host in India grimace when, in crossing your legs, you point your soles toward him or her? (An insult.)

7. How should you handle the whole matter of *language and translation*? It bears looking into before entering upon business relations in another culture. What

ETIQUETTE LESSONS IN THREE COUNTRIES

Companies all over the world are gearing up to meet the challenge of the coming decade: prospering in the world market. American companies are waking up to the fact that the world market is four times the size of the domestic one. Are you ready to do business in this environment?

Not only does the product or service you sell have to be adaptable to this market, but you also have the added burden of cultural "response-ability." Well-traveled businesspeople will invariably tell you, "Culture matters." They generally illustrate their point by telling a joke or a story.

What works and what doesn't is often best related through anecdotes. And you can usually hear some good ones being traded over the dinner table in the local Intercontinental Hotel—a great way to end a hard day's work in a different country. This informal "case study" technique has also been adopted by most cross-cultural training program designers, because they tend to stress experiential learning, and because these stories are what people say they enjoy and remember.

Case 1: Why Is No One Eating?

A businesswoman recently asked us why a high-level delegation of visiting Japanese clients had not approached the breakfast buffet table she had taken such great pains to prepare. "I'd gotten out the good china and silverware and even brought in Japanese green tea for them, but no one touched a thing!"

We solicited some advice on this one from both Japanese acquaintances here and returned expatriates, and they offered several possible explanations. First, American hospitality is based on the idea of "serve yourself." But these Japanese gentlemen probably expected to be served and may have misunderstood the hostess's hospitality. As in many cultures, a person who is offered something should, to be polite, refuse several times until the hostess finally serves what she is offering to the person. Also, we have been told that Japanese men seldom eat sweets, such as danishes, and would certainly never eat them with green tea, which is taken only with Japanese food. Here we see a typical example of intercultural mismatch arising from conflicting approaches to politeness.

The only cues she'd gotten were nonverbal ones.

She wasn't able to bring herself to verbalize the problem, but even if she had, their Japanese face-saving values would have prevented them from embarrassing the hostess by telling her what was wrong. Besides, she couldn't have served them herself even if she had become aware of their expectations at that point. Such behavior would have been inconsistent with her formal role.

The irony of the entire situation is that the American businesswoman consulted her Japanese assistant about the menu!

Case 2: What Does He Mean?

The following incident was sent in by a marketing manager whose area of responsibility is the Middle East.

Mike Johnson was visiting in Saudi Arabia. He was the youngest member of a negotiating team that had been sent over to develop relationships with established local firms. Ahmad al Suwaidi was one of several Saudis Mike had met on this trip. One day, during the small talk after a meeting at Ahmad's office, the topic of deep-sea fishing had come up. Mike said that he really enjoyed fishing, and Ahmad offered to take him on a fishing trip in the Red Sea on his own boat. Mike was delighted and accepted.

Their outing went very well. Mike met Ahmad's American wife, and he was quite surprised to see that she wore a bikini on the boat, not at all what he had expected the wife of a Saudi to do. He and Ahmad talked about many things, including American football, a sport Ahmad had grown very fond of since his days at a Texas university.

Soon after the fishing trip, Mike wanted to return the hospitality and invited the Saudis to dinner at a Riyadh restaurant. Only Ahmad came. When the bill was placed on the table, Ahmad took it saying, "But you are a guest in my country." Mike was confused. It was certainly his invitation. He protested, but weakly, as he didn't want to upset Ahmad, and he wasn't sure that he fully understood Saudi customs.

On the team's last day in Saudi Arabia, members were all invited to Ahmad's house. Ahmad drew Mike away from the group on the pretext of showing him his prayer-bead collection. When they were out of earshot, Ahmad said, "Mike, I think we could do business together, you and I."

Mike answered, "Yes, our companies do seem to be perfectly suited to be partners for this venture and many others, I hope."

"No, I mean I think we could do business, you and I," said Ahmad.

Taken aback, Mike replied, "I'm afraid I don't quite understand. Do you mean independently? I couldn't leave my company. . . ."

Many things are going on here, but one of the main problems is not even culturally specific to Saudi Arabia. Mike has allowed himself to be lulled into a false sense of security. Just because some of the host national's behaviors seem very modernized, Westernized, or Americanized (the excellent spoken English, the American wife in the bikini, the football talk), we mustn't let ourselves fall into the trap of assuming, "oh, they are just like us." Most awkward incidents like this one occur because we have overgeneralized or stereotyped the other person. The mischief comes from the fact that we've gotten lazy and have stopped paying attention to very real differences. This greatly limits the amount of information we will take in. We have to pay attention to our own perceptions and never forget the cultural "lenses" we are seeing the world through. That prism tends to distort and reorganize reality.

Some of the cultural specifics in this example are: Saudis, and many other nationals, will rarely come right out and say "no" to your face. They won't refuse a verbal invitation, like Mike's invitation to dinner, but they also won't feel obligated to show up when the offer was made like this. Once again Mike assumed too much. He took for granted that "yes" meant yes. Never assume anything.

Mike could have gotten around the problem of Ahmad's insistence on picking up the check by intervening earlier. Using the pretext of having to make a phone call, he could have gone to the maitre d', given him his credit card, and signed the slip in advance. In some cultures an older person doesn't like to be seen letting someone his junior pay the bill, especially in public. Mike was also acting very "American" by feeling pressured to return Ahmad's hospitality so immediately and directly. This *quid pro quo* mentality can be taken offensively by others who may sense, rightly or wrongly, that the person is trying to discharge an obligation that's making him or feel uncomfortable. Americans are often criticized for this, as well as being in too much of a hurry in general, coming on too strong, or acting too familiar too fast.

In the final encounter between Mike and Ahmad,

Mike's mistake is in looking at the situation in black and white and, ergo, naïve terms. All Ahmad may really mean to do is flatter him and "make a friend." He might be testing the waters, in which case Mike could have responded by merely thanking him for the compliment and leaving things open.

Unfortunately, Mike overreacted to this "feeler." Ahmad had not suggested that Mike leave his company, but the result of Mike's assumption was that the whole relationship cooled. A better response on Mike's part could have created a bond that would have accomplished both sets of goals.

Case 3: Did She Put a Curse on Me?

The next example will be left for you to try your hand it. It was contributed recently by a German who lived and worked in Brazil for several years.

"I'd already been in São Paulo for about a year when this happened, so I'd already heard about these macumba, or voodoo, practices that had come over from Africa. For example, I knew that all sorts of people would go to the beaches on the night of the new year to throw flowers and whatnot into the waves. They would wait to see if their offerings would be carried out to sea, meaning good luck for the year, or be washed back in, bringing bad luck.

The following incident, however, still puzzles me. We had a woman who cooked and cleaned for our family. We liked her. She had her own living quarters in the backyard, separate from the house, and we never invaded her privacy. We had no reason to because nothing was ever missing—rare in Brazil where light-fingered servants are a fact of life that most employers resign themselves to if the thefts are petty. It's a poor country, after all.

"But for some reason, when the woman was away for a week's vacation, my wife went into the room, probably just to let some air into the place. She found a kind of altar, with the typical signs of macumba around: chicken bones, melted wax, and stuff. But she also found a picture . . . of herself. It really upset us both. And we don't know to this day whether the woman meant her well or not. But it certainly changed the way we regarded her after that. I'm happy to say nothing bad ever happened, but it still haunts us."

words can you learn to indicate your interest in another culture? Should you supply your own translator? Will he or she be trusted? What should you conclude if your host insists on providing his or her own translator for you?

8. How should you *dress* for business and social occasions in the host country? Before "going native" in dress, consider the risks of losing your identity as a foreign visitor and hence your immunity to some forms of criticism. In our own country, no one expects the visitor wearing Tibetan ceremonial gowns to cope well with cabs, train schedules, and all the other hassles of urban life. We bend to help. However, the same visitor in typical American street clothes may be treated with irritation and impatience. Similarly, your clear identification as an American abroad may bring a modicum of helpfulness from the host country.

9. How do your foreign hosts handle *persuasion*? Do your hosts favor direct propositions supported by evidence? Do they wish to consider your reputation, your family roots, your personal success, your age, your sex, your educational attainments? Do they want to hear your arguments or merely to share your friendship? Do they base a business relation on rational analysis or on trust?

10. What aspects of the host country's *religious or political life* must be understood for effective business relations? Are certain times of the day set aside for worship, not work? Is work automatically canceled on some holidays, or is it optional? Must certain work groups be separated due to political differences? Are some jobs tasks disliked for religious or political reasons?

11. What *prejudices* against you as an American must you overcome in the culture? Do your hosts automatically assume that you throw money around in a careless and tasteless way? Do they assume that your appetites for food, alcohol, and sex are out of control? Do they look upon you as a steamroller, who believes that might makes right? In all these matters, you may have to exert your imagination and energies to show yourself as you are, not as you are thought to be.

CATEGORIES OF CULTURAL DIFFERENCE

Not all differences create major misunderstandings or offenses between persons of different cultures. Nonetheless, these differences must be understood to enhance intercultural communication. The Language Research Center at Brigham Young University suggests several key areas for exploration for those getting to know another culture.

The following list shows general ways in which cultures can differ. In reading the list, compare your own culture in each category to another culture with which you are familiar.

1. **Greetings**—appropriate or inappropriate gestures (such as handshake or touching), verbal greetings (what to say), how close together persons stand when greeting or conversing, conversation topics, etc.
   a. meeting a person the first time
   b. everyday acquaintances
   c. close friends
   d. elderly people
   e. women
   f. youth

    g. children

    h. leaders in the culture

    i. to show special respect

    j. from a distance:

    k. use of family name or first name

    l. use of titles (such as Mr. or Dr.)

    m. compliments with greetings (what to compliment, how to give and receive compliments, and when)

2. **Visiting a family at home**—what should and should not be done in the following situations.

    a. greeting

    b. entering the house

    c. gifts and flowers (what is appropriate: when and how to give, receive, and open gifts)

    d. compliments on possessions, decor, or to family members

    e. proper conduct (in the living room, parlor, or guest welcoming area)

    f. conversation (what topics are best and when people usually talk)

    g. table manners (seating arrangements, when a guest should begin to eat, excusing oneself from the table, etc.)

    h. utensils and how to use them

    i. conversation at the dinner table

    j. compliments on the food

    k. saying farewell and leaving

    l. parties and social events (What should be remembered by a guest to best interact with the host and other guests? What is expected of the guest?)

    m. words to avoid

3. **Talks, speeches, and public addresses** to groups of people.

    a. subjects or topics that these people are especially fond of or those which should not be referred to

    b. gestures that help or hurt communication

    c. the way the speaker stands or sits in front of the group

    d. hints on using an interpreter

4. **Meetings**—punctuality, best ways to begin and end the meeting, seating arrangement, eye contact, and using an interpreter.

    a. large formal meetings

    b. small group sessions (about 3–15 people)

    c. private interview with an individual

5. **Gestures**—those that help to carry a message and those that should be avoided.

    a. with hands

    b. head

    c. eye and eye contact, eyebrows, face (Is it customary to look a person directly in the eyes when speaking? What would be the reaction to this by a person in this culture?)

    d. legs (such as crossing the legs when sitting down)

    e. feet (moving things with them, pointing them at people, gesturing with them, putting them on one's desk, etc.)

    f. posture (standing and sitting down, hands on hips, etc.)

g. touching (another person, male and female, etc.)
h. shoulders
i. arms (such as folding them or putting them around another's shoulders)
j. smiling and laughing customs (When is a smile appropriate or inappropriate? In what situations does a smile mean something other than happiness and goodwill?)
k. yawning
l. calling someone to you with your hands (palm facing up or down, etc.)
m. handing, passing, or giving things to another person

6. **Personal appearance.**
   a. clothing
   b. eyeglasses and sunglasses
   c. hats
   d. other

7. **General attitudes** of (1) adults, a. male b. female: (2) teenagers, a. male b. female, about
   a. nature and [the human] role in it
   b. society, groups, and the individual, self
   c. wealth, clothes, possessions
   d. work, success, failure, and fate
   e. government, politics, taxes, police, welfare assistance
   f. personality traits that are considered good or bad in a person
   g. role of men and women
   h. sexual promiscuity, abortion
   i. time, punctuality
   j. youth, teenagers
   k. elderly people
   l. physically or mentally handicapped
   m. business and economic progress
   n. war and the military
   o. crime and violence
   p. majority groups, races, and minority groups (special likes, dislikes, or problems)
   q. other nations and their people (special likes, dislikes, or problems)
   r. longevity, retirement, and death
   s. political systems (socialism, communism, imperialism, democracy, etc.)
   t. humor
   u. promises, agreements, and trust
   v. community participation
   w. revenge, retributions, repayment of wrongs received
   x. animals, pets
   y. showing emotions
   z. gambling, drinking alcoholic beverages, drugs
   aa. giving and receiving criticism
   bb. making decisions in business, among peers
   cc. education
   dd. what possessions or achievements indicate status (for men and women, adult and youth)

8. **Language**—dialects, use of English, etc.
9. **Religions**—general attitudes toward religion, predominant beliefs.
10. **Special holidays**—specific dates and how these holidays are celebrated.
11. **The family**
    a. average size of family
    b. attitudes about the family and its role in society
    c. teenagers' role in the family
    d. role of the elderly in the family
    e. authority, obedience, roles of father, mother, and children (making decisions in the family)
    f. system of family inheritance
    g. milestone experiences in life for a male
    h. milestone experiences in life for a female
    i. special activities that are used to show that a person has become an adult (or otherwise changed social status)
    j. who in the family works (father, mother, children)
    k. average daily schedule and activities for fathers, mothers, children
12. **Dating and marriage customs.**
    a. from what age does dating begin? How important is dating? Why?
    b. is dating in larger groups or individual couples?
    c. common dating activities
    d. chaperones
    e. acceptable and unacceptable dating behavior
    f. engagement customs
    g. attitude about marriage
    h. age at which most men marry
    i. age at which most women marry
    j. how much influence the family has in deciding about marriages
    k. prerequisites to marriage (such as completion of education or financial independence)
    l. desirability of children (birth control)
    m. attitude about divorce
    n. attitude toward displaying affection in public (such as between husband and wife or parents and children)
13. **Social and economic levels**—including size of different general classes, average income and what it provides for the family, general housing conditions and possessions (such as refrigerator, range, toaster, cars, radios, telephones, televisions, etc.).
14. **Distribution of group**—rural or urban, what cities or areas, group population for areas concerned and what ratio group population is to total population in these areas.
15. **Work.**
    a. the economy of the group (What are the main occupations of the people, industries, and important products?)
    b. individual work schedules (hours per day, days per week)
    c. age at which people begin working
    d. choosing a job

16. Diet.
   a. average diet, size of meals when they are eaten
   b. special foods which are usually given to guests
   c. Is mealtime important for some other reason than just nutrition?

17. Recreation, sports, arts, music, leisure time.
   a. family cultural and physical recreation and sports activities (including vacations)
   b. individual recreation, games, sports of children, youth, adults, and elderly
   c. distinctive arts of the culture which a visitor should know about

18. History and government.
   a. history of the group, including facts and events considered most important by the people and why
   b. heroes, leaders of the group and why they are esteemed
   c. group government systems, differences from regular local government

19. Education.
   a. education in the group
   b. any private education systems within the group

20. Transportation and communication systems—their use and significance to the group.
   a. bicycles
   b. individual cars and road system
   c. buses
   d. taxis
   e. other
   f. mass communication (such as TV, radio, newspapers, magazines)
   g. individual interpersonal communication (such as telephones, postal service)
   h. any special or unusual methods of trade, exchange, communication or transportation

21. Health, sanitation, medical facilities—including general attitude about disease.

22. Land and climate—including geographical effects on the history of the group, problems posed today by the geography or climate where these people are located.

23. "Universal" signals or nonverbal cues a newcomer should know that indicate approval or disapproval, acceptance or rejection in this society.

Source: "Categories of Cultural Difference," Language Research Center, Brigham Young University, 1996. Reprinted with permission.

This list is a partial summary of some aspects of culture which can unite people who share the same basic attitudes, backgrounds, and lifestyles. Since these characteristics can vary widely between cultures, they can be a source of misunderstanding and miscommunication.

EXAMINE YOUR OWN LANGUAGE AND CULTURAL HABITS

While you investigate your host country's customs and language, remember to examine your own ways of speaking and writing. You can aid your hosts in understanding your business communications in three key ways:

1. Avoid slang and idioms
2. Slow down your speech
3. Check your listener's understanding of what you're saying or writing.

Avoid Slang and Idioms

Learn to cut out slang and idioms (including local or regional colloquial expressions) from the words you use for international business. Robert Bell, a magnetic resonance specialist, comments:

> When I travel to business meetings abroad, I have to remember that my ordinary mode of friendly conversation contains many idioms (such as "right on the money") that foreign colleagues will find strange and uninterpretable. I remind myself to speak "plain vanilla" English around those who don't know the language well.

An American manager wrote the following sentence to a foreign businessman with limited English skills. "By the way, I've shipped the computer order we discussed last week." The American manager was shocked to receive a telex from his foreign client: "What is 'the way' you refer to? Urgent to know."

The English language is rich in such innocent idioms and Americanisms. For the sake of clear business dealings abroad, try to become aware of words and phrases that might be misunderstood.

Slow Down Your Speech

Adjust the pace of your speaking to match the rate of comprehension of your foreign host. You will often do business with men and women abroad who have, through hard work, acquired quite a bit of English. If you rush ahead at the same speaking pace you would use with a native speaker, you unintentionally dash these people's efforts to communicate with you. Before leaving for an international trip, practice slowing down your speech without sounding patronizing. Look directly at the person to whom you are speaking, so that he or she can see the words as they form on your lips and notice your facial and hand gestures.

Check for Comprehension

Some Americans, in speaking to foreign persons, frown quizzically as a visual way of asking, "Are you following me?" Try not to use the frown in this way. Unfortunately, this puzzled frown will often be misinterpreted as anger, criticism, or impatience.

Instead, when you want to check for comprehension, raise your eyebrows and give an inquiring smile. That visual gesture will produce either a nod of comprehension from your foreign friend or an indication that he or she has not understood. Learn to check often (in polite ways) to see whether your listener is comprehending. In a telephone conversation, for example, pause to ask "Am I being clear?" or "Do you understand?" or simply "O.K.?"

In face-to-face conversations, do not mistake a courteous smile on your listener's face or a nod as a sign of complete comprehension. Particularly in Asian and Latin American cultures, your listener will give you a smile simply as a polite gesture. Asian listeners may even nod and say "yes" (*hai*) repeatedly, all in an effort to show respect to you. All the while, they may almost entirely misunderstand what you are saying. Good barometers of such misunderstanding are the eyes. Watch to see whether your listener's eyes respond to your words. If you notice a glazed, lost look, back up and begin again in a simpler fashion. Another helpful technique is to politely ask the other party to say back (or write back) what he or she understood you to say. In working with a translator, this process is called "back translation."

WHERE TO LEARN ABOUT OTHER CULTURES

From the preceding discussion, it's clear that no businessperson can afford to learn about other cultures through personal blunders and insults.There are many ways to learn about other cultures before you step into your first intercultural business meeting or send off an important report to an international office. These techniques include visiting a country's embassy or consulate, participating in cultural training, asking people who have lived in or visited the country of interest, and studying the language.

Visit the Country's Embassy or Consulate

Most trade-seeking nations maintain experienced ambassadors and consuls with extended staffs in major U.S. cities, particularly New York, Washington, DC, and Los Angeles. You can make an appointment with the commerce secretary at the embassy to learn how to approach businesses—and often whom to approach—when you visit the foreign country. If you cannot visit the person, write a letter describing your business interests. Solicit the help of the embassy in making your venture mutually profitable.

Seek out Cultural Training

Many schools, clubs, and organizations provide cultural awareness training. The following groups will provide you with information about their services and general advice about cultural preparation.

> Overseas Briefing Associates
> 201 East 36th Street
> New York, NY 10016

> The Business Council for International Understanding
> The American University
> Washington, DC 20016

> The Intercultural Communications Network
> 1860 19th Street, N.W.
> Washington, DC 20009

A benefit of such organizations is that they can acquaint you with such universal business conventions abroad as *name cards*. Similar in size and format to business cards used in this country, name cards contain not only your name, title, and company in English, but also on the reverse side the same information translated into the language of your host country. Especially important in such a translation is the statement of your title. Corporate "president," for example, in English does not signify the same thing in Japan. There, a "president" is an honored, retired, and relatively powerless former leader of industry. Probably your title as "president" would be rendered "senior director" to communicate your status clearly in your host country.

Such name cards are given and taken freely in your business dealings. You may easily dispense a hundred such cards in your first week in a foreign country and take in twice that number. Many countries publish name card collection books, complete with hierarchical interior divisions so you can store your collected name cards in a pecking order of sorts. Without such cards of your own, you may have difficulty establishing your credentials in business contacts that come your way through the day.

Ask People Who Have Been There

Except for your own personal experience, the most valuable information you can get is the helpful hints from someone whose background is similar to your own. Find out whether anyone in your company or another company has visited the country in question. Find time to listen to stories of his or her experiences. The ultimate authorities on a different culture are, of course, the people of that culture. Seek out their advice for how best to handle written and oral communications.

Also, ask questions and seek guidance from secondary resources, such as the country's national airline serving your city (Swiss Air, British Airways, and so forth). At such places, you probably will meet someone here who knows someone over there—and that someone can prove invaluable to you as an initial cultural contact.

American banks that do business abroad and foreign banks in this country can often prove helpful to you. Also, draw on the considerable resources of the United States Chamber of Commerce. It publishes a number of booklets on trade relations. Each foreign country seeking trade will probably also have a chamber of commerce anxious to serve you. In most cases, you can reach this office by writing to the Office or Ministry of International Trade in the capital city of the country that interests you.

Study the Language

Above all, begin *language training* in the tongue of the culture you intend to visit. If you don't at least try to learn the language, you'll be totally dependent on a translator or virtually isolated from the friendly conversations. Don't be concerned that you haven't mastered the language. Your hosts will take it as a compliment that you are at least trying to learn their language at all and will help you at every turn.

WRITING FOR INTERCULTURAL BUSINESS

Business documents in different countries differ not only in form but also in pattern of organization, tone, and level of detail. German documents, for example, are terse and heavily detailed, whereas Latin American documents emphasize a polite style and generalized concepts. Reports for Japanese associates must be prepared with formal, honorific openings. Casual analogies and other non-business-related information get cut from the reports and proposals sent to British colleagues.

Even when you try to follow the style and tone of the documents written by native businesspeople in Latin America, Asia, and Europe, your Americanness will still show. Some of that is fine. Intercultural readers, whether located inside the U.S. or abroad, except American communications to show the features of American document conventions.

Nonetheless, shrewd intercultural communicators still try hard to *bend* their writing habits and assumptions toward the communication needs and expectations of their readers. As a case in point, many European cultures expect significant business correspondence to end with two signatures—the signatures of both the letter writer and his or her superior. Therefore, to get a more positive reaction from a European reader, the American letter writer may decide to use two signatures.

An American writer may even have to learn when not to write at all. As reported in separate studies by Michael Yoshino and William Ouchi, Japanese companies don't use written communication for routine business matters as much as American companies do. If an American writer communicates solely by memo, a Japanese reader may tend to treat the message as being inappropriately serious or important—calling a meeting, for example, to discuss the implications of the memo. Instead, alternate channels of communication should be chosen: a conference telephone call, perhaps, or a face-to-face meeting with selected decision-makers.

A final example involves the use of first names. In American correspondence, it is common after the first two or three business contacts to begin addressing the reader by his or her first name. This practice is generally taken in our culture to be a sign of friendliness and trust. In Germany, however, business readers look upon the use of first names ("Dear Helmut") as a sign of inappropriate chumminess bordering on disrespect. For Germans, friendliness, trust, and respect in correspondence is demonstrated by the writer's willingness to use titles and last names: "Dear Director Schmidt." Figures 18–1 through 18–9 show some examples of international memos and responses.

The memo in Figure 18–1, written by a Mitsubishi manager, and its English translation in Figure 18–3 shows how the American "To/From/Subject/Date" material has been redistributed at the top of the memo page. An official seal—the personal trademark of a Japanese manager—appears beside the name. By Japanese business tradition and Mitsubishi practice, this memo begins with standard language of respect. Following this traditional expression of respect and well-wishing, the memo turns to its specific business—in this case, the hiring of two secretaries. Note that the requested qualifications of these secretaries are appended to the memo in the form of "supplements," a common Japanese way of handling lists and details. The memo ends by turning again to traditional, expected language. No signature appears after the phrase "with our best regards."

Figure 18–3 shows an American response to a Japanese manager's memo. The American memo endeavors to catch the form and spirit of the Japanese memo form without mimicking it in all details. The American writer would probably fail badly, for example, in trying to imitate all the nuances of the traditional Japanese beginning and ending. In this memo, the American writer begins rather formally, addresses the request in a general way, and highlights details by a numbered list. But why go to the trouble to follow Japanese practice in these matters? A typical memo in the succinct, frank American style may have been misunderstood by the Japanese manager as an impatient, glib, or even mildly insulting response. In the Latin American memo and its English translation, Figures 18–4 and 18–5, note the distribution of the message on the page (somewhat lower than American practice); the convention of assigning numbers to memos; the use of "Antecedent"; the respectful tone, particularly in the memo opening; and letter-like conclusion. Figure 18–6 shows an American response to a Chilean memo.

FIGURE 18–1   A Japanese Manager's Memo

テンポラリーワーカーズ株式会社　御中　　　　　　1989年10月 2日

五菱商事株式会社

取締役人事部長

山田　太郎

業務秘書派遣依頼の件

拝啓、

　　貴社益々御隆昌の段お慶び申し上げます。また、平素より格別のお引き立ての程誠に有難く存じます。

　　扨て、頭書の件に関し、弊社に於きましては、今般米国ＧＵ社と合弁企業を設立する運びとなり、新会社の為の業務秘書を二名新規募集致します。就きましては、貴社の幅広い人材の中から、下記条件に適合する候補者を弊社人事第一課宛御推薦戴ければ幸いです。貴社より御推薦戴きました候補者につきまして、追って面談日時等を取り決めさせていただきたく存じます。

　　お忙しい中とは存じますが、本件に就いての御検討を宜しくお願い申し上げます。

敬具

記

弊社希望条件　　1. 英語能力（英検二級以上）

　　　　　　　　2. 和文ワードプロセサー（二級以上）

　　　　　　　　3. コンピュータ経験有り

以上

In the Russian memo and its English translation, Figures 18–7 and 18–8, note the initial gesture of respect, followed by a straightforward—even blunt—statement of the problem. This business seems to contain an emotional message as well, especially in the passage regarding Mashinka's drinking. The memo closes, as it began, on a highly formal note. The writer signs his full name.

Figure 18–9 shows an American response to the Russian memo.

FIGURE 18–2   An English Translation

Messrs: Temporary Workers Corporation   October 2, 1998

Five Diamond Corporation
Director, General Manager
Taro Yamada
(official seal)

Subject: Secretary Recruiting

Dear Sir:

It is our pleasure for serving you. I would like to take this opportunity to thank you for supporting our company for many years.

*(Meantime,) We have finalized a plan to establish a joint-venture with GU Company, our American partner. And we have started looking for two secretaries for this project. Among your numerous capable candidates, we wish you can recommend two people to us with the undermentioned abilities. We will set up interviews with the appointed candidates immediately after receiving your recommendation.

*(We guess that you are busy, however.) We will appreciate your reply as soon as possible.

With our best regards.

Supplements
Requested Conditions
1. Fluent English ability (above JST grade-2)
2. Japanese wordprocessing ability (above grade-2)
3. Experience of computers

*Approximate equivalents for untranslatable Japanese phrases.

CHINA: AN EXTENDED CASE IN MANAGEMENT COMMUNICATION

Geographically, culturally, and economically, China represents a huge footprint on the globe. At its present rate of economic growth, China may surpass the United States in gross national product (GNP) by the second decade of the new century. Even though much of its one billion people now live below the poverty level, the Chinese enjoy a vision of things to come. "One billion people—but 900,000,000 *business*people," goes the popular Chinese saying.

In preparation for writing this chapter on intercultural communication, the authors visited China twice to meet with more than 200 business managers and leaders in several trading regions of that vast country. This narrative sums up what we learned about intercultural communication with businesspeople in China. We offer these comments and suggestions as guidelines for your own communication with and, perhaps, travel to an emerging economic giant.

- *The Chinese (unlike the French, in some cases) appreciate your attempt to speak a bit of their language.* Understand, however, that the Chinese widely spoken in Hong Kong and the Economic Territories is Cantonese. The Chinese spoken in Beijing and most of the rest of China is Mandarin. Strong feelings are attached in some regions to this language difference. Mandarin speakers in Beijing, for exam-

FIGURE 18–3 An American Response to a Japanese Memo

Five Diamond Corporation
Director, General Manager
Taro Yamada

October 3, 1998

Temporary Workers Corporation
Vice President
Richard Matthews

Subject: Your Request for Secretaries

Thank you for contacting Temporary Workers Corporation for your employment needs. We have certainly enjoyed being of service to you for the past four years.

After a careful review of sixteen highly skilled candidates, we have selected two secretaries to meet the needs you describe. Both are available at your convenience for an interview. We believe their considerable skills (listed below) will justify their employment.

We recognize that these are indeed busy times for you. However, we will be most pleased to hear from you as soon as possible to schedule interviews.

With sincere best wishes.

Supplements
Qualifications of Both Candidates

1. Grade 3 English ability in speaking and writing
2. Grade 3 Japanese wordprocessing ability
3. Experience with Japanese and American computer systems

---

ple, may not understand (or pretend not to understand) your tourist phrases spoken in Cantonese. Similarly, Cantonese speakers in Hong Kong may quickly "correct" your Mandarin attempts to their Cantonese equivalent.

- *Food and sociability are intimately linked with business discussions and decision making.* Your Chinese host will offer tea and probably a meal as part of your business visit. (When visiting the United States, your Chinese guest will expect the same from you.) Although topics of conversation at the table may touch on business matters, more often the Chinese prefer to use meal times as periods of relaxation—a chance to ask questions about your country, to talk about food, the weather, customs in different parts of China, family life (they will appreciate seeing pictures of your friends and family), and many other comfortable topics. Especially in your first meals together, the topics of politics and religion are generally out of bounds. Your questions in these areas will probably be greeted by a polite, ambiguous, and short answer.

- *At a format meal with Chinese business hosts, you will probably be given a wrapped gift.* It is customary to thank your host and to set the gift aside for opening later. In response, you may present your host with a small, wrapped gift in return. (Your Chinese hosts will not expect such a gift, however; they know that

FIGURE 18–4 A Chilean Manager's Memo

MEMORANDUM No. 532

Ant.: Su memorandum no.228
de fecha 25.7.98.
Mat.: Solicitud de una
secretaria edicional.

Santiago, 12 de septiembre de 1989

DE: GERENTE DE FINANZAS

A: GERENTE GENERAL

De acuerdo a su memorandum de antecedente, me dirijo a usted con el objeto de solicitarle una secretaria adicional para nuestra gerencia. Como es de su conocimiento, nuestra unided ha tenido un gran crecimiento en los ultimos 5 meses. Se han contratado tres jóvenes profesionales y no se ha aumentado nuestra dotación de personal administrativo. En la actualidad contamos con tres secretarias, muy competentes, pero que no dan abasto con todo el trabajo requerido. Esto no nos permite alcanzar el rendimiento deseado.

La naturaleza de nuestras operaciones hace indispensable que la secretaria que se contrate tenga dominio del idioma inglés, tanto oral como escrito. Adicionalmente, debe estar familiarizada con el uso de procesadores de texto y de Lotus 1-2-3.

Agradezco de antemano su consideración.
Atentamente,

Juan González R.

gift-giving customs differ in the United States.) You need not bring a gift for each businessperson at the table. Presenting one gift to your primary host at the table is considered to be giving a gift to all. The most appreciated gifts are those that represent your country in some way or can be set on a shelf or mantel—a regional bowl, a decorative piece, and so forth. Less appropriate are items of personal jewelry or company products. (One U.S. automobile salesperson presented his Chinese host with a chromed carburetor from his company. It still sits on the host's desk as a standing joke.)

- *The Chinese believe deeply in the value of kuanxi ("relationship").* They want to know you deeply (your history, your motives, your personality, and especially your interaction with others) before committing to business relationships. This process of getting to know you takes time—and often many meals together. Be patient, self-disclosing, and gracious during what may seem to you to be a prolonged period of relationship-building.

- *Most successful contracts with the Chinese involve "behind-the-contract" components.* In a state-supervised economy, few Chinese businesspeople see direct personal results from their successful business relations with you. They typically do not receive commissions or other bonuses based on their performance (although this situation is changing, especially in the new Economic Zone territories). As an incentive to accept your contract, Chinese businesspeople are quite receptive to "behind-the-contract" add-ons such as trips at your expense to visit your company

FIGURE 18–5   An English Translation

MEMORANDUM #532

Antecedent : your memorandum
#228 of 07.25.98

Subject   : request of an
additional secretary

Santiago, september 12, 1998

FROM : FINANCE MANAGER
TO   : GENERAL MANAGER

Regarding your memorandum of antecedent, I am addressing you with the object of requesting an additional secretary for our department. As you know, our unit has had considerable growth during the last five months. Three young professionals have been recruited and the administrative staff has not increased. At present we have three very competitive secretaries, but they are not able to do all the work required. This has not permitted us to obtain the desired performance.

The nature of our operations make indispensable that the secretary that will be hired has proficiency in oral and written English. In addition, she must be familiar with the use of word processors and Lotus 1-2-3.

Thank you in advance for your consideration,

Sincerely yours,

Juan González R.

in the United States, special equipment given to them as a marginal aspect of the contract, and other "perks." Explicit bribes are both unwelcome and illegal in China.

- *Even after friendships have been established, the Chinese maintain a level of formality in address.* One story will make the point: After visiting and traveling with Ming Xian Liu, our Chinese host, over a period years, he asked the authors, "What shall I call you now that we are friends?" We responded, "Art and Dayle." Then we asked in return what we should call him (expecting his answer to be "Ming" or "Ming Xian"). He replied, without smiling, "Mr. Liu." The Mr. and Ms. forms of address are maintained as a sign of respect even in lifelong friendships (and, we are told, within many Chinese marriages!).
- *The Chinese want you to enjoy and approve their culture and country; they are sensitive about discussions of poverty.* Much of China strikes the Western visitor as poor, dirty, and ugly. At the same time, the grandeur of Chinese culture, history, geography, monuments, and recent economic progress is undeniable. As a general rule, Chinese businesspeople will avoid conversations that delve too deeply into the Third World aspects of the country.
- *Finally, the Chinese are excellent negotiators by leaving many details of contracts and business arrangement unspecified.* Although no strict quid pro quo is intended by their hospitality and relationship-building, the Chinese operate on the assumption

FIGURE 18–6   An American Response to a Chilean Memo

Memorandum #541

Antecedent: Your memorandum #534,
Sept. 12, 1998

Material: Response to your request
for an additional sec-
retary

To: Finance Manager
From: General Manager

Regarding your request for additional secretarial support, I wish to suggest an alternate way of resolving the problem you describe. Instead of hiring an additional secretary, I propose that you send overflow typing and accounting work to the General Manager's secretarial pool. These employees are often seeking additional work and should be able to give you the support you require.

I have asked the Word-processing Supervisor to make specific arrangements with you for routing work expeditiously.

Thank you for bringing this problem to my attention and for your cooperation in trying out the solution I suggest.

Sincerely,

Helen Williams

---

that business friends go far beyond the letter of the law to make contracts work to mutual advantage. From a Western perspective, not a little guilt plays a part in this Chinese strategy. We may feel obligated to offer extra services and other accommodations to Chinese hosts who have been so gracious to us. Conversely, Chinese businesspeople often reject business deals that focus too closely on legal recourse, exact specifications of deliverables, and penalties for delays or other interruptions.

As one Chinese business student explained to us, "China is a land of people, not laws." In this brief phrase he was suggesting that the most successful business relationships between China and foreign business interests have been forged as much at the dining table

FIGURE 18–7   A Russian Manager's Memo

Святослав Николаевич Кислородов
Заместитель директора по кадрам

Уважаемый Товарищ Кислородов,

У нас в отделении АСУ не хватает секретаршей. Несколько дней уже у нас нет способности даже выполнять все очередные документы. А сейчас опять-таки запила Машинка. Что нам делать? Пожалуйста, немедленно дайте нам разрешение добавить лишь одну секретаршу.

С уважением,

Борис Иванович Боголюбимов

FIGURE 18–8 An English Translation

9/1/98

Svyatoslav Nikolayevich Kislorodov
Deputy to the Director for Personnel

Respected Comrade Kislorodov,

We do not have enough secretaries in our MIS department. For the last few· days we have not even been able to fill out the regular documents. And now Mashinka has somehow again taken to drink. What are we to do? Please, immediately give us permission to add at least one more secretary.

With respect,

Boris Ivanovich Bogolyubimov

---

as at the boardroom table. In dealing with a relationship-oriented society, communication skills could not be more valuable in achieving bottomline business results.

MAKING PRESENTATIONS IN INTERCULTURAL SETTINGS

Just as American approaches to business writing must be adapted to intercultural conventions, oral presentations must be adjusted to what intercultural audiences expect and prefer. Again, an American presenter's goal is not to be taken for a native speaker but instead to adapt successfully to the culture's expectations, with the goal of delivering a culturally acceptable presentation.

FIGURE 18–9 An American Response

9/2/98

Boris Ivanovich Bogolyubimov
Supervisor, MIS Department

Honored Comrade Bogolyubimov,

Supervisor Kislorodov has asked me to respond to your memorandum of Sept. 1, 1998. Like you, we feel the daily need for additional secretarial support. Our official documents are often prepared less quickly than we would wish. Such delays must be expected for the next several months until we receive final approval for Research Allocation Request #607.

I will look to you for patience and ingenuity in continuing to perform your duties admirably under the current conditions. I request that you send Mashinka to meet with Supervisor Kislorodov at 10 a.m., Sept. 15, 1998.

With great respect,

William Evans Phillips
American Liaison for MIS Reearch

Five elements of the presentation should be reevaluated in preparing for an intercultural address:

1. The introduction
2. The method of presenting an argument
3. The use of visual aids
4. The use of humor
5. The conclusion and recommendation

The Introduction

Many cultures expect the speaker to recognize and pay respect to members of the audience, often in the order of their importance. It may be culturally taboo to start off with business early in the presentation. In some cultures, speakers may be expected to give a great deal of background information about themselves and their company.

How do you know what to do? It's best to discuss your presentation plans with an experienced business speaker who is a member of your audience's culture. Ask advice on what approaches will be most acceptable to your listeners.

The Method of Argumentation

Typical American presentations describe a problem and then go on to suggest possible solutions. This approach may be unpersuasive and even offensive to some cultures. The blatant description of a business problem may be taken as a slight against your audience's country, culture, or company. An intensely proud group of African businesspeople, for example, may rankle at a speaker's opening remarks about starvation or poor rural planning. In many cultures, you may be better off describing your suggestions as a "next step in a glorious heritage." Often, this approach is much more persuasive than the problem-solution approach.

The Use of Visual Aids

American speakers typically rely on sides, graphs, charts, and other visual aids to do much of their communicating. American audiences often take the use of such materials as a sign of the speaker's preparation and expertise. This is not so for some other cultures for which visual aids interrupt the important process of personal evaluation and bonding. To get an idea of this negative effect, think about what your own reaction would be if a new acquaintance who was invited to your home for dinner brought along charts of his educational history and a videotape of his sports prowess. While these matters might come up naturally in conversation, you would probably feel that the visual aids were a bit much. In the same way, some cultures do not place the same importance on visual aids as do American business audiences.

The Use of Humor

For American presenters, keeping an audience awake and alert often involves the periodic use of humor, anecdotal stories, and other attention-getting techniques. These should be checked carefully with a native presenter before you use them in an intercultural speech. There is a fine line between what's funny and what's offensive in all cultures. Even in closely aligned cultures, such as that of Great Britain and America, the types and uses of humor can vary greatly. The British by and large cannot fathom what's funny about Jay Leno or David Letterman; Americans groan at the romping silliness of many BBC sitcoms. Such differences are magnified many times over when the cultures involved do not share common ancestries, religions, or political systems.

The Conclusion and Recommendation

American presenters are often told to ask for the sale—that is, to explicitly tell the audience what should be done. In many cultures, such directness is taken as the worst form of rudeness. Conclusions and recommendations in these cultural settings must be handled with great delicacy so as not to appear high-handed or pushy. Decision-makers in your audience must be credited with the ability to see the implications of your presentation; their agreement or action must be subtly suggested or invited.

YOUR FUTURE AS AN INTERCULTURAL BUSINESSPERSON

As the ability to know—almost instantaneously—transforms lives and cultures around the planet, no businessperson can hide in a regional or national niche and expect to avoid the influence of the Information Revolution. While a hardware store owner in Wichita may not sell hammers to China, he or she will want to be the first to know when hammers imported from Poland are sold 20 percent cheaper than the American variety. Larger corporations will have no reason to limit their marketing horizons to national borders, especially as jet travel and communication devices make the world what McLuhan calls a "global village." "There are no passengers on spaceship earth," he wrote. "We are all crew."

In the words of John Naisbitt, author of the best-selling book, *Megatrends,*

> We are living in the "time of the parenthesis," the time between eras (between the Industrial Era and the Information Era). The time of the parenthesis is a great and yeasty time . . . a time of great change and uncertainty (and we must make uncertainty our friend) . . . and a time of great opportunity. In stable eras everything has a name and everything knows its place . . . and we can leverage very little. But in the time of the parenthesis we have extraordinary leverage and influence . . . individually . . . professionally . . . and institutionally . . . if we can get a clear sense, a clear conception, a clear vision of the road ahead. My God, what a fantastic time to be alive!

SUMMARY

1. Businesspeople must recognize the importance of cultural differences.

2. This chapter suggests 11 key areas in which cultures can be evaluated.

3. Several agencies offer cultural awareness materials and training for businesspeople.

4. Because language is the most important link between people, businesspeople should examine their own use of English in relation to the language needs of their foreign listeners.

5. At all levels, business is becoming internationalized. Business trips to and communications with other cultures will be a reality for more and more businesspeople in the years ahead.

QUESTIONS FOR DISCUSSION

1. What are the 11 areas of cultural sensitivity?

2. How could the use of human time and space affect your business transactions in a foreign country?

3. What are some steps you may take in order to acquaint yourself with a foreign culture?

4. What are name cards? How are they used?

5. How should you rely on a colleague's personal experience in a foreign country you plan to visit?

6. What is probably the most significant way you can prepare ahead for your visit to a foreign country?

7. Why is it important to speak "plain vanilla" English in business meetings abroad?

8. When speaking English with a nonnative speaker, what habits should you avoid?

9. How can visual gestures aid your communication with a foreign businessperson who does not speak your language well?

10. How can you check your listener's comprehension over the phone?

11. In a face-to-face conversation, what are good ways to check for comprehension?

12. Explain Marshall McLuhan's statement, "There are no passengers on spaceship earth. . . . We are all crew."

13. What is the "time of the parenthesis"? What are its advantages?

EXERCISES

1. Pick a country that you would like to visit on business some day. Write a letter to the embassy or consulate of that country, requesting as much information as is available on travel and business opportunities there. Keep this information in your files for future use.

2. Research attitudes on the relationship between men and women in the country of interest to you. How might the relations between the sexes in this country affect your communication with your host?

3. Extend an invitation to a potential business associate in a foreign country. Convey the proper respect for his or her culture.

4. Continue your research on the foreign country of your choice, and identify strict taboos that you'll want to be aware of. What particular taboos might you have violated if you had not taken time to investigate the cultural differences between your country and the foreign country?

5. How should you dress to make the best impression possible in the foreign country that interests you?

6. Identify the religious and political ideologies you would be most likely to find in the country you are researching. How do these ideologies resemble or differ from your own? How will you avoid possible difficulties in these areas?

7. If you are an American citizen, how might you be regarded in the country of interest to you? Investigate current perceptions about America held in that country. If these perceptions are negative, how do you plan to present yourself positively?

8. Compile a list of slang and idioms that might be misinterpreted by a foreign businessperson with limited English skills.

9. Identify part of your town, city, state, or region where intercultural differences may influence how business is conducted. Describe in writing the kind of adjustments you would make if you were doing business in this locale.

10. Reflect on your own travel experiences inside or outside the U.S. In what areas would you be most comfortable doing business? In which areas least comfortable? Why? Write your responses to these questions.

11. Create two dialogues between businesspeople of differing cultures. In the first dialogue, demonstrate successful intercultural communication. In the second, show the symptoms and results of cultural insensitivity.

12. Watch a foreign film. Keep track of the cultural differences that occur in the 11 areas of cultural sensitivity described in this chapter.

13. Interview a businessperson or some other associate who has lived abroad or in a cultural area of this country that differs from your own culture. Determine how your interviewee made intercultural adjustments. How successful were these adjustments? What would the person do differently now?

INTERNET ASSIGNMENT

For the first five years of its existence, your company has extended its market across the continental United States. Now you are ready to "go global" and are preparing marketing teams of managers to travel to Europe, South America, Japan, Korea, and China to explore new marketing opportunities and meet potential trading partners.

You face the problem, however, that very few of your managers have ever worked or traveled abroad. Investigate resources in the Intercultural Communication section of the Internet Guide. Then prepare a short presentation or write a memo in which you tell your managers why and how to use these sites to improve their intercultural communication skills before they set foot in a foreign country.

 **19**

Ethics and Law
for Management
Communication

PERSONAL ETHICS: TOUGH DECISIONS

Each of us has personal moral beliefs, and those beliefs differ somewhat from person to person. It is not our purpose here to discover *where* moral beliefs come from, nor to decide *which* moral beliefs are superior to others. Instead, we focus our discussion on the most common ethical dilemma facing business communicators: the tension between being true to personal moral beliefs and remaining loyal to company goals, procedures, policies, and leadership. We then consider a more limited set of public ethics, as reflected in laws pertaining to business communication.

Let's take a case in point. As a midlevel manager, you are told by your boss that a drastic staff reduction in the company is coming within a matter of months. Most of your subordinates, in fact, will be laid off. Your boss specifically tells you "not to breathe a word" about the coming layoffs to your employees, for fear they will desert the company and accept work elsewhere. They're needed, your boss reminds you, to finish up work on a major contract having to do with safe waste disposal for toxic chemicals.

What would you do in this situation? On one hand, your subordinates trust you not to conceal information crucial to their professional and personal well-being. Many of your people could relocate successfully if they knew a staff reduction was coming. If they don't know, they will be among the masses of the unemployed on termination day. Many will lose their homes and medical insurance.

On the other hand, the company trusts you as a manager to support company goals. The company needs a full roster of workers right up to layoff day in order to finish the major contract. Company profits depend on your silence—even your pretense—to your employees regarding firings and layoffs.

Finally, there's the matter of the contract itself—production of a device that safely disposes of toxic waste. Thousands of citizens will benefit directly and indirectly from the manufacture of this treatment machine. Shouldn't their interests be considered?

CONFLICTING VALUES

Review some of the factors you should consider in making ethical choices. Notice that each of these factors has value, which makes the conflict that much harder.

1. *Should you simply obey authority?* Your boss has told you what to do.
2. *What loyalty do you owe to the company and its goals?* You accepted the job, after all, as a manager of company projects.
3. *What loyalty do you owe to your subordinates?* They trust you.
4. *What do you owe to yourself and your own family?* If you act contrary to company goals, you may very well be terminated yourself.
5. *What do you owe to society?* The waste disposal project, if completed, will improve the life of the community.

This situation can become increasingly complex as other factors affect the decisions you make. Can you, for example, participate in interviews for a new engineer—knowing that she's selling her home in California to travel across country to join your company, all (unbenownst to her) for only a few months of employment before the layoffs? How do you respond in writing to an employee's various requests for promotion or educational support, knowing full well that the employee soon won't have a job? How do you speak on behalf of the company to a group of recently graduated college students looking for employment with your division?

On the other hand, what if you did protest the unfairness of the silence policy to your boss? Does your protest itself relieve you of the responsibility for further ethical decisions and actions? More generally, does your protest get you off the hook for the mistakes of a group? What if you filed a written protest and then still took part in the group's actions?

Choosing a Moral Response

Faced with such ethical dilemmas, an employee can choose to do nothing, quit, work within the system to change things, or blow the whistle on the company's actions. First, by choosing to do nothing (unfortunately, a common choice), the employee passes moral decision making to others. In some cases, unethical business actions have taken place simply because all employees choose to do nothing. Second, the employee can simply quit. This option, while emphatic and attention-getting for a moment, often does little to change the moral mistakes of an organization. Third, an employee can work within company structures to change unethical situations. This process can involve establishing committees, bringing in consultants, and talking to individuals. Finally, an employee can *blow the whistle* on unethical company practices by alerting the press, regulatory agencies, and the general public.

The Process of Making Ethical Decisions

"I'll certainly know right from wrong when the choice comes." Don't let this naïve confidence get you into trouble in the hard world of complex decisions. The result all too often is that you may do nothing instead of actively making a decision.

There are no easy answers for many real-world business dilemmas, and no textbook can define precisely the nature or limits of your loyalty to your company, subordinates, or family. However, it is possible to describe the *process* that many businesspeople use

---

COMMUNICATION FOR A NEW CENTURY

HOW TO UPGRADE ETHICS IN THE WORKPLACE

Ethics in the workplace has become an increasing concern in the wake of a seeming epidemic of unethical behavior among employees, up to and including senior management. Moral considerations aside, much of the concern is based on dollars and cents. Unethical conduct in business can run the full gamut from minor lying and cheating to major indiscretions, including theft of company profits or competitive secrets, and the costs can be staggering.

In our observations of the workplace based on contacts with executives of the personnel industry, the following are current suggestions offered to upgrade the level of ethics in the workplace and to forestall much of the unethical behavior:

Offer classes for employees on ethical conduct. Human resources departments can provide a real service to their organizations by implementing ethics classes in the workplace. Here, examples of what is and is not ethical behavior can be presented and discussed, and the company's outlook on the subject emphasized. Classes can be held prior to or following work shifts. As an added incentive, employees can be paid for the time they spend in the classes.

Provide a presentation on ethics in all new employee orientations. Incoming employees are an important audience for the company's message on ethics. The presentation should include a personal videotape from the chairman and other written material which may be included in the firm's management training sections.

Hold an annual review of compliance with business ethics policies. The review should include the middle and upper management ranks of the company, encompassing all departments. As an alternative, an internal audit of compliance with business ethics policies can be held on an annual basis.

Require managers to sign a letter once a year confirming their understanding and acceptance of ethical practices and guidelines. The letter has the advantage of focusing attention on the importance of ethics in the corporate culture of the organization, and of stimulating adherence to ethical standards because of the regular signing required. An alternative approach is to require signing of conflict of interest statements, a common practice even before the current concern with ethics.

Provide a hotline for the reporting of ethics concerns. This can be established through the company's human resources department, where callers are encouraged to report ethics concerns with the assurance that their calls will be handled on a confidential basis. Without the protection of confidentiality, employees may be reluctant to come forward.

Implement a counseling program on ethics for employees. This approach formalizes the topic through emphasis, education, and discussion at management and employee meetings. Employees can be required to sign an ethics awareness and agreement card.

All of these measures are designed to improve the ethical climate in the workplace. Perhaps the most effective approach, however, is for the company to emphasize quality in its products or services and fairness in its business dealings, transmit this attitude to its employees, and place a high degree of trust in individual responsibility.

when reaching difficult ethical decisions. The following questions suggest the kind of internal dialogue that you might consider during your decision-making process:

1. *How does the decision affect me?* Assess what you have to gain or lose and how you feel about the situation.
2. *How does the decision affect others?* Review as objectively and accurately as possible the impact of your decision on other people, including society at large.
3. *Is there a compelling reason to put the welfare of others ahead of my own welfare?* No one of us is entirely altruistic. What in the situation may lead you either to prefer or to put aside your own interest?
4. *If my decision were repeated by others in comparable situations, what kind of world would emerge?* Picture your decision as one spark touching off other sparks that eventually lead to a bonfire. What kind of society or business climate is eventually created or destroyed by your decision?

The answers that you find in such soul-searching are deeply personal and often can't be rationally defended to someone who does not share your personal system of values. They are nonetheless *your own* ethical conclusions and should form the basis of your communications and other actions.

In the termination case, for example, you might decide to obey your boss's command not to tell the workforce of the coming staff reduction. You might reason (and feel) that your employees are adults who have entered into the management–labor arrangement of the company by their own choice and without coercion. While the disruptions to their lives brought about by the staff reduction are regrettable, you feel that there is no obligation on the part of the company or its managers (including yourself) to give up company projects for the sake of the workers' welfare. Besides, you decide, the nature of the project—a waste disposal system—is itself important for social improvement. The life disruptions of dozens of employees should not stand in the way of safe living conditions for thousands of community members.

On the other hand, you might decide to warn your employees (privately, perhaps) of the coming terminations. You may be willing to take the risk that your boss might find out about your disclosure, particularly as your employees begin to leave the company for other work, but that's a risk you're willing to take.

You might even take a bolder stand, confronting your boss with what you call "deception" being practiced on employees who have been loyal to the company. You insist that you won't use others in this way, even if it means giving up your job. Your boss fires you on the spot, creating hardship for your own family, though your subordinates are now warned about the coming layoffs. As you stand in the unemployment line with your former subordinates, you decide that at least you've had the moral satisfaction of having acted according to your beliefs.

TYPICAL MORAL DILEMMAS CONFRONTING BUSINESS COMMUNICATORS

Sooner or later, you'll probably communicate (through speaking or writing) what you decide to do in an ethically problematic situation. Here are five arenas in which business communicators often have to make ethical decisions:

Cosmetic Half-truths

Through the power of words, a shred of truth can be made to seem larger and more attractive than it really is. A job opening, for example, can be dishonestly described to a candidate as a "sure stepping-stone to promotion," when in fact only two of the six people to hold the position in the past were promoted.

Outright Lies

Managers often feel pressure to tell clients and colleagues blatant lies—usually with the purpose of "buying time" until more favorable results or action is possible. A company with sagging sales, for example, might tell potential investors that business is great, with the goal of gaining the investors' money and producing the promised sales levels. A manager may look his or her boss in the eye and declare that a report is "almost ready for final printing," when the manager really hasn't even started writing the report.

Unethical Company Practices

Employees at all levels may find the actions of their company morally objectionable. The company, for example, may be selling lethal weapons both to an insurgent group fighting dictatorship and to the dictator's forces as well. The company may covertly be gaining unfair advantage over competitors by using industrial espionage and payoffs.

Harmful or Potentially Harmful Actions by the Company

At times, employees may object on ethical grounds to the impact of company products or services on society. Perhaps a corporation markets "Tastes Good!" foodstuffs that have little nutritional value to impoverished, undereducated countries whose citizens don't know what they're buying. Or, as in the case of recent automobile recalls, the manufacturer may save a few dollars per car by leaving off a safety feature crucial to the welfare of the consumer.

Company Allegiances

Employees may also have moral reservations about the causes, regimes, and political or social movements supported by the company. Millions of corporate dollars flow to candidates, organizations, and political action groups from companies each year. It is unlikely that each and every employee in the corporation morally agrees with all of the company's affiliations and allegiances.

ETHICS: MORAL VERSUS LEGAL ISSUES

Most of your ethical decisions in these and other situations will be influenced by the moral choices you make. Note that these are *ethical* decisions, not legal matters. In the case of the unexpected layoffs, no law dictates that senior management must tell its future staffing plans, including layoffs, far in advance to the workforce. Unfortunately, this doesn't make the issues any less urgent: Even to decide *not* to face moral questions is itself an ethical choice.

Some moral decisions do become legal issues. When society reaches consensus about what a person should do, society establishes laws that dictate the behaviors each member of society should follow. Laws are said to be *reactive* because they respond to the presence of undesirable behavior; morals are *proactive* because they attempt to prevent undesirable behavior.

In addition, when evaluating the moral implications of a company's or individual's actions, it is often helpful to distinguish between moral duties and moral ideals. *Moral duties* are rules necessary for the ordinary functioning of society. "Don't steal" and "don't molest," for example, are rules to be followed by all citizens who wish to live in a normal community. By contrast, *moral ideals* are goals that we may strive to reach, but they are seldom reached entirely. "Be understanding" and "be completely truthful" are moral ideals that we may approach but never fully achieve in all situations.

Unfortunately, when you are acting on behalf of a company, your ethical choices and your actions are even more complicated. Your moral choices as a representative (an *agent*) of your company reflect on the integrity and image of your company. What's more, what you say and do on behalf of your company may legally obligate your company in ways that your company wouldn't appreciate. In fact, everything you communicate as a representative agent of your company may have some legal consequences.

THE LEGAL CONSEQUENCES OF GIVING YOUR WORD

Since the signing of the Magna Carta, business law in all Western nations has placed substantial weight on the *giving of one's word*, in oral or written form. Instead of shedding blood or piling up stones, we finalize business transactions and understandings in three ways.

1. *Words of commitment:* we will, we agree to, we promise
2. *Acts of commitment:* the use of signatures and seals
3. *Documents of commitment:* deeds, notes, letters, and contracts

Therefore, businesspeople must take their words seriously, not only as vehicles for communication, but also as significant legal instruments. In a memo, letter, or proposal, your words influence the affairs of others. Sometimes that influence proves negative: you must deny a promotion, file a claim, demand payment, or turn down a proposal. How do people respond? Often, they fight you, sometimes in court. They may cite your words as evidence against you.

If, for example, you call a competitor a "thief" or "liar" in the presence of others, your words can return to haunt you as evidence in a slander suit. At other times, your words may arouse expectations in others. Clients may trust your evaluation of a home for sale as "$20,000 under market price." Buyers may rely on a piece of paper assuring the serviceability of a washing machine. When these expectations are dashed, people return to your words as evidence that they have been misled.

These scenarios of blame, anger, and disappointment are not intended to say that every client wants to sue. The great majority of your words—even those written in hate and poor judgment—will not face legal review or challenge, but some will. Unfortunately, not everyone wins in the real world of business. When your company wins a major contract, several other companies have lost the competition. When you as a salesperson capture 50 percent of your sales territory, other salespersons are falling behind.

People and companies fight for financial survival with every means at their disposal, including legal suit. If your success acts detrimentally upon their survival, they will review the means by which you achieved your success. If they find (or think they find) questionable business practices, they may seek legal actions. Primary evidence in such suits, of course, will be your words, as found in memos, letters, advertisements, contracts, reports, and so forth.

The purpose of this chapter is not to offer specific legal advice for such moments, but instead to suggest areas of legal vulnerability for the business communicator. Learn to avoid these areas of legal hazard through becoming aware and alert to their existence.

The stakes are high. Misspoken and miswritten communications each year cost people their careers and cost companies their profits. Court-awarded damages stemming from ill-chosen words easily run to more than $1 million per day in American courts.

To become more aware of areas of legal vulnerability, we can assess the major laws pertinent to six key areas of interest for every business communicator:

1. You and your employer
2. You and your files
3. You and your customer
4. You and your employees
5. You and the government
6. You and your product or service

In each of these areas, business communicators should weigh the legal implications of their words with care.

You and Your Employer

As an employee, the chances are good that you function as a legal agent for the company. Your status as an agent for the company is implied by your employment. Being a company's *agent* means, simply, that the company is responsible for your work-related actions and words. Your words, especially on paper, are as binding for the company as if they had been penned by the chairperson of the board.

When writing on company letterhead or when identifying yourself by your job title, you probably cannot escape your role as agent even if you use such disclaimers as "speaking unofficially" or "off the record." Nor can the company escape responsibility by claiming that your words did not reflect the will of the management or board of directors. Your employment itself marks the company's implicit obligation to supervise your activities and pronouncements.

For the sake of the company as well as for your career, exercise judgment, discretion, and a high degree of legal awareness when you write memos, letters, proposals, and reports involving any of the following:

• Personnel hiring and firing
• Claims
• Warranties, commitments, assurances

- Contracts
- Labor negotiations
- Tax planning
- Pricing policies
- Interstate trade
- Formal charges, complaints
- Legal questions
- Affirmative Action, Equal Opportunity matters
- Reference letters
- Sales letters representing products and services
- Any topic over which tempers might run high

This long cautionary list is not intended to discourage you from writing entirely. Instead, it is intended to remind you to exercise care in the words you choose. Often, you may decide to seek legal counsel before *publishing* your words (in the legal sense, publishing means to make them known to another party).

Few companies, however, can afford to place a lawyer at the side of each of their business communicators. Therefore, many companies provide their writers with guide letters, to suggest legally approved wording for problematic letters. In the case of a termination guide letter, for example, the legal staff of a company takes time to weigh the legal ramifications of each word in the letter before recommending its use. In Figure 19–1, notice how the guide letter prevents potential legal entanglements when compared to an original letter on the same topic, Figure 19–2. Guide letters, which restrict the writer's freedom, can prevent disastrous legal complications.

When employers do not provide guide letters for legally hazardous areas of communication, the burden falls on the business writer to check out the legal risks involved in his or her words. By the way, simply typing "Personal" or "Confidential" on the envelope or letter in no way shields your words from legal review.

In business dealings for your employer, remember that oral agreements are vastly more difficult to enforce than written agreements. When transacting business, therefore, insist on a written and signed statement describing the terms of the agreement at hand. If the other party is unwilling to give written commitment, you have reason to beware of deception and dishonesty.

In Communispond's survey of 200 executives, managers expressed an almost unanimous desire that business communications be brief. In the light of the legalities of business language, concise business communications have less chance of straying into legally hazardous territory. In Figure 19–3, notice how the longer version of the "no" letter sets the company up for future legal trouble when compared to the shorter letter in Figure 19–4.

Many companies sponsor regular legal seminars in which lawyers discuss current danger areas with business writers. A number of excellent books and articles also deal with the legal aspects of business communications.

You and Your Files

When your company faces suit in court, attorneys for the *plaintiff* (the party pressing charges) will make an effort to gather supporting evidence and documentation, both by *subpoena* and by *deposition* (legal mechanisms to draw pertinent information into the

FIGURE 19–1   Guide Letter Suggested by Legal Staff

LIBRONCHEMICALS

April 9, 199_

Mr. Raymond Duncan
Libron Chemicals
West Trenton Branch
241 Auburn Street
Trenton, NJ 08619-1442

400 Parkway Drive
Newark, NJ 07112-0011
(201) 555-1011

Dear Mr. Duncan:

I must inform you that your employment with Libron Chemicals will be terminated, effective
May 10, 199_

This action has been taken in compliance with company personnel policies and applicable
state, federal, and union regulations. Copies of these policy documents may be obtained
at the company personnel office.

If you have questions regarding this action, please contact Marion Hart at 555-2953.

Sincerely,

Davis Wilborn

Davis Wilborn
Vice President

DW/em

---

open). Your files may contain letters, notes, memos, and other communications which,
though written in good faith, can be turned against you and your company.

A supervising manager at a large accounting firm, for example, hired a young man
who happened to follow a colorful variation of Zen Buddhism. On company stationery,
the manager wrote the following words in a note to her boss, a partner in the firm:

> . . . his occasional facial decoration (the dots of colored ink and bits of glitter) will alienate
> some of our more traditional clients.

A copy of the memo was filed, incorrectly, in the young man's personnel file. When,
two years later, the company tried to fire him for a variety of inadequacies, the man ac-
cused the firm of religious discrimination. The company officials denied that the man's
religious customs or dress ever influenced their decision. However, the man's lawyers, as
you can imagine, were ecstatic to discover, waiting in his personnel file, a memo apparently corroborating the discrimination charge.

Be careful, therefore, not only about what you write, but what you save. Many companies have purge policies, requiring managers to shred business documents more than
three years old (the time expiration for most tax matters). Other companies establish and
enforce strict photocopy rules. Some documents absolutely may not be photocopied and

FIGURE 19–2   Original Letter, Flawed by Potential Legal Snares

---

LIBRONCHEMICALS

April 9, 199_

Mr. Raymond Duncan
Libron Chemicals
West Trenton Branch
241 Auburn Street
Trenton, NJ 08619-1442

400 Parkway Drive
Newark, NJ 07112-0011
(201) 555-1011

Dear Mr. Duncan:

This company has been under pressure from state and federal regulatory agencies to hire more minorities. Unfortunately, you must be terminated, effective May 10, 199_, to make room for these new employees.

In general, your work record here has been superb. You did take more sick days than we expected, though you never exceeded the number provided in your contract of employment. Your large family made it somewhat difficult to send you on extended travel assignments.

For all these reasons, we have reluctantly chosen you as the employee in your work unit to be terminated. Good luck in seeking a career elsewhere.

Sincerely,

Davis Wilborn

Davis Wilborn
Vice President

DW/em

---

hence are marked "For Eyes Only" or "Do Not Copy." These documents frequently contain details of future product planning, marketing strategies, or personnel decisions. Almost all companies take precautions in disposing of documents. Trash bins are hunting grounds for a variety of interested parties: activists, seeking to build a case against a company; industrial spies, looking for product details; and even government agents, trying to establish tax or regulatory violations.

You and Your Customer

Not only good business practice but also the law dictate that you communicate with the customer in a truthful, timely, and unambiguous way.

Warranties and Guarantees

The Consumer Product Warranty Act and Federal Trade Commission Improvement Act of 1975 specifically prohibit companies from using difficult, ambiguous language to hide information or contingencies that a customer needs to know. In the following garble, can you spot the hidden disclaimer in favor of the company?

FIGURE 19–3   Longer Letters Can Stray into Illegal Areas

Appliance Company

May 2, 199_

Ms. Susan Todd
5 Fletcher Road
Baltimore, Maryland 21234-2184

6021 West Belmont Avenue
Garden Grove, California 92645-1486
(209) 555-5033

Dear Ms. Todd:

We can offer no encouragement in your job search because of of your age, 57. We've found that the company's time and money simply are not well spent providing training for people who will soon retire. In the past three years, we've made a companywide effort to hire young in order to capture the newest and best financial ideas coming out of business schools. Although your background and credentials are impressive, they do not suit our current hiring profiles.

Just in case a temporary position becomes available, we will keep your file active for a period of nine months. If an opening develops for which you are suited, we will notify you.

Sincerely,

Reginald Blanchard

Reginald Blanchard
Manager

RB/ss

. . . furthermore, the party of the first part does warrant said product for a period of time not to exceed ninety days, during which time said party shall repair or replace a product proven defective by independent examination, if the putative defect proves, in said party's judgment, not to stem from user-induced causes.

In other words, the company will decide whether or not you abused your widgit. If so, the company will not repair or replace it.

In plain English (and legal English since the 1975 legislation), this warranty speaks clearly:

Acme Industries will stand behind this product for 90 days from the date of purchase. If the product fails to perform properly during this time, return it to Acme Industries. We will promptly repair or replace the product, at our option, and return it to you without charge.

Credit

Since the passage of the Fair Credit Billing Act of 1974, managers have had to exercise extreme care in how they determine creditworthiness and what they put into writing once they make their determination.

FIGURE 19–4   Short Letters Can Avoid Illegal Areas

Appliance Company

6021 West Belmont Avenue
Garden Grove, California 92645-1486
(209) 555-5033

May 2, 199_

Ms. Susan Todd
5 Fletcher Road
Baltimore, Maryland 21234-2184

Dear Ms. Todd:

We appreciate your interest in employment at Gasco Appliance Company.

Although we cannot offer you a position at the present time, we wish to keep your application in our active file for nine months. If a suitable opening occurs, be assured that we will notify you.

Sincerely,

Reginald Blanchard

Reginald Blanchard
Manager

RB/ss

As we would expect, prejudices against color, race, religion, and national origin are strictly prohibited by the legislation. In addition, managers must avoid considering a credit applicant's age (hence, future years of high earning potential) or marital status. Nor may they inquire about future plans for a family. Managers may not ask a married woman to obtain the signature of her husband on the application, if it is her desire to establish credit in her own name.

Credit refusals, according to the law, must be written to the applicant. Here managers do well to state the refusal without detailed explanations and evaluations. Compare the two letters of refusal shown in Figures 19–5 and 19–6.

Collections

In 1978, the Fair Debt Collection Practices Act placed strict limits on collection procedures.

- When you can contact someone who owes you money
- How many times you may call
- To whom you may write (not employers or relatives)
- What you may say
  No false impressions (a collection letter marked "Tax Information")

FIGURE 19–5   Wordy Credit Refusal that May Be Legally Hazardous

Financial   Group
1000 Harbor Way
Baltimore, Maryland 21226-1805
(301) 555-0990

January 22, 199_

Mr. Calvin Stockly
222 Wembley Lane
Fresno, CA 93710-2152

Dear Mr. Stockly:

We must deny your request for credit for the following reasons:

    1. You haven't paid $92 owed to Fresno Furniture since 4/4/9_.

    2. You have a record as a "late payer" with People's Loan and Thrift. Often, your payments are as much as three weeks overdue.

    3. In 1987, action was taken against you in small claims court for the collection of $752. The claim was resolved but still stands as a bad mark against your creditworthiness.

You understand, I'm sure, why our action cannot be more favorable.

Sincerely,

Rhonda Leaver

Rhonda Leaver
Credit Manager

RL/ot

    No threats (". . . or you'll regret it.")
    No slanderous language
• What you must provide
    Timely responses
    Accurate records
    Understandable documents

    Because collection practices have such a marred history, legislation is strict—with potent financial and criminal penalties for violators. Any business writer drawing up collection letters should read the pertinent legislation and also seek legal review for letters before they are mailed out.

FIGURE 19–6   **Effective Credit Refusal**

Financial   Group
1000 Harbor Way
Baltimore, Maryland 21226-1805
(301) 555-0990

January 22, 199_

Mr. Calvin Stockly
222 Wembley Lane
Fresno, CA 93710-2152

Dear Mr. Stockly:

We appreciate your interest in a SeaBreeze credit card. We are unable to grant credit at this time but would welcome reapplication at a future date.

Details of your credit history may be reviewed by calling Lambert Credit Reporting Service, 209-493-5847.

Again, thank you for your application. We look forward to your continued business and do hope to give a more favorable answer regarding credit in the future.

Sincerely,

Rhonda Leaver
Credit Manager

RL/ot

You and Your Employees

As a manager, you will communicate often with and about your employees. In many cases, what you say and how you say it are prescribed in federal and state legislation.

Privacy

Inevitably as an employer, you will hold in your possession employee documents containing personal information—age, marital status, health history, employment performance records, reference letters, and security clearances. Since the passage in 1974 of the Federal Privacy Act and subsequent state legislation, strict regulations guide how you can use this information and to whom you may show it.

Most companies develop personnel policy documents to set forth, both for managers and employees, the ground rules by which confidential information is to be handled. If your company has such policies, follow them. If not, exercise caution when revealing to a third party any fact, opinion, or assumption based on confidential knowledge. When in doubt, seek legal advice. Many managers make a practice of asking the employee in question to grant signed permission before revealing confidential information.

Equal Opportunity and Affirmative Action

A massive body of law now surrounds the landmark Civil Rights Act of 1964 and the Equal Employment Opportunity Act of 1972. Managers are constrained by law not to consider race, religion, age, sex, land of birth, or physical impairments in making hiring and firing decisions. None of these items, therefore, should appear even by innuendo in any business document relating to employment.

Probably the most visible result of these laws has been the establishment of Affirmative Action programs in companies large and small. Contrary to the oversimplifications we sometimes hear, Affirmative Action programs do not hire minorities at all costs. Instead, these programs try to evaluate the hiring and firing policies of the company. Have certain groups been omitted from consideration or been treated unequally once hired? If so, why? The result of this evaluation leads many companies

To advertise job openings more widely

To adjust pay and position inequities within the company

To plan for the inclusion of slighted groups

These goals may seem hopelessly idealistic, but federal and state legislation has put teeth into Affirmative Action reforms by awarding government contracts contingent upon solid progress in bringing minority groups into the company.

The Handicapped

The Vocational Rehabilitation Act of 1973 and the Americans with Disabilities Act of 1995 started a flood of legislation protecting the handicapped individual against discrimination in the workplace. Private and public foundations have made extensive use of radio and television time to remind employers how valuable—in dollar-and-cents terms—the handicapped can be as employees. Some federal grant and tax programs now provide incentives for employers who hire and train the handicapped. The question is now, Can he or she do the job? and no longer, Do I want to hire a handicapped person?

Labor Relations

In all matters related to communication with workers, managers should be guided by the Labor–Management Relations Act as interpreted in the many publications of the National Labor Relations Board. Communications during periods of unionization and strikes are particularly subject to close regulation. Managers, for example, cannot threaten or bribe employees in matters related to labor movements and negotiations. Even subtle suggestions ("You won't ever regret voting 'no' . . .") are strictly prohibited. Before making public statements on labor matters, managers do well to seek legal advice.

Recommendations

Prior to 1974 and the Family Educational Rights and Privacy Act, managers wrote letters of recommendation on the assumption that they would never be seen by the person being evaluated. Too often, falsehoods and half-truths contained in such "carte blanche" letters went uncorrected. Sometimes these negative comments dogged the steps of an employee for years, a secret and unexpungable ledger in his or her employment file.

Legislation now permits virtually all students and many employees to review their own letters of recommendation, unless they have signed a waiver to that right. Therefore, managers writing reference letters must choose words that in no way can be interpreted as libelous (defamation in writing). While no absolute measurement can be taken, letters of recommendation have taken a definite turn away from negative comments since 1974. Some say this development has been less than helpful to employers seeking accurate recommendations. Others welcome the new emphasis on what a prospective employee *can* do rather than what he or she *can't* do. Many managers who feel they must include negative judgments in a letter of recommendation simply turn down the request to write a letter.

You and the Government

Over your business career, you will send hundreds of pages of written commitments to governmental agencies. These pages will include tax documents, regulatory forms, incorporation papers, and a host of other filings. In drawing up these documents, take into account the special challenges posed by the Freedom of Information Act of 1966.

Businesses routinely send product, process, and service descriptions to governmental agencies. These documents are now available for public view—including the close inspection of competitors eager to discover trade secrets, formulas, assembly details, and so forth. The business writer faces the challenge of satisfying government requirements for information without divulging valuable company secrets.

COMMUNICATION FOR A NEW CENTURY

GIVING REFERENCES

It isn't how much or how little you say in a job reference that will most determine whether you're vulnerable to a lawsuit. Rather, it's the content. These are the points to keep in mind:

- Truth is a complete and absolute defense to any defamation claim (though not necessarily to other claims). Try to stick as closely as possible to specific factual statements about a former employee's job performance.
- Avoid subjective generalities, innuendo, and half-truths. They could leave you wide open to a defamation claim or other charge.
- Limit references to information appropriate to the situation and give them only to persons who have a legitimate business use for them. For instance, if someone is applying for a job on a fac-

tory assembly line, you probably don't need to review the trouble he or she had understanding double-entry bookkeeping. Issues such as timeliness, willingness to cooperate with others, and so on are likely to be more useful to the prospective employer.
- Apply your policy on employee references consistently, so you don't find yourself facing subsidiary charges of discrimination.
- Don't allow your job references to be colored by personal animosity. Animosity can result in legal liability when a simple, honest mistake in assessing an employee's abilities might not.

Reprinted, with permission, *Inc.* Magazine, June, 1989. Copyright © 1989 by Goldhirsh Group, Inc. 38 Commercial Wharf, Boston, MA 02110.

A second set of strict government laws involves the use of the mails. The purpose of the dozens of laws pertaining to the mails is to eliminate fraud in its various guises.

The following opening of a come-on letter, for example, defrauds the public by deceitfully and cruelly offering what it cannot deliver:

Dear Health-Conscious Reader,

Has cancer touched your family? If so, rush $39.50 for a six month supply of Vaccitabs—the only tablet guaranteed to drive cancer out of a diseased body and away from a healthy body . . .

Legislators have felt that this kind of communication lures the most vulnerable members of society. When the pills turn out to be mere flour and sugar, the buyer has little recourse. For all practical purposes, he or she cannot sue for $39.50, especially if the company is out of state. Hence, legislation makes it illegal to promote fraud by means of the mail.

While you undoubtedly have no intention of hawking false cures by mail, you may plan to use the post for direct sales or prospect letters. Obtain and read postal regulations that apply to such sales. If you are unsure whether your words match your product in a fair way, seek legal advice.

You and Your Product or Service

With the passage of the Fair Packaging and Labeling Act of 1966 came new standards, particularly for the words that accompany products and services on labels, packages, and instructions. Claims made in these forms may express the manufacturer's enthusiasm for the product ("New! Incredible!"). Labels cannot deceive the consumer by falsehoods, exaggerations, misleading comparisons, and inaccurate specifications. Lined leather gloves, for example, may be advertised to be "as warm as toast," but not as having "rabbit fur lining" when, in fact, synthetic material was used.

To abide by such laws and the wider demands of integrity, managers must often exert a restraining influence on the enthusiasms of ad writers and marketing specialists. What may seem innocent and mild overstatement regarding a product can too easily mushroom into a legally inappropriate deception in court.

Equal care must be taken not to infringe copyright laws. When a document is published, it bears a copyright designation identifying the person or company owning rights to the work. Extended passages from the copyrighted document cannot be reproduced for commercial purposes by others. Your professor, for example, cannot legally mimeograph 30 copies of a good grammar worksheet he or she finds in a copyrighted workbook.

When you need to borrow sections of a copyrighted work, write to the publisher or holder of the copyright for permission to use the passages.

SUMMARY

1. Ethical dilemmas common in business include half-truths, outright lies, unethical practices, harmful actions, and unsavory company allegiances.

2. Responses to ethical dilemmas include tolerance, resignation, and attempts to work within the system for change.

3. Your employer can be held liable for words you write on company stationery or as an agent for the company.

4. Communications involving employment are constrained by many laws and regulations. Business communicators should know these legal provisions before writing employment-related documents.

5. The language of warranties and guarantees must meet legal guidelines.

6. Communications involving credit and collection are especially vulnerable to legal actions. They should be reviewed by an attorney familiar with business law.

7. Language used in letters or documents to federal, state, or city agencies must be evaluated with care for potential legal hazards.

QUESTIONS FOR DISCUSSION

1. Why is it important for business communicators to take their words seriously as legal instruments?

2. Daily, how much money do American courts award in damages stemming from ill-chosen words? What does this figure suggest to you about the legal ramifications of your business communications?

3. Is it possible to escape your role as a legal agent of your company when working on company time?

4. What general topics or writing assignments in particular pose legal hazards for the business writer?

5. What is a *guide letter*?

6. In what way does being brief help to avoid legally hazardous territory?

7. Why should you be especially cautious when writing memos that will be stored in company files?

8. What guidelines did the Consumer Product Warranty Act and Federal Trade Commission Improvement Act of 1975 establish for business communications?

9. How does the Fair Credit Billing Act of 1974 affect managers' decisions about their customers' creditworthiness?

10. What limitations does the Fair Debt Collection Practices Act of 1978 place on writers of collection letters?

11. Why is it important for employers to keep their employees' personnel files private?

12. What effects have Affirmative Action programs had on businesses' hiring and firing policies?

13. What should employers keep in mind when writing letters of recommendation?

14. What is the Freedom of Information Act, and how does it affect the business writer?

15. What guidelines are set forth in the Fair Packaging and Labeling Act of 1966?

EXERCISES

1. Research slander and libel cases in a local law library. Bring a case to class and share it with your classmates. How could litigation have been avoided?

2. Ted Benson, a lathe operator with CDC, Inc., has applied for a newly opened management positive with the company. He seems qualified to do the job. The only spots on his work record are a few late arrivals to work and an unwillingness to work overtime. He also has no college degree. The real problem, however, is his personality. The two managers with whom he'd be working closely, Sandra Samuelson and Don Starman, have to told you that he's an "obnoxious twit." You are assigned to write a letter to Ted turning down his application for advancement in the company. Consider the legal ramifications of the message.

3. Carla Bonoff has applied for credit with your wholesale supply company. However, a quick check with TRW reveals that Ms. Bonoff never pays her bills on time and is delinquent on several accounts. You think it would be unwise to take a chance. Write a letter turning down her application for credit.

4. When Henry Collier worked as plant manager for RanTech Corporation, he contacted your architectural firm, asking you to design a new employee lounge to be added to the company's main building near the cafeteria. Three weeks later, when you called to set up an appointment to present the plans to Mr. Collier, you discovered that he had left RanTech for greener pastures. The Vice President of Operations currently fulfilling Collier's old duties said he knows nothing about the plans, and denied that RanTech owed you any money for your work, since Collier had not gone through the proper channels before contracting you. You argue that Collier was acting as a legal agent for RanTech when he hired you. Write a letter to RanTech asking for your payment.

5. Joel Kincaid has been a valuable employee with your company for more than two years. Recently, you were saddened to discover that he had contracted AIDS. While the disease has certainly affected his usually cheerful personality, his work seems to be up to par. However, his fellow employees don't want to work near him. They fear that they might contract the disease and have written a petition to you asking that Joel be fired. The company has a responsibility to all its employees, and in this case, the needs of the many outweigh the needs of the few, they argue. Consult with the company physician and make a decision. Then write one letter to Joel and another addressed to the petitioners, presenting your decision. What are your legal responsibilities in this situation?

6. Elizabeth Pope is seriously delinquent on her student loan payments. She owes eight months of payments and contact letters have produced no results. It's time for a stronger collection letter. Write one, but consider your legal responsibilities under the Fair Debt Collection Practices Act of 1978.

7. In today's mail, you received a letter from Peter Bagdasarian, a recent job applicant to your company. Apparently Peter has a friend at DataTron; the friend told him that an African American woman had been hired instead of him because of the company's Affirmative Action policy. Bagdasarian's tone in the letter was angry. He feels qualified for the job and is threatening to bring reverse discrimination charges against DataTron. Write him a letter before he takes this unnecessary troublesome action.

8. Leo Musgrove was recently let go from DataTron because of his abuse of sick leave time. Oddly enough, he has asked you, his department manager, to write a letter of recommendation for him. You explain that it would be difficult to recommend him for the exact reason that he was let go. He says that he must have a letter, even if you have to tell the truth. His work for the company was adequate—he just wasn't around to do it often enough. Additionally, you like Leo, so you want to help him out. Write a letter of recommendation, but be honest to your reader, as well as helpful to Leo.

9. Interview a manager or other businessperson about the importance of ethics in work. Ask your interviewee to recount stories of unethical behavior he or she has heard of in business and the results of that behavior. Summarize the interview in writing.

10. Interview a law student or a lawyer about the difference between ethics and laws. Based on your conversation, describe the difference in writing.

11. Does your company or any organization to which you belong publish a recommended code of ethics for students? If so, evaluate that code in writing. If not, try to create a sample code. Explain each of the points you include in this code.

12. Write a dialogue between two businesspeople with differing ethical perspectives. One believes in survival ethics—"I do whatever is necessary to get ahead." The other believes in more altruistic values—"I base my actions on what's good for the whole community."

13. Working together in a writing team with several classmates, create a general ethical code for business. You may want to consult similar codes already in existence for physicians, accountants, and others. In creating this code, note areas of disagreement among team members. Were disagreements resolved by consensus? By vote? Can ethical disagreements be resolved by majority vote?

INTERNET ASSIGNMENT

Managing a major retail auto sales company has proven to be an exciting and profitable career for you. Each day you get to meet new people, solve a wide range of customer problems, and develop better ways to sell the line of cars and trucks you represent.

To date, your company has no code of ethics to guide the actions and conversations of your salespeople with their customers. To see what other companies have done in this area and to find guidelines for setting and enforcing ethical and legal standards within your company, consult the Communication Ethics and Law section in the Internet Guide. Compile a list of sites particularly helpful to you in writing a code of ethics to be taught to each salesperson in your organization and placed in a frame in each salesperson's office. Make up whatever business details you require to complete this assignment.

Management Communication Cases

All names, situations, and locales used in these cases are entirely fictitious. Any similarity to real names, situations, and locales is purely coincidental.

PART 1

Cases 1 through 4 are intended to accompany Chapters 1 through 4.

CASE 1: WORDS, WORDS, WORDS

As a farsighted business leader, you saw the light early in the electronic revolution of the office. At considerable expense, you installed word-processing stations, electronic-mail connections, high-speed printers, and all the rest of the modern marvels available for the office.

Although communication within the company has certainly improved, you now find yourself drowning in an embarrassment of riches: you and most of your managers have too many words to deal with each day. Memos, letters, proposals, and reports fly out of the machines at a flash only to pile up on desks throughout the office.

Writing Activities

1. Write an extended memo to your managers. Suggest practical steps they can take to deal with the new flood of words.
2. Write an information sheet for your employees. The purpose of the sheet is to guide their writing efforts. Suggest practical ways they can do their part to halt the glut of words, words, words. Advise them how to write more effectively, not just to write less.

Speaking Activities

1. You have a reputation for getting through your daily reading matter in record time. A group of executives in the company invites you to speak to them for five to seven minutes about techniques you use to read quickly, to organize, and to remember.

2. A group of secretaries expresses anxiety that new machines will mean a new office staff. Address the group and speak candidly about your estimate of the impact of new electronic office machines upon the present office staff.

CASE 2: NO ONE CAN WRITE AROUND HERE!

Surrounding Washington, DC, are the "Beltway industries"—relatively small companies that provide goods and services to various government agencies. Leaders of these small companies meet each month as members of the Council for Government-related Industries. This group studies common problems shared by member companies.

"Our current problem to solve," says council president Linda Guest, "has more to do with education than with manufacturing or legislation. Our member companies are complaining that they just can't hire people with good writing skills anymore. Most of our companies depend on the writing of proposals for their business. If employees can't write proposals, the company can't win government contracts."

The Beltway industries hire most of their entry-level employees from eight regional community colleges and two area universities. All of these institutions require their students to take one semester of composition and one semester of literature.

The question before the Council for Government-related Industries is what recommendations to offer (and perhaps what assistance to give) to area educational institutions to improve the writing competence of their graduates.

Individual Writing Assignments

1. In the role of Linda Guest, write to Herbert Miller, Academic Dean of Montgomery Community College. Your goal in the letter is to inquire about writing requirements for Montgomery graduates and to express the interest of the council in improving writing competence prior to graduation.

2. In the role of Linda Guest, write a memo to other council members. Ask for their insights into why area graduates have inadequate writing skills. Also ask for their suggestions about what to do.

3. In the role of a council member, respond to the questions of Linda Guest in Assignment 2.

Group Writing Assignments

1. Join with several other members of the council in drawing up a one-page press release regarding the writing problem and the council's resolution to do

something about it. Remember that you do not want to alienate colleges in the region.

2. Working with several other members of the council, develop a questionnaire that can be administered to new employees who are recent graduates of colleges in the area. Your questionnaire should help to determine what went wrong in the instruction of writing for these graduates and what they think can be done about it.

Individual Speaking Assignments

1. As Linda Guest or a member of the council, prepare a short presentation to give before the Montgomery Community College faculty and administrators. They have invited you to present the concerns and views of the council regarding the writing problem.

2. In the role of a Montgomery faculty member, prepare a short oral presentation in which you defend the colleges of the area against any blame regarding the writing problem. If you admit there is a problem, develop an argument that places responsibility elsewhere for it.

Group Speaking Assignments

1. Convene a meeting of the council to discuss what should be done about the writing problem. Discuss, among other agenda items, possible ways to work with area colleges.

2. Assemble interview panels to talk to recent graduates of area colleges. Inquire about their training in writing. Ask for their ideas on how to improve the writing abilities of entry-level employees.

CASE 3: CAN'T GET STARTED

You are understandably excited about your first day as Unit Supervisor in the communications division of Cosmopolitan Insurance Company. You will direct the writing efforts of seven employees, working on such projects as brochures, advertisements, form letters, and reports.

The previous supervisor was dismissed, you learned, for not providing "direction and leadership" for the unit's writers. You resolve, therefore, to be a hands-on supervisor from your very first day.

Your first day begins at 8 o'clock with the customary introductions and well-wishing. You are somewhat surprised by 9 o'clock to see that none of the writers has yet begun to work. You ask several if they have projects to work on. "Oh, yes," they reply, "we all have plenty to do."

By 10 o'clock, you are dumbfounded to see almost every writer still nursing a morning cup of coffee, talking at the water cooler, or flipping through the newspaper. You promptly call a meeting to get to the heart of the problem.

One writer seems to speak for the rest. "Well, you don't start writing the way you start your car. It's an art, and sometimes it takes several hours to get motivated. Most of us experience Writer's Block until about 11 o'clock every morning."

Individual Writing Activities

1. Write a step-by-step guide for overcoming Writer's Block.
2. In a polite but firm memo to the writers in your unit, set forth your expectations of their activity beginning at 8 A.M. every morning.
3. Write up an account of your first day for your journal.

Group Writing Activities

1. After discussing Writer's Block in groups of three or more, each participant writes down his or her own method of overcoming moments of stagnation and frustration in writing.
2. In the role of writers within the unit, meet in small groups to generate a written reply to the new supervisor's outrageous suggestion that actual writing be undertaken before 11 A.M. each day.

Individual Speaking Activities

1. Deliver an informal pep talk to your writers on overcoming Writer's Block in an efficient way.
2. Tell how you manage to break through the blocks and dead ends that so often accompany the writing process.

Group Speaking Activities

1. Meeting together as a unit, discuss the supervisor's suggestion that the morning be spent more productively each day. Assign roles within your group. One person can play the supervisor, another a militant advocate of the writer's freedom to hours of unstructured thinking, another a lazy writer who simply hates to begin work before 11 A.M. each day, and so forth. Your meeting may not produce agreement, but at least the new supervisor will have a clear idea of the issues involved.
2. One of the perpetual problems in the unit is deciding just how long a given writing assignment should take. Meet as a group, again including the supervisor, to devise some guidelines for estimating the amount of time needed for a given writing project. You may want to develop time estimates for each of these projects:

   a one-page sales letter
   a two-page form letter
   a half-page advertisement (text)
   a four-page brochure
   a six-page report

CASE 4: RAYTEX COMPUTERS, INC.

While pursuing a business degree two years ago, you met two classmates who would change your life: Bob Simmons and Kathy Leavitt. After graduation, the three of you pooled your resources, slim though they were, to form Raytex Computers, Inc. In your first six months, you were able to produce the prototype of the Raytex Companion, a lap-sized printer that fit into a briefcase and was capable of printing neat business letters.

On the strength of that prototype, Raytex attracted a sizable venture capital loan and began production.

Now, three years later, the company has reached a plateau of sorts. Certainly, Raytex has been successful in its region of the country. However, you want to market your product nationally before a competitor beats you to the opportunity.

That kind of growth will require more investment capital, more employees, a larger plant, more sophisticated marketing and advertising strategies, and a host of other changes.

As directors of the Raytex Corporation, the three of you have become used to production planning: how many silicon chips to order, how many assembly-line workers to hire, and so forth. Your expansion plans call for a new kind of planning, though—the planning of crucial business communications with banks, advertising agencies, lawyers, accountants, and others. "Once," Bob Simmons jokes, "my years were all spent with a soldering iron in my hand. Now all you'll let me touch is a pen."

Consider the new challenges that face Bob, Kathy, and you as you make the transition from managers of technology (production-line management) to managers of communication (information and persuasion management).

Individual Writing Activities

1. In your role as a director of Raytex, list the major communication activities, both written and oral, that you will face during your national expansion campaign. For example, you will have to make presentations to financial institutions to seek new capital.

2. Write a personal letter to Bob, thanking him for his leadership in the technological sector of the company. Explain to him why he must now get used to using a pen more than a soldering iron as a manager.

3. Write a personal letter to Kathy, thanking her for heading up the difficult area of personnel management at Raytex. Suggest the kinds of changes you foresee in her responsibilities as Raytex begins to penetrate national markets.

Group Writing Activities

1. Meeting in groups of three (representing the three directors of Raytex), draw up a job description for a business communicator to assist the directors. Specify the kind of background you would require of this person, as well as the typical tasks in which the communicator will be involved day to day.

2. Again meeting in groups of three as directors, decide how you can train your managers in communication skills to prepare them for your national expansion

campaign. Devise a plan for such training; specify what will be taught, by whom, and when. Set aside an appropriate amount of money to cover the expense of this training effort.

Individual Speaking Activities

1. Tell a group of assembled Raytex managers why the company has decided to "go national" at this time. Point out the distinct advantages of being the first company to market a lap-sized computer on a national scale.

2. Describe the meteoric growth of Raytex, speaking informally as if addressing a local Rotary Club meeting. Focus on the key ingredients that made for your company's success. Use information contained on the fact sheet accompanying this case.

Group Speaking Activities

1. Participate in a brainstorming session involving other Raytex directors and managers. Try to come up with an orderly and effective plan for national expansion. Present your decisions to a larger group.

2. Participate in a closed-door directors' meeting with Bob and Kathy (in other words, a group of three). Decide through discussion on a fair division of responsibility regarding the major tasks involved in national expansion. Who will speak to the bankers? Who will handle advertising? Who will oversee hiring? Consider these and other topics, then give an oral summary of your decisions to a larger group.

FACT SHEET Raytex Computers, Inc.

Gross Sales

1995	$362,000
1996	$824,000
1997	$1,903,000
1998	$3,852,000

Product Line	**Units Sold**				**Projected**
	1995	**1996**	**1997**	**1998**	**1999**
Raytex Personal Computer	202	409	1082	3277	6279
Raytex Dot Matrix Printer	54	201	804	1203	3079
Raytex Color Monitor	21	54	302	812	1502
Raytex Lap Computer (in production)					2300
Employees	14	28	97	143	166
Earnings per share	−.06	−.02	.21	.54	.85

PART II

Cases 5 through 12 are intended to accompany Chapters 5 through 8.

CASE 5: SHORT AND NOT SO SWEET

At Life Force Insurance, the paper blizzard began in the 1980s with the advent of word processing and grew to crisis proportions as fax, e-mail, and high-speed photocopying arrived in the mid-1990s. Company president Conrad Underwood acted decisively to control the growing volume of memos, letters, reports, and other documents by insisting on brevity from all company writers: "I don't want to see any memo or letter longer than half a page," he ordered. "Keep every message as short as possible. None of us has time to read a novel."

Employees at Life Force responded immediately to the president's order. Within a few weeks, managers noticed with relief that the documents filling their in-baskets now took less than half the time to read. Everyone in the company seemed to approve the president's direction.

Then came the customer complaints, first as a trickle and then as a flood. It seems that, in correspondence to clients, employees had been brief to the point of being blunt. One notorious letter to a grieving spouse of a deceased policyholder said tersely: "Death claim granted, check attached forthwith."

As such letters tar the image of the company more and more each day, the president faces the immediate task of changing the style of letters to clients without bringing on another paper blizzard in the company.

Individual Writing Assignments

1. In the role of Conrad Underwood, write a memo to all employees in which you instruct them not to write terse letters to clients, but to maintain a brief style for in-house communication.
2. Again in the role of Conrad Underwood, write a letter of apology to a policyholder who received an unnecessarily blunt letter from one of your employees.
3. In the role of a policyholder, write a letter of complaint to Life Force Insurance regarding the blunt and even rude tone of recent letters you have received from the company.

Group Writing Assignments

1. Convene a quality circle (a relatively small discussion and problem-solving group) to discuss the stylistic problems described in the case. Decide what to do about the problem.
2. Join with several other employers at Life Force Insurance to draw up several guide letters that can be used by other company writers who are unsure what should and shouldn't be said to clients in correspondence.

Individual Speaking Assignments

1. In the role of Conrad Underwood, prepare a short presentation for delivery to employee groups. Describe the problems caused for the company by unnecessarily blunt correspondence to policyholders. Instruct employees on the kind of writing you want to see in the future.

2. In the role of a company employee, interview a policyholder regarding his or her impressions of Life Force Insurance, based on correspondence received. Prepare a brief oral report for senior management on your findings.

Group Speaking Assignments

1. In the role of company CEO, convene a meeting of company employees to discuss the writing problem. Come up with solutions that will not bring about another paper blizzard in the company.

2. Join with several of your colleagues in convening a focus group (a small discussion group) of company clients to give you their impressions and reactions to recent company correspondence. Take notes on their opinions, then decide with your colleagues how this information can best be presented to senior management.

CASE 6: CHIPS

It has all happened so fast. Eight years ago you were baking chocolate chip cookies out of your home for a local delicatessen. Now you run The Chips Corporation, a complex business supplying the greater New York City area with cookies from your secret recipes. You employ eight bakers, a fleet of delivery trucks, and several managers, supervisors, and accountants to keep the whole operation running smoothly.

Smoothly? You smile sadly, looking at the pile of "communications" piled on your desk (see the fact sheet accompanying this case). In this rapid growth period, no one took time to organize the kinds of communications useful to managers in the business. As a result, everyone jotted notes on whatever paper was available. Even important business letters sometimes went out in handwritten form.

Individual Writing Activities

1. You resolve to end the paper chaos. Choose at least eight forms of business communication. By describing the uses, stationery, routing, and filing requirements for each form, you will be establishing a systematic network for written communication in your company.

2. Write a memo to your office staff, directing that all in-house memos follow a prescribed form. Specify that form.

Group Writing Activities

1. Meet together in groups of three or more to decide on a color code for in-house stationery. Write up a brief information sheet guiding other employees in the use of the color code.

2. Meet together in groups of three or more to chart the flow of written communications within the company. Who writes to whom? Create a list of suggestions to streamline communication.

Individual Speaking Activities

1. Prepare for your appearance on a network talk show by drawing up speaking notes for a three-minute monologue on your company's rise to success. Deliver the monologue into a tape recorder if possible.

2. Your bakers need an occasional pep talk. Develop a short, informal speech emphasizing their importance to the company. Suggest future rewards and opportunities.

Group Speaking Activities

1. Meet with your key managers. Discuss how your company can keep and even extend its share of the market.

2. Sit down with a group of chocolate chip cookie afficionados. Discuss with them the merits and shortcomings of your cookies.

FACT SHEET Chips

Three examples of communications from Chips Corporation prior to efforts to overhaul business writing within the company.

Letter to a supplier:

> 20 # flour by June 2 — no later!
>
> Bill COD
>
>   Owner,
>   Bill Lengol

Letter to an overdue account:

Mr. Ledderer, my records show that you bought several dozen trays of our product over the past three months for sale in your two delicatessens. Have you made payment for these? Did I send you a receipt of any kind? We're trying to straighten out your account, and it appears that you owe us. Please respond.

Letter to a bank president:

Dear Sir/Madam:

For some time, as you may be aware, we have been in your neighborhood in the cookie business in New York. And now we are seeking expansion financing, you see we need a new production oven which will cost more than we are able to raise from our own invested funds and therefore are turning to the excellent reputation of your bank for helping small businesses such as us in these matters. Thank you.

Sincerely,

Bill Lengol

CASE 7: FOR ALL THE RIGHT REASONS

For the past four years, you have built up your retail antique business—the King's Head, on a rural highway outside Sacramento, California. Yesterday, you received word from a real estate agent that a large furniture store had gone bankrupt downtown. The store lease is available to you at an advantageous price (see the fact sheet accompanying this case). To move or not to move, that is the question.

Individual Writing Activities

1. Write a letter to the broker, requesting full details on the property available, including terms of the lease.
2. Make a list of all the reasons you want to move, then all the reasons you don't want to move. Make a second list of all the reasons your customers may want you to move and all the reasons they may not want you to move.
3. Assume for this activity that you do decide to move. Write a goodwill letter to your present customers. Inform them of your move, emphasizing ways in which their interests will be better served (using the "you" perspective).
4. Assume for this activity that you decide not to move. Write a letter to the broker informing him or her of your decision.

Group Writing Activities

1. Together with six other merchants along your stretch of highway, you form the Highway 9 Business Group, a chamber of commerce of sorts to promote trade along Highway 9. Meet with at least three other business leaders (your classmates) to draw up a promotional letter for mailing to 5000 area homes.
2. The Highway 9 Business Group needs a form letter inviting other businesses in the area to join the association. Together with at least three other people, draft the form letter. Focus on what the association can do for the merchant.

Individual Speaking Activities

1. At its first bimonthly meeting, the chairperson of the Highway 9 Business Group calls on you to say a few words about why you decided not to sell out and move into the city. Speak to the group for three to five minutes on that topic.
2. A local service club invites you to speak briefly on antiques. Choose some aspect of that broad topic, and deliver a five- to seven-minute presentation.

Group Speaking Activities

1. A merchant new to the Highway 9 Business Group sits at a conference table with at least three members of the group, including you. The new merchant asks all of you to discuss the future of the Highway 9 area, as you foresee it. Participate in the discussion. The student playing the role of the new merchant can help to gen-

erate discussion by asking a series of lively questions. (For example, "What's going to happen to the swamp behind the antique store?")

2. The Highway 9 Group decides to interview the new merchant for membership. First, decide on the procedure and questions for the interview, then lead the questioning. Last, decide on the new merchant's application.

FACT SHEET The King's Head

Information on 2731 W. Main St., formerly Andrews Furniture

The building

The structure comprises three floors, brick exterior, with office facilities on all three floors and show rooms on floors one and two.
Total Square footage: 20,310.
Breakdown: showrooms 14,500 sq. ft.
          office facilities 5,810 sq. ft.
Heat: oil furnace
Flooring: carpeting (some stains, worn)
Elevator: services all three floors, not working at present
Windows: large show windows facing onto Main St.
Parking: shares private lot with three other merchants on this block. Most customers find public parking.

The lease

Fifteen percent of the annual lease to be deposited up front as damage—refundable if building is restored to condition in which it was leased.

Lease amount: $8,200 per month, fixed rate, for 7 years. No option rights for renewal, though owner indicated interest in renegotiating terms at some future date.

Utility expense

Average heating bills per month: $1,805
Average electrical bills mo: $2,035
Average water/trash per mo: $800

The area

The three blocks surrounding the building include two banks, one furniture store, several clothing stores, three jewelers, eight professional offices, and one light manufacturer (computer parts). The area is served by public bus lines (47 and 89).

CASE 8: VISIT FOR A DAY, STAY FOR A LIFETIME

Together with two partners, you have developed Pebble Brook Shores, a 1000-unit lakeside village of condominiums (see the fact sheet accompanying this case). Your buyers, you project, will come primarily from the neighboring community of Tremont (population 110,000).

Unfortunately, Tremont's citizens are served by only one newspaper, the *Triton*. The editor of the paper has stood staunchly against the development of Pebble Brook Shores and now refuses your advertising.

You must find some other way to advertise your development in Tremont.

Individual Writing Activities

1. Write a promotional letter, with blanks left for the addressee's name to be filled in by word processing.
2. Write a goodwill letter to the Tremont Chamber of Commerce. Represent your development as a healthful addition to the community.
3. Write a letter to your attorney. Rehearse the details of the *Triton's* refusal to accept your advertising. Ask for legal counsel in enforcing your right to advertise.
4. Write a letter of thanks to the first family to buy a lakeside condominium.
5. Respond positively or negatively, as you wish, to a claims letter from a purchaser of a condominium. The purchaser alleges that a malfunctioning dishwasher is your responsibility during its first year of operation.

Group Writing Activities

1. Meet with your partners. Write the text for a full-page newspaper advertisement on the Pebble Brook Shores development.
2. Meet with a group of bankers. Write a brief, accurate statement of the financing that they are willing to make available to approved buyers of your condominiums.
3. Meet with your lawyers. Draft a direct letter to the *Triton*, insisting on your right to place an advertisement.

Individual Speaking Activities

1. Briefly address the Chamber of Commerce. Describe the kind of community you have tried to create at Pebble Brook Shores.
2. In a brief presentation, report to your partners on sales at Pebble Brook Shores during the first six months.

Group Speaking Activities

1. Meet with at least three residents of the condominium development. Listen to what they like and dislike about Pebble Brook Shores. Offer your opinions, projections, assurances, and explanations.
2. Meet with the maintenance staff at Pebble Brook Shores. Explain forcefully that they have not been doing a good job and that residents have been complaining. Listen to any explanations they offer, then work toward a constructive solution.

FACT SHEET Pebble Brook Shores

Nature of development: resort condominium village for upscale second-home buyers and midrange first-home buyers.

Number of units

There are a total of 1000 units. Of these there are 510 one-bedroom units, 200 two-bedroom units, 200 three-bedroom units, and 90 penthouse suites (3/4 bedrooms, 3/4 baths).

Features

Pebble Brook Shores offers the following desirable features:
   membership in Lake Club, with boating/swimming/tennis privileges
   membership in Pebble Brook Golf Association
   gardener provided with monthly association dues (required)
   guard gate with passkey entrance
   all electric kitchens, natural gas heat
   built-in appliances, including microwave oven
   upgraded carpets, fixtures (choice of carpet colors)
   fenced rear yards
   shared swimming pool for every 200 units
   guaranteed parking (two spaces) with one guaranteed space for guest parking
   tasteful use of stained glass in some window areas
   tile floors in kitchen/bath

Price range

Prices range from $79,500 for one-bedroom units (and up) to $269,000 for top-of-the-line penthouse units. Developer will assist buyer in finding suitable financing. Qualifies for VA, FHA purchase.

CASE 9: CONVENING THE CONVENTION

In exactly seven months, two days, and four hours, retailers of cotton products from throughout North America will descend on your city for the 19th Annual Cotton Products Convention, sponsored by your employer, the United Cotton Products Association. As executive assistant to the president of the association, you bear full responsibility for organizing the convention and preparing for the guests.

Individual Writing Activities

1. Using the fact sheet accompanying this case, write a letter of inquiry to the Starflight Hotel. Ask a number of specific questions about their convention facilities. Describe your needs.

2. Write a letter of invitation to Senator Rosa Freeman of Georgia. Invite her to deliver the keynote address. Describe the purpose of the conference, its constituency, and the honorarium and travel funds you can make available to the senator.

3. Write a letter of request to the major of your city. Ask for public services (such as police and paramedic service) that you will require during the convention. Demonstrate, if possible, that the convention is in the interest of the mayor's city.

4. By means of a business letter, place an order for 3000 name tags. Specify the kind of name tag, its advertised price, any pertinent code numbers, and the requested date of delivery. Add any other information necessary for the purchase of the name tags.

5. By means of a business letter, reserve the convention facilities of the Starflight Hotel. Abide by any request the hotel has made for a deposit. Specify the arrangements you expect from the hotel during the convention.

6. Write a letter of refusal to a cotton goods wholesaler who wishes to set up a booth in the main hotel lobby during the convention.

7. Write a letter of refusal to Army General Willard "Pap" Reynolds, retired, who has offered to speak to the convention without charge.

8. Write a letter answering the inquiry of a retailer in New Jersey who wants to know why the convention charges have been raised this year from $35 to $65.

Group Writing Activities

1. Together with a group of association staffers, write a single page welcoming retailers to the convention. The page will appear inside the front cover of the convention program.

FACT SHEET Cotton Products

Membership profile: United Cotton Products Association

Total membership: 5320

Regional distribution: Northeast	1032
South	3021
Midwest	503
Other	754

Average age: 54

Average income: $68,400 per year

Occupations represented retail cotton products merchants, wholesalers, farmers, brokers, researchers, advertisers, marketers, production specialists, government relations experts

Gender distribution of membership: 73% male, 27% female

Annual membership dues: $100

CASE 10: FOOD, GLORIOUS FOOD

For less than two weeks, you have tried to catch on to your new job as Director of Customer Relations for Quantity Foods, Inc. All kinds of duties come your way during the work day; impromptu plant tours for the Girl Scouts, visiting dignitaries from Nepal, consumer activists on the road from Des Moines, and so forth. Mail, too, has been stacking up on your desk. You resolve to answer as many of the letters as possible today.

Individual Writing Activities

1. Write an adjustment letter to Porthfield C. Kaye, who found your chicken soup a bit too salty (and returned the half-used can, wrapped in aluminum foil).

2. Write an adjustment letter to Ms. Brenda Donnelly, who paid 74 cents a can for your cranberry sauce only to discover "an even larger can of cranberry sauce made by Pacific Foods, selling for only 69 cents." She demands a refund of 74 cents.

3. Write an adjustment letter to Herbert Lillian, stock manager of Lincoln Super Market. An order of 600 boxes of powdered sugar arrived in damaged condition; 250 of the boxes were too damaged to be sold.

4. In the role of a grocery customer, write a claims letter to the Customer Relations department. In a can of Quantity Foods' kidney beans, you found a bean-sized stone. Unfortunately, you found it the hard way by biting down and cracking a $750 crown on a tooth. Decide in your claim letter what you want to ask for.

5. In the role of a retailer doing business with Quantity, write a claim letter regarding the undershipment of some 40 cases of canned vegetables. You ordered 260 cases, and you only received 220 cases.

Group Writing Activities

1. Working with other members of the Customer Relations staff at Quantity Foods, draft a one- or two-page document stating the company's policies with regard to customer claims. Be as specific as possible, and try to cover the most predictable cases that will arise.

2. Again working with the Customer Relations staff, draft a one- or two-page document that can be sent to the customer explaining Quantity Foods' attitudes toward its products, its expressed and implied warranties, and its customer service policies.

INDIVIDUAL SPEAKING ACTIVITIES

1. Prepare and deliver a short presentation of two or three of Quantity Foods' newest or most unusual products. Address a group of interested consumers.

2. Explain the steps Quantity Foods takes to ensure freshness. Address your remarks to a group of nutritionists. Take time to answer their questions after your short speech.

3. Propose the elimination of a certain line (of your choice) from the Quantity Foods family. Address an assembled group of company executives. Speak on the basis of complaints received in your department.

GROUP SPEAKING ACTIVITIES

1. Participate in a "future-think" session with other company members. Brainstorm and speculate on what particular foods will be the hot sales items in the coming five years.

2. Lead a panel of two or three other company members in interviewing a candidate for "Radio Chef," a popular program sponsored by your company. The old chef ate his way to an early death, and you're looking for a personable man or woman to replace him.

CASE 11: YOU'RE SITTING ON MY PROFIT

You manage the collections department at Gold Coast Furniture Mart, a huge wholesaler and retailer of midpriced residential and commercial furnishings. While you have several sets of form letters available on word processing and mail merge, you still take time to write some letters yourself to larger accounts. You also supervise the writing of letters by others in your group.

Individual Writing Activities

1. Write a first collection letter to Mr. and Mrs. Gunther Armstrong, who purchased a $2300 living room set last year. The Gunthers have made their agreed-upon monthly payment of $79.69 regularly for the past 11 months. The current payment, however, is now 20 days past due.
2. Write a final collection letter to Betterybuy Waterbeds, Inc., who purchased $6700 worth of office furnishings from you six months ago. The sale was made "Net 30"—all due and payable within 30 days. You haven't received payment. No one from Betterbuy has responded to your previous letters.
3. Write a second collection letter to National Mattress Supply. Their account for $368 is now 40 days past due. The manager of the company phoned ten days ago to say that "a check is in the mail." No check has arrived so far.
4. Write a first collection letter to the Urban Recovery Center for Homeless Teenagers. The Center purchased six inexpensive mattresses and bed frames from you five months ago. The monthly payment is $38.20. All payments except the last have been made on time.
5. Write a first collection letter to the president of the city's chamber of commerce, Ms. Wanda Frank. Ms. Frank purchased an expensive burled walnut dining set and agreed to make monthly payments of $102. She put 20 percent down on the set two months ago and has not sent any payments to date. At last month's chamber meeting, she mentioned to you how much she was enjoying her new table.

Group Writing Activities

1. Together with a group of your collection-letter writers, draft a series of four all-purpose collection letters, to be used in series as an account becomes increasingly delinquent.
2. Working with senior managers and salespeople in the company, develop written profiles of four common types of customers at your furniture store.
3. Together with the sales manager, draft a statement for customers. Explain in the statement what kind of credit is available at your store, and how a customer can qualify. Explain the penalties and consequences of failure to pay.

Individual Speaking Activities

1. Prepare and deliver a short speech (five to seven minutes) for the local Rotary Club. Speak on the topic. "Why Some People Just Don't Pay Their Bills."
2. Prepare and deliver a short speech at a regional meeting of the Account Adjusters Association. Speak on "Powerful Motivators in Debt Collection."

Group Speaking Activities

1. Meet with other staff members in your group to discuss the use of innovative language in bringing about payment of overdue accounts.
2. Together with a vice president in your company, interview a representative of Caldwell Auto Marts, a company that wants to furnish its seven dealerships with your products—purchased on credit, of course. Let a classmate play the part of the Caldwell representative. Supply him or her with some credit data for use in the interview.

PART III

Cases 12 and 13 are intended to accompany Chapters 9 through 11.

CASE 12: INSERT TAB A INTO SLOT B

You have worked at Drayco Toys, Inc., long enough to see tastes come full circle. Parents used to buy model kits and toys they assembled themselves for Johnny and Jill. Then, with fast foods came fast toys—ready to use right off the shelf. Now the pendulum has swung back. You think parents are ripe for your great idea: a kit out of which a parent can build any number of toys for the kids.

Individual Writing Activities

1. Write a memo to your immediate supervisor, asking for time to develop the proposal described in this case.
2. Write a memo to four fellow employees, asking them to participate in the development of the proposal.

Group Writing Activities

1. Divide the task of writing a proposal into several segments, one for each member in the proposal-writing team. Discuss the development of the proposal, then write a rough draft.
2. Play the role of a proposal evaluation team. You have been asked to look over the rough draft developed in Activity 1 above. Read the rough draft, discuss it, then make constructive suggestions for its improvement.
3. On the basis of the evaluation group's suggestions, write a final draft of the proposal. Each member may write a section of the proposal, with one or more members acting as editor for the document as a whole.

Individual Speaking Activities

1. As originator of the idea, prepare and deliver a brief summary of your proposal to an assembled group of managers. Answer their questions after your presentation.
2. Address a group of parents. In a short impromptu presentation, try to make your idea sound attractive.

Group Speaking Activities

1. Choose two class members to play the devil's advocate in speaking against your idea. Defend the proposal as well as you can.
2. Meet with the proposal writing team. Discuss alternative ways in which the proposal could be developed.

CASE 13: SEVEN HUNDRED TODDLERS FOR SALE

In the early 1990s, Ruth and William Pennington saw the need for high-quality child care in Seattle, Washington. They had read that more than 60 percent of families in Seattle required at least three days of child care per week. Working closely with state and local agencies, Mr. and Mrs. Pennington set up a total of 28 child care centers by 1995 throughout the Seattle area.

Now financially secure, this entrepreneurial couple wants to sell all 28 centers. A certified public accounting firm has been retained to prepare financial statements. A separate firm, Genesis Consultants, has contracted to write a report titled "An Overview of Personnel, Facilities, and Child-Care Procedures" for review by potential buyers. The report gives information about the following:

- The number of employees
- Education, training, and experience of employees
- Pay ranges of employees
- A general description of benefits for employees
- Total number of children per center
- Ages of children now under care
- A general description of typical facilities
- A relatively detailed description of care procedures and schedules
- A summary of state and local licenses and permits held by the centers

Individual Writing Assignments

1. In the role of Ruth or William Pennington, write a letter to Genesis Consultants describing the work you would like them to perform. Add any information you think appropriate with regard to deadlines, fees, or other matters.
2. In the role of a potential buyer, write a letter to Mr. and Mrs. Pennington indicating your interest in buying one or more child-care centers. Ask the questions that you will need answered prior to opening serious negotiations.

3. In the role of a Genesis executive, write a letter to Mr. and Mrs. Pennington regarding progress on the work you are doing for them.
4. In the role of a Genesis executive, write a memo to a co-worker inquiring about six details (of your choice) needed for completion of the Pennington report.

Group Writing Assignments

1. Together with several of your colleagues at Genesis, write the report requested by the Penningtons.
2. Imagine that you are part of an investment group that wants to make an offer on several of the Pennington child-care centers. Working together, draft a proposal to purchase the centers.

Individual Speaking Assignments

1. In the role of Ruth or William Pennington, prepare a short presentation to explain to your employees the sale of the child-care centers and to thank them for years of faithful service.
2. In the role of a state official, prepare a short presentation to give to Genesis Consultants regarding the Pennington child-care centers. Make Genesis aware of new state regulations for such centers.

Group Speaking Assignments

1. Convene a meeting of employees at one child-care center. The purpose of the meeting is to determine ways by which the employees themselves may be able to buy and run the child-care center.
2. As part of an interview panel from Genesis, interview several parents of children from Pennington centers. Inquire about what the parents like and dislike about the centers. Gather the information you receive into a short oral report to be delivered to the Penningtons.

PART IV

Cases 14 through 17 are intended to accompany Chapter 12.

CASE 14: I KNOW SOMEONE LOOKING FOR WORK

Top End Audio Outlets began as a large downstore store, then spread over a period of seven years to 11 suburban locations. Floor clerks and salespeople were generally hired at minimum wage plus commissions.

The rapid growth of the company in recent years has required the hiring of many new employees. "It's pretty haphazard," admits company president Sheila Evans. "When we have an opening, one of our employees usually brings in a friend who wants to work. If he or she looks reasonably capable, we hire on the spot."

"Our biggest problem is turnover," she continues. "The new hires brought in by word-of-mouth tend to work for a couple months, then move on to other companies. And we have another related problem: internal theft. I can't prove it yet, but I think a lot of our merchandise is walking out the door with these short-term employees."

"As the company continues to grow, we need to organize our way of hiring new employees. We need to figure out how to attract honest people who are willing to work for a year or more."

Individual Writing Assignments

1. Develop a relatively lengthy help-wanted ad that will attract the kind of employee Top End Audio needs.
2. In the role of Sheila Evans, write a letter to Personnel Associates, a firm specializing in effective hiring. Describe the problems your company is facing, and inquire about what kind of help Personnel Associates can offer.
3. Develop an application form for use by those seeking employment with the company.
4. in the role of an executive from Personnel Associates, write a letter responding to the inquiry (in Assignment 2) by Sheila Evans.
5. In the role of a Top End supervisor, write a memo to all floor managers. Warn them of possible internal shoplifting and inform them of a plan (of your own creation) to apprehend the thieves.

Group Writing Assignments

1. As one of several managers at Top End, work together to write a short report for Sheila Evans on the state of employee turnover in the company and what can be done about it.
2. As part of a writing team at Personnel Associates (see Individual Writing Assignments 2 and 4), write a proposal for Top End Audio describing how you will help them solve their personnel problems.

Individual Speaking Assignments

1. In the role of Sheila Evans, prepare a presentation to deliver at a meeting of company employees. You want to discuss employee turnover, ways to attract and retain employees, and the current theft problem.
2. In the role of an executive from Personnel Associates, prepare an oral presentation to be delivered to senior management at Top End. In your presentation, you will describe how Personnel Associates can help the company solve its personnel problems.

Group Speaking Assignments

1. As part of an interview panel, call in several company employees to discuss with them the problems faced by the company in attracting and retaining employees. Gather together the information you receive into a short oral presentation to be given to senior management.

2. Imagine that you and your co-workers are attending a meeting at which Sheila Evans discusses the company's problems. With one student playing the role of Sheila, let other students play audience members. The goal of the meeting is a frank, open discussion of what's wrong at Top End.

CASE 15: TAKE ME, I'M YOURS

It's April. In less than two months you will graduate with a B.A. in Finance. Uncle Albert and Aunt Rose told you employers would be beating a path to your door as you neared graduation. Well, the path could use a bit more beating. You have no leads at all until you seen an employment ad on the finance department bulletin board:

> National company seeks entry-level financial managers with strong academic preparation in cash-flow analysis and institutional lending practices. Salary commensurate with proven abilities and preparation. Fringe package outstanding. Send résumé to Alfred T. Ross, Seattle *Express*, Drawer 965A, Seattle, Washington 93772.

That's you they're asking for!

Individual Writing Activities

1. Prepare a letter of application to accompany your résumé.
2. Prepare a résumé (chronological or functional, as you wish).
3. Write to Mr. Ross, inquiring about the nature of the company and the job advertised.
4. Write a brief note to a former employer or an instructor. Ask for a letter of recommendation. Mention the kind of position you seek, and suggest some areas of focus for the letter.
5. Assume that you learn which company Mr. Ross represents. Write a letter of inquiry to the company, asking for the kind of information you think you will need in preparing for a possible interview.

Group Writing Activities

1. Together with three or four of your classmates, draw up a two- or three-page informal report. Point out the experiences and activities that seem to make a difference when it comes time to look for a good job. Offer advice and recommendations.
2. Too many of your classmates have chased blind ads in the employment section only to come up disappointed. Join with them in writing an open letter to a newspaper. Suggest in your letter the kinds of substantive evidence a newspaper should require from the advertiser before allowing a blind ad to run.

Individual Speaking Activities

1. In preparation for a possible interview, speak for two or three minutes about the most valuable work-related experience you have had. How can that experience contribute to your success in the job for which you are applying?

2. Present your résumé as if it were a short oral presentation. Introduce, then sell yourself.

Group Speaking Activities

1. In a group of three or four, exchange résumés. Offer advice and constructive criticism.
2. Practice *round-robin interviewing* with a group of your classmates: One person asks an interview-type question of someone else in the group. After giving an answer, it becomes that person's turn to ask an interview question of someone else in the group.

CASE 16: OH MY GOSH, THEY WANT TO INTERVIEW ME

You receive a letter from CTW International praising your qualifications as expressed in your letter and résumé. The manager who wrote the letter invites you for an on-site interview on Friday, May 20, at 9 A.M.

Individual Writing Activities

1. Write a letter accepting the job interview. Make up a name for the manager.
2. Assume that the interview went well. Write a letter of thanks to those who interviewed you.
3. Time passes so slowly when you're waiting for some action on the part of the prospective employer. Write a polite letter of inquiry in an effort to learn where the company is in its decision-making process regarding your application.
4. When it rains, it really rains. On the same day that you receive a job offer from CTW International, you also receive an offer from FinanceWest. You need to decide. Write a polite letter to each company, asking for a period of time (you decide how long to ask for) to respond to their offers.
5. Write a letter of acceptance for one of the two job offers named in Activity 4.
6. Write a "Thanks, but no" letter to the employer whose offer you did not accept.

Group Writing Activities

1. Discuss possible approaches to the following essay topic: "Why do you seek a degree in business?" After discussion, put your best ideas into a short essay answer of about a page or so.
2. Discuss the most difficult moments (experienced or imagined) in interviews. Create a list of important dos and don'ts for interviewing.

Individual Speaking Activities

1. In a short presentation of three to five minutes, describe the range and depth of your preparation for your chosen career. For what aspects of the job were you prepared well? In what areas will you require further preparation?

2. Interviews often conclude with the invitation. "Do you have any questions for us?" Draw together several meaningful questions that might serve well at such a moment. Speak them to a classmate to test their usefulness.

Group Speaking Activities

1. Together with several of your classmates, interview a candidate for a hypothetical position. After the interview, let the candidate listen in on your evaluative discussion.
2. Divide your résumé into its several parts, giving each part to a different classmate. Sit back with the rest of the audience to listen as your chosen group of classmates presents your résumé aloud, trying to make you sound as admirable as possible. Listen for areas of strength and weakness in your résumé.

CASE 17: TAKE ME AWAY FROM ALL THIS!

You manage Shangri-la Tours, a rapidly expanding chain of travel agencies specializing in exotic tours to out-of-the-way places. Business is great—so great, in fact, that you can't continue to manage your own travel agency while supervising the other branches as well. You need to hire someone to manage the home office. He or she must have all the expected background for such a position but must also possess a flair—a magnetism that makes middle-class customers want to leave the safe world behind and venture (profitably for you) to steaming jungles and windy peaks. In other words, you're looking for a very special person.

Individual Writing Activities

1. Write a letter to an executive employment agency. Describe the kind of manager you seek, and the terms of employment.
2. Write advertising copy for a two-page brochure on one of your exotic vacations.
3. Write a letter to all other branch supervisors, letting them know that applications are being taken for the office manager's job.
4. Write a short report for the directors of your corporation. Describe the specific ways in which you plan to restructure management of the various branch offices once you have hired a replacement for your own position as an office manager. Argue that the changes you propose will benefit the company.

Group Writing Activities

1. Meet with at least three of your branch supervisors. Brainstorm about several new exotic vacation possibilities. Write down a list of tasks for each member of the group so that your ideas become reality.
2. Ask each of your branch supervisors to write one or two pages profiling the kind of person you should hire as the home office manager. Work together as a group to combine the various profiles into one written description of Mr. or Ms. Right.

Individual Speaking Activities

1. Address a group of senior citizens (your classmates will do). Try to interest them in "the vacation of their wildest dreams."
2. Prepare and deliver a short presentation addressed to the directors of your corporation. Argue for the need to replace you as home office manager to free up your valuable time.
3. Pretend that you are the special person Shangri-la Tours seeks for home office manager. Speak about your unique qualifications and background, as if in an interview situation.
4. Using a dictaphone or tape recorder, dictate a letter to Shangri-la Tours. Indicate your interest in the position of office manager, and suggest the range and depth of your qualifications.

Group Speaking Activities

1. With one person playing the role of job applicant, assemble a group of three or four company representatives to interview the candidate.
2. In a group made up primarily of past travel clients, lead a discussion of the values of exotic, risk-filled vacations.
3. Working with a company group of three or four members, divide the typical exotic vacation into stages. Assign one stage to each member of your group. Together, make a short presentation that endeavors to "sell" the vacation to a local travel club.

PART V

Cases 18 through 20 are intended to accompany Chapters 13 through 17.

CASE 18: TRUCKS TO REMEMBER

As Creative Director for Right Now Advertising, Inc., you have taken personal charge of finding an advertising theme for Cross-country Trucking, one of your larger accounts. The president of the trucking firm wants an image the public can remember easily. That image has to reflect friendliness, reliability, and a certain degree of charm.

Individual Writing Activities

1. Write a memo to your advertising staff. Call a meeting to discuss the Cross-country account and other matters. Include a brief agenda in your memo.
2. Write a business letter to the president of Cross-country Trucking. Assure the president that your firm is working hard on the matter of an advertising theme and that you will have results no later than (you specify a time).
3. You have a bright idea for a slogan befitting the trucking company. Write up the idea in the form of a short proposal.
4. The president of your company wants to know how work is proceeding with the

Cross-country account. Write a short report summarizing the steps you have taken and any results you have achieved.

5. In developing your advertising campaign, you need some hard facts about the trucking industry. Write a letter of inquiry to the American Trucking Association.

6. The American Trucking Association proves helpful beyond your expectations, all without charge. Write a thank-you letter to the director of the association.

7. You have come up with a logo for Cross-country Trucking. Before proposing it to the trucking company, you have to make sure another company is not now using the logo. Write a letter to your lawyer, asking that a search be undertaken to check out the availability of the logo.

Group Writing Activities

1. After a particularly productive brainstorming session, you and your creative colleagues are ready to write a rough outline to use to develop a short presentation of your chosen theme for the Cross-country account. Write the outline, noting places where visual aids can be used effectively.

2. You have one minute on national television for a Cross-country advertisement. Work with your creative colleagues to write the text for the commercial. Describe the scenario of action and scenery that takes place along with your words.

Individual Speaking Activities

1. Prepare a short presentation on your chosen advertising concept for Cross-country Trucking. Deliver the presentation to a group of executives in your advertising company. Ask their advice, then rework the presentation accordingly.

2. Deliver the presentation of the Cross-country advertising concepts to a group of Cross-country executives. Use visual aids to make your points in a memorable way.

3. Develop and read the text of a one-minute television or radio commercial for Cross-country Trucking. Ask a group of listeners to give you feedback on the content and delivery of the message.

4. Prepare and deliver a short speech of five to seven minutes on the methods you used to come up with the advertising package for Cross-country Trucking. Your speech will be given to the American Trucking Association at their annual convention and probably will produce a flood of new business for your firm.

Group Speaking Activities

1. Brainstorm with at least three other members of your company about a workable and exciting advertising concept for Cross-country Trucking. It will be your responsibility to summarize ideas and points of view for the group at the end of the brainstorming session.

2. Assume that you have developed an advertising package for Cross-country Trucking. Assign one portion of the package to each member in your group. Together, you will present the entire package to Cross-country management. Use visual aids appropriately.

3. Three representatives of your advertising company meet with three representatives of Cross-country Trucking. Each side gives ideas, reactions, preferences, and possibilities. At the end of the session, try to reach consensus on the areas of agreement and disagreement in the group.

CASE 19: THE TONGUE-TIED PRESIDENT

Springfield Medical Supply began with a $200,000 bank loan, guaranteed by the Small Business Administration. Its gross sales of medical supplies and small equipment topped $8 million last year. The company employs 42 people. Its president and chief executive officer is Bernard Springfield, founder of the company.

Springfield began his career in medical supplies as a warehouse supervisor. His genius for minimum inventory and on-time delivery of orders attracted the attention of two physicians, who helped Springfield attract an S.B.A. loan for his own company.

As president and CEO, Bernard Springfield maintains a hands-on style of leadership, particularly with regard to ordering, warehousing, and delivery. There are days, in fact, when his managers in these areas wish he wasn't so directly involved in their tasks. "I don't know how he finds time," one manager says, "to do my job and also his own as president."

Springfield Medical Supply is in the initial stages of planning to go public with a stock offering on the American Stock Exchange in the near future. This move will give the company badly needed capital for expansion into new product lines. It will also require that Bernard Springfield make a number of crucial presentations to bankers, stock analysts, and stock market regulators.

Unfortunately, there's a problem. Bernard Springfield, for all his expertise in medical supply, has no experience in making major business presentations. On the few occasions in the past when he has made speeches, he has tended to mumble, ramble, and perspire profusely. Employees and investors at Springfield worry that the president won't inspire the confidence of Wall Street.

Individual Writing Assignments

1. In the role of Bernard Springfield, write a letter to First National Bank describing, in general, the business mission and success of Springfield Medical Supply. In your letter, express interest in opening a line of credit with the bank.
2. In the role of a Springfield customer, write a letter of thanks for prompt deliveries and flexibility in solving ordering problems.
3. In the role of Bernard Springfield, write a memo to all company employees informing them of plans for a public stock offering and future changes in the company.

Group Writing Activities

1. Together with other major investors at Springfield, draft a tactful letter to Bernard Springfield suggesting that he seek help in public speaking before facing Wall Street Analysts.
2. Join with other co-workers at Springfield in writing a proposal to Bernard Springfield. In it, suggest specific ways by which employees can acquire company stock at attractive prices before the company goes public.

Individual Speaking Assignments

1. Instead of writing a letter to Bernard Springfield, as in Group Writing Assignment 1, prepare the information for delivery as an oral presentation. One student should play the role of Bernard Springfield at the meeting where the presentation is delivered.
2. You have been selected to present the employee stock proposal (Group Writing Assignment 2) to Mr. Springfield. Make the presentation by arguing as persuasively as possible for the employee plan.

Group Speaking Assignments

1. Participate as part of a meeting of business leaders who share fears about public speaking. Bernard Springfield is attending at the request of his company's investors. Discuss the causes of speakers' nervousness and possible solutions.
2. Participate as a member of an employee committee invited by Mr. Springfield to discuss the employee stock-ownership plan. Divide various aspects of the plan among your group for discussion.

CASE 20: LIES, LIES, LIES

Your company's product—Dreamboat cream-filled cupcakes—has fierce competitors. While you don't mind a fair fight for market dominance, you do despise the cheating, lying advertisements appearing on nationwide television during the last two weeks: "An independent survey revealed that children from Oregon to Vermont are switching from Dreamboat cupcakes to Super Spongies. Why? Probably because Dreamboat cupcakes contain absolutely no dairy products: no milk, no cream, no butter. Growing kids need good nutrition. Join the thousands who would rather have a Spongie."

FACT SHEET Anti-Dreamboat Advertisements by Spongie Corporation

These ads appeared in nationwide magazines:

1. What's your child putting in his or her mouth?

(picture of a child putting a small boat toward mouth)

Boats are for sailing, not for eating. Dreams won't make them taste any better (especially when they contain absolutely no nutritional value for growing young bodies).

Say goodbye to the Dreamboats, Mom, and hello to Spongies—the snack that cares about what your child eats.

2. It looks like cream. It isn't. It looks like cake from whole wheat flour. It isn't.

(picture of child examining a squished Dreamboat)

Only a child could be fooled by Dreamboats. That's just the point.
Introducing Spongies—real nutrition from real milk, flour, eggs.

3. Getting ready to launch another Dreamboat . . .

(picture of cluttered chemical laboratory with bubbling vats)

Next time, Mom, reach for Spongies. The snack food made from milk, eggs, and flour, not artificial ingredients and laboratory chemicals.

Individual Writing Activities

1. Prepare an advertising counterattack by listing those claims you can refute, those claims you can explain away, and those claims you must admit. Develop your own set of claims against Spongies. For additional background information, use the fact sheet accompanying this case.

2. Pay particular attention to Spongies' "independent survey." In a one- or two-page memo, demonstrate (by making up whatever evidence you require) that the Spongies company is using statistics in a deceptive way.

3. In a page or two, compare the ingredients of Dreamboat cupcakes with Spongies. Argue that Dreamboats have superior nutritional value.

4. In the role of Dreamboat CEO, write a letter to the National Advertising Division (NAD) of the Better Business Bureau. After explaining your position on the Spongie ads, solicit the NAD's assistance in resolving the problem.

Group Writing Activities

1. Meet with at least three other company members to write the text of a television ad to counteract the effect of the Spongie advertising.

2. Meet with several other company members to plan for a new product in the Dreamboat line. Write a one- or two-page description of the new product.

Individual Speaking Activities

1. Deliver a short presentation on Dreamboat cupcakes to your stockholders' meeting. They need to be reassured that the popular Spongie ads are not correct and can be counteracted.

2. Speak briefly and informally to your advertising group on the importance of absolute truthfulness in the treatment of statistics.

Group Speaking Activities

1. Meet with other company members to devise a strategy to counteract the Spongie advertisements.

2. Hold a news conference at which you and other company members answer questions about the impact of the Spongie ads on the Dreamboat line of pastries. Have some of your classmates play the parts of newspaper and television reporters.

3. Play the role of president of Dreamboat Corporation on the telephone with another class member playing the part of the president of Spongie Corporation. State your charges frankly and try to work toward a solution.

PART VI

Cases 21 through 25 are intended to accompany Chapters 18 and 19.

CASE 21: MIRROR, MIRROR

You work as a manager for Associated Chemical Products, a multinational corporation with a wide product line, ranging from chemicals for the production of plastics to pharmaceuticals. Your particular responsibility lies in the area of personnel management. You hire and sometimes participate in the firing of administrative personnel for your foreign operations. You claim, in fact, to know more people in more foreign countries than the Secretary of State.

Writing Activities

1. Write a guide for use by your company's foreign visitors when they visit the United States. Of course, you cannot write a complete history or geography text. Instead, try to indicate some of the subtle customs or cultural habits of our people. Foreign visitors might be interested in knowing, for example, what the "thumbs up" sign means in this country. Choose 15 or 20 such cultural items for your guide.

2. Write a letter in English to a foreign company executive about to visit the home office for the first time. Present in your letter an agenda of events for the day of his or her visit, adding any other information the visitor may find helpful.

Speaking Activities

1. You are invited to speak to a foreign exchange club, as a person knowledgeable about foreign travel and business. You agree to speak for seven to ten minutes on the topic, "What to do and say when you don't know what to do or say in a foreign culture."

2. Your boss pooh-poohs the idea of a short training seminar for employees going abroad to work. In a presentation of five to seven minutes, argue that the seminar is important. Address your remarks to a group of company executives, including the boss who's opposed to the seminar.

CASE 22: GET READY, GET SET, GET EDUCATED

As marketing director for Teletronics Video Systems, you oversee the company's new sales effort: sending 20 bright, personable salespeople abroad to establish the Teletronics image and product line in foreign countries. Each company representative will have specialized training for the country of his or her destination. Before they go off to such seminars, you gather the group together for a general presentation on cultural differences.

Writing Activities

1. Write an agenda for the presentation, pinpointing your major points in a memorable way. The agenda will be kept by participants as a summary of the presentation.

2. Your immediate supervisor, a vice president in the company, has asked you to write a worst-case scenario for the kinds of things that might go wrong when 20 Teletronics salespeople go abroad. Consider various aspects of cultural differences, then write a short report to the vice president on the topic.

Speaking Activities

1. Address the assembled salespeople on the topic, "Keeping Your Eyes and Ears Open to New Experiences and Surroundings."
2. Join with two or three other company members in interviewing candidates for foreign service. Devise an insightful list of interview questions that will let you determine which candidates are most likely to succeed abroad.

CASE 23: WOULD YOU BUY A USED CAR FROM THIS PERSON?

The used-car display areas for Executive Auto run for more than three blocks along Main Street in Phoenix, Arizona. The dealership specializes in upscale automobiles, including Cadillac, Lincoln, Mercedes, BMW, Audi, and Volvo. Last year, the company sold 3300 cars, an average of almost 10 per day.

In the competitive Phoenix market, Executive Auto works hard to maintain customer confidence. The company has tried to disassociate itself from the usual stigma attached to used-car lots by telling the truth about each car on its lot. In fact, the dealership's motto is "A Square Deal Every Time."

No wonder, then, that company president Ralph Owens flew into a rage when he saw the front page headline in the *Arizona Republic*: "Investigation of Auto Swindles Likely." Several auto companies, including Executive Auto, were named in the article as likely targets for a state investigation of illegal business practices. Specifically, the article alleged, used-car dealers were destroying records and other evidence of repairs done by previous owners of the cars they were selling.

Owens called an immediate meeting of sales managers and read the article to them. The truth came out slowly in the meeting. Finally, one manager blurted out, "A lot of our used cars come to us with the glove compartment stuffed with old repair bills, gas receipts, and other papers. We just clean them out and throw them away." When Owens asked specifically what was done with a car's service and repair record, the manager described the typical cleaning process: "We look through any service or repair book we find in the car. If it's going to hurt the sale, we trash it. If it looks clean, we leave it in the glove compartment for the new buyer to see. There's nothing illegal about that."

The manager was right, of course. No law requires that a dealer save repair receipts or transfer them to the buyer of a used car. It's also true that a buyer would be leery of purchasing a car with a documented history of transmission, engine, or electrical problems. The question facing Ralph Owens is whether his company should destroy records found in the automobile, when those records may discourage a buyer from purchasing the car. The issue, Owens recognizes, is an ethical one.

Individual Writing Assignments

1. In the role of an Executive Auto customer, write a letter complaining of preexisting mechanical problems in a car you purchased from Executive Auto. From a previous owner of the car, you have learned that Executive Auto knew of the problems. Describe what you want done about the situation.
2. In the role of Ralph Owens, write a letter of protest to the *Arizona Republic* for their story naming Executive Auto as a possible target for investigation.
3. In the role of Ralph Owens, write a memo to all sales employees. Try to determine what they know about disposing of papers and service books containing negative information about the condition or history of cars on the Executive Auto lot. Word your memo in such a way that employees will not be afraid to respond.

Group Writing Assignments

1. As part of the sales group at Executive Auto, write a short report for Mr. Owens on how receipts, papers, and service books found on trade-in cars are handled when the cars are prepared for resale.
2. As part of an investigative team from the Arizona State Consumer Protection Agency, write up a list of questions you will ask senior management at Executive Auto to answer in writing.
3. As a member of senior management at Executive Auto, respond in writing to the questions posed in Assignment 2.

Individual Speaking Activities

1. In the role of Ralph Owens, prepare a speech for all sales employees in which you emphasize the importance of following ethical standards as well as legal standards in the sale of used automobiles. Be specific about the procedures and practices you want your employees to follow.
2. In the role of an irate customer, meet personally with Mr. Owens to describe the problems you have experienced with a car you purchased from Executive Auto and to suggest ways to resolve the problem.

Group Speaking Experiences

1. Participate, as a salesperson, in a group discussion with Mr. Owens about the limits of a salesperson's responsibility in telling potential buyers about automobiles for sale. Discuss ethical as well as legal issues.
2. Participate as a member of a state consumer protection panel in interviewing disgruntled customers of Executive Auto. Draw up the results of your interviews into a short oral presentation to be delivered to the State Attorney General.

CASE 24: BUT THAT'S WHAT YOU SAID

For the past ten years, you have directed Automagic Specialties. With corporate offices now in six states, you can usually live up to your claim of finding rare and exotic automobiles for upscale clients. Much of your promotional work is done through the mails. Your employees—auto brokers—send out letters advertising the specific characteristics of the cars they have available.

Writing Activities

1. Write a guide letter to suggest wording for the promotional letters mailed out by your employees.
2. Write a list of legal and ethical no-nos for your employees. Describe by example the kind of representations they should not make about the cars they advertise. In each case, explain why.

Speaking Activities

1. One of your more expensive cars will go up for auction soon. The auctioneer asks you to prepare a two- or three-minute promotional presentation on the car, to be delivered at the auction. Prepare and deliver the short speech.
2. A dissatisfied customer, Cal Vinegard, writes to tell you that his expensive Cord purchased from your company has turned out to be a lemon. He expects you to refund his money or face legal suit. Place a telephone call to Cal in an effort to reach a mutually acceptable resolution to the problem. A classmate can play the role of Cal, with the telephone arrangements simulated.

CASE 25: HAVE WE GOT A DEAL FOR YOU

At Diversified Investment Group, your active staff makes oral and written representations regarding a wide variety of investment vehicles, ranging from blue-chip equities to precious metals, mutual funds, growth stocks, and even speculation in commodities such as soybean futures and pork bellies.

Writing Activities

1. Draft a general, commonsense guide to business ethics for your employees to read and follow.
2. To demonstrate the difference between enthusiastic sales presentations and misleading deception, write side-by-side descriptions of an investment possibility of your choice. One description should be straightforward and honest; the other description should illustrate how words can be used to distort facts and deceive readers.

Speaking Activities

1. You yourself were burned by a clever con artist. In a presentation of five to seven minutes, tell how you were deceived and describe the reparations you want. Present your case as if you were speaking to the judge in a civil suit.

2. The local Rotary Club has invited you to speak for a few minutes on the most spectacularly successful investments you have ever heard of. Agree to give a five-to seven-minute talk. Use visual aids to illustrate your points.

Guidelines for Grammar, Mechanics, Usage, and Documentation

This concise guide limits its scope to practical problems faced by business writers. For a more complete grammar of the English language, refer to one of the comprehensive handbooks available.

SENTENCES MUST BE COMPLETE

English sentences are composed of a subject (a noun or pronoun) and a predicate (containing a verb).

(noun)	—	(verb)
Western Electric		*explored fiber optics*
(subject)	—	(predicate)

Nouns name people (Clark Kent), places (Cincinnati), things (boxes), ideas (freedom), and activities (thinking).

Verbs describe action (pushes, sends, reaches) and states of being (is, are, was, were).

Commands ("Go for coffee.") are complete sentences, though they seem to be missing a subject. The subject *you* is implied:

(You)	*Go for coffee*
(implied subject)	(predicate)

When a group of words lacks either a subject or a predicate, the result is a sentence fragment, not a sentence.

Fragment: And walked aimlessly for hours. (no subject)
Fragment: Waking from a bad dream. (no predicate)
Fragment: The man who left his briefcase in the car. (no predicate)

While advertising and magazine writers use sentence fragments freely, traditional business prose does not usually allow sentence fragments.

SENTENCES MUST BE DISTINCT

When two sentences run together as one, the result is a run-on sentence.

> *Error:* Sandra gave creative energy to the company, she sparked the imaginations of others by using her own.

When a writer unsuccessfully tries to repair a run-on sentence by using only a comma, the result is a **comma splice.**

> *Error:* Sandra gave creative energy to the company, she sparked the imaginations of others by using her own.

Run-on sentences and comma splices can easily be repaired in any one of six ways.

1. Separate the two sentences with a period.

   > *Error:* The mills needed raw materials the workers needed jobs.
   > *Correct:* The mills needed raw materials. The workers needed jobs.

2. Join the two sentences with a semicolon.

   > *Example:* The mills needed raw materials; the workers needed jobs.

3. Join the two sentences with a comma and a conjunction.

   > *Example:* The mills needed raw materials, and the workers needed jobs.

4. Join the two sentences with a semicolon and a conjunctive adverb followed by a comma.

   > *Example:* The mills needed raw materials; however, the workers needed jobs.

Common conjunctive adverbs

accordingly	besides	hence	likewise	otherwise
also	consequently	however	moreover	still
anyhow	finally	indeed	nevertheless	then
anyway	furthermore	instead	next	therefore

5. Join the two sentences with a subordinate conjunction.

   > The workers needed jobs because the mills needed raw materials.

Common subordinating conjunctions

> Time: before, after, since, until, till, when, whenever, while, as
> Place: where, wherever
> Manner: as if, like
> Reason: because, as, so that
> Contrast: though, although, even though
> Condition: if, unless, whether

6. Join the two sentences together with a relative pronoun.

Error: Bernard Clay is an engineer, he banished the slide rule from our offices.
Correct: Bernard Clay is the engineer who banished the slide rule from our offices.

Common relative pronouns

Who	Whose
Whom	That
Which	

SENTENCES MUST BE ORDERLY

Sentences must have their parts in the right places to work properly.

Error: Sarah placed both hands on the lectern, rising to speak. (The lectern is not rising to speak!)

Correct: Rising to speak, Sarah placed both hands on the lectern.
Sarah, rising to speak, placed both hands on the lectern.

Phrases such as "rising to speak" add extra meaning to (or modify) the subject of the sentence, Sarah. Always keep such modifiers close to the word they modify, to prevent distorted and silly meanings.

Error: He left his car behind, smoking a cigar.
Correct: Smoking a cigar, he left his car behind.

A modifier is said to "dangle" when added incorrectly at the beginning or end of a sentence:

Error: You can buy the watch at a discount price, which has a platinum bracelet.
Error: Together with the platinum bracelet, you can buy the watch at a discount price.
Correct: You can buy the watch with the platinum bracelet at a discount price.

SUBJECT AND VERB MUST AGREE

By acquired habit as speakers of English, we usually choose verbs that agree with the subjects in our sentences.

Factories sometimes cost (*not* costs) too much in the suburbs.
Each of the workers leaves (*not* leave) at 5 P.M.
(singular)   (singular)

Sometimes, however, we trip up by attaching a singular subject to a plural verb or vice versa.

Other easily mistaken singular subjects are

- Either/or
  Example: Either Jill or Mary answers our needs.

- Everyone
  Example: Everyone of them knows the head supervisor.

- Subjects separated by or
  Example: The computer or the teletype causes (not cause) static on the telephone.

Some plural nouns have singular meanings.

Economics is difficult but enlightening.
  (singular)

Other plural nouns include *aesthetics*, *checkers*, *mathematics*, *mumps*, *physics*, *politics*, and *statistics* (when referred to as a field of study).

Collective nouns can take singular or plural verbs, depending on whether they refer to a group as a unit or as a collection of individuals.

The team was organized by Henderly. (a group)
The team play their hearts out every game. (individuals)

Pronoun Choice

Pronouns in a sentence must agree with the noun to which they refer.

Every one of the packages lost its wrapper.
  (*not* their)

1. Use a plural pronoun to refer to two nouns joined by *and*.

   Wilson and Anderson gave their resignation speeches together.

   Use a singular pronoun to refer to subjects preceded by *each* or *every*.

   Each manager and each supervisor gave his or her approval to the project.

2. Use a singular pronoun to refer to nouns separated by *either/or* or *neither/nor*.

   Either the door or the hallway needs its annual coat of paint.

   When a singular and a plural noun are separated by or, the pronoun reference (and verb form) agrees with the noun closest to the verb.

   Common stock or apartments seem to be likely investment vehicles if their value remains steady this year.
   Apartments or common stock seems to be a likely investment vehicle if its value remains steady this year.

3. Use a singular or a plural pronoun to agree with collective nouns such as committee, crew, group, majority, number, and team, depending on whether it refers to a group as one unit or as a collection of independent individuals.

   The crew wins another of its many races.
   The crew are ready to receive their ribbons.

4. Use a singular pronoun to refer to *everyone*.

> Everyone has a right to express his or her own opinion.

5. Use a singular or plural pronoun to refer to *some* or *most*, depending on whether *some* or *most* refers to singular or plural nouns.

> Some of the sport has lost its excitement.
> Some of the sports have lost their excitement.

6. Use *I*, *we*, *you*, *he*, *she*, *it*, and *they* as subjects,

> He, she, and I went to the personnel office.

Note that these same forms are used after linking verbs:

> The best worker is she. (She is the best worker.)

7. Use *me*, *us*, *you*, *him*, *her*, *it*, and *them* as direct objects, indirect objects, and objects of prepositions.

> The job affected him and her in positive ways.
> Send Tom and me the bill.
> Send the bill to Tom and me.

8. Use *who* as a subject.

> Who tells the boss what to do?
> I want to meet the person who tells the boss what to do.

9. Use *whom* as an object.

> Give the package to whom you wish.

10. The indefinite pronouns *few*, *several*, and *all* take plural verbs and pronoun references.

> Few of the employees dislike their bosses.
> Several of her friends board their pets.
> All the boxes still sit in their appropriate places.

Indefinite pronouns such as *none* and *someone* take singular verbs and pronoun references.

> None of the men knows his grandfather's place of birth.
> Someone continues to leave his or her coat on my chair.

Comma

Use a comma

1. To set off an introductory phrase or subordinate clause from the independent statement

> When she saw the computer display, she noticed how little space it took on the top of the desk.

2. Before a coordinating conjunction (*and*, *or*, *but*, *for*, *yet*, or *nor*) linking two independent clauses; if the independent clauses are very short, the comma may be omitted

Landscaping for company headquarters may prove to be expensive, but first impressions of the company are often important for new clients.

3. After a conjunctive adverb following a semicolon

The staff members agreed to work extra hours for three weeks; however, they requested overtime pay.

4. To set off nonrestrictive (or nonessential) phrases or clauses

One of our managers, who knew PASCAL, offered to help debug the program.

5. To set off phrases or words in apposition

John Wilson, candidate for Congress, spoke at the luncheon.

6. To set off a name directly addressed

We will expect your letter, Ms. Jones, no later than September 5.

7. To set off an interjection

Well, I see your point.

8. To separate adjectives in a series

For our service truck, we sought an inexpensive, dependable vehicle.

9. To set off quoted material from the rest of a sentence

"We can meet our goals," proclaimed the new president.

10. To precede the conjunction when a list of three or more items is given.

The clips, brads, and fasteners were in the drawer.

SEMICOLONS

1. Use semicolons to separate closely related main clauses.

Creative business managers know how to delegate authority; they give their employees a sense of importance by involving them in significant ways.

2. Use semicolons to separate items in complex lists.

The assembly line faced a variety of problems: workers who, left by themselves, wasted time; machinery that dated from the Eisenhower years; and rushed schedules that brought perpetual panic.

COLONS

1. Use colons to signal the introduction of an example, an explanation, a quotation, or a list. Colons should always follow complete sentences.

Error: The ingredients of the concrete: Portland cement, lime, sand, pea gravel, and water.

Correct: The ingredients of the concrete were the following: Portland cement, lime, sand, pea gravel, and water.

2. Use colons in time designations and after greetings in formal letters.

> The workday begins promptly at 8:00 A.M.
> Dear Ms. McCoy:

APOSTROPHES

1. Use apostrophes to mark missing letters in contractions.

> isn't   they've   she's

2. Use apostrophes to form some plurals.

> Ph.D.'s   C.O.D.'s

3. Use apostrophes to indicate possession.

> *Singular:* business's   boss's   manager's   woman's
> *Plural:*   businesses' bosses'   managers'   womens'

> a. It's = it is   It's important to me.
>   Its = belongs to it   The table is missing its leg.

> b. Personal pronouns (hers, theirs, ours) do not take apostrophes.
>   The job is hers if she wants it.

> c. The impersonal pronoun *one* uses an apostrophe.
>   One's work can also be one's recreation.

QUOTATION MARKS

1. Use quotation marks to separate others' words from your own.

> He called out, "Please step forward if you wish to bid."

2. Use quotation marks to set off titles of short poems, short stories, songs, chapters, essays, or articles.

> "How to Write a Résumé"   "The Lake Isle of Innisfree"

3. Use quotation marks to indicate irony.

> His "university degree" was in fact a diploma purchased for $300.

Be careful not to overuse quotation marks in this way.

ITALICS

1. Use italics (or underlining) to mark the titles of books, plays, movies, newspapers, and magazines.

> The *Wall Street Journal* reviewed the financial aspects of *Star Wars*.

2. Use italics to identify foreign words and phrases.

> The visitor used the German word for work, *arbeiten*.

3. Use italics to give special emphasis.

> We asked the supervisor not only *how* to do the job, but *why* it should be done at all.

4. Use italics to set off words that you wish to call attention to as words.

> Tell the technical writers they use *is* too often.

PARENTHESES

1. Use parentheses to enclose explanation or details.

> The 507 press (a fabrication press for plywood) saved the company $82,000 in one year.

2. Use parentheses to enclose publisher information in a footnote.

> John Renley, *Common Stock Investment Strategies* (New York: Williams Press, 1983).

DASHES

1. Use dashes to separate a series from the rest of the sentence.

> The essential materials of the automobile—steel, rubber, plastic, and glass—can be stockpiled in almost unlimited quantities.

2. Use dashes to mark off an afterthought.

> Her resignation came only after repeated attempts to get the raise she wanted—and deserved, for that matter.

3. Use dashes to separate a parenthetical comment.

> Ledger books—the kind used for professional bookkeeping—were being sold at half price.

HYPHENS

1. Use hyphens to mark divisions within hyphenated words.

> editor-in-chief   twenty-one   (but one hundred and five)

2. Use hyphens to divide words into syllables when division is necessary at a line-end.

> cor-   corpo-   corpora-
> poration   ration   tion

CAPITALIZATION

1. Use a capital letter to begin sentences, direct quotations, and most lines of poetry.

> Let your employees feel that they matter.
> He asked, "Why did you call?"

2. Capitalize the names and initials of persons, places, and geographical areas.

   Henry Higgins   Hinton, Iowa   the South

3. Capitalize the names of organizations and their members.

   Rotary Club   Rotarians

4. Capitalize the names of ships, planes, and spacecrafts.

   Voyager II   the Queen Elizabeth II

5. Capitalize the names of ethnic groups, races, nationalities, religions, languages, and historical periods.

   Jewish   Romanian   Native American   English   Renaissance

6. Capitalize the names of days, months, holidays, and historical periods and events.

   Friday   October   the Roaring Twenties   Memorial Day

7. Capitalize the first word and all other major words in titles of books, plays, poems, musical compositions, films, and works of art.

   "Some Enchanted Evening"
   The Sound and the Fury
   Star Wars

Documentation

Documentation refers to the practice in professional and academic writing of citing sources for ideas, specific language, graphic illustrations, and other materials borrowed from the work of others. The two documentation systems used most often in contemporary academic communication are the Modern Language Association (MLA) system and the American Psychological Association (APA) system. These widely used documentation systems undergo periodic revision. For reference in future years, the reader is therefore advised to check the latest documentation publications of these organizations, usually available at public and university libraries.

Some businesses publish their own guides to documentation, including IBM, NASA, and TRW. In addition, many associations specify a particular set of style and documentation guidelines for their membership and publications. Among such associations are the American Chemical Society, the American Mathematical Society, and the American Institute of Physics. Technical communicators working within these disciplines or submitting to the professional journals of these organizations should determine which documentation system is expected.

THE PURPOSES OF DOCUMENTATION

Business writers document material borrowed from the work of others for at least three reasons:

1. Appropriate citation adds credibility to the writer's assertions. In effect, expert testimony or supportive facts are summoned by the writer to support his or her argument. Lacking such cited sources, the writer's claims could seem merely a matter of individual opinion.

2. Documentation also helps the writer avoid plagiarism. Just as physical property should not be stolen from others, so intellectual property (in the form of ideas,

graphic illustrations, statistics, and other material) should not be borrowed without appropriate acknowledgment.

3. Accurate citation guides the reader to sources for further reading or investigation about a topic. In many cases, business writers will include references not only to works actually cited, but also to other works germane to the topic.

ITEMS TO DOCUMENT

Business writers must provide appropriate documentation for

- verbatim material cited in their work;
- paraphrased versions of the ideas and language of others;
- points of fact not established by the writer's own research and not held as common knowledge;
- borrowed or adapted graphic aids and tables.

AVOIDING PLAGIARISM

Business writers have varying degrees of understanding regarding the nature of plagiarism. By defining and describing plagiarism, this brief discussion is intended to help writers avoid a serious breach of academic and professional integrity.

The *MLA Handbook for Writers of Research Papers*, third edition (1988), by Joseph Gibaldi and Walter S. Achtert, defines plagiarism as "the act of using another person's ideas or expressions in your writing without acknowledging the source. . . . In short, to plagiarize is to give the impression that you have written or thought something that you have in fact borrowed from someone else" (p. 21).

Examples

1. Repeating more or less verbatim someone else's words without acknowledging the source.
The following passage occurs in *Basics of Qualitative Research* (1990), by Anselm Strauss and Juliet Corbin.

> "In axial coding our focus is on specifying a category (*phenomenon*) in terms of the conditions that give rise to it; the *context* (its specific set of properties) in which it is embedded; the action/interactional *strategies* by which it is handled, managed, carried out; and the *consequences* of those strategies" (p. 97).

Plagiarism occurs if this passage is repeated without a source acknowledgment, even if several words are changed:

> In axial coding we specify a category in terms (a) of the conditions that give rise to it; (b) the context in which it is embedded; (c) the action or interactional strategies by which it is managed; and (d) the consequences of those strategies.

This passage must be footnoted, with appropriate reference in the notes and bibliography to Strauss and Corbin's work.

2. Paraphrasing someone else's terms, ideas, or argument without acknowledging the source.

Plagiarism of the Strauss and Corbin passage occurs if their ideas are used without source credit:

> To perform axial coding correctly, researchers begin by specifying a coding category. Next, they describe the context of that category as well as the strategies by which it is managed. Finally, they define the consequences of those strategies.

Plagiarism could be avoided in this passage by inserting the phrase "according to Strauss and Corbin" and footnoting the reference appropriately.

MODERN LANGUAGE ASSOCIATION (MLA) DOCUMENTATION GUIDELINES

Prior to 1988, the MLA documentation system was based on footnotes or endnotes, with superscripted (raised) numbers within the text to indicate reference locations. Examples of this system can be seen in many pre-1988 books, particularly those in the humanities. This older system is still used in some companies.

In general, however, most business and professional organizations using the MLA system have switched to the new MLA documentation guidelines summarized here. This new system is much like the APA documentation style, with in-text citations of author and page information coordinated with full citations listed in a bibliography or "Works Cited" section.

In-text Citation

Follow these guidelines in placing reference citations within the text.

Citing a Single Author

When an author is named in the text, cite only the page reference:

According to Norman Victor, price fluctuations in copper "depend directly upon political conditions in South America" (152).

When an author is not named in the text, include both author and page reference without a separating comma in parentheses:

Price fluctuations in copper "depend directly upon political conditions in South America" (Victor 152).

If the author is not known for a report, magazine article, or similar publication, use the short title of the work in place of the author's name.

"Preferred provider organizations (PPOs) continue to lobby vigorously for their political agenda" (*HMO Report* 321).

Citing Multiple Authors

When citing a reference with multiple authors, cite the authors' last names without a separating comma between the names and the page reference:

"Profits from personal computer sales have been distributed much more widely in the 1990s than in the 1980s" (Woodruff, Lincoln, and Todd 243).

When citing a reference to more than one work, separate the works by a semicolon:

Several authorities point to the economic rise of South Korea as a key factor in moderating world-wide steel prices (Andrews 142; Wilson 304; Kent 102).

When citing more than one work by the same author, use short title citations for the works, separating them from one another by a semicolon:

Franklin Evert found that CEOs typically distinguish themselves as top performers within the first two years of their careers (*Leadership* 133; *At the Top* 231).

Citations are placed before the period (as illustrated above) or, in the case of longer, indented quotations, two line spaces below the last line, flush with the right margin:

Legal expenses for American corporations exceeded $6 billion in 1993, a figure that could be reduced by at least half through mutually agreed-to arbitration. The American Arbitration Association holds regular informational seminars for companies interested in seeking low-cost alternatives to litigation.

(Brown 322)

Bibliography or Works Cited

The term "Bibliography" may be used for a list of works cited or an extended list that also includes relevant works not actually cited. The term "Works Cited" is used only for a list of works referenced in the text.

The list of works cited should be placed at the end of the paper, beginning with a new page. Page numbers should continue consecutively from the last page of the text. The words "Works Cited" are centered on the first line after the top margin. The list of works begins at the left margin, two line spaces down from this heading. Each entry begins at the left margin. If the entry is longer than one line, indent the second and following lines five spaces from the left margin.

Entries are listed alphabetically by the last name of author or, if the author's name is not known, by the first word (other than "A," "An," or "The") in the title.

Required Citation Information for Books

Author, title, and publication information are the minimal information requirements for book citation:

Burton, Philip Ward. *Advertising Copywriting.* 6th ed. Lincolnwood, IL: NTC Publishing Group, 1991.

A Book by Multiple Authors

Cite the authors' names in the order they appear on the title page of the work. Reverse only the name of the first author:

Hovland, Roxanne, and Gary B. Wilcox. *Advertising in Society.* Lincolnwood, IL: NTC Publishing Group, 1989.

Multiple Books by the Same Author

Name the author only for the first work listed. Thereafter, type three hyphens followed by a period. List multiple books alphabetically by first main word:

Burton, Philip Ward. *Advertising Copywriting.* 6th ed. Lincolnwood, IL: NTC Publishing Group, 1991.

———. *Which Ad Pulled Best?* 7th ed. Lincolnwood, IL: NTC Publishing Group, 1993.

Organization Author

If only an organization is listed as the author of a work, treat the organization name as an author name. List it alphabetically by first main word:

Plastics Institute. *Polymer Research, 1993.* New York: Plastics Institute Publications, 1994.

Anonymous Author

If the author of a work is unknown, list the title of the work in the place reserved for the author:

Encyclopedia of Magnetic Resonance Imaging. New York: Urban Publishing, 1993.

Pamphlet Citation

Cite pamphlets in the same way books are cited.

Understanding the Communication Revolution. New York: Western Digital, 1993.

Jenson, R. Edward. *Accessing the Internet.* Chicago: Technology Publications, 1993.

Citation of an Article in a Collection

Foster, Conrad. "Management Training." *New Horizons for Leadership.* Ed. C. Walton Smith. New York: Academy Publishers, 1992.

Citation of a Government Publication

If the author of the work is unknown, state the name of the government followed by the agency.

Arizona. Department of Land Management. *Water Conservation for the 1990s.* Phoenix: State Publications, 1993.

Citation of Association Proceedings

Technical Education: A Review of Approaches. Proceedings of the Society for Technical Education. Atlanta: STE Publications, 1993.

Required Citation Information for Periodicals

Periodicals include magazines, journals, newspapers, and other publications that appear at regular intervals. Required publication information includes author, title of the article cited, title of the publication, and publication data.

Citation of a Newspaper Article

"Super-Computer Access Opens Up." *San Francisco Chronicle.* 8 June 1994: D1.

Lincoln, Robert L. "Evaluating Mortgage Rate Fluctuations." *Banking News.* 16 May 1994: 4.

Citation of a Magazine or Journal Article

Steward, Thomas A. "Reengineering: The Hot New Management Tool." *Fortune.* 23 Aug. 1993: 40–48. [magazine]

"Ethics Policies Help Reduce Internal Control Costs." *Journal of Accountancy.* 4 (1994): 14–16. [journal]

Citation of a Review

Holzhauer, Ronald. "Reengineering to Success." Rev. of *Reengineering: Leveraging the Power of Integrated Product Development,* by V. Daniel Hunt. *Plant Engineering.* Dec. 1993: 20.

Citation of Other Sources

Software

Rosenberg, Victor, et al. *Pro-Cite.* Vers. 1.3. Computer software. Personal Bibliographic Software, 1987. IBM PC-DOS 2.0, 256 KB, disk.

TV and Radio

Teleconferencing for Business. Narr, Robert Trent. KNBC, Los Angeles, 6 May 1994.

Recordings

Lloyd Webber, Andrew. *Cats.* Cond. David Firman. Geffen, 2GHS 2017, 1981.

Videotapes and Films

High-Impact Communication Skills. D. E. Visuals, 1992. [videotape]

What Makes Rabbit Run? Dir. David Chesire and R. Eaton. Centre Productions, 1985. (16 mm, 29 min.) [film]

Interviews

Richardson, Linda C. Personal Interview. 19 May 1994.

Wolfe, Tom. Interview. *The Wrong Stuff: American Architecture.* Videocassette. Dir. Tom Bettag. Carousel Films, 1983.

Lectures and Speeches

Sidney, Collin. Address. Opening General Session, ABC Convention. New York, 14 June 1994.

[See the last page of this Appendix for Internet documentation advice.]

AMERICAN PSYCHOLOGICAL ASSOCIATION (APA) DOCUMENTATION GUIDELINES

APA documentation style for in-text citation is similar to MLA guidelines, with these key differences:

1. All in-text references to authors or sources are by last name only:

   Frederickson (1993) reported an increase in polio among Hispanic Americans.

2. The year in which the cited source was published is enclosed in parentheses immediately after the name of the author. (See example above.)

3. Page numbers of cited only in the case of a direct quotation, not for paraphrased material.

   Woodward (1993, p. 122) predicted "comet fragments larger than a kilometer in size will strike Jupiter in the summer of 1994."

   Woodward (1993) predicted that mile-sized comet fragments will collide with Jupiter in the summer of 1994.

4. Use "p." (for single pages) or "pp." (for multiple pages).

APA Guidelines for References

The page(s) called "Works Cited" in MLA documentation style are titled "References" in APA style. As with MLA style, all items listed are placed flush left, with second and following lines for each entry indented three spaces.

Observe the following differences with regard to book citations:

1. List the last name of the author and initials for given name(s), followed by year of publication in parentheses, then title (with only the first word and all proper nouns capitalized) and publication information:

   Shelton, J. (1994). *Handbook for technical writing.* Lincolnwood, IL: NTC Publishing Group.

2. List multiple works by the same author in chronological (not alphabetical) order:

   James, C. (1988). *Econometrics.* New York: Technical Publications.

   James, C. (1991). *The new markets.* New York: Seager Press.

3. Multiple authors are listed by last name and initials, separated by "&":

   Brown, H. & Buskirk, B. (1989). *Readings and cases in direct marketing.* Lincolnwood, IL: NTC Publishing Group.

Observe the following differences in periodical citations:

1. For journals, list the authors by last name, initial(s), publication date, article title, publication title, and publication information.

   Rieseman, R. (1994). Position emission tomography. *Medical Diagnostics,* **41,** 238–244.

2. For magazines, add the month after the year:

   Forest, K. (1994, August). Preparing for a technical career. *Technical Careers,* pp. 20–34.

3. For newspapers, add the day after the year and month:

   Victoria, L. (1994, May 1). Locating blood donors in an emergency. *Los Angeles Times,* p. A4.

Other forms of citation follow these same general principles.

Review

Jacobs, E. (1993, January 8). Effective speaking for technical managers. [Review of *Professional Speaking*]. *The Technical Manager,* p. 17.

Software

Andrews, L. (1994). *Hyperion* [computer program]. St. Louis, MO: Legacy Software.

Videotapes and Films

Person, S. (Producer). (1993). *Diversity in the workplace.* [Videotape]. Miami, FL: Media House.

Interviews

Osborn, W.K. (1994). [Personal interview]. New York.

Lectures and Speeches

Amandson, L. (1994). "Exploring Alaska's hidden heartland" [Lecture]. University of Arizona, Tucson, AZ.

DOCUMENTING INTERNET SOURCES

The Internet presents special problems for documentation. First, many Internet sources have little recognized validity. Information they contain may not have gone through a review process of any kind to check for accuracy; as the saying goes, "You can put anything on the Internet." Second, Internet sources have an annoying habit of going out of existence without notice—and leaving no record of their previous contents behind. Finally, these sources often fail to update their information in a timely way, or even to specify when the information was placed on the Internet.

For all these reasons, business writers have the obligation of providing enough information to assure accessibility and suggest credibility for the Internet materials they cite. Do so by specifying the following in your References section:

- the full Website address and title (if any), including all extensions and icons

    www.buscomm.html, The Writer's Helper, icon: "Style"

- the date you accessed the Website

    Accessed Jan. 9, 1998

- brief information on the individual or group who authors or supervises the Website

    This site is maintained by the Department of Communication at the University of Oregon. The site supervisor is Dr. Allen Forbes. [If you can find no such information, say: "No site author or supervisor information available."]

- place Internet sites alphabetically by address, not title, within your References

- within your body text, cite only the Internet address and title within parenthesis:

    Magazine editors expect professional writers to avoid "is" and "are" when possible in favor of more vivid verbs (www.buscomm.html, The Writer's Helper).

Index